The culture of film and the viewing experience

The Film Experience recognizes that the world of cinema doesn't stop with film's formal elements. It consistently explains the larger cultural contexts that shape the ways that viewers experience films and contribute to film's presence, power, and indeed its "magic."

A focus on film culture ▶ explores the connections between film fans and the movie industry, how technology is shaping today's moviegoing experience, multiple views of film history, and much more.

Tools that foster critical viewing and analysis

The Film Experience offers a vast array of learning tools including helpful Viewing Cues in every chapter, clear coverage of various approaches to film studies, bold key terms throughout, and the very best coverage of writing about film from Tim Corrigan, a recognized master of the form.

Marginal Viewing Cues ▶ highlight key concepts in the main text and encourage readers to consider these concepts while viewing films on their own.

SECOND EDITION

THE FILM EXPERIENCE
An Introduction

Timothy Corrigan
University of Pennsylvania

Patricia White
Swarthmore College

Bedford/St. Martin's
Boston • New York

or Bedford/St. Martin's

Executive Editor for Communication: Erika Gutierrez
Developmental Editor: Lai T. Moy
Associate Editor: Ada Fung
Project Editor: Peter Jacoby
Senior Production Supervisor: Dennis J. Conroy
Marketing Manager: Adrienne Petsick
Art Director: Lucy Krikorian
Text Design: Jerilyn Bockorick
Copy Editors: Alice Vigliani and Pat Phelan
Indexer: Melanie Belkin
Art Editor: Ada Fung
Photo Research: Julie Tesser
Cover Design: Billy Boardman
Cover Art: Composite photograph. Drive-in movie theater, 1958; photo by J. R. Eyerman;
   © Time Life Pictures/Getty Images. Scene still from *Blade Runner*, 1982; © Ladd
   Company/Warner Brothers/The Kobal Collection.
Composition: Nesbitt Graphics, Inc.
Printing and Binding: RR Donnelley and Sons

President: Joan E. Feinberg
Editorial Director: Denise B. Wydra
Director of Development: Erica T. Appel
Director of Marketing: Karen R. Soeltz
Director of Editing, Design, and Production: Marcia Cohen
Assistant Director of Editing, Design, and Production: Elise S. Kaiser
Managing Editor: Shuli Traub

Library of Congress Control Number: 2008931065

Manufactured in the United States of America.

3 2 1 0
f e d

For information, write: Bedford/St. Martin's, 75 Arlington Street,
Boston, MA 02116   (617-399-4000)

ISBN-10: 0-312-44585-7
ISBN-13: 978-0-312-44585-0

Acknowledgments

Acknowledgments and copyrights appear at the back of the book on pages
558-559, which constitute an extension of the copyright page.

Published and distributed outside North America by PALGRAVE MACMILLAN
Houndmills, Basingstoke, Hampshire RG21 6XS Companies and representatives
throughout the world.

ISBN-13: 978-0-230-22329-5
ISBN-10: 0-230-22329-X

A catalogue record for this book is available from the British Library.

This book is dedicated to Kathleen and Lawrence Corrigan and Marian and Carr Ferguson, and to Max Schneider-White.

Preface

"Experience is not what happens to you; it is what you do with what happens."

—Aldous Huxley

Virtually all of us have enjoyed the experience of watching movies, and we are well aware of the many pleasures they bring: of becoming captivated by imaginary worlds brought to life, of observing our favorite stars, of delving into different film genres, and of witnessing the enthralling moments in film history projected onto the big screen. Yet these moments of enjoyment are usually scattered impressions that we rarely coordinate into a working knowledge of film and film form—a knowledge that would inevitably add to our understanding of the movies. Cultivating and encouraging that knowledge in a way that is accessible to beginning film students is the primary aim of this book.

The Film Experience: An Introduction offers students a serious, comprehensive introduction to the art, industry, culture, and—above all—the *experience* of movies, and it gives instructors enough scope and flexibility to use the book to complement a range of approaches to film and media-studies courses.

In publishing the first edition of *The Film Experience*, our goal was to introduce a new approach to film studies, one that simultaneously treated students as the avid movie fans they are while surpassing other texts in helping students understand the art form's full scope. To do so, we strove to create a book that paid careful attention to formalist concepts—from mise-en-scène, cinematography, editing, and sound to narrative structure and genre—while also going further than competing texts by situating this formal knowledge in the larger cultural contexts that inform the ways that we view films: the surrounding historical, social, and theoretical influences. Based on our firsthand experience as teachers, we have found that this holistic approach enables students to view films from multiple angles with a more perceptive eye.

Our overall aspiration, then, has been to teach students *how* to think about film, presenting them with different lenses through which they could analyze movies on their own. In short, we wanted to create a book that would help transform students from avid movie fans into critical film viewers. And given this goal, we were gratified when instructors teaching with the first edition of *The Film Experience* reported that we had succeeded.

About the New Edition

One of the true pleasures of writing and publishing *The Film Experience* has been the opportunity to bring out a new edition and thereby take a very good learning tool and make it even better. Thus, when it came time to prepare the second edition, we spoke with a wide range of instructors from two- to four-year institutions across the United States, and we asked students what they thought made *The Film Experience* so special and how it could be improved. Overall, our instructor and student reviewers reported how much they liked the book's coverage and approach. To make the book even better, though, they suggested that we build upon the perspective of the first edition by streamlining the text, clarifying key concepts, expanding and sharpening the focus on the culture of film, and making the text even clearer and easier to use. With these helpful comments in mind, we focused the revisions that culminated in the second edition on three key areas:

The Best Coverage of Film's Formal Elements

Formalist concepts gives students an understanding of the practices and techniques that make film meaning possible; therefore, clear presentation of formal content is vital in an introductory text. Thus *The Film Experience* offers the strongest coverage available of mise-en-scène, cinematography, editing, and sound plus extensive coverage of the structure of narrative film, genre, documentaries, and experimental films. Each chapter offers clear explanations of major concepts and numerous definitions of bolded key terms, plus a plethora of useful learning tools and special features.

To improve the new edition, we've focused on the following areas:

- **A fresh, dynamic, four-color design.** Film is fundamentally a *visual* art; to capitalize on this essential aspect of cinema, the new edition of *The Film Experience* boasts a fresh and dynamic new full-color look. The overall design creates a contemporary feel that will capture students' interest and pull them into the text. By using full-color reproduction of frame enlargements from actual films, we can show images as they first appeared onscreen—whether in color or black and white—so that students can perform close analysis on specific frames as they were intended to be seen by the filmmakers, analysis that is impossible with books offering only black-and-white images.

- **Streamlined text and enhanced chapter structure.** Along with the new color design, we have incorporated numerous changes to make the book easier to navigate and to highlight the most important concepts. In particular, the overall text is about 10 percent shorter while a more clearly defined head structure in every chapter helps students keep track of where they are in the overall discussion and identify key formal and cultural topics.

- **The best art program—now even better.** With more than seven hundred images—the strongest and most extensive art program in any introductory film text—*The Film Experience* visually reinforces all the major techniques, concepts, and film traditions discussed in the text. Taking advantage of the new design, this edition includes more than two hundred new full-color images that illustrate the discussion better than ever. The vast majority of the images are actual film frames from digital sources, not publicity or production stills. We have selected the best available source versions and preserved the aspect ratios of the original films whenever possible. Our aim was to reproduce images that accurately reflect the films from which they are taken—in both color and black and white—giving students precise visual reference points for discussion and analysis.

■ **New chapters on documentary and experimental cinema.** Because of increasing interest in the dynamic worlds of documentary and experimental film, this new edition now offers a full chapter on each. These chapters examine films from the birth of each form through today and offer sections on history, elements, and significance.

Chapter 8 on documentary focuses on a wide range of approaches and rhetorical positions, from the early actualities of the Lumière brothers, the foundational work of Robert Flaherty and Dziga Vertov, and the films of Leni Riefenstahl through more contemporary offerings such as Michael Apted's *7 Up* series and the work of Michael Moore, plus elements of the documentary tradition incorporated into the reality television craze and the rise of the mockumentary.

Chapter 9 on experimental cinema explores antecedents in the fine arts; examines crossover cinematic experimentation of artists such as Jean Cocteau, Fernand Léger, Luis Buñuel, and Salvador Dalí; and features a healthy discussion of more recent works such as *Symbiopsychotaxiplasm* and *Tongues Untied*, along with thoughtful exploration of digital approaches.

■ **A broad range of films—now even broader.** Each generation of students that takes the introductory course (from eighteen-year-old first-year students to returning adults) is familiar with its own recent history of the movies; hence we have updated this edition with a number of new examples that reflect the diverse student body, from *The Simpsons Movie, Match Point,* the *Bourne* series, and *Juno* to *There Will Be Blood, Curse of the Golden Flower, The Devil Wears Prada,* and *Grizzly Man.*

And though we understand the importance of connecting with students through films they already know, it is also our profound responsibility to help students understand the rich history of film—recent and classic, blockbuster and independent, Hollywood and foreign—while promoting the diverse practices, audiences, and histories that define the film experience. Thus, our overall range of films includes classic and contemporary films from Hollywood (*Citizen Kane, The Searchers, Vertigo, Do the Right Thing*), experimental and challenging films outside the mainstream (*Meshes of the Afternoon, Sunless, Daughters of the Dust, Orlando*), and international films (*The Battleship Potemkin, Rashomon, The 400 Blows,* and *The Apple*), along with a vast array of new films added in this edition such as *Take One, Dilwale Dulhania Le Jayenge, I'm Not There,* and so many more. (It is important to note that because films are not always released in the same year in which production is completed, the correct release year for certain films is debatable. Throughout this text, we have used the most widely agreed upon release dates for students' historical reference.)

■ **New Transforming Film sequences.** These sequences illustrate historical, cultural, and technical evolutions in film practice through multiple images and clear juxtaposition; they appear at least once in each of the formal and genre chapters. For example, one sequence reveals a formal evolution: the transformation of actors into their cinematic roles from the simple application of make-up to the more sophisticated use of computer-generated imaging. Another sequence reflects an evolution in film culture: the transformation of viewing spaces from the single-roomed Nickelodeon theaters to the high-definition IMAX multiplexes.

Comprehensive Coverage of the Culture of Film

At the core of *The Film Experience* story is its focus on the relationship among viewers, contexts, and industry and how these connections shape the ways that we all view films. Although recent technological advances including DVD extras and Web sites such as the Internet Movie Database (IMDb) have expanded the layperson's *potential* access to insider information about films and the film industry, our experience in the classroom indicates that most students are still unfamiliar with the larger processes that underpin viewership; and of course, students are even less familiar with the history and rationale behind the practice of film studies itself. Therefore, this new edition of *The Film Experience* offers even more coverage that will help students understand the structure and impact of film culture on their own viewing experiences:

- **A new first chapter offers a powerful rationale for thinking seriously about film.** Through this new introductory chapter, students learn how to engage in the formal study of film, to recognize some of the histories and debates that shape *how* we define film culture, and to take a closer look at how *other* students and scholars have studied film in the past and continue to do so in the present.

- **New coverage of going to the movies.** Today, the movie experience means more than a ticket, a theater, and a bag of popcorn. IMAX theaters and 3-D viewing, HDTVs, and video iPods are some of the technological innovations that are transforming our viewing experiences, while cell phone ringtones, viral marketing, and video-on-demand via cable and Internet platforms represent the convergence among formerly distinct media forms. New coverage in Chapter 2 and throughout considers how increasing interest in changing viewing spaces and advanced viewing technologies are affecting the overall film experience.

- **Expanded coverage of the film industry, fandom, and spectatorship.** Chapter 2 also offers expanded coverage of the film industry and now includes an extensive new section on film production—ranging from discussions on how a film is financed to concrete explorations of the role of directors and editors. This coverage of the production process helps frame a deeper look at the experience of movie fandom and shows how industry strategies of exhibition, marketing, and advertising shape the overall viewing experience. In addition, more coverage of the cultural meanings of stars, genres, and fan activity shows how the industry recognizes that without avid movie fans, there would be no film experience.

- **More coverage beyond Hollywood.** Throughout the text, students are continually reminded that the Hollywood blockbuster is not the only type of movie out there and that many movie cultures exist. In this new edition, we have bolstered coverage of several cinema traditions, including Chinese and Hong Kong films, New German cinema, Japanese anime, Bollywood, and Iranian cinema, along with adding more on New Queer Cinema and orphan films.

- **Improved and streamlined coverage of history.** In keeping with the book's holistic approach to film, two full chapters explore the diverse range of historical models and perspectives that influence how we watch and evaluate movies. Chapter 11 examines the "traditional" history of Hollywood cinema from 1895 to the present. Chapter 12 introduces a series of alternative and more inclusive approaches to film history, including global cinema from the pre–World War II period to the present, African American film history, American women film history, and gay and lesbian film history.

  Beyond these two full chapters, we have also streamlined and restructured the Short History sections within each chapter to read more chronologically, providing students with digestible overviews of critical events in each area of film history. This restructuring helps to emphasize the importance of historical context when learning the analytical terms, formal vocabulary, and critical methods of film studies.

- **Stronger coverage of multiple approaches to film.** We introduce readers to the widest variety of theoretical models, giving them a complete picture of both the medium and the discipline. Chapter 13 presents students with the core schools and debates within film theory, including realism and formalism, Marxism, semiotics and structuralism, poststructuralism and feminism, cultural studies, film philosophy, postmodernism, and more.

Tools That Foster Critical Viewing and Analysis

The Film Experience helps students translate theoretical understanding into analytical insight, with the concrete result that their analyses in class discussions and in their written work will become clearer and more perceptive. The tools we offer include:

- **Clear explanations and definitions of fundamental film terms.** Comprehension of formal film vocabulary goes beyond memorizing definitions; it requires context. Therefore, key terms appear in boldface and terms useful in the context of a specific discussion are italicized throughout the book. All bolded terms are also defined in an extensive end-of-book glossary.

- **Viewing Cues—now even more useful.** A favorite feature carried over from the first edition, these prompts—now appearing as marginal notes adjacent to relevant discussions in the main text—highlight key concepts and encourage students to consider these concepts while viewing films on their own or in class.

- **New and compelling chapter-opening vignettes.** Each chapter now opens with a narrative vignette that focuses on actual scenes from real movies, immediately placing students inside a film and helping them understand the thinking required of critical viewers; each vignette connects what students know as movie fans to the chapter's formal discussion. For example, Chapter 3 opens with a detailed description of the unusual narration styles of *Stranger than Fiction* and then segues into discussing the cultural impact of storytelling in film.

- **Revised Film in Focus essays in each chapter.** Film in Focus essays demonstrate how certain techniques or concepts inform and enrich particular films. Examples include a new, detailed analysis in Chapter 2 of the distribution of Charles Burnett's *Killer of Sheep* that helps students understand the close link between industry and the viewing experience and a close examination in Chapter 6 of *The Piano* that illustrates the effects of sound in establishing cinematic meaning.

- **New Concepts at Work activities at the end of each chapter.** These include brief chapter summaries followed by questions that give students creative opportunities to think more deeply about film concepts. For example, in Chapter 8 on documentary, an end-of-chapter question asks students to imagine the steps they would take to create a mockumentary film about a particular documentary area such as a travelogue.

- **More advice on writing about film than any other text.** *The Film Experience* offers more detailed instruction and more student writing examples than any other introductory text. Praised by instructors and students as a key reason they love the book, Chapter 14, "Writing a Film Essay," is a step-by-step guide to writing papers about film, from taking notes, choosing a topic, and developing an argument to incorporating film images and completing a polished essay. It includes a sample student essay on *Citizen Kane* annotated with film captures.

Resources for Students and Instructors

- Book companion site at bedfordstmartins.com/filmexperience by James Fiumara, University of Pennsylvania. A free resource for all users of *The Film Experience*, this fully revised site includes links to other film resources, downloadable versions of all the Viewing Cues, the unabridged glossary, quizzes, and other support material. The chapter quizzes and chapter summaries have been streamlined to provide students with comprehensive practice and study of major film concepts discussed in the book.

- Instructor's Resource Manual (ISBN 0-312-53711-5) by Amy Monaghan, Clemson University. Although a great deal of revision, thought, and creativity have gone into the development of the second edition of *The Film Experience*, there is no doubt that a strong text deserves an equally strong Instructor's Resource Manual that can supplement that text and suggest ways for teaching the course. The Instructor's Resource Manual for this edition therefore recommends methods for teaching the course using the chapter-opening vignettes, the Viewing Cues, the Film in Focus, and the Transforming Film features. In addition, it offers such standard teaching aids as chapter overviews, questions to generate class discussion, ideas for encouraging critical and active viewing, supplemental analyses of films, and an appendix of sample syllabi. Each chapter of the manual also features a complete, alphabetized list of films referenced in each chapter of the main text.

- Video resources. For qualified adopters, Bedford/St. Martin's is proud to offer in DVD format a variety of short and feature-length films discussed in *The Film Experience* for use in film courses, including films from the Criterion Collection. For more information, please contact your local publisher's representative.

Acknowledgments

A book of this scope has benefited from the help of many people. A host of reviewers, readers, and friends have contributed to this edition, and Timothy Corrigan is especially grateful to his students and his University of Pennsylvania colleagues Karen Beckman, Peter Decherney, Meta Mazaj, and Nicola Gentili for their hands-on and precise feedback on how to make the best book possible. Patricia White thanks Amelie Hastie and Ed O'Neill for well-timed advice; her colleagues in Film and Media Studies at Swarthmore, Bob Rehak and Sunka Simon; her students and assistants, especially Mara Fortes, Robert Alford, Brandy Monk-Payton, and Willa Kramer; and, in memoriam, Jim Lyons.

Instructors throughout the country have reviewed the book and offered their advice, suggestions, and encouragement at various stages of the project's development. For the second edition we would like to thank Kellie Bean, Marshall University; Christine Becker, University of Notre Dame; David Berube, University of South Carolina; Yifen Beus, Brigham Young University Hawaii; Jennifer Bottinelli, Kutztown University; Donna Bowman, University of Central Arkansas; Barbara Brickman, University of West Georgia; Chris Cagle, Temple University; Shayna Connelly, Columbia College; Jill Craven, Millersville University; Eli Daughdrill, Santa Monica College; Clark Farmer, University of Colorado–Boulder; William Ferreira, Houston Community College–Southwest; Anthony Fleury, Washington and Jefferson College; Rosalind Galt, University of Iowa; Neil Goldstein, Montgomery County Community College; Thomas Green, Cape Fear Community College; Ina Hark, University of South Carolina; Elizabeth Henry, Eastern Oregon University; Mary Hurley, St. Louis Community College; Christopher Jacobs, University of North Dakota; Brooke Jacobson, Portland State University; Kathleen Rowe Karlyn, University of Oregon; David Laderman, College of San Mateo; Peter

Limbrick, University of California–Santa Cruz; William Long, Camden County College; Cynthia Lucia, Rider University; Glenn Man, University of Hawaii at Manoa; Jayne Marek, Franklin College; Kelli Marshall, University of Texas–Dallas; Adrienne McLean, University of Texas–Dallas; Jeffrey Middents, American University; Stuart Noel, Georgia Perimeter College; Dann Pierce, University of Portland; Dana Renga, Colorado College; Susan Scheibler, Loyola Marymount University; Matthew Sewell, Minnesota State University–Mankato; Steven Shaviro, Wayne State University; Kathryn Shield, University of Texas–Arlington; Christopher Sieving, University of Notre Dame; Ed Sikov, Haverford College; Philip Sipiora, University of South Florida; Dina Smith, Drake University; Cristina Stasia, Syracuse University; Nickolas Tanis, New York University–Tisch School of the Arts; Kirsten Moana Thompson, Wayne State University; John Tibbetts, University of Kansas; Willie Tolliver, Agnes Scott College; Chuck Tryon, Fayetteville State University; Kenneth Von Gunden, Penn State University–Altoona College; and Greg Wright, Kalamazoo College.

For the first edition, we are grateful to Nora M. Alter, University of Florida; Constantin Behler, University of Washington, Bothell; J. Dennis Bounds, Regent University (Virginia); Richard Breyer, Syracuse University; Lucy Fischer, University of Pittsburgh; Jeremy Butler, University of Alabama; Jill Craven, Millersville University; Robert Dassanowsky, University of Colorado, Colorado Springs; Eric Faden, Bucknell University; Stefan Fleischer; State University of New York, Buffalo; Brian M. Goss, University of Illinois at Urbana–Champaign; Mark Hall, California State University–Chico; Tom Isbell, University of Minnesota–Duluth; Christopher Jacobs, University of North Dakota; Jonathan Kahana, Bryn Mawr College; Joe Kickasola, Baylor University; Arthur Knight, College of William and Mary; Gina Marchetti, Ithaca College; Ivone Margulies, Hunter College, City University of New York; Joan McGettigan, Texas Christian University; Mark Meysenburg, Doane College (Nebraska); Charles Musser, Yale University; Mark Nornes, University of Michigan; Patrice Petro, University of Wisconsin–Milwaukee; Kimberly Radek, Illinois Valley Community College; Frank Scheide, University of Arkansas; Jeff Smith, Washington University (St. Louis); Vivian Sobchack, University of California, Los Angeles; Maureen Turim, University of Florida; Leslie Werden, University of North Dakota; Jennifer Wild, University of Iowa; Sharon Willis, University of Rochester; and Sarah Witte, Eastern Oregon University.

Special thanks go to the following individuals and organizations for their assistance and expertise in acquiring photo stills: Anthology Film Archives, Robert Haller, Jessica Rosner at Kino International, Beth and Margaret at Narberth Video & Entertainment; the McCabe Library acquisitions and circulation staff and the Instructional Technology and Media Services staff at Swarthmore College, Rob Epstein and James Chan at Telling Pictures, TLA Video (especially Jon Krumbiegel and Gary Berenbroick), and Joseph Yransky. James Fiumara provided assistance in many ways, most notably for his comprehensive revision of the chapter summaries and introductions on the book companion Web site accompanying the second edition of the text, as well as for his work assembling the material for the glossary in the first edition. Thanks also go to Amy Monaghan for her excellent work on the first edition's Instructor's Resource Manual and to Benjamin Platt for his thoughtful and inspired guidance during the manual's development.

At Bedford/St. Martin's, we thank Erika Gutierrez, executive editor of communication, for her belief in and support of this project from the outset. We are grateful to former editor Vik Mukhija for his guidance during the project's earlier stages. We are especially grateful to editor Lai T. Moy for guiding us with patience and good humor throughout this project and to associate editor Ada Fung for her precise work on the art program and for her help coordinating the numerous reviews and other tasks, big and small. We are indebted to photo researcher Julie Tesser for her extraordinary work acquiring every piece of art in this book; the art program

was a tremendous undertaking, and the results are beautiful. We are also grateful to Willa Kramer and Lisa Hermes for all their work capturing the film grabs for this edition. The handsome page layouts were created by Jerilyn Bockorick. We thank Erica Appel, director of development, and Simon Glick, executive editor, for their support of this book, as well as Peter Jacoby, project editor, and Shuli Traub, managing editor, for their diligent work on the book's production; we thank Lucy Krikorian, art director, for overseeing a beautiful design and Billy Boardman, designer, for a dynamic new cover. We also express thanks to new media associate Allison Hart for her work on the companion Web site.

We are especially thankful to our families, Marcia Ferguson and Cecilia, Graham, and Anna Corrigan, and George and Donna White, Cynthia Schneider, and Max Schneider-White. Finally, we are grateful for the growth of our writing partnership and for the rich experiences this collaborative effort has brought us. We look forward to ongoing projects.

Timothy Corrigan
Patricia White

Brief Contents

Brief Contents

Contents

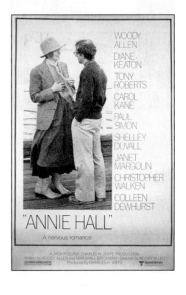

PART 2
COMPOSITIONS: film scenes, shots, cuts, and sounds   58

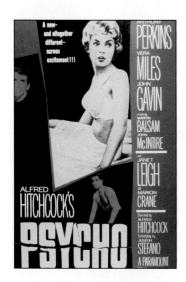

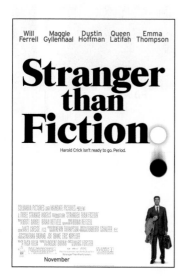

PART 5
REACTIONS: reading and writing about film 454

THE FILM EXPERIENCE

PART 1

CONTEXTS
making, watching, and studying movies

In 1997, thousands of viewers lined up for the much-anticipated re-release of George Lucas's intergalactic blockbuster, *Star Wars: Episode IV—A New Hope*. Although many people had already seen the classic version on videotape or DVD, they nevertheless found themselves caught up in the fanfare of the ballyhooed re-release. Advertisements, stories about the new technology, and reviews circulated widely, and distribution extended to all corners of the world. By contrast, the popularity of Mike Leigh's *Secrets and Lies* (1996), a modestly budgeted British film that was released around the same time, was based on two factors having little to do with extravagant production or promotion. Many viewers wanted to see the film because of Leigh's Oscar nomination for best director, an honor that led to the film's wider distribution in the United States. Still others were influenced by their enjoyment of his earlier movie, *Life Is Sweet* (1991). These social and institutional forces—promotion, distribution, and exhibition—are what organize the film experience, and it is the thoughtful investigation of these forces that encompasses the study of film culture.

Part 1 of this book identifies the institutional, cultural, and industrial shifts in and contexts of the film experience and shows us how to turn our personal movie practices into a critical perspective on film. Chapter 1 discusses how and why studying film is a significant part of cultural life worldwide. Chapter 2 introduces the movie production process within the frameworks of distribution, promotion, and exhibition. Understanding these different contexts will help us to develop a broad and analytical perspective on the film experience.

CHAPTER 1

Introduction to the Film Experience

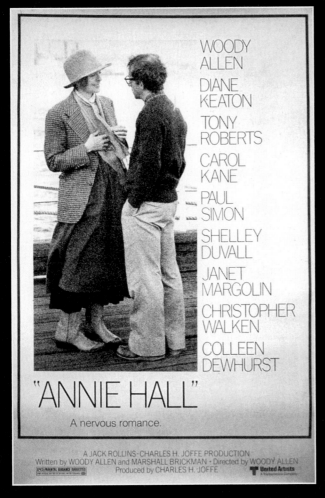

- Why film studies?
- Film culture and practices
- Film experiences

CHAPTER 2

Preparing Viewers and Views: Production, Distribution, Promotion, and Exhibition

- Changing viewing technologies
- Stages of filmmaking
- Mechanisms of film distribution
- Practices of promotion and exhibition

WOODY
ALLEN

DIANE
KEATON

TONY
ROBERTS

CAROL
KANE

PAUL
SIMON

SHELLEY
DUVALL

JANET
MARGOLIN

CHRISTOPHER
WALKEN

COLLEEN
DEWHURST

"ANNIE HALL"

A nervous romance.

A JACK ROLLINS-CHARLES H. JOFFE PRODUCTION
Written by WOODY ALLEN and MARSHALL BRICKMAN · Directed by WOODY ALLEN
Produced by CHARLES H. JOFFE

PG PARENTAL GUIDANCE SUGGESTED
SOME MATERIAL MAY NOT BE SUITABLE FOR PRE-TEENAGERS

United Artists
A Transamerica Company

Introduction to the Film Experience

In Woody Allen's 1977 film *Annie Hall*, Alvy Singer and Annie Hall stand in line to see the 1972 French documentary *The Sorrow and the Pity*. Next to them in line is a film and media professor who pontificates about the work of media theorist and counterculture critic Marshall McLuhan, author of *Understanding Media* and *The Gutenberg Galaxy*. As Alvy grows more irritated by the conversation, he finally interrupts the professor and tells him he knows nothing about McLuhan's work, as Annie looks on, embarrassed. When the professor objects, pointing out that he teaches McLuhan's books, Alvy counters by bringing McLuhan himself out from a corner of the lobby to confirm that the professor is all wrong about McLuhan's writings. While this encounter between moviegoers comically exaggerates a secret wish about how to end an argument about the interpretation of movies, it also dramatizes, with typical Allen humor, the many dimensions of film culture—from scholarship to dating—that take place outside the movie theater itself and that drive a seemingly necessary pleasure in thinking and talking, both casually and seriously, about film. For Alvy and many of us, going to the movies is a golden opportunity to converse, think, and disagree about film as a central part of our everyday lives.

The availability of movie types, the devices with which they can be viewed, and the venues within which they are shown have increased in the twenty-first century. More than ever before, different film cultures—groups of people defined by their particular tastes, habits, or environments—in the United States and around the world engage in an expanding variety of ways of seeing, understanding, and enjoying movies. We can watch the short silent films of Charlie Chaplin on a portable DVD player, see a televised release of the epic *Lawrence of Arabia* (1962) on consecutive Sunday and Monday nights, join lines of viewers to see a premiere of *Harry Potter and the Order of the Phoenix* (2007) on a large screen in an old movie palace [Figure 1.1], or start watching a downloaded feature film on an iPod during a subway ride. Our encounters with and responses to these films—how and why we select, like or dislike, understand or are challenged by them—are a product of the diverse attitudes, backgrounds, and interests that we, the viewers, bring to the movies.

1.1 *Harry Potter* **fans in line**. Experiencing the premiere of a movie becomes a singular social event with friends and other fans.

The Film Experience aims to introduce the movies from the points of view of these multifaceted personal and social experiences. The text demonstrates that viewers and viewing situations represent a dynamic plentitude of perspectives that need to be considered seriously and rigorously if those experiences are to be fully understood and appreciated.

KEY CONCEPTS

In this chapter, we explore

- what motivates us to study film and how this approach can be both important and enjoyable
- how a long history of film study supports and helps explain our interests in analyzing and thinking carefully about film
- how the film experience and studying that experience are not simply about movies themselves but reflect cultural and historical dynamics and issues central to our lives
- how film studies offers various points of view and points of emphasis that may concentrate on the technological, educational, political, aesthetic, or economic dimensions of film practice

Because the movies have been such an important part of everyday experience for more than a century, most of us already know a great deal about them. We know which best-seller will be adapted for the big screen, what new releases can be anticipated in the summer; we can identify a front-runner for a major award and which movie franchise a child's Halloween costume comes from. Such items of entertainment news are considered trivia, not the basis for academic insight;

nevertheless, as references that are more or less shared, they can form the basis for an inquiry into the role of movies in cultural life. For example, our opinions about casting attest to our understanding of common character functions; our curiosity about new technology is piqued by the degree of successful illusion created by new kinds of special effects; and our expectations of genre formulas (such as those found in a horror movie) may provoke an audience outburst when a character decides to explore a sudden noise. Studying movies includes formalizing such knowledge of narrative patterns, technology, and the classification of movie types in the context of movie histories and possible futures.

Students bring a lifetime of exposure to the movies to the classroom, where their knowledge can be built upon in systematic ways. In other words, the study of movies takes common knowledge and pleasure seriously while acknowledging that film culture is richer, more varied, and more challenging than most of us realize. It introduces economic, technological, and aesthetic models. It provides us with the vocabulary for approaching the film industry and its products while raising theoretical questions that stretch our common reactions. These questions include psychological ones about perception, comprehension, and identification; philosophical ones about the nature of the image and the viewer's understanding of it; social and historical ones about what meanings and messages are reinforced and excluded in a culture's films. Far from destroying our pleasure in the movies, studying them increases the ways we can enjoy them thoughtfully.

Why Film Studies?

Film studies is a critical discipline that promotes serious reflection on the movies. It is part of a rich and complex history that overlaps with critical work in many other fields, such as literary studies, philosophy, and art history. From the beginning, the movies have elicited widespread attention from scientists, politicians, and writers of many sorts, all attempting to make sense of the movies, their efforts to describe the world, their artistic value, or their place in society [Figure 1.2]. Even before the first public projection of films in 1895, scientists Étienne-Jules Marey and Eadweard Muybridge embarked on studies of human and animal motion that would lay the groundwork for the invention of cinema as we know it. In the early twentieth century, poet Vachel Lindsay and psychologist Hugo Münsterberg wrote essays and books on the power of movies to change social relationships and the way people perceive the world. By the 1930s, the Payne Fund Studies and later Margaret Farrand Thorp's *America at the Movies* (1939) offered sociological accounts of the patterns and impact of movies on young people and other social groups. Eventually, courses about the art of the movies began to appear in universities, even as elite cultural institutions like the Museum of Modern Art began to take the new art form seriously.

1.2 **Mon ciné**. Since the 1920s, *Mon ciné* and other movie magazines from around the world have promoted movies not just as entertainment, but also as objects of serious study with important sociological and aesthetic value.

1.3 **Cahiers du cinéma**. Appearing first in 1951, *Cahiers du cinéma* remains today one of the most influential journals of film criticism and theory.

After World War II, new kinds of filmmaking emerged in Europe along with passionate, well-informed criticism about the history and art of the movies, including Hollywood genre films **[Figure 1.3]**. Such criticism fueled film studies, which attained a firm foothold in North American universities by the 1970s. Today the study of film represents a wide spectrum of approaches and points of view, including studies of different historical periods or national cinemas, studies of how race and gender play a part in the kinds of movies made and audiences' responses to them, and studies of particular aesthetic or formal features of films. (See Chapter 13 for an in-depth account of central issues in film theory.) *The Film Experience* aims to introduce many of these approaches as part of a holistic perspective on the formal and cultural dynamics of watching movies. It does not privilege any one mode of film study over another but provides the critical tools and perspectives that will allow individuals to approach film study according to their different needs, aims, and interests.

Despite the rich past and present of film studies, many moviegoers question why we bother to *study* film, since most of us associate the movies with entertainment and relaxation. On closer examination, however, most of us would admit that the line between the pleasure of watching movies and the pleasure of studying them is not so clear-cut. With other so-called entertainments, we do, after all, enhance our enjoyment by increasing our knowledge of that entertainment form and by thinking more deeply about our experience of it. Whether we find pleasure in music, a sporting event, or fashion, our delight in these entertainments is made richer by honing our analytic thinking, furthering our depth of knowledge, and broadening our technical and formal vocabularies. Recognizing the subtle nuances of lighting in a particular movie scene is like recognizing significant chord changes in a Radiohead song, the defensive strategies in a college basketball game, or the ingenuity of a young fashion designer.

One sign of the popularization of a kind of film study today is the demand for DVD supplements—what one writer has called "film studies on a disk" **[Figure 1.4]**. Many of us now rent or purchase

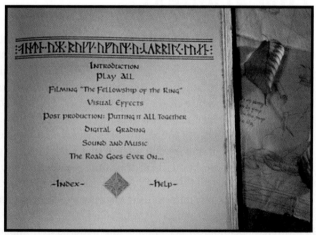

1.4 **Lord of the Rings DVD supplement index**. Expanded DVD formats and extras can now provide self-guided study tours of technical and even scholarly issues.

DVDs not just for the movies themselves but also for the extra features; these may include a film expert's commentary, a director's discussion of some of the technical decisions she made during filming, or historical background on the story behind the film. Some DVD editions address issues that are central to film studies: preservation of the filmic materials that give audiences access to the best possible print, inclusion of promotional materials such as trailers and posters that provide a glimpse of film culture at the time of the film's release, even scholarly commentary. In the *Treasures from American Film Archives* series, early films, hard-to-find gems, and restored classics have been preserved and contextualized with scholars' voiceovers, making accessible to consumers works that were previously only available to experts [Figure 1.5].

Another important reason for studying the movies is the undeniable prominence of film and media in the values and ideas that permeate our social and cultural lives [Figure 1.6]. Even in the context of a classroom, film study makes clear that the movies are not simply a mechanical art but a practice or experience that centrally engages numerous aspects of our daily lives. Public debates about violence in the movies, the crossover of movie stars into positions of political power, and the technological and economic shifts that have led to the vigorous marketing of new formats and playback devices are only some of the constant reminders of how movies spread throughout the fabric of our everyday experiences. To think seriously about film and to study it carefully is therefore to take charge of one of the most influential forces in our lives. Expanding our knowledge of the histories and kinds of film and their range of influences connects our everyday knowledge to wider sociocultural patterns and questions.

1.5 *Treasures from American Film Archives* **DVD collection**. Like the best film archives, some DVDs now recover, restore, and contextualize gems from film history.

1.6 *Star Wars* **marketing**. The movies surround and enter our everyday experiences.

The Film Experience: Film Spectators and Film Cultures

While certain critical approaches to the movies look first at the formal construction of films or the historical background of the production of a film, in *The Film Experience* we approach such questions through an emphasis on the dynamics of viewing movies: our approach foregrounds movie spectators and how they respond to films [Figures 1.7a–1.7d]. Some may study film to learn the nuts and bolts of how to make a film. If so, there is much to be found in *The Film Experience* that addresses these interests and needs. Yet, for most of us, our past, present, and future experience of the movies involves the way we watch them—how we enjoy and understand them, and how that viewing experience makes a meaningful impact on our lives. We may be interested in stories of producers, stars, and directors; but more often than not, that interest leads back to how we think about a particular movie, why it excites or disappoints us. The significance of the movies, in short, may not be primarily about how a movie is made but about how we, as viewers, respond to it.

1.7   The film experience describes the many ways we watch movies: (a) a drive-in theater, (b) a movie theater, (c) an open-air cinema, and (d) a suburban cineplex.

To situate film study in the context of viewers and spectators is to celebrate the activity and power of those viewers. Movie spectators are not passive audiences who simply absorb what they see on the screen. We respond actively to films, often in terms of our different ages, backgrounds, educational levels, and even geographical locations—all these factors make film viewing and film study a profoundly cultural experience.

Studying film should thus offer us many ways to "read" a film, or to interpret it. This is not to say that studying film allows a movie to mean anything one wants, which is why this book insists on a precise understanding of film forms, practices, and terminologies. Studying film through the cultural dynamics of viewing does, though, encourage viewers to tactically choose and explore different pathways into a film, pathways that reflect both individual and social concerns that emphasize the different ways movies can be meaningful.

Some of the pathways emphasized and explored here are the technological, the economic, the aesthetic, the historical, and the social. Some viewers and some films, for instance, may find importance in the technological or economic features of a film; others may highlight the aesthetic or formal innovations; and still others may emphasize a film's historical or social significance as its most meaningful quality [Figures 1.8a–1.8d]. The same film, in fact, could lead different moviegoers to any one of these (or other) critical pathways, and it is less a question of which is the most important way to engage the film than a question of which provides the most productive and rigorous encounter for that viewer.

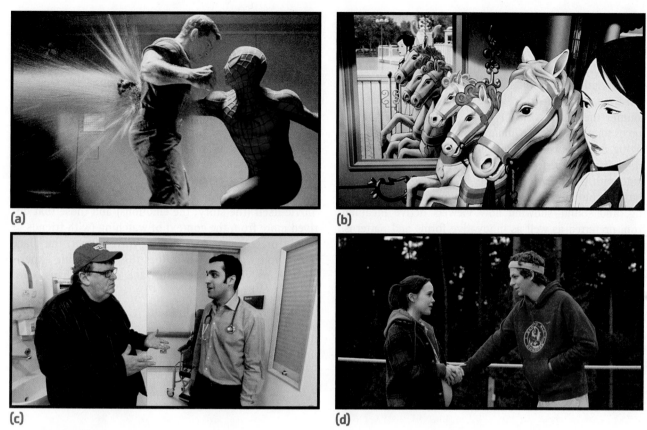

1.8 While different films draw different viewers, viewers also look at films in different ways: (a) *Spider-Man 3* (2007) may offer unique technological wonders and comic-book spectacle, (b) *Paprika* (2006) an unusually strange adventure in animated fantasy, (c) *Sicko* (2007) an oddly funny political awakening, and (d) *Juno* (2007) an especially contemporary and sassy coming-of-age story.

Certainly the artistic and commercial choices that shape a film—what a movie looks and sounds like—are the starting point of any film experience. But the experience culminates in the audiences, in all their diversity, who process those choices in ways that bring meaning to their lives. For example, the visual and audio complexities of *Citizen Kane* (1941) are technically the same for each person, but they provoke different responses in every viewer. Newspaper tycoon William Randolph Hearst reacted negatively to the film and claimed it to be an inflammatory portrait of himself, refusing to allow his papers to carry ads for it. He was far from a typical viewer, however. In recent decades, the film's consistent ranking at the top of critics' polls has served as the primary influence for the increased viewing of *Citizen Kane*, thus illustrating how viewers respond to both the movie and its perceived place in film history [Figure 1.9].

Throughout *The Film Experience*, we are attentive to the fact that readers of the text and viewers of films situated in the United States have wide exposure to mainstream Hollywood films that are studio produced. Meanwhile, there are audiences in countries outside the United States that see a mix of films produced in their own country and films from other cultures, as well as Hollywood films. Such significant differences among viewers and viewing communities exist within the United States as well. While film viewers don't make the movie, their varying cultural experiences of film bring it into a dynamic circulation that makes film meaningful.

1.9 *Citizen Kane* (1941). Even canonized films offer multiple entryways and the possibility of various responses for careful viewers.

Viewers' experiences with the movies are the starting point of this text's approach to the study of film. Patterns of distribution and exhibition that present film in particular ways create the social context in which audiences encounter the movies. Part 1 of the text introduces these forces together with the film production process itself, implying that the meanings of films do not all derive from filmmaking; they derive also from the ways viewers engage with films. Part 2 presents the four formal systems that structure films—mise-en-scène, cinematography, editing, and sound—showing how viewers derive meaning from preferred as well as innovative forms and patterns. Part 3 introduces and analyzes the primary modes through which viewers' encounters with the movies are shaped: through narrative, genre, and nonfiction and experimental forms. Multiple ways that the history of film

can be approached are described in Part 4, showing that the viewer's perspective is key even when analyzing the significance of historical narratives. Finally, Part 5 centers on the viewer's perspective in its presentation of tools for approaching film theory and writing about films.

Activity

Write a journal entry describing a movie-going or movie-watching experience that was important to your childhood. Reflect on elements that were specific to the movie itself (the story; the emotions) and those that derived more from the context of watching (with friends or family present; as a holiday or travel ritual; the place where you watched). How does this memorable experience shape your movie tastes and even, perhaps, your sense of self today?

chapter

2

Preparing Viewers and Views

Production, Distribution, Promotion, and Exhibition

In the year 2000, *Crouching Tiger, Hidden Dragon* became the highest-grossing foreign-language film in U.S. history, suggesting that in the new millennium the film experience would be characterized by a new emphasis on the global. Made by Taiwan-born director Ang Lee, *Crouching Tiger, Hidden Dragon* belongs to the *wuxia*, or martial arts, genre widely popular in Asia, and it features popular Chinese stars who all spoke the film's Mandarin dialect with a range of different accents. But the film would not have been so successful in the United States had it not drawn on other factors: a subculture of Hong Kong film and *wuxia* fans including, but by no means limited to, Asian Americans; an art-house audience built up by Lee's previous films that were U.S.-based and produced by the independent company Good Machine; admirers of the classical cellist Yo Yo Ma, who created the score; and, perhaps most important, the backing of multinational media giants Columbia and Sony, which gave the film a major release on par with any Hollywood blockbuster. In short, the global film experience today is economic as well as aesthetic and linguistic; the production, release, and reception of a film are part of an integrated cycle with many dimensions. Since the film's theatrical release in the United States, it has achieved international success both in theaters and on DVD. The ambiguous last image of *Crouching Tiger, Hidden Dragon,* in which the heroine leaps into the clouds, might prompt a viewer to see the film again. Read another way, this open-endedness is indicative of the many ways films are open to interactions with viewers across space and time.

15

What draws us to a film? What makes us enjoy or not enjoy it? How do movies attract us both emotionally and intellectually? What exactly is *film culture*—the social and historical environment permeated with certain ideas, values, and expectations about movies? And how does film culture prepare us for different ways of seeing a film before we actually watch it? Film culture comprises the varied practices associated with moviemaking as well as viewing or spectatorship. These practices include calculated, studio-launched publicity campaigns, ads and trailers on the Internet, celebrity gossip, and activities as benign and habitual as going to the movies with friends on weekends. In this chapter, we explore how the cultural parameters of our experience of a movie—that is, where and when we see a movie—can shape our responses, enjoyment, and understanding of it as much as the production of the film itself. Today, more than ever before, the film experience involves numerous viewing technologies (HDTV, iPods), changing social environments (from IMAX to home theaters), and multiple cultural activities (reading about films, directors, and stars, or consuming video games or special DVD editions connected to a film franchise). These significantly different ways of seeing a film lead to potentially different ways of understanding it and how it was made.

KEY CONCEPTS

In this chapter, we look carefully at

- how our experience of movies and our taste for certain films have both personal and public dimensions
- how changing viewing technologies have affected our overall film experience
- how the stages of filmmaking, from preproduction to postproduction, inform what we see on the screen
- how the mechanisms of film distribution determine what we see
- how film promotion attempts to predispose us to see films in certain ways
- how film exhibition—whether in cineplexes, at film festivals, or on television or a personal computer—can structure our response to films
- how, throughout these different commercial and industrial processes, cultural and social forces determine the many different ways movies are positioned before us

The Many Ways of Viewing Films

As we have noted, the technological and social variations in viewing movies are many. The multitude of situations in which we view film emphasizes how our engagement with a movie goes beyond determining whether we like or dislike it. As *active viewers*, our involvement is far more energetic and dynamic. Not only do we embrace film for its narrative, performances, and message, but we also consider it in specific cultural, social, and historical contexts. In the wake of rapid transformations in the technology of exhibition, we must ask ourselves: Can we determine what an authentic or authorized experience of a film should be, or which way of seeing a movie should be

privileged? How might these different venues and formats for watching a movie change our experience of it? To what extent are our experiences of movies today defined and redefined by changing cultural contexts and environments?

Films from a wide range of places and moments in cinema history focus on the rich and varied dynamics of moviegoers, their passions, and their often unpredictable activities. In Buster Keaton's *Sherlock, Jr.* (1924), for instance, a bumbling projectionist walks into the movie he is showing transformed into a Sherlock Holmes–like detective. In Belgian filmmaker Chantal Akerman's *Meetings with Anna* (1978), a young woman filmmaker's travels with her recent movie become a complex and tangled voyage into herself and her society. In Spike Lee's bitter comedy *Bamboozled* (2000), racist **stereotypes** found in movies of the past return and, disturbingly, still make audiences laugh [**Figure 2.1**]. These three examples— a silent film highlighting the magic of the movies, a European art film dramatizing the longing for personal connections, and an American **independent film** satirizing the power of movies to manipulate race—together suggest the varied and dynamic culture of viewers and their interactions with the movies. This variety and nuance lies at the heart of the drama that is the film experience.

2.1 *Bamboozled* (2000). The uncomfortable histories of racist stereotypes and viewers' reactions to them are interrogated in Spike Lee's controversial film.

Private and Public Tastes

Movies are always both a private and a public affair. Since the beginning of film history, the power of movies has derived in part from viewers' personal and sometimes idiosyncratic responses to a movie and in part from the social and cultural contexts that surround their experience of that film. Early viewers of the Lumière brothers' *Train Arriving at a Station* (1894) were rumored to have fled their seats to avoid the train's oncoming rush; new interpretations of such first-encounter stories suggest that viewers attended the screening precisely for the visceral entertainment [**Figure 2.2**]. In a more contemporary example, some individuals reacted on a personal level to *Crouching Tiger, Hidden Dragon* (2000), breathlessly absorbed in the balletic fights and intrigued by the feminist implications of the film's powerful female warriors [**Figure 2.3**]. Other viewers dismissed the film because they found *Crouching Tiger* to be a watered-down, Americanized version of Hong Kong martial arts movies, a reaction that drew on the more contextual factors of genre conventions.

Thus our individual reactions to films have public and social dimensions. When *Crouching Tiger, Hidden Dragon* was released, many viewers were predisposed to appreciate it because of critics' reviews and word-of-mouth praise that followed the

▶ **VIEWING CUE**

Examine your tastes in movies by jotting down your thoughts in a journal entry. What kind of films do you enjoy? Why?

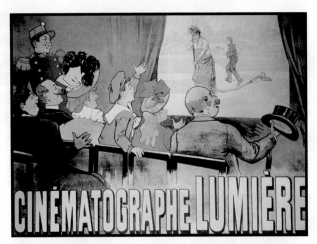

2.2   Poster for public screening of early films by the Lumière brothers. The audience's reaction is as important an advertisement for the novelty as is the film onscreen, which represents their short comic sketch, *L'Arroseur arrosé* (*The Waterer Watered*, 1895).

2.3   *Crouching Tiger, Hidden Dragon* (2000). Viewers' perceptions of this film's female fighters will vary depending on their degree of familiarity with genre conventions, among other factors.

film's appearances at the Cannes and New York film festivals. As the film continued to play, its Academy Award nominations and later wins for cinematography and score also influenced audiences' reactions to it. The social context—watching the film on a large theater screen, thereby experiencing the visual effects as much more spectacular—encouraged the energetic cheers of the audience and helped shape the overall film experience. For some, *Crouching Tiger* became like a sporting event in which viewers fed off the enthusiasm of the entire audience and the larger social situation. Press coverage that connected the film to the increased global success of Asian action films intrigued new audiences, drew on an extensive subcultural fan base, and mediated between art-house and genre-oriented filmgoers.

At the intersection of these personal and public experiences, each of us has developed different tastes—cultural, emotional, intellectual, and social preferences or interests—that influence our expectations and lead us to like or dislike particular movies. Some tastes vary little from person to person; most people prefer good characters to bad ones and justice served to justice foiled. Yet many tastes are unique products of our experiential circumstances or experiential histories. *Experiential circumstances* are the material conditions that define our identity at a certain time and in a certain place, such as our age, gender, race, socioeconomic background, and the part of the country or world in which we live. *Experiential histories,* such as our education, relationships, travels, and even the other films we have seen, are the personal and social encounters through which we have developed our identities over time. These encounters help determine individual tastes and taste cultures. For example, American college students who are fans of television news parodies and of Wes Anderson's debut film *Rushmore* (1998) may find themselves drawn to his offbeat independent film *Life Aquatic with Steve Zissou* (2004). A World War II veteran, because of his experiential history, might have a particular taste for WWII films, ranging from such sentimental favorites as *Mrs. Miniver* (1942) to the harder-hitting dramas *The Longest Day* (1962) and *Flags of Our Fathers* (2006) [**Figure 2.4**]. African American audiences interested in the historical significance of Motown music or familiar with the original Broadway musical or the stars of the big-screen **adaptation** may be particularly attracted to *Dreamgirls* (2006) [**Figure 2.5**]. A culture's taste in films can also be tied to historical events, such as the Watergate scandal depicted in *Nixon* (1995) or the September 11 terrorist attacks on the United States addressed in Michael Moore's *Fahrenheit 9/11* (2004).

2.4   *Flags of Our Fathers* (2006). World War II remains a fascinating subject for many American viewers. In the same year, Clint Eastwood explored the period in this film and in *Letters from Iwo Jima* (2006).

2.5   *Dreamgirls* (2006). Musicals often draw their fan base from audiences familiar with the Broadway productions from which they are adapted or the singers featured in the cast.

Identification

At the movies, our tastes and responses relate indirectly to two viewing activities that interact when we watch a film: identification and cognition. Clearly, the movies we like are not only the ones we can personally identify with or fully understand. Simultaneous activities of identification and cognition also provide a framework that can shape our tastes. Commonly associated with our emotional responses, *identification* at the movies suggests a complex process by which we empathize with, project onto, or participate in a place, an action, or a character—whether separately or as these elements interact. Both adolescent and adult viewers can respond empathetically to the portrayal of the social electricity and physical awkwardness of teenage sexuality in *American Graffiti* (1973) [Figure 2.6], *The Breakfast Club* (1985), or *Superbad* (2007), though different generations might resonate more to the music of one movie or the fashions of the other, and male viewers are likely to relate more easily—or uneasily—to the high school boys at the center of *Superbad* than are female viewers [Figure 2.7]. Each of us may identify with different minor characters (such as the nerd Brian and the prom queen Claire in *The Breakfast Club*), but the success of a film often depends on eliciting audience identification with one or two of the main characters (such as Curt and Steve, the two boys who are about to leave for college in *American Graffiti*). While watching *An American in Paris* (1951), one viewer may instantly participate in the carefree excitement of the opening scenes by identifying with the street life of the artistic Montmartre neighborhood [Figure 2.8] where she had lived as a college student; another viewer who has never been to Paris may participate vicariously in that romantic setting because the film so effectively re-creates an atmosphere with which he can identify, in part through exposure to similar portrayals.

Cognition

Identifying with a movie is largely an emotional experience. Like dreams, film can relate to our basic urges, desires, and memories. However, our pleasure in watching movies derives not just from our emotional responses but also from our rational reactions. These latter responses can be described as forms of comprehension, or *cognition*. In other words, watching a movie is both an emotional experience that involves identifying through processes of participation and empathy and a cognitive process that involves the intellectual activities of comparison and comprehension. We bring assumptions about a given location or setting to most films, we expect events to change or progress in a certain way, and we measure characters against similar characters encountered elsewhere. Engaged by our emotional identification with the

2.6   *American Graffiti* (1973). Viewers may empathize with adolescent awkwardness despite—or because of—period settings.

VIEWING CUE

How do your personal circumstances shape your tastes in movies? Describe how your tastes have changed over the years and what you believe accounts for those changes.

VIEWING CUE

What is your understanding of films? Do you know about films from a particular country or era, particular genres, soundtracks, stars, or literary sources?

2.7   *Superbad* (2007). Gender is an important, though not necessarily predictable, aspect of viewer identification.

2.8   *An American in Paris* (1951). The setting of a film may be a source of identification.

2.9 *Gladiator* (2000). Watching this epic may combine historical knowledge, narrative recognition, and visceral response.

2.10 *The Bridges of Madison County* (1995). Clint Eastwood's role portrays a different sort of masculinity than usually associated with his persona as a star.

▶ **VIEWING CUE**

Does the movie rely on easily understood actions and characters? If not, how do you make sense of what you see?

terrors or triumphs of Russell Crowe's character in *Gladiator* (2000), for example, we also find ourselves engaged cognitively with other aspects of the film. We recognize and distinguish the Rome in the movie through particular visual **cues**—the Coliseum and other Roman monuments—known perhaps from studies in world history, pictures, or other movies. We expect we will know who will win the battles and fights because of what we've learned about such skirmishes, but even that knowledge won't necessarily prepare us for the extreme and graphic violence depicted in the film [**Figure 2.9**]. Because of other experiences, we arrive at the film with certain assumptions about Roman tyrants and heroes, and we appreciate and understand characters like the emperor Commodus or the gladiator Maximus as they successfully balance our expectations with surprises.

What we like or dislike at the movies can often relate to what we understand as part of the evolving processes of identification and cognition. Even as we are drawn to and bond with places, actions, and characters in films, we must sometimes reconsider how those ways of identifying have (or could be) developed and changed by our intellectual development. Indeed, this process of cognitive realignment and reconsideration determines to a large degree our reaction to a movie. In *The Bridges of Madison County* (1995), for example, Clint Eastwood, best known for playing physically tough and intimidating characters, plays a reflective and sensitive lover, Robert Kincaid [**Figure 2.10**]. Viewers familiar with Eastwood's other roles who expect to see the same type of character played out in *The Bridges of Madison County* must reconsider what had attracted them to that star, as well as assess how those expectations have been complicated and are now challenging their understanding of *The Bridges of Madison County*. Does this shift suggest that the film is about a human depth discovered within older masculinity or about the maturing of that masculinity through the encounter with an equally strong woman (Meryl Streep as Francesca Johnson)? Whether we are able to engage in that process and find the realignment convincing will lay the foundation for our response to the movie.

The Technologies of Viewing Films

Technology itself draws attention to historical, cultural, and contextual differences in experiencing a film. Today watching movies on a television screen is the norm, and for many of us, watching on a personal computer or a portable device has become even more typical. However, the technological difference between watching a film on a public movie screen and on a private medium significantly alters the experience. Differences in the sound and image quality of a film, for instance, indicate a dramatic (though narrowing) technological gap between movies exhibited in a theater and those seen on a television or computer monitor. Increasingly, the technical language for speaking about sound and image quality has entered into common parlance, as manufacturers have recently sought to introduce new technologies to eager consumers. However, such technical comparisons do not capture the qualitative differences between public and home viewing and the differences be-tween a medium produced using light and celluloid and its consumption through electronic means.

Film Gauge

Early in film history (by 1909), the width of the strip of film used for filming and exhibiting movies was stan-dardized as 35mm. This **film gauge** is still dominant for theatrical exhibition worldwide. Other common gauges

2.11 *Lawrence of Arabia* (1962). The film's 70mm widescreen format is suited to panoramic desert scenes and military maneuvers.

are 16mm, used with smaller, lighter cameras and favored for newsreels, docu-mentaries, experimental, independent, and amateur films; and 70mm, used for in-creased visual impact in films ranging from *Oklahoma!* (1955), which introduced the patented Todd-AO 70mm format, to the widescreen epic *Lawrence of Arabia* (1962) [**Figure 2.11**]. Since its introduction in the 1970s, IMAX technology, which uses a horizontal variant of 70mm film, has provided the most spectacular exhi-bition format.

Film formats used for theatrical exhibition offer a high-quality picture. For decades, viewers of films broadcast on television saw a significantly inferior version of the original cinematic image; moreover, such broadcasts would be interrupted by television commercials and were often edited to accommodate such interruptions. The advent of HDTV (high-definition television) and DVD (digital video disc) are part of an attempt to close the gap between the film experience in the theater and the one available at home. Such technologies improve the quality of the image appre-ciably by creating higher resolutions of digital reproduction. Discussions of the dif-ference between seeing a movie in a theater and watching it at home have become an aspect of film culture and the ever-altering film experience as individuals con-tinue to consume new viewing technologies at an unprecedented rate.

Aspect Ratio

A related dimension of the viewing experience is the size and shape of the image onscreen. The size of the screen is relative to the type of movie theater—whether the converted storefront of cinema's early days, the vast movie palace of the 1920s, the drive-in of the 1950s, or the multiplex of the 1980s. The shape of the screen is meas-ured by the ratio of width to height, denoted by the term **aspect ratio**. Borrowing from painting and classical aesthetics that valued symmetry and balance, the rec-tangular proportions of the movie image were standardized at a ratio of 1.37:1 by the Academy of Motion Picture Arts and Sciences in 1932. These dimensions are known as **academy ratio**, and they dominated movie production until 1952.

Since the 1950s, movie screens and television have developed changing aspect ratios. From the 1930s television prototypes until the extensive marketing of widescreen digital models in the late 1990s, television monitors used a 1.33:1 (or 4.3) ratio, which closely approximates the movie industry standard. Since the 1950s, how-ever, movies themselves have commonly used **widescreen ratios** (1.85:1 or 2.35:1)—initially to compete with television by providing a more spectacular viewing experience. As a consequence, movies converted for standard television viewing are subjected to a **"pan-and-scan" process** to allow the film image to fit the television format: with this process, a computer-controlled scanner determines the most impor-tant action in the image and then crops peripheral action and space so that the cen-tral action is reproduced as one image or is perhaps re-edited to two images. (**Fullscreen** versions of widescreen films on video and DVD are similarly produced.) With the rise of the home video market, **letterbox** formats that imitate the widescreen formats of theatrical projection became regular options, appealing particularly to

2.12 *Artaud Double Bill*
(2007). With an image from *The
Passion of Jeanne d'Arc* (1929) on
screen and captured on a cell phone,
Atom Egoyan's short film (a contribution
to the Cannes Film Festival project *To
Each His Own Cinema*) acknowledges
the many ways today's viewers may
encounter even classical film images.

cinephiles, or film connoisseurs. But it was not until digital televisions finally adapted the shape of the screen to widescreen presentation that the specialized knowledge of different aspect ratios became more culturally pervasive, as did increased expertise in sound technology–a corollary to individuals' desire to achieve a full "home theater" experience. DVD editions of theatrical blockbusters rich in special effects, elaborate sound mixes, and spectacular big-screen images warrant this movement. But does this mean that the public dimension of theatrical exhibition will eventually disappear? How will this change affect film culture and the film experience?

New Media and Media Convergence

In contrast to viewing technologies that attempt to imitate the big-screen experience are those that try to maximize (sometimes by literally minimizing) the uniquely personal encounter with the film image, such as the individual screens of portable media players, iPods, and personal computers. In such cases, consumers have adapted quickly to **media convergence [Figure 2.12]**, the process by which formerly distinct media (such as cinema, television, the Internet, and video games) and viewing platforms (such as television, computers, and cell phones) become commercially, technologically, and culturally interdependent. With the rapid introduction of new viewing technologies, the issues associated with the differences among film, television, and digital technologies have become more complex and variable.

Sometimes, viewing is a multiplatform process: viewers may learn and spread the word about a new film release through **viral marketing**–which describes any process of advertising that relies on social networks such as word of mouth or Internet links–and play an online game set in the film's fictional world on the film's Web site, all before attending the movie in a theater. A viewer who enjoys the film and its soundtrack might download a ring tone for her cell phone and place the title in her Netflix queue in anticipation of its release on DVD months later. Increasingly, television programs and feature-length films can be digitally downloaded and exported to a television–or home theater–for viewing. The distinctions between viewing technologies are more easily bridged even as the boundaries of media texts become less clearly drawn.

Producing Views: How Films Are Made

Film production is, quite literally, about the process of "producing views"–as in "things to look at." The aim at each step of film production is to create an artistic and/or commercial product that will engage, please, or provoke viewers. In short, film **production** is a multi-layered activity in which industry, art, technology, and imagination entwine. It describes the different stages–from the financing and scripting of a film to its final edit and, fittingly, the addition of production **credits**–that contribute to the construction of a movie. Movies are quintessentially a collaborative art and business; making a movie is a complex, lengthy, and often expensive process that involves numerous individuals with a wide range of tasks and responsibilities. Although production may not seem a central part of our film experiences as viewers, the making of a film anticipates an audience of one sort or another and implies a certain kind of viewer. Does the film highlight the work of the director or the screenwriter, the cinematographer or the composer of the musical score? Does the answer determine our perspective on the film? Understanding contemporary commercial filmmaking in its many dimensions contributes to a more fully integrated film experience. Later chapters on film form build on these brief accounts of the filmmaking process.

Preproduction

Although the term "production" is used (often in distinction from **distribution** and *exhibition*) to define the entire process of making a film, a great deal happens—and often a long time passes—before a film begins to be shot. **Preproduction** designates the phase when a project is in development. At this stage, movies typically develop between the efforts of the screenwriter and the producer, often in the context of a studio or an independent production company. Frequently with the director's participation, these individuals work together to conceive and continually refine an idea for a film in order to realize it onscreen.

Screenwriters

A **screenwriter** or scriptwriter is often the individual who generates the idea for a film, either as an original concept or as an adaptation of a story, novel, or historical or current event. The writer presents that early concept or material in a **treatment**, a short prose description of the action and major characters of the story. The treatment is then gradually revised as several versions of a complete **screenplay**, from the *temporary screenplay* submitted by the screenwriter to the *final shooting script* that details exact scenes and camera setups. As these different scripts evolve, one writer may be responsible for every version, or different writers may be employed at each stage, resulting in minor and sometimes major changes along the way. Even with a finished and approved script, an uncredited **script doctor** may be called in to do rewrites. From *Sunset Boulevard* (1950), about a struggling screenwriter trapped in the mansion of a fading silent-film star, to *Adaptation* (2002), about (fictional) screenwriter Charlie Kaufman's torturous attempt to adapt Susan Orlean's book *The Orchid Thief*, numerous films have focused on screenwriters [Figure 2.13]. One reason may be the dramatic shifts and instabilities in the process of moving from a concept to a completed screenplay to a produced film, a process that highlights the initial dream and attendant difficulties of trying to communicate with an audience.

Producers and Studios

The key individuals in charge of movie production and finances are the film's producers. A **producer** oversees all of the different operations in putting a film together. His-

torically this role has changed regularly: at times, a producer may be fully involved with each step of film production from the selection and development of a script to the creation of an advertisement campaign for the finished film; at other times, a producer may be an almost invisible partner who is responsible principally for the financing of a movie.

During the heyday of the Hollywood studio system in the 1930s (see pp. 334–335), producers were extremely powerful studio personnel. MGM was identified with the creative vision of such powerful producers as Irving B. Thalberg, who worked closely with studio mogul Louis B. Mayer. After leaving MGM to found his own studio, producer David O. Selznick controlled all stages of production beginning with the identification of the

2.13 *Adaptation* (2002). As its title indicates, screenwriting is the very topic of this inventive film, in which Charlie Kaufman is both a character and the credited writer.

2.14 **James Schamus and Ang Lee**. Ang Lee's best-director Oscar for *Brokeback Mountain* (2006) was the fruit of a long collaboration with producer James Schamus.

2.15 *Tarnation* (2003). As Jonathan Caouette's debut film shows, even an ultra-low-budget independent production can be released theatrically if it lands an adequate distribution deal.

primary material for the film (for instance, a "property" such as the best-seller *Gone with the Wind*, purchased before the book was published). He supervised every aspect of the 1939 film, even changing directors during production—a process documented in his famous "memos." With the rise of the independent film movement in the 1990s, independent producers have worked to facilitate the creative freedom of the writer and director, arranging the financing for the film as well as seeing the film through casting, hiring a crew, scheduling, shooting, **postproduction**, and distribution sales. For example, producer James Schamus first worked with Ang Lee on the independent film *Eat Drink Man Woman* (1994) and co-wrote the screenplays of *Sense and Sensibility* (1995), *Crouching Tiger, Hidden Dragon,* and *Lust, Caution* (2007). As vice president of Focus Features (a specialty division of Universal), Schamus shepherded Lee's *Brokeback Mountain* (2006) through all stages of production [**Figure 2.14**]. Within all such systems, there are finer distinctions among the tasks and roles of producers: an **executive producer** may be connected to a film primarily in name, playing a role in financing or facilitating a film deal and having little creative or technical involvement, while a co-producer credit may designate an executive with a particular production company partnering in the movie. The **line producer** is in charge of the daily business of tracking costs and maintaining the production schedule of a film; and a **unit production manager** is responsible for reporting and managing the details of receipts and purchases.

The budget of a film, whether big or miniscule, is handled by the producers. In budgeting, **above-the-line expenses** are the initial costs of contracting the major personnel, such as directors and stars, as well as administrative and organizational expenses in setting up a film production. **Below-the-line expenses** are the technical and material costs—costumes, sets, transportation, and so on—involved in the actual making of a film. *Production values* is an evaluative term about the quality of the film images and sounds that reflects the extent of these two expenses; in both subtle and not-so-subtle ways, production values often shape viewers' expectations about a film. High production values suggest a more spectacular or more professionally made movie. Low production values do not necessarily mean a poorly made film. In both cases, we need to adjust our expectations to the style associated with the budgeting.

Financing Film Production: The Industry and the Independents

Of the many screenplays written and the many treatments sold, few in fact become movies, as movies are generally made to generate money. Certainly some films are made primarily as personal or artistic expressions. For instance, Jonathan Caouette's *Tarnation* (2003) recounts the filmmaker's childhood and adolescence through a collage of snapshots, Super-8 footage, answering machine messages, video diaries, and home movies [**Figure. 2.15**]. It does not use a conventional screenplay, and it was edited on a home computer with an alleged production budget of about $200. Subsequently producers came on board, and their financial support enabled the production of a theatrical release print and screening at the Sundance Film Festival. The publicity at the festival led to landing a distributor, limited theatrical exhibition, and considerable critical attention. Accrued costs for making and distributing a larger, mainstream movie like *The Good Shepherd* (2006, starring Matt Damon and Angelina Jolie) came to more than $100 million—a significant investment that assumed a significant financial return. Concomitant with the conception of a film, therefore, is a plan to find a large enough audience to return that investment and, ideally, a profit.

2.16 *Freedom Writers* (2006). Financing a modest film is much easier with the commitment of a major star; two-time Oscar-winner Hilary Swank led a cast of unknowns in this drama based on the writings of youth following the 1992 Los Angeles riots.

Financing and managing production expenses is a critical ingredient in making a movie. Traditionally studios and producers have worked with banks or large financial institutions to acquire this financing, and the term "bankable" has emerged as a way of indicating that a film has the necessary ingredients—a famous star or well-known literary source—to make that investment worth the risk. In recent years, financing a film has sometimes been a more personal or creative process. Kevin Smith made *Clerks* (1994) by charging expenses to various credit cards. *Freedom Writers* (2006) took six years to finance and produce, an accomplishment sustained mainly through the efforts and commitment of the film's star, Hilary Swank [**Figure 2.16**]. Indeed, as much as the rise of the so-called independent film since 1990 has to do with innovations in cinematic style, it has perhaps just as much to do with financing strategies; that is, instead of relying on a single source such as a bank or a studio, independent filmmaking relies on organized groups of individual investors or pre-sales of distribution or broadcast rights in different markets.

Casting Directors, Agents, and Super Agents

With the increasing costs of films and the necessity of attracting money with a bankable project, the roles of casting directors and agents have become more important. **Casting directors,** who identify the actors who would work best in particular scripted roles, emerged during the advent of the star system around 1910. It was around this time when the exceedingly popular "Biograph Girl," Florence Lawrence, first demanded to be named and given a screen credit. Casting directors have since become bigger and more widely credited players in determining the look and scale of films. Representing actors, directors, writers, and other major individuals in a film production, **agents** negotiate with casting directors and producers and enlist different personnel for a movie. The significance and power of the agent extends back at least to the 1930s, when talent agent Lew Wasserman, working as a publicist for the Music Corporation of America (MCA), began to create independent, multiple-movie deals for Bette Davis, Errol Flynn, James Stewart, and many others. By the mid-1950s, Wasserman and others had established a **package-unit approach** to film production whereby the agent, producer, and casting director determine a script, stars, and other major personnel as a key first step in a major production, establishing the production model that would dominate after the demise of the traditional studio system. By the mid-1970s, so-called super agents would sometimes predetermine a package of stars and other personnel from which the film must be constructed. Michael Ovitz is perhaps the most famous of these; he co-founded the powerful Creative Artist Association (CAA) in 1975, where he represented Tom Cruise and Barbra Streisand, and in 1995 was named president of the Walt Disney Company, serving for only fourteen months.

2.17   *Henry V* (1944). The film's sets move from onstage at the Globe Theatre to more realistic ship sets.

Locations, Production Design, Sets, and Costumes

From the beginning of the twentieth century through the rise of contemporary documentary filmmaking, **location scouting** has determined places that provide the most suitable environment for different movie scenes. The simple pragmatics of a location may be one factor: Does the place fit the requirements of the script? How expensive would it be to film on this location? Since the interaction between a character and the physical location of the action is often a central dimension of a film, choosing the correct physical location is critical. Although many films rely on constructed sets that re-create a specific place, the power of movie realism has demanded the use of actual locations to invigorate a scene. Few films more explicitly demonstrate the magic of movie set design than Laurence Olivier's *Henry V* (1944), where the drama shifts from the stage of Shakespeare's Globe Theatre to the comparatively realistic sets of ships leaving for war in France. In recent decades, the cinematic task of re-creating real-seeming environments has shifted to computer-graphics technicians. These technicians design the models to be digitally transferred onto film, becoming, in a sense, a new kind of location scout.

By 1915, **art directors**, those individuals responsible for supervising the conception and construction of movie sets in collaboration with **set designers**, became an integral and important part of filmmaking—although in those early years, they were "technical directors" doing "interior decoration" [**Figure 2.17**]. Today the term **production designer** is widely used for the person in charge of the film's overall look. As the movie business expanded through the 1930s, the role of **costume designers**, those who plan and prepare how actors will be dressed for parts, greatly increased. Costume designers such as Adrian ensured the splendor, the suitability, and sometimes the historical accuracy of their characters' appearance, and their work was often as influential on clothing trends as that of fashion designers [**Figure 2.18**]. Indeed, for those films in which costumes and settings are central to the story—films set in fantasy worlds or historical eras, such as *Pan's Labyrinth* (2006), which uses both kinds of settings—one could argue that the achievement of the film becomes inseparable from the decisions about the art and costume design. In the end, successful films aim to integrate all levels of the design from the sets to the costumes, as in Zhang Yimou's *Curse of the Golden Flower* (2006), an operatic tale of intrigue, spectacle, and deceit set in tenth-century China [**Figure 2.19**].

2.18   **Greta Garbo, George Cukor, and Adrian on the set of *Camille*** (1936). Costume designer Adrian contributed significantly to the sumptuous style of MGM films of the 1930s and 1940s.

Production

Most mythologized of all phases of movie making is production itself—the weeks or months of actual shooting, on set or on location, known as a **film shoot**. Countless films, from *The Bad and the Beautiful* (1952) to *Beware of a Holy Whore* (1971), *Irma Vep* (1996), and *Sex Is Comedy* (2002), dramatize inspired or fraught interactions among cast, crew, and the person in charge of it all, the director [**Figure 2.20**]. The reality of production varies greatly with the scale of the film and its budget; but the director, who has been involved in all of the creative phases of preproduction, must now work closely with the actors and production personnel—most notably, the camera units headed by the cinematographer—to realize a collaborative vision.

The Director

Although every film will afford a director a different degree of control, the **director** has been commonly regarded as the chief creative presence or the primary manager in film production, responsible for and overseeing virtually all the work of making a movie—from the placement of the actors to the position of the camera and the selection of which images appear in the finished film. The earliest films of the twentieth century involved very few people in the process of shooting a film, with the assumption that the cameraman was the de facto director. By 1907, however, a division of labor separated production roles, placing the director in charge of all others on the film set.

Directors have different methods and degrees of involvement. Alfred Hitchcock claimed he never needed to see the action through the camera viewfinder since his script directions were so precise that there would be only one way to compose the shot; others are comfortable relinquishing important decisions to their assistant director (A.D.), cinematographer, or sound designer; still others, like Woody Allen, assume multiple roles (from screenwriter to actor and editor) in addition to that of director [**Figures 2.21 and 2.22**]. In Hollywood during the studio era, directors' visions were often subordinated to "house style" or a producer's vision; yet directors worked so consistently, and honed their craft with such skilled personnel, that critics have claimed to detect a given director's "signature" style across routine assignments, elevating directors like Howard Hawks and Nicholas Ray to the status of **auteurs** (directors considered "authors" of their films). Today a company backing a film will choose or approve a director for projects that seem to fit with his or her skills and talents; for example, Chris Columbus's success with family films like *Home Alone* (1990)

2.19 *Curse of the Golden Flower* (2006). Spectacular use of color and opulent costume and set design characterize this period epic.

2.20 *Irma Vep* (1996). Maggie Cheung stars in a film about making a film—starring Maggie Cheung.

2.21 **Woody Allen**. Allen stands behind the camera as director.

2.22 *Manhattan Murder Mystery* (1993). Woody Allen in front of the camera in an acting role.

2.23   *Zodiac* (2007). Movie actors' performances must be constructed in conjunction with camera work, editing, and elements of mise-en-scène.

2.24   *The Departed* (2006). Cinematographer Michael Ballhaus suggests interpretations of the characters' motives through shot setup.

led to his involvement with the Harry Potter franchise. Because of the control and assumed authority of the director, contemporary viewers often look for stylistic and thematic consistencies in films by the same director, and filmmakers like Quentin Tarantino have become celebrities.

The Cast, Cinematographer, and Other Production Personnel

The director works with the actors to bring out the desired performance, and of course these collaborations vary greatly. Mike Leigh is known for a long improvisational rehearsal period with his ensemble cast, from which his scripts and particular actors' roles emerge. David Fincher's exacting directorial style requires scores of **takes**, a grueling experience for *Zodiac* (2007) actors Jake Gyllenhaal and Robert Downey Jr. [**Figure 2.23**]. **Blocking**, or the planning of actors' movements in relation to each other, the camera, and the set, may take precedence over the director's concern for the actors' emotional preparation. Because films are shot out of order and in a variety of shot scales, a film actor's performance must be delivered in bits and pieces. Some actors prepare a technical performance; others rely on the director's prompting or other, more spontaneous inspiration.

The **cinematographer**, also known as the director of photography or D.P., selects the cameras, film stock, lighting, and lenses to be used as well as the camera setup or position. In consultation with the director, the cinematographer determines how the action will be shot, the images composed, and, later, the kind of exposure needed to print the takes. The cinematographer oversees a **camera operator** and other camera and lighting crew. Many films may owe more to the cinematographer than to any other individual in the production: the scintillating *Day of Heaven* (1978) no doubt profits as much from the eye of cinematographer Nestor Almendros as from the direction of Terrence Malick; and the consistently stunning work of cinematographer Michael Ballhaus, from R. W. Fassbinder's *The Marriage of Maria Braun* (1979) to Martin Scorsese's *The Departed* (2006), displays the artistic singularity and vision that are usually assigned to film directors [**Figure 2.24**].

Also on set are many other personnel, from the **production sound mixer** and other sound crew including the boom operator, to the **grips** who install lighting and dollies, to the special effects coordinator, scenic, hair, and make-up artists, to catering staff. A production coordinator helps this complex operation to run smoothly. A film shoot is an intense, concentrated effort in which the contributions of visionary artists and professional crew mesh with the imperatives to keep on schedule and remain within budget.

Postproduction

Some of the most important aspects of the finished film, including editing, sound, and visual effects, are achieved after **principal photography** is completed and production is over. How definitive or efficient the process is depends on many factors—a documentary may be constructed almost entirely during this phase, or a commercial feature may have to be recut in response to test screenings or the wishes of a new executive with authority over the project.

Editing, Sound, and Special Effects

The director works closely with the editor and his or her staff to select, trim, and assemble shots into a finished film with a distinctive style and rhythm, a process that is now often carried out with digitized footage and computer editing. **Editing** is anticipated in preproduction with the preparation of a shooting script, and in production it is recognized in the variety and number of takes provided. Only a fraction of the footage that is shot and developed makes it into the finished film, however, making editing crucial to its final form.

2.25 *Sky Captain and the World of Tomorrow* (2004). While the aesthetic of this film's visual effects was derived from the past, the technology used to achieve them was state of the art at the time of its release.

Postproduction also includes complex processes for editing sound and adding special effects. A sound editor oversees the work of creating audio patterns and relationships with the visual image. Less apparent than the editing of images, editing of sound can create noises that relate directly to the action of the image (such as the image and sound of a dog barking), underpin those images and actions with music (such as the pounding beats that follow an army into battle), or insert sounds that counterpoint the images in ways that complicate their meanings (such as using a religious hymn to accompany the flight of a missile).

Special effects are techniques that enhance a film's realism or surpass assumptions about realism with spectacle. Whereas some special effects are prepared in preproduction (such as the building of elaborate models of futuristic cities), others can be generated in production with special camera filters or setups, or created on set, such as the use of pyrotechnics. Most special effects today are created in postproduction and are distinguished by the term **visual effects**. For most of film history, teams of technicians and artists worked in postproduction to create elaborate optical effects with expensive equipment. In the contemporary digital age, computer technicians have virtually boundless postproduction capabilities to enhance and transform the reality of an image. *Sky Captain and the World of Tomorrow* (2004), a film set in 1939 and giving that period's vision of the future, is an early example in which the entire world of the film (except the actors, whose performances were filmed using **blue screen technology**) was generated in postproduction [**Figure 2.25**].

There are many ways that the process of film production is linked to our experience as film viewers. Film production prepares us in the most literal way for viewing a film. The films that are produced, the visions of the stars, directors, and other personnel who work on them, and the developments of film language that they reflect are all shaped by larger cultural patterns. Because the process involves the industry's consideration of the public, including individual viewers, it inevitably places film in a specific cultural context.

Distribution: What We Can See

We noted earlier that the viewing experience involves acts of identification and cognition; in this section, we discuss the dimension of film culture known as distribution and, following that, promotion and exhibition. These three dimensions, along with film production, prepare us to identify with and think about a film prior to our actual viewing of it. Whether we recognize it or not, our tastes, avenues of identification, and cues for understanding a film frequently come in advance. Furthermore,

text continued on page 32 ▶

Producing
The 400 Blows (1959)

When it appeared in 1959, François Truffaut's *The 400 Blows* was immediately recognized as one of the signature films of what became known as the **French New Wave**, not only because of its fresh and innovative style and themes but, less obviously, because of production methods that were equally unusual. The film was made in opposition to the sometimes cumbersome industrial methods of both Hollywood production and what Truffaut disparaged as the "Tradition of Quality" produced by France's studio system. Accurately or not, Truffaut and his fellow directors of the French New Wave are frequently credited with and defined by these shifts in production methods. These directors were not conventionally trained as assistant directors working in the industry, and film schools had yet to be established; their training came largely through watching films—by the hundreds at the Cinémathèque Française—and writing about them in the pages of such journals as *Cahiers du cinéma*. Their filmmaking methods were influenced by this point of entry: they employed an open-ended and more spontaneous realism, elevated and isolated the director as an *auteur*—a presumed independent artist who controls the film production as a kind of personal expression (see p. 27)—and, finally, integrated a reflexivity within the film that calls attention to film production itself **[Figure 2.26]**.

Certainly one of the most noticeable features of *The 400 Blows* is its realistic portrayal of a rebellious adolescent's daily life and routines. *The 400 Blows* tells the tale of Antoine Doinel, whose search for identity on the streets of Paris is saturated with questions about sexuality, authority, family, economics, and education. Fittingly, the film relies extensively on location shooting across Paris to create a world that seems true to life as it is lived, not as it is portrayed in glossy, studio-produced films. Focusing this realism further, the **protagonist** of the film is played by Jean-Pierre Léaud, a

2.26   **François Truffaut**. The director is closely identified with the French New Wave.

young teenager with no acting experience who brings an unrehearsed energy to the character of a young boy constantly confronting a seemingly endless variety of authority figures and institutions—schoolteachers, parents, police—bent on controlling him. The gritty street realism and the naive energy of the actors that underpin this production are the essence of what the film aims to communicate.

A second variation on traditional mainstream film production is the notion that the director is an auteur, producing his or her own perspectives and experiences on film and, in this case, creating a semi-autobiographical movie scripted by Truffaut from events in his life. Like the protagonist of the film, filmmaker François Truffaut was himself both a bad boy and a writer, in both cases known for "raising hell"—which is an idiomatic translation of the film's French title, Les quatre cents coups. The film features more than a few autobiographical signals referring to Truffaut's own unhappy childhood, his discovery at age twelve that his legal father was not his biological father, and his constant trouble with virtually every kind of authority. Truffaut's own life, like that of Antoine Doinel, can be summarized as that of a troubled truant and sometimes thief ultimately redeemed by the cinema and writing about the cinema. Like Antoine, he was weaned on the cinema, and as a teenager he started his own cine-club, The Film Addicts Club. Shortly after this, he enlisted in the army, but after another of many "escapes" from various institutions, he was released because of an "unstable character." During this period, Truffaut found a surrogate father figure in the great film critic and scholar André Bazin, to whom The 400 Blows is dedicated in its credits and to whom Truffaut's parents even gave legal guardian rights. Truffaut quickly became one of the most vociferous and polemical writers about film of the 1950s, and he was recognized as the primary scholar and archivist for the journal Bazin co-founded, Cahiers du cinéma, as well as the magazine Arts.

Truffaut entered film culture as a writer for Cahiers du cinéma at the age of twenty-six and quickly established himself as a notorious troublemaker whose mission was to verbally assault what he considered the worn-out practices of mainstream film production, a "cinema of papa" for whom, he claimed, movies were simply illustrations of literary screenplays. In 1954, Truffaut wrote his best-known essay, "A Certain Tendency in the French Cinema," in which he loudly attacks the prevalence of film adaptations of literary screenplays and proclaims an irreconcilable conflict between the French "Tradition of Quality" and "an auteur's cinema"—auteurism being the crucial critical framework that argues that the filmmaker is tantamount to the literary author and expresses his personal vision with moving images. In 1958, in response to his scathing attacks on the French cinema, the Cannes Film Festival refused Truffaut press accreditation; in the following year The 400 Blows, his first feature film, would provoke a full-blown scandal in the French film community when it became France's official entry in the Cannes festival and then won the prize for best director. With it, the French New Wave was launched, and 1959 would become one of the most important years in film history. Truffuat's film was joined that year by the release of Alain Resnais and Marguerite Duras's Hiroshima, mon amour and Godard's

Breathless, a trio of movies that made it unmistakable that a new cinematic vision had arrived.

The success of The 400 Blows in 1959 brought with it several ironies (or, at least, complexities) regarding the relation of the film's themes to its production history—specifically as an emblem of Truffaut's rebellion against the literary formulas of paternal predecessors. In the light of the film's production, for instance, Truffaut's vociferous attack on old father figures appears a bit less intractable, less about overthrowing those figures than about manipulating them and their tools. However financially independent Truffaut was, with a production budget of less than $100,000, The 400 Blows was in fact bankrolled by producer/distributor Ignace Morganstein, one of Truffaut's newly acquired father figures through his 1957 marriage to Morganstein's daughter. Morganstein not only funded the film but, in a sense, provoked it when, after his own films suffered repeated attacks by critic Truffaut, he challenged the young critic and son-in-law with the dare, "If you know so much, why don't you make a film?" Truffaut did just that, while also continuing to write scathing reviews of his father-in-law's films.

Paralleling and supporting the emphasis on a more personal production process aligned with auteur cinema is a third, stylistic, distinction of the film: the use of a discontinuous editing style (often with "jump cuts"; see Chapter 5 for more on editing styles) and lightweight, handheld camera equipment to produce a sense of freshness, energy, and immediacy. Numerous examples of Truffaut's experimentation with these kinds of innovations with cinematic language appear throughout the film, often as a subtle but significant way to reflexively call attention to film production itself. There is, for instance, the sequence toward the conclusion of The 400 Blows when a female therapist interviews Antoine: here the lack of a countershot of the therapist, the static position of the camera, and a stream of jump cuts through the entire sequence highlights Antoine's spontaneity and Léaud's extraordinary facial expressivity, as he is neither cowed nor contained by the question-answer format. One of the central scenes in the entire film is a dense and explicit presentation of Truffaut's new film syntax embedded in a historical reflection about cinema's heritage and novelty. Situated in the longer sequence when Antoine and René skip school and make a quick trip to the cinema, Antoine climbs aboard the spinning carnival ride called the "Rotor" [Figure 2.27]. For film historians especially, the scene becomes an unmistakable metaphor for the cinema itself, as the construction of the ride resembles that nineteenth-century precursor of the cinema, the zoetrope, and contains another historical reference to the paternity of Alfred Hitchcock (specifically the climactic carousel sequence in Strangers on the Train [1951]). More important, perhaps, Truffaut's cameo presence in this scene announces a new and more personal cinematic idiom. The rollicking celebration of movement is

2.27 *The 400 Blows* (1959). The carnival ride is a metaphor recalling the disorienting, exhilarating machinery of film.

2.28 *The 400 Blows* (1959). The film ends with a famous, ambiguous freeze-frame in which Jean-Pierre Léaud as Antoine Doinel gazes directly at the camera.

not just a vehicle for narrative but also the expression of energy and delight, both Antoine's and the filmmaker's. Antoine and René's wild ramble as they play hooky through the streets of Paris highlights the unpredictable realism of the film's aesthetic but simultaneously visually liberates the characters and the images from conventional laws of nature and cinematic realism.

No two sequences in the film better map Truffaut's personal syntax of imagistic movement than the relationship between the opening tracking shot of the film through the anonymous streets of Paris and the celebrated closing track that follows Antoine's flight to the sea. Here the parallel tracks of the opening and closing frame the entire film as a narrative version of the film frame that freezes Antoine's look directly into the camera as the film's concluding image [Figure 2.28]. The opening track describes an anonymous point of view wandering the streets of Paris, with unpopulated streets and a continual line of building walls creating a relatively uncomfortable shallow depth of field—except, significantly, for glimpses of that most renowned image of Paris, the Eiffel Tower. Lasting more than a minute, twenty seconds and climaxing in a closing freeze frame, the final tracking shot becomes a determined movement to the sea that is less about an escape from the Observation Center for Delinquent Youth than about the flight to a perspective on the sea only imagined in Antoine's childhood. Antoine says earlier in the film that he's "never seen the ocean," and his flight to the ocean becomes the pursuit of a vision never before encountered. The challenge of describing Antoine's expression at this moment—as defiant, angry, frightened, or confused—is superseded by the formal triumph of a personal expression directly confronting the authority of the film frame—and the authority of traditional film production itself.

our choices and attitudes can also be influenced, directed, and (to some extent) controlled by aspects of film culture and the movie industry—such as, most dramatically, when a particular film is never released. When producing movies, the industry does not just focus its attention on selecting actors or finding locations before filming begins. It also considers its audience and, therefore, prepares individuals for their film-viewing experience. The discussion that follows begins by detailing how viewers and views of movies are prepared by the social and economic machinery of distribution (with an emphasis on the U.S. distribution system, which often controls even foreign theaters) and, as we will see later, promotion and exhibition.

Distributing Different Views

At the beginning of cinema history, from about 1895 to 1910, audiences flocked to see machines like the Vitascope (bought and marketed by Thomas Edison) project virtually any moving images, whether a couple kissing or a crowd walking across the Brooklyn Bridge. There they found and enjoyed a constant supply of short one-reel films, such as historical reenactments found in movies like the gruesome *Execution of Czolgosz* (1901) and topical versions of fairy tales of films like *The "Teddy"*

Bears (1907). Today we consume movies made available through different paths of distribution to theaters, video stores, television, and Internet sites. Our tastes for and knowledge of films frequently rely first on these avenues of distribution.

Distributors and Distribution

Distribution is the practice and means through which certain movies are sent to and placed in theaters and video stores, on television and cable networks, on airlines or in hotels, and in libraries and classrooms.

A distributor is a company that acquires the rights to a movie from the film-makers or producers (sometimes by contributing to the costs of producing that film) and then makes that movie available to audiences by renting, selling, or licensing it to theaters or other exhibition outlets. The availability of a film is, of course, depen-dent upon which films are produced by moviemakers, but the inversion of that logic is central to the economics of mainstream movie culture: Hollywood and many other film cultures produce movies that they assume can be successfully distributed. Film history has accordingly been marked with regular battles and compromises be-tween filmmakers and distributors (for example, when studios ensured that only their films were seen in first-run theaters, or when the canny independent distribu-tor Miramax suggested or imposed cuts on its filmmakers' work during the height of its success in the 1990s) about what audiences are willing to watch and which films can be successfully distributed. Indeed, a more negative situation is also true: viewers never see many good films that are produced but not distributed.

The Feature Film

Consider the following examples of how the prospects for distrib-uting and exhibiting a film can influence and often determine the content and form of a movie, including decisions about its length. From around 1911 to 1915, D. W. Griffith and other filmmakers struggled to convince movie studios to allow them to expand the length of a movie from roughly fifteen minutes to over one hun-dred minutes. Although longer films imported from Europe achieved some success, most producers felt that it would be im-possible to distribute longer movies because they believed audi-ences would not sit still for more than twenty minutes. Griffith persisted and continued to stretch the length of his films, insist-ing that new distribution and exhibition patterns would create and attract new audiences—those willing to accept more complex stories and to pay more for them. The commercial and financial success of *The Birth of a Nation* (1915), Griffith's three-hour epic distributed as a major cultural event comparable to a legitimate theatrical or operatic experience [**Figure 2.29**], thus became a benchmark and a major force in overturning one distribution for-mula, which offered a continuous program of numerous short films, and establishing a new one, which concentrated on a sin-gle **feature film**, a longer movie that is the primary attraction for audiences (see p. 47). After 1915, most films would be distributed with 90- to 120-minute running times, rather than in their previ-ous 10- to 20-minute lengths, though different combinations of accompanying shorts or double-bills were prevalent at different times.

Since 1915, this pattern for distribution has proved quite durable. In 1924, Erich von Stroheim handed his studio a nine-hour adaptation of Frank Norris's *McTeague,* retitled *Greed.*

VIEWING CUE

How might a distribution strategy determine a response to a film? Does knowing this strategy help you understand the film's aims better?

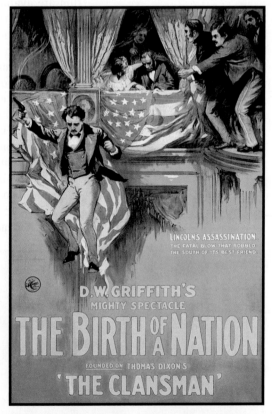

2.29 **Advertisement for *The Birth of a Nation*** (1915). The ambitious nature of D. W. Griffith's epic was apparent in advertisements and its unprecedented three-hour running time.

2.30   *Heaven's Gate* (1980). A disastrous theatrical release was later tempered when Michel Cimino's film was re-cut, re-released, and eventually restored for successful home-video distribution.

Appalled by the length, studio executives re-cut the film to about two hours, emaciating the story but allowing them to distribute it for a profit. In 1980, United Artists decided to reduce the length of Michael Cimino's massive epic *Heaven's Gate* (1980) from over four hours to 149 minutes in order to come closer to the standard film length [**Figure 2.30**]. After the catastrophic failure of its **first release** to movie theaters, and as a result of the flexible viewing conditions of home video, much of the original version was eventually restored. The recent trend toward longer running times, especially for "prestige" or "epic" films, acknowledges the flexible contexts in which films are now viewed.

Our experience of a movie—its length, its choice of stars (over unknowns, for example), its subject matter, and even its title—is partly determined by decisions made about distribution even before the film becomes available to viewers. Because most movies are produced specifically to be distributed to certain kinds of audiences, distribution patterns can make or shape a movie and our expectations of it. Whether a movie is available everywhere for everyone at the same time, released during the holiday season or available only in specialty video stores or on Internet sites, distribution patterns bring expectations that a particular film either fulfills or frustrates.

Release Strategies

As one of its primary functions, distribution determines how many copies of a film are available and the number of locations at which the movie can be seen. A movie can thus be distributed for special **exclusive release**, premiering in only one or two locations. A particularly dramatic example of this strategy is the restored version of Abel Gance's classic *Napoléon* (1927), an epic tale of the life of the French emperor that periodically presents the action simultaneously on three screens. The original film premiered in April 1927 (although the film was not shown in its entirety until a month later to a private audience and was subsequently distributed in the United States as a single-screen presentation). In 1981, the exclusive release of the restored film was accompanied by an orchestra, and it appeared in only one theater at a time. In this most recent incarnation, *Napoléon* toured the country showing in only a very select group of cities and theaters so that seeing it became a privileged event. Although each film will use an exclusive release in its own way, we generally approach these films expecting an unusual or singular experience created by a daring subject matter (such as the history of a nation) or a remarkable technological or formal achievement (such as a three- or four-hour running time).

2.31   *Rocky Balboa* (2006). As a major studio release and the sixth and final installment in the Rocky series, Stallone's film received a saturated release.

A film with a mass circulation of premieres, sometimes referred to as **saturation booking** or a saturated release, is screened in as many locations as possible in the United States—and sometimes abroad—as soon as possible. For a potential blockbuster such as Sylvester Stallone's *Rocky Balboa* (2006) [**Figure 2.31**], the distributors immediately release the movie in a maximum number of locations and theaters to attract large audiences before its novelty wears off. In these cases, distribution usually promises audiences a film that appeals to most tastes (offering, perhaps, action sequences or breathtaking special effects rather than controversial topics) and is easy to understand (featuring uncomplicated plots and characters). A **wide release** may premiere at as many as two thousand screens, whereas a **limited release** may initially be distributed only to major cities—Quentin Tarantino's *Reservoir Dogs* (1992), first appeared in only seventy-five theaters—and then expand its distribution, depending on the film's success. The expectations for films following a limited release pattern are generally less fixed than for wide releases: they will usually be recognized in terms of the previous work of the director or an actor but will offer a certain novelty or experimentation (such as a controversial subject or a strange plot twist) that will presumably be better appreciated the more the film is publicly debated and understood through the reviews and discussions that follow its initial release. The Weinstein Company's decision to limit the release of Todd Haynes's experimental biopic of Bob Dylan, *I'm Not There* (2007), to major cities despite its well-known cast, was a bid to maximize critical attention to the film's daring and the intriguing promise of its performances, which include Cate Blanchett playing Dylan in the 1960s [**Figure 2.32**].

2.32 *I'm Not There* (2007). Todd Haynes's experimental Bob Dylan biopic built up critical attention through a limited release pattern.

As part of these more general practices, the history of distribution has developed other strategies that can shape or respond to the interests and tastes of intended audiences. **Platforming** involves releasing a film in gradually widening markets and theaters so that it slowly builds its reputation and momentum through reviews and word of mouth. With **block booking**, a common practice until it was limited by court order in 1948 yet still practiced in some ways today, a studio/distributor pressures a movie theater to accept and show smaller, less expensive films in order to gain the opportunity to show more popular movies. For instance, a cineplex might need to book a smaller, more subtle film like *True Romance* (1993) for a number of weeks in order to show the blockbuster *Jurassic Park* (1993) during the same period. Although block booking allows us to see films other than blockbusters, it also establishes a hierarchy of quality by which distributors identify for us—whether we are aware of it or not—which movies are considered the most important ones to see.

Target Audiences

Since the latter part of the twentieth century, movies have also been distributed with an eye toward reaching specific target audiences—viewers who producers feel are most likely to want to see a particular film. Producers and distributors aimed *Shaft* (1971), an action film with a black hero, at African American audiences by distributing it primarily in large urban areas. Distributors positioned *Trainspotting* (1995), a hip tale of young heroin users in Edinburgh, to draw art-film and younger audiences in cities, some suburbs, and college and university towns. The *Nightmare on Elm Street* movies (1984–1989), a violent slasher series about the horrific Freddy Krueger, were aimed primarily at the male teenage audience who frequented cineplexes and, later, video stores. The initial success of *Transformers* (2007), one of many films based on cartoons, occasioned a later release of an extended IMAX version in which the special effects were even more dominant.

The various distribution strategies all imply important issues about how movies should be viewed and understood. First, by controlling the scope of distribution, these strategies determine the quality and importance of an audience's interactions with a film. As a saturated release, *Godzilla* (1998) aimed for the swift gratification of an exciting onetime event with a focus on special effects and shocks. Platformed gradually through expanding audiences, *Driving Miss Daisy* (1989) benefited from growing conversations and more careful reflections on the relationship between an

2.33 *Driving Miss Daisy* (1989). Platforming this modestly budgeted film cultivated audiences and critical responses.

2.34 *Scream* (1996). The franchise targeted the teenage audience for slasher films and expanded it through parody.

older white woman and her black chauffeur [**Figure 2.33**]. No distribution pattern produces a single set of expectations, nor does the distribution method determine the meaning of a film. Yet distribution methods can lead viewers, overtly or subtly, to look at a film in certain ways. We come to a saturated release perhaps prepared to focus on the performance of a star, on the relationship to a best-selling novel, or on the new use of computer technology. With a platformed release, ideas and opinions about the film are already in the air, and any controversy or innovation associated with it informs our initial viewing.

Second, in targeting audiences, distribution can identify primary, intended responses to the film as well as secondary, unexpected ones. *Scream* (1996) [**Figure 2.34**] and *Scream 2* (1997) would probably offend or confuse most elderly audiences unfamiliar with teenage **horror films**, but the targeted teenage audiences come prepared, knowing the formulas and clichés associated with this kind of movie, and are likely to see these films as spoofs and parodies of contemporary slashers. One set of responses is not necessarily better or more correct than another, but recognizing the part played by distribution targeting does allow a viewer to think more precisely and productively about the many social and cultural dynamics of responding to a movie. At the very least, this awareness indicates how our identification with and comprehension of films are as much a product of our social and cultural location as they are a product of the film's subject matter and form.

Ancillary Markets: Television, Video/DVD, and Internet Distribution

In recent decades, movie distribution has increasingly taken advantage of television, home video, and DVD as avenues for distribution, with more of a film's revenue being generated by such **ancillary markets** than by initial theatrical release. From network to premium channels, and from On-Demand options to digital recording devices, more and more movies are presented through television distribution—the selection and programming, at carefully determined times, of films made both for theaters and exclusively for television. Normally, there is a lag time between a theatrical release in a cinema and cable or network releases, but some movies are distributed directly to video or cable, such as the two sequels to the film *From Dusk till Dawn* (1996). Whether a movie is released later for television or is made expressly for video and television, this type of distribution usually aims to reach the largest possible audience and to raise revenues. Part of the motive in these cases may be to reach more people with its message, such as when *Schindler's List* (1993) was featured as a primetime commercial-free (though corporate-sponsored) television movie years after its original theatrical release. In a recent bid to reach specialized audiences through subscription cable, IFC Films has made critically acclaimed foreign and

U.S. independent films available on demand the same day they are released to urban art-house theaters, allowing television audiences in markets outside such cities access to such works as the Romanian *4 Months, 3 Weeks, 2 Days* (2007), winner of the Cannes Film Festival's top prize.

Guaranteed television distribution can reduce the financial risk for producers and filmmakers and thus, in some situations, allow for more experimentation. This was certainly the case with the BBC's daring production of Dennis Potter and Jon Amiel's eight-hour *The Singing Detective* (1986), an extraordinary cinematic/televisual combination of musical and mystery genres that twists tales of World War II, childhood trauma, and the skin disease of a detective writer [**Figure 2.35**]. Sometimes the flow between television and theatrical distribution is reversed. Premium (subscription) cable channels such as HBO increasingly produce their own films that include riskier documentary subjects for presentation on their networks, sometimes allowing a theatrical window for the film to receive reviews and become eligible for awards. Finally, foreign television sales, often made while a film is in production, constitute an aspect of distribution that can help finance a film.

2.35 *The Singing Detective* (1986). This eight-hour BBC production changed assumptions about the made-for-TV movie when it was broadcast in the United States.

Television distribution has both positive and negative implications. In some cases, films on television must adjust their style and content to suit the formats of time and space: scenes might be cut to fit a time slot, or, as with *Schindler's List*, the film may be shown on two different nights, thus potentially breaking the flow and temporal impact of the movie. The size of the image might also be changed so that a widescreen film image will fit the shape of the television monitor. In other cases, television and video distribution may expand the ways a movie can communicate with its audience and experiment with different visual forms. *The Singing Detective* uses the long length of a television series watched within the home as the appropriate format to explore and think about the passage of time, the difficulty of memory, and the many levels of reality and consciousness woven into our daily lives. Indeed, these questions can be asked of virtually any film: What about it seems best suited for distribution in movie theaters or distribution on television? What about it seems least suited?

As with cinema and television distribution, video and DVD distribution determines the availability of films on videotape or DVD for rental or purchase in stores or from Web sites such as Netflix or independent video distributors such as Kino. Since the selection in video rental stores is based on a market perspective on local audiences as well as the tastes of the individual proprietors, movies on video and DVD can wind up being distributed to certain cities or neighborhoods and excluded from other locations. Asian American neighborhoods are likely to have more Asian films in their local video stores than are other neighborhoods. Chain stores such as Blockbuster are likely to focus on high-concentration family-oriented shopping sites, offering numerous copies of current popular mainstream movies and excluding daring subject matter or older titles. Some independent video stores specialize in art films, cult films, or movie classics such as those released on DVD by the Criterion Collection.

For viewers, there are two clear consequences to these patterns of video distribution. First, video distribution can control—perhaps more than does theatrical distribution—local responses, tastes, and expectations: as part of a community anchored by that video store, we see and learn to expect only certain kinds of movies when the store makes five or six copies of one blockbuster film available but only one or none of a less popular film. In fact, the control of video outlets extends even to altering or censoring a film when scenes or lines of dialogue considered

▶ VIEWING CUE

If the movie just viewed were shown on television, how might such distribution have significantly changed the look or feel of it? ⏸

2.36   **Local video store**. DVD stores bring mass media to local communities.

offensive to the local community are edited out. The second consequence highlights the sociological and cultural formations of film distribution. As a community outlet, video stores become part of the social fabric of a neighborhood: the movies made available in rental stores tend to reflect the community, and the community tends to see itself in the kinds of movies it regularly watches. Viewers are consumers, and video stores can become forums in which the interests of a community of viewers—in children's film, Latino cinema, or less violent movies, for instance—can determine which films are distributed [**Figure 2.36**].

An innovator in DVD distribution, Netflix has provided another model for distributing films (followed by Blockbuster and other companies). As part of a subscription system that offers viewers a steady stream of DVDs, Netflix members can select and return films as rapidly or as slowly as they are seen. Because the DVDs arrive and are returned through the mail, this distribution arrangement emphasizes the rapidity of contemporary consumption of movies. And because preselected DVDs are sent automatically, it also reflects a kind of passivity in movie consumption. Streaming video rentals and downloading for purchase or rental are increasingly popular. The success of such models may indicate an audience's desire to see a growing variety of films that may not be available through theatrical distribution or neighborhood video stores, as Netflix, iTunes, and other sources expand their offerings of foreign, classic, and documentary films. This emphatic attention to a new ease and freedom of film consumption raises different questions about changing viewing patterns and their implications. These new paradigms undermine the social and communal formations of the overall film experience, from browsing the video store to watching movies with an audience? Does increased ease of access to film traditions remote in time or location make for a richer film culture? Or does the fragmented audience make a shared movie culture a more remote possibility? How might these patterns influence and change the kinds of movies that are made?

Distribution Timing

Distribution timing—when a movie is released for public viewing in certain locations—is another prominent feature of distribution (and, as we will see later in the chapter, of exhibition). Adding significantly to our experience of movies, timing can take

▶ **VIEWING CUE**

How might the distribution of a film that has been released in the last year have been timed to emphasize certain responses? Was it a seasonal release?

2.37   ***Speed*** (1994). Action movies intended as summer amusements have become central to the release calendar.

2.38   ***Miracle on 34th Street*** (1947). Annual television broadcasts of classic Christmas movies compete with theatrical fare timed to the season.

advantage of the social atmosphere, cultural connotations, or critical scrutiny associated with particular seasons and calendar periods. The summer season and the December holidays are the most important in the United States because audiences usually have more free time. Offering a temporary escape from hot weather, a summer release like *Speed* (1994) also matches the thrills of the film with rides at an amusement park [Figure 2.37]. Christmas movies like *Miracle on 34th Street* (1947) promise a celebration of goodwill and community [Figure 2.38]. The Memorial Day release of *Pearl Harbor* (2001) immediately attracts the sentiments and memories of Americans remembering World War II and other global conflicts. The film industry is calculating releases ever more carefully—for example, holding a promising film for a November release in order to vie for prestigious (and business-generating) awards nominations.

Mistiming a film's release can prove to be a major problem, as was the case with *A Little Princess* (1995), whose release unfortunately coincided with the more aggressively distributed *Pocahontas* (1995). Both films aimed for the same target audience of families with children, but *Pocahontas* was able to take advantage of Disney's large distribution system and was put in so many theaters that *A Little Princess* was virtually lost to audiences. As one would expect, avoiding unwanted competition with a film can be a key part of a distributor's timing: distributors accelerated the timing of the opening of *The Matrix* (1999) [Figure 2.39] precisely to avoid competition with *Star Wars: Episode I—The Phantom Menace* (1999) [Figure 2.40].

2.39

2.40

2.39   *The Matrix* (1999), **2.40** *Star Wars: Episode I—The Phantom Menace* (1999). The summer 1999 release of *The Matrix* was moved up to avoid competition with the much-anticipated opening of the first *Star Wars* prequel, *The Phantom Menace*.

Multiple Releases

Of the several other variations on the tactics of timing, movies sometimes follow a *first release* or first "run" with a *second release* or second "run"; the first describes a movie's original premiere, while the second refers to the redistribution of that film months or years later. After its first release in 1982, for example, *Blade Runner* made a notable reappearance in 1992 as a longer "director's cut." While the first release had only modest success, the second (supported by a surprisingly large audience discovered in the home video market) appealed to viewers newly attuned to the visual and narrative complexity of the movie. Audiences wanted to see, think about, and see again oblique and obscure details in order to decide, for instance, whether Deckard was a replicant or a human [Figure 2.41].

For the film's twenty-fifth anniversary in 2007 a **final cut** was released theatrically, but it catered primarily to DVD customers. With second releases, financial reward is no doubt a primary goal, and the trend to reissue films like *Return of the Jedi* in 1997 testifies to the success of this formula: reappearing in 2,111 theaters, *Return of the Jedi*'s reissue earned another $46 million. Re-releases of either classic or popular films such as animated Disney fare can also create new points of view, predisposing viewers to certain kinds of responses, such as appreciation for the techniques of animation before computers. They can initiate an emotional nostalgia for past experiences

 **VIEWING CUE**

Try to identify the target audience of one of the films you've discussed in class. How might this movie have gained different audiences through DVD distribution?

2.41   *Blade Runner* (1982, 1994, 2007). While its initial opening was disappointing, Ridley Scott's dystopian "future noir" was an early success on home video. Releases of a director's cut for its tenth anniversary and a final cut for its twenty-fifth make the question of the film's definitive identity as interesting as the questions of human versus replicant identity posed by its plot.

2.42   *Lawrence of Arabia* (1962). Originally released in 1962, this spectacular 70mm epic was restored and successfully re-released theatrically in 1989 (and later released in a DVD "director's cut").

2.43   *It's a Wonderful Life* (1946). A box-office disappointment when it was initially released, Frank Capra's film became a ubiquitous accompaniment to the holiday season on television. In recent years, NBC's broadcast restrictions attempted to restore the film's status as an annual family viewing event.

associated with an old film (ideally to be shared with new generations) or, in some instances, provoke curiosity about fresh material added to the re-release or about new information a viewer has acquired about a feature of the film such as its director or star.

With a film that may have been unavailable to viewers during its first release or that simply may not have been popular, a re-release can lend it new life and reclaim viewers through a process of rediscovery. When a small movie achieves unexpected popular or critical success or a major award, for example, it can then be redistributed with a much wider distribution circuit and to a more eager, sympathetic audience that is already prepared to like the movie. For example, the initial distribution of Werner Herzog's *The Mystery of Kaspar Hauser* (1975) in Germany proved unsuccessful; after it garnered film festival prizes and was acclaimed overseas, the film was successfully redistributed in Germany. A re-release may occur in the attempt to offer the audience a higher-quality picture, or to clarify story lines by restoring cut scenes, as was done in 1989 with Columbia Pictures' re-release of the 1962 Oscar award–winning *Lawrence of Arabia* [**Figure 2.42**]. Similarly, television distribution can re-time the release of a movie to promote certain attitudes toward it. *It's a Wonderful Life* did not generate much of an audience when it was first released in 1946. Gradually (and especially after its copyright expired in 1975), network and cable television began to run the film regularly, and the film became a Christmas classic shown often and everywhere during that season [**Figure 2.43**]. In 1997, however, the television network NBC reclaimed the exclusive rights to the film in order to limit its television distribution to one showing each year and to try to make audiences see the movie as a special event.

Day-and-Date Release

Steven Soderbergh's *Bubble* (2006) drew attention to a new experiment in release timing. *Day-and-date release* refers to the period of time between the theatrical release of a film, its broadcast or cable premiere, and its distribution on video or DVD. Commonly this window has been about three to six months, but with *Bubble*, an offbeat, low-budget murder mystery about a slacker working in a doll factory, director Steven Soderbergh and producers Mark Cuban and Todd Wagner of HDNet Films and 2929 Entertainment effectively closed this window by releasing the film almost simultaneously to three different venues: four days following its theatrical release in January 2006 (in only thirty-two theaters), the film appeared in stores on DVD and on the HDNet Cable station [**Figure 2.44**]. Director M. Night Shyamalan immediately denounced this strategy, claiming that it would dilute the fundamental experience of the movies as a singular, larger-than-life encounter with the fantasies of storytelling, an experience more in keeping with the aesthetics of Shyamalan's own films, such as *The Sixth Sense* (1999) and *Lady in the Water* (2006) [**Figure 2.45**].

Whether or not this kind of distribution strategy actually announces a radical change in film distribution, it does signal the kinds of experimentation that digital production and distribution can allow and the inevitable changes and adjustments that will occur in the future in response to shifting markets, tastes, and technologies.

2.44 **Bubble** (2006). Steven Soderbergh experimented with releasing this modest digital film about a murder's impact on small-town workers at a doll factory simultaneously to theaters, cable, and DVD.

2.45 **Lady in the Water** (2006). M. Night Shyamalan insists on the magic of encountering the movies on a big screen. Unfortunately, his fairy-tale film was a critical and box-office failure.

Across the exchange between Soderbergh and Shyamalan, it also suggests larger concerns about how these changes can affect our responses to films and the kinds of films that will be made.

The Repeat Viewer

As viewers, we are an inevitable part of the distribution path. Distributing a movie through one or more releases thus anticipates and capitalizes on an increasingly common variation in contemporary movie culture: the repeat viewer who returns during a first release to see the same movie more than once. *Love Story* (1970), a tale of tragically doomed young love, was among the first modern movies to draw viewers back to the theater for multiple viewings, but films from Rudolph Valentino's *The Sheik* (1921) and *Gone with the Wind* (1939) to *Toy Story* (1995) and *The Sixth Sense* (1999) have each exploited this viewing pattern somewhat differently. Women returned with women friends to share their adoration of Valentino; adults returned with children to *Toy Story,* more interested in the inside jokes than the story; and fans of *The Sixth Sense* returned to spot early clues that anticipate the surprise ending [**Figure 2.46**]. Data taken from repeat viewings of *Titanic* (1997) revealed the extent of business brought to moviegoing by teenage girls—with repeat viewers like these, timing becomes more a function of the viewers' choices, not the distributor's. However, it also demonstrates the changing variety of experiences at the movies for the same individual: how a different time and place, different companions, and more knowledge about a movie can alter or enrich how a viewer comes prepared to see a film with different expectations and assumptions.

▶ **VIEWING CUE**

What film have you seen recently that might attract repeat viewers? What elements or dimensions of this film suggest that the film-makers would or would not have expected repeat viewings?

Whether with an exclusive Christmas release or an experimental film classic, the distribution path implicitly identifies viewers as a certain kind of audience (in terms of age, gender, and other characteristics), watching the movie in a certain place (in a theater, or at home on a television), and as a moviegoer with certain habits (a midnight movie fan who avidly looks for the unusual film, or the family that goes out during the holidays for inoffensive Hollywood fare). Thinking about a movie means considering carefully how it attempts to position us in a particular place and time because these positions can significantly influence how we understand the movie.

Distribution's influence on film culture runs the gamut. A studio can easily "dump" a film directly into the video market because it does not think the film will

text continued on page 43 ▶

2.46 **The Sixth Sense** (1999). Repeat viewers may detect clues to this film's surprise ending in encounters like this one, in which a troubled boy's mother, played by Toni Collette, fails to meet the gaze of the main character, played by Bruce Willis.

Distributing
Killer of Sheep (1977)

Distribution is almost invisible to the public and hence much less glamorous than film production or exhibition, but it determines whether a film will ever reach an audience. Whether influenced by taste, economics, or even politics, distribution performs a crucial gate-keeping function, shaping audiences' tastes and tolerances. Independent filmmakers often bring new perspectives to mainstream, formulaic filmmaking, but their visions need to be shared. African American filmmakers, who have historically been marginalized within the system of production, often encounter additional challenges in getting their films distributed. The career of Charles Burnett, considered one of the most significant African American filmmakers despite his relatively small oeuvre, is marked by the vicissitudes of distribution. The recent successful release of his first feature, *Killer of Sheep* (1977), more than thirty years after it was made, not only illuminates black American filmmakers' historically unequal access to movie screens but also illustrates the multiple levels on which current distribution campaigns function. The way the film's distributor, Milestone Films, handled the film's theatrical, non-theatrical, and DVD release in order to maximize critical attention and gain significant revenue serves as a model for similar endeavors [Figure 2.47].

Produced in the early 1970s as a master's thesis film, Burnett's *Killer of Sheep* emerged amidst a flowering of African American filmmaking talent at the University of California, Los Angeles Film School; these filmmakers were dubbed the "L.A. Rebellion" by critic Clyde Taylor. Less an organized oppositional movement than a collaborative, creative moment, the films created by these young filmmakers, including Burnett, countered dominant images of African Americans onscreen. In place of the two-dimensional stereotypes of past classical Hollywood films, the almost-too-good-to-be-true characters played by Sidney Poitier in the 1960s, or the often cartoonish, street-smart characters of the so-called **blaxploitation** films that Burnett saw on urban screens at the time, he depicted his protagonist, Stan, as the father of a black family living in the impoverished Watts neighborhood—residence of the filmmaker's own

2.47 *Killer of Sheep* (1977). Strikingly poetic realism characterizes Charles Burnett's legendary independent film about an African American family in Los Angeles's Watts neighborhood. The film was finally distributed theatrically thirty years after it was made.

family. A decent man whose slaughterhouse job and daily struggles have numbed and depressed him, Stan nevertheless gets by, and his bonds with his family and community, depicted in grainy, beautifully composed black-and-white images, are profoundly moving. In the film's final scene, Stan and his wife slow dance to a song by Dinah Washington, getting through another day.

Killer of Sheep was never distributed theatrically. Essential to the mood and meaning of the film is its soundtrack, composed of blues and R&B music by Paul Robeson, Washington, and Earth, Wind, and Fire. Without the resources to clear the music rights for public presentation, Burnett circulated his film over the years in occasional festivals and museum and educational settings. His artistic reputation became firmly established: in 1990, the film was among the first fifty titles named to the National Film Registry by the Library of Congress. But audiences never got to see the film. Only when Burnett was able to complete *To Sleep with Anger* in 1990 due to the participation of Danny Glover and Burnett's receipt of a prestigious MacArthur Fellowship, did one of his films receive theatrical distribution. Although the early 1990s saw an unprecedented boom in commercially successful black filmmaking, *To Sleep with Anger*, a family drama that lacked violence and unambiguous resolutions, was overlooked amid the media's attention to more sensationalized depictions of ghetto culture set to hip hop soundtracks, such as *Boyz N the Hood* (1991).

Eventually, however, Burnett's critical reputation helped secure the restoration of *Killer of Sheep* by the UCLA Film and Television Archives just when its original 16mm elements were in danger of disintegrating beyond repair. The restoration, one of several planned for independent films of historical significance, was funded by Turner Classic Movies and filmmaker Steven Soderbergh, whose own debut feature *sex, lies, and videotape* (1989) changed the landscape for the distribution of independent film. In March 2007, the specialty, or "boutique," distributor Milestone Films, whose founders (Dennis Doros and Amy Heller) have long been in the business of releasing important classic and contemporary films theatrically,

opened the film in a restored 35mm print in New York. Excellent reviews that positioned the film in relation both to African American history and to such filmmaking movements as **Italian neorealism**, and the grassroots support of the Harlem-based organization Imagenation, made the opening a record-breaking success, and the film soon opened in art cinemas around the country. The next phase was release on DVD to institutions such as universities that did not have the facilities to show *Killer of Sheep* on 35mm but might want to have a public screening. Finally, the film was released on DVD for the consumer market, packaged with another unreleased early feature by Burnett, *My Brother's Wedding*, along with a commentary track and other features. Although Milestone, unlike non-theatrical distributor California Newsreel, is not primarily known as a distributor of African American films, its experience as a "niche" distributor helped land a thirty-year-old film on critics' top-ten lists, a special prize from the New York Film Critics Circle, and a place in public memory about film aesthetics, American culture, and everyday experience.

be profitable; an art film distributor can create a market for foreign films in postwar America; non-theatrical distributors can circulate independent, experimental, educational, or special interest films to libraries, colleges, and media arts centers; and public television networks can distribute their films to home viewers. Access to movie culture determines viewers' experience of it, and distribution thus determines filmmakers' ability to communicate with those audiences.

Marketing and Promotion: What We Want to See

Why and how we are attracted to certain movies is a slightly different but equally important matter. Just as a film can be distributed in various ways, a movie can be marketed and promoted in ways that specifically shape and direct our interests. A film might be advertised in newspapers as the work of a great director, for example, or it might be described as a steamy love story and illustrated by way of a sensational poster. A film trailer might emphasize the romantic story line in an otherwise cerebral spy film like *The Lives of Others* (2006). Although these preliminary encounters with a film might seem marginally relevant to how we experience the film, promotional strategies, like distribution strategies, prepare us in important ways for how we will see and understand a film.

Generating Our Interest

Marketing and promotion aim to generate and direct interest in a movie. Film **marketing** involves identifying an audience in order to bring a product (the movie) to the attention of buyers (viewers) so that they will consume (watch) that product. Film **promotion** refers to the specific ways a movie can be made an object that an audience will want to see. No doubt the **star system** (see p. 65) is the most common and potent component of the marketing and promotion of movies around the world. One or more well-known actors (popular at a specific time and within a specific culture) act as the advertising vehicle for the movie, and, like other marketing and promotional practices, the star system aims to create, in advance, specific expectations that will draw an audience to a film. Quite often, these marketing and promotional expectations—that Tom Cruise stars or that Mexican filmmaker Alejandro González Iñárritu directs, for example—subsequently become the viewfinders through which an audience sees a movie.

Long a part of film culture, the methods of marketing and promotion are many and creative. Viewers find themselves bombarded with everything from newspaper and billboard advertisements to previews shown before the main feature to tie-in games featured on the official movie Web site. Stars make public appearances on radio and television and are profiled in fan magazines; newspaper critics attend early screenings and write reviews that coincide with the release of a film—all these actions contribute to movie promotion. In addition, while movies have long been promoted through prizes and gifts [Figure 2.48], modern distributors are especially adept at marketing films through **tie-ins**: ancillary products such as T-shirts, CD soundtracks, toys, and other gimmicks made available at stores and restaurants that advertise and promote a movie. *The Little Mermaid* (1989), for example, was anticipated with the replica toys of Ariel and the frequently performed song "Under the Sea."

A marketing blitz of note is that which accompanied *Independence Day* (1996). Given its carefully timed release on July 3, 1996, following weeks of advertisements in newspapers and on television, it would be difficult to analyze first-run viewers' feelings about this film without taking into account the influence of these promotions. Defining the film as a science fiction thriller, the advertisements and reviews drew attention to its status as the film event of the summer, its suitability for children, and its technological wizardry. Promoted and released to coincide with the Fourth of July holiday, *Independence Day* ads emphasized its patriotic American themes. In that light, many posters, advertisements, and publicity stills presented actors Will Smith together with Bill Pullman or Jeff Goldblum, not only to promote the film's stars but also to draw attention to the racial harmony achieved in the film and its appeal to both African American and white audiences [Figure 2.49]. During the first month of its release, when U.S. scientists discovered a meteorite with fossils that suggested early life on Mars, promotion for the movie responded immediately with revised ads: "Last week, scientists found evidence of life on another planet. We're not going to say we told you so. . . . "

Typical Hollywood promotions and advertisements often emphasize the realism of movies, a strategy that promises audiences more accurate or more expansive reflections of the world and human experience. For *Dark Victory* (1939), a Bette Davis film about a socialite dying of a brain tumor, advertisements and press kits drew viewers' attention to the disturbing truth of a terminal illness, a reality that promotions claimed had never before been presented in movies. A related mar-

2.48 **Movie marquee**. Promoting movies through prizes, giveaways, and product tie-ins dates back to the 1920s.

2.49 *Independence Day* (1996). The film's massive promotional campaign for its Fourth of July weekend opening drew on blatant and subtle forms of patriotism, such as the multicultural appeal of its cast.

2.50 *Innocents of Paris* (1929). The marquee promotes the novelty of sound and song and this early musical's singing star.

2.51 *Jarhead* (2005). Topical interest in the Iraq conflict and the best-selling memoir on which it was based fueled interest in this film about a Marine's baffling Gulf War experience.

2.52 **Tom Cruise**. The star's erratic behavior during daytime and late-night talk show appearances to promote *Mission: Impossible III* contributed to Paramount's ending its contract with Cruise.

keting strategy is to claim textual novelty in a film, drawing attention to new features such as technical innovations, a rising star, or the acclaimed book on which the film is based. With early sound films like *The Jazz Singer* (1927), *The Gold Diggers of Broadway* (1929), and *Innocents of Paris* (1929), marketing advertisements directed audiences toward the abundance and quality of the singing and talking that added a dramatic new dimension to cinematic realism **[Figure 2.50]**. Today promotions and advertisements can exploit new technologies, as when *Mask* (1994) touted everywhere the remarkable digital transformations of Jim Carrey's face and body, or when *The Polar Express* (2004) flaunted its novel, motion-capture technology, which used Tom Hanks's movements to animate several of the film's characters; or they can take advantage of current political events, as when Sam Mendes's *Jarhead* (2005) advertised its plot's timely encounter with debates and concerns around the ongoing war in Iraq **[Figure 2.51]**.

Stars are booked to appear on talk shows and in other venues in conjunction with a film's release, as official promotion tactics, but stars may also bring unofficial publicity to a film. Brad Pitt and Angelina Jolie boosted audiences for the film *Mr. and Mrs. Smith* (2005) when they became a couple during its filming. Conversely, unwelcome publicity can cause an actor's contract to be cancelled or raise concerns about the impact on ticket sales, as happened with Tom Cruise's often odd remarks and public appearances preceding the release of *Mission: Impossible III* (2006) **[Figure 2.52]**.

Older films in current release and art and foreign-language films have less access to the mechanisms of promotion than do current mainstream films, and their promotion is not usually in the hands of film companies seeking huge financial

2.53 *Bonnie and Clyde* (1967). Critical accounts may position this film as an updated gangster film or as social commentary on the turbulent 1960s.

profits. Even so, audiences for these films are led to some extent by what we might call *cultural promotion,* academic or journalistic accounts that discuss and frequently value films as especially important in movie history or as aesthetic objects. A discussion of a movie in a film history book or even in a university film course could thus be seen as an act of marketing, which makes clear that promotion is not just about urging viewers to see a film but is also about urging them to see it with a particular point of view. Although these more measured kinds of promotion are usually underpinned by intellectual rather than financial motives, they also deserve our consideration and analysis because they, too, shape our understanding of films. How does a specific film history text, for instance, prepare you to see a film such as *Bonnie and Clyde* (1967) **[Figure 2.53]**? Some books promote it as a modern gangster film. Others pitch it as an incisive reflection of the social history of the turbulent 1960s. Still other texts and essays may urge readers to see it because of its place in the oeuvre of a major U.S. director, Arthur Penn. Even independent and classical movies require publicity: by promoting the artistic power and individuality of the director; by associating them with big-name film festivals in Venice, Toronto, and Cannes; or by calling attention, through advertising, to what distinguishes them from mainstream Hollywood films. For a foreign film, a committed publicist can be crucial to its attaining distribution by attracting critical mention. In short, we do not experience any film with innocent eyes; consciously or not, we come prepared to see it in a certain way.

Advertising and Ratings

Advertising is a central form of promotion that uses television, billboards, film trailers or previews, print ads, banners on Web sites, and other forms of display to bring a film to the attention of a potential audience. Advertising can use the facts in and issues surrounding a movie in various ways. Advertising often emphasizes connections with and differences from related or similar films or highlights the presence of a particularly popular actor or director. The poster for Charles Chaplin's *The Kid* (1921), for example, proudly pronounces it "the great Film he has been working on for a whole year" **[Figure 2.54]**. For different markets, *G.I. Jane* (1997) was promoted as a star vehicle for Demi Moore or as the latest film from Ridley Scott, the director of *Alien* (1979), *Blade Runner* (1982), and *Thelma & Louise* (1991). It is conceivable that these two promotional tactics created different sets of expectations about the movie—one more attuned to tough female sexuality, the other to lavish sets and technological landscapes. As this example reveals, promotion tends not only to draw us to a movie but also to suggest what we will concentrate on as a way of understanding its achievement.

Trailers

One of the most carefully crafted forms of promotional advertising is the **trailer**, which previews carefully edited images and scenes from a film in theaters before the main feature film or on television or a Web site. In just a few minutes, these trailers provide a compact series of reasons why a viewer *should* see that movie. A trailer for Stanley Kubrick's *Eyes Wide Shut* (2000) is

2.54 *The Kid* (1921). Chaplin, unlike in his well-known slapstick comedies, expresses a demeanor in the poster that suggests the serious themes of his first feature film.

indicative: typical of this kind of promotion, it moves quickly to separate large bold titles announcing the names of Tom Cruise, Nicole Kidman, and Kubrick, foregrounding the collaboration of a star marriage and a celebrated director of daring films. Then, against the refrain from Chris Isaak's soundtrack song "Baby Did a Bad Thing," a series of images condenses the progress of the film, including shots of Kidman undressing [Figure 2.55], Cruise as Dr. Harford sauntering with two beautiful women, a passionate kiss shared by the two stars, two ominous-looking men at the gate of an estate (where the orgy would take place), and Cruise being enticed by a prostitute. Besides the provocative match of two, then-married star sex symbols with a controversial director, the trailer underlines the dark erotic mysteries of the film within an opulently decadent setting. It introduces intensely sexual characters and the alternately seedy and glamorous atmosphere of the film in a manner meant to draw fans of Cruise, Kidman, Kubrick, and dark erotic intrigue. That this promotion fails to communicate the stinging irony in the movie's eroticism may, interestingly, account for some of the disappointed reactions that followed its eager initial reception. The availability of trailers on the Internet has increased the novel approaches to this format, and trailers are rated and scrutinized just as are theatrical releases.

VIEWING CUE

Look at the film advertisements around you. What do the billboards, trailers, banners, pop-up windows, and newspaper advertisements communicate to you about this film?

High Concept, A and B Pictures, and Other Marketing Labels

Trailers, posters, and newspaper advertisements carefully select not only their images but also their terminology in order to guide our perspective on a film even before we see it. Parodied brilliantly in Robert Altman's *The Player* (1992), modern Hollywood can often promote a film with the language of **high concept**, a short phrase that attempts to sell the main marketing features of a movie through its stars, its genre, or some other easily identifiable connection [Figure 2.56]: in *The Player,* one film is described as "kind of a psychic political thriller with a heart"; other high-concept movies might be advertised as "Stanley Kubrick's exploration of pornography" or "In *Lara Croft: Tomb Raider* (2001), superstar Angelina Jolie brings the CD-ROM game to life." The rhetoric of movie advertising frequently descends into such silly clichés as "two thumbs up" or "action-packed, fun-filled adventure," yet promotional and marketing language also uses succinct descriptive terms to position a movie for particular expectations and responses. As we have seen, the term "feature film," originating in 1912 but becoming a key promotional strategy in the 1930s, describes a movie that is of a certain length (over seventy minutes), that is promoted as the main attraction or an **A picture** in a theater, and that promises high-quality stars and stories. Conversely, a **B picture** is a less expensive, less important movie that plays before the main attraction and indicates less visual and narrative sophistication. Just as today the term **blockbuster** prepares us for action, stars, and special effects, and **art film** suggests a slower, perhaps more visually and intellectually subtle movie, the terminology used to define and promote a movie can become a potent force in framing our expectations.

2.55 *Eyes Wide Shut* (2000). Advertisements and trailers for Stanley Kubrick's last film emphasized the film's director, its stars—Tom Cruise and Nicole Kidman, who were married at the time—and its sexual content.

2.56 *The Player* (1992). Director Robert Altman and writer Michael Tolkin satirize the movie business; the screenwriter's "pitch" to a studio executive becomes a literal matter of life and death.

The Rating System

Rating systems, which provide viewers with guidelines for movies (usually based on violent or sexual content), are a similarly important form of advertising that can be used in marketing and promotion. Whether they are wanted or unwanted by viewers, ratings are fundamentally about trying to control the kind of audience that sees a film and, to a certain extent, about advertising the content of that film. In the United States, the current ratings system classifies movies as G (general audiences), PG (parental guidance suggested), PG-13 (parental guidance suggested and not recommended for audiences under thirteen years old), R (persons under age seventeen must be accompanied by an adult), and NC-17 (persons under age seventeen are not admitted). Most countries, as well as some religious organizations, have their own systems for rating films. Great Britain, for instance, uses these categories: U (universal), A (parental discretion), AA (persons under age fourteen are not admitted), and X (persons under age eighteen are not admitted). Interestingly, the age limit for X-rated films varies from country to country, the lowest being age fifteen in Sweden.

A movie like *Free Willy* (1993), the tale of a child and a captured whale, depends on its G rating to draw large family audiences, whereas sexually explicit films like *Show Girls* (1995), rated NC-17, and Nagisa Oshima's *In the Realm of the Senses* (1976), not rated and confiscated when it first came to many countries, can use the notoriety of their ratings to attract curious adult viewers. But an NC-17 rating can damage a film's box-office prospects because many newspapers will not carry ads for such films. When promotion casually or aggressively uses ratings, our way of looking at and thinking about the movie already begins to anticipate the film. For example, with an R rating, we might anticipate a movie featuring a degree of sex and violence. A rating of G might promise happy endings and happy families. Such movies as *Men in Black* (1997) [Figure 2.57] eagerly sought a PG-13 rating because it, ironically perhaps, attracts a younger audience of eight-, nine-, and ten-year-olds, who want movies with a touch of adult language and action.

▶ **VIEWING CUE**

How would you summarize the "buzz" that anticipated or surrounded, for example, *Sex and the City* (2008)? Can you analyze how it prepared viewers with certain expectations?

Word of Mouth

Our experience at the movies is directed in advance of our viewing of the film in less evident and predictable ways as well. Word of mouth, the conversational exchange of opinions and information sometimes referred to as the "buzz" around a movie, may seem a somewhat insignificant or at least hazy area of promotion, yet it is an important social arena in which our likes and dislikes are formed and given direction by the social groups we move in. We know our friends like certain kinds of films, and we all tend to promote movies according to a culture of taste whereby we judge and approve of movies according to the values of our particular age group, cultural background, or other social determinant. When marketing experts direct a movie at a target audience, they intend to promote that film through word of mouth, knowing viewers talk to each other and recommend films to people who share their values and tastes.

Examine, for instance, how a group of friends might promote *Titanic* (1997) among themselves. Do they recommend it to one another because of the strength or attractiveness of the female character Rose, the breathtaking special effects, or the confrontation between the rich and the poor [Figures 2.58 and 2.59]? What would each of these word-of-mouth promotions indicate about the social or personal values of the person promoting the movie and the culture of taste influencing his or her views?

2.57 *Men in Black* (1997). A PG-13 rating can suggest a certain edge to a film that makes it attractive to preteens.

2.58 *Titanic* (1997). Word of mouth anticipating the release of James Cameron's film focused on special effects.

2.59 *Titanic* (1997). After the film's release, word of mouth fostered its success among young female fans of Leonardo DiCaprio and the romance plot.

From Fanzines to Web Sites

Fan magazines extend word of mouth as a form of movie promotion and shed light on the sociology of taste. Popular since the 1920s, and sometimes called "fanzines," in recent years fan magazines have evolved into Internet discussion groups and promotional and user-generated Web sites. Web sites, often set up by a film's distributor, have, in fact, become the most powerful contemporary form of the fanzine, allowing information about and enthusiasm for a movie to be efficiently exchanged and spread among potential viewers. In a breakthrough example of this trend, *The Blair Witch Project* (1999) Web site was established in advance of the film's release and used fake documents and clues to help generate word of mouth; the success of this strategy transformed this simple, low-budget horror film ($35,000) into a huge box-office hit ($15 million). In the spring of 2001, Steven Spielberg's *A.I.* and the *Planet of the Apes* remake targeted e-mail accounts and set up Web-based games (in the case of *Planet of the Apes,* a global scavenger hunt called Project A.P.E.) that spread through chat rooms even before the films were released. Notoriously, the title *Snakes on a Plane* (2006) was so resonant with viewers in its very literalness that the Web activity around the film prompted changes to make the film more daring and campier, even before its release. The subsequent box-office disappointment may have been a measure of viewers' reaction to marketing manipulations [**Figure 2.60**].

To encourage and develop individual interest in films, these fanzines and Web sites gather together readers and viewers who wish to read or chat about their ongoing interest in movies like the *Star Trek* films (1979–1994) or cult favorites like *Casablanca* (1942). Here tastes about which movies to like and dislike and about how to see them are both supported and promoted on a far more concrete social and commercial level. Information is offered or exchanged about specific movies, arguments are waged, and sometimes games or fictions are developed around the film. Magazines may provide information about the signature song of *Casablanca,* "As Time Goes By," and the actor who sings it, Dooley Wilson. Chat room participants may query each other about Mr. Spock's Vulcan history or fantasize about his personal life. Even before the release of *The Lord of the Rings: The Fellowship of the Ring* (2001), the filmmakers engaged fans of the Tolkien novel through e-mails and Web sites, trading information about the production for feedback on casting decisions and scene cuts. The Internet promotes word of mouth about a film by offering potential audiences the possibility of some participation in the making of the film, an approach that is increasingly common today.

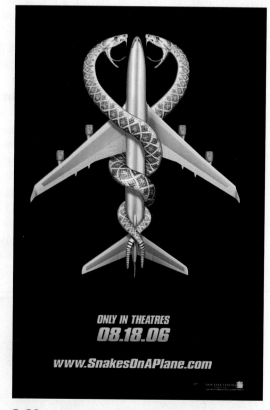

2.60 *Snakes on a Plane* (2006). Potential audiences had great fun with the film's advance publicity on the Web; the box-office performance did not live up to the hype.

text continued on page 51 ▶

Promoting
The Crying Game (1992)

Neil Jordan's *The Crying Game* is an ingenious example of various promotional maneuvers. A hybrid of art film and thriller, its story about the sexual identity crisis of Fergus, a member of the Irish Republican Army (IRA), begins with the capture of Jody, a black British soldier. After witnessing Jody's violent, accidental death, Fergus flees to England, where he seeks out and falls in love with Dil, Jody's former lover [Figure 2.61]. Complicating this plot, Fergus does not realize, during the first part of their courtship, that Dil is transgendered; Dil's female gender presentation leaves Fergus—and some audience members—surprised to discover a male anatomy.

For both British and American audiences, the film was first promoted on the basis of its artistic novelty and integrity, which was associated primarily with Jordan's cultural reputation as a serious director of such inventive British films as *Mona Lisa* (1986). That *The Crying Game* was only moderately successful when first released in England can be attributed, in part, to the social context of its release: renewed IRA activity in England at the time may have made it difficult for British audiences to look past the subplot and concentrate on Jordan's artistry or on the intriguing relationship between Fergus and Dil. The U.S. distributor, Miramax, also recognizing difficulties in distributing and promoting the film, was concerned about three traditional marketing taboos: race, political violence, and homosexuality. How-

ever, removed from the British–Irish political context, Miramax decided it could repackage the movie to promote it by drawing attention away from its political intrigue and focusing on the romantic and sexual "secret" of Dil's masculinity. The film broke box-office records in the United States for a British production. The promotional schemes in Britain and the United States resulted in significantly different ways of seeing and understanding the same movie.

At the center of its promotional history, *The Crying Game* used two different advertising approaches, one for the British release and another for the U.S. release conducted by the then-maverick company Miramax. The differences between these campaigns crystallize in the advertising posters used for the two promotions. In the British poster [Figure 2.62], a large profile of Stephen Rea as Fergus holding a smoking gun centers the image, surrounded by smaller images of Jaye Davidson as Dil and Miranda Richardson as the femme fatale, Jude. Numerous lines of print promote the film as "From the Director of *Mona Lisa*," "Neil Jordan's Best Work to Date," and as

2.61 *The Crying Game* (1992). The novelty of the film was its combination of unlikely subject matter: the IRA and sexual identity.

2.62 *The Crying Game* (1992). The British poster promotes the film's subject matter of political violence.

offering "More Surprises Than Any Film Since *Psycho.*" The American poster features only the image of Miranda Richardson, with a smoking gun, set against a black backdrop [**Figure 2.63**]. The print is equally spare: "Sex. Murder. Betrayal." and, under the film's title, "play it at your own risk." The British poster advertises the cinematic heritage of Jordan, while highlighting the masculine and political violence associated with Fergus's large image. The American poster conversely creates the dark atmosphere of sexual intrigue, notably offering audiences a participatory game rather than a serious political reality.

In the wake of the film's promotion and box-office success in the United States, the Internet continued to promote the film's initial participatory lure. Typically, dozens of Web sites about *The Crying Game* have appeared in numerous languages. Some sites, such as *The Crying Game* Fan Page, feature photos, Boy George's rendition of the title song, and links

2.63   *The Crying Game* (1992). The American poster promotes the film through an emphasis on sexual games, yet the central romance is not depicted.

to movie reviews. Others are devoted to a single star, such as Forest Whitaker or Jaye Davidson.

Ratings and, especially, word of mouth created specific expectations and interests in *The Crying Game*. It received an R rating in the United States (no doubt for its frontal male nudity), where such a rating would more likely suggest sexual content rather than violence. But especially in the United States, word of mouth functioned as the most powerful strategy in the promotion of *The Crying Game*. Viewers, including movie reviewers, were urged to keep the secret of Dil's biological gender as a way of baiting new audiences to see the film. A widely announced word-of-mouth promotion—"Don't tell the secret!"—drew a continuous stream of audiences wanting to participate in this game of secrets. Word of mouth became part of a strategy to entice American audiences who, anticipating a sexual drama of surprises and reversals, would in most instances overlook the political tensions that complicated the film for British audiences.

As they proliferate, promotional avenues like these deserve attention and analysis in terms of deciding how they add to or confuse our understanding of a film. Our different experiences of the movies take place within a complex cultural terrain where our personal interest in certain films intersects with specific historical and social forces to shape the meaning and value of those experiences. Here, too, the film experience extends well beyond the screen.

▶ **VIEWING CUE**

Consider the film you just viewed. Which of the promotional strategies discussed above seem most accurate? Most misleading? What about the film has been ignored or underplayed in any of these promotional strategies? ⏸

Movie Exhibition: The Where, When, and How of Movie Experiences

Distribution and promotion are called extra-filmic dimensions of the movie experience; they describe events that precede, surround, or follow the actual images we watch on a screen or television monitor. The final extra-filmic dimension of the movie experience is **exhibition**, the where and when we can see films. Like distribution and promotion, we tend to take exhibition for granted, forgetting that the many ways we watch movies contribute a great deal to our feelings about, and our interpretations of, film. We watch movies within the normal, cultural range of exhibition venues: in theaters, at home on video monitors, or on a plane or train on computer screens. Not surprisingly, these extra-filmic dimensions are closely related in how they anticipate and condition our responses to movies.

The Changing Contexts and Practices of Film Exhibition

If production, distribution, and promotion already work to anticipate, shape, and direct our tastes, then exhibition contexts and practices can support or alter the intended aims and meanings of a movie. These contexts and practices include the physical environment in which we view a movie, the temporal frameworks describing when we watch a movie and the length of time it takes, and the technological format and devices through which we see the movie.

Seeing the same movie at a cineplex or in a college classroom, watching it uninterrupted for two hours on a big screen or in thirty-minute segments over four days on a computer, can elicit very different kinds of film experiences. A viewer watching a film on an airplane monitor may be completely bored by it, but watching it later in a theater, he or she may find that film much more compelling, appreciating its visual surprises and interesting plot twists.

Movies have been distributed, exhibited, and seen in many different contexts historically. At the beginning of the twentieth century, movies rarely lasted more than twenty minutes and were often viewed in small, noisy **nickelodeons**, storefront theaters where short films were shown continuously to audiences passing in and out, or in carnival settings that assumed movies were a passing amusement comparable to other carnival attractions. By the 1920s, as movies grew artistically, financially, and culturally, the exhibition of films moved to lavish movie palaces like Radio City Music Hall, with sumptuous seating for thousands and ornate architecture. By the 1950s, city centers gave way to suburban sprawl; as the theaters lost their crowds of patrons, drive-ins and widescreen and 3-D processes were introduced to distinguish the possibilities of film exhibition from its new rival, television at home. Today we commonly see movies at home, on a VCR or DVD player, where we can watch them in the normal 90- to 120-minute period or extend our viewing over many nights in a series of episodes; watching films in miniature, portable formats such as iPods has also become increasingly popular. In recent years, as movies continue to compete with home video, film exhibitors have countered with so-called megaplexes—theaters with twenty or more screens, more than six thousand seats, and over a hundred show times per day. These new entertainment complexes may feature not just movies but also miniature golf courses, roller rinks, restaurants, and coffee bars. Home exhibition has responded in turn with more elaborate digital picture and sound technologies.

The Culture of Exhibition Space

Changing exhibition formats parallel many other changes in the ways in which we watch and respond to movies. Informing all of them is a culture of exhibition space; how and where we watch a movie reflects or becomes part of specific social activities that surround and define moviegoing: exhibition highlights a social dimension of watching movies because it gathers and organizes individuals as a specific social group. Further, our shared participation in that social environment directs our attention and shapes our responses in ways that influence how we enjoy and understand a film.

A movie such as *Charlotte's Web* (2006) **[Figure 2.64]** will be shown as a Saturday matinee in suburban theaters (as well as other places) to attract families with children to its famous children's tale of a spider who saves a piglet. The time and place of the showing obviously coordinate with a period when middle-class families can share recreation and amusement, making them more inclined to appreciate this lighthearted tale of family love and affection. Conversely, Peter Greenaway's *The Pillow Book* (1996) **[Figure 2.65]**, a complex film about a woman's passion

▶ **VIEWING CUE**

For the next film you watch, consider how the film was first exhibited. Would it have been shown in a nickelodeon? A movie palace? A cineplex? How would that exhibition context have been appropriate for the movie? ⏸

▶ **VIEWING CUE**

How could the "culture of exhibition" be more or less suited to the film you've just viewed? What would be the ideal audience for the film? Why? What kind of exhibition would most likely draw that audience? ⏸

2.64 *Charlotte's Web* (2006). G-rated family films are distributed widely to theater chains.

for calligraphy, human flesh, poetry, and sexuality, would likely appear in a small downtown theater frequented by single individuals and young couples who also spend time in the theater's coffee bar. This movie would probably appeal to an urban crowd with more experimental tastes, and to those who like to watch more intellectually stimulating and conversation-provoking films. Reversing the exhibition contexts of these two films would indicate how those contexts could generate wildly different reactions.

The Technology of Exhibition

Earlier in this chapter we discussed the technologies of viewing films (pp. 20–22) and how the various viewing options affect our overall film experience. The technological conditions of exhibition–that is, the industrial and mechanical vehicles through which movies are shown–are equally influential. In a large theater, a movie can be shown with a 35mm or even 70mm movie projector that displays large and vibrantly detailed images. We might see another movie in a cineplex theater at a mall with a relatively small screen and a smorgasbord of other movies in the theaters surrounding it. We may watch a third movie on a DVD player that allows us to watch just our favorite scenes. In the past, popular exhibition practices included inserting a short movie within a vaudeville performance or offering double features in drive-in theaters full of teenagers in cars. Today's movies exhibited on a computer screen can share the monitor with other kinds of activities.

Different technological features of exhibition are sometimes carefully calculated to add to both our enjoyment and our understanding of a movie. Cecil B. DeMille's epic film *The Ten Commandments* (1923) premiered in a movie palace, where the plush and grandiose surroundings, the biblical magnitude of the images, and the orchestral accompaniment supported the grand spiritual themes of the film. In most cases, the idea is to match, as here, the exhibition with the themes of the film so that the conditions for watching it parallel the ideas or formal practices in the movie. With a movie that uses special projection techniques for exhibition, such as 3-D glasses [Figure 2.66] for *Creature from the Black Lagoon* (1954), the form and technology of exhibition in which we are meant to watch the film can often relate to its subject matter. Here the appearance of the creature becomes even more shocking with more visual dimensions. Often regarded with nostalgia, 3-D technology made a comeback with Robert Zmeckis's *Beowulf* (2007), which received a wide release and used competing, state-of-the-art 3-D technologies.

The Timing of Exhibition

Overlapping with distribution timing, the timing of exhibition is a more flexible but equally influential part of our movie experience. That is, when and for how long we see a film can shape our experience as much as where we see the film. Although it

2.65   *The Pillow Book* (1996). Art films, especially those that receive an NC-17 rating, are likely to be distributed primarily to specialty cinemas in urban locations.

2.66   3-D exhibition. Viewers enjoy a screening with special 3-D glasses.

▶ VIEWING CUE

Consider how different kinds of exhibition technologies might affect your response to a movie. Do they enhance or shape your understanding of the film in specific ways? If so, how?

▶ VIEWING CUE

Imagine seeing this film at different times of the year or during the week. How would the timing of the exhibition affect your expectations about the movie? What would be the best time to exhibit the film? Why?

text continued on page 55 ▶

Exhibiting
Citizen Kane (1941)

The tale of a man obsessed with power and possessions, *Citizen Kane* is often considered one of the greatest films ever made. It is usually hailed for Orson Welles's portrayal of Charles Foster Kane and Welles's direction of the puzzle-like story, and for the film's complex visual compositions. It is also a movie that ran into trouble even before its release because of its thinly disguised and critical portrayal of U.S. media mogul William Randolph Hearst. Less often is the film seen and understood according to its dramatic exhibition history, one that has colored or even decided the changing meanings of the film.

As the first film of a director already hailed as a "boy genius" for his work as a theater actor and director, *Citizen Kane* was scheduled to open with appropriate fanfare at the spectacular Radio City Music Hall in New York City. Besides highlighting the glamorous and palatial architecture of this building, exhibiting the film in New York first would take advantage of the fact that Welles's career and reputation had been made there. The physical and social context for this opening exhibition would combine the epic grandeur of the Radio City building and a New York cultural space attuned to Welles's artistic experimentation. Already offended by rumors about the film, however, Hearst secretly moved to block the opening at Radio City Music Hall. After many difficulties and delays, the film's producer and distributor, RKO, eventually premiered the film simultaneously at an independent theater in Los Angeles and at a refurbished vaudeville house in New York City [Figure 2.67]. As a final twist, when major theaters such as the Fox and Paramount chains were legally forced to exhibit the film, they sometimes booked *Citizen Kane* but did not screen it for fear of vindictive repercussions from Hearst. Where it was shown in Warner Bros. theaters, its short and tortured exhibition history overshadowed the film itself, making it appear for many audiences strange and unnecessarily confrontational. Clearly the intended opening exhibition would have generated a response quite different from the one that occurred. Would its association with a movie palace like Radio City

Music Hall have highlighted the more traditional features of the film, like its comedy and star performances, and made its complex story less of an obstruction? Or might the scandal of the movie's exhibition problems have added to its notoriety and celebrity?

Changing sociological and geographical contexts for exhibition have continued to follow *Citizen Kane* as its reputation has grown through the years. After its tumultuous first exhibition in the United States, the film was rediscovered in the 1950s by the art-house cinemas of France. There it became less a provocative commentary on an American mogul and his power politics than a brilliantly creative expression of film language. Today many individuals who see *Citizen Kane* watch it in a classroom—say, in a college course on American cinema. In the classroom, we look at movies as students or as scholars, and we are prepared to study them. In this context, viewers may feel urged to think more about the film as an art object than as entertainment or thinly disguised biography. In the classroom, we may fo-

2.67 *Citizen Kane* (1941). The film's premiere was delayed by the objections of William Randolph Hearst to its thinly veiled portrayal of his life.

cus more on the importance of the serious tragedies in the film (such as Kane's real and visual alienation from his best friends) and less on the comic interludes (such as the vaudevillian dance number). This is not to say that someone watching *Citizen Kane* in an academic situation cannot see and think about it in other ways. It's clear, however, that exhibition context can, very importantly, suggest certain social attitudes through which we watch a movie.

The exhibition history of *Citizen Kane* likewise describes significant differences in how the film is experienced through different technologies. Its original exhibition used a 35mm projection providing the rich textures and sharp images needed to bring out the imagistic details and stunning deep focus that made the film famous. The visual magnitude of scenes such as Susan Alexander's operatic premiere and Kane's safari picnic at Xanadu, or the spatial vibrancy and richness of Kane and Susan's conversation in one of Xanadu's vast halls, arguably require the size and texture of a large theatrical image. Since its first theatrical exhibition, the film has been seen on 16mm film and later on videotape, and more recently it has been remastered as a DVD. The content of the film remains the same, but the different technologies often mute the visual power of such images and scenes because the lower quality or smaller size of the images redirect our understanding from the visual dramatics of single images to the events of the story.

The shift in the exhibition context from the theater to the television obviously affects other subtle and not-so-subtle changes in how we see and understand the movie. On television, the image becomes a different size and quality and our level of concentration changes, perhaps from intense concentration to distracted attention. A viewing experience on television or video, moreover, may be broken up because of commercials or because we can start and stop the movie ourselves. In the case of *Citizen Kane,* as with many other films that move between

theaters and television, the basic action of the movie may appear the same, but how we engage that material can change in ways that determine the meaning of the film experience. Whereas the large images in the theater may direct the viewer more easily to the play of light and dark as commentaries on the different characters, a video player might not allow those observations but might instead allow the viewer to replay dialogue in order to note levels of intonation or wordplay. The DVD of *Citizen Kane* gives viewers the added opportunity to supplement the film with rare photos, documents on the advertising campaign, commentaries by filmmaker Peter Bogdanovich and critic Roger Ebert, and a documentary, *The Battle over Citizen Kane* (1996), that describes the history of its script and its exhibition difficulties [Figure 2.68]. To whatever degree these supplemental materials come into play, it is clear that a DVD exhibition of *Citizen Kane* offers possibilities for significantly enriching an audience's experience of the film. Viewers taking advantage of these materials would conceivably watch *Citizen Kane* prepared and equipped with certain points of view: more attuned perhaps to Welles's creative innovation and influence on later filmmakers like Bogdanovich, or more interested in how the film re-creates the connections between Hearst and Kane detailed in the documentary supplement. That the DVD provides material on "alternative ad campaigns" for the original release of the film even allows viewers to investigate the way different promotional strategies can direct their attention to certain themes and scenes.

The fame of *Citizen Kane* as topping critics' polls as the best film ever made and its frequent invocation as the effort of a "boy wonder" contribute to yet another exhibition context through fans posting excerpts on the Internet in a video-sharing site such as YouTube. Would-be filmmakers compare their efforts to Welles's or remix parts of his classic film, introducing new generations to the classic.

2.68   *Citizen Kane* (1941). The supplementary material of DVD distribution and exhibition offer the chance to see Orson Welles and the film's script.

is common to see movies in the early evening, before or after dinner, audiences watch movies according to numerous rituals and in various time slots. Afternoon matinees, midnight movies, or the in-flight movie on a long plane ride give some indication of how the timing of a movie experience can vary and how that can influence other considerations about the movie. In each of these situations, our experience of the movies includes a commitment to spend time in a certain way. Instead of time spent reading, in conversation, sleeping, or working on a business project, we watch a movie. That time spent with a movie accordingly becomes an activity associated with relaxing, socializing, or even working in a different way.

▶ **VIEWING CUE**

Think of a movie you've watched as a "leisure time" versus a "productive time" activity. How might a film be viewed differently in a classroom versus during a long airplane flight?

Vaudeville theater.

Atlanta's Fox Theatre, built in 1929.

Drive-in.

Multiplex theater chain.

IMAX.

On any particular occasion, reflect on the period of time you choose to watch a film. How else might that time be spent, and what is your rationale for using this time to watch a film? Does the choice of that specific day and time to see a film have any bearing on the film you choose to see? More important, how accurate are the conventional assumptions about the time spent watching films as a time to escape the so-called real world?

Leisure Time

Traditionally, movie culture has emphasized film exhibition as *leisure time,* a time that is assumed to be less productive (at least compared to the time spent working a job) and that reinforces assumptions about movies as the kind of enjoyment associated with play and pleasure. To some extent, leisure time is a relatively recent historical development. Since the nineteenth century, when motion pictures first appeared, modern society has aimed to organize experience so that work and leisure could be separated and defined in relation to each other. We generally identify leisure time as "an escape," "the relaxation of our mind and body," or "the acting out of a different self." Since the early twentieth century, movie exhibition has been associated with leisure time in these ways. Seeing a comedy on a Friday night promises relaxation at the end of a busy week. Playing a concert film on a DVD player while eating dinner may relieve mental fatigue. Watching a romantic film on television late at night may offer the passion missing from one's real life.

Productive Time

Besides leisure time, however, we can and should consider film exhibition as *productive time,* meaning time used to gain information, material advantage, or knowledge. From the early years of the cinema, movies have been used to illustrate lectures or introduce audiences to Shakespearean performances. More strictly educational films, such as those shown in health classes or driver education programs, are less glamorous versions of this use of film. Although less widely acknowledged as part of film exhibition, productive time continues to shape certain kinds of film exhibition. For a movie reviewer or film producer, an early morning screening may be about "financial value" because this use of time to evaluate a movie will presumably result in certain economic rewards. For another person, a week of films at an art museum represents "intellectual value," as it helps explain ideas about a different society or historical period. For a young American, an evening watching *Schindler's List* can be about "human value" because that film aims to make viewers more knowledgeable about the Holocaust and more sensitive to the suffering of other human beings.

Film exhibitions usually try to provide a variety of time periods to accommodate many different temporal values, and different viewers can certainly find different values in the same exhibition. Still, the timings of exhibitions do tend to frame and emphasize the film experience according to certain values. The Cannes Film Festival introduces a wide range of films and functions both as a business venue for buying and selling film and as a glamorous showcase for stars and parties. The May timing of this festival and its Riviera location ensure that the movie experience will be about pleasure and the business of leisure time. In contrast, the New York Film Festival, featuring some of the same films, has a more intellectual or academic aura. That it occurs in New York City during September and October, at the beginning of the academic year, associates this experience of the movies more with artistic value and productive time. The premiere of Sofia Coppola's *Marie Antoinette* (2006) at the Cannes festival exploited both the high-profile glamour of that festival's party atmosphere and a French context that would certainly draw the kind of attention it would not receive at the New York event. That many French critics hostilely denounced the film indicates either a tactical error in the choice of an opening exhibition or the truism that all publicity is good publicity **[Figure 2.69]**.

Classroom, library, and museum exhibitions tend to emphasize understanding and learning as much as enjoyment. When students watch films in these kinds of situations, they are asked to attend to them somewhat differently from the way they may view films on a Friday night at the movies. They watch more carefully, perhaps; they may consider the films as part of historical or artistic traditions; they may take notes as a logical part of this kind of exhibition. These conditions of film exhibition do not necessarily change the essential meaning of a movie; but in directing how we look at a film, they can certainly shade and even alter how we understand that film. Like other changes in viewing conditions, exhibition asks us to engage and think about the film not as an isolated object but as part of the expectations established by the conditions in which we watch it.

2.69 *Marie Antoinette* (2006). At the Cannes Film Festival, *Marie Antoinette* had a premiere as sumptuous as its mise-en-scène.

CONCEPTS AT WORK

Behind virtually every movie is a complex set of decisions, choices, and aims about how to make, distribute, market, and exhibit a film to reach audiences. Here we've highlighted some of the most important parts of that work as they anticipate and position viewers in specific ways to respond to a film. Keeping in mind the way viewers both identify with movies and learn to understand them, we've seen how production methods, distribution strategies, marketing techniques, and exhibition places have responded to and created different kinds of movie experiences and can often fashion how those films are enjoyed and understood.

Activities

- Compare a story about a film in the arts section of your local paper with a discussion of the same film in the online version of the industry "trade" paper *Variety* or the independent film online source Indiewire.com. What does this tell you about the cultural priorities of the film industry today? How is film production valued and viewed in these different examples?
- Imagine that you and a group of investors plan to open a state-of-the-art movie theater in your hometown. Describe your plans for its design and its location. What kind of films would you exhibit there? How would you use the timing of their distribution and exhibition to your advantage? How would these decisions reflect your intentions for the kinds of film you would show and the audience you'd hope to attract?

THE NEXT LEVEL: ADDITIONAL SOURCES

Acland, Charles R. *Screen Traffic: Movies, Multiplexes, and Global Culture.* Durham, NC: Duke University Press, 2003. Examining the changes in the movie business since the mid-1980s, this book explores the new global reach of the cinema today and the changing production, distribution, and exhibition structures of business enmeshed in the economics of megaplexes, pay-per-view distribution, and accelerating viewing patterns.

Gomery, Douglas. *Shared Pleasures: A History of Movie Presentation in the United States.* Madison: University of Wisconsin Press, 1992. A well-researched and discriminating history of the many changes in film exhibition from 1895 to 1990, this study provides a wealth of detail about the evolution of distribution in U.S. movies.

Lukk, Tiiu. *Movie Marketing: Opening the Picture and Giving It Legs.* Los Angeles: Silman-St. James, 1997. Less a scholarly work than a series of case studies, this book concentrates on a variety of contemporary movies—from *Four Weddings and a Funeral* to *Mrs. Doubtfire*—and describes the different marketing and promotion strategies used today.

Mayne, Judith. *Cinema and Spectatorship.* New York: Routledge, 1993. This excellent book summarizes and rethinks models of identification at the movies to develop more varied and dynamic descriptions that account for different audience responses.

Stokes, Melvyn, and Richard Maltby. *American Movie Audiences: From the Turn of the Century to the Early Sound Era.* London: BFI, 1999. This excellent collection of essays maps the remarkable diversity of moviegoing patterns in the first part of the twentieth century. Arguing the diverse social compositions of early film audiences, the book presents convincing evidence of those audiences often resisting the homogenization and standardization being promoted by a corporate Hollywood.

Vachon, Christine, with Austin Bunn. *A Killer Life: How an Independent Producer Survives Deals and Disasters in Hollywood and Beyond.* New York: Simon and Schuster, 2006. A lively account of the production process by a founder of New York–based independent film company Killer Films, which produced such innovative films as *Boys Don't Cry* and *I'm Not There.*

Williams, Linda, ed. *Viewing Positions: Ways of Seeing Film.* New Brunswick, NJ: Rutgers University Press, 1995. This varied collection of essays on spectatorship at the movies presents critical discussions addressing a range of viewing experiences, from early cinema to postmodern malls.

PART 2

COMPOSITIONS

film scenes, shots, cuts, and sounds

To some extent, a movie mimics how we commonly use our senses to experience our real world. Most often, films activate our senses of sight and sound; to a lesser extent, films also stimulate our sense of touch. D. W. Griffith's *Broken Blossoms* (1919) re-creates the claustrophobic sensations of being trapped in a small room; in the Taviani brothers' Italian film *Padre Padrone* (1977), we hear the breezes whisper through tree limbs as if we were alone in a strange, almost mystical, landscape; in Rob Marshall's *Chicago* (2002), we visually experience the robust energies and physical power of dance. As a gimmick in conjunction with the release of *Scent of Mystery* (1960), theaters activated an audience's sense of smell by releasing rose and tobacco fragrances from pipes under viewers' seats. By manipulating the senses, film images and sounds create experiences viewers recognize and respond to—physically, emotionally, and intellectually.

In the next four chapters, we identify the formal and technical powers associated with the different elements of film form. In each chapter, we provide a short historical, industrial, and cultural background for that formal element. We then detail the specific properties and strategies of each particular aspect of film form. Finally, we suggest some of the cultural values and traditions that have influenced and evolved around these formal mechanisms and that help determine our points of view on, and interpretations of, scenes, shots, cuts, and sounds at the movies.

CHAPTER 3

Exploring a Material World: Mise-en-Scène

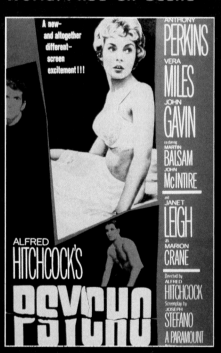

- Sets and settings
- Actors and performance styles
- Lighting
- Costumes and make-up

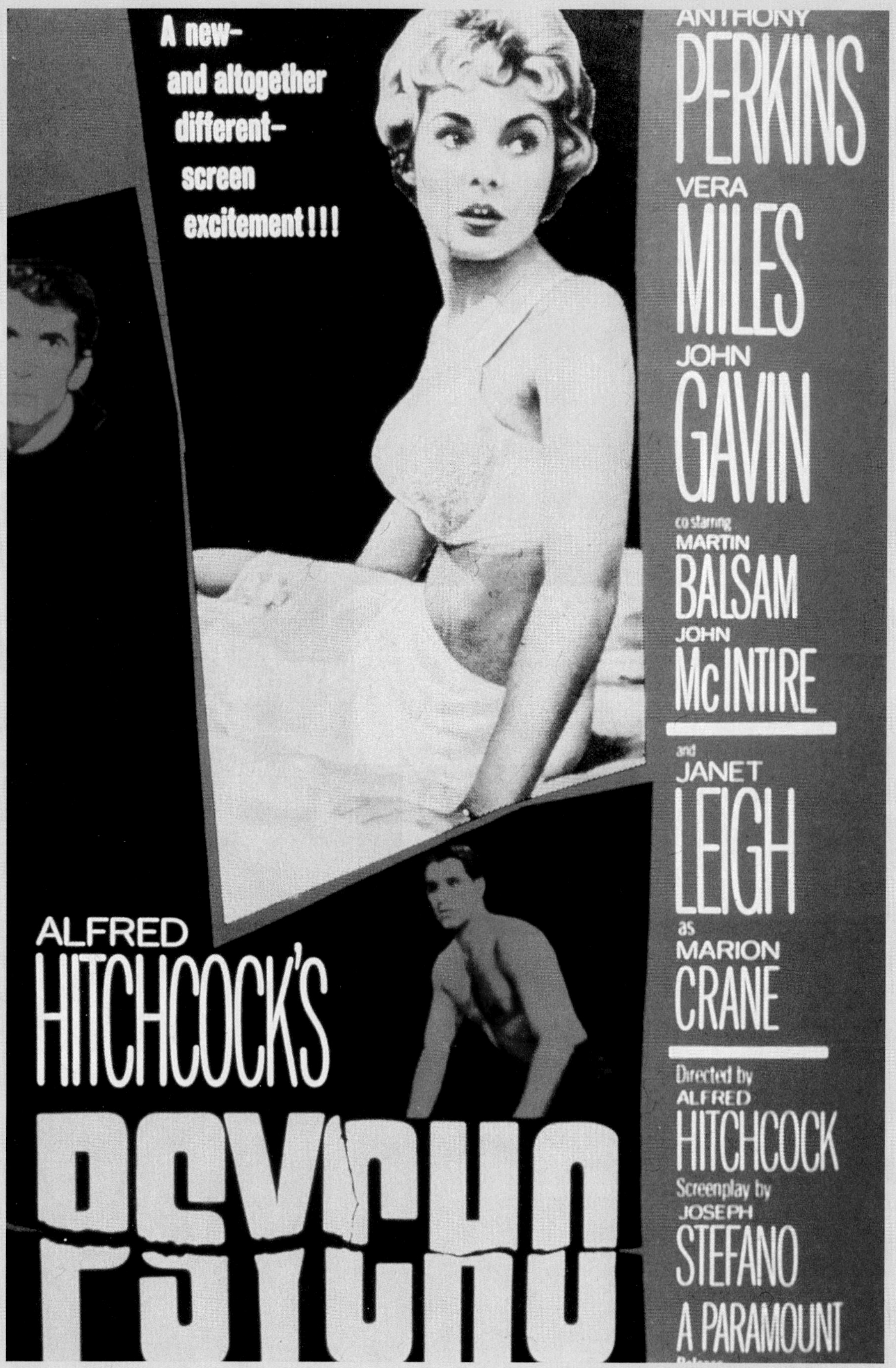

A new-
and altogether
different-
screen
excitement!!!
ANTHONY
PERKINS
VERA
MILES
JOHN
GAVIN
co starring
MARTIN
BALSAM
JOHN
McINTIRE
and
JANET
LEIGH
as
MARION
CRANE
Directed by
ALFRED
HITCHCOCK
Screenplay by
JOSEPH
STEFANO
A PARAMOUNT
ALFRED
HITCHCOCK'S
PSYCHO

Exploring a Material World

Mise-en-Scène

In the trailer for his 1960 film *Psycho*, director Alfred Hitchcock takes the viewer on a
tour of the film's now-legendary sets, treating them as actual locations. Walking
through the ordinary-looking Bates Motel and the sinister old house behind it,
Hitchcock blandly points out a steep staircase where a murder occurs, darkly hints at
the significance of a picture on the wall, and finally reaches to pull back the shower
curtain. The viewer enjoys the trailer's manufactured suspense, which is more than
likely enhanced by familiarity with the shocking events that occur in each of these
sites, either because the viewer has already seen the film (this trailer postdates its
release) or knows it by reputation. But outside the fictional world of the story, these
settings don't quite carry the same charge of dread. Evoking the centrality of mise-en-
scène to a film's mood, the trailer also shows how meticulously its effects are coordinated. But the full impact of these settings and props is not achieved until they are
experienced in the course of watching *Psycho* itself.

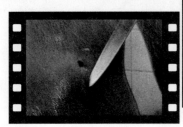

From the French term meaning "placed in a scene" or "onstage," **mise-en-scène** refers to those elements of a movie scene that are put in position before the filming actually begins and are employed in certain ways once it does. Mise-en-scène orchestrates a rich and complex variety of formal and material elements inherited from theater, using principles of composition derived from painting and photography. The mise-en-scène contains the scenic elements of a movie, including actors, aspects of lighting, sets and settings, costumes, make-up, and other features of the image that exist independently of the camera and the processes of filming and editing.

Outside the movies, our surroundings function like mise-en-scène. The architecture of a town might be described as a public mise-en-scène. How a person arranges and decorates a room could be called a private mise-en-scène. Courtrooms construct a mise-en-scène that expresses institutional authority. The placement of the judge above the court, of the attorneys at the bar, and of the witnesses in a partially sequestered area expresses the distribution of power. The flood of light through the vast and darkened spaces of a cathedral creates an atmospheric mise-en-scène aimed to inspire contemplation and humility. The clothes, jewelry, and make-up a person chooses to wear are, in one sense, the functional costuming all individuals don as part of inhabiting a particular mise-en-scène: businessmen wear suits, clergy dress in black, and service people in fast-food restaurants wear uniforms with company logos. This chapter describes how mise-en-scène organizes and directs much of our film experience by putting us in certain places and by arranging the people and objects of those places in specific ways.

KEY CONCEPTS

In this chapter, we consider

- how settings create meaningful environments for a film
- how theatrical and other traditions affect the history of cinematic mise-en-scène
- how sets and props relate to a film's story
- how actors and performance styles function in a mise-en-scène
- how lighting is used to evoke certain meanings
- how costumes and make-up contribute to our understanding of a character
- how mise-en-scène puts in play values associated with specific film traditions

3.1 *The Elephant Man* (1980). Recognizing the human beneath the power of make-up.

3.2 *Panic Room* (2002). The stress and fear of being enclosed becomes a formal structure of both old and new films.

62

In many ways, we respond not only to physical settings and material surfaces and objects, but also to the sensations associated with them. Whether we respond by actually touching the materials or simply imagining their texture and volume, this tactile experience of the world is a continual part of how we engage and understand the people and places around us. Such is also the case with the movies. Characters attract or repulse us through the clothing and make-up they wear: in *Some Like It Hot* (1959), Marilyn Monroe's eroticism is inseparable from her slinky dresses; in *The Elephant Man* (1980), the drama hinges on Joseph Carey Merrick's deforming make-up and the recognition that he is a sensitive human being inside a hideous shape [Figure 3.1]. Actions set in open or closed spaces can generate feelings of portent or hopelessness: in *Lawrence of Arabia* (1962), the open desert shimmers with possibility and danger; in *Panic Room* (2002), as its title indicates, emotion is created almost entirely through the constricted setting in which its heroine is trapped [Figure 3.2]. In *Vertigo* (1958), when the protagonist relives again and again the dizzying fear of heights that he first discovers when he watches a partner fall from a roof, viewers share his perspective. These tactile experiences can be culturally modified, influenced, or emphasized in very different ways by specific films. For instance, rarely has a taste for the texture and smell of food (especially chocolate) been re-created as intensely as it is in *Like Water for Chocolate* (1992) [Figure 3.3].

Setting the artistic precedent for cinematic mise-en-scène is the theatrical stage, where our sensual and tactile engagement is based on the presence of real actors performing in real time on a physical stage. Film engages us in a different way. A film's material world may be actual objects and people set in authentic locations, like the stunning slopes of the Himalayas in *Seven Years in Tibet* (1997). Or it may include objects and settings constructed by set designers to appear fantastic or realistic, such as the cramped spaces within a submarine in *U-571* (2002) [Figure 3.4]. In all its variation, mise-en-scène—a film's places and spaces, people and objects, lights and shadows—has evolved as a key dimension of our movie experience.

3.3 *Like Water for Chocolate* (1992). Dark, luxuriant colors draw attention to the texture of the food.

3.4 *U-571* (2002). Realistic sets create the claustrophobic mise-en-scène of a submarine.

A Short History of Mise-en-Scène

TRANSFORMING FILM:
Changing Stages
of Mise-en-Scène

From early silent dramas to contemporary fantasies, mise-en-scène moved swiftly across stages, through elaborately posed costumes and sets, to spectacular, realistic backgrounds, and onto the stages of the imagination.

Athalie (1910).

Intolerance (1916).

My Fair Lady (1964).

Manhattan (1979).

Charlie and the Chocolate Factory (2005).

The first movies were literally "scenes." Sometimes they were quaint public or domestic scenes (a baby being fed or a couple kissing); often they were dramatic scenes re-created on a stage for a movie camera. The ancient sites and holy objects seen in *The Passion Play of Oberammergau* (1898) fascinated audiences with their realistic appearance. A mixture of slides and short films, *Old Mexico and Her Pageants* (1899) used scenes and costumes to enliven and illustrate a lecture. While such films usually presented what could be accomplished in a one-room studio or a confined outdoor setting, by 1907 mise-en-scène had become more elaborate. Movies like *The Automobile Thieves* (1906) and *On the Stage; or, Melodrama from the Bowery* (1907) began to coordinate two or three interior and exterior settings, using make-up and costumes to create different kinds of characters and exploiting the stage for visual tricks and gags. In D. W. Griffith's monumental *Intolerance* (1916), the sets that reconstructed ancient Babylon were, in many ways, the main attraction **[Figure 3.5]**. In the following section, we will sketch some of the historical paths associated with the development of cinematic mise-en-scène throughout more than a century of film history.

Theatrical Mise-en-Scène and the Prehistory of Cinema

The clearest heritage of cinematic mise-en-scène lies in the Western theatrical tradition that began with early Greek theater around 500 B.C. and evolved through the nineteenth century. The first stages served as places where a community's religious beliefs and truths could be acted out. Centuries later, European medieval theater celebrated Christian stories—of Adam and Eve or the nativity—in mystery plays using a small cast with costumes, props, and scenery. During the Renaissance of the late sixteenth and early seventeenth centuries, the sets, costumes, and other elements of mise-en-scène that were used to stage, for example, the plays of William Shakespeare reflected a secular world of politics and personal relationships through which individuals and communities fashioned their values and beliefs.

By the beginning of the nineteenth century, lighting and other technological developments rapidly altered the nature of mise-en-scène and began to anticipate the cinema. On the English stage, eighteenth-century actor and theater manager David Garrick is credited with unifying and professionalizing the theatrical experience and setting the stage apart from the audience with spectacular sets, costumes, lighting, and new norms of audience behavior. In contrast to the drawing-room interiors of the eighteenth century, stages and sets grew much larger; they could now support the massive panoramic scenery and machinery developed by innovators such as P. J. de Loutherbourg, whose scenic illusions and breathtaking spectacles were designed to overwhelm audiences. At about the same time, an emphasis on individual actors (such as Fanny and John Kemble and Ellen Terry in England) influenced the rising cult of the star, who became the center of the mise-en-scène.

1900-1912: Early Cinema's Theatrical Influences

The subjects of the first films were limited by their dependence on natural light. But by 1900, films revealed their theatrical influences. *The Downward Path* (1901), a melodrama familiar from the popular stage, used five tableaux—brief scenes presented by sets and actors as "pictures" of key dramatic moments—to convey the plight of a country girl who succumbs to the wickedness of the city. One of many early films that turned to famous playwrights for movie material was the 1904 release *Damnation of Faust*, which adapted Goethe's *Faust*. Further encouraging this theatrical direction in mise-en-scène was the implementation of mercury-vapor lamps and indoor lighting systems around 1906 that enabled studio shooting. By 1912, one of the most famous stage actors of all time, Sarah Bernhardt, was persuaded to participate in the new medium, starring in the films *Queen Elizabeth* (1912) and *La dame aux camélias* (1912). Besides legitimate theater, other aspects of nineteenth-century visual culture influenced the staging of early films. The famous "trick" films of Georges Méliès, with their painted sets and props, were adapted from the magician's stage shows. In the United States, Edwin S. Porter's *Uncle Tom's Cabin* (1903) imitated the staging of familiar scenes from the "Tom Shows," seemingly ubiquitous regional adaptations for the stage of Harriet Beecher Stowe's novel.

1915–1928: Silent Cinema and the Star System

The 1914 Italian epic *Cabiria*, which included a depiction of the eruption of Mount Etna, established the taste for movie spectaculars. Feature-length films soon became the norm, and elaborately constructed sets and actors in carefully designed costumes defined filmic mise-en-scène. By 1915, art directors or set designers (called "technical directors" doing "interior decoration" at the time) became an integral part of filmmaking. The rapid expansion of the movie industry in the 1920s was facilitated by the rise of studio systems in Hollywood, Europe, and Japan. Studios had their own buildings and lots on which to construct expansive sets and personnel under contract to design and construct them. Erich Kettelhut's famous, futuristic set designs for Fritz Lang's film *Metropolis* (1926), constructed on the soundstage of the German Ufa studios, were influenced by the modernist architecture of the Manhattan skyline.

Beginning in the late 1910s, cinema developed and promoted its own stars, and the star system often identified an actor with a particular genre that had a distinctive mise-en-scène. Rudolf Valentino's films, for example, were set in a romantic version of the Middle East [**Figure 3.6**], and Douglas Fairbanks starred in swashbuckling adventure tales. Charlie Chaplin's "Little Tramp" was instantly recognizable by his costume. Costume also helped shape an individualized glamour for female stars; designers such as MGM's Adrian developed a very specific look for actresses Greta Garbo and Joan Crawford, whose films were showcases for clothing and décor that reflected the art deco style of the 1920s even when their settings were historical.

3.5 *Intolerance* (1916). Epic sets often make an epic movie.

3.6 *The Sheik* (1921). The charismatic power of Rudolf Valentino is often linked to the romance of specific settings.

1930s–1960s: Studio-Era Production

The rapid introduction of sound at the end of the 1920s was facilitated by the stability of the studio system, in which a company controlling film production and distribution had sufficient capital to invest in production facilities and systems. **Soundstages**—large soundproofed buildings—were designed to move and construct with new efficiency elaborate sets, which were often complemented by an array of costumes, lighting, and props. Art directors were essential to a studio's signature style. During his long career at MGM, Cedric Gibbons was credited as art director on 1,500 films, including *Grand Hotel* (1932), *Gaslight* (1944), and *An American in Paris* (1951); he supervised a large number of personnel charged with developing each film's ideal mise-en-scène from the studio's resources. Producer David O. Selznick coined the title production designer for William Cameron Menzies's central role in creating the look of the epic *Gone with the Wind* (1939), from its dramatic historical sets, décor, and costumes to the color palette that would be highlighted by the film's Technicolor cinematography. Studio backlots enabled the construction of entire worlds: the main street of a western town or New York City's Greenwich Village, for example. Other national cinemas invested considerable resources in central studios. Cinecittà (cinema-city) was established by Italian dictator Mussolini in 1937, bombed during World War II, then subsequently rebuilt and used for Italian and international productions (including, in 2002, Scorsese's *Gangs of New York*). The expense lavished on mise-en-scène during the heyday of the studio system shapes contemporary expectations of "movie magic."

► **VIEWING CUE**

Can you identify any historical precedents for the primary mise-en-scène of the film you've just seen? A specific kind of theater? A cityscape? An architectural or painting style?

1940–1970: New Cinematic Realism

Photographic realism and the use of exterior spaces and actual locations—identifiable neighborhoods and recognizable cultural sites—complement cinema's theatrical heritage. Although the Lumières' earliest films were of everyday scenes and their operatives traveled all over the world to record movies, location shooting did not influence mainstream filmmaking until World War II. Ever since postwar Italian neorealist films that were shot on city streets (as refugees were housed in the Cinecittà studios) (see pp. 411–412), fiction and documentary filmmaking have come to depend on location scouting for suitable mise-en-scène. Few films more explicitly demonstrate the transformation within the history of mise-en-scène than Laurence Olivier's *Henry V* (1944), where the drama shifts from the stage of Shakespeare's Globe Theatre to the comparatively realistic sets of ships leaving for war in France [Figure 3.7]. *Naked City* (1948) returned U.S. filmmaking to the grit of New York's crime-ridden streets. By the 1960s, cinematic realism in the United States was associated with youth rebellion. Italian filmmaker Michelangelo Antonioni used amateur actors and sensual desert locations in the counterculture classic *Zabriskie Point* (1970). Realistic mise-en-scène was central to many of the new cinema movements of the 1970s that went beyond the established studio styles, including the postrevolutionary cinema in Cuba and the emergence of feature-filmmaking in sub-Saharan Africa in such films as Ousmane Sembène's *Xala* (1975).

3.7   *Henry V* (1944). Produced in the midst of World War II, Laurence Olivier's film charts within its own frame an important shift from a theatrical mise-en-scène to a more realistic setting.

1975–Present: Mise-en-Scène and the Blockbuster

Since the mechanical shark created for Spielberg's *Jaws* in 1975, the economics of internationally marketed blockbuster filmmaking have demanded an ever more spectacular emphasis on mise-en-scène, enhanced by photographic and computer-generated special effects. Spielberg's *Close Encounters of the Third Kind* (1977), for example, combined elaborate, built sets with special effects by Douglas Trumbull. Since the 1980s, the cinematic task of re-creating realistic environments and fantastical mise-en-scène alike has shifted to computerized models and computer-graphics technicians, who design the models to be digitally transferred onto film. *Pan's Labyrinth* (2006) portrays the internal world of its lonely child heroine in a rich mise-en-scène constructed from actual sets, costumes, prosthetics, and computer-generated imagery [**Figure 3.8**]. Certainly, realism remains a priority in many contemporary films, like *There Will Be Blood* (2007), and many films today benefit from the technical capacity of computers to re-create the exact details of historical eras, such as the nineteenth-century New York streets of Martin Scorsese's *Age of Innocence* (1993). In a sense, many contemporary audiences look for and many contemporary movies provide an experience that is "more real than real," to adapt the motto of *Blade Runner*'s Tyrell Corporation.

3.8 *Pan's Labryinth* (2006). Computer-generated imagery often creates realistic nightmares.

The Elements of Mise-en-Scène

In this section, we will identify the elements of mise-en-scène and introduce some of the central terms and concepts underpinning the notion of mise-en-scène. These include the settings and sets and how they contribute to scenic and atmospheric realism, as well as the other important elements including props, actors, costumes, and lighting.

Settings and Sets

Settings and sets are the most fundamental features of mise-en-scène. The **setting** refers to a fictional or real place where the action and events of the film occur. The **set** is, strictly speaking, a constructed setting, often on a studio soundstage; but both the setting and the set can combine natural and constructed elements. For example, one setting in *Citizen Kane* (1941) consists of a fictional mansion located in Florida (based on the actual Hearst estate in San Simeon, California), which, in this case, is a set constructed on an RKO soundstage.

Historically and culturally, sets and settings have changed regularly. The first films were made either on stage sets or in outdoor settings, using the natural light from the sun. Films gradually began to integrate both constructed sets and natural settings into the mise-en-scène. Today's cinematic mise-en-scène continues to use elaborate stages, such as the studio re-creation of Vietnam

VIEWING CUE

Describe, with as much detail as possible, one of the sets or settings in the next movie you watch for class. Other than the actors, which features of the film seem most important? Explain why.

VIEWING CUE

Examine the interaction of two important sets or settings in the film. What is their relationship? Does that interaction suggest important themes in the film?

3.9 *The Day after Tomorrow*
(2004). A digital mise-en-scène
becomes a futuristic New York City.

battlefields for *Full Metal Jacket* (1987), as
well as actual locations, such as the
Philadelphia streets and neighborhoods of
The Sixth Sense (1999) or the highways and
small western towns of *Little Miss Sunshine*
(2006). Models and computer enhancements
of mise-en-scène are popular for such
movies as *The Day after Tomorrow* (2004),
which digitally depicts a futuristic New
York City that has been destroyed by rising
ocean waters **[Figure 3.9]**.

Scenic and Atmospheric Realism

Settings and sets contribute to a film's mise-en-scène by establishing scenic realism and atmosphere. One of the most common, complicated, and elusive yardsticks
for the cinema, **realism** is the term most viewers use to describe the extent to which
a movie creates a truthful picture of a society, person, or some other dimension of
life. Realism can refer to psychological or emotional accuracy (in characters), recognizable or logical actions and developments (in a story), or convincing views and
perspectives of those characters or events (in the composition of the image). The
most prominent vehicle for cinematic realism, however, is the scenic realism of the
mise-en-scène, which enables us to recognize sets and settings as accurate evoca-
tions of actual places. A combination of selection and artifice, scenic realism is
most commonly associated with the physical, cultural, and historical accuracy of
the backgrounds, objects, and other figures.

Indeed, our measure of a film's realism is often more a product of the authenticity of this scenic realism than of the other features of the film, such as the psychology or actions of characters. Movies like the animated *Beauty and the Beast*
(1991) and the comic-book adaptation *Spider-Man 3* (2007) dramatize authentic
human emotions (the blossoming of an unexpected love in the first, and the inner
turmoil of a divided soul in the second), but these films would probably not be considered realistic because of the fantastic nature of their settings in magical castles
and futuristic laboratories. Other movies, such as *Michael Collins* (1996), which depicts the Irish revolution at the turn of the century, establish a convincing realism
through the physical, historical, and cultural verisimilitude of the sets and settings
(in *Michael Collins,* Dublin and the Irish
countryside), regardless of how the characters or story may be exaggerated or roman-
ticized **[Figure 3.10]**. Recognition of scenic
realism frequently depends, of course, on
the historical and cultural point of view of
the audience. *The Stepford Wives* (2004),
for example, set in an affluent white American suburb may at first seem realistic to
many affluent Americans but would appear
as a fantastic other world to farmers living
in rural China.

In addition to scenic realism, the mise-
en-scène of a film creates atmosphere and
connotations, those feelings or meanings associated with particular sets or settings. The
setting of a ship on the open seas might sug-

▶ **VIEWING CUE**

In the film you just watched for
class, what were the scenic connotations created by one of the most
important sets or settings? What
aspects of the sets helped you
better understand the scene?

3.10 *Michael Collins* (1996). The Irish countryside at the turn of the century creates
a convincing scenic realism.

gest danger and adventure; a kitchen set may connote comfortable, domestic feelings. Invariably these connotations are developed through the actions of the characters and developments of the larger story: the early kitchen set in *Mildred Pierce* (1945) creates an atmosphere of bright, slightly strained warmth; in *E.T.* (1982), a similar set describes the somewhat chaotic space of a modern, single-parent family; in *Marie Antoinette* (2006), the opulence of Versailles conveys the heroine's loneliness as well as her desires [Figure 3. 11].

Props, Actors, Costumes, and Lights

Unlike other dimensions of film form such as editing and sound, mise-en-scène was in place with the first films; hence the early decades of film history were explorations in how to use the materials of mise-en-scène. By 1906, mercury-vapor lamps for indoor lighting added new possibilities to mise-en-scène, making lighting as flexible to manipulate as furniture and sets. Eventually, as in *Titanic* (1997), movies would travel the globe and search the seas for settings; set builders turned into computer model makers; and costuming became not only more elaborate but also obsessed with the historical accuracy of dresses, shoes, and even buttons. Here we will examine the multiple physical objects and figures that speak through cinematic mise-en-scène.

Props

A **prop** (short for *property*) is an object that functions as a part of the set or as a tool used by the actors. *The Maltese Falcon* (1941) is named after its central prop, which its characters strive to possess or safeguard; *The Wizard of Oz* (1939) will be forever identified with the ruby slippers (they were silver in the book) that Dorothy acquires upon accidentally killing the Wicked Witch of the East. Props acquire special significance when they are used to express characters' thoughts and feelings, their powers and abilities in the world, or the primary themes of the film. In *Singin' in the Rain* (1952), when Gene Kelly transforms an ordinary umbrella into a gleeful expression of his new love, an object whose normal function is to protect a person from rain is more expressively used as an extension of a dance: the pouring rain makes little difference to a man in love [Figure 3.12]. In Alfred Hitchcock's *Suspicion* (1941), an ordinary glass of milk, brought to a woman who suspects her husband of murder, suddenly crystallizes the film's unsettling theme of malice hiding in the shape of innocence; in his *Spellbound* (1940), parallel lines in the pattern of a bathrobe trigger a psychotic reaction in the protagonist, John Ballantine, and in this film, too, a glass of milk suddenly appears ominous and threatening [Figure 3.13]. Even natural objects or creatures can become props that concentrate the meanings of a movie: in the 1997 Japanese film *The Eel,* the main character's bond with the eel becomes the vehicle for his poignant redemption from despair about human society.

Props appear in movies in two principal forms. *Instrumental props* are those objects displayed and used according to their common function. *Metaphorical props* are

3.11 *Marie Antoinette* (2006). Against a scenic background of extravagance, discontent and desire come into sharp relief.

▶ **VIEWING CUE**

For your next assigned film, turn off the sound and analyze a single scene in the movie. What is communicated through the elements of the mise-en-scène alone? ⏸

3.12 *Singin' in the Rain* (1952). An umbrella transformed as dancing prop.

3.13 *Spellbound* (1940). An ordinary but ominous glass of milk that may or may not have been poisoned.

VIEWING CUE

Distinguish two props: one instrumental and the other metaphorical. Describe how the props reflect certain themes in the film.

VIEWING CUE

Identify the single most important prop in this film. Why is it significant?

those same objects reinvented or employed for an unexpected, even magical, purpose—like Gene Kelly's umbrella—or invested with metaphorical meaning. The distinction is important because the type of prop can characterize the kind of world surrounding the characters and the ability of those characters to interact with that world. In *Babette's Feast* (1987), a movie about the joys of cooking in a small Danish village, a knife functions as an instrumental prop for preparing foods; in *Psycho* (1960), that same prop is transformed into a hideous murder weapon [**Figures 3.14a and 3.14b**]. *The Red Shoes* (1948) might be considered a film about the shifting status of a prop, red dancing slippers: at first, these shoes appear as an instrumental prop serving Victoria's rise as a great ballerina, but by the conclusion of the film they have been transformed into a darkly magical prop that dances the heroine to her death [**Figure 3.15**].

In addition to their function within a film, props may acquire significance in two prominent ways. *Cultural props*, such as a type of car or a piece of furniture, carry meanings associated with their place in a particular society. In *Herbie Fully Loaded* (2005), a sequel to the "flower-power" era's *The Love Bug* (1969), the heroine fixes up a tiny Volkswagen Bug and the comedy revolves around associations with this inexpensive, "retro" car model and its remarkable magical powers; in *Easy Rider* (1969), the two protagonists ride low-slung motorcycles that clearly suggest a countercultural rebellion [**Figure 3.16**]. *Contextualized props* acquire a meaning through their changing place in a narrative. *The Yellow Rolls-Royce* (1964) and *The Red Violin* (1998) focus fully on the changing meaning of the central prop: in the first film, three different romances are linked through their connection to a beautiful Rolls-Royce; the second film follows the path of a Nicolo Bussotti violin from seventeenth-century Italy to an eighteenth-century Austrian monastery, to nineteenth-century Oxford, to the Chinese cultural revolution in the twentieth century [**Figure 3.17**], and finally to a contemporary Montreal shop. Some films play specifically with the meaning a contextual prop comes to acquire. In *Ronin* (1998), a mysterious briefcase unites a group of mercenaries in a plot about trust and betrayal, but its secret significance becomes ultimately insignificant; Alfred Hitchcock's famous "McGuffins"—props that only appear to be important, like the stolen money in *Psycho* (1960) and the uranium in *Notorious* (1946)—are props meant to move a plot forward but are of little importance to the real drama of love, fear, and desire.

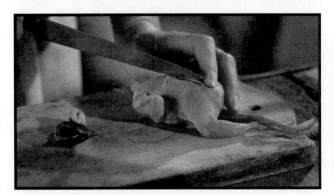

3.14a *Babette's Feast* (1987). A knife is a simple instrumental prop.

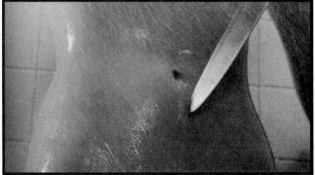

3.14b *Psycho* (1960). A knife can also be a murder weapon with possible metaphorical meanings associated with male sexuality.

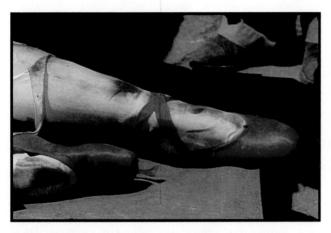

3.15 *The Red Shoes* (1948). Brilliantly red shoes: a prop that dominates a tragic story of passion and obsession.

3.16 *Easy Rider* (1969). The motorcycles stand out as countercultural icons.

3.17 *The Red Violin* (1998). The changing significance of a contextualized prop.

Staging: Performance and Blocking

At the center of the mise-en-scène is most often a flesh-and-blood **actor** who embodies and performs a film character through gestures and movements. A more intangible yet essential part of mise-en-scène, **performance** describes the actor's use of language, physical expression, and gesture to bring a character to life and to communicate important dimensions of that character to the audience. Because characters help us see and understand the actions and world of film, and because performance is an interpretation of that character by an actor, many films are made or broken by an actor's performance. In a film like *Kind Hearts and Coronets* (1949), in which Alec Guinness plays eight different roles, the shifting performances of the actor may be its greatest achievement.

In a performance, we can distinguish two primary elements: voice, which includes the natural sound of an actor's voice along with the various intonations or accents he or she may create for a particular role; and bodily movement, which includes physical gestures and, especially important to the movies, eye movements and eye contact. (As in many elements of mise-en-scène, these two features of performance also rely on other dimensions of film form such as sound and camera positions.) Woody Allen has made a career of developing characters through the performance of a strident, panicky voice and bodily and eye movements that dart in uncoordinated directions. At the heart of such movies as *The Blue Angel* (1930) and *Shanghai Express* (1932) is Marlene Dietrich's sultry voice, complemented by drooping eyes and languid body poses and gestures [**Figure 3.18**].

Additionally, different acting styles define performances. With *stylized acting*, an actor employs emphatic and highly self-conscious gestures or speaks in pronounced tones with elevated diction; the actor seems fully aware that he or she is acting and addressing an audience. Much less evident today, these stylized performances can be seen in the work of Lillian Gish in *Broken Blossoms* (1919), in Joel Grey's role as the master of ceremonies in *Cabaret* (1972) [**Figure 3.19**], and in virtually any Monty Python movie. More influential since the 1940s, **naturalistic acting** requires an actor to fully and naturally embody the role that he or she is playing in order to communicate that character's essential self. Sometimes associated with a practice called "method acting" taught by Lee Strasberg and based on the innovations of Russian

3.18 *The Blue Angel* (1930). The body and eyes of Marlene Dietrich.

VIEWING CUE

Focus on a central character or actor. How would you describe his or her acting style in the film? Does that style seem compatible with the story?

acting teacher Konstanin Stanislavski, it is famously demonstrated by Marlon Brando as Stanley in *A Streetcar Named Desire* (1951), a role in which the actor and character seem almost indistinguishable [**Figure 3.20**].

Types of Actors. As part of the usual distribution of actors through mise-en-scène, **leading actors**—the two or three actors who appear most often in a film—play the central characters. Recognizable actors associated with particular character types or minor parts are sometimes referred to as **character actors**. They usually appear as secondary characters playing sinister or humorous roles, such as the bumbling cook in a western. **Supporting actors** play secondary characters in a film, serving as foils or companions to the central characters. Supporting actors and character actors add to the complexity of how we become involved in the action or pinpoint a movie's themes. In the hands of a strong actor, such as James Earl Jones in a supporting role in *Field of Dreams* (1989) or Tatum O'Neal as a Bible salesman's precocious daughter in *Paper Moon* (1973), these supporting roles frequently balance our perspective on the main characters, perhaps requiring us to rethink what the main character means and what distinguishes him or her. In *Field of Dreams*, the writer that Jones plays, Terence Mann, fulfills his fantasy of joining the baseball game that lead actor Kevin Costner's character does not choose to enter because of a more important commitment to his family [**Figure 3.21**].

The Stars. The leading actors in many films are, of course, stars—those individuals who, because of their cultural celebrity, bring a powerful aura to their performance, making them the focal points in the mise-en-scène. Unlike less famous actors, star performers center and often dominate the action and space of the mise-en-scène; bring the accumulated history and significance of their past performances to each new film appearance; and acquire a status that transforms their individual physical presence into more abstract or mythical qualities, combining the ordinary and extraordinary.

The star's performance focuses the action of the mise-en-scène and draws attention to important events and themes in the film. In *Casablanca* (1942), there

3.19 *Cabaret* (1972). Joel Grey's stylized performance.

3.20 *A Streetcar Named Desire* (1951). Marlon Brando becomes Stanley.

are a multitude of individual dramas about different characters trying to escape Casablanca, but Humphrey Bogart's (as the character Rick Blaine) is, in an important sense, the only story: the many other stories become more or less important only as they become part of his life. In *The Bridges of Madison County* (1995), the story of a male photographer and a female immigrant who meet and fall in love in the isolated farmlands of Iowa, there are no characters other than those played by the stars Clint Eastwood and Meryl Streep for most of the film; this focus on their interactions intensifies the story. In a way, this film becomes the story of two stars creating an exclusive world bracketed off from other lives and characters [Figure 3.22]. Johnny Depp's tongue-in-cheek performance as Jack Sparrow in *Pirates of the Caribbean: The Curse of the Black Pearl* (2003) contributed to the film's unexpected success and generated sequels highlighting the character's antics.

3.21   *Field of Dreams* (1989). James Earl Jones as Terence Mann, the supporting character with opportunities unavailable to the protagonist.

Moreover, in all three of these films, much of the power of the characters is a consequence of the star status of the actors, recognized and comprehended in relation to their other roles in other films—and in some cases, in relation to a life off the screen. Recognizing and identifying with Rick in *Casablanca* implies, especially for viewers in the 1940s, a recognition on some level that Rick is more than Rick, that this star-character in *Casablanca* is an extension of characters Bogart has portrayed in such films as *High Sierra* (1941) and *The Maltese Falcon* (1941). A similar measuring takes place as we watch Eastwood and Streep. Streep's performance in *The Bridges of Madison County* impresses viewers because the character she plays is so unlike the characters she plays in *Sophie's Choice* (1982) and *Out*

3.22   *The Bridges of Madison County* (1995). A film about two star performances.

of Africa (1985); part of our appreciation and understanding of her role is the performative skill and range she embodies as a star. Depp's pirate captain builds on the actor's association with eccentric characters and on the persona of rock star Keith Richards of the Rolling Stones. We understand these characters as an extension of and departure from other characters associated with the star.

As a result of this extended presence, stars acquire a mythical power whereby we understand and expect from their characters larger-than-life accomplishments and abilities. Star performers are capable of astonishing acts of intelligence and physical or emotional strength; they can commit acts of kindness and acts of evil that typical individuals would be incapable of. Rick is nobler than the usual individual, more compassionate, braver, and ultimately able to sacrifice his merely human tendencies to the grander, mythical self that closes the film. Because he is a star, we accept Robin Williams in *Dead Poets Society* (1989) as both wittier and probably more passionate than the average high-school English teacher; in *It Happened One Night* (1934), we expect Clark Gable to be far more charming and self-confident than a regular reporter would be. Certainly this mythic stature is part of what drives us to identify desires and dreams with stars; it also allows movies to engage in particular confrontations with a viewer's expectations, such as when a film turns on stars' mythical immortality: in *Psycho*, star Janet Leigh

text continued on page 75 ▶

Sets and Settings in
Meet Me in St. Louis (1944)

Vincente Minnelli's *Meet Me in St. Louis* is a frolicking historical musical that, on one level, could be said to be about settings and sets: it foregrounds these elements of mise-en-scène that may appear less visibly in other movies. The film takes place in St. Louis in 1903 as the city prepares to host a World's Fair. Within this setting, the film concentrates on a family's large Victorian house whose elaborate stairways, porches, and parlors are the sets that contain most of the film's action. The narrative describes the family harmony of five siblings, their parents, grandfather, and jovial cook, and then follows the various crises precipitated when romances disturb this tranquility and the father's career threatens to move them all to New York City. The setting and sets for these actions become the film's center and its stabilizing context: the palpable hominess of the kitchen stove and pots in scenes of ketchup-making, the comfortable chair that anchors the father, and the spacious entryway and oak staircase that signal the solidity and financial comfort the family enjoys in a period of history that the film imagines as traditional and carefree.

In part because it is a musical that requires spaces to perform, *Meet Me in St. Louis* creates a special self-consciousness about the importance of sets. During a party, for example, the parlor becomes an impromptu set for staging song-and-dance performances. Here Esther (played by Judy Garland) and her sisters and brother perform for their guests, and the creation of this stage in the home represents a way of bonding people through the entertainment value of a set. Later, when the family seems about to leave for New York, Tootie, the youngest sister (played by Margaret O'Brien), visits the staged scene of snow people she has built on the lawn. It is a family—snowmen, -women, and -children (and a snow-pet!) set in the yard outside the house. For Tootie, this set probably represents the harmony of her own family; but in her anger at the impending departure from St. Louis, she smashes and destroys the figures [Figure 3.23]. In both

scenes, *Meet Me in St. Louis* underlines how important sets and settings are to the meaning of the characters' lives and the themes of the film.

However accurate they are in fact, the sets of *Meet Me in St. Louis* aim at historical and scenic realism. Besides the architecture of the house and the costumes of the characters, another set stands out: the trolley car, which is the scene of another song. It creates the illusion of a set in motion and reminds us that at the turn of the century the trolley was one of the many remarkable new mechanical and technological progressions in the history of cities. As the site of budding love and adolescent excitement, the crowded, clanging trolley suggests that the place of American progress can also easily accommodate the energy of young love.

Through its historical setting in 1903, *Meet Me in St. Louis* calls attention to the inherited history of mise-en-scène as a way of mapping different community relation-

3.23 *Meet Me in St. Louis* (1944). Tootie knocks the heads off of her family of snow people.

ships, of reflecting social institutions, and of measuring the powers of individuals to interact with their world—of creating, in short, certain scenic atmospheres and connotations. As a geographical place, St. Louis suggests the center of the United States, and the affluence of the house sets nostalgically connotes middle-class midwestern, white America at the turn of the century. The film's location comes to represent a global centrality: one character remarks during the opening of the World's Fair that St. Louis has now become the center of the world. The platform from which the family gazes out at the fair becomes the last set foregrounded by the film. Made in 1944, when Americans were spread around the world fighting World War II, *Meet Me in St. Louis* presents the enduring institutions of America in and as its mise-en-scène.

Within this setting, the splendor of the house serves to represent the institutional magnificence of the family, a large and varied family that, in this case, corresponds to the many rooms that act as a fluid set through which the characters (mostly women) sing, dance, cry, and love each other. Indeed, *Meet Me in St. Louis* is most intriguing as it

weaves a group of confined, melodramatic settings (the rooms within the house) until they eventually open out as a spectacular mise-en-scène (at the harmonious gathering at the World's Fair). Between these two kinds of scenes, the female characters of the film learn, above all else, how to take control of their situations, to overcome fear, to act on desires—in short, to stage their world to serve their emotions and needs. Esther's initial flirtation with John, for example, begins with her conscious and careful orchestration of mise-en-scène. After a party, she asks him to help extinguish the gas lamps in the foyer of the home, and as she moves him around the set, from lamp to lamp, she brings a new romance to light [Figure 3.24].

Accordingly, the concluding mise-en-scène at the World's Fair becomes a marvelous spectacle that, in terms of the narrative, rewards the family for staying put in St. Louis with a stupendous light show and theatrical display of buildings, restaurants, and monuments. As all the characters rejoice, the setting of St. Louis now becomes, through the global connotations of this glowing World's Fair set, the figurative center of the world [Figure 3. 25].

3.24 *Meet Me in St. Louis* (1944). Esther setting the scene for romance.

3.25 *Meet Me in St. Louis* (1944). The World's Fair as the climactic stage and set, the vivid Technicolors now helping to create the fantasy.

is unexpectedly killed halfway through the movie; in *Arlington Road* (1999), the protagonist, Jeff Bridges, does not, as we expect, survive.

The meaning and importance of stars is only part of the process through which we come to comprehend films. Sometimes we come to a film without knowledge of a featured actor and come away from it impressed by the star persona it is building, as with newcomer Michelle Rodriguez in *Girlfight* (2000). Some movies, such as Robert Altman's *Nashville* (1975), may populate the story with an ensemble of actors rather than one or two stars. The result is a movie that is not so much a story as it is a collage of different episodes that parodies our desire for stars in the movies. In François Truffaut's *The 400 Blows* (1959), a then-unknown actor, Jean-Pierre Léaud, plays the main character, Antoine Doinel, and the innocence of the

> ▶ **VIEWING CUE**
>
> How does the presence of stars control the mise-en-scène and your understanding of the film? How do they contribute to the meaning of the movie?

3.26   *The 400 Blows* (1959). An unknown Jean-Pierre Léaud (*right*) grows into his role.

3.27   *On Golden Pond* (1981). A career of different roles embodied in Katharine Hepburn's complex performance. Here, with co-star Henry Fonda, the low-contrasting browns and tans suggest both aging and enrichment.

young actor matches perfectly with the story of a growing boy who must struggle to find an identity on the streets of Paris [**Figure 3.26**]. (Truffaut would continue the relationship between Léaud and Doinel through a series of films that matched the growth of the character with that of the actor.)

Performative Development. Whatever the status of the actor, mise-en-scène usually highlights *performative development,* changes in a character described through an actor's performance. An actor's performative development may take place from one movie to another, or it may occur within the same movie. We may remark on how an actor changes or develops his or her performative style over the course of several movies as a way of understanding each different character. Alternatively, we may note how one performance allows us to comprehend the development of a character through one movie. Katharine Hepburn's many performances developed a spectrum of characters, from *Stage Door* (1937) through *Long Day's Journey into Night* (1962); this stylistic flexibility in her acting allowed her to depict a host of personalities, from the saucy rebel to the weary, drug-addicted mother, a performative range that potentially comes into play in our expectations when we watch any of her roles. In a single film, *On Golden Pond* (1981), a sharp viewer may map Hepburn's development of several of these performative skills: her role as the aging wife of a lonely, confused man communicates, through the changing carriage of her body and facial expressions, a struggle to maintain the strength of a once-youthful rebel despite her own weariness [**Figure 3.27**].

Actors are frequently cast for parts precisely because of their association with certain **character types** (see p. 72) that they seem especially suited to portray because of their physical features, acting style, or previous roles. Tom Hanks portrays "everyman" characters, while Helen Mirren played both Queen Elizabeth I and Queen Elizabeth II in the same year. To appreciate and understand a character can consequently mean recognizing this intersection of a type and an actor's interpretation or transformation of it. Arnold Schwarzenegger's large and muscular physical stature and clipped voice and stiff acting style suit well the characters he plays in *The Terminator* (1984) and *Total Recall* (1990), but in *Kindergarten Cop* (1990), his performance and character become more interesting precisely because he must develop that performance type in the role of a kindergarten teacher.

VIEWING CUE

Are there specific scenes in which the blocking is especially important? How?

Blocking. The arrangement and movement of actors in relation to each other within the single physical space of a mise-en-scène is called blocking. *Social blocking* describes the arrangement of characters to accentuate relations among them. In

Little Women (1994), family and friends gather around the wounded father who has just returned from the Civil War, suggesting the importance of the familial bonds at the center of this society [**Figure 3.28**]. *Graphic blocking* arranges characters or groups according to visual patterns to portray spatial harmony, tension, or some other visual atmosphere. Fritz Lang, for instance, is renowned for his blocking of crowd scenes: in *Metropolis* (1927), the oppression of individuality appears instantly in the mechanical movements of rectangles of marching workers [**Figure 3.29**]; in *Fury* (1936), a mob lynching in a small town creates graphic-blocked patterns whose directional arrow suggests a kind of dark fate moving against the lone individual.

3.28   *Little Women* (1994). Blocking the family tightly around the father.

Costumes and Make-Up

Costumes are the clothing and related accessories that a character wears or that define the character and contribute to the visual impression and design of the film overall. These can range from common fashions, like a dark suit or dress, to historical or more fantastic costumes. Cosmetics, or *make-up* applied to the actor's face or body, highlight or even disguise or distort certain aspects of the face or body.

How actors are costumed and made up can play a central part in a film as well, describing tensions and changes in the character and the story. Sometimes a

3.29   *Metropolis* (1927). Rectangular masses of futuristic workers.

character becomes fully identified with one basic look or costume: through his many movie incarnations, James Bond has always appeared in a tuxedo; in *Crocodile Dundee* (1986), the singularity of Paul Hogan in New York City is underlined by his Australian bush hat, rugged clothing, and suntanned skin. Moreover, the dynamic of costuming can be highlighted in a way that makes costuming the center of the movie. *Pygmalion* (1938) and its musical adaptation as *My Fair Lady* (1964) are essentially about a transformation of a girl from the street into an elegant socialite [**Figure 3.30**]; along with language and diction, that transformation is indexed by the changes of costume and make-up from dirt and rags to diamonds and gowns.

Costumes and make-up function in films in three different ways. First, when costumes and make-up support scenic realism, they reproduce, as accurately as possible, the clothing and facial features of people living in a specific time and place. Thus Napoleon's famous hat and jacket, pallid skin, and lock of hair across his brow are a standard costume and the basic make-up for the many films featuring this character, from Abel Gance's 1927 *Napoléon* to Sacha Guitry's 1955 *Napoleon*. Second, when make-up and costumes function as character highlights, they draw out or point to important parts of a character's personality. Often these highlights are subtle, such as the ascot a pretentious visitor wears; sometimes they are pronounced, as when villains in silent films wear black hats and twirl their moustaches. In William Wyler's black-and-white film *Jezebel* (1939), Bette Davis's character shocks southern

text continued on page 80 ▶

VIEWING CUE

How do costuming and make-up add scenic realism, highlight character, or mark the narrative development?

3.30   *My Fair Lady* (1964). A flower girl transformed through costume and set design by Cecil Beaton.

From Props to Lighting in *Do the Right Thing* (1989)

In Spike Lee's *Do the Right Thing,* characters wander through the theatrical space of Bedford-Stuyvesant, a gentrifying African American neighborhood in Brooklyn. Here life becomes a complicated negotiation between private mise-en-scène (apartments, bedrooms, and businesses) and public mise-en-scène (city streets and sidewalks crowded with people). With Lee in the role of Mookie, who acts as a thread connecting the different characters, stores, and street corners, the film explores the different needs that clash within a single urban place by featuring a variety of stages—rooms, stores, and restaurants—with personal and racial associations. On the hot summer day of this setting, lighting creates an intense and tactile heat, and this sensation of heat makes the mise-en-scène vibrate with energy and frustration.

However much it appears to use a real location, *Do the Right Thing* carefully constructs a setting of interlocking sets. From her window frame, Mother Sister "sees all" of this highly public place, where interior lives are constantly on display and frequently in conflict when they meet on the street. Walls and windows become especially significant for the sets of this film: DJ Mister Señor Love Daddy's window is a window to the entire neighborhood; a bright-red wall acts as a backdrop for the lounging, fast-talking Sweet Dick Willie and his two pals, who rhetorically perform as if on stage; and other building walls are painted with political slogans ("Dump Koch," "Tawana Told the Truth," and "*Our* Vote Counts"). Most important to the plot, the movie's mise-en-scène contains the pizzeria's "wall of fame" where Sal hangs his photos of celebrated Italian Americans.

The central crisis of *Do the Right Thing* turns on the drama of instrumental props that become loaded with cultural meanings and metaphorical powers. Early in the film, Smiley holds up a photograph of Martin Luther King Jr. and Malcolm X as a call to fight against racism with both nonviolence and violence. Shortly thereafter, Da Mayor nearly instigates a fight because the Korean grocer has not stocked a can of his favorite beer, Miller High Life. It is the photographs of famous Italians in Sal's pizzeria—photos of Frank Sinatra, Joe DiMaggio, Liza Minnelli, Al Pacino, and others—however, that ignite the film [Figure 3.31]. When Buggin' Out complains that there should be photos of African Americans on that wall because Sal's clientele is all black, Sal angrily responds that he can decorate the walls of his pizzeria however he wishes. Later, when Radio Raheem refuses to turn down his boom box (an object that has become synonymous with who he is), he and Buggin' Out confront Sal with the cultural significance of the photo-props and their social rights within this mise-en-scène: why, they demand, are there no photographs of African Americans on the wall? Finally, at the climactic moment in the film, Mookie tosses

3.31 *Do the Right Thing* (1989). The political flashpoint of props: nostalgic black-and-white photos of Italian Americans on the pizzeria wall.

a garbage can through the window of the pizzeria, sparking the store's destruction but saving the lives of Sal and his son.

The film's performances mobilize faces and bodies as active forces in the mise-en-scène. Rather than highlighting two or three star performers, *Do the Right Thing* features numerous supporting roles: Ossie Davis as Da Mayor, John Turturro as Pino, Rosie Perez as Tina, Danny Aiello as Sal, Richard Edson as Vito, and Giancarlo Esposito as Buggin' Out, to name a few. Although they appear to work in a naturalistic style that accurately re-creates realistic figures from the streets of Brooklyn, the people in this neighborhood must constantly and consciously perform for each other in order to communicate and establish their identities. This leads to the often-exaggerated stylized acting found in the gestures and grimaces of Turturro's portrayal of an angry Italian son and in Esposito's theatrical movements, declamatory speeches, and wild eyes as his character tries to provoke actions.

3.32 *Do the Right Thing* (1989). Mookie in the heritage of Jackie Robinson.

Lee's performance as Mookie is certainly the central role, one that draws on his then-emerging status as a star actor and a star filmmaker (a combination found in the work of such other director-actors as Clint Eastwood, Woody Allen, and Barbra Streisand). In fact, this double status as star and director indicates clearly that what happens in the mise-en-scène is about him. Physically unimposing, restrained, and cautious throughout the film, Lee's performance seems to shift and adjust depending on the character he is responding to: he is confrontational with Pino, defensive with Tina, and generous with the stuttering Smiley, for example. As the central performer in a neighborhood of performers, Lee's Mookie is a chameleon, surviving by continually changing his persona to fit the social scene he is in. By the end of the film, however, Mookie must decide which performance will be the real self he brings to the mise-en-scène—how, that is, he will "act" in a time of crisis by taking responsibility for the role he is acting.

Do the Right Thing features costumes that reflect the styles of dress in U.S. cities in the 1980s, and make-up that intends to suggest natural faces, thus adding to the scenic realism of the film. Yet their significance exceeds scenic realism because the costumes both highlight characters and mark the movie's narrative development. Da Mayor's dirty, rumpled suit contrasts sharply with the costumes that define the personalities of younger characters, such as Mookie's Brooklyn Dodgers shirt with the name and number of the legendary African American baseball player Jackie Robinson on the back [**Figure 3.32**], and Pino's white, sleeveless tee-shirt with its white working-class connotations. Jade, Mookie's sister, stands out in her dramatic hats, skirts, earrings, and noticeably more elegant make-up and hairstyles, calling attention perhaps to the individuality and creativity that allow her, uniquely here, to casually cross racial lines.

Two other examples in *Do the Right Thing* underline the cultural and political forces of costuming. When a white man on a bicycle accidentally runs over Buggin' Out's Air Jordan sneakers, his apology doesn't sufficiently counter the effect of his Boston Celtics tee-shirt featuring the name of its white star-player, Larry Byrd, and the incident nearly results in a violent conflict. Besides the cultural play of clothing in instances like this one, among the more complicated pieces of costuming is Radio Raheem's hand jewelry, huge "love" and "hate" rings that recall *The Night of the Hunter* (1955), in which the central **antagonist** has those words tattooed on his knuckles. Among other resonances, Radio Raheem's rings transform the mysterious and psychotic connotations of the earlier movie into an explicit political message, akin to the opposing ideologies personified by Martin Luther King Jr. and Malcolm X.

Both social and geometrical blockings become dramatic calculators in a film explicitly about the "block" and the arrangement of people in this neighborhood. Mother Sister sits in her window looking down at Da Mayor on the sidewalk, suggesting her dominance over and distance from the confusion in the street. In one scene, Pino, Vito, and Mookie stand tensely apart in a corner of the pizzeria as Mookie calls on Vito to denounce his brother's behavior and Pino counters with a call for family ties; their bodies are quietly hostile and territorial simply in their arrangement and their movements around the counter that separates them. This orchestration of bodies climaxes in the final showdown at Sal's pizzeria. When Buggin' Out and Radio Raheem enter the pizzeria, the screaming begins with Sal behind the counter, while Mookie, Pino, Vito, and the group of kids shout from different places in the room. When the fight begins, the bodies collapse on each other and spill onto the street as a mass of undistinguishable faces. After the arrival of the police and the killing of Radio Raheem, the placement of his body creates a sharp line between Mookie and Sal and his sons on one side and the growing crowd of furious blacks and Latinos on the other. Within this blocking, Mookie suddenly moves from his side of the line to the other and then calmly retrieves the garbage can to throw through the window. The riot that follows is a direct consequence of Mookie's decisions about where to position himself and how to shatter the blocked mise-en-scène that divides Sal's space from the mob.

Do the Right Thing employs an array of lighting techniques that at first may seem naturalistic but through the course of the film become directional in particularly dramatic ways. Especially through the lighting, heat becomes a palpable feature of this mise-en-scène. From the beginning, the film juxtaposes the harsh, full glare of the streets with the soft morning light that highlights the interior spaces of DJ Mister Señor Love Daddy's radio station, where he announces a heat wave for the coming day, and the bedroom where Da Mayor awakens with Mother Sister. Here the lighting of the interior mise-en-scène emphasizes the rich and blending shades of the dark skin of the African American characters, while the bright, hard lighting of the exterior spaces draws out the sharp distinctions in the skin colors of blacks, whites, and Asians. This high-key lighting of exteriors, in turn, accentuates the color of the objects and props in the mise-en-scène as a way of sharply isolating them in the scene: for example, the blues of the police uniforms and cars, the yellows of the fruits in the Korean market, and the reds of the steps and walls of the neighborhood [Figure 3.33].

Other uses of lighting in the film are more specifically dramatic and complex. For example, the dramatic backlighting of Mookie, as he climbs the stairs to deliver the

3.33 *Do the Right Thing* (1989). The high-key lighting against a glaringly red wall adds to the intensity and theatricality of these otherwise casual commentators on the street.

pizza, adds an almost religious and certainly heroic/romantic effect to the pizza delivery. When Pino confronts Vito in the storage room, the scene is highlighted by an overhead light that swings back and forth, creating a rocking and turbulent visual effect. In the final scene, Mookie walks home to his son on a street sharply divided between the bright, glaring light on one side and the dark shadows on the other.

More charged with the politics of mise-en-scène than many films, *Do the Right Thing* turns a relatively small city space into an electrified set where props, actors, costumes, and lighting create a remarkably dense, jagged, and mobile environment. Here the elements of mise-en-scène are always theatrically and politically in play, always about the spatial construction of culture in a specific time and place. To live here, people need to assume, as Mookie eventually does, the powers and responsibilities of knowing how and when to act.

3.34 **Fellini's *Roma*** (1972). Costumes give shape to the excessive fantasies of a childhood memory.

society when she appears in a red dress; her performance and the blocking of her entrance convey the tension without the actual use of color. In Fellini's *Roma* (1972), an autobiographical panorama of the title city becomes a bombastic fashion show peopled by the fantasy characters and memories of childhood [Figure 3.34]. Third, when costumes and make-up act as narrative markers, their change or lack of change becomes a crucial way to understand and follow a character and the development of the story. Often a film, such as *Citizen Kane* (1941) or *The Age of Innocence* (1993), develops through the aging face of the protagonist, gradually whitened and lined, and changing styles of clothing, appearing more modern, as the story advances. In Alan Rudolph's offbeat *Trouble*

3.36   *Rocky* (1976). The hats and jackets of South Philadelphia.

3.35   *The Picture of Dorian Gray* (1945). Facial make-up and costume help create an extremely composed and proper surface for a character with a dark secret.

in Mind (1985), Coop's hairstyles grow increasingly outlandish as he becomes more and more absorbed in the surreal plot. In the adaptation *The Picture of Dorian Gray* (1945), the entire story concentrates on the lack of change in the facial appearance of the protagonist, who has sold his soul for eternal youth [Figure 3.35].

Costumes and make-up that appear as natural or realistic in films carry important cultural connotations as well. In *Rocky* (1976), the title character dresses to reflect his working-class background in South Philadelphia, and his somewhat clownish hat particularly accentuates his bumbling but likeable personality [Figure 3.36]. When Rocky boxes in the championship fight, however, he becomes a bare and powerful form whose simple trunks and cape contrast with the glitzy costumes of his opponent. As the bout progresses, facial make-up exaggerates the gruesome violence of the fight, yet he continues to deliver his lines with an almost humble dignity and determination. After his valiant and heroic effort, his plain girlfriend in nerdy eyeglasses becomes more attractive through the power of make-up and costuming.

Lighting

One of the most subtle and important dimensions of mise-en-scène is **lighting**. Our daily experiences outside the movies demonstrate how lighting can affect our perspective on a person or thing, as when a room hidden in dark shadows evokes feelings of fear, while the same room brightly lit suggests warmth and comfort. Lighting is a key element of cinematography that we will discuss in Chapter 4, but the effects of lighting are visible on screen and thus appropriate to this discussion. *Mise-en-scène lighting* refers specifically to light sources—both natural light and electrical lamps—located within the scene itself. It is used to shade and accentuate the figures, objects, and spaces of the mise-en-scène, but the primary sources of film lighting are usually not visible onscreen.

**TRANSFORMING FILM:
The Power of Costume
and Make–Up**

In *The Godfather* (1972), make-up draws out the colors, lines, and features of Marlon Brando (a) to create a character that is and is not Brando (b). In *The Lord of the Rings: The Fellowship of the Ring* (2001), Gollum begins with the reality of actor Andy Serkis's face and body (c) that is then aligned with an imagined face (d) and finally transformed beyond the human through computer generated images (e).

(a)   (b)

(c)

(d)

(e)

3.37

3.38

3.39

3.40

3.41

3.42

3.43

3.44

3.37–3.45 *Sweet Smell of Success* (1957). Lighting makes meaning: from the glare of a coffee shop and the shadows of a sexual encounter to the highlighting of power and the threatening underlighting of a policeman.

3.45

The interaction of lighting, sets, and actors can create its own drama within a specific mise-en-scène. How a character moves through light or how the lighting on the character changes within a single mise-en-scène can signal important information about the character and story. In *Back to the Future* (1985), the suddenly illuminated face of Marty McFly, from an unseen source, signals a moment of revelation about the mysteries of time travel. More complexly in *Citizen Kane,* the regular movement of characters, particularly of Kane, from shadow to light and then back to shadow suggest Kane's moral instability.

The mise-en-scène can use both natural and directional lighting. **Natural lighting** usually assumes an incidental role in a scene; it derives from a natural source in a scene or setting, such as the illumination of the daylight sun or the lamps of a room. Spread across a set before more specific lighting emphases are added, **set lighting** distributes an evenly diffused illumination through a scene as a kind of lighting base. **Directional lighting** is more dramatically apparent; it may create the impression of a natural light source but actually directs light in ways that define and shape the object or person being illuminated. As illustrated in the scenes presented here from *Sweet Smell of Success* (1957) [**Figures 3.37–3.45**], the lighting used in the mise-en-scène has developed an even more specific technical grammar to designate its variety of strategies:

- **Key lighting** is the main source of lighting from a lamp; it may be bright with few contrasts (known as "high") or shadowy with sharp contrasts between light and dark (known as "low"), depending on the ratio of key to fill lighting and the effect desired [**Figures 3.37 and 3.38**].
- **Fill lighting** can be used to balance the key lighting or to emphasize other spaces and objects in the scene [**Figures 3.39 and 3.40**].
- **Highlighting** describes the use of the different lighting sources to emphasize certain characters or objects or to charge them with special significance [**Figure 3.41**].
- **Backlighting** (sometimes called **edgelighting**) is a highlighting technique that illuminates the person or object from behind; it tends to silhouette the subject [**Figure 3.42**].
- **Three-point lighting** combines key lighting, fill lighting, and backlighting to blend naturally the distribution of light in a scene [**Figure 3.43**].
- **Frontal lighting**, **sidelighting**, **underlighting**, and **top lighting** are used to illuminate the subject from different directions in order to draw out features or create specific atmospheres around the subject [**Figures 3.44 and 3.45**].

▶ **VIEWING CUE**

Consider a film in which lighting dramatically adds to a scene. Where does it work less obtrusively but in an equally important way?

The effects of lighting in the mise-en-scène range from a **hard** to a **soft lighting** surface that, in conjunction with the narrative and other features of the mise-en-scène, elicit certain responses. *Shading*, the use of shadows to shape or draw attention to certain features, can explain or comment on an object or person in a way the narrative does not. Hard and soft lighting and shading can create a variety of complex effects through highlighting and the play of light and shadow that enlighten viewers in more than one sense.

The Italian romance *Under the Tuscan Sun* (2003) depends on the soft natural light referred to in the title, and the shaded eyes of Jake in *Chinatown* (1974) indicate problems with his perspective well before the plot describes them. In a movie like *Barry Lyndon* (1975), the story is conspicuously inseparable from the lighting techniques that illuminate it: extraordinarily low and soft lighting, with sharp frontal light and little fill light on the faces, creates an artificial intensity in the expressions of the characters, whose social desperation hides their ethical emptiness [**Figure 3.46**]. One particular version of this play of light is referred to as **chiaroscuro lighting**, a pictorial arrangement of light and dark that can create the uneasy atmospheres found in German expressionist films such as Paul Wegener's 1920 tale of magic and supernatural creatures, *The Golem*. None of the elements of mise-en-scène—from

3.46 *Barry Lyndon* (1975). Low candle lighting and a murky color scheme add an eerie atmosphere to the ghostlike appearance of the characters.

props to acting to lighting—can be assigned standard meanings because they are always subject to how individual films use them. They have also carried different historical and cultural connotations at different times. While the shadowy lighting of **German expressionist cinema**, as in the 1924 horror film *Waxworks*, may be formally similar to that found in 1950s film noir, such as in *Kiss Me Deadly* (1955), the lighting has a very different significance, reflecting the distinctive perspective of each film and the cultural context that produced it. The metaphoric darkness that surrounds characters like Dracula and Jack the Ripper in the first film suggests a monstrous evil that may also be psychological; in the second, that shadowy atmosphere describes a corruption that is entirely human, a function of brutal greed and sexualized violence.

The Significance of Mise-en-Scène

How does mise-en-scène "signify" in a film? Whether mise-en-scène presents authentic places or ingeniously fabricates new worlds, audiences invariably look for and find particular meanings in sets, props, acting styles, lighting, and other elements of mise-en-scène. From the miniaturized reenactment of Admiral Dewey's naval victory in *The Battle of Manila Bay* (1898) and Georges Méliès's fantastic stage for *The Man with the Rubber Head* (1901) to the futuristic ductwork of *Brazil* (1985) [**Figure 3.47**], located "somewhere on the Los Angeles–Belfast border," and the contemporary streets of Tehran in *The Circle* (2000), movie audiences have recognized the significance of and specific meanings created by a film through views of real lands and landscapes as well as through the sets, props, and costumes created with astonishing verve and style for fantasized worlds. In this final section, we explore how the changing places in film help us identify and assign meaning to a film in different ways through different cultures.

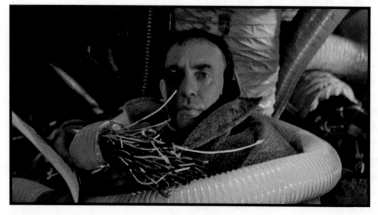

3.47 *Brazil* (1985). The twisted mise-en-scène of future life.

Defining Our Place in a Film's Material World

Whereas earlier we examined the historical foundations and formal strategies of mise-en-scène, here we will argue how those formal elements often impart emotional and intellectual values and meanings through a film. For most movie viewers, recognizing the places, objects, and arrangements of sets and settings has never been simply a formal exercise. The mise-en-scène has always been the site where viewers measure human, aesthetic, and social values, recognize significant cinematic traditions, and, in those interactions, identify and assign meaning to the changing places of films.

The most fundamental value of mise-en-scène is that it defines our location in the material world: the physical settings and objects that surround us indicate our place in the world. Some people crave large cities with bright lights and active crowds; others find it important that their town have a church as the visible center of the community. Much the same holds true for cinematic mise-en-scène, in which the place created by the elements of the mise-en-scène becomes the essential condition for the meaning of the characters' lives. As part of this larger cultural context, cinematic mise-en-scène helps to

- describe the physical conditions and limits of our natural, social, or imaginary worlds
- measure the ability of individuals and social groups to control and arrange their world in a meaningful way

On the one hand, mise-en-scène describes the limits of human experience by indicating the external boundaries and contexts in which people live. On the other, it reflects the powers of the characters and groups that inhabit it by showing how people can have an impact on the space in which they live. While the first set of values can be established without characters, the second requires the interaction of characters and mise-en-scène.

▶ **VIEWING CUE**

Examine the mise-en-scène of the film you are studying in class. Does it emphasize the force of the physical conditions of society or how those conditions can be transformed? ‖

Mise-en-Scène as an External Condition

Mise-en-scène as an *external condition* indicates surfaces, objects, and exteriors that define the material possibilities in a place or space. One mise-en-scène may be a magical space full of active objects; another may be a barren landscape with no borders. In *King Solomon's Mines* (1937) and *The African Queen* (1951), deserts and jungles create landscapes of arid plains and dense foliage threatening the colonial visitors, whereas in films like *The Lady Vanishes* (1938) and *The American Friend* (1977), the interiors of trains and subways consist of long, narrow passageways, multiple windows, and strange, anonymous faces. An individual's movements are restricted as the world flies by outside [**Figure 3.48**]. In each case, the mise-en-scène describes the material terms of a film's physical world; from those terms, the rest of the scene or even the entire film must develop.

3.48 *The American Friend* (1977). The crowded anonymity of a subway.

Mise-en-Scène as a Measure of Character

Mise-en-scène as a *measure of character* dramatizes how an individual or group establishes an identity through interaction with (or control of) the surrounding setting and sets. In *The Adventures of Robin Hood* (1938), the mise-en-scène of a forest becomes a sympathetic and intimate place where the outlaw-hero can achieve justice and find camaraderie; in *A Company of Wolves* (1934), a similar mise-en-scène becomes an environment fraught with psychological significance. In *Brokeback Mountain* (2005), the wide open space of the mountain expands the characters' horizons [**Figure 3.49**]. In the science fiction film *Donovan's Brain* (1953), the vision and the personality of a mad scientist are projected and reflected in a laboratory with twisted, mechanized gadgets and wires; essentially, his ability to create new life forms from that environment reflects

3.49 *Brokeback Mountain* (2005). An expansive country provides the space for new identities.

both his genius and his insane ambitions. In both these interactions, the character and the elements of the mise-en-scène may sometimes determine more about each other's meaning than even the interactions between the characters do.

Keep in mind that our own cultural expectations about the material world determine how we understand the values of a film's mise-en-scène. To modern viewers, the mise-en-scène of *The Gold Rush* (1925) might appear crude and stagy; certainly the make-up and costumes might seem more like circus outfits than realistic clothing. For viewers in the 1920s, however, it was precisely the fantastical and theatrical quality of this mise-en-scène that made it so entertaining: for them, watching the Little Tramp perform his balletic magic in a strange location was more important than the realism of the mise-en-scène.

Interpreting Film through Context

Two prominent contexts for eliciting certain interpretations, or readings, of films include naturalistic mise-en-scène and theatrical mise-en-scène. A *naturalistic mise-en-scène* appears realistic and recognizable to viewers. A *theatrical mise-en-scène* denaturalizes the locations and other elements of the mise-en-scène so that its features appear unfamiliar, exaggerated, or artificial. Throughout their history, movies have tended to emphasize one or the other of these contexts, although many films have moved smoothly between the two. From *The Birth of a Nation* (1915) to *Amadeus* (1984), settings, costumes, and props have been selected or constructed to appear as authentic as possible in an effort to convince viewers that the filmmakers had a clear window on a true historical place: the first movie re-creates the historical sites and elements of the Civil War, whereas the second reconstructs the physical details of Wolfgang Amadeus Mozart's life in eighteenth-century Europe. In other films, from *The Cabinet of Dr. Caligari* (1919) to *The Golden Compass* (2007), those same elements of mise-en-scène have exaggerated or transformed reality as most people know it: *Caligari* uses sets painted with twisted buildings and nightmarish backgrounds, while talking animals inhabit the fantastical settings of *The Golden Compass*.

The Naturalistic Tradition

Naturalism is one of the most effective and most misleading ways to approach mise-en-scène. If mise-en-scène is about the arrangement of space and the objects in it, as we have suggested, then naturalism in the mise-en-scène means that how a place looks is the way it is supposed to look. We can, in fact, pinpoint several more precise characteristics of a naturalistic mise-en-scène:

- The world and its objects follow assumed laws of nature and society.
- The elements of the mise-en-scène have a consistently logical or homogeneous relation to each other.
- The mise-en-scène and the characters mutually define each other, although the mise-en-scène may be unresponsive to the needs and desires of the characters.

Naturalistic mise-en-scène is consistent with accepted scientific laws and cultural customs. Thus in a naturalistic setting, a person would be unable to hear whispers from far across a field, and a restaurant might have thirty tables and several waiters or waitresses. This kind of realistic mise-en-scène also creates logical or homogeneous connections among different sets, props, and characters. Costumes, props, and lighting are appropriate and logical extensions of the naturalistic setting, and sets relate to each other as part of a consistent geography. *Battle of Algiers* (1966) is an attempt to re-create with documentary realism the revolution

▶ **VIEWING CUE**

How does thinking about the movie in terms of naturalistic or theatrical mise-en-scène help you to better understand it?

fought in the city's streets a decade earlier. In the submarine film *Das Boot* (1981), the individual sets are necessarily small, cramped rooms, and the characters wear the uniforms of World War II German sailors. Naturalism in the movies also means that the mise-en-scène and the characters mutually define or reflect each other. The gritty streets and dark rooms of a city reflect the bleak attitudes of thieves and femmes fatales in *The Killers* (1946); in *The Perfect Storm* (2000), the ferocious bat-

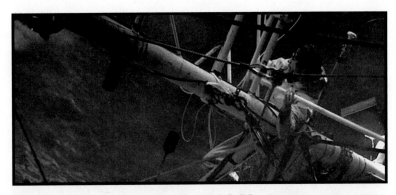

3.50 *The Perfect Storm* (2000). A ferocious battle at sea uses naturalistic mise-en-scène to define character.

tle with the sea reflects the personal turmoil and struggles of the characters and allows them to reach their full physical and psychological potential as human beings **[Figure 3.50]**.

Two specific traditions have emerged from naturalistic mise-en-scène. A *historical mise-en-scène* re-creates a recognizable historical scene, highlighting those elements that call attention to a specific location and time in history: *All Quiet on the Western Front* (1930) can still stun audiences with its brutally accurate representation of trench warfare in World War I; *A Man for All Seasons* (1966) re-creates the sumptuous robes and august chambers of Parliament in the sixteenth-century England of martyr Thomas More. Calling attention to the ordinary rather than the historical, in contrast, an *everyday mise-en-scène* constructs commonplace backdrops for the characters and the action. In *Louisiana Story* (1948), a swamp and its rich natural life are the always-visible arena for the daily routines of a young boy in the Louisiana bayous. In the Brazilian film *Central Station* (1998), a railroad station in Rio de Janeiro and a poor rural area in the Brazilian countryside are the understated stages in a touching tale of a woman's friendship with a boy in search of his father.

The Theatrical Tradition

In contrast, theatrical mise-en-scène creates fantastical environments that display and even exult in their artificial and constructed nature. Films in this tradition define themselves in one or more of these terms:

- Elements of the mise-en-scène tend to violate or bend the laws of nature or society.
- Dramatic inconsistencies appear within one or between two or more settings.
- The mise-en-scène takes on an independent life that requires confrontations or creative negotiations between the props and sets and the characters.

Often violating the accepted laws of how the world functions, theatrical mise-en-scène can call attention to the arbitrary or constructed nature of that world. Horses change colors and witches melt in *The Wizard of Oz* (1939), and in movies from *Top Hat* (1935) to *Silk Stockings* (1957), Fred Astaire somehow finds a way to dance on walls and ceilings and transform spoons and brooms into magical partners. Dramatic inconsistencies within a film's mise-en-scène indicate the instability of those scenes, costumes, and props—and the world they define. The films of Monty Python offer innumerable examples. In *Monty Python's The Meaning of Life* (1983), a pirate ship sails through the streets of Manhattan and a darkly costumed grim reaper interrupts a classy dinner party to announce that all of the chatting friends have died of food poisoning. In a theatrical mise-en-scène, props, sets, and even bodies assume an independent (and sometimes contradictory) life that provokes regular confrontations or negotiations between the mise-en-scène and the

3.51 *Monty Python's The Meaning of Life* (1983). A dinner party is suddenly disturbed by the theatrical entry of Death.

characters [**Figure 3.51**]. Martin Scorsese's *After Hours* (1985) describes the plight of Paul when he finds himself lost at night in the SoHo neighborhood of New York City. Characters suddenly die, a woman surrounds herself with the objects and clothing of a 1960s lifestyle, and a vigilante group mistakes Paul for a robber; in this film, each apartment or street corner seems to be another individual's personal stage, and Paul becomes an unwilling participant in the play.

Two historical trends—expressive and constructive mise-en-scène—are associated with the theatrical mise-en-scène. In an *expressive mise-en-scène*, the settings, sets, props, and other dimensions of the mise-en-scène assert themselves independently of the characters and describe an emotional or spiritual life permeating the material world. Associated most commonly with the German expressionistic films of the 1920s, this tradition is also seen in surrealism, in horror films, and in the magic realism of Latin American cinema. Since Émile Cohl's *Fantasmagorie* (1908) depicted an artist surrounded by sketches and drawings whose life and activity are independent of him, expressive mise-en-scène has enlivened the terrifying, comical, and romantic worlds of *The Birds* (1963), in which birds become demonic; *Barton Fink* (1991), in which wallpaper sweats; and *The Secret of Roan Inish* (1994), in which the natural world of Ireland becomes a magical kingdom.

In a *constructive mise-en-scène*, the world can be shaped and even altered through the work or desire of the characters. Films about putting together a play or even a movie are examples of this tradition as characters fabricate a new or alternative world through their power as actors or directors. In François Truffaut's *Day for Night* (1973), for example, multiple romances and crises become entwined with the project of making a movie about romance and crises, and the movie set becomes a parallel universe in which day can be changed to night and sad stories can be made happy. Other films, however, have employed constructive mise-en-scène to dramatize the wishes and dreams of their characters. In *Willy Wonka and the Chocolate Factory* (1971), the grim factory exterior hides a wonderland where, as one character sings, "you can even eat the dishes." In *Batman* (1989), spectacular costumes and electronic gadgets create a comic-book mise-en-scène in which good and bad characters battle each other for control, whereas the mise-en-scène of *Being John Malkovich* (1999) constantly defies the laws of spatial logic, as Craig the puppeteer and his co-worker Maxine struggle for the right to inhabit the body of the actor Malkovich.

We rarely experience the traditions of naturalistic and theatrical mise-en-scène in entirely isolated states. Naturalism and theatrics sometimes alternate within the same film, and like our experience of mise-en-scène in general, following the play and exchange between the two can be one of the more exciting and productive ways to watch movies and to understand the complexities of mise-en-scène in a film—of how place and its physical contours condition and shape most experiences. In this context, Preston Sturges's *Sullivan's Travels* (1941) is a remarkable example of how the alternation between these two traditions can be the very heart of the movie. In this film, Hollywood director John L. Sullivan, after a successful career of making films with titles like *So Long, Sarong*, decides to explore the realistic world of suffering and deprivation (as material for a serious realistic movie he intends to title *O Brother, Where Art Thou?*). He subsequently finds himself catapulted into a grimy world of railroad boxcars and prison chain gangs, where he discovers, ironically, the power of those fantastic places and people he once filmed to delight and entertain others [Figure 3.52]. The theatrical mise-en-scène of Hollywood, he learns, is as important to human life as the ordinary worlds people must inhabit.

Spectacularizing the Movies

Throughout film history, audiences have often gone to the movies simply to see spectacular places and sights. The most notable example of the movie industry catering to this thirst for magnificent scenes is the advent of the IMAX theater, where panoramas of nature and space appear through the extraordinary size and scope of the screen. But cinema's history and its use of mise-en-scène abound with examples of movie spectaculars that aim, first and foremost perhaps, to thrill audiences with sights they have never seen before and can barely imagine.

3.52 *Sullivan's Travels* (1941). Leaving Hollywood to explore the "real" world.

Movie spectaculars are films in which the magnitude and intricacy of the mise-en-scène share equal emphasis with or even outshine the story, the actors, and other traditional focal points for a movie. Certainly many kinds of films have employed spectacular sets and settings as part of their narrative, but what distinguishes a movie spectacular is an equal or additional emphasis on the powers of the mise-en-scène to create the meaning of the film or even overwhelm the story. If small art-house films usually concentrate on the complexity of character, imagistic style, and narrative, movie spectaculars attend to the stunning effects of sets, lighting, props, costumes, and casts of thousands.

The history of movie spectaculars extends back to the 1914 Italian film *Cabiria,* an epic about the Second Punic War [Figure 3.53], which became a clear inspiration for the making of D. W. Griffith's *Intolerance* (1916), with its four historical tales and sensational sets of ancient worlds. Since then, there have been many successful movie spectaculars and many colossal failures. Some of the most notable successes include *Napoléon* (1927), *The Ten Commandments* (1923, 1956), *Metropolis* (1926), *Alexander Nevsky* (1938), *Gone with the Wind* (1939), *The Adventures of Baron Munchausen* (1943, 1989), *Lawrence of Arabia* (1962), *2001: A Space Odyssey* (1968), *Apocalypse Now* (1979), *Gandhi* (1982), *The Last Emperor* (1987), and *Gladiator* (2000).

Movie spectaculars fit squarely into two cultural traditions: that of the sublime and that of the epic. The aesthetic tradition of the sublime has a long history, beginning with the writings of Roman philosopher Longinus and continuing with late-eighteenth-century and nineteenth-century thinkers, poets, and painters—from Immanuel Kant and Edmund Burke to Samuel Taylor Coleridge and J. M. Turner. The *sublime* usually suggests the power of scenes and places to dizzy (or simply humble) the human mind before their

text continued on page 92 ▶

3.53 *Cabiria* (1914). In perhaps the first movie spectacular, the eruption of Mount Etna begins a cinematic tradition using mise-en-scènes to show disaster.

Naturalistic Mise-en-Scène in *Bicycle Thieves* (1948)

The setting of Vittorio de Sica's *Bicycle Thieves* is post–World War II Rome, a mise-en-scène whose stark and impoverished conditions are the most formidable barrier against the central character's longing for a normal life. Antonio Ricci finds a job putting up movie posters, a humble but adequate way to support his wife and his son Bruno in an economically depressed city. When the bicycle he needs for work is stolen, he desperately searches the massive city on foot, hoping to discover the bike before Monday morning, when he must continue his work. The winding streets and cramped apartments of Rome appear as bare, crumbling, and scarred surfaces, describing a frustrating and impersonal urban maze through which Ricci walks asking questions without answers, examining bikes that are not his, and following leads into strange neighborhoods where he is observed with hostile suspicion. In what was once the center of the Roman Empire, masses of people wait for jobs, crowd onto buses, or sell their wares. The most basic materials of life take on disproportionate significance as props: the sheets on a bed, a plate of food, and an old bike are the center of existence. In the mise-en-scène, the mostly bright lighting reveals mostly blank faces and walls of poverty.

Individuals have little power to change or even fully understand this mise-en-scène. When Ricci reaches a point of extreme desperation, he visits a woman—"The Santona," or "the one who sees"—who is supposed to have visionary powers and who he hopes will tell him where to find his bike. Of course, in a room filled with more impressive furniture

and props than anywhere else in the film, she can only offer bromidic and useless advice: "Find it now or not at all" **[Figure 3.54]**. Neither visionary nor even human powers can affect the material reality and force of this mise-en-scène. Characters must mostly watch without affecting the world around them.

Bicycle Thieves is among the most important films within the naturalistic tradition of mise-en-scène, associated specifically with the Italian neorealist movement of the late 1940s. The laws of society and nature follow an almost mechanical logic that cares not at all for human hopes and dreams. Here, according to a truck driver, "Every Sunday, it rains." In a large city of empty piazzas and anonymous crowds, physical necessities

3.54 *Bicycle Thieves* (1948). The Santona: distinguished more by her furnishings than her vision.

reign: food is a constant concern; most people are strangers; a person needs a bicycle to get around town; and rivers are more threatening than bucolic. Ricci and other characters become engulfed in the hostility and coldness of the pervasive mise-en-scène, and their encounters with Roman street life follow a path from hope to despair to resignation. In the beginning, objects and materials, such as Ricci's uniform and his bed linens, offer promise for his family's happiness in a barren and anonymous cityscape. However, the promise of these and other material objects turns quickly to ironic emptiness: the bicycle is stolen; the marketplace overwhelms him with separate bicycle parts that could never be identified; and settings (such as the church into which he pursues one of the thieves) offer no consolation or comfort. Finally, Ricci himself gets caught in this seemingly inescapable logic of survival when, unable to find his bike, he tries to steal another one [**Figure 3.55**]. Only at the end of the day, when he discovers his son is not the drowned body pulled from the river, does he give up his search for the bicycle. Realizing that this setting and the objects in it will never provide him with meaning and value, he returns sadly home with the son he loves.

Bicycle Thieves's very purpose is to accentuate the common and everyday within a naturalistic tradition. Ricci and his neighbors dress like the struggling working-class population, and the natural lighting progresses from dawn to dusk across the various sets that mark Ricci's progression through the day. This film's everyday mise-en-scène is especially powerful because without any dramatic signals, it remains permeated by World War II. Even within the barest of everyday settings, objects, and clothing, *Bicycle Thieves* suggests the traces of history—such as Mussolini's sports stadium—that have created these impoverished conditions.

Along with these traces of history within its everyday mise-en-scène, we are reminded of a theatrical tradition that ironically counterpoints the film's realism. While performing his new duties in the first part of the film, Ricci puts up a glamorous poster of the movie star Rita Hayworth [**Figure 3.56**]. Later the sets and props

3.55 *Bicycle Thieves* (1948). Bare streets and a bicycle to steal.

3.56 *Bicycle Thieves* (1948). Reminders of different values and traditions.

change when Ricci wanders from a workers' political meeting to an adjacent theater where a play is being rehearsed. In these instances, a poster prop and a stage setting become reminders of a world that has little place in the daily hardships of this mise-en-scène—a world where, as one character puts it, "Movies bore me." For many modern tourists, Rome might be represented by that other tradition—as a city of magnificent fountains, glamorous people, and romantic restaurants.

For Ricci and his son, however, that tradition is only a strange place and a fake set like the restaurant filled with rich patrons eating ravenously before returning to face the reality of the streets. For Europeans who lived through World War II (in Rome or other cities), the glaring honesty of the film's mise-en-scène in 1948 was, understandably, a powerful alternative to the glossy theatrical tradition of Hollywood sets and settings.

> ▶ **VIEWING CUE**
>
> Describe why the mise-en-scène of the film you just watched fits best with a naturalistic or a theatrical tradition. Explain how this perspective helps you to experience the film. Illustrate your position using two or three scenes as examples. ⏸

breathtaking size, beauty, or magnificence. Epics, from poetry like John Milton's *Paradise Lost* to novels like Herman Melville's *Moby Dick,* tell heroic tales of nations or spiritual communities and the moments and events that defined them. More often than not, *epics* are about the importance of cultural place as a large national or spiritual mise-en-scène. Movie spectaculars often set epic stories about the birth or salvation of communities in a sublime mise-en-scène whose magnitude of place overwhelms and supersedes individual desires and differences. Through the last century, these sublime epics have tended to expand from spectacles of cities (*Metropolis*) to visions of nationhood (*Gone with the Wind*) to the stellar landscapes that surround our globe (*2001: A Space Odyssey*) and fantastic places within our globe (*The Lord of the Rings*). In all their differences, however, movie spectaculars exploit one of the central traditions of film viewing: the desire to be awed by sublime worlds beyond our normal views.

CONCEPTS AT WORK

Mise-en-scène is what we actually see at the movies, and thus it is central. Yet as it is used in the service of the film as a whole, it can also be overlooked—think of the numerous times Universal has used the *Psycho* house in other movies and TV shows. It is the juxtaposition of its ordinary appearance with unthinkable horror that made the Bates Motel one of the screen's most memorable examples of mise-en-scène and emphasized the decisive role it played in film's meaning. Viewers are sometimes even afraid to take showers after seeing *Psycho*! But, just as Hitchcock anticipated in the film's trailer, moviegoers actually enjoy being scared in this way. The motel remains one of the main attractions of the backlot tour at Universal Studios in Hollywood, which, when it began operating just four years after the release of Hitchcock's film, already included the *Psycho* house. These creepy three-fifths scale sets and facades remind viewers both of the movie's thrills and chills and of the artifice and manipulation that went into generating them.

Activity

Imagine a film, such as *The Wizard of Oz*, in which setting seems to determine plot ("follow the yellow brick road," for example) and transpose its characters to the world of another film: a mystery film or a social drama, for example. How would you design the new setting, and how would you rethink the plot based on a new setting?

THE NEXT LEVEL: ADDITIONAL SOURCES

Affron, Charles and Mirella. *Sets in Motion: Art Direction and Film Narrative.* New Brunswick, NJ: Rutgers University Press, 1995. Concentrating on the work of set designers, this study examines a number of films to demonstrate how sets do far more than embellish a film, often becoming the center of its meaning.

Brewster, Ben, and Lea Jacobs. *Theatre to Cinema: Stage Pictorialism and the Early Feature Film.* Oxford: Oxford University Press, 1997. The book is a careful, scholarly investigation of the transition from stage to screen in early film history.

Dyer, Richard. *Stars.* Rev. ed. London: BFI, 1998. A landmark study of the many ways that stars organize and focus a reading of film, this work explores both their onscreen presence and their offscreen activities.

Gaines, Jane M., and Charlotte Herzog, eds. *Fabrications: Costume and the Female Body.* London: Routledge, 1990. This collection of essays addresses the role of costume and costume design in defining film narrative, shaping female star images, and appealing to women audiences.

Gibbs, John. *Mise-en-Scène: Film Style and Interpretation.* New York: Columbia University Press, 2002. A book devoted exclusively to the importance of mise-en-scène, it is a historical survey of this critical dimension of film and a detailed examination of its aesthetic powers.

Neumann, Dietrich. *Film Architecture: Set Designs from Metropolis to Blade Runner.* Munich and New York: Prestel Art Press, 1999. The book is a lavishly illustrated study of modernist architecture and urbanism's influence on set design that accompanied an art exhibition.

Williams, Christopher. *Realism and the Cinema.* London: Routledge, 1980. A wide-ranging examination of the arguments about film realism, this book also looks at different filmic practices of realism and the ideological stakes implicit in those movies.

Seeing through the Image
Cinematography

Buster Keaton's silent classic *The Cameraman* (1928) celebrates the daring of the newsreel cinematographer, who shoulders a camera and follows the action—into the trenches or atop the scaffolding of a skyscraper under construction. Selling old-fashioned tintype portraits on the streets, Keaton's character is literally pushed aside by the newsreel cameramen, whose technology is much better suited to the speed and transformations of the modern city. So the hapless Keaton trades in his outdated still camera for a secondhand movie camera, and misadventures with the almost lifelike apparatus, an organ-grinder's monkey, and accidental (and quite avant-garde) double exposures ensue, until finally he gets his footage. At the same time, he wins the love of the heroine, but only when he's caught behaving heroically in front of the camera. Made just when synchronized sound would temporarily tie down the motion-picture cameras that had become so fluid during the silent era, *The Cameraman* balances the documentary and storytelling impulses of cinematography in the astonishing stunts Keaton performs, captured as evidence of his ingenuity by *The Cameraman*'s own cameraman.

Visual stimuli determine a significant part of our experience of the world around us: we look left and right for cars before we cross a busy street, we watch sunsets in the distance, we focus on a face across the room. The visual dynamics by which we encounter our world vary. Sometimes we are caught up in the close-ups of a crowded sidewalk; sometimes we watch from a window high above the street. Vision allows us to distinguish colors and light, to evaluate the sizes of things near and far, to track moving objects, or to invent shapes out of formless clouds. Vision allows us to project ourselves into the world, to explore objects and places, and to transform them in our minds. In the cinema, we know the material world only as it is relayed to us through the filmed images (and recorded sounds) that we process in our minds.

This chapter describes the feature at the center of most individuals' experiences of movies: film images. Although film images may sometimes seem like transparencies or open windows on the world, they are carefully constructed and filmed. Here we will detail the subtle and complex ways cinematography composes individual movie images in order to communicate feelings, ideas, and other meanings.

KEY CONCEPTS

In this chapter, we examine

- how the film image develops from a long historical heritage of visual spectacles
- how the frame of an image positions our point of view according to different distances and angles
- how film shots use the depth of the image in various ways
- how the film image moves according to certain patterns in order to achieve certain effects
- how film stock, color, lighting, and compositional features of the image can be employed in a movie
- how visual effects are achieved through an array of camera techniques
- how digital technology has transformed cinematography
- how the movie image assumes significance in different cinematic traditions

We go to the movies to enjoy stimulating sights, share other people's perspectives on the world, and explore that world through the details contained in a film image. In Ingmar Bergman's *Persona* (1966), a woman's tense and mysterious face suggests the complex depths of the person behind it. At the beginning of *Saving Private Ryan* (1998), we share viscerally the perspective of confused and wounded soldiers as bullets zip across the ocean surface during the D-Day invasion **[Figure 4.1]**. In *Walkabout* (1971), an empty horizon in the Australian wilderness vibrates with heat and light, becoming a vision of a new and unknown world **[Figure 4.2]**.

Vision occurs when light rays reflected from an object strike the retina of the eye and stimulate our perception of that object's image in the mind. Photography, which means "light writing," mimics vision in the way it registers light patterns onto celluloid film. Yet whereas vision is continuous, photography is not; rather, it freezes a single moment in the form of an image. Movies connect a series of these single moments and project them above a particular rate of frames per second to create an illusion of movement. For decades, a phenomenon known as **persistence of vision** explained this illusion as a delay in human perception that occurred when the retina retained a visual imprint, or afterimage, for a fragment of a second. Each imprint in a sequence of images was thought to overlap briefly with the previous one, creating the illusion of movement. More recent studies of perception suggest that humans process the incremental differences among sequential still images just as we process actual motion—this effect is called short-range **apparent motion**, and it is now considered the psychological process that explains our perception of movement when watching films [**Figure 4.3**]. In brief, the brain is actively responding to visual stimuli exactly as it would in actual motion perception, rather than passively processing sequential impressions received on the retina. The analogy between human and mechanical vision (in which an image is imprinted on the retina as if on a strip of film) appealed to early film theorists who were excited by the potential of new technology to expand perception. Perhaps this analogy explains why "persistence of vision" has endured as an account of how the brain perceives continuous movement from rapidly projected still images.

Such technological and physiological mechanisms suggest that the magic of the film image comes from its power to re-create how we see the world through imagistic compositions that direct, expand, and even transform our natural vision.

4.1 *Saving Private Ryan* (1998). The film uses visceral camera work to bring viewers close to the dying on D-Day.

4.2 *Walkabout* (1971). Striking images of the Australian outback are integral to this mysterious coming-of-age tale.

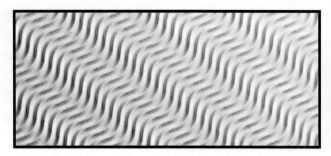

4.3 **Optical illusion**. The difference between images on a strip of film is so slight that when they are projected at sufficient speed the viewer perceives continuous motion. Short-range apparent motion can be illustrated with optical illusions like this one.

4.4 *Blade Runner* (1982). The technology imagined to explore unseen elements of a photograph anticipates developments in computer imaging.

In the science fiction film *Blade Runner* (1982), Rick Deckard (Harrison Ford) uses a computer to explore unseen spaces in a photograph, using visual technology to offer perspectives that surpass the powers of human vision [**Figure 4.4**]. Through that image, he sees a room in a way that the traditional human perspective never could. Even the conventional film image, however, manifests similar power and art. Whether in the slow-moving precision and clarity of the single forty-five-minute zoom image of Michael Snow's *Wavelength* (1967) or in the glowing and nostalgic textures of Frederico Fellini's *Amarcord* (1974), through the film image we can see and understand the world with fresh eyes.

A Short History of the Cinematic Image

The human fascination with creating illusions is an ancient one; in the *Republic*, Plato wrote of humans trapped in a cave who mistake the shadows on the wall for the actual world. Leonardo da Vinci described how a light source entering a hole in a *camera obscura* (literally, "dark room") projected an upside-down image on the opposite wall, offering it as an analogy of human vision and anticipating the mechanism of the camera. One of the earliest technologies that used a light source to project images was the magic lantern. In the eighteenth century, showmen developed elaborate spectacles called *phantasmagoria* [**Figure 4.5**]. The most famous of these were Étienne-Gaspar Robert's terrifying mobile projections of ghosts and skeletons on columns of smoke in an abandoned Paris crypt. These fanciful devices provided the basis for the technology that drives modern cinematography and the film image's power to control, explain, and entertain. In this section, we will examine the historical development of some of the key features in the production and projection of the film image.

1820s–1880s: The Invention of Photography and the Prehistory of Cinema

The components that would finally converge in cinema—photographic recording of reality and the animation of those images—were central to the visual culture of the nineteenth century. Combining

4.5 **Phantasmagoria**. This engraving from 1831 shows Étienne-Gaspar Robert's elaborate performances using magic lanterns and other effects.

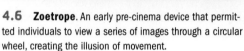

4.7   Eadweard Muybridge's motion studies. Experimenting with still photographs of motion, Muybridge laid the groundwork for cinematography.

4.6   Zoetrope. An early pre-cinema device that permitted individuals to view a series of images through a circular wheel, creating the illusion of movement.

amusement and science, the *phenakistiscope* (1832) and the *zoetrope* (1834) [**Figure 4.6**], among other such pre-cinema contraptions, allowed a person to view a series of images through slits in a circular wheel, a view that creates the illusion of a moving image. In 1839, Louis Jacques Mandé Daguerre produced the first still photograph (although Joseph Nicéphore Niépce laid the groundwork in 1826). Photography's ability mechanically to produce images of reality and to make them readily available to the masses was among the most significant developments of nineteenth-century culture. Photography permeated everything from family albums to scientific study to private pornography collections. In the 1880s, both Étienne-Jules Marey in France and Englishman Eadweard Muybridge, working in the United States, conducted extensive studies of human and animal figures in motion using **chronophotography**, series of still images that recorded incremental movement and formed the basis of cinematography [**Figures 4.7 and 4.8**]. Muybridge's Zoopraxiscope, introduced in 1879, enabled moving images to be projected for the first time.

4.8   Étienne-Jules Marey's chronophotographic gun. Developed in 1882, this device took rapid, consecutive images of birds in flight and other moving objects.

1890s–1920s: The Emergence and Refinement of Cinematography

Inventor W. L. K. Dickson invented the first motion picture camera, patented by his employer, Thomas Edison, as the Kinetoscopic camera in 1891. But the official birth date of the movies is widely accepted as 1895, when the brothers Auguste and Louis Lumière successfully joined two key elements: the ability to record a sequence of images on a flexible, transparent medium, and the capacity to project the sequence.

4.9   *Niagara Falls* (1897). One of the Lumière brothers' nonfiction moving snapshots (or actualities) shows the wonder and balance of a single moving image.

4.10   *The Kiss* (1896). From the Edison company, one of the most famous early films regards an intimate moment.

The Lumières debuted their Cinématographe at the Grand Café in Paris on December 28, 1895, showing ten short films, including the famous scene of workers leaving the Lumière factory.

The very first movies consisted of a single moving image. The Lumières' early film *Niagara Falls* (1897) simply shows the famous falls and a group of bystanders, but its compositional balance of a powerful natural world and the people on its edge draws on a long history of painting that infuses the film with remarkable energy and beauty that the addition of motion renders almost sublime [Figure 4.9]. Referred to in one newspaper as "The Anatomy of a Kiss," the early Edison film *The Kiss* (1896) titillated viewers by giving them a playfully analytical snapshot of an intimate moment [Figure 4.10].

In the early years of film history, technical innovations in the film medium and in camera and projection hardware were rapid and competitive. Eastman Kodak quickly established itself as the primary manufacturer of **film stock,** which consists of a flexible backing or base such as celluloid and a light-sensitive emulsion. The standard **nitrate** film base was highly flammable, and its pervasive use (it was not definitely replaced by **safety film** until 1952) is one reason why so much of the world's silent film heritage is lost. Early black-and-white film's emulsion was **orthochromatic,** sensitive only to blue and green light and processed using a red safety-light. **Film speed** is a measure of film's sensitivity to light: a slow film is less sensitive and requires a longer exposure than a fast film. *Film gauge,* or the width of film stock, varied in the early years until it was fixed at 35mm by the Motion Picture Patents Trust in 1909, a gauge that is still standard today [Figure 4.11a–4.11c]. Also agreed upon at that time was the *aspect ratio* of image height to width of 1:1.33. By the 1920s, the rate at which moving images were recorded (and later projected) increased from sixteen frames to twenty-four frames per second (fps), offering more clarity and definition to moving images.

The silent-film era saw major innovations in lighting, mechanisms for moving the camera and varying the scale of shots, and the introduction of much more sensitive **panchromatic** stock, which responded to a full spectrum of colors and became the standard for black-and-white movies after 1926. Such cinematographers as Billy Bitzer, working with D. W. Griffith in the United States, and Karl Freund, shooting such German expressionist classics as *Metropolis* (1927), brought cinematographic art to a pinnacle that was adversely affected by the introduction of sound and attendant restrictions on outdoor and mobile shooting.

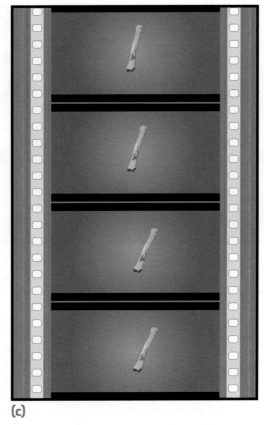

(a) (b)

(c)

4.11 Common film gauges drawn to scale.
(a) **16mm film gauge.** The lightweight cameras and portable projectors used with this format have been effective for documentary, newsreel, and independent film as well as for prints of films shown in educational and home settings.

(b) **35mm film gauge.** The standard gauge for theatrically released films, introduced in 1892 by Edison.

(c) **70mm film gauge.** A wide, high-resolution gauge, in use since the early days of the film industry, but first used for feature films in the 1950s. A horizontal variant of 70mm is used for IMAX formats.

1930s–1940s: Developments in Color, Wide-Angle, and Small-Gauge Cinematography

Technical innovations increased even as the aesthetic potential of the medium was explored. By the 1930s, color processes, by which a single or a wide range of colors become part of the film image, had evolved from the individually hand-painted frames or tinted sequences of silent films to colored stocks and, finally, the rich **Technicolor** process that would dominate color film production until the 1950s. The Disney cartoon *Flowers and Trees* (1932) **[Figure 4.12]** was the first to use Technicolor's three-strip process, which recorded different colors separately, using a dye transfer process to create a single image with a full spectrum of color. The process offered new realism but was often used to highlight artifice and spectacle, as in *The Wizard of Oz* (1939).

Meanwhile the **camera lens**, the piece of curved glass that redirects light rays in order to focus and shape images, also changed significantly—in terms of lens speed, which determines how much light an aperture allows to be gathered (that is, the "f-stop"), and the introduction of new lenses—wide-angle, telephoto, and zoom. Each lens produces a different **focal length**—the distance from the center of the lens to the point where light rays meet in sharp focus—that alters the perspective relations of an image. Wide-angle lenses have a short focal length, telephoto lenses have a long one, and a zoom is a variable focus lens. The range of perspectives offered by these advancements allowed for better resolution, more **depth of field**, wider angles, and more frame movement.

4.12 *Flowers and Trees* (1932). The first film to be released that used the full-color, three-strip Technicolor process was one of the *Silly Symphony* series of short subjects produced by Walt Disney.

4.13 *The Heiress* (1949). Gregg Toland's cinematography made use of the wide-angle lens and faster film stocks to create images in which both foreground and background are in sharp focus.

4.14 *House of Wax* (1953). This popular horror film made Vincent Price the "king of 3-D" as film in the 1950s strove for ever more spectacular cinematographic effects. The film also featured stereophonic sound.

During the 1920s, filmmakers used gauzy fabrics and, later, special lenses to develop a so-called soft style, through which the image could highlight the main action or character. From the mid-1930s through the 1940s, the development of the **wide-angle** lens (commonly considered a lens of less than 35mm in focal length) allowed cinematographers to explore a depth of field that could show different visual planes simultaneously. Cinematographer Gregg Toland is most closely associated with refinements in wide-angle cinematography, characterized by the dramatic use of deep focus in his work on Orson Welles's *Citizen Kane* (1941) and William Wyler's *The Heiress* (1949) **[Figure 4.13]**.

Camera technology also developed, with the introduction of more lightweight **handheld cameras** (such as the Arriflex camera) that were widely used during the war for newsreels and other purposes. Small-gauge production also expanded during this period, with the 8mm film developed in 1932 for the amateur filmmaker and the addition of sound and color to the 16mm format. In fact, 16mm's portability and affordability encouraged its use in educational films and other documentaries, as well as in low-budget independent and avant-garde productions.

1950s–1960s: Widescreen, 3-D, and New Color Processes

The early 1950s witnessed the arrival of several **widescreen processes**, which changed the size of the image—its aspect ratio (see p. 21)—by dramatically widening it (in part, to distinguish the cinema from the new competition of television). One of the most popular of these processes in the 1950s, CinemaScope used an **anamorphic lens**, which squeezed a wide-angle view onto a strip of 35mm film and then "unsqueezed" it during projection. Other widescreen films, such as *Lawrence of Arabia* (1962), used a wider film gauge of 70mm. This period, during which the popularity of television urged motion-picture producers to more spectacular displays, also saw a craze for 3-D movies such as *House of Wax* (1953) **[Figure 4.14]**. By now most movies were shot in color, facilitated by the introduction of Eastmancolor as an alternative to the proprietary Technicolor process. In the 1960s, Hollywood began to court the youth market, and cinematographers experimented more aggressively with ways to distort or call attention to the image through the use of **filters** (transparent sheets of glass or gels placed in front of the lens), **flares** (created by directing strong light at the lens), **telephoto lenses** (lenses with a focal length of at least 75mm and capable of magnifying and flattening distant objects), and fast motion, among other effects.

▶ **VIEWING CUE**

Think about the cinematography of this week's screening in relation to the larger history of the image. Are there shots that seem like paintings, photographs, or other kinds of visual displays? To what effect? ⏸

1970s–1980s: Cinematography and Exhibition in the Age of the Blockbuster

As we have seen, the history of film images is to a great extent that of film stock, cameras, and other recording and projection equipment. In the 1970s, the flexibility of **camera movement** was greatly enhanced with the introduction of the **Steadicam**, a camera stabilization device that allows the operator to follow action smoothly and rapidly, as evidenced in the uncanny camera movements in *The Shining* (1980). Special effects technology also developed rapidly in the era of the blockbuster ushered in by *Jaws* (1975). The spectacular qualities of motion pictures are on display in modern **IMAX** and **Showscan** projection systems developed in the 1970s [Figure 4.15]. IMAX systems store approximately three times as much information as a 70mm film image when projected horizontally rather than vertically. Showscan, developed by Douglas Trumbull and marketed in 1983, projects at sixty frames per second (rather than twenty-four frames) and creates remarkably dense and detailed images.

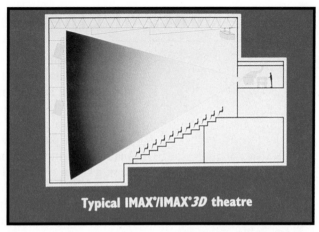

4.15 **IMAX theater design.** The IMAX format requires a special projection system for its spectacular cinematography.

1990s and Beyond: The Digital Future

Television, documentary filmmakers, and artists in the 1970s first used video as an alternative medium to celluloid, and with the development of camcorders in the 1980s, it spread widely among consumers. Although the succession of broadcast and consumer formats (including Portapak reel-to-reel, U-matic, Beta, and VHS) were analogue formats, they paved the way for the consumer embrace of such digital technologies as Mini-DV in the 1990s. The film industry developed digital technology for special effects and nonlinear editing before **digital cinematography** became a viable alternative to 35mm film. *Star Wars: Episode II—Attack of the Clones* (2002) was the first high-profile film to be shot in high-definition (HD) digital video. Distribution and exhibition using digital technology (satellite distribution and hard drive projection, for example) are currently the focus of as much technical, aesthetic, and entrepreneurial activity as existed in similar periods of change in film history. But whether the base is celluloid or not, they are still *moving* images: cinema.

Although the film image will continue to develop in new directions, traces of its past constantly resurface. Russian iconography permeates the images of Tarkovsky's *Andrei Rublev* (1969) [Figures 4.16a and 4.16b]. The Japanese tradition of *ukiyo-e* woodblock prints appears in the films of Kenji Mizoguchi, including *Utamaro and His Five Women* (1946). And in Raoul Ruiz's *Time Regained* (2000), rich color tones re-create the vibrancy of magic lanterns [Figures 4.17a and 4.17b]. In virtually every movie we see, our experience of the film image is permeated by its history.

(a)   (b)

4.16 **(a) Russian icon painting from the sixteenth century, (b)** *Andrei Rublev* (1969). The composition and lighting of Tarkovsky's film about the great Russian icon painter evokes Rublev's medieval art.

(a)   (b)

4.17 **(a) Magic lantern slide** (1905), **(b)** *Time Regained* (2000). Raoul Ruiz's adaptation of Marcel Proust's work evokes the past through lighting that recalls the rich color of magic lantern slides.

The Elements of Cinematography

Cinematography means motion-picture photography—literally, "writing in movement." The basic unit of cinematography is the shot. The **shot** is the visual heart of the cinema: it is a continuous point of view (or continuously exposed piece of film); it may move forward or backward, up or down, but it does not change, break, or **cut** to another point of view or image. A film depicting a hotel room the morning after a wild party may "shoot" the scene, or employ cinematographic shots, in many different ways. One version might show the entire room with its broken window, a fallen chair, and a man slumped in the corner as a single shot that depicts the scene from a calm distance. Another version might show the same scene in a rapid succession of images made by multiple shots—the window, the chair, and the man—creating a visual disturbance missing in the first version.

Points of View

VIEWING CUE

Identify a subjective point-of-view shot from the movie you are watching for class. Describe what marks it as such.

In cinematographic terms, **point of view** refers to the position from which a person, an event, or an object is seen (or filmed). All shots have a point of view: a **subjective point of view** re-creates the perspective of a character through camera placement; an **objective point of view** represents the more impersonal perspective of the camera. A point of view may be discontinuous—for instance, in *The Natural* (1984) the perspective changes dramatically from the position behind home plate [Figure 4.18] to a point of view positioned on the field—or it may change as part of a continuous point of view. In the same film, the perspective from behind home plate shifts gradually to follow the ball into the stands. While the first is edited, cutting between two shots, the second is a single shot whose point of view is continuous. The specific object highlighted within a point of view is the shot's **focus**, the point in the image that is most clearly and precisely outlined and defined by the lens of the camera. In our example, while the point of view may move continuously, the focus may remain constantly on a single player or even on the small baseball that appears in the image.

4.18   *The Natural* (1984). To see a baseball game from directly behind home plate offers a different point of view on the game than to watch it from center field.

Four Attributes of the Shot

Every shot orchestrates four important attributes: framing, depth of field, color, and movement. The **framing** of a shot contains, limits, and directs the point of view within the borders of the rectangular frame. Usually framing is even, but sometimes it can appear unbalanced or askew, as in the **canted frame** that famously recurs in *The Third Man* (1949) [Figure 4.19]. Framing determines the image size by correlating with the camera's distance from its subject. In *A League of Their Own* (1992), the framing at one point depicts only the face of the batter and, shortly thereafter, the entire ballpark. Film images also create a depth of field, the range or distance before and behind the main focus and within which objects remain relatively sharp and clear: sometimes an image may create a short or shallow range and sometimes a long range or deep focus. From a viewing position in the center-field bleachers, for example, a film image may focus primarily

4.19   *The Third Man* (1949). Suspicions about Orson Welles's character Harry Lime are reinforced by the canted framing.

on a play at second base but create a depth of field that keeps the players before and behind that action—the pitcher and an outfielder—in focus. Finally, a film image or shot may depict or incorporate movement. The subject of the shot may move, and the **mobile frame** of the image may follow an action, object, or individual, or it may move to show different actions, objects, or individuals. (Such movement requires the camera or lens to move during filming.) During the championship game in *A League of Their Own,* the mobile frame of the shot shows the younger sister as she races around the field on her way to scoring the winning run, the movement of the shot capturing the strength and dexterity of her strides in a single motion [**Figure 4.20**].

4.20 *A League of Their Own* (1992). A mobile camera increases the viewer's excitement during the winning run.

Framing

Although we may not attend to every individual image in a movie, its cinematography involves careful construction by filmmakers and rewards close observation by viewers. Abel Gance's *Napoléon* (1927) [**Figure 4.21**] orchestrates images to appear simultaneously on multiple screens; to shoot single scenes in *Dancer in the Dark* (2000), Lars von Trier used numerous digital cameras placed at different angles and distances in order to capture the exact images needed. Films have experimented with and refined ways to manipulate and use the film image and its properties for over one hundred years. The three dimensions of the film image—the height and width of the frame, and the apparent depth of the image—offer endless opportunities for representing the world and how we see it. Here we will examine and detail the formal possibilities inherent in the cinematic image, possibilities that, when recognized, enrich our experience of the movies.

Aspect Ratio. Like the frame of a painting, the basic shape of the film image on the screen determines the film composition. The *aspect ratio* describes the relation of width to height of the film frame as it appears on a movie screen or television monitor. *The Grand Illusion, Citizen Kane* (1941), and other classic films employ the 1.33:1 image ratio standardized in 1932 by the American Academy of Motion Picture Arts and Sciences and used by most films until the 1950s. Technically, *academy ratio* is 1.37:1, which includes the portion of the filmstrip used for the optical soundtrack, which is not visible when projected [**Figure 4.22a**]. These dimensions are closely approximated by the television screen and are rendered as 4:3 in DVD formats and draw on associations between film frame and window or picture frame. The standard U.S. *widescreen ratio* [**Figure 4.22b**], which has largely replaced academy ratio since the 1950s, is 1.85:1. (The standard European widescreen ratio is 1.66:1, and the digital equivalent is the compromise of 16:9.)

Aspect ratios often shape our experience to align with the themes and actions of the film. For example, CinemaScope, which uses an anamorphic (or compressed) lens to achieve a widescreen ratio of 2.35:1 [**Figure 4.22c**], was first used for religious epics and musicals. In Nicholas Ray's 1955 drama of teenage frustration and fear, *Rebel without a Cause,* the elongated horizontal CinemaScope frame depicts the loneliness

text continued on page 108 ▶

▶ **VIEWING CUE**

While watching the next film shown in your class, choose two or three distinctive shots, sketching and then describing them as precisely as possible. Why do you consider them important?

4.21 *Napoléon* (1927). Abel Gance's historical tour-de-force juxtaposed images on multiple screens.

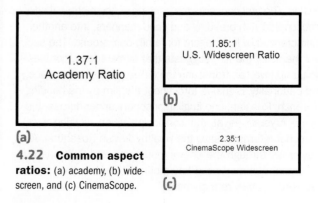

1.37:1
Academy Ratio

(a)

1.85:1
U.S. Widescreen Ratio

(b)

2.35:1
CinemaScope Widescreen

(c)

4.22 **Common aspect ratios:** (a) academy, (b) widescreen, and (c) CinemaScope.

Frames and Movements in *The Grand Illusion* (1937)

Jean Renoir's *The Grand Illusion*, set during World War I, focuses on a group of French aviators who are moved from one German prison camp to another. Certainly the horror, devastation, and loss of war impact the lives of these soldiers, but the achievement of the film is to reveal how a common humanity can transcend this war setting. *The Grand Illusion* demonstrates that its brutal and repressive mise-en-scène is only part of the drama and that the point of view from which events are revealed often tells the richer tale. Here, especially, it is possible to imagine the influence of Renoir's father, the French impressionist painter Pierre-Auguste Renoir, for whom the frame of a painting (such as *The Boating Party*) harmonized the points of view of so many kinds of people, watching each other's humanity unfold. In the catastrophes of war since the *belle époque* of his father's France, Renoir the son still finds the power of framing to portray human compassion.

Appropriate to this attention to the image, a smudge in a reconnaissance photograph opens the film, and the two French officers who fly off to investigate that blur are soon captured. Brought to a German barracks after their plane is shot down, the captured officers are treated with the special deference due aristocrats by the German Captain von Rauffenstein. Two main themes are apparent in *The Grand Illusion*. The first concerns the passing of one historical age, preoccupied with breeding and good manners, into another, characterized by less regard for family background. The second theme of the film suggests that camaraderie, compassion, and love can transcend the differences of class, race, and nationality. Signaled throughout the film by the bonding of French, Russian, and English prisoners under duress, the theme crystallizes at the conclusion when working-class Maréchal returns to save the wealthy Jewish Rosenthal. As they cross through the snowy mountains into Switzerland, Rosenthal summarizes a key motif in the film: "You can't see borders; they're man-made."

These themes of a lost age and a new humanity shape the visual compositions of *The Grand Illusion*, where subjective point-of-view shots and framings designate the confrontations between personal perspectives and the world. Immediately after his capture, the wounded Maréchal dines with a German officer who tries to uphold the illusions of social etiquette, politely offering to cut his food while they chat about their pasts as auto mechanics. Suddenly, they both become silent and look beyond the film frame [Figure 4.23]. The next shot shows the object of the somber point of view—a funeral wreath for a French flier recently gunned down by the Germans.

Similarly, frame compositions in *The Grand Illusion* describe subtle relations and tensions in the interaction of the characters. Late in the film, for instance, Boeldieu and Maréchal plan the latter's escape: Boeldieu stands on the right side of the frame, elevated to the top corner;

4.23 *The Grand Illusion* (1937). The characters' gazes direct our attention beyond the frame.

Maréchal squats in the lower left-hand corner; and occupying the majority of the frame's center is a pet squirrel in a birdcage [**Figure 4.24**]. Frequently, depth of field creates powerful compositions; when Rauffenstein realizes, during the escape episode, that Boeldieu will not surrender and will have to be hunted down by his soldiers, one shot shows Rauffenstein climbing wearily and sadly up the castle steps in the background while lines of German troops race through the foreground in pursuit of Boeldieu [**Figure 4.25**]. More often, though, the movement of the frame, from side to side or front to back, makes the crucial points and renders the major themes while capturing the flux of reality. One powerful sequence begins with three village women at the gate of the prison, with men working in an open field in the deepest plane of the image. As the women stare past a wagon entering the gate, the camera follows their gaze to a group of young German soldiers marching in formation. One woman remarks, "Poor boys." In the next image, Boeldieu, Maréchal, and other French prisoners watch through a window frame as the same German soldiers march rapidly across the background of the image. With his men making costumes for a prison play, Boeldieu sighs, "Out there, children play soldier. In here, soldiers play children." In the foreground, inside the window frame now, the camera frame momentarily isolates several prisoners, and each comments on what the war means to him. In the background, the Germans continue to exercise, suddenly drawing the French prisoners to the window as they begin to march. As the frame moves, right to left, across the prisoners' faces, we watch as they recognize a dark and violent reality much greater than their private lives.

The *Grand Illusion* presents an intricate story rooted in the traditional human values of compassion and respect. The power of the film is its ability to dramatize those values in the context of modern war, where they are tested in

4.24 *The Grand Illusion* (1937). The composition suggests the breach between the two comrades ("we've got nothing in common," Maréchal claims), but it also connects them through the squirrel's caged predicament that resembles theirs.

ways that threaten their survival. At the heart of this drama, the film analyzes the many ways in which individuals and groups interact across different and often combative points of view. At the conclusion, Maréchal's chance meeting with a German countrywoman leads to a moment of unexpected love [**Figure 4.26**]. Able to see outside the frames that have divided nations and individuals, this French man and German woman fall in love, and with her help, the two men escape to Switzerland beyond the boundaries that confined them. Throughout the film, Renoir uses mobile framing and shots of sufficient duration to correlate the compositions of his images with these themes, refusing to cut when connections in time and space can be revealed to an attentive spectator.

4.25 *The Grand Illusion* (1937). Rauffenstein fades into the depths of the frame.

4.26 *The Grand Illusion* (1937). Although framed in the composition, the lovers move beyond national borders.

and isolation of Jim Stark (played by James Dean) and his friends, Judy and Plato. Outside the planetarium, Ray's cinematography conveys the city below as an unreachable place for these small-town youths [**Figure 4.27**]. While the more confined frame of *Citizen Kane* fits a film about a man driven to control the world, the widescreen space in *Rebel without a Cause* suits the fitful search of restless teens, and both films use carefully composed frames that highlight screen dimensions. Although aspect ratio may not be such a crucial determinant in every movie, it does not escape the consideration of the filmmaker. For instance, Stanley Kubrick shot his war film *Full Metal Jacket* (1987) in academy ratio rather than widescreen, which had evolved into the standard ratio by the time he shot his film. With this choice, Kubrick emphasizes a central theme: that the Vietnam War entered world consciousness through the box-like screen of television.

The changes in film ratios over the years have presented interesting challenges when movies appear on television or are recorded to tape or disc. Most television broadcasts of movies now announce that they have been "formatted to fit your screen," and a videotape or DVD version of a film may be *letterboxed* by blocking off the top and bottom strips of the square frame to accommodate the widescreen image, or digitally altered and offered in several formats. In recent years, televisions themselves have taken on the horizontal proportions of widescreen cinema frames, even though much television programming does not utilize these dimensions. But before these innovations, and frequently even now, movies shown on television will have been altered through the *"pan-and-scan" process*. This process chops off outer portions of the image that are not central to the action or reconstitutes a single widescreen image into two consecutive television images. Reframing the image can alter our perception of the film and its story. In movies like *Rebel without a Cause* and *The Lord of the Rings: The Return of the King* (2003), to name just two, the surrounding space of the frame is an important part of the drama that helps us understand the characters and their actions [**Figure 4.28**]. Even when these changes seem minor or barely noticeable, they can subtly influence our perceptions and responses to a film. In *Badlands* (1973), a letterboxed image (rather than one formatted to fit the television frame) more appropriately displays the horizontal space that is so important to this road movie and the isolated wanderings of its criminal protagonist.

Masks. Besides the proportions determined by the aspect ratio, a film frame can be reshaped by various **masks**, attachments to the camera that cut off portions of the frame so that part of the image is black. Mostly associated with silent films—like D. W. Griffith's *Intolerance* (1916) [**Figure 4.29**]—or modern movies recalling that earlier period, a masked frame may open only a corner of the frame, create a circular effect, or leave just a strip in the center of the frame visible. An **iris shot** masks the frame so that only a small circular piece of the image is seen: in Harold Lloyd's *The Freshman* (1925), a shot of a timid collegian first appears in an **iris-in** (opening the circle to reveal more of the image) to show his seemingly safe location surrounded by a crowd

4.27 *Rebel without a Cause* (1955). Nick Ray uses the exaggerated width of the CinemaScope frame to show Jim Stark (James Dean) cornered despite the expanse of Los Angeles below.

4.28 *The Lord of the Rings: The Return of the King* (2003). Epic films that use widescreen for elaborate visual compositions and effects are reduced in impact when seen in other formats.

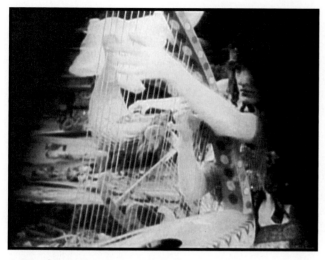

4.29   *Intolerance* (1916). A triangular mask isolates the triangular harp.

4.30   ***The Night of the Hunter*** (1955). An iris-out emphasizes the threat of a figure of evil.

of hostile football players. Conversely, a full image may be reduced, as an **iris-out** (closing the circle), to isolate and emphasize a specific object or action in that image: a shot of a courtroom, for example, might iris-out to reveal the nervous hands of the defendant's mother. In *The Night of the Hunter* (1955), an iris-out follows the demonic preacher as he walks toward the house of the children he threatens [**Figure 4.30**].

Onscreen space refers to the space visible within the frame of the image, whereas **offscreen space** is the implied space or world that exists outside the film frame. Onscreen space is often carefully framed for compositional effect, with the position, scale, and balance of objects or lines within the frame directing our attention or determining our attitude toward what is being represented. Usually the action in offscreen space is less important than the action in the frame (as when a close-up focuses on an intimate conversation and excludes other people in the room). Offscreen space does, however, sometimes contain important information that will be revealed in a subsequent image (as when one of the individuals engaged in conversation looks beyond the edge of the frame—toward a glaring rival shown in the next shot). Offscreen spaces in horror films like *Alien* (1979) seethe with a menace that is all the more terrifying because it is not visible [**Figure 4.31**]. In Robert Bresson's films, offscreen space suggests a spiritual world that exerts pressure on but eludes the fragmented and limited perspectives of the characters within the frame [**Figure 4.32**].

Camera Distance.
A significant aspect of framing is the distance of the camera from its subject, which determines the **scale** of the shot, signals point of view, and contributes a great deal to how we understand or feel about what is being shown. **Close-ups** show details of a person or object, such as the face or hands or a flower on a windowsill, perhaps indicating nuances of the character's feelings or thoughts or suggesting the special significance of the object. An **extreme close-up**

> **VIEWING CUE**
>
> Consider the relation of onscreen and offscreen space in a shot from the film you are studying. How does offscreen space add to your understanding of that shot?

4.31   *Alien* (1979). The horror genre makes significant use of offscreen space to generate suspense: what is Ripley (Sigourney Weaver) going to see?

4.32   *L'Argent* (1983). The agency of characters in Robert Bresson's films often seems to be limited by external forces signified by the emphasis on offscreen space.

4.33 *The Passion of Joan of Arc* (1928). Carl Theodor Dreyer captures the intensity of religious faith through frequent close-ups of actress Renée Falconetti's portrayal of Joan of Arc.

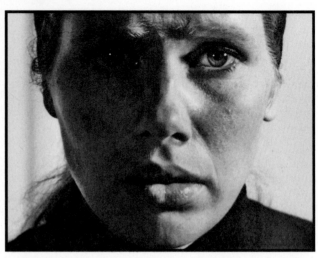

4.34 *Persona* (1966). Existential questions are evoked by the use of close-ups and extreme close-ups in Ingmar Bergman's film.

▶ **VIEWING CUE**

Look for a pattern of framing distances in this film. Do there seem to be a large number of long shots? Close-ups? Explain how this pattern reinforces themes of the film. ⏸

moves in even closer, singling out, for instance, the person's eyes or the petal of the flower. Carl Theodor Dreyer's *The Passion of Joan of Arc* (1928) and Ingmar Bergman's *Persona* (1966) are well-known examples of films that use close-ups and extreme close-ups to depict religious fervor and existential agony, respectively, through the heroines' facial expressions [**Figures 4.33 and 4.34**].

At the other end of the compositional spectrum, a **long shot** places considerable distance between the camera and the scene, object, or person filmed. A human figure remains recognizable but is defined by the large space and background that surrounds it. An **extreme long shot** creates an even greater distance between the camera and the person or object, so that the larger space of the image dwarfs small objects or human figures, such as with distant vistas of cities or landscapes. Most films feature a combination of these long shots, sometimes to show distant action or objects, sometimes to establish a context for events, and sometimes, as with the introduction and conclusion of *Shane* (1953), to emphasize the isolation and mystery of a character as he arrives in the distance [**Figures 4.35a and 4.35b**]. Between close-ups and long shots, a **medium shot** describes a middle ground in which we see the human body from the waist or hips up, as in *The Maltese Falcon* (1941) [**Figure 4.36**], while a **medium long**

4.35a *Shane* (1953). Barely seen, Shane approaches through an extreme long shot.

4.35b *Shane* (1953). The mysterious figure becomes more recognizable in a long shot.

4.36 *The Maltese Falcon* (1941). A medium shot of Sam Spade (played by Humphrey Bogart).

4.37 *Red River* (1948). The medium long shot was often used in westerns to keep weapons in view. French critics dubbed it the "plan American" or "American shot."

shot slightly increases the distance between the camera and the subject, showing a three-quarter-length view of a character (from approximately the knees up), a framing often used in westerns when a cowboy's weapon is an important element of the mise-en-scène **[Figure 4.37]**. A very common framing, the **medium close-up** shows a character's head and shoulders and is frequently used in conversation scenes. Melodramatic or romantic films about personal relationships often feature a predominance of medium close-ups and medium shots to capture the facial expressions of the characters, such as the story of a new bride's haunting by the memory of a former wife in *Rebecca* (1940) **[Figure 4.38]**. Open-air adventures, such as *The Seven Samurai* (1954), the tale of a sixteenth-century Japanese village that hires warriors for protection, tend to use more long shots and extreme long shots in order to depict the battle scenes **[Figure 4.39]**. As these descriptions imply, framing is defined relatively; there is no absolute cut-off point between a medium and a medium long shot, for example. As we have seen, the most common reference point for the scale of the image is the size of the human figure within the frame, a measure that is not a universal element of the cinematic image.

Although many shots are taken from approximately eye level, the camera height can also vary, as an element of a film's style, to present a particular compositional

4.38 *Rebecca* (1940). The melodramatic tension of a medium close-up on the heroine Joan Fontaine's face.

4.39 *The Seven Samurai* (1954). An extreme long shot in an epic.

4.40 *Tokyo Story* (1953). A camera placed low to the ground presents characters sitting on tatami mats.

4.41 *Far from Heaven* (2002). The height of the opening shot establishes the setting and introduces a sense of distance.

element or to evoke a character's perspective. Japanese director Yasujiro Ozu's signature camera level is low to the ground, an ideal position for filming Japanese interiors, where characters sit on the floor [**Figure 4.40**]. A camera might be placed higher to show larger-scale objects, such as tall buildings or landscapes. The opening shot of *Far from Heaven* (2002) takes a god's-eye view of its New England village setting, mimicking the opening of Douglas Sirk's *All That Heaven Allows* (1956) in its vision of 1950s small-town repression [**Figure 4.41**].

Camera Angles. Film shots are positioned according to a multitude of angles, from straight on to above or below. These are often correlated with camera height, as demonstrated by the series of shots presented here from Jane Campion's *The Piano* (1993), a powerful film about a mute Scottish woman who travels with her daughter to New Zealand to complete an arranged marriage. **High angles** present a point of view directed at a downward angle on individuals or a scene [**Figure 4.42**], while **low angles** view the subject from a position lower than it is [**Figure 4.43**]. In either case, the exact angle of the shot can vary from very steep to slight. An **overhead shot** (sometimes called a **crane shot** because of the machinery on which the camera is mounted) depicts the action or subject from high above, sometimes

4.42 *The Piano* (1993). A high-angle long shot of the arrival on the beach.

4.43 *The Piano* (1993). An extreme low-angle shot, slightly canted, shows the farmer/husband as he furiously descends toward his unfaithful wife.

4.44 *The Piano* (1993). With this overhead shot, the film depicts a rare moment of contentment and harmony at the piano.

4.45 *The Shop on Main Street* (1965). A crane shot from a bird's nest.

looking directly down on it **[Figure 4.44]**. In the Czech film *The Shop on Main Street* (1965) **[Figure 4.45]**, a clever opening crane shot looking down on the town reflects the point of view of a stork nesting on a chimney.

Shots change their angle depending on the physical or geographical position or point of view, so that a shot from a tall adult's perspective may be a high-angle shot, whereas a child's view may be seen through low angles. Such shots are often **point-of-view (POV) shots**, which are defined as shots that re-create the perspective of a character and may incorporate camera movement or optical effects as well as camera angle in order to do so. Camera angles can sometimes indicate psychological, moral, or political meanings in a film, as when victims are seen from above and oppressors from below, but such interpretations must be made carefully because formal features like these do not automatically assume particular meanings.

▶ **VIEWING CUE**

Select one or two shots in which depth of field seems especially important. How does depth of field distribute the objects or characters in a way that helps you understand the shot better? ⏸

Depth of Field

Depth of field (see pp. 101–105) is a measure that can be applied to any photographic image; **deep focus** means that multiple planes in the image are all in focus. A film about three physically and psychologically brutalized veterans returning home from World War II, William Wyler's *The Best Years of Our Lives* (1946) is a superior example of how deep focus can create relationships within a single image: the two grown children in the foreground frame the happy reunion of their parents in the background, all in harmonious balance and focus, with just a hint of the theme of isolation that will be developed after the homecoming **[Figure 4.46]**. In **shallow focus**, only a narrow range of the field is focused, but here, too, the choice of a depth of field indicates what is significant in an image. A shot can direct its focus at a specific plane within the image, such as in this medium shot from *The Best Years of Our Lives* **[Figure 4.47]**. With a **rack focus** (or *pulled focus*), the focus shifts rapidly from one object to another, such as refocusing from

4.46 *The Best Years of Our Lives* (1946). The deep focus and balance indicate restored family harmony at a soldier's homecoming.

4.47   *The Best Years of Our Lives* (1946). The focused foreground of embracing lovers leaves the blurred background of the veteran's artificial arms barely visible.

4.48   *L.A. Confidential* (1997). The shot refocuses to highlight the detective's expression against a blurry background.

the face of a woman to the figure of a man approaching from behind her. During a dramatic scene in *L.A. Confidential* (1997), a young self-righteous police officer, Ed Exley, assures his captain he can force the criminal suspect to confess, and the shot rack focuses from the captain to Exley to catch the latter's determined expression as he turns toward the interrogation room [**Figure 4.48**].

Color

▶ VIEWING CUE

How is color (or values of black and white) used in the film? For realism or for other purposes? Identify colors that strike you as dominant, and explain their importance. ⅠⅠ

Color profoundly affects our experience and understanding of a film shot, and black-and-white films also use contrast and gradations to create atmosphere or emphasize certain motifs. In F. W. Murnau's *Nosferatu* (1922), black and white and tones of gray create an ominous world where evil lives, not in darkness but in shading [**Figure 4.49**]. In *The Third Man* (1949), black-and-white contrasts glisten on the slick surfaces of a morally slippery world [**Figure 4.50**]. No longer a necessity, the black-and-white format is used in such modern films as *Raging Bull* (1980) and *Pleasantville* (1998) self-consciously. In the first film, it suggests the violent extremities in the life of prize fighter Jake LaMotta as well as the style of films of the period and milieu in which it is set [**Figure 4.51**]; in the second film, it parodies the superficial and simplistic lives of 1950s television, a world suddenly confused when emotional colors enter the characters' lives [**Figure 4.52**]. Cinematographer Christopher Doyle, well known for his work with Hong Kong filmmaker Wong Kar-wai, shifts between black-and-white and color cinematography in less predictable ways, highlighting the surface of the image, the exposure, and the grain of the stock [**Figure 4.53**].

Beginning with the colors of the mise-en-scène (natural colors, painted sets, locations, or actors' costumes), color describes the spectrum of color grades and hues used by a film, while **tone** refers to the shading, intensification, or saturation of those colors (such as metallic blues, soft greens, or deep reds) in order to

4.49   *Nosferatu* (1922). Diffuse shadows and shades of gray create an atmosphere of dread.

4.50 *The Third Man* (1949). Sharply contrasting blacks and whites, with scintillating greys, intensify the drama of good and evil in Vienna.

4.51 *Raging Bull* (1980). Scorsese's boxing film deliberately uses black and white to highlight bare violence and to evoke newspaper and film images from the period of the film's setting.

sharpen, mute, or balance them for certain effects. Color film stocks allow a full range of colors to be recorded to film. Once colors are recorded on film stocks, that film can be manipulated to create **color balances** that range from realistic to more extreme or unrealistic palettes: these may appear as either *noncontrasting balances* (sometimes called a *monochromatic color scheme*), which can create a more realistic or flat background against which a single color becomes more meaningful, or *contrasting balances*, which can create dramatic oppositions and tensions through color.

In the first decades after the 1895 arrival of the cinema, before color film stock was available, some movies, like the 1910 version of Shakespeare's *King Lear,* used laboriously hand-tinted colored frames that appeared like moving paintings. In the 1930s, the introduction of Technicolor aided the construction of both more realistic and more fantastic worlds. The costume drama *Becky Sharp* (1935) was the first feature film to use the process, and Disney's popular *Snow White and the Seven Dwarfs* (1937) followed soon thereafter. But it wasn't until the 1950s, with the introduction of the less elaborate Eastmancolor stock, that the

4.52 *Pleasantville* (1988). This film makes the shift from black-and-white to color cinematography a metaphor for the characters' emotional awakening.

4.53 *Happy Together* (1997). Cinematographer Christopher Doyle's work for director Wong Kar-wai is characterized by a creative use of different film stocks, including black and white.

majority of films were produced in color. Former animator Frank Tashlin brought a comic-book look to such live-action films as *The Girl Can't Help It* (1956). Color is a key element in the composition of the image, with certain films being justly famous for the expressive use of color. For example, Nestor Almendros filmed Terence Malick's *Days of Heaven* (1978) at the "magic hour" just before sunset to capture a particular quality of light for the historical setting in the Great Plains. Michael Mann's urban crime drama *Miami Vice* (2006) uses eerie blues.

Selection of film gauge and stock, which can vary in speed (a measure of a stock's sensitivity to light), manipulation of exposure, and choices in printing can all affect the color and tone of a particular film. Cinematographer Rodrigo Prieto used different stocks and cameras to achieve the looks of the three interconnected stories in *Babel* (2006). Lighting, a full discussion of which is included in Chapter 3 on mise-en-scène, is clearly crucial to a film's palette and color effects, and it comes under the direction of the cinematographer during the production process.

Movement

When the film frame begins to move, a film shot re-creates a quality of vision that has always been a part of the human experience but that could be adequately represented only with the advent of film technology. In our daily lives, we anticipate these movements of a shot: when, for instance, we focus on a friend at a table and then refocus beyond that friend and toward another at the door; when we stand still and turn our head from our left shoulder to our right; or when we watch from a moving car as buildings pass. Like these adjustments within our field of vision, the film image can move its frame and focus through changes in the view of the camera (such as pans or tracking shots) or through changes in the focus of the camera lens (such as zooms).

Reframing refers to the movement of the frame from one position to another within a single continuous shot. One extreme and memorable example of reframing is an early shot in *Citizen Kane* (1941). Here the camera pulls back from the boy in the yard to reframe the shot to include his mother observing him from inside the window; it then continues backward to reframe the mother as she walks past her husband and seats herself at a table next to the banker Thatcher who will take charge of their son [Figures 4.54a–4.54c]. Often such reframings are much more subtle, such as when the camera moves slightly upward to keep centered in the frame a character who is rising from a chair.

Pan and Tilts. In these mobile frames, the camera mount remains stationary. A **pan** moves the frame from side to side without changing the placement of the camera. In other words, the camera rotates on its vertical axis,

4.54a–4.54c *Citizen Kane* (1941).

as if a character were turning his or her head. For example, the long shot that scans the rooftops of San Francisco for a fugitive at the beginning of *Vertigo* (1958) is a pan (short for panorama), as are many similar establishing shots of a skyline. Or a pan may re-create a character's point of view. The opening sequence of *Rear Window* (1956) includes a pan around the courtyard of the protagonist's building—and we are surprised by the revelation that the man whose view we apparently share is in fact asleep. During the last scene of *Death in Venice* (1970), a slow pan leaves the main character, Gustav

4.55   *Death in Venice* (1970). A pan starts from the protagonist, crosses the beach, and scans the horizon, suggesting his state of mind as he calmly embraces suicide.

von Aschenbach, as he walks onto the beach and then swings past a jetty to settle the shot on the turbulent ocean and the glowing horizon. The movement of this pan suggests the romantic yearning and searching that characterize the entire film and that now culminate in von Aschenbach's death **[Figure 4.55]**.

Less common, **tilts** move the frame up or down on a horizontal axis as the camera rotates on its mount, as when the frame swings upward to re-create the point of view of a man following a skyscraper from the street into the clouds. In Wim Wenders's *Paris, Texas* (1984), a story about a father and son searching for the boy's mother, repeated tilt shots become a rhetorical action, moving the frame up a flagpole with an American flag, along the sides of Houston skyscrapers, and into the sky to view a passing plane. In this case, vertical tilts seem to suggest an ambiguous hope to escape or find comfort from the long quest across Texas.

Tracking Shots. A **tracking shot** changes the position of the point of view by moving the camera forward or backward or around the subject, usually on tracks that have been constructed in advance. Max Ophuls used fluid tracking shots extensively in his films, for example, following a waltzing couple in *The Earrings of Madame de . . .* (1953). In a **dolly shot**, the camera is moved on a wheeled dolly that follows a determined course. The term *traveling shot* is sometimes used interchangeably with both tracking and dolly shots. In the remarkable first shot of Jean-Luc Godard's *Contempt* (1963), a camera on tracks moves forward into the foreground of the image, following a woman reading. When the track reaches that foreground, the camera turns and aims its lens directly at us, the audience. When these two moving camera shots follow an individual, they are sometimes called **following shots**. In *The 400 Blows* (1959), a single following shot tracks the boy, Antoine Doinel, for eighty seconds as he runs from the reformatory school toward the edge of the sea.

Handheld and Steadicam Shots. Even greater mobility is afforded when the camera is carried by the camera operator. Encouraged first by the introduction of lightweight 16mm cameras and later by the use of video formats, **handheld shots** are frequently used in news reporting and documentary cinematography or to create an unsteady frame that suggests the movements of an individual point of view. *The Blair Witch Project* (1999) uses handheld shots so that the audience participates in the characters' frightened flight through the haunted forest **[Figure 4.56]**. Thomas Vinterberg's *The Celebration* (1998) also employs handheld digital video techniques to express the tension, anger, and confusion at a family gathering. In both of these cases, the handheld point of view involves the audience more immediately and concretely in the action.

To achieve the stability of a tripod mount, the fluidity of a tracking shot, and the flexibility of a handheld camera, cinematographers may wear the camera on a

TRANSFORMING FILM: Changing Color Processes

Color processes evolved from early hand tinting to three-color Technicolor experiments to spectacular color process to faster stocks to digital cinematography.

King Lear (1910).

Becky Sharp (1935).

The Girl Can't Help It (1956).

Days of Heaven (1978).

Miami Vice (2006).

4.56 *The Blair Witch Project* (1999). Handheld video viscerally brings the viewer into the horror and confusion in this low-budget sensation.

4.57 *Goodfellas* (1990). The long and winding trail of power behind the scenes is depicted in a three-minute Steadicam shot.

special stabilizing mount often referred to by the trademarked name Steadicam. In *Goodfellas* (1990), a film about mobster Henry Hill, a famous Steadicam shot, lasting several minutes, twists and turns with Hill and his entourage through a back door, a kitchen, and into the main room of a nightclub, suggesting the bravura and power of a man who can go anywhere, who is both onstage and backstage [Figure 4.57].

Zooms. Sometimes confused with a track-in or track-out, a zoom is technically not the result of a moving camera at all, but rather of adjustments to the camera lens during filming that magnify portions of the image. **Zoom lenses**, which employ a variable focal length of 75mm or higher, thus accomplish a different kind of compositional reframing and apparent movement. During a **zoom-in**, the camera remains stationary as the zoom lens changes focal length to narrow the field of view on a distant object, bringing it into clear view and reframing it in a medium shot or close-up. Less noticeable in films, a **zoom-out** reverses this action, so that objects that appear close initially are then distanced from the camera and reframed as small figures. One of the significant side effects of a zoom-in is that the image tends to flatten and lose its depth of field, whereas a track calls attention to the spatial depth that it moves through.

Although camera movements (tracking or Steadicam shots) and changes in the lens's focal length (zooms) may look similar, there are differences in the image and in the historical development of these technologies and practices. In two very different films, *An Occurrence at Owl Creek Bridge* (1962) and Ján Kádar's *Adrift* (1969), zoom-outs are combined with forward tracking shots, so that the respective protagonists appear to be running forward but never making any progress.

Digital Technology

Digital technology, which does not use film stock and thus does not require processing in a laboratory, is transforming cinematography in a number of ways from the amateur to the blockbuster level. Technically, the digital image offers advantages and disadvantages. Besides the economic advantage of lightweight and mobile cameras, the sharpness of the digital image suggests a kind of immediacy that distinguishes it from traditional celluloid images. The tale of a family gathering that is shattered through the horrifying revelation of a grown son, *The Celebration* (1998) uses the digital image to dramatize a stark reality with edgy directness. Director of such Hollywood films as *Leaving Las Vegas* (1995), Mike Figgis experimented with digital recording equipment in *Timecode* (2000). In a frame that contains four different quadrants, four stories are presented simultaneously in real time in a manner reminiscent of surveillance footage [Figure 4.58]. This ninety-three-minute film juxtaposes four continuous shots without any edits, a feat that would be impossible with celluloid, whose reels are of fixed length (approximately ten minutes in 35mm).

VIEWING CUE

Examine one or two shots in which camera movements (tracks, pans) or mobile framings (zooms) are important. Why is a moving frame of a single shot used here instead of a series of shots?

4.58 *Timecode* (2000). Real-time images made possible by digital cinematography are fractured in the gridlike presentation.

4.59 *Personal Velocity* (2002). Three intertwined stories are told in three different styles, all shot in intimate mini-DV format.

Digital moviemaking can be more intimate than 35mm cinematography, which involves large cameras and more crew members. Independent filmmakers quickly adapted to shooting on DV (digital video); for example, in Rebecca Miller's *Personal Velocity* (2002), cinematographer Ellen Kuras films three women's stories with emotional immediacy using mini-DV **[Figure 4.59]**. Sophisticated camera systems have made shooting on DV an option even for large-budget films such as Bryan Singer's *Superman Returns* (2006) or David Fincher's *Zodiac* (2007). Well outside mainstream film culture, "machinima" has become one of the more interesting offshoots of digital cinema. With this practice, filmmakers (such as Hugh Hancock, the creator of *Ozymandias* [2000]) manipulate the digital graphics of popular computer video games in order to create original images and stories (*Ozymandias* is a free interpretation of the Percy Bysshe Shelley sonnet).

Digital image processing also has several disadvantages. While a cinematographer could predict how a particular film stock responds to light, shooting digitally depends more on familiarity with the camera's capabilities. Digital images are recorded and displayed in pixels (densely packed dots), rather than the crystal array or grain produced by the celluloid emulsion used for film. When converted to a digital file, a 35mm film frame contains about ten million pixels. A sophisticated digital camera, such as the Sony Panavision HD 24, records about two million pixels for each of the primary colors. This difference may not make one kind of image better than the other, but the digital image has less range and lacks the grains and tones found in the film emulsion. In addition, traditional film equipment outperforms digital equipment in difficult outdoor conditions.

However, cinematographers have adapted to such challenges by experimenting with color palettes unique to the technology and by taking advantage of ways of altering the image. Digital images are capable of presenting even the most implausible events with starkly convincing realism. One of the most celebrated instances of this is *Forrest Gump* (1994), in which the eponymous slow-witted hero (Tom Hanks) drops his pants in front of President Lyndon Johnson and famously tells John F. Kennedy "I gotta pee" **[Figure 4.60]**. Gump is digitally blended into existing footage of these historical characters, creating a thoroughly realistic depiction of a fictional meeting. Indeed, the use of digital effects has blurred traditional lines between production and postproduction in contemporary filmmaking.

4.60 *Forrest Gump* (1994). Gump with George Wallace: digitally blending fiction and history.

4.61 *Alice* (1988). Jan Svankmajer's animated interpretation of Lewis Carroll's classic is considerably darker than the Disney version.

Animation and Special Effects

Our visual experience is not just naturalistic; it is also fantastical, composed of pictures from our dreams and imaginations. These kinds of images can be re-created in film through two important manipulations of the image, animation and special effects, which can be used to make film seem even more realistic or completely unreal. Both practices have been employed since the earliest days of cinema, but digital technologies have profoundly transformed them.

Animation traditionally refers to moving images drawn or painted on individual animation **cels**, which are then photographed onto single frames of film. In fact, animation includes several variations on that formula, as witnessed in films like *Chicken Run* (2000), the comic story of a chicken rebellion, and Czech filmmaker Jan Svankmajer's *Alice* (1988) **[Figure 4.61]**, which combines live action, puppets, and stop-motion animation to re-create the dizzying events of Lewis Carroll's story. With both these films, **stop-motion photography** records, as separate frames in incrementally changed action, inanimate objects or actual human figures that are then synthesized on film to create the illusion of motion and action: **claymation** accomplishes this effect with clay figures (as in *Chicken Run*), while **pixilation** employs this technique (or instead simply cuts out images from a continuous piece of filmed action) to transform the movement of real human figures into rapid, jerky gestures. If films from *Snow White and the Seven Dwarfs* (1937) to *Shrek* (2001) create graphic cartoon narratives through traditional frame-by-frame drawings and colorizing and filming, today's animation is accomplished more and more through computer graphics. Films such as *Toy Story* (1995) **[Figure 4.62]** and *Finding Nemo* (2003), both produced by the pioneering Pixar studio, are composed entirely of **computer-generated imagery (CGI)**. The striking advances in animation represented by such sophisticated techniques have contributed to the wide popularity of such films. The renewed appreciation for the medium was reflected in the introduction in 2002 of a new Academy Award category: feature-length animated films. Richard Linklater's *Waking Life* (2001) and *A Scanner Darkly* (2006) recorded real figures and action on video as a basis for painting individual animation frames digitally in a technique known as **rotoscoping [Figure 4.63]**.

Special effects is a term encompassing many practices, only some of which actually involve the camera or image processing (for example, many films employ pyrotechnics and other mechanical effects). Since early cinema, filmmakers have employed such basic manipulations as **slow motion or fast motion** to make the

4.62 *Toy Story* (1995). Pixar's first feature and the first computer-animated feature film to be released. The exaggerated crayon colors leap from the more balanced, natural tones of the realistic background.

4.63 *A Scanner Darkly* (2006). For this Philip K. Dick adaptation, Richard Linklater had his actors filmed digitally and then animated using a rotoscope technique.

action move at unrealistic speeds (achieved by filming the action faster or slower than normal and then projecting it at normal speeds); **color filters** that change the tones of the recorded image with different tinted lenses; and **miniature** (or other) **models** used to stage disasters or fantastic landscapes of the kind seen in the monstrous seas of *The Perfect Storm* (2000), which combined the use of models with CGI.

Another common special effect that remakes more than one shot into a single image is a **process shot**, a term that describes many different ways that the image can be set up and manipulated during filming. A process shot might project a background for the action on a screen in order to add another layer to the reality of the image (such as a large dinosaur bearing down on a screen behind an unaware scientist who appears to be only inches away) or to intentionally undermine the realism of the image by suggesting two or more competing realities. Hans-Jürgen Syberberg's film *Our Hitler* (1977), for example, shows Hitler quietly eating dinner while, in the background, Jews arrive at concentration camps; at other times, the film reduces Hitler to a puppet onstage [**Figure 4.64**]. Finally, a **matte shot**, such as the ominous church tower in *Vertigo* (1958) [**Figure 4.65**], joins two pieces of film, one with the central action or object and the other with the additional background, figures, or action (sometimes painted or digitally produced) that would be difficult to create physically for the shot.

4.64 *Our Hitler* (1977). Puppets and process shots are a few of the special effects used in this film to unravel the illusion of a fascist dictator.

4.65 *Vertigo* (1958). The tower that haunts the characters in Hitchcock's film was added to the actual church through a matte shot.

Some special effects use a combination of cinematography and computer techniques, such as the celebrated "bullet time" used to great effect in *The Matrix* (1999), in which images taken by a set of still cameras surrounding a subject are put together to create an effect of suspension or extreme slow motion [**Figure 4.66**]. Current blockbusters are driven more and more by spectacular visual effects, additional sequences and explanations of which often fill their DVDs. The viewer experiences Harry Potter's ride on the mythical hippogriff in *Harry Potter and the Prisoner of Azkaban* (2004) through a combination of techniques including **3-D modeling**. The fantasy world of Peter Jackson's *Lord of the Rings* trilogy was created through a range of special effects—from simple forced perspective to put characters in the proper scale [**Figure 4.67**] to the imaginative work of the New Zealand–based Weta Digital company that used **motion capture** technology to incorporate actor Andy Serkis's physical features into the computer-generated character Gollum.

4.66 *The Matrix* (1999). Neo's (Keanu Reeves's) extraordinary grace in battle is rendered with an effect called "bullet time," also used in commercials.

4.67 *The Lord of the Rings: The Return of the King* (2003). The third film in the trilogy contained 1,448 visual effects shots, nearly three times as many as the first.

The Significance of the Film Image

▶ **VIEWING CUE**

Describe and analyze one important instance of special effects or animation in the film you just viewed. Why is it used? ⏸

From the chariot races in Enrico Guazzoni's *Quo Vadis?* (1913) to the spectacular descent of an alien spaceship in *Close Encounters of the Third Kind* (1977), movie images have been valued for their beauty, realism, or ability to inspire wonder. Often these qualities are found in their production values because of the skill and money invested to generate such experiences. But film images carry other values in what they preserve and say about the world. French filmmaker Jean-Luc Godard's remark that film is truth at twenty-four frames a second is one way to describe the power and importance of the film image. Yet as Godard's many films themselves demonstrate, this "truth" is not just the truth of presentation but also the truth of representation. In short, film images are prized both for their accuracy in showing or presenting us with facts, as well as for how they interpret or represent those facts.

Image as Presentation or Representation

In earlier sections of this chapter, we investigated the cultural and formal structures of cinematography. In this section, we will examine how people intellectually and emotionally interact with film images. Having earlier addressed the historical background of the image and the compositional details we see, we turn to how we respond to film images according to the cultural and historical values and traditions that make images meaningful.

Images hold a remarkable power to capture a moment. Flipping through a photo album provides glimpses of past events. The morning newspaper collapses a day of war into a single poignant image. However, images can do far more than preserve the facts of a moment. They can also interpret those facts in ways that give them new meanings. A painting by Norman Rockwell evokes feelings of warmth and nostalgia, while the stained-glass windows lining a cathedral aim to draw our spiritual passions. Add motion, and the power of images to both show and interpret information magnifies exponentially. More often than not, a film image is designed to do both at once: to realistically and reliably show, or *present*, the visual truth of the subject matter, and to color that truth with shades of meaning, or to *represent* it in order to obtain an emotional or intellectual response.

The *image as presentation* reflects our belief that film communicates the details of the world realistically, even while showing us unrealistic situations. We prize the stunning images of the ancient Forbidden City in *The Last Emperor* (1987) **[Figure 4.68]** as well as the point-of-view shots of an insect in *Honey, I Shrunk the Kids* (1989) for their veracity and authenticity in depicting realities or perspectives. In pursuing this goal, cinematography may document either subjective images, which reflect the points of view of a person experiencing the events, or objective images, which assume a more general accuracy or truth. In *Little Big Man* (1970), images from the perspective of a 101-year-old pioneer raised by Native Americans succeed, for many, in both ways: they become remarkably convincing displays of known historical characters and

4.68 *The Last Emperor* (1987). The sumptuous cinematography gives access to the Forbidden City, illustrating the power of the cinema to "authenticate" through the image.

events—such as General George Custer at the Battle of Little Bighorn—and they poignantly re-create the perspective of the pioneer as he lived through and now remembers those events.

The image also has an instrumental power to influence or even determine the meaning of the events or people it portrays by *re*-presenting reality through the interpretive power of cinematography. The *image as representation* is an exercise in the power of visual stimuli. The way in which we depict individuals or actions implies a kind of control over them, knowledge of them, or power to determine what they mean. When we frame a subject, we capture and contain that subject within a particular point of view that gives it definition beyond its literal meaning. This imagistic value to represent permeates the drama of *Vertigo,* in which Scottie tries so desperately to define Madeleine as an image, and the cinematography aids him by framing her as a painting. It can also be found at the heart of films as diverse as *Blonde Venus* (1932) and *Fight Club* (2000), which in different ways show the ability of the film image to capture and manipulate a person or reality in the service of a point of view. In *Blonde Venus,* as in many of the films directed by Josef von Sternberg starring Marlene Dietrich, the heroine is depicted as a self-consciously erotic figure, whether in an outrageous costume as a showgirl or as a housewife and mother at home; in *Fight Club,* the main character projects and represents himself, undetected for much of the film, as a violently sadomasochistic alter-ego image. In *Pan's Labyrinth* (2006), the viewer is invited into a young girl's fantasy world through artful cinematography, including special effects [**Figure 4.69**].

4.69 *Pan's Labyrinth* (2006). A lonely child's fantasy world is shared by the viewer.

Part of the art of film is that these two primary imagistic values are interconnected and can be mobilized in intricate and ambiguous ways in a movie (as indeed they are in all of these examples). When Harry Potter speaks in the language of snakes in *Harry Potter and the Chamber of Secrets* (2002), the cinematography highlights the fear and confusion among Harry's classmates. Is the image an objective presentation of the perspective of the Hogwarts students, or is it an interpretive representation on the part of the film itself, trying to make the viewer think Harry is deserving of fear? A perceptive viewer must consider the most appropriate meanings for the shot—whether it reflects the students' position or the film's position. Watching closely how images carry and mobilize values, we encounter the complexity of making meaning in a film and the importance of our own activity as viewers.

▶ **VIEWING CUE**

In the film shown for class, look for shots that aim "to present" certain experiences and two or three shots that seem "to represent" different realities. Analyze one shot of each type carefully, and relate them to the film's themes.

Image as Presence and Text

Traditional perspectives of the image in film reflect expectations about the imagistic values encountered in different movies, and these expectations, in turn, influence how we respond to certain kinds of shots and framings in other movies. For some kinds of movies, like documentaries and historical fiction films, we have learned to see the film frame as a window on the world, seeking accuracy. For others, such as avant-garde or art films, we learn to approach the images as puzzles, perhaps revealing secrets of life and society. Here we will designate two conventions in the history of the film image: the convention of image as presence, and the convention of image as text. In the first case, we identify with the image; in the second, we read it.

text continued on page 127 ▶

From Angles to Animation in *Vertigo* (1958)

Alfred Hitchcock's suspense film *Vertigo* is a useful guide into the world of film images because the plot hinges so dramatically on seeing and on the attempt to possess the world through images. In this complex tale, a wealthy businessman named Gavin Elster hires Scottie (played by James Stewart), a retired police detective who suffers from acrophobia (fear of heights), to watch his wife. Madeleine (Kim Novak), he claims, is troubled by her obsession with Carlotta, a woman from the past. After Scottie rescues Madeleine during an apparent suicide attempt, he falls in love with her, and when his acrophobia prevents him from stopping her as she races to leap from a mission tower, her death sends Scottie into a spiral of guilt. Later he believes he sees his lost love on the streets of San Francisco, and his pursuit of a look-alike woman, Judy (also played by Novak), entangles him in another twist to this psychological murder mystery in which the central crisis involves distinguishing reality from fictive images of it.

In this story about Scottie being "framed" for failing to save a life, *Vertigo* takes advantage of almost every possibility in the film frame. Employing a particular brand of widescreen projection called VistaVision, the aspect ratio of Hitchcock's film is one of its immediately recognizable and significant formal features: the especially open space that the widescreen frame creates becomes a fitting environment for Scottie and his anxious searches

through the wide vistas of San Francisco. Although *Vertigo* does not employ masks in the artificially obvious way of older films, at times Hitchcock cleverly creates masking effects by using natural objects within the frame: at several points, for instance, the frame of the car windshield masks and so intensifies Scottie's perspective as he follows Madeleine; at other times, the film uses doors or other parts of the mise-en-scène to create masking effects that isolate and dramatize Scottie's intense gazing at Madeleine [Figure 4.70].

Like many other Hitchcock films, *Vertigo* continually exploits the edges of the frame to tease and mislead us with what we (and Scottie) cannot see. In Scottie's pursuit of Madeleine, she frequently evades his point of view, disappearing like a ghost beyond the frame's borders (as when Madeleine suddenly vanishes from the

4.70 *Vertigo* (1958). In this striking composition, Scottie's previously masked point of view becomes graphically juxtaposed with the mirror image of the woman he pursues.

frame while she and Scottie visit the Sequoia forest). The mystery of Madeleine's fall to her death is especially shocking because it occurs offscreen, revealed only as the blurred body flashes by the tower window, which acts as a second frame limiting Scottie's perception of what has happened [Figure 4.71].

Scottie's fascination with the image of Madeleine also draws attention to the importance of the distance between the subject and the viewer. The different distances between the frame and the object of Scottie's sight reflect his longing for Madeleine. As he follows her from a distance, undetected, his desire to know the mysteries she conceals and his obsession with Madeleine's face create a continual drama of looking. Frequent close-ups and even extreme close-ups concentrate on significant details of her image, such as Madeleine's face in profile, her bouquet of flowers, or the twisted swirl in her hair [Figure 4.72].

The angles of shots are crucial in *Vertigo*. The hilly San Francisco setting naturally accentuates high and low angles as Scottie follows Madeleine through the streets, and the film's recurring motif about the terror of heights informs even the most commonplace scenes, as high angles and overhead shots ignite Scottie's panicked paranoia: whether attempting the steep steps of the church tower, looking down from the stepladder in Midge's apartment, or driving on a steep street, the angles trigger Scottie's anguish and suggest danger. Especially when these sharp angles reflect Scottie's point of view, they suggest complex psychological and moral concerns about power and control as well as about desire and guilt, perhaps dramatizing those moments when Scottie's desires leave him in positions where he is most out of control and threatened.

Deep focus and color are less flamboyant than other elements but equally important to the film. When Scottie discovers Madeleine on the shoreline, for instance, she appears as a small figure in the middle ground. The massive Golden Gate Bridge recedes into the background, and the depth adds to her fragile appearance. *Vertigo* also uses shallow focus as a key feature. Whereas the deep-focus images may suggest mysterious relations and personal conflicts, *Vertigo* frequently uses images whose surfaces seem almost two-dimensional. When Madeleine leaves Ernie's restaurant, there is virtually no depth in the close-up as she turns her profile, so that her image becomes a kind of flat, moving portrait—certainly an ap-

4.71 *Vertigo* (1958). The window frames Scottie's uncertain view of a falling body.

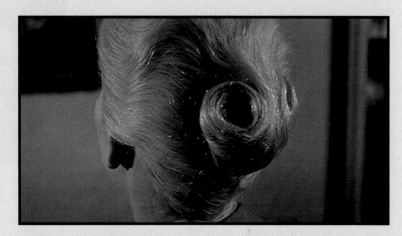

4.72 *Vertigo* (1958). A close-up of the vertiginous swirl of white-blonde hair emphasizes this detail.

propriate way to introduce a character who is associated with a painted portrait and who will haunt Scottie's mind as a drifting image. Finally, while there is a realistic balance of rich colors in the skin tones of the characters and the hues of the buildings, reds, blues, and greens stand out sharply in exaggerated or unnatural ways, as when curtains seem to emanate a green glow that suffuses Judy's room. Like the repetition of red, this eerie green echoes throughout the film, as in Madeleine's metallic-green car and Scottie's green sweater. Indeed, one might claim a symbolic or metaphoric meaning for this green in the film: one renowned admirer of Hitchcock, director François Truffaut, associates that color with death in his film *The Green Room* (1978), drawing on a theatrical tradition of such associations.

Certainly among the more striking dimensions of *Vertigo* is its moving frame. One casual scene demonstrates how common shot movements not only describe events in a complex way but also subtly invest those events with nuance and meaning. The scene takes place early in the

4.73   *Vertigo* (1958). A low-angle, backward tracking shot emphasizes the aggressive Gavin.

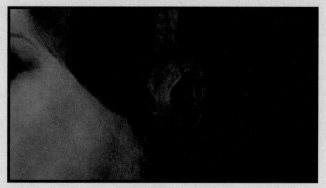

4.74   *Vertigo* (1958). Restless camera movement combining zooms and tracking shots traces Scottie's gaze at the portrait.

film in the business office of Scottie's former schoolmate, Gavin. With the activity of the shipyard continuing outside the picture window, Gavin works to enlist Scottie's help to follow his wife. The scene begins with Gavin sitting in his chair, but Scottie soon sits and Gavin stands and moves around the room: a pan of Gavin walking to a higher position in the room is followed by a low-angle shot of Gavin and a complementing high-angle shot of Scottie; a backward track then depicts the more aggressive Gavin as he moves to the front of the image toward the stationary Scottie [Figure 4.73]. As the moving frame continues to focus on Gavin trying to convince Scottie to help him track his wife, the framing and its movement indicate that this is not quite a conversation between equals: the moving frame makes clear that Gavin directs the image and controls the perspective.

A more clearly central series of camera movements takes place when Scottie finds Madeleine standing before a portrait of Carlotta in an art museum. Here the camera executes several complex moves that simulate Scottie's perspective: it simultaneously zooms in and tracks first on the swirl in Madeleine's hair and then reframes by tracking and zooming out on the same hair design in the painting of Carlotta [Figure 4.74]. Indeed, these reframings in the museum resemble the opening sequence in which Scottie hangs from the gutter and his frightened glances at the street below are depicted through a quick, distorting combination of zooming-in and tracking-out that describes his intense panic and spatial disorientation. Entirely through these camera movements, the film connects Scottie's original trauma and guilt with his mysterious attachment to Madeleine.

Although *Vertigo* seems to be a realistic thriller, it employs—dramatically and disconcertingly—both animation and special effects as a part of its story and description of Scottie's state of mind. An eerie matte shot re-creates a tower that is missing from the actual church at San Juan Bautista; its goal is perhaps largely to add a crucial element to the setting where Scottie's fear of

4.75   *Vertigo* (1958). The special effects of a nightmare: an abstracted black figure against the roof on which another body had fallen.

heights will be exploited. Yet along with the nightmarish significance of that tower, in the final scene the matted image appears as an eerily glowing surface and color as the surreal tower looms over yet another dead body. More obvious examples of special effects include the rear projections and animation when Scottie begins to lose his grip on one reality and become engulfed in another: in one scene, Scottie and Judy's kiss spins free of the background of the room; earlier, during a nightmare triggered by his psychotic depression, an eruption of animation depicts the scattering of the mythical Carlotta's bouquet of flowers and a black abstract form of Scottie's body falling onto the roof of the church [Figure 4.75].

Rather than mimicking or supplementing reality, these instances of animation and special effects in *Vertigo* point out how fragile the photographic realism of the cinematographic shot can be. *Vertigo* describes the obsessions of a man in love with the image of a woman (echoed from Carlotta to Madeleine to Judy). The film contains inordinately long periods without any dialogue, almost as a way to insist that Scottie's (and the film's) interest is primarily in images—in all their forms (from paintings to memories) and from many angles (high, low, moving, stationary, onscreen, and offscreen).

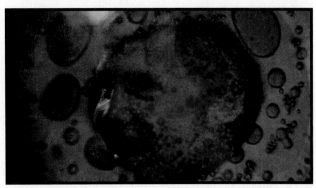

4.76 *9-1/2 Weeks* (1986). The film's sensual images affect the viewer viscerally.

4.77 *Midnight Cowboy* (1969). Special effects and blurred, colored contrasts create a psychological representation of the cowboy's drug experience.

Image as Presence

The compositional practices of the film image that we call the conventions of *presence* imply the following:

- a close identification with the point of view of the image
- a response to the image that is primarily emotional
- an experience of the image as if it were a lived reality

Part of a varied history, images in this tradition fascinate us with a visual activity we participate in, overwhelm us with their beauty or horror, or comfort us with their familiarity. Although not entirely separable from the story and other elements of the film form, imagistic presence is what principally entertains us at the movies, what elicits our tears and shrieks. A shot of horses and riders dashing toward a finish line or of a woman embracing a dear friend communicates an immediacy or truth that engages us and leads us through subsequent images.

Two variations upon this convention are the phenomenological image and the psychological image. The *phenomenological image* refers to filmmaking styles that approximate the physical activity according to which we normally see the world and visually participate in it—such as a shot that re-creates the dizzying perspectives from a mountaintop. As old as film history itself, this tradition appears in vastly different movies: from the remarkably visceral and physically chaotic battle scenes in Orson Welles's *Chimes at Midnight* (1966) to the erotic film *9-1/2 Weeks* (1986) [**Figure 4.76**], phenomenological shots convey a sensual vitality in the image itself. The *psychological image*, in contrast, creates images that reflect the state of mind of the viewer or a more general emotional atmosphere in a scene: in *10* (1979), a middle-aged man fantasizes the image of his dreams coming true as a beautiful woman running toward him in slow motion; in *Midnight Cowboy* (1969), disorienting, blurry images at a party re-create Joe's mental and perceptual experience after taking drugs [**Figure 4.77**]. Both traditions appear regularly in film history and in many different cultures, but certain film movements emphasize one over the other. Westerns—such as *High Noon* (1952)—tend to rely on phenomenological images to imbue movement and conflict with energy [**Figure 4.78**], whereas movies that concentrate on personal crises—such as the melodramatic *Written on the Wind* (1956), a tale of wealth and unhappiness in which high-strung emotions and mental stress are everywhere—often employ psychological images to reflect the states of mind of the characters [**Figure 4.79**].

4.78   *High Noon* (1952). Bodies in motion and pain are rendered immediately through cinematography.

4.79   *Written on the Wind* (1956). Color, angles, composition, and deep focus contribute to the image's depiction of the character's emotional extremes in Douglas Sirk's melodrama of the unhappy rich.

Image as Text

Textuality refers to a different kind of film image, one that demands

- an emotional distancing of the viewer from the image
- a reaction to the image that is primarily analytic
- an experience of the image as artifice or as constructed like a written statement or an aesthetic object to be interpreted

We stand back to look at textual images from an intellectual distance. They seem loaded with signs and symbols for us to decipher. They impress us more for how they show the world than for what they show. So-called difficult, abstract, or experimental films—from Germaine Dulac's surrealist film *The Seashell and the Clergyman* (1928) to *Pi* (1998) [Figure 4.80]—enlist viewers most obviously within this tradition, but many films integrate images that test our abilities to read and decipher. A canted framing of an isolated house or a family reunion shot through a yellow filter may stand out in an otherwise realistic movie as a puzzle image that asks for more reflection: How do we read this image? Why is this unusual composition included? In *The Seashell and the Clergyman,* apparently about a priest in love with a beautiful woman, images resemble the cryptic language of a strange dream, requiring viewers to struggle to decipher them, perhaps as a way of understanding the film's complex drama of repression and desire [Figure 4.81].

Two specific versions of the tradition of textuality can be referred to as the aesthetic image and the semiotic image. The *aesthetic image* asks to be contemplated and to be appreciated for its artistic re-creation of a world or a perspective through texture, line, color, and composition. While aesthetic images can be expected in art films like *The Seashell and the Clergyman,* they also surface in many other kinds of films: in the luxurious close-ups of Greta Garbo in *Queen Christina* (1933), in the elaborate patterns of the choreography of Busby Berkeley's musical *Dames* (1934), and in such films as *Run, Lola, Run* (1998) and *Requiem for a Dream* (2000). In *Run, Lola, Run,* for

4.80   *Pi* (1998). An ordinary image of cream in coffee becomes a visual and mathematical puzzle through the eyes of a math genius.

4.81   *The Seashell and the Clergyman* (1928). Extreme angles, shadows, and highlighted patterns in the pavement suggest a complex dream image.

4.82   *Run, Lola, Run* (1998). The film image changes from live-action to animation, inviting viewer participation in the film's aesthetic world.

instance, a realistic shot of the mother watching a television tracks into the television itself, at which point it becomes an imaginatively animated tracking shot that follows the cartoon image of Lola as she dashes down the stairs. The transformation signifies the malleable world of this movie [**Figure 4.82**].

The *semiotic image* presents images as signs (*seme* means "sign") to be interpreted like language or to be read like a poem. The puzzle-like paintings of René Magritte are a good example [**Figure 4.83**]. Although such semiotic images are associated with experimental or new-wave movies like Glauber Rocha's *Antonio das Mortes* (1969) and Jean-Luc Godard's *Numéro deux* (1975), they may also be found in historical avant-garde films like Sergei Eisenstein's *The Battleship Potemkin* (1925) and Dziga Vertov's *The Man with the Movie Camera* (1929) in which realistic and unrealistic images form strange compositions that demand a reflective reading. In R. W. Fassbinder's *In a Year of Thirteen Moons* (1978), a medium close-up shows the transsexual Elvira being violently forced to look at herself in a mirror. This painful image becomes inscribed with emotional and social divisions, hostilities, and imbalances [**Figure 4.84**].

Recognizing the dominance of either the image as presence or the image as text within a single film or part of a film is one way to begin to appreciate and understand it. A romance like *Under the Tuscan Sun* (2003), suffused with the Italian sunshine of its title, exudes the presence of location shooting, and recognizing how it engages a larger tradition of presence allows us to see its distinctions and differences. A visually dense and complex film about an underground gang of Nazi "werewolves," Lars von Trier's *Zentropa* (1991) asks us to decipher images constructed with special effects and

text continued on page 132 ▶

4.83   *The Treachery of Images* (1929). René Magritte's paradoxical painting shows the difference between how images and words refer to objects.

4.84   *In a Year of Thirteen Moons* (1978). The complexity and drama of the film image mirror the character's struggles.

Meaning through Images in *M* (1931)

Set in Germany around 1930, Fritz Lang's *M* constantly calls attention to its powers to present both objective and subjective experiences. *M* tells the gruesome tale of a child murderer, Franz Becker, whom both police and criminals pursue in an attempt to regain each group's stable, if corrupt, social situation. Throughout the film, objective images alternate with subjective ones: images seem at some points to describe the facts of a dark and anxious German society in 1930; at other points, they reproduce that world through the perspective of individual characters. Even in a fiction film such as this one, the images document a history of facial expressions, cultural products, and social activities, such as the uniforms of the German police and the raucous criminal dens. At still other points in this film, the images present personal perspectives, such as the anxiety of a mother as she waits for her daughter, glances at the clock several times, and stares at an empty seat before a table setting [Figure 4.85].

In *M*, the boundaries between these objective and subjective images regularly blur, and the film occasionally leaves unclear whether the images are a factual record of German street life or descriptions of anxious or even deranged minds. Early in the film, an extreme high-angle shot presents an apparently objective view of children playing in a courtyard, but the angle of the shot also suggests the uneasy and oppressive feeling that suffuses the atmosphere. Soon afterward, a medium shot tracks laterally left to right as it follows the young girl, Elsie Beckmann, as she walks home bouncing a ball, straightforwardly depicting her carefree journey but also suggesting that someone might be following and watching her. Later a descriptive tracking shot of a man walking with a young girl is transformed into a

scene of chaos, fear, and anger when the shot suddenly becomes identified with the subjective perspective of a crowd that sees the man as the murderer.

There are numerous examples in *M* of the power of the image to represent individuals by assigning them meanings and values, often in a self-conscious fashion that dramatically calls attention to this power. These representations are sometimes the common kind one finds in many films: a dark low-angle shot defines a criminal as dangerous, whereas a close-up of a mother emphasizes her internalized sorrow and pain. At other times, the structure of an image suggests more elaborate commentary: the detective Karl Lohmann is shot from an extreme low angle that not only describes him sitting in a chair but also depicts him as a grotesque, slovenly, and comical caricature. Sometimes other, darker judgments and

4.85 *M* (1931). A seemingly benign shot of a child's place setting becomes ominous when it conveys the point of view of a mother whose daughter is missing.

meanings appear through the image. As part of a complex maneuver in that early tracking shot of Elsie, the image shifts subtly from being a description of her perspective to an ominously threatening point of view. When Elsie stops and bounces her ball off a poster warning of the murderer, the low camera angle assumes her point of view; but when, suddenly, the dark shadow of a man drifts across the poster and her perspective, the image acquires a darker and more threatening point of view that literally takes over Elsie's perspective with its own [Figure 4.86]. In a more diabolical way than in most films, vision is equated with control, and here the power of the unseen man's perspective over Elsie anticipates her murder. When, at the conclusion of the film, Becker stumbles into a vacant warehouse, he ironically finds himself the object of the same representational power in the image, the source of the perspective now being a large crowd rather than a troubled individual. He suddenly finds himself literally captured by the gaze of a mob of street thieves and criminals prepared to judge him as the target of their eyes, just as he had done to Elsie.

4.86 *M* (1931). A poster offering a reward for information on a child murderer becomes infused with horror when an anonymous shadow falls over it.

M appears at the end of what is commonly called the "golden age" of German cinema, generally identified with two specific movie traditions: German expressionist films and German "street films." In street films, the movie image documents the tough and unglamorous social realities of criminals, prostitutes, or other desperate individuals. In German expressionism, film images often investigate emotional, psychological, and subconscious realities. *M* engages both these German film movements: while its documentary-like shots of criminals, tools, and weapons suggest the realism of street films, the expressionistic tradition allows Lang to use the textuality of the image to explore a different kind of presence, one associated with desires and fears.

One set of images is especially indicative of expressionism: the images of spirals that appear throughout *M* suggest the power of an image to mesmerize and absorb the viewer. Early in *M*, a high-angle shot of a staircase from above (reflecting the point of view of the anxious mother) creates a dizzying perspective that draws the eye into the receding spiral composition; later the same imagistic figure of absorption recurs in a shop window as a mechanical circle spins hypnotically [Figures 4.87 and 4.88]. These visual metaphors suggest a loss of consciousness that seems to describe Becker's madness,

4.87 *M* (1931). German expressionism: dizzying overhead shot of a staircase.

4.88 *M* (1931). German expressionism: a spiral figure and the mesmerizing loss of consciousness.

but other, less dramatic images draw viewers into compositions that are similarly absorbing.

Midway through the escalating drama, after the criminals pursue Becker into a factory, a medium close-up focusing on his face as he picks at the lock of a storeroom intensifies Becker's emotional desperation through the very proximity and size of the image, making it difficult for us not to empathize with the pain of this villainous character. Indeed, sometimes an image may point toward off-screen realities that are not fully shown but still fire the viewer's imagination with a powerful consciousness of that reality. When the criminals interrogate the factory guard, the camera pulls back from the room and stops outside, where we hear but cannot see the torture. The horrible presence of that torture becomes more immediate and disturbing through the suggestive force of the composition.

A tradition of textual images that can be linked to German expressionism is both conveyed *in* the film, in which characters are often preoccupied with scrutinizing images for the mysteries they hold, and *by* it, as viewers detect the secrets within the film's own images. At one point, Becker examines his close-up reflection in a mirror, pulling his mouth down in a distorted frown, perhaps as a bizarre attempt to see and comprehend the madman inside himself. At another, the police examine a note from Becker in close-up in order to analyze "the very particular shape of the letters," and several times they assemble images of fingerprints and maps to try to identify and locate the killer. In both cases, images become explicit instruments for investigating the crime and thus, the police hope, instruments with which to capture Becker. Finally, the plot turns dramatically when the criminals trailing Becker surrepti-

tiously mark the back of his jacket with the letter *M*, thereby identifying this anonymous figure of a man on the street as the killer by making his image a legible text. Less directly, the film creates complex visual metaphors that ask viewers to decipher their significance: a balloon purchased by Becker for Elsie later appears in a medium shot tangled in telephone wires to suggest her death and perhaps the twisted person of Becker (whose body resembles the balloon figure) **[Figure 4.89]**.

The cinematography in *M* draws on both realist and expressionist traditions to create a mixture of documentary-style images and more symbolic representations that engage the viewer's powers of detection even as the crimes in the film are investigated. The exploration of the powers and limitations of the image in *M* link looking and seeing to matters of life and death.

4.89 *M* (1931). Reading a visual metaphor.

mixed media, but part of its success lies in how it engages the complexities of a tradition of textuality. Film compositions communicate information and tell tales, yet we experience and process—and enjoy—film images most fully by recognizing the values and traditions that underpin them and our expectations of them. The initial hostile reception of *Bonnie and Clyde* in 1967, for instance, turned to admiration several months later. One way of understanding the dynamics of this change is to note that viewers realized that the film's images belong not to a tradition of presence but to a tradition of textuality. At first, many viewers may have seen the film as glamorizing 1930s violence; only later did they recognize the distance of those images as an ironic commentary on 1960s violence. Film, like chance, favors the prepared mind.

CONCEPTS AT WORK

The experience and the art of the cinema are inseparable in cinematography—the moving image selected, framed, lit, tinted, and manipulated through effects. The emergence of cinema at the end of the nineteenth century joined a long-standing impulse to create moving images with the technological capacity to make such images and present them to audiences. Framing (variations in distances and angles), compositions that explore the depth of the images, and camera movements are some of the ways that cinematographers create and explore cinematic worlds. Technical developments in film stock, cameras and lenses, color processes, and eventually digital technologies allowed greater range in cinematic expression. Finally, moving images use all of the aspects specific to the language of film as well as the contexts and traditions in which the medium is imbedded to generate meanings enriched by each viewer's experience.

Films tell their stories through moving images, adding dimension to a flat screen and allowing viewers to locate themselves in the narrative, follow its action, decode significance, and experience emotion. As we have detailed in this and the previous chapter, the properties of the film shot are determined by the infinite range of possibilities of mise-en-scène and cinematography and their interaction. In the next chapter, we learn how the juxtaposition of images enriches the experience and meanings of the film image.

Activity

Imagine Buster Keaton's character from *The Cameraman* filming a newsworthy event like a burning building for a fiction film. Imagine shooting this mise-en-scène through as many different cinematographic "lenses" as possible: both literal lenses such as wide-angle and zoom, and through variations in setups, lighting, framing, film stock, camera movement, and use of special effects. As you reflect on your particular cinematographic choices, note what specific film traditions (that is, image as presence, image as text) your "scenes" draw upon and why.

THE NEXT LEVEL: ADDITIONAL SOURCES

Belton, John. *Widescreen Cinema*. Cambridge, MA: Harvard University Press, 1992. This book examines the technical, economic, social, and aesthetic forces that have been a part of widescreen cinema since 1896, shaping and reshaping the film image to respond to different cultures and audiences.

Berger, John. *Ways of Seeing*. Harmondsworth: Penguin, 1972. Small and well illustrated, Berger's book offers a remarkably broad perspective on how images of all kinds—from paintings to television advertisements—are informed by powerful historical and cultural values.

Manovich, Lev. *The Language of New Media*. Cambridge, MA: MIT Press, 2001. This book presents an influential theory of the philosophy, technology, and impact of digital cinema.

Pierson, Michele. *Special Effects: Still in Search of Wonder*. New York: Columbia University Press, 2002. Pierson's work is an important contribution to theorizing this persistent and ever more dominant dimension of the moving image.

Schaefer, Dennis, and Larry Salvato. *Masters of Light: Conversations with Contemporary Cinematographers*. Berkeley: University of California Press, 1984. Fascinating discussions with acclaimed directors of photography give insight into their art and craft.

Smoodin, Eric. *Animation Culture: Hollywood Cartoons from the Sound Era*. New Brunswick, NJ: Rutgers University Press, 1993. This book offers an examination of not only the technical strategies in film animation (from 1930 to 1960) but also the complex political and ideological agendas that often drove those strategies.

Winston, Brian. *Technologies of Seeing*. London: BFI, 1997. A critical review of the development of the technological image—from 16mm film to HDTV to holography—this study emphasizes the logic behind these changes and how they engage other historical and social shifts.

Passion
Temptation
Obsession

Brian Cox
Matthew Goode
Scarlett Johansson
Emily Mortimer
Jonathan Rhys Meyers
Penelope Wilton

Ein Film von
Woody Allen
MATCH
POINT

BBC FILMS und THEMA PRODUCTION SA PRÄSENTIEREN EINE JADA PRODUCTION "MATCH POINT"
MIT BRIAN COX MATTHEW GOODE SCARLETT JOHANSSON EMILY MORTIMER
JONATHAN RHYS MEYERS PENELOPE WILTON CASTING JULIET TAYLOR GAIL STEVENS C.D.G.
PATRICIA KERRIGAN DICERTO KOSTÜME JILL TAYLOR SCHNITT ALISA LEPSELTER
PRODUKTIONSDESIGN JIM CLAY KAMERA REMI ADEFARASIN B.S.C.
CO-EXECUTIVE PRODUCERS JACK ROLLINS CHARLES H. JOFFE
EXECUTIVE PRODUCERS STEPHEN TENENBAUM COMPOSITEURS HELEN ROBIN NICKY KENTISH BARNES
PRODUZENTEN LETTY ARONSON GARETH WILEY LUCY DARWIN
BUCH UND REGIE WOODY ALLEN © JADA PRODUCTIONS 2005

5

Relating Images
Editing

In Woody Allen's *Match Point* (2005), a tale of infidelity and murder, tennis becomes a metaphor for much of the film's psychological and physical action. Like the back-and-forth volleying of a tennis match, characters' desires, conversations, and movements move back and forth in dangerous games of romance and social power. Indeed, woven within the action and often sustaining it, is a cornerstone of classical film editing: the shot and reverse-shot exchange. This editing method describes the way the image cuts back and forth between two characters, as between Chris (Jonathan Rhys Meyers) and Nola (Scarlett Johansson) as they talk or look at each other. In *Match Point,* this common way of editing two images does not simply describe action; it becomes loaded with the psychological tensions of a highly competitive tennis match and, more disturbingly, the illicit desires and social dangers under its surface.

A
s we move through the world, we witness images that are juxtaposed and overlapped: in store windows, on highway billboards, or on television when we channel surf. As we recognize these different sights as part of a series of related images, we experience something like the logic of film editing, the process that links different images or shots. Yet editing is a departure from the way we normally see the world. In our everyday seeing experience, discrete images are unified by our singular position and consciousness. There are no such limits in editing. And unless we consciously or externally interrupt our vision (as when we blink), we do not see the world as separate images linked in selected patterns. The construction of image patterns specifically intended to access particular emotions or ideas makes the illogical appear logical. Thus we find that a film consisting of eight hundred or more discrete images makes sense.

KEY CONCEPTS

In this chapter, we will examine

- how the art and technologies of editing reflect cultural and historical contexts, and how they have opened up new possibilities for film form
- the ways editing organizes images as meaningful scenes and sequences
- how edited images are based on a material cut or break in the film
- the ways editing constructs different spatial and temporal relationships between images
- how editing establishes continuity in a film
- how editing emphasizes particular graphic or rhythmic patterns
- how editing strategies engage certain filmic traditions of continuity or disjuncture

How does a film connect separate images to create or reflect certain patterns through which viewers see and think about the world? This chapter describes what many consider the most unique dimension of the film experience: editing, or the linking of different images that imitate how we see the world or that create patterns unlike our customary visual experiences.

A Short History of Film Editing

Long before the development of film technology, different images were linked to convey perceptions of the world. Ancient Assyrian reliefs show the different phases of a lion hunt, while the Bayeux tapestry, a 230-foot-long embroidery, chronicles the Norman Conquest of England in 1066 in invaluable historical detail. In the twentieth century, comic strips and manga continued this tradition in graphic art: each panel presents a moment of action in the story, much like a storyboard sketches out the shots of film [Figures 5.1a–5.1c].

Indeed, a long history of cultural practices anticipates the structures of editing, reflecting an impulse to see beyond the limitations of human perception. Religious triptychs, connecting three panels with different pictures to convey spiritual ideas, anticipated the symbolic dimensions of juxtaposed images in editing. This brief history shows how other practices of juxtaposing images have left their traces on editing and how editing has evolved into its modern film forms.

Traditions anticipating film editing were expanded in new ways, especially in early photography. One of the early mechanical and perceptual breakthroughs in the development of the cinema was Eadweard Muybridge's successful 1877 experiment to break down the movement of a galloping horse by taking a series of

5.1 From ancient Assyrian reliefs (a) and the eleventh-century Bayeux tapestry (b) to such modern graphic art as this page from a Korean manhwa comic (c), cultures have told their stories in successions of images.

5.2 *Fencing Pose,* **Étienne-Jules Marey**. Early photographic experiments in human and animal motion, known as chronophotography, anticipate the sequencing of two or more images through editing.

photographic images. Presented together, these images resemble an edited sequence of shots of a horse in motion. Such *chronophotography* was produced by Muybridge and by the French scientist Étienne-Jules Marey to study human and animal motion [**Figure 5.2**].

While the movies juxtaposed images through editing, still photography often found ways to exploit this impulse. Photographs might be deliberately arranged to highlight the relationship among the different images. Eugène Atget, for example, photographed specific views of Paris buildings and streets at different times or in different phases of construction in order to convey the lapse of time. As photography continued to evolve as an art medium, artists would often connect separate photographs by particular motifs or visual patterns. In the photomontages of German artist Hannah Höch, produced in the 1920s, different images were combined into a new composition to suggest conceptual connections and to establish novel visual effects [**Figure 5.3**]. More recently, artist David Hockney has combined separate Polaroid photographs to create one overall image.

1895–1920: Early Cinema and Classical Editing Style

Films quickly evolved from showing characters or objects moving within a single image to connecting different images. Magician and early filmmaker Georges Méliès used stop-motion photography and, later, editing to create delightful tricks,

5.3 *Astronomy and Movement Dada* (1922). Photomontages, such as this one by Hannah Höch, combined images to produce novel visual effects.

like the rocket striking the moon in *Trip to the Moon* (1902) [**Figures 5.4a and 5.4b**]. While basic editing techniques were introduced by other filmmakers, Edwin S. Porter, a prolific employee of Thomas Edison, synthesized these techniques in the service of storytelling, as in *Life of an American Fireman* (1903) [**Figure 5.5**]. One of the most important films in the historical development of cinema, Edwin S. Porter's *The Great Train Robbery* (1903) tells its story in fourteen separate shots, including a famous final shot of a bandit shooting his gun directly into the camera [**Figure 5.6**]. By 1906, the period now known as "early cinema" gave way to cinema dominated by narrative, a transition facilitated by more codified practices of editing.

D. W. Griffith, who began making films in 1908, is a towering figure in the development of what is known as classical editing style. Griffith is closely associated with the use of **crosscutting**, or **parallel editing**, alternating between two or more strands of simultaneous action, which he used in the rescue sequences that conclude dozens of his films. In *The Lonely Villa* (1909), shots of female family members isolated in a house alternate with shots of villains trying to break in and with shots of the father rushing to rescue his family. The infamous climax of Griffith's *The Birth of a Nation* (1915) uses crosscutting to promote identification with the white characters whom the film construes to be "victims" of Reconstruction. Griffith cuts among a white family trapped in an isolated cottage and black soldiers trying to break in, a white woman threatened with rape by a mixed-race politician, and

 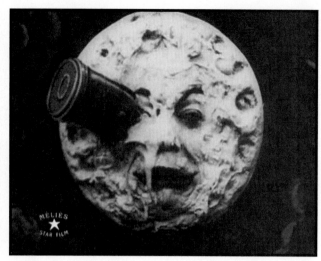

5.4a and 5.4b   *Trip to the Moon* (1902). Stop-motion photography and edited images create fantastic and humorous tricks in one of the earliest science-fiction films.

the Ku Klux Klan riding to the rescue of both [**Figures 5.7a–5.7c**]. The controversial merging of technique and ideas exemplified in Griffith's craft is a strong demonstration of the power of editing. After Griffith's *The Birth of a Nation*, feature filmmaking became the norm, and Hollywood's editing practices followed the classical style that remains the basis for many films today.

1924–1929: Soviet Montage

Within a decade after *The Birth of a Nation*, Soviet filmmaker Sergei Eisenstein's first film, *The Strike* (1924), developed the craft of editing in a different although equally dramatic fashion. Eisenstein's films and writings center on the concept of **montage** (the French word for editing), which has come to signify a style emphasizing the breaks and contrasts between images joined by a cut. To depict the mass

5.5   *Life of an American Fireman* (1903). In an early development of the powers of editing, this six-minute film combines multiple shots to convey the urgency and suspense of a fireman's rescue attempt. Still images are reproduced here from left to right.

5.6   *The Great Train Robbery* (1903). The film's last cut is used to enhance the shock effect of the image rather than to complete the narrative.

5.7a–5.7c *The Birth of a Nation* (1915). In this sequence of images, Griffith's white supremacist views are supported by the parallel editing, which positions the viewer to root for the Ku Klux Klan to arrive in time.

shooting of workers in *The Strike,* Eisenstein interspersed, or **intercut**, long shots of gunfire and of the fleeing and falling crowd with gruesome close-ups of a bull being butchered in a slaughterhouse [**Figures 5.8a and 5.8b**]. The effect of his montage is visceral and provocative.

Eisenstein and such other filmmakers as Lev Kuleshov, Vsevolod Pudovkin, and Dziga Vertov advanced montage as the key component of modernist, politically engaged filmmaking in the Soviet Union of the 1920s. One of the most fascinating self-reflexive sequences in film history is the editing sequence in *The Man with the Movie Camera* (1929) [**Figures 5.9a and 5.9b**], which features the film's own editor, Yelizaveta Svilova. With her husband, director Dziga Vertov, and the latter's brother (and the film's cameraman) Mikhail Kaufman, Svilova was part of the "kinoki" (Kino-Eye) documentary filmmaking group. (In fact, a fascinating aspect of the social history of editing is its relative

5.8a and 5.8b *The Strike* (1924). The workers' massacre compared to the slaughter of a bull.

5.9a and 5.9b   *The Man with the Movie Camera* (1929). Montage under construction, from still frame to moving image.

openness to the participation of women, even in Hollywood.) Other avant-garde movements in the 1920s and thereafter continued to explore the more abstract and dynamic properties of editing employed by the Soviets.

1929–1950: The Studio Era—From Continuity Editing to New Realisms

With the coming of sound and the full development of the Hollywood studio system, film editing expanded and refined the storytelling style known as **continuity editing** while integrating the new demands of simultaneously editing sound and image tracks. Indeed, the complexity of editing with a soundtrack initially resulted in fewer camera movements and fewer cuts, but by the early 1930s editors succeeded in establishing an integrated editing style that extended the continuity system through a more expansive sense of film realism.

Beginning in the 1940s, cinematic realism became established as one of the primary aesthetic principles in film editing. The influence of Italian neorealism, which used fewer cuts to capture the integrity of stories of ordinary people and actual locations, was evident in other new-wave cinemas and even in Hollywood. For example, Nicholas Ray's 1950 *In a Lonely Place* developed an editing style that emphasized imagistic depth and longer takes by cutting less frequently between images [Figure 5.10]. Yet the continuity editing style would remain dominant until the decline at the end of the 1950s of the studio system, whose stable personnel, business models, and genre forms lent consistency to its products.

1959–1989: Modern Disjunctive Editing

The post-World War II period impacted almost every dimension of film form, and editing was no exception. Both in the United States and abroad, alternative editing styles emerged and aimed to fracture classical editing's illusion of realism. Anticipated to some extent by the editing experiments of the Soviet montage movement of the 1920s, these new styles reflected the temporal disjunctions, or disconnections, of the modern world. Disjunctive editing visibly disrupted continuity by creating ruptures in the story, radically condensing or expanding time, or confusing the relationships among past, present, and future. The French new

TRANSFORMING FILM:
Editing Techniques

Early Moviola editing (a) demanded the attention of craftsmen who carefully evaluated and connected different images. Flatbed editing (b) made this process more efficient and less laborious, whereas contemporary digital systems (c), with their ability to store large amounts of visual and sound information, made nonlinear film editing possible.

(a)

(b)

(c)

5.10   *In a Lonely Place* (1950). The heightened realism of postwar cinema tended to explore the depth of images by cutting less frequently between them.

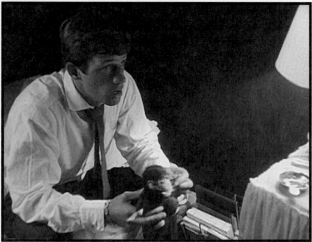

5.11   *Breathless* (1983). The fragmentations created by jump cuts become the visual vehicle for the distractions and disjunctions in a petty criminal's life.

wave of Jean-Luc Godard and Alain Resnais produced some of the first and most dramatic examples of disjunctive editing. Godard's *Breathless* (1983) used **jump cuts**, edits that intentionally created gaps in the action [**Figure 5.11**]. In the 1960s and 1970s, American filmmakers like Arthur Penn and Francis Ford Coppola incorporated disjunctive styles within classical genres. In the 1980s, the fast-paced editing style of commercials and MTV began to appear in mainstream films. Two popular and successful films are indicative, both made by former directors of television commercials: Adrian Lyne's *Flashdance* (1983), about a Pittsburgh woman who doubles as a welder and exotic dancer, and Tony Scott's *Top Gun* (1986), about fighter pilots competing in flight school. Both combine an upbeat pop soundtrack with flashy, rapid editing to suggest the seductive energy of their respective worlds.

1990s–Present: Editing in the Digital Age

One of the most significant changes to film editing is the emergence of nonlinear digital editing in the later part of the twentieth century. Whereas for decades editors cut actual film footage by hand on a Moviola or flatbed editing table, most editors today use computer-based nonlinear digital editing systems. In nonlinear editing, film footage is stored as digital information on high-capacity computer hard drives. Individual takes can be organized easily and accessed instantaneously, sound editing options can be simultaneously combined with picture editing, and such optical effects as dissolves and fades (see p. 145) can be immediately visualized on the computer rather than added much later in the printing process. Because of the flexibility and efficiency of the new technology, the majority of feature films are now edited with nonlinear computer-based systems regardless of whether they are shot on 35mm film or digital video. The duration of a shot on digitally shot films is virtually limitless; *Russian Ark* (2002) is a feature-length film with no cuts at all [**Figure 5.12**].

5.12   *Russian Ark* (2002). Wandering through the Hermitage Museum in St. Petersburg, a single shot comprises the entire film, which combines the past and the present in a meditation on art, politics, and Russian history.

The Elements of Editing

Film editing is the process through which different images or shots are linked. In terms of the movie's finished version, a **shot** can be defined simply as a continuous length of film, regardless of the camera movement or changes in focus it may record. Editing can produce meaning by combining shots in an infinite number of ways. One shot is selected and joined to other shots by the editor to guide viewers' perception. For example, the opening sequence of *Crooklyn* (1994) describes the Brooklyn block where the film is set by editing together a high-angle moving crane shot, an overview of the neighborhood and its inhabitants, and a series of short medium-shots of people and their activities [**Figures 5.13a–5.13c**].

If a shot presents mise-en-scène from a single perspective, film editing extends and redefines that perspective by linking images in various relationships. Some of these relationships mimic the way an individual looks at the world (for example, a shot of someone looking off in the distance linked to another shot of an airplane in the sky), but often these relationships exceed everyday perception. Edited images may leap from one location to another or one time to another and may show different perspectives on the same event. Editing is one of the most significant developments in the syntax of cinema because it allows for a departure from both the fixed perspective and the continuous duration of perspective.

The Cut and Other Transitions

The earliest films consisted of a single shot, which could run only as long as the reel of film in the camera lasted. In the early trick films of pioneer Georges Méliès, this limitation was manipulated by stopping the camera, rearranging the mise-en-scène, and resuming filming to make objects and people seem to disappear. It was a short step to achieving such juxtapositions by physically cutting the film. In Méliès's 1903 film *Living Playing Cards,* a magician, played by Méliès himself, seems to make his props come alive [**Figures 5.14a and 5.14b**].

While these early transformations emphasized cutting, in films transitions between shots are often obscured, along with the technical labor of editing. Rarely can viewers describe or enumerate the edits. Learning to watch for this basic element of film language is a rewarding way to experience the art of film as a medium.

The foundation for film editing is the **cut**, which describes the break and the common border that separate two shots from two different pieces of film. A single shot

▶ **VIEWING CUE**

Do a shot-by-shot breakdown of one scene from a film screened in class. What is the motivation behind each cut? What overall effect do these cuts have on the scene and the film?

5.13a–5.13c   ***Crooklyn*** (1994). The opening of Spike Lee's film juxtaposes a continuous overhead tracking shot with a series of short takes of daily activities to describe the neighborhood where the film is set.

5.14a and 5.14b   *Living Playing Cards* (1903). Pioneer George Méliès anticipated later editing techniques with magical transformations.

(a)

(b)

(c)

can depict a woman looking at a ship at sea by showing a close-up of her face and then panning to the right, following her glance to reveal the distant ship she is watching. A cut renders this action in two shots, with the first showing the woman's face and the second showing the ship. While the facts of the situation remain the same, the single-shot pan and the cut joining two shots create different experiences of the scenario. The first might emphasize the distance that separates the woman from the object of her vision. The second might create a sense of immediacy and intimacy that transcends the distance. In a key scene from *The Best Years of Our Lives* (1946), we first see several characters occupying different spaces of the same shot [**Figure 5.15a**]. After the character on the right shifts his attention to the character in the background, we are presented with a cut isolating them [**Figures 5.15b and 5.15c**]. As these examples illustrate,

5.15a–5.15c   *The Best Years of Our Lives* (1946). The logic of the cut first introduces the space and the characters and then isolates the most significant action by following one character's point of view on another character.

5.16   *The Scarlet Empress* (1934). Extended dissolves were a favorite device of director Josef von Sternberg. The layering of a conversation and the approach of a carriage appear almost as an abstract pattern.

5.17   *Broken Blossoms* (1919). The iris was often used in films by D. W. Griffith to highlight objects or faces. Here it focuses our attention and emphasizes the vulnerability of Lillian Gish's character.

the use of a cut usually follows a particular logic, in this case emphasizing the significance of an action. The less frequently used **shock cut** juxtaposes two images whose dramatic difference creates a jarring visual effect. Samuel Fuller's *Shock Corridor* (1963) surprises viewers with color footage sequences in a black-and-white film. Later in this chapter we will investigate additional ways that editing may create logical or shocking links among different images.

Edits can be embellished in ways that guide our experience and understanding of the transition. For example, **fade-outs** gradually darken and make one image disappear, while **fade-ins** do the opposite. Alfred Hitchcock fades to black to mark the passing of time throughout *Rear Window* (1954). A **dissolve** (sometimes called a *lap dissolve* because two images overlap in the printing process) briefly superimposes one shot over the next, which takes its place: one image fades out as another image fades in [**Figure 5.16**]. Usually these devices indicate a more definite spatial or temporal break than do straight cuts, and they often mark breaks between sequences or larger segments of a film. A dissolve can take us from one part of town to another, while a fade-out, a more visible break, can indicate that the action is resuming the next day.

A number of other transitions between shots or scenes are most often found in older films, especially silent films. The *iris-out* begins by masking the corners of the frame in black and gradually obscuring the image as if a camera shutter were closing; an *iris-in* opens on a small, usually circular, portion of the frame and gradually expands to reveal the entire image [**Figure 5.17**]. **Wipes** join two images by moving a vertical, horizontal, or sometimes diagonal line across one image to replace it with a second image that follows the line across the frame. Modern films, from *Star Wars* (1977) to the independent feature *Desert Hearts* (1985), have used wipes to reference an obsolete film style [**Figure 5.18**]. These transitional devices are traditionally known as **optical effects** because before digital editing they were created in the printing process with an **optical printer**.

Although editing can generate an infinite number of combinations of images, as we will see, rules have developed within the Hollywood storytelling tradition to limit the number of combinations. Other film traditions, most notably those of avant-garde and experimental cinema (see Chapter 9), can be characterized by their degree of interest in exploiting the range of editing possibilities as a primary formal property of film.

text continued on page 148 ▶

▶ **VIEWING CUE**

Make a list of transitional devices besides cuts that are used in a film you've just watched for class. What spatial, temporal, or conceptual relationship is being set up between scenes joined by a fade, dissolve, iris, or wipe?

5.18   *Desert Hearts* (1985). Editing an image with a wipe creates a nostalgic reference to earlier editing techniques, but also may suggest a certain kind of transience in the world of the characters.

Cutting to the Chase in *The General* (1927)

Buster Keaton's classic comedy *The General* is a tour-de-force demonstration of cinema as a medium of movement, and it is the film's editing, along with Keaton's own astonishing agility, that keep it going. Set during the Civil War, *The General* features Keaton as Johnnie Gray, a Confederate train engineer in pursuit of the Union raiders who have stolen his locomotive, named "the General," and unwittingly kidnapped heroine Annabelle Lee, who is trapped inside. *The General* was produced at the end of the silent era, when editing had already been developed in sophisticated ways. In the absence of dialogue, editing is even more important as a narrative and visual language. The editing is not as fast-paced as that of a contemporary action film, but current films with chases at their core, like *Speed* (1994), are a tribute to Keaton's ingenuity. Johnnie's train moves inexorably on its tracks, pursuing another moving train. The camera, too, is constantly moving—on tracks or in vehicles like those it films. It is the film's editing that dynamically juxtaposes these shots, keeping the film itself in motion.

This comical pursuit takes place primarily on Johnnie's locomotive. But, as with any chase film, crosscutting shapes the central action of *The General,* pacing the audience's response to Johnnie's misadventures by returning constantly to the object he pursues. Johnnie chases the locomotive first in a handcart, then on an old-fashioned tricycle (which he jumps on just as its owner parks it). The humor derives from the parallel editing between the powerful engine and these lowly human-powered conveyances.

In the first chase sequence from the train, Johnnie gives the thieves the impression that they are outnumbered. A long shot from the side shows a cannon, which Johnnie had commandeered and loaded, becoming separated from his engine [Figure 5.19]. When it stalls on the tracks, the increasing distance makes it seem inevitable that the cannonball will hit Johnnie instead of the enemy [Figure 5.20]. But a fortuitous bend in the road diverts the cannon blast, and the Union soldiers believe they are under attack. However, the film's cutting gives viewers a picture of the actual situation [Figure 5.21]. It is again through editing that we learn the Union soldiers have realized their mistake; a cut to an extreme long shot shows their train passing over a trestle bridge, while Johnnie, alone with his diminutive locomotive, is visible on a track far beneath.

In *The General*, many sequences are hilarious precisely because the subtlety of their editing complements Keaton's performance, as when Johnnie continues to chop wood atop his train while the Confederate army marches behind him. When the Union army appears on the other

5.19 *The General* (1927). An impending mishap with the cannon.

5.20 *The General* (1927). The film makes a point about the cannonball's threat by cutting to a straight-on angle of Johnnie as seen from the cannon.

5.21 *The General* (1927). A miraculous turn of events as the engine rounds a bend in the track.

side of the tracks, Johnnie finally turns and notices what he has gotten himself into [**Figures 5.22a and 5.22b**]. Much later, Johnnie pretends he is a Union soldier and hides Annabelle in a gunnysack [**Figure 5.23**]. A long shot shows him being ordered to load the sack slung over his shoulder onto the train [**Figure 5.24**]. In a view of the same action from the rear, we see that Annabelle is busy behind Johnnie's back, uncoupling the train car so that they can both escape with the General [**Figure 5.25**]. Again, the editing delivers the punchline. Often a seemingly inevitable situation is miraculously averted, such as when a cannon Johnnie fumblingly shoots straight into the air de-

stroys a dam and thwarts the enemy, rather than falling directly down on Johnnie's head as he anticipates. The execution of each of these gags depends on a very clear setup defined by editing among the various elements: the upright cannon, Johnnie's quizzical gaze upward waiting for the cannonball, a cut to the dam.

Most of the film follows editing conventions and relies on straight cuts between shots, and on fades between segments. For example, the first fade is motivated by the train entering a dark tunnel. A later transition humorously illustrates the temporal ellipsis implied by a fade. A tableau of Johnnie with his arms around Annabelle in the

5.22a and 5.22b *The General* (1927). Oblivious to everything but the chase, Johnnie (played by Buster Keaton) finally notices the tide of history.

5.23 *The General* (1927). Hiding Annabelle in a gunnysack.

5.24 *The General* (1927). Pretending to assist the Union soldiers in loading the train.

5.25 *The General* (1927). The editing shows Annabelle uncoupling the train cars.

rain fades out for the night, only to fade in on the two figures in the exact same posture the next morning. The conventional use of the fade-out to indicate the passage of time is upheld, while the narrative conventions to which it corresponds, the discreet handling of a love scene, are disappointed.

The General celebrates the kinetic nature embodied in the words "motion picture" and "cinema" (from the Greek for "I move"), proceeding as an almost nonstop action sequence. It sums up the fluidity of silent-era filmmaking and, in the continuity of space and time demanded by the chase framework, illustrates the principles that would govern studio filmmaking for decades to come. The entire film is organized around trains moving relentlessly forward on a mechanical path—like film itself, in which one edited shot follows another to guide our perception through the story.

When watching movies, we manage to make sense of a series of discontinuous, linked images (by understanding them according to conventional ways of interpreting space, time, story, and image patterns). We understand the action sequences in *Mission: Impossible III* (2006) despite the improbable feats performed by the hero. Likewise, we make connections among the three separate narratives from three separate periods in *The Hours* (2002). As noted earlier, most of these patterns were established early in the course of film history; as we shall see in Chapter 7, editing patterns anticipate and form the foundation for numerous structural patterns in narrative organizations. The next three sections will explore the spatial and temporal relationships established by editing and will introduce the rules of the Hollywood continuity editing system, a dominant method of editing narrative films. Subsequent discussion will examine patterns of editing images based on graphics, movement, and rhythm in order to show how different techniques provide very different experiences.

Editing Narrative Space

In both narrative and non-narrative films, editing is a crucial strategy for ordering space and time. Two or more images can be linked to imply spatial and temporal relations to the viewer. **Verisimilitude** (literally, "the quality of having the appearance of truth") in fictional representations allows readers or viewers to accept as plausible a constructed world, its events, its characters, and the actions of those characters. In cinematic storytelling, clear, consistent spatial and temporal patterns greatly enhance verisimilitude (although dialogue, acting, sets, costumes, and other elements are also important). In the commercial U.S. film industry, these patterns are constructed through conventions of editing that form part of Hollywood's **continuity style**. Because its constructions of space and time are so codified and widely used, we will devote special consideration to this style.

Continuity Style

Continuity editing is a system that uses cuts and other transitions to establish verisimilitude and to tell stories efficiently, requiring minimal mental effort on the part of viewers. The basic principle of continuity editing is that each shot has a continuous relationship to the next shot. Two particular strategies constitute the heart of this style:

■ using an establishing shot to construct an imaginary 180-degree space in which the action will develop
■ approximating the experience of real time by following human actions

Continuity editing has developed and deployed these patterns so consistently that it has become the dominant method of treating dramatic material, with its own set of rules that narrative filmmakers learn early. Minimizing the perception of breaks between shots, it is often called **invisible editing**. The rules of continuity can be broken, however. Such variations may appear less "realistic" simply because they allow us to notice the editing that is normally hidden.

Spatial patterns are frequently constructed by the use of an **establishing shot**, generally an initial long shot that establishes the setting and orients the viewer in space to a clear view of the action. A scene in a western, for example, might begin with an extreme long shot of wide-open space and then cut in to a shot that shows a stagecoach or saloon, followed by other, tighter shots introducing the characters and action.

The standard practice for filming a conversation presents a relatively close shot of both characters (also known as a **two-shot**) in a recognizable spatial orientation and context, and it then displays the character who is speaking in the next shot before cutting again to show the other character. The editing may proceed back and forth, with periodic returns to the initial view. Such **reestablishing shots** restore a seemingly "objective" view, making the action perfectly clear to the viewers. Early in Howard Hawks's *The Big Sleep* (1946), when detective Philip Marlowe (played by Humphrey Bogart) is hired by General Sternwood, the scene opens with an establishing shot, and their conversation follows this pattern [**Figures 5.26a–5.26h**]. Although many shots are edited together in the course of the conversation, the transitions remain largely invisible because the angle from which each character is filmed remains consistent. Such editing practices are ubiquitous; we have learned to expect the coordination of conversations with medium close-ups of characters speaking and listening, just as we expect that these figures will be situated in a realistic space.

Another device that is used in continuity editing is the **insert**, a brief shot, often a close-up, such as a shot of a hand slipping something into a pocket or a smile another character does not see. The use of inserts helps overcome viewers' spatial separation from the action, pointing out details significant to the plot or underscoring verisimilitude—for example, showing us a ringing telephone. An insert that breaks continuity is referred to as a **nondiegetic insert**—such as the display of printed

5.26a–5.26h *The Big Sleep* (1946). The simple interview, which provides a great deal of plot information, is broken down by many imperceptible cuts that eventually focus our attention on the protagonist's face. Alternating shots of the two characters cut in closer and closer. Finally, the space is reestablished at the end of the interview.

text in a Jean-Luc Godard film. More specifically, a nondiegetic insert introduces an object or view from outside the film's world or makes a comparison that transcends the characters' perspectives, as in a famous nondiegetic insert of clucking chickens in Fritz Lang's *Fury* (1936) [**Figure 5.27**].

Exceptions tend to prove the rules of continuity editing. In *Natural Born Killers* (1994), extraneous and disorienting cuts interrupt interactions among characters. The film's opening sequence dispenses with an establishing shot: a shot of a pot of coffee introduces the location and is followed by some exterior shots of the diner. The waitress's response to Mickey's order is repeated, and the second shot is in black and white [**Figures 5.28a and 5.28b**]. This disorienting introduction conveys a skewed perception of the diner's space, foreshadowing the eruption of violence later in the scene.

5.27 *Fury* (1936). Lang dissolves from one shot of women chatting to another of chickens clucking to illustrate the concept of gossip; this is an example of a nondiegetic insert.

In continuity editing, after the establishing shot provides the initial view of a scene, subsequent shots typically follow the logic of spatial continuity. If a character appears at the left of the screen looking toward the right in the establishing shot, it is likely that he or she will be shown looking in the same direction in the medium shot that ensues. Movements that carry across cuts will also adhere to a consistent screen direction. A character exiting the right of a frame will probably enter a new space from the left. Similarly, a chase sequence covering great distances is likely to provide spatial cues. The breakdown of a scene will proceed as if the action were traversed by an imaginary line that the camera will not cross—a key characteristic of continuity editing.

180-Degree Rule. The **180-degree rule** is the primary rule of continuity editing and one that many films and television shows consider sacrosanct. The diagrams in **Figure 5.29** illustrate the 180-degree rule. In the scene from *The Big Sleep* discussed earlier in this chapter, Marlowe and the general are consistently filmed as if bisected by an imaginary line known as the **axis of action**. All of the shots illustrated by the still images from *The Big Sleep* in **Figures 5.26a–5.26h** were taken from one side of this axis. In general, any shot taken from the same side of the axis of action will ensure that the relative positions of people and other elements of mise-en-scène, as well as the directions of gazes and movements, will remain consistent. If the camera were to cross into the 180-degree field on the other side of the line (represented in Figure 5.29, Diagram A, by the shaded area), the characters' onscreen positions would be reversed. During the unfolding of a scene, however, a new axis of action may be

▶ **VIEWING CUE**

How are spatial relationships among images established by the film's editing patterns in a scene from the movie you just viewed?

5.28a and 5.28b *Natural Born Killers* (1994). This scene uses overlapping editing, two shots in which the waitress repeats the same line. Violating continuity through this device and the use of different film stocks, the editing establishes a threatening mood.

Diagram A

Diagram B

5.29   **Diagram A** illustrates the 180-degree rule by showing the space of the conversation scene from *The Big Sleep* bisected by an imaginary line called the axis of action. All shots of the scene were taken from the white portion of the diagram. If the camera were to cross over to the shaded portion, the position of the characters onscreen would be reversed. **Diagram B** illustrates the editing of the conversation with references to Figures 5.26a–5.26h on page 150. Each character is depicted in tighter framings from a consistent camera angle.

established by figure or camera movement. Some directors even break the 180-degree rule and cross the line, either because they want to signify chaotic action or because conventional spatial continuity is not their primary aim.

30-Degree Rule. Although less frequently reiterated, the **30-degree** rule illustrates the extent to which continuity editing attempts to preserve spatial unity. This rule specifies that one shot must be followed by another shot taken from a position greater than 30 degrees from that of the first. The rule aims to emphasize the motivation for the cut by giving a substantially different view of the action. A transition between two shots less than 30 degrees apart is perceived as unnecessary largely because the cut itself is likely to be visible. Joseph Cornell's experimental film *Rose Hobart* (1936) is a re-editing of the Hollywood film *East of Borneo* (1931); the original film's continuity editing principles are broken in Cornell's reassemblage, defying spatial and temporal logic [**Figures 5.30 and 5.31**].

Shot/Reverse Shot. One of the most common spatial practices within continuity editing, and a regular application of the 180-degree rule, is the **shot/reverse-shot** (sometimes called *shot/countershot*) pattern. Often used during conversations, such as in the example from *The Big Sleep*, this pattern begins with a shot of one character taken from an angle at one end of the axis of action, continues with a shot of the second character from the "reverse" angle at the other end of the axis, and proceeds back and forth.

5.30   ***Rose Hobart*** (1936). Joseph Cornell re-edited and re-scored the 1931 Hollywood adventure film *East of Borneo*, naming his film after its star.

5.31   ***Rose Hobart*** (1936). Mismatched eyelines, abrupt changes in mise-en-scène, and violations of the 30-degree rule wreak havoc with continuity.

A scene from *Clueless* (1995) in which the protagonist, Cher, and her friends, Dionne and Tai, converse in a coffee-shop booth provides another example of a shot/reverse-shot sequence. The scene begins with a tracking establishing shot that depicts the overall environment and shows who is sitting where [Figure 5.32a]. Then the scene cuts back and forth across the booth, usually to depict the character who is speaking [Figure 5.32b]. Cher has the majority of the scene's shots, indicating that she is the focal point of our identification [Figure 5.32c]. Sometimes Dionne and Tai, sitting opposite, are depicted in a two-shot; occasionally these secondary characters receive individual shots [Figure 5.32d].

▶ **VIEWING CUE**

Does the film follow continuity patterns, such as the 180-degree rule? Can you identify other ways that spatial continuity is maintained?

⏸

5.32a–5.32d   ***Clueless*** (1995). This scene follows the 180-degree rule and favors the film's heroine, Cher (played by Alicia Silverstone), as it alternates among characters.

5.33 *Silence of the Lambs* (1991). An eyeline match establishes the position of Clarice (played by Jodie Foster) in relation to Hannibal Lecter (Anthony Hopkins) in his cell.

5.34 *Silence of the Lambs* (1991). The reverse shot.

Eyeline Match. Frequently the shots and reverse shots used in conversation scenes are taken over the shoulder of the participants, which helps remind viewers of their shared physical space. In general, continuity editing often implies spatial contiguity; in other words, it gives the impression that consecutively depicted spaces are adjacent ones. If a character looks offscreen toward the left, the next shot will likely show the character or object that the character is looking at in a screen position that matches the gaze. This is referred to as an **eyeline match** [Figures 5.33 and 5.34]. Shot/reverse-shot sequences of characters in conversation often use eyeline matches. Eyelines give the illusion of continuous offscreen space into which characters could move beyond the left and right edges of the frame.

Point-of-View Shots. Many of Alfred Hitchcock's most suspenseful scenes are edited to highlight the drama of looking. Often a character is shown looking, and the next shot shows the character's optical point of view, as if the camera (and hence the viewer) were seeing with the eyes of the character. Such point-of-view shots are often followed by a third shot in which the character is again shown looking, which reclaims the previous shot as his or her literal perspective. In a tense scene from *The Birds* (1963) in which the heroine, Melanie, sits on a bench outside a school as threatening crows gather on the playground behind her, Hitchcock uses both eyeline matches and point-of-view sequences. Eventually a bird flying high overhead catches her attention [Figure 5.35]. When she turns her head to follow its flight, the shots are matched by her eyeline [Figure 5.36]. Next

5.35 *The Birds* (1963). A low-angle shot of a flying bird . . .

5.36 *The Birds* (1963) . . . is matched to Melanie's eyeline.

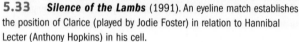

5.37   *The Birds* (1963). Following its flight, she registers shock at what she sees.

5.38   *The Birds* (1963). A point-of-view shot of the gathering birds.

comes a point-of-view sequence in which Melanie—and the viewer who shares her perspective—is horrified by the sinister sight of congregating birds [**Figures 5.37 and 5.38**]. The editing of this scene serves both to construct a realistic space and to increase our identification with Melanie by focusing solely on the act of looking.

Elsewhere in the film, the point of view of Melanie's romantic interest, Mitch, is conveyed by partially masking the frame as if we were looking along with him through his binoculars. Similarly, when we share the point of view of a character waking from a knock on the head, we may see a blurry image. In contrast, over-the-shoulder shots used in a shot/reverse-shot sequence are not point-of-view shots because they do not show exactly what the characters see. However, if, as the conversation intensifies, the scene proceeds in tighter framings of characters' faces as if from the direct perspectives of the participants, then the film has introduced point-of-view shots.

These components of the continuity system—shot/reverse-shot patterns, eyeline matches, and point-of-view shots—construct space in order to highlight human subjectivity. An emphasis on human perspective is also visible in the **reaction shot**, which depicts a character's response to something that viewers have just been shown [**Figure 5.39**]. The cut back to the character "claims" the view of the previous shot as subjective. Continuity editing constructs spatial relationships to create a plausible and human-centered world onscreen.

Although continuity editing strives for an overall effect of coherent space, films can reject continuity and use editing to construct less predictable spatial relations. For example, in Michelangelo Antonioni's film *L'Avventura* (1960), cuts join spaces that are not necessarily contiguous. The landscapes the characters move through express their psychological state of alienation; a realistic use of space is rejected.

Editing Narrative Time

Editing is one of the chief ways that temporality is manipulated in the time-based medium of cinema. A two-hour film may, for instance, condense centuries in a story. Through the power to manipulate **chronology**—the order according to which shots or scenes convey the temporal sequence of the story's events—editing organizes narrative time (see pp. 249–253). Sequences of shots or scenes may describe the linear movement of time forward as one event follows another in temporal order. Often human activity directs the selection and ordering of events in this way.

5.39   *The Way We Were* (1973). Barbra Streisand's face registers her character's emotion in this reaction shot, which records her response after catching sight of her former lover.

5.40 *Sunset Boulevard* (1950). The entire story of *Sunset Boulevard* unfolds in flashback, introduced by the narrator's voiceover. The twist is that the narrator dies in the first few moments of the film.

5.41 *Don't Look Now* (1973). Images of a small figure in red prove to be flashforwards to a horrifying encounter with the past.

Flashbacks and Flashforwards

Editing may also create nonlinear patterns in which events are juxtaposed out of their temporal order. Within the continuity system, such nonlinear constructions are introduced with strict cues about narrative motivation. A **flashback** follows one or more images of the present with one or more of the past; it may be introduced with a dissolve conveying the character's memory or with a voiceover in which the character narrates the past. In one sense, *Citizen Kane* (1941) uses a linear structure, organizing itself around a series of interviews and investigations conducted by a reporter looking for an angle on a great man's death. However, the story of Kane's life is provided in a series of lengthy flashbacks that make the film's chronology complex. Like the typical film noir that relies on the instability of appearances, *Sunset Boulevard* (1950) uses flashbacks motivated by voiceover narration. The film presents a particularly interesting case: continuity is maintained even though the protagonist-narrator is shown to be dead in the first sequence [**Figure 5.40**].

The less common **flashforward** connects an image of the present with one or more future images. Flashforwards present a serious challenge to realistic motivation: how can the characters we are asked to identify with "see" the future? The technique is thus usually reserved for works that intentionally challenge our perceptions. In the countercultural film *Easy Rider* (1969), for instance, the protagonist has a brief flashforward vision of an aerial image of the accident that will be his demise at the end of the film. In Nicolas Roeg's *Don't Look Now* (1973), a couple is tormented by the recent death of their daughter, and haunting images of a small figure in a red rain slicker prove to be flashforwards to a revelatory encounter [**Figure 5.41**]. In *Memento* (2000), the chronology of scenes is completely reversed, but the maintenance of continuity within each scene allows us to follow the film.

Descriptive and Temporally Ambiguous Sequences

Certain edited sequences cannot be located precisely in time. The purpose of such a sequence is often descriptive, such as a series of shots identifying the setting of a film. In *An American in Paris* (1951), as one character describes the heroine to another, we see a series of shots depicting her different qualities (with different outfits to match). These little vignettes are descriptive; they do not follow a linear or other temporal sequence.

Art films often manipulate temporality through editing, defying realism in favor of psychological constructions of time. Writer Marguerite Duras and director Alain Resnais make time the subject of their film *Hiroshima Mon Amour* (1959), which constantly relates the present-day story set in Japan to a character's past. An image of her lover's hand sparks the female protagonist's memory of being a teenager in France during World War II, and the flashback begins with a matching image of another hand.

But temporality is such an important dimension of film narration that even more traditional narratives explore the relationship between the order of events onscreen and those of the story. Steven Soderbergh's *The Limey* (1999) ingeniously inserts shots of the activities of the protagonist, played by Terence Stamp, into the narrative but out of sequence, keeping us guessing about temporal relations **[Figures 5.42a and 5.42b]**.

Duration and Pace

Duration denotes the temporal relation of shots and scenes to the amount of time that passes in the story. Mike Figgis's *Timecode* (2001) is an experiment in filmic duration. In this film, the story time is identical to the screen time, whereas in most narrative films the story time is radically condensed and temporal relations constructed through editing are complexly related to the temporality of the film's story. Temporal continuity is maintained by cutting that constructs a sequence of cause-and-effect events. Editing is one of the most useful techniques for manipulating narrative time. Although actions may seem to flow in a continuous fashion, editing allows for significant temporal abridgement, or **ellipsis**. Cutting strategies both within scenes and from scene to scene attempt to cover such ellipses. Grabbing a coat, exiting the front door, and turning the key in the ignition might serve to indicate a journey from one locale to the next. As we have seen, transitional devices such as dissolves and fades also manipulate the duration of narration. Without the acceptance of such conventions, time would be experienced in a disorienting fashion.

5.42a and 5.42b *The Limey* (1999). Different shots of the protagonist (Terence Stamp) appear in the film without a clear sense of when they occurred.

A specific continuity editing device used to condense time is the **cutaway**: the film interrupts an action to "cut away" to another image or action—for example, a man trapped inside a burning building—before returning to the first shot or scene at a point further along in time. We are so accustomed to such handling of the duration of depicted events that a scene in real time, such as the central character's taking a bath in *Jeanne Dielman, 83 quai du Commerce, 1080 Bruxelles* (1975), seems unnaturally long. Less frequent than the condensation of time, the extension of time through **overlapping editing** occurs with the repetition of an action in several cuts. In *The Battleship Potemkin* (1925), a sailor, frustrated with the conditions aboard ship, is shown repeatedly smashing a plate he is washing. The onscreen passage of time in this scene is longer than that of the action. Overlapping editing is a violation in a continuity system, and while it can be used for emphasis or for foreshadowing, it often appears strange or gimmicky.

The duration of individual shots helps determine the **pace** of a film's editing. What defines relative shot length and hence the experience of pacing can be personally subjective and culturally relative. The quick pacing characteristic of action sequences has become more prevalent in contemporary cinema. One obvious example of controlling pace is the use of **long takes**, or shots of relatively long duration; the image is sustained for what can seem an inordinate amount of time. In Claude Lanzmann's nearly ten-hour-long documentary about the Holocaust, *Shoah* (1985), the camera films an interview subject speaking and then holds on the subject while an onscreen translator conveys his or her words to Lanzmann, who is also present on camera. The long take, often filmed in deep focus with a wide-angle lens, became a significant aesthetic tool in William Wyler's *The Best Years of Our Lives* (1946). For film theorist André Bazin, an advocate of Wyler's aesthetic and the use of the **sequence shot**, in which an entire scene plays out in one take, this type of filmmaking more closely approximates human perception and is thus more realistic than montage. Because of the preponderance of long takes, such films rely more heavily on mise-en-scène, including acting, and camera movement than editing to focus viewers' attention. Yet the extended duration of shots fundamentally affects a film's rhythm and pace. Most films use shot duration to follow a rhythm that relates to the particular aims of the film. In *Flowers of Shanghai* (1998) by contemporary Taiwanese filmmaker Hou Hsaio-hsien, long takes evoke the city's past and vanished way of life. In contrast, the notorious shower murder sequence from *Psycho* (1960) uses seventy camera setups for forty-five seconds of footage, with the many cuts launching a parallel attack on viewers' senses.

As we have seen, continuity editing strives for a realistic space and time that approximate recognized perspectives, such as the crowded movement of a city street. Some narrative films aim to construct psychological space and time, creating such emotional and imaginative perspectives as the anxiety and suspense associated with horror films. In some films, the two may overlap: in *The Crowd* (1928), for example, images of New York City convey a specific setting as well as the hero's psychological impression of an overwhelming, disorienting sensory experience.

Earlier in this chapter, we introduced the term "montage" in relation to Soviet filmmaking of the 1920s. In the Hollywood tradition, montage is usually reserved to denote thematically linked sequences and sequences that show the passage of time by using quick sets of cuts or other devices, such as dissolves, wipes, and superimpositions, to bridge spatial or temporal discontinuities. In studio-era Hollywood, Slavko Vorkapich specialized in such sequences and lent them his name. For example, a Vorkapich sequence might show a series of opening-night triumphs of an actress in a "success montage"; a "roaring twenties montage" might show flappers, beaver coats, and Model Ts; or a "dairy industry montage" might depict in quick succession cows being milked, conveyor belts transporting milk cartons, and schoolchildren drinking milk. In this specialized sense and in its use simply as a synonym for "editing" (Alfred Hitchcock, for example, often discussed it in this way), montage emphasizes the creative power of editing—especially the potential to build up a sequence and augment meaning, rather than to remove the extraneous as the term "cutting" implies.

▶ **VIEWING CUE**

What is the temporal organization of the film you've just viewed for class? Does the film follow a strict chronology? How does the editing abridge or expand time? ⏸

Editing Narrative Shapes and Surfaces, Movements and Rhythms

In addition to temporal and spatial narrative patterns, editing may link images according to more abstract similarities and differences that make creative use of space and time. Here we distinguish among three abstract patterns in editing: graphic editing, **movement editing**, and rhythmic editing. Often these patterns work together to support or complicate the action being shown.

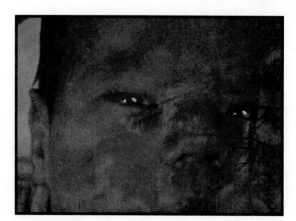

5.43   ***Dog Star Man*** (1964). Graphic editing and superimpositions characterize this film and other experimental films.

Graphic Editing

Linking or defining a series of shots in **graphic editing** are such formal patterns as shapes, masses, colors, lines, and lighting patterns within images. Graphic editing may be best envisioned in abstract forms: one pattern of images may develop according to diminishing sizes, beginning with large shapes and proceeding through increasingly smaller shapes; another pattern may alternate the graphics of lighting, switching between brightly lit shots and dark, shadowy shots; yet another pattern might make use of lines within the frame by assembling different shots whose horizontal and vertical lines create specific visual effects. Many experimental films highlight just this level of abstraction in the editing. Among Stan Brakhage's hundreds of experimental films, *Dog Star Man* (1964) **[Figure 5.43]** uses graphic matches and superimposition extensively. Frequently, narrative films employ graphic editing as well. Graphic elements of the mise-en-scène such as arches are incorporated in Sergei Eisenstein's editing design for *Ivan the Terrible, Part One* (1945) and *Ivan the Terrible, Part Two* (1946) [**Figure 5.44**]. Coherence in shape and scale often serves a specific narrative purpose, as in the continuity editing device called a **graphic match**, in which a dominant shape or line in one shot provides a visual transition to a similar shape or line in the next shot. One of the most famous examples of a graphic match is from Stanley Kubrick's *2001: A Space Odyssey* (1968) [**Figures 5.45a and 5.45b**].

Editing through Movement

To connect images through movement means that the direction and pace of actions, gestures, and other movements are linked with corresponding or contrasting movements in one or more other shots. Cutting on action, or editing during an onscreen movement, quickens a scene or film's pace. A common version of this pattern is the continuity editing device called a **match on action**, whereby the direction of an action (such as the tossing of a stone in the air) is edited to a shot depicting the continuation of that action (such as the flight of that stone as it hits a window). Often a match on action obscures the cut itself, such as when the cut occurs just as a character opens a door; in the next shot, we see the next room as the character shuts the door from the other side.

In *Meshes of the Afternoon* (1943), Maya Deren depicts a continuous movement across diverse backgrounds by strictly matching the action of her character walking forward. The character's first stride is on the beach; her next strides are on dirt, among tall grasses, on concrete, and finally on carpet [**Figures 5.46a and 5.46b**]. As an example of graphic matching as well, because the scale and distance are precisely matched in each shot, this series of cuts demonstrates film editing as a unique way of seeing. (Similarly, the example from *2001: A Space Odyssey,* cited in the preceding section, is also a match on action following the movement of the bone through the air.) Leni Riefenstahl's extraordinary editing in her documentary *Olympia* (1938) has become a model for editing athletic performances, associating the superhuman mobility of athletes with that of the cinema [**Figure 5.47**].

5.44   *Ivan the Terrible, Part Two* (1946). Strong graphic components of Sergei Eisenstein's image create forceful impressions in juxtaposition.

▶ **VIEWING CUE**

What graphic patterns are constructed through the editing of the film you've just viewed? What effects do these patterns have on your viewing of the film?

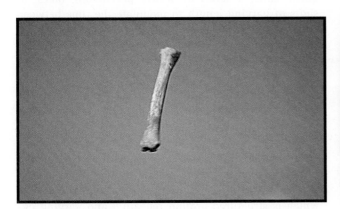

5.45a and 5.45b   *2001: A Space Odyssey* (1968). A famous graphic match from a prehistoric bone to a spaceship transcends millennia of history in one cut.

5.46a and 5.46b   *Meshes of the Afternoon* (1943). The power of cinema illustrated by matching the protagonist's steps across changing backgrounds.

▶ **VIEWING CUE**

Consider the last film you just viewed in class. What is the relationship between figure and camera movement within specific shots and the film's cutting? ⏸

Movement editing can, however, resist matching and instead create other patterns of movement in a series of images: rapid and slow movements, movements into various spaces of a shot, or different styles of movement can be edited together for visual effects. This is often the case in music videos. In pioneering experimental filmmaker Shirley Clarke's *Bridges-Go-Round* (1958), bridges—stationary structures—come alive and achieve a balletic movement through the editing. Chaotic movement editing appears in the climax of *Strangers on a Train* (1951) [**Figures 5.48a and 5.48b**]. Action sequences such as fights and chases also exploit the possibilities of movement editing, both relying on the spatial consistency of continuity editing to convey what's happening, and using variation to increase the surprise and excitement.

Rhythmic Editing

Finally, **rhythmic editing** describes the organization of the editing according to different paces or tempos determined by how quickly cuts are made. Like the tempos that describe the rhythmic organization of music, editing in this fashion may link a rapid succession of quick shots, a series of slowly paced long takes, or shots of varying length to modulate the time between cuts. Since rhythm is a fundamental property of editing, it is often combined with graphic, movement, or continuity aims. The early French avant-garde filmmaker Germaine Dulac defined film as "a visual symphony made of rhythmic images." In *Ballet Mécanique* (1924), her contemporaries Dudley Murphy and Fernand Léger used cutting to create rhythmic and graphic patterns by juxtaposing objects in motion (see Film in Focus, pp. 314–316). Frequently, experimental films find their formal coherence in a rhythmic editing pattern, as in Hollis Frampton's *Zorn's Lemma* (1970), which is structured around repeating and varying cycles of twenty-four 1-second shots. However, narrative

5.47   *Olympia* (1938). The dynamism of human movement is highlighted in this film's editing.

5.48a and 5.48b *Strangers on a Train* (1951). The movements of a carousel around, up and down, and finally out of control are intercut chaotically with the two characters' physical struggle in the climactic sequence of Alfred Hitchcock's *Strangers on a Train*.

films also depend on editing rhythms to underpin the emotion and action of a scene, as depicted in the harrowing opening sequence of *Vertigo* (1958), for example [**Figures 5.49a and 5.49b**]. Directors in different genres and traditions work with their editors to achieve distinctive editing rhythms in their films.

As we have stressed, these different editing patterns are not easily separated: continuity principles are found in many traditions, and spatial, temporal, and abstract patterns are often successfully combined.

Editing from Scene to Sequence

The coordination of temporal and spatial editing patterns beyond the relationship between two images results in a higher level of cinematic organization found in both narrative and non-narrative films. The shot is the single length of film, and combining it with another shot leads to an edited unit such as a scene or a sequence.

While these two terms for edited units are not always strictly distinguished, it may be helpful to conceive of them separately. One can think of a **scene** as one or more shots that describe a continuous space, time, and action, such as the return

text continued on page 165 ▶

▶ **VIEWING CUE**

Time the shots of a specific sequence from any film you've viewed for class thus far. How does the rhythm of the editing in the sequence contribute to the film's mood or meaning?

5.49a and 5.49b *Vertigo* (1958). This sequence uses almost no dialogue, relying on the rhythmic alternation of shots of Scottie looking down from the rooftop, where he hangs from his hands, and shots of the view below.

Patterns of Editing in *Bonnie and Clyde* (1967)

Arthur Penn's *Bonnie and Clyde* represented a new kind of filmmaking in the late 1960s, in part because of its complex spatial and temporal patterns of editing. Based on the famous outlaws from the 1930s, the film describes the meeting of the title characters and their violent but clownish crime wave through the South. Clyde enlists Bonnie in her first robbery because she is bored with her small-town life. As their escapades continue, they are naively surprised by their notoriety. Soon the gaiety of their adventures gives way to bloodier and darker encounters: Clyde's accomplice/brother is killed, and eventually the couple is betrayed and slaughtered.

Dede Allen's editing of this tragicomedy creates both realistic and psychological patterns of time and space. The film's opening shots are presented as snapshots edited together as a documentary photomontage, freezing time rather than making images move [Figure 5.50], almost as if to suggest that only by animating these images can the history come alive.

5.50 *Bonnie and Clyde* (1967). Still photographs will come alive in the course of this film.

Indeed, temporal and spatial realism are constructed by the links between moving images. The scene depicting the outlaw couple's first small-town bank robbery begins with a long shot of a car outside the bank [Figure 5.51a].

The next shot, from inside the bank, shows the car parked outside the window [Figure 5.51b]. Spatially, this constructs the geography of the scene; temporally, it conveys the action that takes place within these linked shots. The scene creates verisimilitude.

At other points in *Bonnie and Clyde*, the logic of the editing describes psychological or emotional patterns. When Bonnie is introduced, for example, the first image we see of her is an extreme close-up of her lips; the camera pulls back as she turns right to look in a mirror. This is followed by a cut on action as she stands and looks back over her shoulder to the left in a medium shot and then by another cut on action as she drops to her bed, her face visible in a close-up through the bedframe, which she petulantly punches. With another cut, she rises from the bed with her back turned toward us and reaches to the right for her dress. Not only is this central character described by a series of jerky shots, but her boredom and frustration are also built into the editing [Figures 5.52a and 5.52b]. Bonnie's restless movements back and forth while dressing are mimicked by a moving camera and by cutting on action. Next Bonnie goes to her window and, in a point-of-view

(a)

(b)

5.51a and 5.51b *Bonnie and Clyde* (1967). Spatial and temporal continuity during the first robbery.

construction, spots a strange man near her mother's car. She comes downstairs to find out what he is doing, and her conversation with Clyde is handled in a series of shot/reverse shots, starting with long shots as she comes outside and proceeding to closer pairs of shots. The two-shot of the characters together is delayed. The way this introduction is handled emphasizes the inevitability of their pairing.

Because *Bonnie and Clyde* is a gangster film in which cars and guns figure prominently, complex spatial connections are repeatedly set up between the pursuers and the pursued. Editing on movement pervades the film; its stop-and-go rhythm is probably one of its most striking features. As the Barrow gang flees from the police in one car chase, shots alternate between the police and the gang. Intercut, as a parallel action, are interviews with witnesses to the robbery (who brag about having been part of a Bonnie and Clyde caper), a pattern that introduces competing temporalities [**Figures 5.53a and 5.53b**].

As a summary of the patterns and logic of editing, the strategies used in the climactic sequence of *Bonnie and Clyde* are instructive. At the film's conclusion, Bonnie and Clyde are in hiding at the home of the father of their accomplice, C. W. Moss. In the scene immediately preceding the ambush, the couple waits in their car for C. W. to finish up some errands in town. A complex series of cuts, several bridged by graphic matches on the actions of opening and shutting of car doors, depicts Bonnie and Clyde spotting a police car and pulling out, while C. W. hides behind a shop door, watching them go; their departure is intercut with C. W.'s point-of-view shots as we

5.52a and 5.52b *Bonnie and Clyde* (1967). The lack of an establishing shot combines with the multiple framings to emphasize the claustrophobic mise-en-scène, taking us right into the character's psychologically rendered space.

5.53a and 5.53b   *Bonnie and Clyde* (1967). As the outlaws' reputation spreads, the linear
temporality and spatial organization of the chase are interrupted by interviews with the witnesses.

realize he is up to something. Two discrete scenes, distinguished by changes in action and characters, are edited together to form the concluding sequence of the film. Bonnie and Clyde see C. W.'s father beside his broken-down truck and pull up next to him. His anxiety about being a part of the frame-up is signaled by his quick glance at the bushes, followed by a point-of-view shot in which a flock of birds suddenly rises. Bonnie and Clyde are each shown following his gaze in eyeline matches. As he takes cover, a remarkable series of rapid-fire shots ensues, alternating rhythmically between close-ups of the lovers' faces as they register alarm, realizing they are surrounded [**Figures 5.54a and 5.54b**]. Then the shooting begins.

The final scene of the sequence is the film's most famous and influential. Accompanied by the staccato of machine-gun bullets, Bonnie's and Clyde's deaths are filmed in slow motion, their bodies reacting with almost balletic grace

to the impact of the gunshots and to the rhythm of the film's shots, which are almost as numerous. In nearly thirty cuts in approximately forty seconds, the film alternates between the two victims' spasms and re-establishing shots of the death scene. Clyde's fall to the ground is split into three shots, overlapping the action [**Figures 5.55a–5.55d**]. The hail of bullets finally stops, and the film's final minute is comprised of a series of seven shots of the police and other onlookers gathering around, without a single reverse shot of what they are seeing. Like most films, *Bonnie and Clyde* matches the duration of scenes and editing rhythms to the actions and themes of the story, yet one of the more creative and troubling dimensions of the film is the striking combination of slow, romantic scenes and fast-paced action sequences, which culminate in this memorable finale.

For linking sex with violence, glamorizing its protagonists through beauty and fashion, and addressing itself to

5.54a and 5.54b   *Bonnie and Clyde* (1967). Quick, rhythmic close-ups convey the characters'
realization that they have been caught.

5.55a–5.55d   ***Bonnie and Clyde*** (1967). Scenes from Clyde's famous death sequence use slow-motion cinematography with movement and overlapping editing.

the anti-authoritarian feelings of young audiences, *Bonnie and Clyde* is among the most important U.S. films of the 1960s. Together with other countercultural milestones such as *The Graduate* (1967) and *Easy Rider* (1969), it heralded the end of studio-style production and the beginning of a new youth-oriented film market, one that revis-ited film genres of the past with a modern sensibility. However, as we have seen, it was not only the film's content that was innovative; *Bonnie and Clyde*'s editing and the climactic linkage of gunshots with camera shots also influenced viewers—ranging from French new-wave filmmakers to the American public.

of Ethan Edwards at the beginning of *The Searchers* (1956). Edwards's brother's family spies his arrival on the horizon and gathers on the porch to await his approach. He arrives, dismounts, and enters the homestead with them, at which point the scene ends. In contrast, a **sequence** is any number of shots that are unified as a coherent action (such as a walk to school) or as an identifiable motif (such as the expression of anger), regardless of changes in space and time. Later in *The Searchers,* one sequence covers several years' time as Ethan and Martin Pawley search for their abducted relative, Debbie, in a series of shots of them traversing different landscapes at different seasons.

Sequences can be constructed of one or more scenes, such as parallel actions during a chase or characters conversing in a restaurant, hailing a cab, and continuing their conversation, with continuity editing condensing the time of the actions. Editing using cuts or other transitions governs the immediate juxtaposition of shots as well as the relationship between such larger units as scenes and sequences.

One way to relate editing on a micro level to editing on a macro level is to attempt to divide a film into large narrative units, a process referred to as narrative **segmentation**. A film may have forty scenes and sequences but only ten large segments. Often locating editing transitions such as fades and dissolves will point to these divisions, which occur at significant changes in narrative space, time, characters, or action. Tracing the logic of a particular film's editing on this level also gives insight into how film narratives are organized. For example, the setting of a film's first scene may be identical to that of the last scene, or two segments showing the same characters may represent a significant change in their relationship. Sometimes the "seam" between segments will itself reveal something significant to viewers about the larger organization of the film. In *Imitation of Life* (1959), director Douglas Sirk starkly contrasts a very upsetting scene in which Sarah Jane is beaten by her boyfriend after he discovers her mother is black with another scene in which her mother massages the feet of her white employer, Lora. Lora's exclamation—"That feels so good!"—acquires sickening irony in the juxtaposition. Here two scenes of black and white intimate relationships, one violent, one apparently benevolent, are deliberately contrasted. Once again, the connections among narrative units demonstrate how editing extends from the juxtaposition of shots to structure the film as a whole.

▶ **VIEWING CUE**

Focus on the editing between scenes and sequences by segmenting the entire film into large narrative units. Often fades and dissolves can help you locate these breaks. ‖

The Significance of Film Editing

The editing styles we have discussed so far are not simply neutral ways of telling stories or conveying information; applied in different contexts—Hollywood or the avant-garde—each style conveys a different perspective on art and realism. Cutting to a close-up in a silent film such as *The Cheat* (1912) was an innovative way of smoothly taking the viewer inside the film's world [**Figure 5.56**]; it served the psychological realism of Hollywood storytelling. Early documentary films—*Song of Ceylon* (1934), for example—developed conventional editing patterns based on connections between the progression of the images linked and a presumed objective voiceover narration motivating the editing according to a "voice of God" perspective. Experimental films like *The Flicker* (1965) employed various patterns of alternation or accumulation that generated aesthetic and structural values like those found in paintings or poetry. The continuity editing that evolved in Hollywood during the 1910s remains the dominant language of narrative cinema (including animation) and television today, with the very word "continuity" representing the powerful and far-reaching value associated with spatial and temporal coherence and narrative clarity.

5.56   *The Cheat* (1912). An early use of the close-up to increase audience involvement.

Just as other formal film elements—including mise-en-scène and cinematography—help create filmic meaning, so too does editing. In the 1960s, a "jumpy" kind of editing was introduced, one that simulated the freewheeling style of pop icons like the Beatles in Richard Lester's *A Hard Day's Night* (1964). Such modern editing often reinforced or promoted the counter-cultural or even revolutionary film themes from this and later periods. By the 1980s, the influence of the commercial editing found in advertising made its mark on MTV music videos; these, in turn, influenced numerous feature films from *Flashdance* (1983) to *Do the Right Thing* (1989) to *Fight Club* (1999). The rapid sequencing of images found in the first two films was related to the prominent role of music in the films; in the third, the fragmentation of identity and the punishment of the body are conveyed in the cutting [Figures 5.57, 5.58a, and 5.58b].

5.57   **MTV.** By the 1980s the influential mark of commercial editing made its way into music videos.

How Editing Makes Meaning

In contemporary culture, images provide a collage of different perspectives, figures, and objects. Disparate billboards create a montage of images on highways to attract us to products and places, while television generates a rhythmic collage of violence and comedy as we surf through different channels. As a concentrated and careful version of these different experiences of the dynamics of images in our lives, film editing can assume one or both of the following general aims:

- to generate emotions and ideas through the construction of patterns of seeing
- to move beyond the confines of individual perception and its temporal and spatial limitations

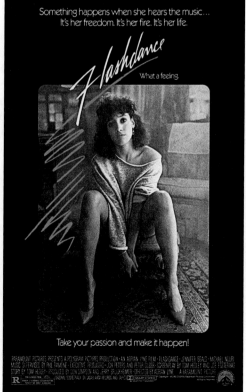

5.58a and 5.58b   *Flashdance* (1983). The MTV aesthetic: the rapid sequencing of images echoes the energy and fragmentation found in contemporary music and life.

5.59a and 5.59b *Stagecoach* (1939). The editing of John Ford's classic *Stagecoach* uses humanizing close-ups of the passengers, medium-long shots of the coach under siege, and long shots of the attackers to keep the viewers' sympathy with the stagecoach passengers.

▶ **VIEWING CUE**

In the film you've just viewed for class, what different emotional and intellectual responses are evoked by the editing choices? Be sure to jot down specific examples from the film to support your response. ⏸

In John Ford's *Stagecoach* (1939), for instance, we experience the approach of pursuing Indians and the subsequent battle and escape of the stagecoach's white passengers [**Figures 5.59a and 5.59b**]. Audience members almost involuntarily hope for the vanquishing of the pursuers, who are shown in long shots. We feel palpable relief, along with the surviving passengers, when their pursuers give up the chase. The editing also constructs feelings of tension. Since we are not confined to the interior of the stagecoach, we see the initial threat and the close calls that the characters cannot see. Through logic and pacing, the editing does more than just link images in space and time; it also generates emotions and thoughts.

This potential of editing is well illustrated in the legendary editing experiments led by Soviet filmmaker Lev Kuleshov in the 1920s. A shot of an actor's face followed by a bowl of soup signified "hunger" to viewers, while the link between the same face and an image of a baby created feelings of delight. In the absence of an establishing shot, viewers took these pairs of images as linked in space and time. Editing a shot of a powerful leader with a shot of a peacock encouraged the audience to identify the leader with the concept of vanity, a more specifically conceptual association. Sergei Eisenstein referred to this intentional juxtaposition of two images in order to generate ideas as intellectual montage. In an example from his *October* (1927), the slogan "In the Name of God" is followed by a series of images from different religious traditions to show the relativity of the concept of the divine and the hypocrisy of the depicted action.

In addition, editing has the power to move beyond the temporal and spatial confines of the individual's perception. With a full array of editing techniques and strategies, film may allow a viewer to see the world, not just from other angles but also more quickly and with greater complexity than normal human vision allows. This type of vision overcomes the physical limitations of human perception, such as great separations in time and space, so that viewers might be treated to a series of shots showing observers all over the world awaiting a visitation from outer space. In *2001: A Space Odyssey,* no individual character's consciousness anchors the film's journey through space and time. Instead, our experience of the film is largely governed by the film's editing—including its long-shot images that show crew members floating outside the spaceship accompanied by Johann Strauss's *The Blue Danube* waltz and its montage of psychedelic patterns that erases all temporal borders [**Figure 5.60**]. Our almost visceral response to these sequences is a result of the cinema's ability to defy our perceptual limits.

Of course, the two central aims of film editing often overlap. The abstract images in *2001: A Space Odyssey* make us think about the boundaries of humanity and the vastness of the universe—and, perhaps, about cinema as a manipulation of images in space and time. Many of Alfred Hitchcock's climactic sequences generate emotions of suspense—achieved in *Saboteur* (1942) by literally suspending the character from the Statue of Liberty [**Figures 5.61a and 5.61b**]. The scene also transcends the confines of perception by showing us details that would be impossible to see without the aid of the movie camera.

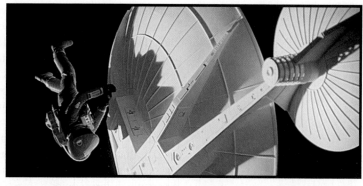

5.60   *2001: A Space Odyssey* (1969). From beginning to end, the editing of this film defies the limits of human perception.

Our responses to these editing patterns are, of course, never guaranteed. We may feel emotionally manipulated by a cut to a close-up or cheated by a cutaway. Additionally, across historical periods and in different cultures, editing styles can seem vastly different, and audience expectations vary accordingly. Older transitional devices such as irises and wipes might generate laughter from audiences today. The slow, meditative editing of Iranian director Abbas Kiarostami's *A Taste of Cherry* (1997) may appear boring to a viewer who has been raised on Hollywood action film sequences. However we respond, editing generates an experience unique to film and television.

▶ **VIEWING CUE**

How is the film's cutting used to extend one's perspective?

Continuity and Disjunctive Editing Styles

Since the beginning of the twentieth century, continuity editing has been paralleled and sometimes directly challenged by various alternative practices that we refer to collectively as disjunctive editing. It is useful to distinguish these two styles to obtain more precise ways of discussing film form and to remark on philosophical differences in editing styles. However, in modern filmmaking it is quite possible to find these two editing methods converging in the editing style of a single film.

Hollywood Continuity Editing

As noted earlier, continuity editing is not an inevitable or a "correct" style of cutting films. Rather, it creates shot patterns that shape space and time to approximate a closed and coherent fictional world, and it constructs a logic and rhythm that mimic human

5.61a and 5.61b   *Saboteur* (1942). Suspense is made literal—and visceral—as a man's fate hangs by a thread.

perception. In this section, we will focus on the Hollywood tradition of continuity editing and a specific practice of continuity called analytical editing, and we will also show how art cinema creates a different variant of continuity through editing.

In *Vertigo,* a close-up of Scottie staring off to the right of the frame, followed by a medium long shot of Madeleine, constructs the illusion of continuous space despite the cut and derives its logic from the human look. It is something of an irony that emulating human perspective entails departing from it—most notably, to show the person who is looking. Continuity editing seems to proceed as a continuous action organized around human perception—even if there is no clearly identified person driving that perception, as in a series of establishing shots of decreasing distance. In the opening shots of *Rear Window* (1954), Hitchcock makes a kind of joke about how cinematic vision mimics human vision. An elaborate camera movement shows us the courtyard view from L. B. Jefferies's room while his protagonist sleeps. When Jefferies later wakes up and looks out the window, Hitchcock cuts from images of him to isolated views of the windows opposite, using editing to re-map the space with which we have already been made familiar in accordance with Jefferies's now-alert gaze.

Hollywood film editing is part of a systematic approach to filmmaking. Continuity style refers to an even broader array of technical choices that support this principle of effacing technique to clarify the narrative and its human motivation. Lighting highlights the face. Mise-en-scène is scaled to the human figure and generally does not distract from the action. Plot is oriented to the perceptions and goals of a clearly drawn protagonist. The soundtrack also plays a major role, as we will see in Chapter 6. But it is editing that best exemplifies the principle of seamlessness in continuity style by incorporating many other aspects. Lighting must be consistent from shot to shot, and other aspects of mise-en-scène—such as costumes and make-up, props, and figure behavior—must be meticulously monitored from setup to setup by following the **continuity script** (for example, the person in charge of continuity would ensure that a cigarette almost burned down in one shot is not freshly lit in a later shot) [**Figures 5.62a and 5.62b**].

In a Hollywood film, editing a scene in the service of narrative continuity and clarity is called **analytical editing**. In other words, the scene is analyzed or broken down by the camera to direct viewers' attention from the general perspective of an establishing shot to increasingly more specific views. Closer shots show character speech (shot/reverse-shot sequences) or denote the position of significant props or

5.62a and 5.62b   *Plan 9 from Outer Space* (1959). The principles of continuity editing are illustrated by their failed execution in a film by notorious B-filmmaker Edward D. Wood Jr. When actor Bela Lugosi died before filming was complete on this low-budget sci-fi horror film, the director replaced him with another actor in a cape. But props alone do not create continuity.

gestures (inserts, cutaways, reaction shots). Again, it is paradoxical that "continuity" traditionally depends on a large number of cuts. Indeed, this paradox prompted André Bazin's praise for William Wyler's use of long, continuous takes. Despite Bazin's claim that such choices heighten realism, cuts in films using long takes are often especially noticeable. Alfred Hitchcock reflects on these questions in *Rope* (1948), in which he allows the camera to run out of film before cutting and then concealing the cuts; a ten-shot film is in many ways an "unnatural" viewing experience.

Spatially, the relationships set up in the Hollywood continuity tradition follow the logic of human interaction. Analytical editing cuts the world to the measure of the body, and camera distance is measured in anthropomorphic scale (a close-up is a shot in which the human face would be seen in its entirety). Point-of-view editing registers the impact of the world on humans, literally sandwiching a view between two shots of a person looking. The 180-degree rule outlines a field of interaction well illustrated by the shot/reverse-shot sequence, in which the camera takes turns "seeing" from different characters' perspectives.

Film theorists speculate that such spatial practices hide a source of potential anxiety for the viewer. If the conversation from *Clueless* illustrated earlier [**Figures 5.32a–5.32d, p. 153**] proceeded without cutting back to the protagonist, Cher, we might remember that in order to film her friends, the camera occupies her seat. Our human perception actually proceeds from what Dziga Vertov and his associates call the "camera eye," a fact we are supposed to forget. In a subjective shot from a horror film that is not anchored by a reverse shot, we are forced to wonder whose point of view the camera is assuming. The mechanical eye becomes associated with that of a monster—perhaps the genre recognizes that being forced to share the point of view of an unknown entity (ultimately the camera itself) can make us anxious.

It is worth underscoring in this connection that every time a shot is shown, an infinite number of other possible shots are *not* shown. By making each cut seem natural, by anchoring it to the perception of an onscreen character or in an analytical breakdown of space, continuity editing typically covers up how much is excluded by each shot. The borders of the frame exclude everything around it; the choice of a particular shot excludes all other shots; and the "natural" world onscreen excludes all the technology that filmmakers use to construct it. Film theorists note that every cut is a potential reminder of these exclusions (after all, anything could come next) and postulate that continuity editing strives to give us the satisfying sensation of knowing what to expect in the editing sequence. The term **suture**, literally referring to stitching up a wound, is used to refer to our sense of being inserted in a specific place in a film, a place from which to look at its fictional world. This reassuring sense is accomplished through devices such as the shot/reverse-shot sequence, which brings us back to a human surrogate within the film whose gaze can stand in for our own—until the next shot. If a human gaze motivates each successive view, we have no need to speculate how the illusion is created. Critics of suture urge exposure of the illusion, not just to make the viewer aware of the filmmaker's craft but also to challenge the viewer's passivity.

The temporal patterns of continuity editing follow human rhythms of growth, memory, and desire. The temporality of editing is determined by character motivation in a narrative framework. The progression of a biographical film from the protagonist's childhood through significant contributions until death is one example. Temporal progression is often linear in order to follow characters' actions, but a character's subjective memory can motivate a flashback structure. Cutting follows the pursuit of the protagonist's goals and desires; in a "deadline" film such as *Lara Croft: Tomb Raider* (2001), the temporal presentation makes the central action clear. The time of intervening actions is omitted (for example, the heroine is never shown getting a good night's sleep). In the chase sequences, parallel editing or crosscutting between the endangered party and the potential rescuer creates the impression of simultaneity. Crosscutting has remained a complex and favored device of the continuity system since D. W. Griffith used it obsessively to set up his last-minute

▶ VIEWING CUE

In the film you just viewed, at what point is continuity editing used? How does this practice encourage you to identify with the characters or to believe in the story's world?

rescues. As we have seen, continuity style organizes the film as a whole into a consistent spatial and temporal world, one that is shaped around the consciousness and agency of its characters.

Continuity style is so pervasive that it is often regarded as natural. Even technicians—from lighting directors and costume designers to (especially) editors—talk about striving for invisibility in their craft. One of the fundamental ways to identify how narrative films are constructed is to train ourselves to notice editing, both within and between scenes and sequences, and to pay attention to how it serves the narrative and its human agents. Continuity editing practices in art cinema are often noticeable to viewers who take Hollywood continuity for granted. Loosely defined, *art cinema* includes narrative feature films from outside Hollywood that are exhibited in specialty cinemas. Art films construct a fictional world, center on human perspective, and direct our view of unfolding events, but they construct space and time differently through editing. Although they provide a form of continuity between cuts, they are not governed by Hollywood continuity style. Analytical editing, with its precise and often-redundant orientation to the spatial unfolding of a scene, is avoided in art films like Carl Theodor Dreyer's *The Passion of Joan of Arc* (1928), in which a series of close-ups against a white background conveys the psychological intensity of Joan testifying before the Inquisitors while never giving an overview of the space. Japanese director Yasujiro Ozu often uses graphic elements to provide continuity across cuts, and although in his *Early Summer* (1951) he conveys his characters' situations poignantly, he is more likely to set up his camera near the ground to show them sitting on the floor than he is to use their optical point of view. Cutting between handheld shots in films, U.S. independent pioneer John Cassavetes follows characters' conversations and reactions but disorients viewers' perception of the overall space in favor of immediacy of emotion. Art cinema conveys a powerful storytelling to Hollywood analytical editing.

Disjunctive Editing

Alternative, less dominant and codified editing practices can be traced back even to very early developments in film syntax. In the 1910s and 1920s, filmmakers were very excited by the possibilities of film art. Sophisticated editing philosophies were applied in various countries and schools, often directly challenging the principles of continuity editing. As noted earlier, we refer to these alternatives as **disjunctive editing**—practices that structure cutting through oppositional relationships or formal constructions based on organizational principles other than the human vision of the world. Disjunctive editing might be deemed *visible editing* because it links shots in less predictable relationships than does continuity editing. To that extent, it confronts viewers with juxtapositions and linkages that seem unnatural or unexpected and has two main functions: to call attention to the editing for aesthetic, conceptual, ideological, or psychological purposes, and to disorient, disturb, or viscerally affect viewers. When the viewer is asked, or even forced, to reflect on the meaning of a particular cut because it is so jarring, many filmmakers and theorists believe, he or she is not only participating more fully in the film experience but may also develop a critical perspective on the film's subject matter or on the process of representation itself.

Disjunctive editing is not a single system with rules and manuals like Hollywood continuity editing. It may be organized around any number of different aspects of editing, such as spatial tension, temporal experimentation, or rhythmic and graphic patterns. Such practices require a comparative or reflective position to make sense of a sequence or scene. Emphasizing the pervasiveness of disjunctive editing is an important way to disrupt an account of film history that implies that the continuity style is inevitable. As we will see, disjunctive editing can even coexist with continuity editing in the same film. The following section will discuss two subtraditions of disjunctive editing: distantiation and montage. **Distantiation**

5.63a and 5.63b   *Michael Clayton* (2007). Today, even mainstream Hollywood films have appropriated jump cuts not primarily to alienate viewers but to emphasize disjunctions and disorientations within a film.

is identified with the plays and critical writings of 1920s German playwright Bertolt Brecht, who advocated showing the parts that were put together to form the completed work so that it could not be consumed without thinking. As noted earlier, **montage** is one of the most systematic practices of disjunctive editing, primarily identified with Soviet filmmakers but also applicable to other aesthetic traditions.

Distantiation. Brecht believed that a seamless work, such as a Hollywood film, was viewed uncritically. A critical distance on both the work of art and the social world on which it commented was achieved when the viewer had to think about the play's structure. This was accomplished through distantiation techniques, also known as *alienation effects*. A distantiation technique specific to film is the *jump cut*, a disjunctive cut that interrupts a particular action and, intentionally or unintentionally, creates discontinuities in the spatial or temporal development of shots. Used loosely, the term "jump cut" can identify several different disjunctive practices. Cutting a section out of the middle of a shot causes a jump ahead to a later point in the action. Sometimes the background of a shot may remain constant, while figures shift position inexplicably. Two shots from the same angle but from different distances will also create a jump when juxtaposed. Such jumps are considered grave errors in continuity editing; films of the French New Wave, notably Jean-Luc Godard's *Breathless* (1961), reintroduced this disjunctive technique into the editing vocabulary, but contemporary films such as *Michael Clayton* (2007) have since appropriated this technique [**Figures 5.63a and 5.63b**].

Jump cuts illustrate the two primary aims of disjunctive editing. In a contemporary film such as Wong Kar-wai's *Happy Together* (1997), they draw attention to the editing. Jumps in distance and time are combined with changes in film stock within a supposedly continuous scene [**Figures 5.64a and 5.64b**]. The viewer

5.64a and 5.64b   *Happy Together* (1997). Here, jump cuts draw attention to the restlessness and displacement of two men who have moved from Hong Kong to Buenos Aires.

5.65a and 5.65b *Last Year at Marienbad* (1961). Delphine Seyrig strikes poses against various backgrounds, challenging our perception of time and place. The same technique was later used in music videos.

notices *how* the action is depicted, rather than simply taking in the action. The viewer may reflect on how the disjointed shots convey the characters' restless yet stagnant moods, recognize in them the film's theme of displacement, or appreciate the aesthetic effect for its own sake.

The jump cuts in Alain Resnais's *Last Year at Marienbad* (1961) are a central device through which the viewer is disoriented in space and especially in time. The major conceit of this classic art film is the characters' confusion between the present and the past (the previous year of the film's title); this diegetic confusion is inseparable from the viewer's disorientation through editing, because the viewer cannot tell whether shots of the two characters in the Marienbad resort depict the present or the past. Finally, the strategy becomes a reflection on the process of viewing a film. How can we assume that the action we are viewing is happening now, when recording, editing, and projection/viewing are all distinct temporal operations? Numerous images show the female protagonist striking poses around the hotel and gardens [**Figures 5.65a and 5.65b**]. The temporal

5.66a–5.66c *The Battleship Potemkin* (1925). Sergei Eisenstein rouses stone lions through montage.

relationship among such shots is unclear, as differences in costume and setting are countered by similarities in posture and styling.

The jump cut can also be used to explore the magical properties of the medium, a trick that goes back to the trick films of Georges Méliès at the beginning of the twentieth century. Maya Deren's *Meshes of the Afternoon,* for example, begins with a hand lowering a flower into the frame. In the film's second shot, the hand abruptly disappears. Later a hand reaches forward to remove a key from the table; then the key suddenly reappears in its original position. This action is repeated; we are invited to engage in existential reflection, enhanced by the fact that the disjunctive nature of these cuts is underscored in the film by a distinctive, synchronized note on the soundtrack.

In addition to jump cuts, other distantiation devices are highlighted throughout the films of Jean-Luc Godard. By foregrounding the ideological effects of continuity breaks, Godard assaults viewers' complacency and asks them to understand disruption as an opportunity for critical thinking. Godard's work emphasizes fragmentation and distance on many levels, from shot and sound/image juxtaposition to the organization of the narrative into "chapters." (The device of introducing chapters with text or numbers is borrowed directly from Brecht's plays.) For example, Godard's *Two or Three Things I Know about Her* (1966) disrupts continuity by cutting between images and printed texts, by having characters and bystanders address the camera directly in the middle of sequences, and by cutting to ever-closer views of a cup of coffee during a meditative voiceover, until finally the entire widescreen image is engulfed by espresso. Calling attention to the editing in film through distantiation foregrounds both the actual labor that goes into constructing the piece and the conventions and assumptions that are challenged in the work.

Montage. The aim of grabbing viewers' attention through collision is at the center of Sergei Eisenstein's work on montage, which is the heart of the second subtradition. Eisenstein's writings, undertaken until his death in 1945, have secured him a place as one of the foremost theorists of cinema. He first developed his concept of montage in conjunction with his work in theater before beginning his film experiments with *The Strike* in 1924. For Eisenstein, montage is a dialectical process. Two shots linked dialectically (that is, contrasted or opposed to one another) become synthesized into something greater, a visual concept. In *The Battleship Potemkin* (1925), the shots of stone lions juxtaposed in sequence suggest that one stone lion is leaping to life [**Figures 5.66a–5.66c**]. According to Eisenstein, the concept of awakening, connected to revolutionary consciousness, is thus formed in viewers' minds even as they react viscerally to the lion's leap. The association of aesthetic fragmentation with a political program of analysis and action has persisted in many uses of disjunctive editing.

Whereas Hollywood films traditionally avoid a disjunctive style, alternative and experimental films often employ it as the foundation of the film. The fragmentation of time and space (which is germane to editing) is an important aesthetic aim of artistic **modernism.** (Think, for instance, of cubism in painting, which aims to show different facets of an object through a distorted depiction of its shape, color, and composition, a very cinematic concept.) Experiments in film using distantiation, montage, and other alternative practices characterize modernist filmmaking; in contrast, Hollywood classicism strives for balance and wholeness. Modernist filmmaking—like that of Godard and Eisenstein—may have a political agenda, seeking to use art to promote a critical consciousness and to break with the status quo. But editing that goes against the grain of continuity values is central to avant-garde film movements that have primarily aesthetic aims. In the 1920s, for example, experimental filmmakers in France organized their films' montage around the rhythms of poetry and music. In Germaine Dulac's surrealist film *The Seashell and the Clergyman* (1928), the central figure is as surprised as we are when his head suddenly appears on the seashell. During the same period, an

Les Demoiselles D'Avignon,
Pablo Picasso (1907).

Kinoglaz, a poster by Alexander Rodchenko (1924).

Two or Three Things I Know about Her, directed by Jean-Luc Godard (1967).

international genre of "city symphony" films emerged. Walter Ruttmann's *Berlin: Symphony of a City* (1927) and Dziga Vertov's *The Man with the Movie Camera* (1929) both create a conceptual whole through montage. In both films, the life of the metropolis is depicted through rhythmic patterns of images that emulate the condensed time and space of modernity. Vertov's film even combines footage from different cities. In the documentary film style developed by British producer John Grierson in such films as *Drifters* (1929), images were cut together in a poetic montage.

Later modernist filmmakers also used montage. American filmmaker Kenneth Anger explores the ritual aspects of film in *Scorpio Rising* (1964), which edits the cult behavior of bikers to a rock-and-roll soundtrack. (In contrast, Andy Warhol's films are distinct for their lack of editing. *Empire* [1964], an eight-hour shot of the Empire State Building using a stationary camera, might be seen as a very prolonged homage to the first films of the Lumière brothers.) The **structural film** movement eschewed narrative and mise-en-scène and explored properties specific to film, including the potential of editing. Part of the experience of watching such films is reflecting on their principles of construction. The very title of Trinh T. Minh-ha's *Reassemblage* (1982) **[Figure 5.67]** references the process of editing. In this short experimental documentary shot in Senegal, Trinh critiques ethnographic filmmaking's presumption that an image can tell the truth of another culture to an outsider. Her film makes use of disjunctive editing by repeating shots, using jump cuts, and refusing to synchronize the picture to a complex soundtrack. Films made from found footage, such as Bruce Conner's *A Movie* (1958), rely on montage to create humorous, sinister, or thought-provoking relationships among seemingly random images.

Video art has also made significant use of disjunctive editing through montage. With the use of effects, video editing can be layered as well as sequential, developing one of Eisenstein's principles: "each shot is a montage cell." In other words, relationships of contrast and opposition exist not only between shots, but within shots as well. Cecelia Barriga's low-budget video art piece *Meeting of Two Queens* (1991) is ingeniously constructed by recutting brief clips from the films of Greta Garbo and Marlene Dietrich. The montage creates comparisons between the glamorous movie star rivals, engineers a meeting, and suggests a romance between the two by making use of viewers' expectations of continuity editing and altering mise-en-scène through superimposition **[Figure 5.68]**. Barriga thereby introduces disjunction to classical films originally edited for continuity.

▶ **VIEWING CUE**

Does the editing of the film you've just viewed for class call attention to itself in a disjunctive fashion, setting up conflicts or posing oppositional values? If so, how and to what end? ⏸

5.67 *Reassemblage* (1982). Disjunctive editing questions the truth of images.

5.68 *Meeting of Two Queens* (1991). Re-editing on video puts Greta Garbo and Marlene Dietrich, stars from rival studios, in the same film.

Converging Editing Styles

It is important to stress that many films and videos employing disjunctive editing are obliged to employ continuity editing techniques as well. More and more frequently, commercial film and television incorporate disjunctive editing techniques, including those formerly restricted to the avant-garde. It is no longer possible—if indeed it ever was—to assign specific responses, such as passive acceptance or political awareness, to specific editing techniques.

As digital video cameras and editing equipment become more commonly used for theatrical features, different kinds of juxtapositions will also become more common. Lars von Trier's use of one hundred small digital video cameras to film *Dancer in the Dark* (2000) presented an editing challenge that an editor working with footage from one film camera would never face. Fortunately, nonlinear digital editing on a computer system allows the editor and director to sample many possibilities without affecting the original materials. Von Trier's film breaks down actions much more minutely than standard analytical editing, so that the arbitrariness of the cutting becomes apparent rather than hidden [**Figures 5.69a and 5.69b**]. However, there is no clear indication that the viewers' distantiation is intended.

It is evident from all of the examples just cited that a great deal of the formal expressive potential of moving-image media such as film and video lies in the exploitation of the disjunctive powers of editing. While this capacity has been emphasized in non-narrative traditions, it is also key to mainstream forms such as the television commercial. Disjunctive editing is an extremely useful tool in the condensed time frame and gut-level appeal of advertising, helping viewers make associative connections between the products and values. In music videos, such as David Fincher's video for Madonna's 1990 hit song "Vogue," space and time are defied for a more immediate effect, as the cutting interacts with the music and the rhythms of the dancers. Viewers remain unable to orient themselves in space. Music video's contribution to contemporary editing conventions in feature films and television is profound, and directors such as Fincher (who went on to make *Fight Club* [1999] and *Zodiac* [2007], among other films) have used their experience creating music videos to make some of the most aesthetically innovative contributions to recent commercial cinema, routinely dispensing with establishing shots, breaking the 180-degree rule, and otherwise bending the rules of continuity editing. As the two formal traditions of continuity and disjunctive editing converge, the values associated with each tradition become less distinct. For Eisenstein, calling attention to the editing was important because it could change the viewers' consciousness. For contemporary filmmakers, disjunctive editing may serve more as an innovative "look."

text continued on page 182 ▶

5.69a and 5.69b   ***Dancer in the Dark*** (2000). The use of many digital cameras makes it possible to intercut close shots from multiple perspectives.

Montage from *The Battleship Potemkin* (1925) to *The Untouchables* (1987)

Soviet filmmaker Sergei Eisenstein's *The Battleship Potemkin* is one of the most renowned examples of daring and innovative editing in film history. A 1925 silent classic based on a 1905 historical event, *The Battleship Potemkin* describes the revolt of maltreated sailors aboard their ship, the sympathetic response of townspeople on shore, and the violent repression of those people by czarist soldiers. Although the story itself is quite direct and relatively brief, Eisenstein employs a variety of disjunctive cutting techniques to charge specific incidents with powerful energy and meanings, emphasizing the breaks and contrasts between images joined by a cut.

In a film with no single protagonist, numerous cuts join small groups to show the participation of the masses in anti-czarist sentiment, moving our perspective beyond the confines of individual perception and its temporal and spatial limitations. To give heightened drama or dynamic tension to an action, Eisenstein uses more shots than a Hollywood film would find necessary, sometimes overlapping the same action from one shot to the next in several points of view. When the ship's doctor is thrown overboard by sailors, the gesture is repeated from overhead and side angles, expanding the screen time of the action and "showing the seams" of the editing through distantiation in order to engage viewers' emotions and to lead them to a particular idea: the desperation of the sailors resulting in a mutinous act [Figures 5.70a and 5.70b]. After the doctor hits the water, Eisenstein employs an insert of the maggot-infested meat that the doctor had approved for the sailors' consumption. Appearing out of

5.70a and 5.70b   *The Battleship Potemkin* (1925). Overlapping cuts of the same action.

temporal sequence, this shot reminds us of the narrative justification of the doctor's treatment and underscores the intertitle: "now he'll feed the fishes."

The centerpiece of *The Battleship Potemkin* is the famous Odessa steps sequence in which innocent citizens are shot and trampled by the czar's soldiers. The sequence is justly celebrated for its dynamic cutting, which makes dramatic use of movement and graphic patterns within shots to bring about Eisenstein's favored interaction between shots: collision. The sequence begins with the intertitle "Suddenly"; townspeople then begin to run from the imperial soldiers down the vast steps toward the camera. This action moves generally from left to right. Several different figures are isolated and intercut throughout the sequence: a boy without legs propelling himself forward with his arms, a group of women, a mother running with her child. When the orderly rows of troops are shown entering from top left, the shot provides a dramatic graphic contrast to the chaos of the mass of people. In

the first major crosscutting episode within the sequence, the mother becomes separated from her son in the crowd, and shots of her turning back for him are intercut with shots of him falling and being trampled by the crowd. Her movement against the crowd to retrieve his body in her arms, from right to left across the screen, is vigorously contrasted with shots of the oncoming crowds and with shots of the soldiers' inexorable progression behind them. Finally, the mother climbs high enough and enters a shot from the bottom left, which positions the soldiers across the top. The film cuts to peasants looking on, and in the next shot she is fired on and falls as the troops continue marching down. The use of movement in opposing directions is one of the key elements that organizes this complicated editing sequence [**Figures 5.71a–5.71d**].

As if this dramatic episode has not raised enough tension and pathos, after an intertitle announces the arrival of the Cossacks, Eisenstein embarks on one of the most famous editing sequences in film history. A young

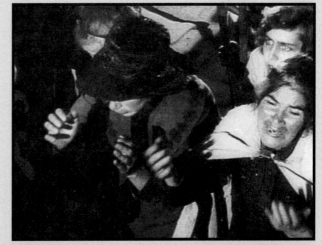

5.71a–5.71d *The Battleship Potemkin* (1925). The conflict between the organized troops and the frightened masses is heightened by graphic collisions among shots showing different screen directions, patterns of light and shadow, and figure movement in the first part of the Odessa steps sequence.

mother is shot and falls in several overlapping cuts. The baby carriage she had been clutching begins to roll down the stairs. Intercut with its descent (in changing screen directions) are repeated shots of onlookers who seem to be mimicking our own powerless, horrified gaze. No establishing shot puts these figures in spatial context. Just as the carriage reaches the bottom and begins to overturn, Eisenstein cuts to quick shots of a Cossack striking directly at us and then to the briefest of shots of the face of a woman wearing pince-nez. In a famous shock cut, her glasses are instantly shattered and bloodied. The sequence fades out [Figures 5.72a–5.72c]. As our vision is assaulted by the shock cut, the image of shattered glasses mirrors our own"injury," even as it stands in for an even more horrific, absent image of the baby's fate.

The Battleship Potemkin, Eisenstein's second film, made a similarly strong impact when it was released in the West in 1926. Threatened with political censorship, it was hailed by artists, activists, and intellectuals as a sig-

nificant advance in film art. It brought international acclaim to Eisenstein and to the extraordinary Soviet cinema of the 1920s. In the long term, Eisenstein's stylistic legacy has survived even as the revolutionary purpose he associated with his aesthetic innovations has become questioned or abandoned. His work has provided the occasion for more than one homage.

Director Brian De Palma emerged among a generation of U.S. filmmakers who were trained in film schools and familiar with film history. He is particularly well known for paying tribute to—or stealing from, depending on one's perspective—other great directors in his films. His *Obsession* (1976) borrows motifs from Alfred Hitchcock's classic *Vertigo,* for example. In his tale of Chicago's crime world in the 1930s, *The Untouchables* (1987), De Palma fashions a tense showdown in a train station that "quotes" the Odessa steps sequence from *The Battleship Potemkin,* sometimes shot for shot. Audiences familiar with the original sequence recognize the endangered baby carriage at the top of the steps. Some see a tour de force of suspenseful editing; others think the sequence is a distracting self-indulgence.

In De Palma's "version" of the sequence, federal agent Eliot Ness (Kevin Costner) and his sharpshooter sidekick, George Stone (Andy Garcia), are collecting evidence of Al Capone's financial mismanagement by intercepting his bookkeeper as he attempts to catch the 12:05 train. Cutting from the station's giant clock to Ness scoping out the staircase, to a mother struggling to climb the stairs with her luggage and her child in a carriage, De Palma and his editor, Jerry Greenberg, set up what will be a most effective action sequence in continuity style. They carefully establish a believable space and a linear, deadline-oriented time frame.

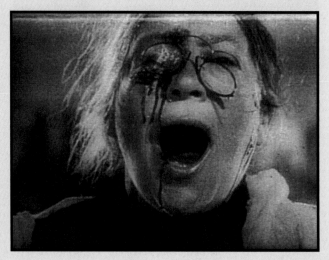

5.72a–5.72c *The Battleship Potemkin* (1925). Horrified onlookers and repeated details of the baby carriage's descent convey a universal sense of helplessness in one of the most famous editing sequences in film history.

Tension mounts as the clock nears noon. The mother makes her way laboriously up the vast staircase. At one point, a trainload of passengers sweeps down, stepping over her. A few sailors cross her path—De Palma's nod to the subject matter of Eisenstein's film. After an extreme close-up of the clock at noon, Ness finally goes to help the mother, but as he pulls the carriage up the stairs (a sequence punctuated by several shots of the boy smiling up at him), Capone's men begin to descend. Ness, almost at the top and sensing himself surrounded, turns to shoot at one of the goons. A detail shows Ness as he lets go of the carriage; then, amidst the chaotic gunfire that ensues, De Palma exploits the carriage's slow descent, intercutting shots of the mother failing to catch the handle and of her view of the carriage from the top of the stairs, an overhead shot of the boy, a shot of the wheels hitting the stairs, and a shot of one of the bad guys shooting at Ness right over the top of the carriage. Finally, Ness runs down, still shooting, to try to catch the carriage, but Stone arrives in the nick of time, diving to stop it with his body at the last step [Figures 5.73a–5.73d]. The boy smiles calmly up at Ness. In the final phase of the action, Stone aims his gun at the final gang member even as he is bracing the carriage from beneath. "You got him?" Ness asks, his question referring both to the boy and to the villain, summing up the way the scene's visual elements play off each other as well as the individual heroism that contrasts so markedly with the ethos of Eisenstein's film. Stone makes the shot. We never see the boy returned to his mother.

Like the sequence from *The Battleship Potemkin,* the protracted climax of *The Untouchables* proceeds nearly without language through several peaks of action by way of its complex editing. The dynamism of contrasting upward and downward movement is also retained, as is the pathos of the mother confronted by gunfire at the top of the stairs (elements of both movements of the *Potemkin* scene are incorporated into this one). But De Palma's set piece differs from Eisenstein's in that it serves the film's narrative goals through spatial and temporal coherence and, in particular, emphasizes its focus on the perceptions and motivations of individuals.

In Eisenstein's film, the conflict was between state power and the righteousness of the people, and the cutting reinforces this objectively rendered polarity. In *The Untouchables,* tension is raised by Ness's struggle with the choice between helping the mother (and later attempting to save the child) and completing his single-minded quest to bring down Capone by apprehending the only man who can give evidence to convict the mob boss. This centrality of character psychology is conveyed by relying on subjective points of view that "suture" our perspective to that of the protagonist. Ness's face is seen before the first shot of the mother and carriage: his gaze conveys the danger of her being on the stairs at the wrong time. Again, it is Ness who looks into the carriage after its fall has been broken to see a smiling child. The individuals whom Eisenstein singles out are types; their faces are not rendered in close-ups marking a subjective point of view. Eisenstein's film makes us helpless witnesses like the massacred people, whereas De Palma's version gives us the illusion of agency. Through its spatial construction, the Odessa steps sequence makes the slaughter of innocents a public spectacle. In the train station shootout, strict spatial continuity is preserved in rendering the virtuosic performance of the heroes.

5.73a–5.73d *The Untouchables* (1987). This film unmistakably quotes and reuses a part of the Odessa steps sequence in Eisenstein's *Potemkin,* but transforms the disjunctive nature of that original montage to serve the point of view of the main character and the overall continuity of the film.

Temporality is also oriented to human goals as we watch the clock and study Ness's expression. Eisenstein's temporal scheme emphasizes disruption: the abstract but urgent intertitle "Suddenly" introduces the extraordinary event and the disjunctive editing sequence that renders it. Repetition in *The Battleship Potemkin* seems to have a didactic function, underscoring the unjust suffering of the people. In *The Untouchables,* multiple shots of the boy's face as his carriage bumps down the steps through the crossfire blatantly, and almost humorously, manipulate our emotions.

More than sixty years after Eisenstein used montage in a modernist film to shock and prod his viewers to ac-

tion, De Palma incorporated the central image of threatened innocence provided by a baby carriage tumbling down stairs into a genre film, showing off all of the resources of continuity editing. Eisenstein's political objective lay as much in his subject matter as in the editing techniques he innovated to convey them. De Palma's style has been called postmodernist because it emphasizes surface effects over subject matter and borrows from other styles. Editing in the disjunctive tradition is about opening up multiple meanings, whereas the continuity tradition favors closure. In *The Untouchables,* the baby survives the precipitous plunge.

One filmmaker, Oliver Stone, is closely associated with both Hollywood filmmaking and disjunctive editing. A major source of controversy over his *JFK* (1991) is the way the film cuts back and forth among diverse "sources"– historical footage, re-created black-and-white scenes, and the investigation, which was filmed in color–to support his fictionalized vision of a conspiracy behind the presidential assassination, a real event that was experienced to an unprecedented degree through the media. An 8mm home movie was the most reliable witness, and the footage, recorded by bystander Abraham Zapruder, has received more frame-by-frame analysis than film scholars have given *The Battleship Potemkin*. Stone's film draws on the "authenticity" lent by newsreel-like footage. Still, if one attends to the disjunctive editing of *JFK*–its seemingly random range of film stocks and bafflingly high number of cuts–it is evident that far from presenting a seamless conspiracy theory or evidence that the image does not lie, the form of Stone's film testifies to the mediated nature of all recent historical events.

Editing is perhaps the most distinctive feature of film form. Editing leads viewers to experience images through particular emotions and ideas, and it remains one of the most effective ways to create meanings from shots. These interpretations can vary from the almost automatic inferences about space, time, and narrative that we draw from the more familiar continuity editing patterns, to the intellectual puzzles posed by the unfamiliar spatial and temporal juxtapositions of disjunctive editing practices.

▶ **VIEWING CUE**

If both continuity and disjunctive editing are present, how do they interact, and how does that interaction shape your understanding of the film?

Ⅱ

CONCEPTS AT WORK

Perhaps the most distinguishing technical and formal element of film practice, editing describes the art of connecting two different shots or film images. This fundamental practice has produced a vast array of strategies associated with different historical, cultural, and aesthetic perspectives. Against the background of a brief history highlighting changes in editing practices, we have detailed the many formal figures available in editing a film: from shot/counter-shot exchanges and continuity styles to graphic matches and disjunctive jump cuts. In conclusion, this chapter has emphasized how

editing does not merely create formal patterns but produces patterns associated with certain values, traditions, and meanings.

Activity

Imagine that you've been asked to remake a mainstream Hollywood movie as a provocative art film. To demonstrate how this would happen, re-edit one piece of that film by redoing the continuity logic of the editing as a disjunctive style. How does this alter the meaning and the relationship between the viewer and the film?

THE NEXT LEVEL: ADDITIONAL SOURCES

Bazin, André. *What Is Cinema?* Edited and translated by Hugh Gray. Two vols. Berkeley: University of California Press, 2005. Originally published in 1967. This translation of Bazin's own selection of critical essays on the language of cinema, published posthumously, includes his classic theorizations of montage and the long take. This new edition includes forewords by Bazin scholar Dudley Andrew.

Bordwell, David. *The Way Hollywood Tells It: Story and Style in Modern Movies.* Berkeley: University of California Press, 2006. An examination of Hollywood films since the 1960s, this study looks at the changes in narrative style to argue, among other issues, that continuity editing has evolved dimensions of what the author calls "intensified continuity."

Burch, Noel. *Theory of Film Practice.* Translated by Helen Lane. Princeton: Princeton University Press, 1981. In this influential study originally published in 1973, a contemporary French theorist and filmmaker considers the construction of space and time in Hollywood and avant-garde films.

Dancyger, Ken. *The Technique of Film and Video Editing: Theory and Practice.* 4th ed. Boston and London: Focal Press, 1997. Aimed at directors and focusing on the history, theory, and practice of film editing, this highly readable book is de-

signed as an update to Karel Reisz's 1953 classic, *The Technique of Film Editing,* and to its 1968 revision by Gavin Miller.

Eisenstein, Sergei. *The Eisenstein Reader.* Edited by Richard Taylor. London: BFI, 1998. A collection of shorter writings by the Soviet filmmaker that illuminate his film practice and his theories of montage, this work covers his entire career from 1923 to 1947.

Figgis, Mike. *Digital Filmmaking.* London: Faber & Faber, 2007. This book is a guide to the dramatic changes and opportunities ushered in by the digital revolution and nonlinear editing, written by a filmmaker who took early and creative advantage of that revolution.

Metz, Christian. *Language and Cinema.* The Hague: Mouton de Gruyter, 1974. Outlining the field of film semiotics in this dense but influential work, Metz presents his framework for analyzing the syntagmatic components of the narrative film (the *grand syntagmatique*). He sees editing as being crucial to supporting the comparison of film with language via the definition of a grammar of film.

Oldham, Gabriella. *First Cut: Conversations with Film Editors.* Berkeley: University of California Press, 1992. Editors share secrets of their craft.

THE PIANO

CIBY 2000 PRESENTS A JAN CHAPMAN PRODUCTION

HOLLY HUNTER HARVEY KEITEL SAM NEILL
A JANE CAMPION film

WITH ANNA PAQUIN KERRY WALKER GENEVIEVE LEMON — COSTUME DESIGNER JANET PATTERSON — SOUND DESIGNER LEE SMITH — MUSIC BY MICHAEL NYMAN — EDITOR VERONIKA JENET — PRODUCTION DESIGNER ANDREW McALPINE — DIRECTOR OF PHOTOGRAPHY STUART DRYBURGH — ASSOCIATE PRODUCER MARK TURNBULL — EXECUTIVE PRODUCER FOR CIBY 2000 ALAIN DEPARDIEU — PRODUCER JAN CHAPMAN — WRITTEN AND DIRECTED BY JANE CAMPION — DEVELOPED WITH ASSISTANCE OF THE AUSTRALIAN FILM COMMISSION AND NEW SOUTH WALES FILM AND TELEVISION OFFICE © 1992 JAN CHAPMAN PRODUCTIONS AND CIBY 2000

DOLBY STEREO

CiBy sales

Listening to the Cinema

Film Sound

Jane Campion's 1993 *The Piano* opens with the sound of Ada McGrath's voiceover: "The voice you hear is not my speaking voice; it is my mind's voice." Thus begins an exploration not simply of the plight of this mute nineteenth-century woman, but also of the relation of sound to personal expression, music, gender, and social politics. The film tells the tale of a woman who does not speak but who is defined by sound—specifically, the music she plays on her piano. With more emphasis than most movies, *The Piano* recognizes from the start that film sound does not simply play a supporting role; rather, as dialogue, background music, or simply noise, film sound can create a drama as complex as mise-en-scène, editing, or cinematography.

The cinema is an audiovisual medium, one among many that saturate our contemporary media experience. Many of the visual technologies we encounter in daily life are also sound technologies: your computer informs you that "you've got mail," the beeps from your little sister's PlayStation Portable (PSP) drive you from the room, or you notice that your television's volume soars when a program is interrupted by a commercial. These devices all use sound to encourage and guide interaction, to complement the visuals, and to give rhythm and dimension to the experience. The cinema works similarly, using complex combinations of voice, music, and sound effects. Too often given secondary status, sound engages viewers perceptually, gives key spatial and story information, and affords an aesthetic experience of its own. This chapter explores how speech, music, and sound effects are constructed and how they are perceived by the film's audience.

KEY CONCEPTS   In this chapter, we will examine

- the importance of sound to the film experience
- how the use and understanding of sound reflect different historical and cultural influences
- how sounds convey meaning in relationship to images
- how sounds are recorded, combined, and reproduced
- the functions of the voice
- the principles and practices that govern the use of music
- the principles and practices that govern the use of sound effects
- the cultural, historical, and aesthetic values that determine traditional relationships between sounds and images

Sound is a sensual experience that potentially makes cinema's deepest impression. Viewers might cover their eyes during the infamous shower scene in *Psycho* (1960), but to lessen the scene's horror, they would have to escape from the shrieking violins that punctuate each thrust of the knife. To perceive an image, we must face forward with our eyes open, but sound can come from any direction. Listening to movies, just as much as watching them, defines the filmgoing experience, and with the advent of advanced technologies, sound has helped to make that experience even more immersive.

A Short History of Film Sound

Topsy-Turvy (1999) tells the story of the collaboration between Gilbert and Sullivan, the late-nineteenth-century British lyricist-composer duo, as they brainstorm, quarrel, and finally witness the first production of their operetta *The Mikado*. The behind-the-scenes story culminates in a performance of the operetta that brings together sound and image for the theater audience within the film and extends this experience to the film's viewers. As this film dramatizes, many of the traditions and

technologies that became synthesized in the institution of the cinema combined sound, especially music, and visual spectacle in public performances.

Theatrical and Technological Prehistories of Film Sound

It is difficult to think of a theatrical tradition that does not have its own distinctive musical conventions. The practice of combining music with forms of visual spectacle goes back at least as far as the use of choral odes in classical Greek theater. Perhaps most relevant to the use of sound in early cinema is the tradition of **melodrama**. Popularized in eighteenth-century France, melodrama, literally meaning "music drama," originally designated a theatrical genre that combined spoken text with music. In England, during a time when laws restricted "legitimate" theater to particular venues, melodrama permitted the mounting of popular theatrical spectacles. Stage melodrama became increasingly more spectacular throughout the nineteenth century and eventually came to dominate the American stage, where melodrama had an incalculable influence on cinematic conventions. Not only was the aural component of the form very important, but the up-and-down rhythms of melodrama's sensational plots also drew on the strongly felt but inexpressible emotions that music so powerfully conveys. All of these qualities were adopted by film melodramas like D. W. Griffith's *Way Down East* (1920), an adaptation of a nineteenth-century play.

Technological breakthroughs that led to such inventions as the phonograph were also important precursors of film sound. As far back as the end of the eighteenth century, inventors were engaged in the problems of sound reproduction. Edison's phonograph, introduced in 1877, had an irreversible impact on the public and on late-nineteenth-century science. Such inventions were often spoken about in terms of writing. "Phonography" means "sound writing," and Edison first thought of recorded sound as a way to record business letters.

1895–1927: The Sounds of Silent Cinema

Edison was also one of the primary figures in the invention of the motion-picture apparatus; the eventual coming together of film and sound haunted the medium from its inception. One of the first films made by Edison Studios in 1895 is a sound experiment in which Edison's chief inventor, W. L. K. Dickson, plays a violin into a megaphone as two other employees dance [Figure 6.1]. Sound cylinders provided a way of synchronizing image and sound very early in film history, and inventors continued to experiment with means of providing simultaneous picture and sound throughout the silent-film era.

6.1   Edison Studios' *Sound Experiment* (1895). A rare film fragment with synchronized sound from the dawn of cinema.

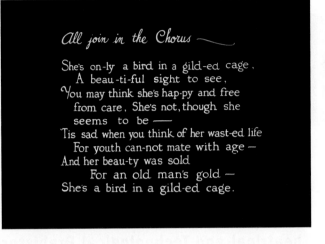

6.2a–6.2c **Early nickelodeon slides**. Films were interspersed with sing-alongs, and slides like these provided the lyrics.

The term "silent drama" was sometimes used to distinguish film from stage drama that used spoken language. But, in fact, so-called silent cinema was often loud and noisy. Loudspeakers lured customers into film exhibitions that were accompanied by lecturers, pianos, organs, small ensembles, or, later, full orchestras. In nickelodeons and other movie venues, audiences themselves customarily made noise, joining in sing-alongs between films [**Figures 6.2a–6.2c**] and talking back to the screen. Often sound effects were supplied by someone standing behind the screen or by specially designed machines. Occasionally actors even provided dialogue to go along with the picture.

Music halls in Great Britain and vaudeville theaters in the United States lent early cinema popular talents, proven material, and formats such as the review, delivering audiences with specific expectations of sound and spectacle to the new medium. Because of the preexisting popularity of specific performers and styles in vaudeville, many ethnic voices were heard in cinema that might otherwise have been excluded from entertainment directed at mass audiences. For his sound film debut at MGM, director King Vidor chose to make *Hallelujah!* (1929), a musical with an all-black cast, capitalizing on the cultural association of African Americans with the expressive use of song [**Figure 6.3**]. Not only musical talent but also stage performers with training and experience were now in demand in Hollywood, and they soon displaced many of the silent screen's most beloved stars.

1927–1930: Transition to Synchronized Sound

No event in the history of Hollywood film was as cataclysmic as the rapid incorporation of synchronized sound in the period 1927–1930. Many dynamics were at work in the introduction of sound, from the relationship of cinema to radio, theater, and vaudeville, to the economic position of the industry as the United States headed into the Great Depression, to the popularity of certain film genres

6.3 *Hallelujah!* (1929). With the coming of sound, musicals abounded, including this film that capitalized on the association of African Americans with the expressive use of song.

and stars. Yet exhibitors needed to be convinced to adopt the relatively untested new technology. The expense of converting a sufficient number of theaters to make the production of sound films feasible was considerable, and the studios had to be willing to make the investment.

From 1926 to 1927, two studios actively pursued competing sound technologies. Warner Bros. aggressively invested in sound and, in 1926, premiered its Vitaphone sound-on-disk system with a program of shorts, a recorded speech by Hollywood censor William Hays, and the first feature film with a recorded score, *Don Juan*. Fox developed its Movietone sound system, which recorded sound optically on film, and in 1927 introduced its popular Movietone newsreels, which depicted everything from ordinary street scenes to exciting news (such as aviator Charles Lindbergh's take-off for Paris) and were soon playing in Fox's many theaters nationwide **[Figure 6.4]**. The new technology became impossible to ignore when it branched out from musical accompaniment and sound effects to include synchronous dialogue. Public response was enthusiastic.

The Jazz Singer, Warner Bros.' second feature film with recorded sound, released in October 1927, is credited with convincing exhibitors, critics, studios, and the public that there was no turning back. Starring vaudevillian Al Jolson, the country's most popular entertainer of the time, the film tells a story, similar to Jolson's own, of a singer who must turn his back on his Jewish roots and the legacy of his father, a cantor in a synagogue, in order to fulfill his show-business dreams. He introduces dialogue to the movies with a famous promise that came true soon thereafter: "You ain't heard nothing yet!" **[Figure 6.5]**. Talking pictures, or "talkies," were an instant phenomenon. In the wake of *The Jazz Singer*'s phenomenal success, the studios came together and signed with Western Electric (a subsidiary of AT&T) to adopt a sound-on-film system in place of the less flexible Vitaphone sound-on-disk process. The studios also invested in the conversion of their major theaters and in the acquisition of new chains to show sound films.

6.4   Program for *Fox Movietone News*. Fox Studios developed a system to record sound optically on the film itself and then produced newsreels to show it off in its vast theater holdings.

1930–1941: Challenges and Innovations in Cinema Sound

The transition to sound was not entirely smooth. The troubles with exhibition technology were more than matched by the difficulties posed by cumbersome sound recording technology. Despite such problems, the transition was extremely rapid: by 1930, silent films were no longer being produced by the major studios; only a few independent filmmakers, such as Charlie Chaplin, whose art grew from the silent medium, held out.

The ability of early films to cross national borders and be understood regardless of the local language, a much-celebrated property of the early medium, was also changed irrevocably by the addition of monolingual spoken dialogue. Film industries outside the United States acquired national specificity, and Hollywood set up European production facilities. Exports were affected by conversion-standard problems and patents disputes. For a time, films were made simultaneously in different languages. Marlene Dietrich became an international star in *The Blue Angel* (1930), produced in

6.5   *The Jazz Singer* (1927). Warner Bros.' Vitaphone sound-on-disk system became a sensation because of Al Jolson's singing and spontaneous dialogue.

6.6   *Dracula* (1931). Tod Browning's classic is one of a cycle of early sound-era horror films made by Universal.

6.7   *Dracula* (1931). The Spanish-language version was shot on the same sets, with cast and costumes for the export market. This version was directed by George Melford.

▶ **VIEWING CUE**

What musical and theatrical traditions seem to have influenced the use of sound in the film you've just screened for class? Are any traces of the history of sound technology apparent? ⏸

Germany in French, English, and German versions. Comparing variations in these films is fascinating, for they demonstrate material dimensions not only of language but also of music and other sounds on the different soundtracks. The Spanish-language *Dracula* (1931), directed by George Melford, used the same sets and the translated script of Tod Browning's Hollywood classic but with a Spanish-speaking cast and more provocative women's costumes [Figures 6.6 and 6.7]. With adequate dubbing technology and other strategies, Hollywood's dominance of foreign markets was eventually reestablished, and foreign films, already dwindling on U.S. screens, became increasingly rare.

By this period, the Radio Corporation of America had entered the motion-picture production business, joining with the Keith-Orpheum chain of vaudeville theaters. The new studio, RKO, quickly became one of five studios known as the "majors" that would dominate sound-era cinema, and RKO's *King Kong* (1933) and *Citizen Kane* (1941) both contributed significantly to sound techniques.

1950–Present: From Stereophonic to Digital Sound

As we have seen, the traditions of spectacle enhanced by music and the human dream to "store" sounds converged in the sound practices that the cinema adopted. The establishment of representational norms in sound recording and mixing practices proceeded rapidly after the introduction of sound. How movies sound—the crispness of voices, the lush quality of orchestral background music, the use of sound effects in conjunction with what is onscreen—supports ideas about the complementary relationship of sound and image, listening and viewing, and about the value of verisimilitude. Further technological innovations in the 1950s (stereophonic sound), the 1970s (Dolby and surround sound), and the 1990s (digital sound) brought the aural experience of Hollywood cinema to the fore but did little to challenge these ideas. More than simple technological "improvements," these changes corresponded with historical shifts in film's social role, as television, home video, and computer games became competitive entertainments.

The most recent and radical change in sound reproduction, **digital sound**, has yet to be standardized into one system, and the competitive formats recall the period of sound's introduction in the late 1920s. Just as in the 1950s, when new film technologies such as CinemaScope and stereophonic sound were used to lure customers back to the theaters, today's digital sound systems attract audiences to theatrical exhibition. Audiophiles lead the companion trend toward home theaters with digital sound systems and speakers configured like those of movie theaters to emulate surround sound. Although cinema's mimetic capacity to reproduce images and sounds from the natural world is one of its strongest appeals, the perpetual quest for images and sounds that are bigger, louder, and better indicates that part of cinema's appeal is its ability to provide a heightened sensory experience that intensifies the ordinary.

The Elements of Film Sound

Despite our habitual references to motion *pictures* and to film *viewers*, sound is fully integrated into the film experience. In fact, one aspect of sound—human speech—is so central to narrative comprehension and viewer identification that we can often follow what happens even when the picture is out of sight. Sounds can interact with images in infinite ways, and strategies used to combine the two fundamentally affect our understanding of film. The song "We'll Meet Again"—a nostalgic 1940s song used to boost troop morale during World War II—that accompanies footage of H-bombs dropping in *Dr. Strangelove, or: How I Learned to Stop Worrying and Love the Bomb* (1964) makes it impossible to read these images as noble or tragic; instead, a frame of dark satire determines our view of war [Figure 6.8].

6.8 *Dr. Strangelove, or: How I Learned to Stop Worrying and Love the Bomb* (1964). An image of aggression set to nostalgic 1940s music sets the film's dark satirical tone.

The relationship between the original sound and its reproduction differs from that between an object and its filmed image. Although a sound is altered when it is recorded, engineered, and reproduced, we feel that we are hearing a real sound in real time. With images, we readily recognize that we see only a two-dimensional copy of the original. Sound effects of footsteps to accompany an image of a character walking are not really necessary; such an image is easily interpreted. However, the sound of footsteps heightens the sense of immediacy and presence. In recent years, improvements in sound technology and developments in sound recording practices have pursued goals of ever greater "realism" and intensity, making contemporary films sound much richer than those of the past. Sound has also led the way toward digitization, with digital image manipulation and picture editing following in turn. In what follows, we will explore the relationship of sound and image and the often-unperceived meanings of sound, before considering more fully the technology and aesthetics of film sound.

▶ VIEWING CUE

How did the format and venue of the last film you watched affect your experience of its sound? ⏸

Sound and Image

Any consideration of sound in film entails discussion of the relationship between sounds and images. Some filmmakers, such as the comic actor and writer-director Jacques Tati, have consistently given equal weight to the treatment and meaning of sound in their films. In *Playtime* (1967), as in Tati's other films, comic gags take place in long shots, and sounds cue us where to look [Figure 6.9]. In his unique films *The Umbrellas of Cherbourg* (1964) and *The Young Girls of Rochefort* (1967), filmmaker Jacques Demy pursues a vision of film's musicality. All of the dialogue is sung to Michel Legrand's music, while the candy-colored sets and costumes are designed to harmonize with this heightening of experience. Derek Jarman's *Blue* (1993), made after the filmmaker had lost his vision through an AIDS-related illness, combines an image track consisting solely of a rich shade of blue with a soundtrack featuring a complex mix of music, effects, and voices reading diaries and dramatic passages. Gazing into a vast blue screen allows viewers to focus more carefully on a soundtrack that conveys particular emotions and ideas [Figure 6.10].

For many filmmakers, however, as for viewers, sound functions more as an afterthought, being there to enhance the impact of the image. Many possible reasons

6.9 *Playtime* (1967). Jacques Tati's comic film emphasizes sound as much as image, often cuing the gag through sound effects.

exist for this disparity. Film is generally considered to be a predominantly visual medium rather than an aural one, following a more pervasive hierarchy of vision over sound. The artistry of the image track is perceived to be greater, as the image is more clearly a conscious rendering of the object being photographed than the recording is of the original sound. The fact that sound came later in the historical development of cinema has also been offered as an explanation of its secondary status. Yet the importance and variety of aural experiences at the movies were great even before the introduction of synchronized soundtracks. Since the early years of sound cinema, certain directors and composers have struggled against a too-literal, and too-limited, use of sound in film, arguing that the infinite possibilities in image and sound combinations are germane to the medium and its historical development. French filmmaker René Clair feared that the introduction of sound would diminish the visual possibilities of the medium and reduce it to "canned theater." In his musical film *Le Million* (1931), for example, in which crowds pick up and sing songs integral to the plot, Clair demonstrates that sound's potential is more than additive; it transforms the film experience viscerally, aesthetically, and conceptually.

6.10 *Blue Monochrome*
(1961), Yves Klein. Derek Jarman's film *Blue* (1993) is inspired by Klein's blue canvasses. A single blue image is accompanied by a complex soundtrack of voiceover, effects, and music, poetically reflecting on the director's life and AIDS-related illness.

Synchronous and Asynchronous Sound

Because sound and image always create meaning in conjunction, film theorists attentive to sound have looked for ways to talk about the possibilities of their combination. In his book *Theory of Film* (1960), Siegfried Kracauer emphasizes a distinction between **synchronous** and **asynchronous sound**. The former has a visible onscreen source, such as when dialogue appears to come directly from the speaker's moving lips, while the latter does not. (Some analysts prefer to call this distinction **onscreen** versus **offscreen sound**.) Kracauer goes on to differentiate between **parallelism** in the use of sound, which occurs when the soundtrack and image "say the same thing," and **counterpoint** (or contrapuntal sound), which occurs when two different meanings are implied by these elements. The two pairs of terms are distinct from each other. A shot of a teakettle accompanied by a high-pitched whistle is both synchronous and parallel.

The teakettle accompanied by an alarm bell would be a synchronous yet contrapuntal use of sound. A voiceover of a nature documentary may explain the behavior of the animals in an asynchronous use of parallel sound. Idyllic images accompanied by a narration stressing the presence of toxins in the environment and an ominous electronic hum would be a contrapuntal use of asynchronous sound. A familiar example of how relationships between sound and image can achieve multiple meanings comes at the end of *The Wizard of Oz* (1939). The booming voice and sound effects synchronized with the terrifying image of the wizard are suddenly revealed to have been asynchronous sounds produced by an ordinary man behind the curtain. When we see him speaking into a microphone, the sound is in fact synchronous, and what was intended as a parallel has now become a contrapuntal use of sound [Figure 6.11].

6.11   *The Wizard of Oz* (1939). The source of the wizard's voice is revealed.

In 1928, the dawn of the motion-picture sound era, radical Soviet directors embraced the creative possibilities of sound montage. Sergei Eisenstein, Vsevolod Pudovkin, and Grigori Alexandrov wrote in their "Statement on Sound" that "only a contrapuntal use of sound in relation to the visual montage piece will afford a new potentiality of montage development and perfection." Their endorsement of counterpoint, invoking principles of musical composition, can be opposed to filmmaking practices that emphasize parallelism—the mutual reinforcing or even the redundancy of sound and image. In Hollywood films, for example, it seems remiss not to accompany a shot of a busy street with traffic noises, although viewers immediately understand the locale through the visuals. This parallelism is also an aesthetic choice, one striving for clarity and harmony.

Diegetic and Nondiegetic Sound

One of the most frequently cited and instructive distinctions in sound is between the **diegetic sound**, which has its source in the narrative world of film, and the **nondiegetic sound**, which does not belong to the characters' world. Materially, the source of film sound is the actual soundtrack that accompanies the image, but diegetic sound implies a visible onscreen source. **Diegesis** (a term derived from literary analysis but now more commonly used in film studies) refers to the world of the film's story, including not only what is shown but also what is implied to have taken place. ("Diegesis" comes from the Greek word meaning "telling" and is distinguished from "mimesis," meaning "showing." The implication is that while mimetic representations imitate or mimic, diegetic ones use particular devices to tell about or imply events and settings.) One question offers a simple way to distinguish between diegetic and nondiegetic sound: can the characters in the film hear the sound? If not, the sound is likely to be nondiegetic. This distinction can apply to voices, music, and even sound effects. Conversations among onscreen characters, the voice of God in *The Ten Commandments* (1956), a voiceover that corresponds to a confession a character is making to the police, and the radio music that accompanies Mr. Blonde's sadistic assault of a police officer in *Reservoir Dogs* (1992) are all diegetic. Nondiegetic sounds do not follow rules of verisimilitude. For example, the voiceover narration that tells viewers about the characters in *The Magnificent Ambersons* (1942), background music that accompanies a love scene or journey, or sound effects such as a crash of cymbals when someone takes a comic fall are all nondiegetic. Audio practitioners refer to diegetic music, such as a shot of a band performing at a party or characters listening to music, as **source music** [**Figures 6.12a and 6.12b**].

However useful, this distinction can sometimes be murky. Certain voiceovers, though not spoken aloud to other characters, can be construed as the thoughts of

text continued on page 196 ▶

▶ **VIEWING CUE**

Distinguish an example of synchronous sound (with an onscreen source) from an example of asynchronous sound (with an offscreen source) in the film you are studying. Are these sounds easy to distinguish?

▶ **VIEWING CUE**

Find an example of diegetic sound in the film you are studying, and one of nondiegetic sound. What would the movie be like without the latter?

6.12a and 6.12b *Written on the Wind* (1956). Source music provides the dramatic soundtrack when Marylee's dance is intercut with her father's heart attack.

Sound and Image in
Singin' in the Rain (1952)

Hollywood has furnished its own myth about the introduction of synchronized sound in *Singin' in the Rain.* Directed by Stanley Donen and Gene Kelly, *Singin' in the Rain* demonstrates an escapist use of sound in film while also being *about* how sound in film achieves such effects. It addresses the relationship of sound to image, the history of film sound technologies, and the process of recording and reproducing sound.

In the 1940s and 1950s, MGM's "Freed Unit," working under the supervision of producer Arthur Freed (a former songwriter whose songs are used in *Singin' in the Rain*), produced a series of lavish musicals. Set in Hollywood at the end of the 1920s, *Singin' in the Rain* follows efforts at the fictional Monumental Pictures to make the studio's first successful sound film. Although the film's self-consciousness about the filmmaking process invites the audience into a behind-the-scenes perspective, the film itself continues to employ every available technique to achieve the illusionism of the Hollywood musical. One of the lessons of the film is that a "talking picture" isn't just "a silent picture with some talking added," as the studio producer assumes it to be. The film shows that adding sound to images enhances them with all the exuberance of song and dance, comedy, and romance. It also suggests that a great deal of labor and equipment are involved in creating such effects.

From the very beginning of *Singin' in the Rain,* the technology responsible for sound reproduction—technology that is usually hidden—is displayed. The film opens outside a Hollywood movie palace where crowds have gathered for the premiere of the new Lockwood and Lamont picture. Our first orientation is aural: "Ladies and gentlemen, I am speaking to you from. . . ." The

asynchronous announcer's voice carries across the crowds and seems to address us directly. The second shot opens directly on a loudspeaker, underscoring the parallelism of image and soundtrack, and then begins to explore the crowd of listeners. When we first see the radio announcer, the source of the synchronous voice, the microphone is very prominent in the mise-en-scène [Figure 6.13]. Referring to the bygone days of radio and silent movies, the film celebrates its modern audience's opportunity to watch sound and image combined in a sophisticated MGM musical.

Singin' in the Rain immediately begins to exploit the resources and conventions of studio-era sound cinema. When star Don Lockwood (Gene Kelly) begins to tell the story of his past in a diegetic voiceover to the assembled crowds and the radio listeners at home, this is a contrapuntal use

6.13 *Singin' in the Rain* (1952). A concern with sound recording technology is evident in the microphone's prominence in the first scene.

of sound because the series of flashback images belie his words. When his onscreen image gives way to his off-screen voice speaking of studying at a conservatory, we see him and his buddy, Cosmo Brown (Donald O'Connor), performing a vaudeville routine instead. The scene shows that images and voices can be out of sync, a theme that will become prominent in the film as a whole. It also shows the multiple ways the soundtrack can interact with the images. The comic vaudeville routine is, in turn, accompanied by lively music and humorous sound effects—the diegetic sound of the flashback world—encouraging our direct appreciation of the number. Next we hear the crowd's appreciative reactions to Lockwood's narration, a narration that we know to be phony. However, we do not experience these two different levels of sound—Don's self-serving narration and the debunking synchronized sound of the flashbacks—as confusing. It is clear that the film's unveiling of the mechanisms of sound technology will not limit its own reliance on the multiple illusions of sound and image relationships.

Later, when Don wants to express the depth of his feelings to Kathy Selden (Debbie Reynolds), he takes her to an empty soundstage. Ironically, his sincerity depends on the artifice of a sunset background, a wind machine, and a battery of mood lights, which together render the very picture of romance [Figure 6.14]. Yet the corresponding sound illusion is conjured without any visible sound recording or effects equipment, much less an onscreen orchestra. Indeed, each of Don's touches, such as switching on the wind machine, is synchronized with a nondiegetic musical flourish. It is possible to ask us to suspend our disbelief in this way because, in the film's world, music is everywhere.

The film pits the stilted, overblown style of silent costume drama against the rhythms of a vital, contemporary musical—a form so spontaneous that song even erupts backstage. In the "Make Them Laugh" sequence, Cosmo extemporizes a dance with props available on the set. When he begins to sing, an unseen orchestra starts up; when he takes a pratfall, cymbals crash in a parallel but asynchronous use of sound. The world in which illusions are made is itself illusory. In the course of the film, Don Lockwood will learn to incorporate his true self—the one who enjoys "singin' and dancin' in the rain"—into his onscreen persona. Lina Lamont (Jean Hagen), who represents image without the animating authenticity of sound (she's a beautiful woman with a comical accent, and ironically, her hilarious performance is one of the greatest aural pleasures of the film), will be replaced by Kathy, who dubs Lina's

voice. Kathy is depicted as genuine *because* she can sing. Image and sound go together.

Nothing illustrates the film's paradoxical acknowledgment of the sound–image illusions constructed by Hollywood and its indulgence in them better than the contrast between the disastrous premiere of the non-singing *The Dueling Cavalier* and the film's final scene at the opening night of the musical *The Dancing Cavalier*, in which the truth of Lina's imposture comes out. In the former, a noisy audience laughs at and heckles the errors of poor synchronous sound recording: the actors' heartbeats and rustling costumes drown out their dialogue (for us, of course, the laughter and the heartbeats are both sound effects, the latter mixed at comically high levels). The film they have created fundamentally misunderstands the promise of "talking pictures." Don's lines "I love you, I love you, I love you" are vapid and roundly mocked. The falseness is fully on display when the film goes out of sync: the villain nods his head as Lina's high-pitched "No, no, no" comes out. The potential deceptiveness of technology is mocked. At the premiere of the musical *The Dancing Cavalier*, in contrast, the film finally makes the proper match, not only between sound and image (thus correcting the humorous synchronization problems of the first version) but also between Don and Kathy. After she's forced to dub Lina "live" at the premiere, and the hoax is exposed when the curtains are drawn for all the audience to see [Figure 6.15], the humiliated Kathy runs from the stage. Don gets her back by singing "You Are My Lucky Star" to her from the stage (thus demonstrating before the audience in the film that unlike Lina, he used his own singing voice during the film within a film). Cosmo conducts the conveniently present

6.14 *Singin' in the Rain* (1952). The illusion of romance is visibly created on the soundstage, but the music the characters dance to has no apparent source.

6.15 *Singin' in the Rain* (1952). The dubbing deception is revealed.

6.16 *Singin' in the Rain* (1952). The film's final reflexive moment is accompanied by an invisible chorus on the soundtrack.

orchestra (the premiere is of a sound film that should not require accompaniment), and Kathy joins Don in a duet. The core characters finally have both a public stage for a "live" performance of their formerly behind-the-scenes musical and emotional sincerity.

Lest we read the film as suggesting that the on-screen orchestra is more genuine than the romantic background music of the earlier scenes because it is synchronous, we must note that the film ends triumphantly with asynchronous music. A full, invisible chorus picks up "You Are My Lucky Star" as the camera takes us out into the open air, to pause on the bill-

board announcing the premiere of *Singin' in the Rain*, starring Lockwood and Selden (who, of course, are represented by images of the stars of the movie by the same name that we are watching, Gene Kelly and Debbie Reynolds) **[Figure 6.16]**. This patently fake chorus and the billboard advertising the film we are watching are the culmination of the film's effort to render Hollywood illusionism—so aptly represented by extravagant musicals such as *Singin' in the Rain*—natural. *Singin' in the Rain* dramatizes the arrival of sound in Hollywood as the inevitable and enjoyable combination of sound and image.

a character and thus as arising from the narrative world of the film. Film theorist Christian Metz has classified these as **semidiegetic sound**; they can also be referred to as **internal diegetic sound**. The uncertain status of the dead character's voice-over in *Sunset Boulevard* (1950) is an example. Diegetic music—such as characters' singing of "Happy Birthday"—is often picked up as a nondiegetic theme in the film's score. Such borderline and mixed cases, rather than frustrating our attempts to categorize, are illustrative of the fluidity and creative possibilities of the sound-track as well as of the complex devices that shape our experience of a film's spatial and temporal continuity.

Sound Production

As early as the preproduction phase of a contemporary film, a **sound designer** may be involved to plan and direct the overall sound through to the final mix. During production, **sound recording** takes place simultaneously with the filming of a scene. When the slate is filmed at the beginning of each take, the **clapboard** is snapped; this recorded sound is used to synchronize sound recordings and camera images **[Figure 6.17]**. Microphones for recording synchronous sound (radio microphones) may be placed on the actors, suspended over the action outside of camera range on a device resembling a fishing pole called a **boom**, or placed in other locations on set. The placement of microphones is often dictated by the desire to emphasize clarity and intelligibility of dialogue, especially the speech of the stars, in the final version of a film. **Direct sound** is sound captured directly from its source, but some degree of **reflected sound**, captured as sounds bounce from the walls and sets, may be desired to give a sense of space. The production mixer (or sound recordist) combines these different sources during filming, adjusting their relative volume or balance. In the multitrack sound recording process, introduced in Robert Altman's *Nashville* (1975), as many as twenty-four separate tracks of sound can be recorded on twelve tracks.

When a cut of the film is prepared, the crucial and increasingly complex phase of **postproduction sound** work begins. **Sound editing** interacts with the image track to create rhythmic relationships, establish connections between sound and onscreen sources, and smooth or mark transitions. When a sound carries over a visual transition in a film, it is termed a **sound bridge**. For example, music might continue over a scene change or montage sequence, or dialogue might begin before the speaking characters are seen by the audience. The director consults with the composer and the picture and sound editors to determine where music and effects will be added, a process called **spotting**. Sound effects may be gathered, produced by sound-effects editors on computers, retrieved from a sound library, or generated by **foley artists**. Named for the legendary sound man Jack Foley, these members of the sound crew watch the projected film and simultaneously generate live sound effects—footsteps, the rustle of leaves, a key turning in a lock—on what is called a foley stage. These effects are eventually mixed with the other tracks. The film's composer begins composing the score, which is recorded to synchronize with the film's final cut [**Figure 6.18**]. The composer may actually conduct the musicians in time with the film. **Postsynchronous sound**, recorded after the fact and then synchronized with onscreen sources, is often preferred for the dialogue used in the final mix—natural sound recorded during production may be indistinct due to noise, perspective, or other problems, and much of the actor's performance will depend on intelligibility of dialogue.

During **automated dialogue replacement (ADR)**, actors watch the film footage and re-record their lines to be dubbed into the soundtrack (a process also known as **looping** because actors watch a continuous loop of their scenes). Although dubbing can violate verisimilitude, in Italy and other countries it is used for all of a film's dialogue. Dubbing often replaces the original language of a film for exhibition in another country. Other common practices, such as assembling extras to approximate the sound of a crowd (known as **walla**, the word they were instructed to murmur) or recording **room tone** (the aural properties of a location when nothing is happening), may be used to cover any patch of pure silence in the finished film. Such practices show the extent to which the sound unit goes to reproduce "real-seeming" sound.

Sound mixing (or re-recording), an important stage in the postproduction of a film, can occur only after the image track, including the credits, is complete (this is referred to as *locking picture*). All three elements of the soundtrack—music, sound effects,

6.17 **Production still,** *Oliver Twist* (1918). Clapboards are used to synchronize sound and image takes.

6.18 *Far from Heaven* (2002). Director Todd Haynes and composer Elmer Bernstein recording the film's score, which re-creates the sound of 1950s Hollywood movies.

6.19 *Barton Fink* (1991). Incorporating or exaggerating unusual sounds in the mix adds to the unreality of the film.

and dialogue—that have been recorded on separate tracks will now be combined. As the tracks are mixed, they are cut and extended, adjusted and "sweetened" by the sound editor with the input of the director and perhaps the sound designer and picture editor. There are no objective standards for a sound mix. Besides making sure it is complete and clear, the director and technicians will have specific ideas for the film's sound in mind. The final mix might place extra emphasis on dialogue, modulate a mood through the volume of the music, or punch up sound effects during an action sequence. In a film like *Barton Fink* (1991), much of the sense of inhabiting a slightly unreal world is generated by a sound mix that incorporates sounds such as animal noises into the effects accompanying creaking doors [**Figure 6.19**]. At a film's final **mix**, a sound mixer produces a master track to match the final cut of the film. Optical tracks are "married" to the image track on the film print, whereas digital tracks may be printed on the film or recorded on separate disks.

Sound reproduction is the stage in the process when the film's audience (literally, those who listen) experiences the film's sound. During projection, optical soundtracks are illuminated and read by a solar cell that transfers the light to electrical energy, which is then amplified and transferred to the speaker system. Magnetic and digital soundtracks are also converted back to sound waves by the sound system during projection.

The reproduction of a sound is undoubtedly a copy. But it seems to have the same presence or effect on the ear as the original sound, even if its source, directionality, tonality, or depth has changed. We believe we are hearing the sound right here, right now, and indeed we are, but we are hearing a recording of an airplane engine, not an actual airplane engine. Sound perspective enhances this impression of presence and can be manipulated with great nuance in digital sound mixing. The placement of speakers in the actual three-dimensional space of the theater may be used to suggest sounds emanating from the left or right of the depicted scene or from behind or in front of the audience.

▶ **VIEWING CUE**

In the film you've just viewed, from what direction do particular sounds come? Are the words of major actors the most audible elements of the film's sound mix? Is the mix full, or are there relatively few sounds? ⏸

Voice, Music, Sound Effects

Glengarry Glen Ross (1992), adapted by David Mamet from his own play, is dominated by the sound of actors' voices. *The Terminator* (1984) keys us to events in its futuristic world by noise, while the title of *The Sound of Music* (1965) announces what one can expect to hear on its **soundtrack**. Voice, music, and sound effects are the three elements of the film soundtrack, and they are often present simultaneously. In some sense a film's image track, composed of relatively discrete photographic images and text, is simpler and more unified. Nevertheless, although the three sound elements can all be present and combined in relation to any given image, conventions have evolved governing these relationships. Usually dialogue is audible over music, for example, and only in special cases does a piece of music dictate the images that accompany it. (Disney's *Fantasia* [1940] was an experiment in allowing the music to "go first.") Here we will examine each of the basic elements of the soundtrack and its potential to make meaning in combination with images and other sounds. We will uncover conventional usages of soundtracks and how they have both shaped the film experience and given direction to theorists' inquiries into the properties and potential of film sound.

Voice in Film

Human speech is often central to narrative film's intelligibility, primarily in the form of dialogue (film scenarios became known as scripts when there were words for the actors to say). Acoustic qualities of the voices of actors make a distinct contribution to a film: Jimmy Stewart's drawl is relaxed and reassuring; Robin Williams's cadences let us know we are watching something more antic and comic. But of course *what* actors say is crucial: speech establishes character motivation and goals and conveys plot information.

Making an intelligible record of an actor's speech quickly became the primary goal in early film sound recording processes, although this goal required some important concessions in the otherwise primary quest for realism. For example, think about how we hear film characters' speech. While the image track may cut from a long shot of a conversation to a medium shot of two characters to a series of close-up, shot/reverse-shot pairings, the soundtrack does not reproduce these distances accurately through changes in volume or the relationship between direct and reflected sound. Rather, actors are miked so that what they say is recorded directly and is clear, intelligible, and uniform in volume throughout the dialogue scene. **Sound perspective**, which refers to the apparent distance of a sound source, remains close.

Dialogue. A great deal of humor is derived from the depiction of early solutions to the miking of actors in *Singin' in the Rain*. First only every other word is caught as the actress Lina Lamont moves her head while speaking; then hiding the microphone in her bodice amplifies the sound of her heart, drowning out the words she speaks. Director Robert Altman's innovations in multitrack film sound recording in *Nashville*, mentioned earlier in this chapter, allowed each character to be miked and separately recorded. One stylistic feature of this technique is Altman's extensive use of **overlapping dialogue**, mixing characters' speech simultaneously, a technique Orson Welles had attempted with less sophisticated recording technology. In *Nashville*, characters constantly talk over each other [Figure 6.20]. This technique, which may make individual lines less distinct, is often used to approximate the everyday experience of hearing multiple, competing speakers and sounds at the same time. Dialogue is also given priority when it carries over visual shifts, such as shot/reverse-shot patterns of editing conversations. We watch one actor begin a line and then watch the listener as he or she continues. Sound preserves temporal continuity as the scene is broken down into individual shots. As commentators on film sound have noted, in the Western philosophical tradition speech is endowed with the capacity to signify presence, and films defer to this capacity. Speech occurs here and now, and thus it is a key support of verisimilitude. Sometimes the most outlandish plot premises and settings can be anchored by dialogue. Given the importance and authority we accord the spoken word, it is interesting that film sound often has second-class status in relation to the image.

The Voice-Off. The voice can be seen to originate from an onscreen speaker, or it may originate from a speaker who can be inferred to be present in the scene but who is not currently visible. This technique is referred to as **voice-off**, and it is a good example of the greater spatial flexibility of sound over image. The opening shot of *Laura* (1944) follows a detective looking around a fancy apartment as a **narrator**

6.20   *Nashville* (1975). Robert Altman's twelve-track recording process captures each character individually, and overlapping dialogue is used in the final mix.

6.21 *M* (1931). Use of offscreen sound and space imply the murderer's presence.

introduces the film's events. Abruptly, the same voice addresses the detective from an adjacent room, telling him to be careful what he touches, a striking use of voice-off. It may also be used in a genre such as the horror film to generate suspense. Early in the film *M* (1931), the murderer's offscreen whistle is heard, followed by an onscreen shadow of a man, combining the expressive possibility of sound (just recently introduced when the film was made) with that of lighting and mise-en-scène (which had already been available to silent cinema) [Figure 6.21].

In an experimental film, voice-off may also serve to make the viewer/listener think about different levels of the film's fiction. How do we know that an offscreen voice shares the same space and time as the onscreen figures? The soundtrack of Chantal Akerman's *News from Home* (1976) consists of the director's voice reading letters in French from her mother back home in Belgium [Figure 6.22]. The images depict sparsely populated New York streets and lonely subway platforms and cars. The disjunction between voice and image reinforces the distance remarked in the correspondence. In Jean-Luc Godard's *Two or Three Things I Know about Her* (1966), characters frequently address the camera directly as if they are being interviewed. In fact, they are responding to questions from Godard that are inaudible to us, but the lack of a voice-off makes the sequences function on a different level from that of the film's more obviously fictional (although equally verbose) episodes. A more conventional example of voice-off appears in *Sin City* (2005), where the voice of "Yellow Bastard" precedes the revelation of the disfigured body and so creates a more disturbing effect when the two are joined.

While use of the voice-off in a classical film is a strong tool in the service of film realism, implying that the mise-en-scène extends beyond the borders of the frame, the illusion of realism can be challenged if the origins of the voice-off are not clear. The voice-off of HAL 9000, the computer in *2001: A Space Odyssey* (1968), is consistent with realism because the voice has a known source. However, the even level of volume makes it seem to pervade the spaceship even as it retains its intimate quality. In the film's uncanny combination of humanity and technology, it suggests how the voice-off can introduce distance into the customary match of sound and image.

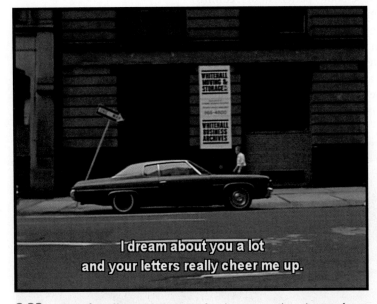

6.22 *News from Home* (1976). Letters from home are read over images of a lonely New York City.

The Voiceover. Although both are uses of the human voice whose source is not visible in the frame, a voice-off is distinguished from the familiar technique of **voiceover** by the simple fact that characters within the diegesis cannot hear the latter. The voiceover is an important structuring device in film: a text spoken by an offscreen narrator can act as the organizing principle behind virtually all of the film's images, such as in a documentary film, a commercial, or an experimental video or essay film. The unseen narrators of the classic documentaries *Night Mail* (1936) and *The Plow*

That Broke the Plains (1936) offer a poem about the British postal service and an account of the U.S. government's agricultural programs, respectively, while the filmmaker's voiceover in Alex Gibney's *Taxi to the Dark Side* (2007) offers a somber description of contemporary torture in Afghanistan and Guantánamo Bay [**Figure 6.23**]. The voiceover device soon became the cornerstone of the documentary tradition, in which the voiceover "anchors" the potential ambiguity of the film's images. The sonic qualities of such voiceovers—usually male, resonant, and "unmarked" by class, regional, or foreign accent or other distinguishing features—are meant to connote trustworthiness (although today they can sound propagandistic). The traditional technique of directing our interpretation of images through a transcendent voiceover is sometimes referred to as the "voice of God." A similar confident male voice can still be heard in nature shows, commercials, and trailers seen in movie theaters.

6.23 *Taxi to the Dark Side* (2007). The somber and matter-of-fact voiceover in this documentary makes the realities it describes seem even more disturbing.

In the newsreel segment early in *Citizen Kane,* Orson Welles emulates, and gently mocks, this genre's characteristic sound, in particular the March of Time series shown in movie theaters from 1935 to 1951. The volume even increases notably at the start of the segment to emphasize the voiceover's booming authority. This sanctioned story of Kane's life remains impersonal, in contrast to the multiple on-camera narrators whose recollections organize the film's other segments. In the introduction to *History of the World: Part I* (1981), Mel Brooks casts Orson Welles himself as God the narrator, parodying precisely the theological transcendence with which voiceovers have been associated. More recently, *Stranger than Fiction* (2006) plays with many of the traditional assumptions when the main character, IRS agent Harold Crick, suddenly begins to hear a voiceover narration describing and directing his life and ultimately confronts the female author-narrator, Karen Eiffel, convincing her to alter her plans for his death [**Figure 6.24**]. What at first seems like a nondiegetic voiceover suddenly becomes discovered within the diegesis.

Voiceover narration has multiple functions in fiction films. *The Royal Tenenbaums* (2001) begins with a "once upon a time" voiceover as a way of introducing the world of the story. Voiceovers can also render characters' subjective states. Much of the humor of *Bridget Jones's Diary* (2001), for instance, comes from viewers' access to the heroine's internal (semidiegetic) comments on the situations she encounters [**Figure 6.25**]. But voiceover can also be an important

6.24 *Stranger than Fiction* (2006). Here voiceover ironically appears within the protagonist's world.

6.25 *Bridget Jones's Diary* (2001). The subjective voiceover of this film humorously articulates the desires and anxieties of the heroine.

6.26 *Laura* (1944). Shown writing in a tub, Waldo Lydecker (Clifton Webb) opens the film with a voiceover narration. His account of the heroine's death proves him unreliable when she is discovered to be alive.

6.27 *Mildred Pierce* (1945). The voiceover of Mildred (played by Joan Crawford) increases our sympathy for her situation as a wife and mother in the flashback.

structural device in narration, orienting viewers to the temporal organization of a story by setting up a flashback or providing a transition back to the film's present. The sound and image tracks can relate to each other with considerable temporal complexity. For example, a voiceover narration in the present can accompany a scene from the past that uses both images and sounds from within the depicted world. Use of voiceovers to organize a film's temporality is prevalent in certain genres such as film noir, in which the voiceover imitates the hard-boiled, first-person investigative style of the literary works from which many of these stories are adapted. Sometimes, in keeping with the murky world of film noir or the limited perspective of the investigator, such voiceovers prove unreliable. For example, the account of the heroine's death given by the narrator's opening voiceover in *Laura* is contradicted later in the film when she proves to be alive [**Figure 6.26**]. At the end of *Laura,* the villain's offscreen voice is heard on a radio broadcast, tricking the characters about his whereabouts, a plot twist that seems to refer to this unreliability of the voice.

Michael Curtiz's *Mildred Pierce* (1945) is a "woman's film"—featuring a female star whose character faces exaggerated versions of the problems many women encounter—but it is given a film noir framework, and the voiceover is an important element in this clash of styles. In the beginning, Mildred (played by Joan Crawford) confesses to a crime we eventually learn she did not commit. However, her voiceover's credibility is compromised by her gender as well as by genre conventions. Several flashbacks are introduced by scenes in which Mildred is interrogated by the police. "It seems as if I was born in a kitchen," she narrates [**Figure 6.27**]. These voiceovers are quickly abandoned as the flashback segments revert to and play out in synchronized sound. Eventually Mildred's version of events is discredited by the police, who use her words to convict her daughter; her voiceover ultimately confirms their point of view. In fact, critics note that in **women's pictures** such as *Mildred Pierce* and Alfred Hitchcock's *Rebecca* (1940), female voiceovers rarely carry through to closure, violating the symmetry we have come to expect from a classical Hollywood film.

The authoritative connotations of the voiceover tradition have been modified by identifying the filmmaker's voice or introducing a voice with distinct, embodied qualities, what some theorists call "grain." When a filmmaker's own

VIEWING CUE

Identify specific uses of voice in the film you will screen next in class. Is dialogue abundant? If voiceovers are used, what are their function and diegetic status?

voiceover narration is used in a work that is autobiographical, or in one that reflects on the filmmaking process, it may increase documentary "truth" even as it eschews the objectivity the "voice of God" tradition once conveyed.

Talking Heads. Theorist Bill Nichols looks at the different ways the voices of filmmakers and subjects can be used in documentaries to discuss what he terms the "voice" of the film itself. At one end of the spectrum is the authoritative, anonymous voiceover that sets up and interprets the film's images. At the other, **talking heads**—on-camera interviews, usually shot in medium close-up—tell the documentary's story. In Lynne Fernie and Aerlyn Weissman's documentary about lesbian life in the 1940s to 1960s, *Forbidden Love* (1992), there is no voiceover, printed text, or on-camera presence to lead the viewer through the material. The interviewed subjects are the authorities. In between lies a spectrum of possibilities. In *Roger and Me* (1989), director Michael Moore's own voiceover is heard, and he interacts on camera with his subjects, while in other documentaries filmmakers may interview subjects on camera but not attempt to draw attention to themselves. In his documentary *Lumumba: Death of a Prophet* (1992), Raoul Peck speaks about the process of making his film, showing black **leader** (the strip attached to the beginning of a reel of film sometimes used to project a black image onscreen) as he speaks about how the images that he needs to tell his story about the controversial death of the African leader are missing. Given this broad spectrum, "voice," in Nichols's sense of the word, then refers to how the film's overall perspective correlates with the status of specific speakers in the film.

In their book *Unthinking Eurocentrism* (1994), Robert Stam and Ella Shohat introduce "voice" as an analytic category in order to challenge both the primacy of the visual in film theory and the Eurocentric perspective of film history. They argue that traces of non-European voices and cultures persist in documentaries and fiction films in such elements as music or performance styles. This dialogic, or double-voiced, quality means that films convey multiple messages. For example, a film like Spike Lee's *Do the Right Thing* (1989) relies as much on the verbal styles of its characters and the emotions and meanings of its music as on its visual elements, and neither of these levels is definitive.

Synchronization. Synchronization, the visible coordination of the voice with the body from which it is emanating, tends to be a valued practice in Hollywood films. It anchors sound that might otherwise seem to be autonomous or even call into question the seamless illusion of reality that Hollywood films strive for. Film theorist Kaja Silverman argues that synchronization is especially enforced for characters who are culturally more closely identified with the body, such as women and African Americans; these characters have not been allowed to achieve authoritative presence through speech alone. Thus Morgan Freeman's voiceover narration of *The Shawshank Redemption* (1994) is unusual precisely because it validates the experience of an African American character. *Eve's Bayou* (1997) is narrated by a child, a device that infuses the film with wonder and a sense of having to decipher the narrative; the fact that Eve is female and African American makes the film's emphasis on untold stories even more urgent [**Figure 6.28**].

Ever since "the talkies" were introduced, the human voice has organized systems of meaning in various types of film: narrative films are frequently driven by dialogue, documentaries by voiceover; and experimental films often turn voice into an aesthetic element. As noted above, some writers suggest that a theory of "voice" can open up cinema analysis to more meanings than a model devoted to the image alone. Although we have stressed how frequently film sound

TRANSFORMING FILM:
The Changing Role of Music

The significance of the role of music has shifted through movie history.

The pianos, organs, and even orchestras of silent film were often as much of an attraction as the movie itself.

The Girl Can't Help It (1956). Little Richard performs within the film story.

Beauty and the Beast (1991). The animated musical has resurged in recent decades.

Across the Universe (2007). Julia Taymor adapts Beatles tunes in an inventive musical about the 1960s.

6.28 *Eve's Bayou* (1997).
A little girl's version of events gains
credence by the voiceover device.

is subordinated to the image, certainly the realm of the voice shows us how central sound is to cinema's intelligibility. In fact, the prevalence of the human voice is a measure of just how focused the universe of classical cinema is on depicting human experience. From recording to mixing to reproduction, sound practices privilege the human subject. Contrasting a Hollywood drama with a film whose dialogue is dubbed demonstrates how sound mixing favors the human voice. The flatness of the postsynchronized sound used in dubbed films confirms our belief in a more "natural" way of syncing up voices and bodies. Ironically, the Hollywood soundtrack is likely to have used postsynchronized dialogue in the form of ADR, a technology that strives for an illusion more perfect than the original sound it replaces.

Music in Film

Music is a crucial element in the film experience; among a range of other effects, it provides rhythm and deepens emotional response. Music has rarely been absent from film programs, and many of the venues for early film had been musical ones first. The piano, an important element of public and private amusements at the turn of the twentieth century, quickly became a cornerstone of film exhibition. Throughout the silent film period, scoring for films steadily developed from the distribution of collections of music cues that accompanists and ensembles could play to correspond with appropriate moments in films to full-length compositions for specific films. When D. W. Griffith's *The Birth of a Nation* premiered in 1915, a full orchestra, playing Joseph Carl Breil's score in which the Ku Klux Klan rallied to Wagner's "Ride of the Valkyries," was a major audience attraction. The architecture of the large movie palaces constructed during this period was acoustically geared to audiences familiar with listening to orchestral music in a concert setting. *The Jazz Singer* and other early sound films were conceived to show off the musical performances of their stars. As mentioned previously, speech made it to the screen as an afterthought—and thus the introduction of dialogue presented problems of scale and volume in the movie palaces.

Although the term "talkies" for the new sound films soon took over, movies of every genre—westerns, disaster films, science fiction films—relied on music from the beginning. Often this music contributes to categorizing such films *as* genre films. Vangelis's music for *Blade Runner* (1982), for example, distinctly marks it as a science fiction film. In contrast, Max Steiner's score for *Gone with the Wind* (1939) sets its nostalgic, romantic tone.

Narrative Music. When we think about the conventions of film sound, background music comes most immediately to mind. Music is the only element of cinematic discourse besides credits that is primarily nondiegetic. It can also move easily back and forth from the level of the story world to the nondiegetic level on which that world can be commented upon. In the back of our minds, we are aware that the practice of scoring films with music that has no source in the story violates verisimilitude, and yet we readily accept this convention. The gag in Mel

Brooks's *Blazing Saddles* (1974), in which the musical soundtrack turns out to be coming from Count Basie's jazz orchestra playing in the middle of the desert, is entertaining because it shows the absurdity of the convention [Figure 6.29]. Occasionally we are jolted out of absorption in a film because the music is simply too overblown, its commentary on the action too obvious. Nevertheless, normally we value the musical score as a crucial element of our affective, or emotional, response to a film. The scoring for narrative films thus presents a notable paradox: much of what is valued in classical cinema—verisimilitude, cause-and-effect relationships—is completely ignored in even the most admired examples of film music.

6.29 *Blazing Saddles* (1974). Soundtrack music finds its onscreen source in Count Basie's orchestra playing in a desert in Mel Brooks's spoof.

The conventions of musical scoring, composition, orchestration, and mixing contribute to a particular kind of experience at the movies. Film music encourages us to be receptive to the information being conveyed by the visual as well as by the other acoustic dimensions of the film. It opens us to experience the movie as immediate and enveloping. It encourages us to let our barriers down. Many commentators speculate that these effects are psychologically related to the fact that the earliest human sensory experience is auditory. Because music is nonrepresentational—it is not a copy of something specific in the world the way an image is—it can be more suggestive. Set apart from the diegesis and taking place right there in the theater, music eases our transition into the fictional world.

Because many of the practices of musical scoring were developed in tandem with the dominant form of narrative film, we will focus this discussion on narrative film music. In Hollywood and related mainstream film practices, the musical score has a direct connection to the story. However complex or lush it may be, it serves a dramatic purpose. The term **underscoring**, also referred to as *background music* (in contrast to source music, which is diegetic), already emphasizes this status. Music quite literally underscores what is happening dramatically. A piece of music composed for a particular place in a film is referred to as a **cue**. When recording the score, the conductor watches the film for the cue to begin playing that particular piece of music. Often music reinforces story information through recognizable conventions. Action sequences in the *Indiana Jones* series are introduced by the inescapable "dum da-dum dum" as a parody of and a tribute to these recognizable themes. Through the use of motifs, themes assigned to particular figures, music also participates in characterization. We know when the main character has entered the scene not only visually but also aurally, because principal characters usually have a musical motif. The presence of "bad girl" Marylee Hadley in *Written on the Wind* (1956) is signaled by a distinctive sultry theme. Most notably, music is subordinate to that part of the narrative that competes in the realm of sound—the dialogue. A music cue will usually be audible during sequences in which there is no dialogue, often helping to smooth a spatial or temporal transition. When dialogue predominates, however, it will fade, its volume will drop, or it will change to be less "competitive."

Composers for classical cinema, such as Erich Korngold, Dimitri Tiomkin, and Max Steiner, generated their own set of musical styles to suit the accepted function of film music, and many of these principles are still dominant in contemporary practice. In Steiner's more than three hundred scores, including those for *King Kong*, *Gone with the Wind*, *Now, Voyager* (1942), and *Mildred Pierce*, musical accompaniment was notable for being almost continuous. He composed using a **click track**—holes punched in the film to keep the beat of the action—and his style was highly illustrative, emphasizing what happens on the screen through music.

Much of Hollywood film music composition is derived from nineteenth-century, late romantic orchestral music. Here the term "classical" is undoubtedly appropriate for studio-era Hollywood style, for popular music was rejected in favor of classical music. The work of such composers as Wagner and Strauss was rich in its ability to convey narrative information; reliant on compositional principles such as motifs assigned to different characters, settings, or actions; and lushly emotive, tonal, and euphonic. As such, it was perfectly suited to the musical experience that Hollywood was striving for with the integration of sound. This type of music was compatible with Hollywood storytelling not only because of its purely musical qualities but also because of the associations and values this music carried for audiences. These associations ranged from the high cultural status conferred on symphonic music of European origin (as opposed to the status of American jazz or pop) to the recognizable connotations of a particular instrumentation, such as somber horns for a funereal mood, violins for romance, and a harp for an ethereal or heavenly mood.

In her book *Unheard Melodies: Narrative Film Music* (1987), Claudia Gorbman lists the "principles of composition, mixing, and editing" that classical film music follows. The first is invisibility, which refers to the predominance of nondiegetic music (over the actual depiction of musicians) and to the fact that the technical apparatus that produces film music, like the camera and the projector responsible for the image we see, is never seen. The boom mikes visible in a film like *Red Rock West* (1992) violate this principle and are clearly accidental. The principle of inaudibility is analogous to the "invisible" editing style of the continuity system. This principle dictates that conscious attention not be paid to the score. Volume does not interfere with dialogue, the mood and rhythm of the music do not contradict those of the action, and compositions are matched to the narrative flow rather than allowed to follow their own progression. Ironically, screen music is at its best if we do not "hear" it.

6.30 *Spellbound* (1945). Gregory Peck's character is stricken by an episode of vertigo, signaled by the theremin on the soundtrack.

Gorbman next stresses film music's function as a signifier of emotion. Dialogue and action fall short in their capacity to convey not only particular feelings but also the experience of feeling itself. Music is subjective, whereas the image is perceived as objective. A close-up of the heroine's face matched with a great swell of music in *Now, Voyager*, a convention readily seen today in the soap opera, provides a good example of how music supplements visuals when emotions are at stake. Gorbman isolates three common ways music's connotation of emotion are used. First, music conveys the irrational. In Hitchcock's *Spellbound* (1945), for example, the mental state of the hero is conveyed by the sound of the theremin, an unusual electronic instrument whose spooky sound is also used in science fiction films [Figure 6.30]. Second, music is associated with women, who are already culturally associated with emotion. Our pejorative idea of sappy music is derived from the sound of women's genres, where tears and musical notes fall with the same abundance. The music accompanying a brief scene in an empty bedroom in Gillian Armstrong's *Little Women* (1994) gives the viewer time to cry after Beth's death. Third, lush orchestration ennobles the ordinary and makes the specific timeless. In *The Cider House Rules* (1999), the milestones of one young man's coming of age are made grand by Rachel Portman's score.

The next principle Gorbman discusses, narrative cueing, refers to how music tells us what is happening in the plot. It is heavily relied on in classical scores. Cues may be denotative: a return of the main theme signifies that *Gone with the Wind* is about to conclude; a western song over the credits of *Rancho Notorious* (1952) signifies the setting of a film of that genre. Narrative cueing is also connotative: violins on the soundtrack may indicate that the characters are falling in love; a few notes of "Deutschland über alles" in the score of *Casablanca* (1942) signifies the looming Nazi threat. Music's role in relation to narrative may be to point something out or emphasize its significance; the most noticeable examples are called **stingers**, sounds that force us to notice the significance of something onscreen, such as the ominous chord struck when the villain's presence is made known. The highly effective soundtrack of *The Shining* (1980) includes a stinger when a mirror held up to letters written backwards on the wall reveals the word "murder." Scores can also musically imitate what happens on the screen—a soufflé falls, a doorbell rings. Overillustrating the action through the score, such as accompanying a character walking on tip-toe with plucked strings, is referred to as **mickey-mousing**. (This term is a reference to the way cartoons often use the musical score to follow or mimic every action in synchronization, narrating through music rather than language.) Max Steiner is particularly noted for his habit of pointing out everything in his soundtracks in this manner.

We have already indicated how important the soundtrack as a whole is to a film's continuity, another principle of film music. Continuity is also valued in the music itself. Discontinuities in visual information represented by cuts and scene changes are frequently bridged by the durational aspect of sound, and this function is most easily served by music. Various arrangements of the theme song of *High Noon* (1952) carry characters across space and help bridge transitions between scene changes. Critics of studio-style film music complain that the composer's job involves nothing more than filling up any gaps in the film with the soundtrack.

Gorbman notes that musical scores follow the principle of unity, which is also a basic tenet of classical film style. Composing a score around themes provides built-in unity through its structure of repetition and variation. Often critics attribute the classical film score's stress on unity to the influence of composer Richard Wagner's notion of the *Gesamtkunstwerk*, or "total work of art." Finally, Gorbman concludes her list of principles for narrative film scores with the acknowledgment that any one of these rules may be violated, but only, she emphasizes, in the service of another rule. Her list of points is extremely helpful in identifying what makes narrative film scores, despite considerable range, so consistent and recognizable.

Although musical scoring conventions have evolved and changed since the classical era of studio filmmaking, we can hear in the orchestral scores of John Williams, the most well-known composer of films of the 1980s and 1990s, an homage to the romantic styles of the studio composers of earlier decades. Williams composes heroic, nostalgic scores that support and sometimes inflate the narrative's significance in films from *Star Wars* (1977) to *Home Alone* (1990). His five Academy Awards and more than forty nominations suggest that the film industry recognizes his style's consistency with Hollywood studio practice.

In Hollywood cinema of the studio era, nonclassical musical styles, such as jazz, popular, and dance music, might be used as source music and featured in

6.31 **Lena Horne**. Most of the actress's appearances in mainstream films were restricted to cameo numbers.

musicals, but their incorporation into background music was gradual. One of the effects of the neglect of American musical idioms in favor of European influences was that African American artists and performers were rendered almost as inaudible as they were invisible in mainstream movies. African American performers were frequently featured in musicals, but they were there to provide entertainment and were rarely integrated into the narrative. Lena Horne's talent, for example, was shamefully underutilized because there were almost no leading roles for African American women in the 1940s and 1950s [Figure 6.31].

As jazz music became more popular, jazz themes began to appear in urban-based film noirs of the 1940s. Henry Mancini's music for Orson Welles's *Touch of Evil* (1958) effectively connotes themes of crime, violence, and sexuality in the exaggerated border-town setting. Occasionally dissonance appeared in studio scores, but usually only when diegetically motivated—for example, to signify a psychological disturbance. In keeping with this connotation, the first atonal score was composed by Leonard Rosenman for *The Cobweb* (1955), a movie set in a home for the mentally ill. With other changes in the U.S. film industry in the postwar period, musical conventions shifted as well. Modernist and jazz-influenced scores, such as Leonard Bernstein's score for *On the Waterfront* (1954), became more common as different audiences were targeted through more individualized filmmaking practices. At the end of the studio era, the great tradition of the Hollywood musical also began to wane, but a closer look at the genre will underscore how central music is to the narrative film experience, even at the cost of verisimilitude.

The Hollywood Musical. It was fitting that the last effort of the studios to dominate movie screens was the big-budget, spectacular musical, because in many ways the musical epitomizes Hollywood entertainment. Despite the phenomenal success of *The Sound of Music* in 1965, however, further attempts at studio-produced blockbuster musicals, such as *Doctor Dolittle* (1967) and Francis Ford Coppola's *Finian's Rainbow* (1968), were box-office disappointments, their failures indicative of a change in movie culture.

The musical had been a perennial favorite, from the early sound era's backstage musicals featuring elaborate Busby Berkeley numbers [Figure 6.32] to later musicals that integrated songs and narrative, such as *An American in Paris* (1951). Rogers and Hammerstein's *Oklahoma!* (1955) formed abiding myths of the U.S. character. The musical genre often followed the principles of classical narrative film scoring with the addition of production numbers that positively reveled in film music's audibility. The opening tune of Rouben Mamoulian's early sound film *Love Me Tonight* (1932) is picked up by character after character, as if they can all actually hear the background music. The manner in which music connotes emotion or "spirit" in Hollywood films is perhaps best illustrated by the musical genre, in which this feeling erupts in a story world where song and dance are expected.

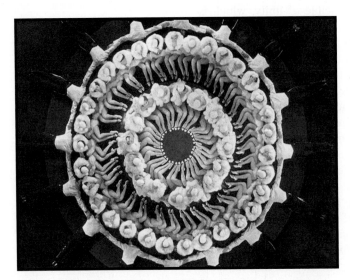

6.32 ***42nd Street*** (1933). Busby Berkeley choreographed outrageous musical numbers designed for the unique perspective afforded by the movie camera.

Even as the studios tried to prolong their dominance with spectacular musicals, Richard Lester's films with the Beatles, *A Hard Day's Night* (1964) and *Help!* (1965), successfully revised the genre for an era geared toward youth and dominated by popular music. At the end of the twentieth century, films from directors notable for their stylization, such as Todd Haynes's *Velvet Goldmine* (1998), the Coen brothers' *O Brother, Where Art Thou?* (2000), Lars von Trier's *Dancer in the Dark* (2000), and Baz Luhrmann's *Moulin Rouge!* (2001), updated the genre. But by this time, songs had found their way onto soundtracks through means that often did not require the suspension of disbelief demanded by the often-utopian world of the musical.

Prerecorded Music. Popular songs have long had a place in the movies, promoting audience participation and identification by appealing to tastes shared by generations or ethnic groups. Sheet music and recordings sales were profitable tie-ins even before sound cinema. In the 1980s, however, the practice of tying the affective (and commercial) response of the audience to popular music on a film's soundtrack was so well established that the pop score began to rival originally composed music. *American Graffiti* (1973) helped inaugurate this trend with its soundtrack of nostalgic 1960s tunes, and *The Big Chill* (1983) captures the zeitgeist of its characters' and viewers' generation through popular music. The centrality of prerecorded music is reflected in the increasing importance of the **music supervisor**, who selects and secures the rights for songs to be used in films. In youth-oriented, MTV-influenced films with pop music scores, such as *Save the Last Dance* (2001), the promotion of the soundtrack is as important as that of the film [Figure 6.33]. In the 1990s, the proliferation of the pop soundtrack drew the film experience outside the theater to the record store, and music videos began to include scenes from upcoming films. Although theme songs have been composed for and promoted with films for decades, as in *Love Is a Many-Splendored Thing* (1955) to name one hit, the contemporary movie and recording industries have such close business relationships that even films without pop soundtracks often feature a tie-in song in their end-credits sequences. The extremely successful film careers of musicians like rapper-actor Will Smith demonstrate the increasing symbiosis of these entertainment media.

 VIEWING CUE

As you watch the film for your next class, pay particular attention to its music. Is the film's score drawn from the classical tradition? Is popular music used? How do scoring choices contribute to the film's meaning?

Sound Effects in Film

Although the movies can represent the world in many ways, their capacity for successful mimesis, or imitation, has always fascinated audiences. Much of the mimetic impression in cinema comes from the use of sound effects, although like other aspects of the soundtrack they may not be consciously noticed by viewers. Dialogue in film is deliberate; it tells a story and gives information. Background music is a clear enhancement, "unrealistic" if we pay attention to it. But sound effects appear unmanufactured, even accidental. This sense of the naturalness of effects is ironic because the sound texture of a film is so deliberately crafted and because in daily life we hardly notice such ubiquitous sounds as fluorescent lights humming, crickets chirping, and traffic going by—sounds that might be added to achieve a "realistic" sound mix.

6.33   *Save the Last Dance* (2001). The promotion of a film's soundtrack has become crucial for its success.

In most films, every noise that we hear is selected, and these effects generally conform to our expectations of movie sounds. Virtually nothing appears on-screen that does not make its corresponding noise: dogs bark, babies cry. A spaceship that blows up in outer space will usually produce a colossal bang even though in fact there is no sound in space. If a recording of a .38 revolver sounds like a cap gun on film, it will be dubbed with a louder bang. These expectations vary according to film genre. Traffic noise will be loud in an action film, in which we remain alive to the possibilities of the environment. In a romance, the sound of cars will likely fade away unless traffic is keeping the lovers apart. The extraordinary density of contemporary soundtracks does not necessarily mean that they are more "realistic" than the less dense soundtracks of classical Hollywood; they simply make more extensive use of the particular properties of sound to convey a visceral experience of the cinema. The change in the texture of contemporary soundtracks is based in new technological capabilities, but, as in other instances of "improved" technologies, this progress is not inevitable but rather a development that follows particular ideas and goals, although these are likely to remain unstated.

Sound effects are one of the most useful ways of giving an impression of depth to the two-dimensional image when they are reproduced in the three-dimensional space of the theater. Although the screen is itself only an illusory space of action, film presentation makes use of the directional properties of sound—a gunshot may come from the lefthand side of the screen, for example. In the mix, additional diegetic sounds such as thunderclaps can be added that were not present on set at all, adding significantly to a film's illusionism. Asynchronous sound effects, such as the hoot of an owl in a dark-woods setting, both expand the sense of space and contribute to mood, often in very codified, even clichéd ways. Adding the clank of utensils and snatches of offscreen conversation to the soundtrack when two characters are shown at a table conjures a restaurant setting without having to shoot the scene in one.

The very manner in which noises are produced for a soundtrack illustrates their function in constructing, rather than reproducing, a particular experience. As we detailed earlier, incidental sounds—footsteps, the rustle of clothing, a punch in the stomach—are not even recorded at the same time as the film's dialogue. Rather, they are added later by the **foley artist** by walking on gravel, rubbing together different pieces of fabric, hitting a rolled-up telephone book, and so on. Our acceptance of these simulated synchronous sounds testifies to the strength of our impulse to perceive effects realistically. The process is a meticulous reconstruction of some but not all of the sounds that would have been present on set. The sounds selected are those that are deemed significant, if only because they establish a particular mood. Dramatic effects such as explosions are quite deliberately placed, and often enhanced, because of their narrative significance.

At the same time that they serve a mimetic function, sound effects have become part of how the cinema experience is distinguished from the ordinary. THX is a standards system devised by director George Lucas and named after his first feature film, *THX 1138* (1971), for evaluating and ensuring the quality of sound presentation. THX theaters promise to deliver an intense aural experience that is identical in each certified venue. Sound effects, like visual effects, draw in viewers. How crucial a film's sound is to the Hollywood illusion is marked in the relatively recent Academy Award category for sound effects editing. Audiences are increasingly trusted to discern things aurally. In the films of master action film director John Woo, for example, each character may have a particular gunshot noise assigned to him or her so that the action can be followed throughout a protracted sequence without dialogue. The distinctive soundtrack of *Jaws* (1975) lent us not only what has now become the cliché of the shark's musical motif but also a rich new standard of sound-effects use. The film acknowledges a predecessor in the genre—and

▶ **VIEWING CUE**

To what extent do sound effects add to the film's sense of realism? Can you locate an example in which sound effects are primarily responsible for creating a particular impression of location, action, or mood?

```
          SHREK
       (loud belch)
Buuurrrpppp!

          DONKEY
       (admonishing)
Shrek!

          SHREK
What?!  It's a compliment.  Better out
than in, I always say.

          DONKEY
Well it's no way to behave in front of a
princess.

          FIONA
       (belches)
Buuurp!
```

6.34a and 6.34b *Shrek* (2001). In most animated films, soundtracks and dialogue are prepared in advance of the animations.

in the ingenious use of sound—when the death of the shark is accompanied by a sound effect of a prehistoric beast's death from *King Kong.* In these monster movies, sound effects take us beyond everyday events while also relying on their capacity to refer to familiar experience.

As with music, the animated film illustrates the deliberately designed nature of film sound effects particularly well. In fact, most cartoon soundtracks are prepared in advance of the images, the reverse of live-action filmmaking [**Figure 6.34a and 6.34b**]. Cartoons thus demonstrate especially well the synchronization of sound effects to onscreen actions. Drawings do not "naturally" make sounds of their own; every sound in an animated film is conventionalized. In *Duck Amuck* (1953), for example, Daffy Duck is baffled by the cartoon he finds himself in and cannot follow the logic of his mischievous animator. All sorts of mishaps befall him, and the abrupt termination of the soundtrack is one of the most disturbing of these mishaps. So unused are we to complete silence, that we are likely to look around us to see whether the theater's sound system really has gone out. Daffy holds up a sign demanding "Sound please!" and begins to play the guitar with which his animator has provided him. But the sound it "emits" is that of a machine gun, demonstrating with this synchronization error the arbitrary nature of the standard of matching image and sound. As Daffy's misadventures suggest, sound effects appeal to the audience subtly and viscerally.

The Signficance of Film Sound

The sounds of the film experience build on viewers' everyday social and leisure activities to contribute to the movies' immediacy and sensory richness. Whether it is the pathos lent by Louis Gottschalk's score for D. W. Griffith's *Broken Blossoms* (1919), the stimulating interactions between the musical quotations of *2001: A Space Odyssey* and Alex North's original music for the film, the indelible aural record of Laurence Olivier's performance of *Hamlet* (1948), or the comical sounds of Jacques Tati's *Playtime,* movie soundscapes intensify our experience of what the world sounds like while attesting to sound's power to convey what seem like essential truths and meanings.

text continued on page 214 ▶

Subjectivity through Sound in *The Piano* (1993)

The fact that Jane Campion's film—a tale of a nineteenth-century woman who travels from Scotland to New Zealand with her young daughter to marry a man she's never met—takes its title not from the central character but from an object, a musical instrument, cues us in to the importance of sound in this film. The heroine Ada McGrath's grand piano, which she transports on her long journey, is a central element in the film's plot and mise-en-scène. It is no surprise that piano music on the soundtrack echoes this importance, carrying a great deal of the film's emotion, sensuality, and drama. Because Ada is mute, our understanding of voice as a medium of subjectivity extends to the metaphor of music as voice, powerfully conveying the story of a headstrong woman shaping her own experience. In addition, sound effects are used expressively to make Ada's psychological experience accessible to us.

Although Ada cannot speak, the film paradoxically begins with her voiceover: "The voice you hear is not my speaking voice; it is my mind's voice." This innovative use of the voiceover device allows us access to Ada's inner world even before we have seen her, powerfully connecting us to her subjectivity. The voiceover will not return until the very end of the film, when she speaks of the silence of her piano, lying at the bottom of the sea, as a "weird lullaby" [Figure 6.35]. In the interim, Ada's "voice" makes itself heard through written notes and sign language, which her daughter, Flora, translates so that others can understand. Flora also uses her own voice to express a will as strong as her mother's. She makes up stories to shock the women in their new town, and she eventually reveals to her step-father, Stewart, that her mother is having an illicit affair. Ada's lover, George Baines, the overseer on her husband's plantation, indicates another level of the film's use of voice by speaking with the Maori in their own language.

Ada's voiceover declares, "I don't think of myself as silent because of my piano." She speaks most directly and expressively through her music. When Ada and Flora first arrive in New Zealand, they are stranded on the beach overnight. Ada breaks open the piano's wooden crate just enough to reach in to play with one hand. The music fills the soundtrack, although we hear the sound effects of a key plunking and of waves lapping at the shore in the mix. The piano is associated with Ada's desire and individuality and with the freedom of the seascape. As she is led away by her husband the next day, the piano is temporarily abandoned on the beach. Ada looks back at the instrument, and her visual point of view is accompanied by nondiegetic music, which then provides continuity during the shots of their progress

6.35 *The Piano* (1993). The mute heroine's voiceover describes the piano's underwater grave.

6.36 *The Piano* (1993). Nondiegetic music accompanies the heroine's thoughts of her piano.

6.37 *The Piano* (1993). The music seems to conjure this insert of the piano, abandoned on the beach.

across the lush but difficult terrain, always connecting her back to the piano on the beach even when she can no longer see it. Later, during a rainstorm, Ada goes to the window of her new home, and we see a shot of the piano on the beach [Figures 6.36 and 6.37]. This is not a literal point-of-view shot but a subjective insert. The nondiegetic piano music that accompanies the shot reprises the piece Ada had begun on the beach, following the principle of unity. As space seems to be transcended by the soundtrack, the close interplay between nondiegetic and diegetic music helps to make Ada the subjective center of the film.

The Piano's nineteenth-century setting motivates the use of a romantic musical idiom that functions, as it would in the score of a classical Hollywood film, to signify emotion. For example, in the dramatic scene in which her husband brutally punishes Ada for her affair with Baines, music swells (the theme from her journey away from the beach), only to terminate abruptly when Flora screams out, "Mother!" Interestingly, however, the music Ada plays is not by well-known nineteenth-century composers but her own original compositions. This strengthens both the metaphor of music as voice and its association with female transgression in the film. As a town busybody comments, "She does not play music as we play it. . . . To have a sound creep inside you is not at all pleasant." Early in the film, Baines takes Ada back to the beach and to her piano. Music comes in as a sound bridge before the scene transition. We then see Ada playing on the beach, as the sounds of waves, birds, and Flora's voice reinforce the fact that the music is now diegetic. Although these sound effects add realism, they also have psychological dimensions, conveying Ada's passion as well as her connections with her daughter and with the wildness of the waves and the freedom of birds in flight. It gets dark; Flora joins Ada at the keyboard, but the music remains continuous over the ellipsis.

After witnessing this scene, Baines purchases the piano from Stewart and makes a proposition to Ada. In exchange for erotic favors, he will give the piano back to her, key by key. Music remains associated with eroticism when their attraction becomes mutual. Ada's husband eventually catches her with Baines (he overhears and then spies on them). But what the film shows us at this point is a scene in which reciprocal passion, removed from Baines's initial objectification and Stewart's voyeurism, is indicated by the beautiful nondiegetic piano accompaniment.

Throughout *The Piano*, the heroine's point of view and audio perspective are central. This is powerfully conveyed by the soundtrack even though Ada never uses the synchronized speech that is usually associated with characters' desires and intentions. The film's soundscape is filled with the rich noises of the New Zealand landscape. The suck of mud on the characters' shoes combines with the rustle of petticoats. Birds sing and screech, rain and wind clamor for attention. These wild elements are associated with Ada's wildness and the sharpness of her hearing. When she leaves Stewart and orders her piano thrown overboard, these sounds culminate with quiet, mysterious underwater noises as she herself is pulled into the sea. She breaks free and surfaces as her voiceover returns to narrate the film's ending. She has followed her desires; she and Flora go to live with Baines, and she teaches piano and begins learning to speak. But most important, the music Ada feels compelled to play—when she hears Baines is leaving, when she walks in her sleep—and the music that accompanies significant moments in the film, assisting transitions and narration, are associated with her own will and sensuality. In a medium that often visually objectifies women, Campion uses soundtrack elements to endow her heroine with subjectivity.

VIEWING CUE

Isolate a particular scene in which sound seems especially responsible for conveying information to the spectator. How do voice, music, and sound effects work together?

Authenticity and Experience

While vision depends on an objective distance between the viewer and the viewed, sound comes to meet us. Although we traditionally place a premium on seeing over the other senses, as in "seeing is believing," we can also express a strong current of mistrust: "the eyes deceive." Hearing can then seem more reliable, especially when it is associated with the voice. The voice comes from within, and this interiority gives it depth and authenticity. We tend to trust what we hear, to enter into the perceptual experience fully. Film sound, because it seems to permeate the body of the viewer in a way that images alone cannot, contributes to the authenticity and emotion we experience while viewing a film. Sound in film can indicate a real, multidimensional world and give the viewer/listener the impression of being authentically present in space. Additionally, sound encourages the viewer to experience emotion, depending on the kind of sound, such as a particular piece of music.

The assumption that sound gives the viewer/listener the impression of being authentically present in space is supported by the preferences established in the standard techniques of sound recording, mixing, and reproduction. As previously mentioned, though the cinematic images and sounds that we see and hear were both captured at some other moment and are being reproduced for us, sounds feel immediate. Hearing the taps on Eleanor Powell's shoes in *Born to Dance* (1936) makes us witnesses to her virtuosity [**Figure 6.38**]. Foregrounding actors' voices through close miking and sound perspective and mixing that emphasizes dialogue also authenticates our perception. We are "in on" the characters' most intimate conversations. Sounds that are synchronized with the action by the depiction of their sources in the image, or even sounds that support the action while not being themselves "authentic"—for example, background music—all give us a central place in the fictional world that begins to seem present and real. The zither theme of *The Third Man* (1949) makes us feel disoriented in the streets of postwar Vienna, just as the film's characters are.

Sound encourages the viewer to experience emotion and to see the world in terms of particular emotions. Sound tends to connote interiority and the ineffable. When the lovers in *Now, Voyager* cannot really say what they mean to each other, the string section, performing Max Steiner's score, eloquently takes over. Sound reaches the viewer viscerally, seeming to involve the body directly. Excruciating suspense is generated in *Jurassic Park* when we hear the sound of the menacing tyrannosaurus rex [**Figure 6.39**]. Simply watching the dinosaur progress would be a less emotional experience.

The film environment attempts to duplicate our acoustic experience of the world, to orient us in this new

VIEWING CUE

How does the soundtrack of the next film you view "authenticate" the image? Would the absence of sound affect the film's authenticity? How?

6.38 *Born to Dance* (1936). Eleanor Powell's tap dancing is a perfect display of synchronized sound.

6.39 *Jurassic Park* (1993). On the digital soundtrack, the T-Rex's footsteps can be heard approaching the truck where the children are hiding, generating keen suspense.

space in a way that feels genuine and genuinely gets us to *feel*. This is not necessarily measured by strict realism. The sense of presence at the dance contest in *Saturday Night Fever* (1977) is better achieved through a sound mix that sacrifices background noise to focus on the Bee Gees' music.

Although film sound can have a great deal of complexity, and realism is thrown out the window every time background music appears, authenticity and emotion are often served by a subordination of the autonomy of sound to the cues given by the image. In contrast to this practice of sound–image continuity, however, a competing approach explores the concrete nature of sounds and their potential independence of the images and of each other. This practice of sound montage, which characterizes the films of Jean-Luc Godard and others, does not *serve* the values of authenticity and emotion; rather, it makes us conscious of their violation by calling attention to the actual sound recording process or asking us to be aware of and reflect on emotional cues.

VIEWING CUE

How is emotion introduced to the viewing experience through the qualities of a particular sound?

Sound Continuity and Sound Montage

Sound continuity describes the range of scoring, sound recording, mixing, and playback processes that strive for the unification of meaning and experience by subordinating sound to the aims of the narrative. **Sound montage** reminds us that just as a film is built up of bits and pieces of celluloid, a soundtrack is not a continuous gush of sound from the real world; rather, it is composed of separate elements whose relationship to each other can be creatively manipulated and reflected upon. The theme song from *Doctor Zhivago* (1965) is extremely lush and romantic, but it reinforces the big emotions of the film's characters at appropriate points in the plot and thus achieves continuity. In Andrei Tarkovsky's *Nostalgia* (1983), though the sound of an electric saw can be heard at different times and in different settings, the source is never revealed. This ambiguous sound functions as an element of montage. Most assumptions, shared by technicians and viewers, about what constitutes a "good" soundtrack emphasize a continuity approach. However, since the introduction of sound, many filmmakers have used it as a separate element for a montage effect. With the increasing sophistication of audio technology, it is possible that sound montage will find more practitioners.

Analyzing a film that adheres to sound continuity can be rewarding precisely because really hearing the soundtrack demands such attentiveness. As we have seen, matching up actors' voices with their moving lips and ensuring the words are intelligible were among the early goals of sound technology. Audiences were thrilled just to *see* the match. Despite our familiarity with film sound today, the degree of redundancy between image and sound in the continuity tradition still makes it difficult to analyze the soundtrack autonomously. From the priority granted to synchronization, we can define several compatible continuity practices:

- The relationship between image and sound and among separate sounds is motivated by dramatic action or information.
- With the exception of background music, the sources of sounds will be identifiable.
- The connotations of musical accompaniment will be consistent with the images (for example, a funeral march is unlikely to accompany a high-speed chase).
- The sound mix will emphasize what we should pay attention to.
- The sound mix will be smooth and will emphasize clarity.

Films that adhere to the principles of verisimilitude will use sound to amplify, as it were, what is taking place on the screen. Attention will be directed back to the characters, actions, and mise-en-scène by sound that supports it. In *The Big Sleep* (1946), a conversation in a car between the two protagonists, Marlowe and Vivian, begins with engine noise in the background. We see that there is a dog on the porch in the opening scene of *The Searchers* (1956), but when we hear it bark, the image comes alive. The relationship between image and sound and among separate sounds will also be motivated by dramatic action or information. In *The Big Sleep,* the engine noise will soon disappear so we can focus on the characters' avowal of love. The continuous use of music to cover a sequence of character activity draws our attention away from discontinuity in the image track. For example, continuous orchestral music links the "training montage" in *Rocky Balboa* (2006).

It may be easier to think of what sound continuity seeks to avoid than what it positively pursues. Sound should not intrude on the narrative. Unmotivated or unidentified sounds will not have a prominent place on the soundtrack. Nor will unidentified speakers be heard, unless in a conventional context such as a documentary, in which the voiceover explanation will demonstrate its own continuity with the content of the image. Characters' speech will not break with the diegesis to offer commentary or non sequiturs. Technology and techniques have developed in consort with these aims. Dolby noise-reduction technology improves frequency response and gives an almost unnatural clarity. Noise interferes with the sound signal and can call attention to the fact that the sound was recorded and, thus, to how the film was made. These are goals of continuity rather than of strict realism. As film scholar John Belton has observed, film conventions have developed in accordance with what the *image*, not the world, sounds like. Both documentary and narrative traditions tend to rely on sound continuity.

Exploring the infinite possibilities of sound and image interactions, and interactions among sounds and images, is the province of montage. Often deriving its practices in direct opposition to the principles of sound continuity, sound montage calls attention to the distinct, autonomous elements that make up a film. Because sound continuity is so pervasive, many of the examples of its violation are from less familiar art and experimental films and from very recent cinema. Bertolt Brecht, whose writings about theater are discussed in Chapter 5, called for "the separation of elements" that would make audiences aware of each element of a theatrical production and thus of the work that went into creating it. Separating sound from image in film is one of the most concrete illustrations of Brecht's principle. Like disjunctive image editing practices, sound montage does not smooth over juxtapositions. In sound montage, sound may "come first," and the borders between the nondiegetic and the diegetic may be difficult to establish. In addition, the expectation that every element of the mise-en-scène will make a naturalistic noise is frustrated, and voices, whether diegetic or nondiegetic, do not always preserve the illusion of a closed world. The music might appear and disappear, giving it a more material presence, and sound effects can be "synchronized" to arbitrary sources.

When motivated relationships—for example, the image of a dog motivates the sound effect of barking—are given up, we see and hear something onscreen that is different from an attempted extension of our natural world. This can be directly critical, as in a disturbing sequence in *Natural Born Killers* (1994) when Mallory's life at home with her abusive father is presented as if it were a situation comedy, complete with laugh track, applause, and perky theme music, directly commenting on how the media uses sound to manipulate emotion. In a very different use of sound montage, the succession of still images that

▶ **VIEWING CUE**

Identify two or three instances of sound continuity in a film you have watched for class. How do they support either the narrative action or the thoughts and feelings of a character?

⏸

constitutes Chris Marker's *La Jetée* (1962) is anchored by a voiceover that tells of the time experiments in which the protagonist is participating, identifying the film as science fiction [**Figure 6.40**]. Prioritizing sound makes us listen to the film's structure; the image track accompanies or provides counterpoint to what we hear.

The use of the voice can be opened up to include direct address to the viewer or the use of recitation or reading instead of naturalistic dialogue, as in Godard's *Weekend* (1967) or Isaac Julien's *Looking for Langston* (1988). The sensual quality of sounds can be explored as it might be in a musical composition, or poetic effects can be achieved by combining different sound "images." Voices are layered in Marguerite Duras's *India Song* (1975). A film can deliver ideas through multiple channels; the sound can contradict the image. Interview texts printed on the screen are read aloud with slight alterations by the voiceovers in Trinh T. Minh-ha's *Surname Viet Given Name Nam* (1989) [**Figure 6.41**].

Overall, sound montage stresses the fact that images and sounds communicate on two different levels; rather than trying to make them equivalents, montage calls attention to what each contributes differently. Sergei Eisenstein, the primary theorist of montage, extended his ideas to sound even before the technology was perfected. In his first sound film, *Alexander Nevsky* (1938) [**Figure 6.42**], he experimented with what he called "vertical montage," which emphasized both the simultaneity of and the difference between image and sound. He also collaborated closely with composer Sergey Prokofiev to make a film in which every picture edit was influenced by the accompanying soundtrack. German filmmaker Ulrike Ottinger's *Madame X: An Absolute Ruler* (1977) makes ingenious use of postsynchronous sound. Her film's motley crew of

6.40 *La Jetée* (1962). The fluidity of a voiceover accompanying a montage of still images creates a reflective distance between the two elements.

6.41 *Surname Viet Given Name Nam* (1989). The qualities of the film's voices—they are often accented and seem to belong to nonactors reciting—convey information that could not be gathered from images.

6.42 *Alexander Nevsky* (1938). The editing of Sergei Eisenstein's first sound film was planned with the score in mind.

6.43 *Madame X: An Absolute Ruler* (1977). Sound montage without dialogue defines the characters' actions.

female pirates do not speak; instead, their movements are "synchronized" with noises like animal growls or metallic clanking [**Figure 6.43**].

Experimentation with sound montage began with the introduction of sound. Filmmakers such as Jean Vigo and René Clair in France and Rouben Mamoulian and King Vidor in the United States are identified with the early sound era because of the lyrical and creative ways sound and image are combined in their films. In films such as Mamoulian's *Applause* (1929), for instance, music and effects do not duplicate the image but create a more subjective and atmospheric setting. French director Robert Bresson takes apart the usual fit between sound and image by a minimalist use of sound. In spare films such as *Pickpocket* (1959) and *L'Argent* (1983), which explore themes of predestination and isolation through scrutiny of details, Bresson achieves an uncanny presence of select sounds while refusing realistic indicators of space [**Figure 6.44**]. In "Notes on Sound," Bresson sums up his ideas: "what is for the eye must not duplicate what is for the ear." Belgian filmmaker Chantal Akerman also achieves a hyperrealist use of sound in films such as *Jeanne Dielman, 23 Quai du Commerce, 1080 Bruxelles* (1975), where the echo of the protagonist's high heels resonates long after the film's images fade. Without the use of room tone or other techniques to give spatial cues or to make sounds warmer, the minimalist sounds in the films of Bresson and Akerman become very concrete.

Other filmmakers layer sounds in ways that collide with images and other sounds. Dziga Vertov's early sound film *Enthusiasm* (1931) innovates the collection of documentary sounds, juxtaposing them as if in a collage. The sounds are not harmonized with each other or with the images but rather create disruptions or even shocks. A clock ticks over the image of a tolling bell, for example. The Soviet filmmaker was keenly interested in sound, and his work in radio and even his poetry showed a fascination with industrial noise. Jean-Luc Godard's many experiments with sound collage, which began early in his career, are indebted to Vertov's (for a time, Godard worked in a collective called the Dziga Vertov group). Godard emphasizes music in the organization of many of his films; a favorite technique is to interrupt a music cue so that it literally cannot fade into the background. In *First Name: Carmen* (1983), we actually see a string quartet playing without knowing what its relationship to the story space might be. The abrupt cessation of a soundtrack element may be extended to voices and effects as well. In the café scene in *Band of Outsiders* (1964), one of the characters suggests that if the friends in the group have nothing to say to each other, they should remain silent. This diegetic silence is conveyed by the complete cessation of sound

6.44 *L'Argent* (1983). Robert Bresson's films use sound to explore themes of isolation.

on the soundtrack, something that is rare indeed. By using nonauthoritative or noncontinuous voiceovers as well as frequent voice-offs, and by having on-camera characters address the camera, read, or make cryptic announcements, Godard challenges the natural role of the human voice in giving character and narrative information. Instead, language becomes malleable, an element in a collage of meaning.

Several examples from *Tout va bien* (*All's well*) (1972), made by Godard and Jean-Pierre Gorin, illustrate these strategies. The film opens with an unidentified male voice-off declaring his intention of making a film. A female voice responds that making films costs money. The image shows a hand writing checks for the production of the film *Tout va bien*. In another sequence, one of the film's protagonists speaks directly to the camera about his career as a political filmmaker turned director of commercials, and he is seated next to a camera as he does so. The speech makes us think about Godard's own position. Another memorable scene is set in a supermarket as it is taken over by anarchists. To add another element, the words of the journalist character played by Jane Fonda [Figure 6.45] are introduced by loudspeaker tones, such as those that would normally direct shoppers to a special bargain. This sound element confuses internal and external sound, layering sound in a collage effect. A measure of Godard's emphasis on sound can be detected in the name of his production company, Sonimage (which means either "his image" or "sound/image"), and in the release of an audio version of his television series *Historie(s) du cinéma* (1988–1998). Over a more than forty-year career, Godard has earned a reputation as probably the most exemplary practitioner of sound montage.

6.45 *Tout va bien* (1972). The cacophony of this setting is interrupted by the internal diegetic monologue of the other main character, a journalist played by Jane Fonda.

Other experimental filmmakers such as Yvonne Rainer have developed very interesting montage styles in their work with sound. In Rainer's *Journeys from Berlin/1971* (1980), we are engaged by a voiceover narration that does not correspond to the images we see and by the words on the soundtrack that often sound like unattributed quotations. In German filmmaker Alexander Kluge's *The Patriot* (1979), the narrating voiceover is attributed to a knee. Because of the possibilities of mixing sound electronically, and because of the music and performance traditions on which it draws, video art has also explored sound montage to a great extent. But even in Hollywood films, sound montage can dominate. Although it is narratively motivated by the futuristic setting, the soundscape of Ridley Scott's *Blade Runner* resembles that of an experimental film. Sound is at least as responsible as the mise-en-scène and the storyline for the theme of anxiety in a synthetic, syncretic world. Director David Lynch's sound designs are similarly integral to his disorienting onscreen worlds. In their richness, contemporary soundtracks draw more and more on montage traditions of layering sounds without necessarily encouraging reflection on the discrete functions of sound and image. The continuity tradition that subordinates sound to image and accords with screen realism is still dominant. One of the most interesting films to confront questions of sound practice in Hollywood film is *The Conversation* (1974). Although it does not depart from sound continuity in ways that an experimental film might do, the film asks viewers to consider the meanings and effects of sound as an autonomous element.

text continued on page 222 ▶

VIEWING CUE

Is sound montage used to create meaning at certain points in the film? If so, how and to what effect?

The Ethics and Effects of Sound Technology in *The Conversation* (1974)

In the 1970s, some of the most innovative U.S. films were produced by Francis Ford Coppola's Zoetrope Studios—from George Lucas's *American Graffiti* (1973) to Coppola's own *Apocalypse Now* (1979). Among the director's collaborations with sound designer and editor Walter Murch, *The Conversation* is notable because its very topic is the exploitation of sound technology. While the film's own sound conforms to the principles identified with the continuity tradition, by virtue of its foregrounding of how sound is created and transmitted, it can also illustrate the aims of sound montage practice.

The film, set in San Francisco, follows the activities of a surveillance expert, Harry Caul (played by Gene Hackman), as he goes about what seems to be a routine job: eavesdropping on a pair of lovers in the park. Harry's expertise and interest in technology leave little space for human contact and complement his rather paranoid character. Interestingly, Harry's hobby is playing the saxophone. The warm sound of this instrument foreshadows his eventual awakening to the more human dimensions of the sounds he records for a living.

The first sequence of the film is a tour de force of sound and image counterpoint, which makes us partake in the activity of surveillance as we actively attempt to decode what is happening on the screen. Eavesdropping enhances the sound's quality of presence; we feel we are *right there* in the

scene. Yet the activities of the on-camera sound recordists make us aware of those of the recordist, mixer, and director behind the scenes, just as a sound montage would do.

The film opens with an aerial shot over San Francisco's Union Square; a slow zoom in is accompanied by jazz music, while sound perspective remains constant. As the music shifts from an instrumental theme to the banter of two singers, and as the hubbub of the busy square and then the applause become audible, we recognize that the music is diegetic, coming from the scene even though we cannot at first see the source. The music's festive and emotional connotations are immediately recognizable. Yet electronic interference comes in very early on; we begin to suspect that we are

6.46 *The Conversation* (1974). We eavesdrop on characters that the plot never brings us to know better.

hearing the music through a device "within" the film as well as through the loudspeaker in the theater, and the emotional register turns slightly sinister.

In the next few shots, it remains difficult to tell who the object of the surveillance is and who the object of our attention should be, in part because the sound is not mixed to emphasize the action. Indeed, it is the gestures of a mime, taunting through his mimicry a figure whose crumpled raincoat suggests a desire for anonymity, that we must "listen" to in the first aerial shot if we want to pick out Harry in the crowd. The silent stalker is stalked. Finally, when Harry enters a van where his assistant is stationed, we learn that the target is a young couple, Ann and Mark, played by Cindy Williams and Frederic Forrest [Figure 6.46].

6.47   ***The Conversation*** (1974). Audio technology becomes a pervasive presence in the film.

The sound mix in the scene is quite complicated. The cut to the first shot taken at ground level corresponds to a notable shift in sound perspective with an increase in the diegetic music volume. Quickly a snatch of random conversation is heard, followed by a snippet of another—this time, the targeted couple—but the succession has already identified for us the arbitrariness of continuity sound mixing practices that isolate immediately what we should pay attention to. The closeness of our sound perspective is then given technical justification when we see both Harry and a man with a hearing aid in close proximity to the couple. We stay with Ann and Mark as they continue a conversation about a drunk passed out on the park bench; the volume of the conversation does not change as Harry climbs into the van. Here the continuity in sound perspective signals the importance of this apparently trivial conversation. And once again, what seemed like the film's sound—we hear the conversation—is revealed as sound produced within the story—what we hear is the recording of the conversation as we see the reel-to-reel tape recorder spinning [Figure 6.47]. At other moments, electronic interference comes in, constantly reminding us that what we are hearing is filtered through several sets of equipment and through the aural perspective of other listeners.

In the next scene, as Harry begins to listen to his recording for more than just the quality of the reproduction, he will play these few lines of recorded conversation over and over again, discovering in the captured sounds clues to a suspicious event. Is the "guilty" party the couple, presumably engaged in an affair, or those who pay to have them watched? And what is the ethical role of the "invisible" bystander, the hired sound recordist, and by extension the film viewer? The opening scene of *The Conversation* functions like a puzzle. Harry and the viewer will strive to find the truth behind

the sounds captured in the square. We powerfully feel sound's ability to testify to presence in a particular space and time by the emphasis on the value of Harry's recording.

Toward the end of the scene, a new sound element is introduced. A nondiegetic moody piano theme begins as the couple parts; the music continues, with some street noise in the mix, as Harry starts home. The piano carries over the dissolve to the next scene and ends just as Harry turns the key in his door, when it is abruptly replaced by a shrill sound effect, his alarm being set off. Our newly honed attention to the concrete nature of each sound element encourages us to evaluate this nondiegetic musical theme. Associated almost exclusively with long shots of Harry making his way around town, the wandering theme played on a single instrument underscores his alienation, inviting us as viewers to feel the emotion Harry attempts to keep at bay. After Harry arrives home, we see him playing the sax. The sound of the saxophone is very solitary; it connects Harry to the piano theme we've just heard as well as to the musicians in the park. All three of these musical elements, though distinct, are jazz. Jazz's connotations of the urban night world establish the film in the genre of film noir, although it begins in broad daylight. Interestingly, however, Harry plays his sax along with a record player, syncing up his own performance of the expressive qualities of music with prerecorded sound. This is emphasized by a shot of the record spinning. Such close-ups of sound technology are frequent in the film and remind us of the source of film voices, music, and effects. Often these cutaways are unmotivated by any character's specific attention to the sounds being emitted at that moment.

As the film progresses, Harry becomes increasingly suspicious of his employer's intentions, and he returns again and again to the evidence gathered in the first scene, in the form of the tape. The film's theme of paranoia finds a perfect echo in its setting in the world of sound technology, eavesdropping, and surveillance. Because of the claims to presence of sound, the incriminating audiotape, with the accidental music and noises it captures, appears "real" and convincing even in a film that is constantly showing off the paraphernalia of sound recording, mixing, and playback. By emphasizing that truth lies in the words spoken in that first conversation, the film upholds the privileged relationship between the voice and inner nature, while also facilitating Harry's (and the audience's) identification with other humans *through* technological mediation. Sound is used in service of narrative, but the narrative is about the uses of sound. Despite the period quaintness of the now-obsolete machines the film lingers on—reel-to-reel tape recorders and oversized headphones, the squeaky sound of rewinding, and the mechanical click of old-fashioned buttons—*The Conversation* remains an apt commentary on the values and practices of sound technology.

CONCEPTS AT WORK

Films re-create sounds from the world around us and create new patterns of sound that construct or emphasize meanings and themes in the films. Listening carefully to films is a critical act that engages the films we watch in an audio dialogue that involves film history and culture, as well as specific formal elements and strategies. We listen—consciously or unconsciously—to a film with many layers of sound, from the dialogue to the background score; and depending on our familiarity with other films and film history, we note connections with and distinctions from other films, from off-screen sound to a rock music sound montage, that characterize the use of sound in a particular movie. While film sound may sometimes represent the least visible of the formal and technical elements of the movies, in short, listening to movies can quite often provide the most insightful discoveries about a film's complex vision.

Activity
Select a scene or sequence from a film that uses orchestral music, mute the audio, and try accompanying the scene with other musical choices: jazz, part of a well-known score from a different film, a pop song. How do the changes redirect an understanding of the scene and its meaning?

THE NEXT LEVEL: ADDITIONAL SOURCES

Altman, Richard, ed. *Sound Theory, Sound Practice.* New York: Routledge, 1992. This anthology addresses the undertheorizing of film sound and includes perspectives on the history of film sound and on non-narrative film sound.

Chion, Michel. *Audio-Vision: Sound on Screen.* Edited and translated by Claudia Gorbman. Foreword by Walter Murch. New York: Columbia University Press, 1990. This translated work by a leading theorist of film sound stresses the inseparability of sound and image and introduces original terminology to explore the experience more precisely.

Dickinson, Kay, ed. *Movie Music: The Film Reader.* London: Routledge, 2003. This collection of essays includes a classic statement by Theodor Adorno and Hans Eisler as well as discussions of animation, the record industry, and formal analysis of music.

Donnelly, Kevin. *The Spectre of Sound: Music in Film and Television.* London: BFI, 2005. This study examines the use of music to elicit emotional reactions in both films and television; it explores the use of pop music, horror music, orchestral music, and other types of film music.

Eisenstein, Sergei, Vsevolod Pudovkin, and Grifore Alexandrov. "Statement on Sound," in *The Eisenstein Reader.* Edited by Richard Taylor. London: BFI, 1998, pp. 80–81. Originally published in 1928, this manifesto by Soviet montage theorists anticipates the creative uses of sound in film.

Gorbman, Claudia. *Unheard Melodies: Narrative Film Music.* Bloomington: Indiana University Press, 1987. A thorough examination of how music works in narrative cinema; drawing on narratology and semiology, this book introduces important theories of film music with extensive examples.

Kozloff, Sarah. *Overhearing Film Dialogue.* Berkeley: University of California Press, 2000. A rare comprehensive study of film dialogue, this book examines the critical neglect of dialogue in American movies. The second part of the book analyzes the distinct use of dialogue in four genres: westerns, screwball comedies, gangstger films, and melodramas.

Lastra, James. *Sound Technology and the American Cinema.* New York: Columbia University Press, 2000. Linking practices and rhetoric of film sound in the 1920s and 1930s with nineteenth-century technologies, Lastra demonstrates persistent ways of speaking about the aural dimension and tracks social and sensorial changes wrought by modernity.

O'Brien, Charles. *Cinema's Conversion to Sound: Technology and Film Style in France and the U.S.* Bloomington: Indiana University Press, 2005. This work is an innovative crosscultural analysis of how two different film cultures—those of France and the United States—assimilated the sound revolution in often notably different ways. Unlike traditional studies of sound technology, the book argues less for the common stylistic strategies associated with Hollywood and instead emphasizes the significant role that cultural differences can play in the production of cinematic sound.

Weis, Elisabeth, and John Belton, eds. *Film Sound: Theory and Practice.* New York: Columbia University Press, 1985. A comprehensive anthology covering history, technology, aesthetics, and classical and contemporary sound theory, this work includes a section on practice that comprises essays on the work of directors who have used sound innovatively, from the early sound period to modern Hollywood cinema.

PART 3

ORGANIZATIONAL STRUCTURES

from stories to genres

We go to the movies not just to experience a film's elaborate scenes, brilliant images, dramatic cuts, and rich sounds. We also go for the gripping suspense of a murder mystery, the fascinating revelations of a documentary, the poetic voyage of a musical score set to abstract images and sounds, and the delight of seeing life as if it were a 1930s musical. We turn to films like *Syriana* (2005) for the twists and turns of a story about political and economic intrigue in the Middle East, to *Hoop Dreams* (1994) for the disturbing facts and human costs behind sports recruiting, to *Fantasia* (1940) for rhythms and sounds made into creative animated images, and to *Eternal Sunshine of the Spotless Mind* (2004) for its novel approach to romantic conventions and plots.

Besides the stylistic details found in the mise-en-scène, cinematography, editing, and sound, movie experiences are also encounters with larger organizational structures and attractions. Some of us may look first for a good story; others may prefer documentary or experimental films. Some days we may be in the mood for a melodrama; other days we may feel like watching a horror film. Part 3 explores the principal organizations of movies—narrative, documentary, and experimental films, and movie genres—each of which, as we will see, arouses certain expectations about the movie we are viewing. Each shapes the world for us into a distinctive kind of experience, offering a particular way of seeing, understanding, and enjoying it.

CHAPTER **7**

Telling Stories about Time: Narrative Films

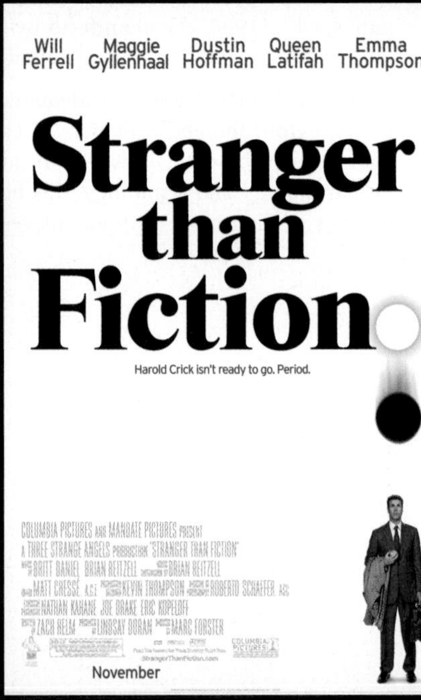

Will Ferrell   Maggie Gyllenhaal   Dustin Hoffman   Queen Latifah   Emma Thompson

Stranger than Fiction

Harold Crick isn't ready to go. Period.

COLUMBIA PICTURES AND MANDATE PICTURES PRESENT
A THREE STRANGE ANGELS PRODUCTION "STRANGER THAN FICTION"
MUSIC BRITT DANIEL · BRIAN REITZELL   MUSIC SUPERVISOR BRIAN REITZELL
EDITOR MATT CHESSE, A.C.E.   MUSIC KEVIN THOMPSON   DIRECTOR OF PHOTOGRAPHY ROBERTO SCHAEFER, A.S.C.
PRODUCED NATHAN KAHANE JOE DRAKE ERIC KOPELOFF
WRITTEN ZACH HELM   PRODUCED LINDSAY DORAN   DIRECTED MARC FORSTER

November

- Stories and plots
- Characters
- Narration and narrative point of view
- Classical and alternative narrative traditions

224

CHAPTER 8
Representing the Real: Documentary Films

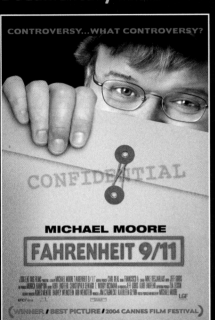

- Cultural practices
- Nonfictional and non-narrative images and forms
- Formal strategies and organizations

CHAPTER 9
Experimental Screens: Avant-Garde Film, Video Art, and New Media

- Defining experimental media
- Aesthetic histories
- Formal strategies and organizations

CHAPTER 10
Rituals, Conventions, Archetypes, and Formulas: Movie Genres

- Genre identification
- Genre as cultural ritual
- Prescriptive and descriptive understanding of film types
- Six genres
- Meaning through genre

Will
Ferrell

Maggie
Gyllenhaal

Dustin
Hoffman

Queen
Latifah

Emma
Thompson

Stranger than Fiction

Harold Crick isn't ready to go. Period.

COLUMBIA PICTURES and MANDATE PICTURES PRESENT
A THREE STRANGE ANGELS PRODUCTION "STRANGER THAN FICTION"
MUSIC BY BRITT DANIEL BRIAN REITZELL MUSIC SUPERVISION BY BRIAN REITZELL
EDITOR MATT CHESSÉ, A.C.E. PRODUCTION DESIGNER KEVIN THOMPSON DIRECTOR OF PHOTOGRAPHY ROBERTO SCHAEFER, ASC
EXECUTIVE PRODUCERS NATHAN KAHANE JOE DRAKE ERIC KOPELOFF
WRITTEN BY ZACH HELM PRODUCED BY LINDSAY DORAN DIRECTED BY MARC FORSTER

November

Telling Stories about Time

Narrative Films

In the surreal comedic drama *Stranger than Fiction* (2006), Will Ferrell plays IRS agent Harold Crick, who begins to hear the voice of a narrator telling the story of his life. While we all may accept the notion that our lives often change and develop like stories, Crick faces the unusual crisis that his life seems to be someone else's story. In this bizarre twist on the role of narration in our lives, Crick seeks out the author, Karen Eiffel. To his chagrin, he discovers she has been researching how to kill off her character, Crick, a standard ending for all her novels. More self-consciously than most movies, *Stranger than Fiction* explores the complex and mutually formative relationship between life, narrative, and the movies.

Movies have thrived on **narrative**, the art and craft of constructing a story with a particular plot and point of view. Narrative film developed out of a long cultural, artistic, and literary tradition of storytelling, showing characters pursuing goals and confronting obstacles to those goals. In general, narrative follows a three-part structure consisting of a beginning, a middle, and an ending; an opening state is disrupted in the middle of the narrative, and that disruption leads to a reestablishment of order in the ending. At its core, narrative maps the different ways we have learned to organize patterns of time and history in our lives.

KEY CONCEPTS In this chapter, we will examine

- the cultural ubiquity of storytelling in film
- the different historical practices that create the foundations for film narratives
- how film narratives construct plots that can arrange the events of a story in different ways
- the way film characters motivate actions in a story
- the way plots create different temporal and spatial schemes
- the power of narration and narrative point of view and how they determine our understanding of a story
- the differences between classical and alternative narrative traditions

Storytelling has always been a central part of societies and cultures. Stories spring from both personal memories and communal memories, through which we reconstruct the events, actions, and emotions of the past through the eyes of the present. Stories pass time, they entertain children before bed and sailors at sea, they communicate ideas about social behavior, they reconcile us to the changing of the seasons or the inevitability of death, and they strengthen both the memory and the imagination of a society. The many stories of the Bible, Hindu scriptures, Icelandic sagas, oral tales of indigenous cultures, and well-known stories of historical events (such as the Civil War) and people (such as Abraham Lincoln) are all driven by these aims. In a sense, stories are both the historical center of a culture and the bonds of a community. More often than not, history itself is recounted in narrative terms.

A Short History of Narrative Film

Over time, stories have appeared in a myriad of material forms and served innumerable purposes, many of which reappear in movie narratives. Some films, like *Little Big Man* (1970) and *Contempt* (1963), make explicit references to the narrative history that precedes them. *Little Big Man*, for instance, acts out the

heritage of Native Americans gathered around the fire listening to storytellers recounting the history of their people; *Contempt*, in contrast, struggles with the narrative forms found in Homer's *Odyssey* and those demanded by commercial filmmaking—between telling a tale as an epic poem and as a Hollywood block-buster [Figures 7.1a–7.1c]. To appreciate the richness of film narrative, viewers must keep in mind the unique cultural history of narrative itself. For example, spoken or recited aloud, oral narratives represent a tradition that extends from the campfire to today's stage performance artists. Written narratives, such as Charles Dickens's *Bleak House* (1853), appear printed in periodicals or books, while visual narratives develop through a series of graphic images, such as the stories told through lithographs in the eighteenth century and through

7.1b *Penelope with the Suitors* (Pinturrichio). Since the time of medieval and Renaissance paintings, the visual arts have incorporated stories and allegories, often orchestrating numerous character actions and events within a single frame, such as in this early sixteenth-century scene from the *Odyssey*.

7.1a **Fifth-century Greek urn**. Ancient Greek epics, including the renowned *Odyssey*, were often depicted as visual narratives.

7.1c *Contempt* (1963). Jean-Luc Godard's film explicitly engages the history of narrative in his modern tale about the struggles to adapt Homer's *Odyssey* to the screen.

7.2a and 7.2b *Spider-Man*
(2002). The transformation of visual narrative from page to screen.

modern comic books like *Spider-Man* [Figures 7.2a and 7.2b]. Musical narratives communicate stories through arrangements that might identify characters by certain musical motifs, as in *Peter and the Wolf* (1934).

In these and other examples, the form and material through which a story is told opens some possibilities and closes others, allowing certain unique expressions and prohibiting others. An oral narrative might offer more direct and flexible contact with listeners, allowing a story to change from one telling to another; a visual narrative might be able to describe the appearance of characters more concretely; and a literary one might be able to represent their thoughts. In the context of these differences, attending to how a particular film narrative might employ an oral form or how a musical narrative (say, from an opera) may work alongside the visual narrative of a movie illuminates the history of storytelling embedded in cinematic form.

1900–1920: Adaptations, Scriptwriters, and Screenplays

While the first movies were usually content to show simple moving images (such as a train arriving at a station), often these images referred to a story behind them. Adaptations of well-known stories were popular with early film audiences; their familiarity with the characters and plot helped them follow emerging motion picture narrative techniques. As early as 1896, the actor Joseph Jefferson represented Rip van Winkle in a brief short. By 1903, there appeared a variety of similar film tableaux (or images) that assumed audiences would know the larger story behind what was shown on the screen—Shakespeare's *King John* (1899), *Cinderella* (1900), *Robinson Crusoe* (1902), and *Ali Baba and the Forty Thieves* (1905) [Figure 7.3]. *Uncle Tom's Cabin,* the most popular novel and stage play of the nineteenth century, was adapted for the screen numerous times in the silent film era, including by Edwin S. Porter [Figure 7.4]. Porter's films were among the first to use editing to tell stories, and by 1906 the movies were becoming a predominantly narrative medium.

These early historical bonds between movies and stories served the development of what we will call an *economics of leisure time.* In the first decades of the twentieth century, the budding movie industry recognized that stories take time to tell and that an audience's willingness to spend time watching stories makes money for the industry. In these early years, most individuals went to the movies to experience the novelty of "going to the movies," of spending an afternoon with friends or an hour away from work. By 1913, moviemakers recognized that by developing more complex stories they could attract larger audiences, keep them in their seats for longer periods, and charge more than a nickel for admission. Along with the growing cultural prestige of attending films that told serious stories, movies could now sell more time for more money through longer narratives. Quickly cinema established itself among the leading sources of cultural pleasures that included museums, art galleries, and traditional theaters. At the same time, cinema's own history came to be governed by the forms and aims of storytelling.

7.3 **Ali Baba and the Forty Thieves** (1905). An early tableau narrative that assumes the audience knows the larger story behind the image.

7.4 **Uncle Tom's Cabin** (1903). One of numerous silent film adaptations of the most popular nineteenth-century novel and stage play.

As narrative film developed, two important industrial events stand out: the introduction of film scripts to prepare movie narratives, and the advancement of narrative dialogue through sound. Whereas many early silent movies were produced with little advance preparation, the growing number and increasing length of movies from 1907 onward required the use of *scriptwriters* (or screenwriters), who created film scenarios or scripts, either original stories or adaptations from short stories, novels, or other sources. (A 1907 copyright lawsuit regarding an early movie version of *Ben-Hur* [1907] underlined the importance of scriptwriters who could develop original narratives.) As part of this historical shift, movies' narratives quickly became dependent on a film script, or **screenplay**, which standardized the elements and structures of movie narratives.

▶ **VIEWING CUE**

For the film you will watch next in class, describe as much of the story as you can. What are the main events, the implied events, and the significant and insignificant details of that story? ⏸

1927–1950: Sound Technology, Dialogue, and Classical Hollywood Narrative

While dialogue had an obviously limited function in silent movies (appearing only as **intertitles**, printed words inserted between the images), the introduction of sound technology and dialogue in the late 1920s proved to be one of the most significant advancements in the history of film narrative. While sound impacted the cinema in numerous ways, perhaps most important was that it enabled film narratives to create and develop more intricate characters, whose often-rich dialogue and vocal intonations signaled new psychological and social dimensions. More intricate characters could, in turn, propel more complex movie plots. In many ways a product of the new narrative possibilities offered by sound, screwball comedies such as *Bringing Up Baby* (1938) feature fast-talking women whose verbal dexterity is a measure of their independence and wit [Figure 7.5]. Other films of this period use sound devices, such as a whistled tune in Alfred Hitchcock's *The Man Who Knew Too Much* (1934), to make oblique connections between characters and events and to build more subtle kinds of suspense within the narrative.

7.5 **Bringing Up Baby** (1938). The dialogue of the fast-talking heroines of screwball comedies reflects their independence and wit.

7.6 *The Best Years of Our Lives* (1946). This postwar narrative questions the usual closure of the return home.

Along with the continuing evolution of the relation between sound and narrative, the 1930s and 1940s solidified and fine-tuned the fundamental shape of classical Hollywood narrative. A trio of movies produced in 1939, often heralded as Hollywood's Golden Year—*Gone with the Wind*, *Stagecoach*, and *The Wizard of Oz*—illustrate sound-era movie narratives as modern-age myths. During these years, the Hollywood studio system grew in size and power, and it provided a labor force, a producer system, and a global financial reach that created an extraordinarily efficient industrial system for storytelling. This system became increasingly identified with narrative genres, such as musicals or westerns (see Chapter 10). During this period, the introduction and advancement of specific movie technologies—for example, deep-focus cinematography and Technicolor processes—offered ways to convey and complicate the narrative information provided by specific images. While the plot structure of the classical narrative remained fully intact, these technologies allowed movies to explore new variations on the narrative atmosphere of a scene or the dramatic tensions between characters.

With growing pressure from the Hays Office, the U.S. organization that determined the guidelines for what was considered morally acceptable to depict in films, and its strict Production Code, film narratives during the 1930s turned more conspicuously to literary classics for stories that could provide adult plots acceptable to censors. These classics included *Pride and Prejudice* (1938) and *Wuthering Heights* (1939). For an industry that needed more verbal narratives, Hollywood looked increasingly to New York and other places where literary figures like F. Scott Fitzgerald could be lured into writing new stories and scripts.

World War II (1939–1945) significantly jolted classical Hollywood narratives. The stark and often horrific events revealed by this conflict raised questions about whether formulaic stories with linear plots, clear-headed characters, and neat endings could adequately capture the period's far messier and more confusing realities. If the narrative of *The Wizard of Oz* (1939) followed the yellow brick road that led a character home, the war-scarred narrative of *The Best Years of Our Lives* (1946) poignantly doubted whether one could ever go home again and, if one could, questioned what path to follow [**Figure 7.6**].

1950–1980: Art Cinema

The global trauma of World War II not only challenged the formulaic Hollywood storytelling style of the time, but it also gave rise to an art cinema in Europe that emerged in the 1950s and 1960s. This new form of cinema questioned many of the cultural perspectives and values that existed before the war. Produced by such directors as Ingmar Bergman, Federico Fellini, and Agnès Varda, these films experimented with new narrative structures and assumptions other than those of the classical model. In *Cleo from 5 to 7* (1962), for instance, Varda restricts the narrative to two hours in the day of a singer, capturing the real-time details of her life. Although the protagonist fears a cancer diagnosis, the narrative eschews melodrama for the joys of wandering through the everyday [**Figure 7.7**]. Influencing

7.7 *Cleo from 5 to 7* (1962). Agnès Varda's narrative restricts itself to two hours of real time as it documents a slice of the life of a young woman in Paris.

later new-wave cinemas such as the New German cinema of the 1970s and the New Hollywood cinema of the 1970s and 1980s, these films intentionally subverted traditional narrative forms such as linear progression of the plot and the centrality of a specific protagonist. In addition, these narratives often turned away from the objective point of view of realist narratives to create more individual styles and tell stories that were more personal than public. These narrative turns toward personal or regional subjects often resulted in self-reflexive styles that called attention to the very mechanisms of storytelling. François Truffaut's *The 400 Blows* (1959), a semi-autobiographical tale of a boy growing up in Paris, is one of the best examples of these new narrative strategies (see Film in Focus, pp. 30–32).

1980–Present: Narrative Reflexivity and Games

Contemporary movies represent a wide variety of narrative practices, but three can be identified as particularly significant. In the practice of *reflexivity*, filmmakers remake and reframe familiar stories or genres with a high degree of self-consciousness, or they approach forms and themes with an attitude of irony. *Grindhouse* (2007), by Quentin Tarantino and Robert Rodriguez, is set up as a double feature imitating two exploitation film styles, and it even includes announcements of upcoming attractions. Movies now are often as much about how stories are told as they are about the stories themselves [**Figure 7.8**].

A second contemporary direction is the appropriation of narratives directly from amusement park rides and the simultaneous attempt to approximate thrills associated with those rides. *Pirates of the Caribbean: Dead Man's Chest* (2006) is a fairly explicit example of this narrative practice (in this case, based on a Disney World ride). However, *Harry Potter and the Order of the Phoenix* (2007), with its narrative series of games, tests, and visceral thrills, seems to aspire just as much to the model of a narrative ride, making its story perfectly suited for IMAX theaters.

As films move toward and into the digital age, a third tendency is to structure stories with the effects of video and digital gaming, making the film a kind of interactive game for audiences. While *Lara Croft: Tomb Raider* (2001) is one of the first narratives to be based on a video game, an increasing number of movies have either implicitly or explicitly constructed stories as an interactive exploration of spaces. *Mortal Kombat* (1995), for instance, is an example of a nonstory game (the objective of which was to become rulers of a specific space, the Earthrealm) being adapted into a nonstory film [**Figure 7.9**]. No longer do the stories all depict the linear plot that an audience simply follows. Indeed, as film narrative evolves into the twenty-first century, the

7.8   *Grindhouse* (2007). Contemporary narratives like this film are highly self-conscious and reflexive about the historical sources and materials that construct their stories.

7.9   *Mortal Kombat* (1995). The nonlinearity of plot transformed from game to film.

convergences and exchanges between these two media may represent one of its most interesting new directions.

The Elements of Narrative Film

While narrative is universal, it is also infinitely variable. The origins of cinema storytelling in other narrative forms and texts, the evolution of narrative strategies across film history, and the distinct narrative traditions across cultures give a sense of this variety. However, we can identify the basic elements of narrative and some of the characteristic ways the film medium deploys them.

Stories and Plots

As a starting point, let us identify the main features of any kind of narrative: story, character, plot, and narration. (Later in this chapter, we will explore and develop each of these four features in more detail.) A **story** is the subject matter or raw material of a narrative, with the actions and events (usually perceived in terms of a beginning, a middle, and an end) ordered chronologically and focused on one or more **characters**, those individuals who motivate the events and perform the actions of the story. Stories tend to be summarized easily, as in "the tale of a man's frontier life on the Nebraska prairie" and "the story of a woman confronting the violence of her past in Pakistan."

The **plot** orders the events and actions of the story according to particular temporal and spatial patterns, selecting some actions, individuals, and events and omitting others. The plot of one story may include the smallest details in the life of a character; another may highlight only major, cataclysmic events. One plot may present a story as progressing forward step by step from the beginning to the end; another may present the same story by moving backward in time. One plot may describe a story as the product of the desires and drives of a character, whereas another might suggest that events take place outside the control of that character. Thus one plot of President John F. Kennedy's life could describe all the specifics of his childhood through the details of his adulthood; another plot might focus only on his combat experience during World War II, the major events of his presidency, and his shocking assassination in 1963. The first might begin with his birth, and the second with his death. Finally, how the plot is formulated can also differ significantly: one version of this story might depict Kennedy's life as the product of his energetic vision and personal ideals, whereas another version might present his triumphs and tragedies as the consequence of historical circumstances.

From early films like Edwin S. Porter's *Life of an American Fireman* (1903), regarded as one of the earliest significant narrative films, to recent movies like Christopher Nolan's *Memento* (2000), with its plot-in-reverse narrative, movies have relied on the viewer's involvement in the narrative tension between story and plot to create suspense, mystery, and interest. Even in the short and simple rescue narrative of Porter's film [**Figures 7.10a–7.10d**], some incidental details are omitted, such as the actual raising of the ladders. To add to the urgency and energy of the narrative, the rescue is actually repeated from two different camera setups. In *Memento*, the tension between plot and story is more obvious and dramatic: this unusual plot, about a man without a short-term memory, begins with a murder and proceeds backward in time through a series of short episodes, as the film unveils fragments of information about who the man is and why he

▶ VIEWING CUE

How do story and plot in a film differ? In what order does the plot in the film you've just viewed present the events of the story? ⏸

7.10a–7.10d *Life of an American Fireman* (1903). The story, though simple, proceeds from a fire alarm sounded, to the racing of the firefighters through the streets, to the rescue.

committed the murder [**Figure 7.11**]. In other films, we know the story (of President Kennedy's life, for instance) or the outcome of the story (that Kennedy was assassinated); in these cases, what interests us is discovering the story through the construction of the plot.

Narration

In addition to character, story, and plot, narration is essential to our understanding of film narrative. **Narration** refers to the emotional, physical, or intellectual perspective through which the characters, events, and action of the plot appear. Sometimes narration is associated primarily with the action of the camera and the selection of images, occasionally reinforced by verbal commentary on that action or other soundtrack cues. In other instances, as in *Memento*, narration becomes identified with the voiceover commentary of a single individual, usually (but not always) someone who is a character in the story; this perspective is called first-person narration, often recognized as one person's subjective point of view. In still other films, such as the epic *Curse of the Golden Flower* (2007), narration may assume a more objective and detached stance vis-à-vis the plot and characters, seeing

7.11 *Memento* (2001). A crisis of memory becomes a crisis of plot.

7.12 *Curse of the Golden Flower* (2007). While third-person narration may maintain a certain objectivity, It can also create a dynamic relationship with the characters and action, infusing scenes with energy and wonder.

events from outside the story; this is referred to as **third-person narration** (which we will later refine as "omniscient" or "restricted"). Even in cases of third-person narration, a presiding attitude or perspective defines the narration as it controls the plot. With third-person narrations like *Curse of the Golden Flower*, it still may be possible to describe a more specific kind of attitude or point of view. Far from being staid and detached, this film's narration is forceful and dynamic, igniting intimate and action sequences alike [**Figure 7.12**].

Narrative across Cultures

None of these dimensions of film narrative—story, plot, character, and narration—functions independently of historical, cultural, and industrial issues. Plots may prompt ready recognition from audiences and be as simple as folktales, westerns, or the *Star Wars* movies. Yet many narratives in Western cultures are more inward, centering on individuals, their fates, and their self-knowledge. Individual heroes are frequently male, with female characters participating in their quest or growth primarily through marriage—a pervasive form of narrative resolution. Moreover, Western narrative models, such as the Judeo-Christian one that assumes a progressive movement from a fall to redemption, reflect a basic cultural belief in individual and social development. Of course, cultural alternatives to this popular logic of progression and forward movement do exist, and in some cultures individual characters may be less central to the story than the give-and-take movements of the community or the passing of the seasons. In *Xala* (1975) for instance, by Senegalese filmmaker Ousmane Sembène, the narration is influenced by oral tradition and the central character's plight is linked to a whole community. This tradition is associated with the griot, storytellers in some West African cultures who recount at public gatherings the many tales that bind the community together.

Another cultural difference in film narrative can appear in the presence, or absence, of narration itself. Consider, for example, how narration in traditional Hollywood films is typically invisible and the mechanisms of storytelling seem to disappear. In dramatic contrast, visible film narration can be found in the Japanese tradition of the *benshi*. Originally associated with the Kabuki theater, which evolved from the feudal period through the beginning of the modern era in Japan, the *benshi* is an actor who stands to the side of the stage and narrates the action that occurs on the stage. Because of the importance and power of this theatrical tradition, the *benshi* became a major figure in Japanese cinema at the start of the twentieth century. Thinking about the evolution from theatrical to cinematic narrative traditions in Japanese culture illuminates continuities and differences in Hollywood's storytelling style and reminds us to listen for the "voice" of narration hidden in the visual and audio cues of contemporary films. And although our example of *benshi* in Japan shows that narrative is subject to different cultural variations, it also confirms that virtually everyone loves stories. It, as well as our earlier examples of the Judeo-Christian model and the African oral-tradition model, also reminds us that when analyzing a film narrative, it is crucial always to question not just the pattern according to which it organizes events, but also the cultural values implied or addressed by that pattern.

Stories permeate our experience of our own culture and our encounters with other cultures. Indeed, from those first movie sketches about bandits and explorers in *The Great Train Robbery* (1903) and *A Trip to the Moon* (1902), to the tales of political history and personal crises in Tomás Gutiérrez Alea's narrative of 1960s Cuba, *Memories of Underdevelopment* (1968), and Stephen Frears's look at the British monarchy, *The Queen* (2006), movie narratives have defined cultural experiences [**Figures 7.13a–7.13d**].

▶ **VIEWING CUE**

From what point of view is the narration of the film you are studying? If not controlled by an individual, how might the narration reveal certain attitudes about the story's logic?

▶ **VIEWING CUE**

Consider the next film you view for class. Identify traces of older narrative traditions in the film. How does it use or transform these traditions to help you understand the film?

7.13a–7.13d Stories and narratives may be an important part of every culture, but diverse and distinctive cultures—such as (a) the America of *Indiana Jones* (1981), (b) the Senegal of *Xala* (1975), (c) the Japan of *Kwaidan* (1964), and (d) the India of *Sholay* (1975)—often create very different stories and very different ways of telling those stories.

Characters

The first characters portrayed in films were principally bodies on display or in motion: a famous actor posing, a person running, a figure performing a menial task. When movies began to tell stories, however, characters became the central vehicle for the actions; and with the advent of the Hollywood star system around 1910, distinctions among characters developed rapidly. From the 1896 *Lone Fisherman* to the 1920 *Pollyanna* (featuring Mary Pickford), film characters evolved from amusing moving bodies to figures with specific narrative functions, portrayed by adored mythic figures. With the introduction of sound films in 1927 and drawing on traditions of literary realism, complex psychologies and social categories began to identify characters and their relations. Today the evolution of character presentation continues, with digitalized figures threatening to replace real-life actors. Through all these historical incarnations, characters have remained one of the most immediate yet under-analyzed dimensions of the movies.

Character Functions

According to the discipline of **narratology**, the study of narrative structure, plots proceed through a fairly limited number of actions or functions—including prohibition,

text continued on page 239 ▶

VIEWING CUE

Examine carefully one or two characters in the film you will watch next for class. How is each character constructed and identified?

Plot and Narration in
Apocalypse Now (1979)

Francis Ford Coppola directed *Apocalypse Now,* one of Hollywood's most ambitious film narratives, not long after his blockbuster successes *The Godfather* (1972) and *The Godfather: Part II* (1974) and his ingenious *The Conversation* (1974). Coppola and his first successful films were part of an American renaissance in moviemaking during the 1960s and 1970s, revealing the marked influence of the French New Wave filmmakers Jean-Luc Godard, François Truffaut, and others who brought decidedly experimental and ironic attitudes to film narrative. *Apocalypse Now* is also one of the first serious attempts by a U.S. director to confront the lingering anger and pain of the Vietnam War, a then-recent and traumatic memory that Americans struggled to make sense of.

The film's story is deceptively simple: during the Vietnam War, Captain Willard (played by Martin Sheen) and his crew journey into the jungle to find a maverick and rebellious U.S. army colonel named Kurtz (Marlon Brando). The story describes Willard's increasingly strange encounters in the war-torn jungles of Vietnam and Cambodia. Eventually he finds and confronts the bizarre rebel Kurtz at his riverside encampment in Cambodia.

As in other film narratives, *Apocalypse Now* constructs its story through a particular plot with a particular narrative point of view. The story of Willard and Kurtz could be plotted in a variety of other ways—by offering more information about the crew that accompanies Willard, for instance, or by showing events from an objective point of view rather than from one man's perceptions and thoughts. However, the film's plot concentrates less on the war or on how Kurtz became what he is (which is the main topic of the characters' conversations) than on Willard and his quest to find Kurtz. The plot begins with the desperate and shell-shocked Willard being given the assignment to seek out and kill Kurtz, to "terminate with extreme prejudice," and then follows Willard on his journey as he encounters a variety of strange and surreal people, sights, and activities [Figure 7.14]. In one sense, the plot's logic is linear and progressive: for Willard, each new encounter reveals more about the Vietnam War and about Kurtz. At the same time, the plot creates a regressive temporal pattern: Willard's journey up the river takes him farther and farther away from a civilized world and a rational truth, returning him to his most primitive instincts.

The mostly first-person voiceover narration of *Apocalypse Now* focuses primarily on what Willard sees around him and on his thoughts about those events. At times, the narration extends beyond Willard's perspective, showing actions from the perspective of other characters or from a more objective perspective, while still representing the other characters and events as part of Willard's confused impressions. Bound mostly to Willard's limited point of view, the narration colors events and other characters with a tone that appears alternately perplexed, weary, and fascinated. As a function of the film's narration, Americans, Vietnamese, and Cambodians appear increasingly bizarre, unpredictable, and even inhuman: rock music merges with the sounds of helicopters; soldiers

7.14 *Apocalypse Now* (1979). This scene depicts Willard's first-person narrative point of view.

(a)

(b)

7.15 *Apocalypse Now* (1979). Here the traditional narrative pattern has been severely challenged.

surf during a violent attack on a village [**Figure 7.15a**]; tigers explode from the jungle; U.S. soldiers riot during a Playboy Bunny extravaganza in the depths of Vietnam [**Figure 7.15b**]. In these and other ways, the narration, linked to Willard's control of the narrative point of view, communicates not just what happens but also the disturbing sense of a world gone awry. In *Apocalypse Now,* the traditional narrative pattern of personal progress and development is both acknowledged and severely challenged.

Indeed, as part of its exploration of the tragedies and horrors of the Vietnam War, *Apocalypse Now* continually raises questions about its own narrative debts and historical influences. Characters tell each other stories about their lives, use the musical narrative of a Wagnerian opera as background for a vicious attack on a village, and (toward the end of the film) even act out a mythic narrative of ritual sacrifice as a bull and Kurtz are simultaneously slaughtered. The film makes no secret of its loose adaptation of Joseph Conrad's novella *Heart of Darkness* (1902), set in the nineteenth-century African Congo. Throughout the movie, passing references are made to various literary practices that question whether a traditional narrative can make sense of the brutality and emptiness of modern life, such as Joseph Campbell's well-known studies of narrative myths and T. S. Eliot's dark meditation in "The Hollow Men" (his 1925 poem that begins with a quote from Conrad's *Heart of*

Darkness, "Mistah Kurtz—he dead"). Deep in Kurtz's dark jungle cavern, we catch glimpses of books on myth [**Figure 7.16**] and hear Kurtz reciting Eliot's poems, as if Coppola is acknowledging a narrative lineage that extends from Conrad's novella to *Apocalypse Now,* mapping the difficult relationship of narrative, modern history, and the darkness of the human heart. Almost a compendium of these narrative materials and traditions, *Apocalypse Now* seems to suggest that the history of war and colonization may well be bound up by a long history of attempts to control life and other people through the power of narrative.

7.16 *Apocalypse Now* (1979). The literary history of a cinematic narrative.

struggle, return, and recognition—each of which is performed by one or more characters. In the Russian folktales studied by narratologist Vladimir Propp, there are also a limited number of characters or *dramatis personae*, which include the villain, the hero, the donor (who prepares the hero), the helper (often an animal), and the princess or sought-for person. These character functions map surprisingly well onto the common narratives of popular cinema and should be kept in mind when we begin to think of film heroes and heroines as unique individuals, as the conventions of realist characterization and the casting of charismatic stars often encourage us to do. In considering the function of character in the movies, it is useful to look at how we are encouraged to accept fictional entities as rounded individuals even while recognizing that familiar character types recur across different plots.

TRANSFORMING FILM: The Evolution of Character Presentation

Character presentation has undergone wide historical incarnations, from the body on display (a) to the live actor transformed by costume and makeup (b, c) and the hybrid human/computer-generated figure (d) to the wholly digitalized figure (e) that threatens to replace the onscreen live actor.

(a) Eugene Sandow as himself in *Sandow* (1894).

(b) Rudolph Valentino as Ahmed Ben Hassan in *The Sheik* (1921).

(c) Marlon Brando as Don Vito Corleone in *The Godfather* (1972).

(d) Bill Nighy as Davy Jones in *Pirates of the Caribbean: Dead Man's Chest* (2006).

(e) Remy (the rat) in *Ratatouille* (2007).

As indicated earlier, characters are either central or minor figures (usually, but not always, human beings) who anchor the events in a film. They are commonly identified and understood as a product of their appearance, gestures and actions, dialogue, and the comments of other characters, as well as such incidental but important features as their names or clothes, in the process referred to as characterization. Characters' thoughts, personalities, expressions, and interactions appear to focus the action of films and propel their narratives—although often the more interior qualities are less available to viewers than they are to readers of verbal narratives. Characters can be seen as motivating the actions of a film's story. Their stated or implied wishes and fears produce events that cause certain effects or other events to take place; thus the actions, behaviors, and desires of characters create the *causal logic* favored in **classical film narrative,** whereby one action or event leads to, or "causes," another action or event. In the 1939 classic film *The Wizard of Oz*, Dorothy's desire to "go home"—to find her way back to Kansas—leads her through various encounters and dangers that create friendships and fears; these events, in turn, lead to others, such as Dorothy's fight to retrieve the witch's broom. In the end, she returns home joyfully. The character of Dorothy is thus defined first by her emotional desire and will to go home and then by her persistence and resourcefulness that eventually allow her to achieve that goal [**Figure 7.17**]. A character's inferred emotional and intellectual make-up motivate specific actions that subsequently define that character.

Most film characters are a combination of both ordinary and extraordinary features. This blend of fantasy and realism has always been an important movie formula: it creates characters that are recognizable in terms of our experiences and exceptional in ways that make us interested in them. Often the differences and complexities of certain film characters can be attributed to this blending and balancing. For example, the title characters of *Gandhi* (1982), *Malcolm X* (1992) and *Million Dollar Baby* (2004) [**Figures 7.18a–7.18c**]—the humble lawyer who became the leader of India, the street hustler who spearheaded a movement for social justice, and the young working-class woman who became a prizefighter, respectively—all combine extraordinary and ordinary characteristics. Even when film characters belong to fantasy genres, as with the tough but vulnerable heroine of *Alien* (1979), understanding them means appreciating how that balance between the ordinary and the extraordinary is achieved.

7.17 *The Wizard of Oz* (1939). Narrative cause-and-effect logic finds Dorothy and her new companions on the yellow brick road toward the Emerald City.

(a)

(b)

(c)

7.18   **(a)** *Gandhi* (1982), **(b)** *Malcom X* (1992), **(c)** *Million Dollar Baby* (2004). These characters, whether based on historical figures or wholly invented, represent a balance of the ordinary and extraordinary.

Character Coherence, Depth, and Grouping

No matter how the ordinary and the extraordinary, the unique and the typical, are blended in characters, narrative traditions tend to construct character behavior, emotions, and thoughts as consistent and coherent. **Character coherence** is the product of different psychological, historical, or other expectations that see people, and thus fiction characters, as fundamentally consistent and unique. We usually evaluate a character's coherence according to one or more of the following three assumptions or models:

▶ **VIEWING CUE**

Focus on a single character in the film you're currently studying. Is the character realistic or extraordinary? Why or why not? Does the character's historical or cultural realism seem at odds with your own cultural or historical situation?

⏸

- *Values.* The character coheres in terms of one or more abstract values, such as when a character becomes defined through his or her overwhelming determination or treachery.
- *Actions.* The character acts out a logical relation between his or her implied inner or mental life and visible actions, as when a sensitive character acts in a remarkably generous way.
- *Behaviors.* The character reflects social and historical assumptions about normal or abnormal behavior, as when a fifteenth-century Chinese peasant woman acts submissively before a man with social power.

Within a realist tradition, the character Charles Foster Kane in *Citizen Kane* (1941) appears inexplicable in many ways: he madly seeks more and more art objects, rejects his friends, and changes from an idealistic and energetic young man into a bitter and reclusive old man [**Figure 7.19**]. A closer examination of his character, however, might suggest that he is unusually complicated but still coherent by virtue of his obsessive determination to control his world, his need for unconditional love, or the historical image of masculine wealth and power in U.S. society in the first part of the twentieth century.

Inconsistent, contradictory, or *divided characters* subvert one or more patterns of coherence. While inconsistent characters may sometimes be the result of poor characterization, a film may intentionally create an inconsistent or contradictory character as a way of challenging our sympathies and understanding. In films like *Desperately Seeking Susan* (1985)—about a bored suburban housewife, Roberta, switching identities with an offbeat and mysterious New Yorker—characters complicate

7.19   *Citizen Kane* (1941). Certainly one of the most complex characters in film history, Charles Foster Kane seems, only at first, to resist simple models of character coherence and behavior.

7.20 *Mulholland Dr.* (2001). The double characters of the amnesiac and the young actress complicate character coherence.

▶

VIEWING CUE

Select a character in the film you're watching for class that you might define as singular. Does that singularity indicate something about the values of the film? Does the character seem coherent? How? ⏸

or subvert the expectation of coherence by taking on contradictory personalities. *Mulholland Dr.* (2001) dramatizes this instability through *character doubling* when its two characters become mirror images of each other. In its tale of an amnesiac woman and a young actress becoming entangled in a mysterious plot, fundamental notions about character coherence and stability are undermined [**Figure 7.20**].

Film characterization inevitably reflects certain historical and cultural values. In Western cultures, movies promote the concept of "the singular character," distinguished by one or more features that isolate the character as a unique personality. Like John Wayne as Ethan Edwards in *The Searchers* (1956), the unique character is a product of a complex mixture of traits. The broad scope of these traits reflects a modern notion of the advanced individual as one who is emotionally and intellectually complex and one-of-a-kind. The consequent **character depth** associated with the unique character becomes a way of referring to personal mysteries and intricacies that deepen and layer the dimensions of a complicated personality, such as Louise in *Thelma and Louise* (1991), whose surface actions clearly hide a deep trauma (a presumed sexual assault) that she tries unsuccessfully to repress. At other times, the unique character may be a product of one or two attributes, such as exceptional bravery or massive wealth, that separate him or her from all the other characters in the film. We should acknowledge that the value placed on singularity represents a social system that prizes individuality and psychological depth in ways that are open to question. After all, Hannibal Lecter in *The Silence of the Lambs* (1991) and its prequel and sequel is one of the most singular and exceptional characters in film history [**Figure 7.21**]; our troubling identification with him (at least in part) goes right to the social heart of our admiration for such uniqueness.

Character grouping refers to the social arrangements of characters in relation to each other. Traditional narratives usually feature one or two protagonists, characters we identify as the positive forces in a film, and one or two prominent antagonists, characters who oppose the protagonists as negative forces. As with the sympathetic relationship between a German officer and a French prisoner in *The Grand Illusion* (1937), this oppositional grouping of characters can sometimes be complicated or blurred. In a film featuring an ensemble cast such as *Crash* (2004), the conflicting relations and competing interests among a group of interrelated characters provide much of the film's drama. Surrounding, contrasting, and supporting the protagonists and antagonists, *minor* or *secondary characters* are usually associated with specific character groups. In *Do the Right Thing* (1989), Da Mayor wanders around the edges of the central action throughout most of the film. Although he barely impacts the events of the story, he becomes importantly associated with an older generation whose idealistic hopes have been dashed but whose fundamental compassion and wisdom stand out amidst racial anger and strife.

Social hierarchies of class, gender, race, age, and geography, among other determinants, also come into play in the arrangements of film characters. Traditionally, movie narratives have focused on heterosexual pairings in which males have claimed more power and activity than their female partners. Another traditional character hierarchy places children and elderly individuals in subordinate positions. Especially with older or mainstream films, characters from racial minorities have existed on the fringes of the action and of social ranks markedly below those of the protagonists: in *Gone with the Wind*, for example, character hierarchy subordinates

7.21 *The Silence of the Lambs* (1991). Hannibal Lecter's dark depth of character is revealed.

7.22 *North Country* (2005). Dynamic and innovative characters, like the working-class female protagonist played by Charlize Theron, alter traditional character hierarchies of class and gender.

7.23 *The Devil Wears Prada* (2006). The "heartless career woman" character type as depicted by Meryl Streep in her role as imperious fashion editor Miranda Priestly.

African Americans to whites. When social groupings are more important than individual characters, the *collective character* of the individuals in the group is primarily defined in terms of the group's action and personality. Sergei Eisenstein's *The Battleship Potemkin* (1925) explicitly fashions a drama of collective characters, crafting a political showdown among the czarist oppressors, the rebellious sailors, and the sympathetic populace in Odessa. Modern films, such as *North Country* (2005) [Figure 7.22], may shuffle those hierarchies noticeably so that classes like blue-collar workers or groups like women and children assume new power and position, as in this story about a female mine-worker's fight against institutionalized sexual harassment in the workplace.

Character Types

Character types share distinguishing features with other, similar characters and are prominent within particular narrative traditions such as fairy tales, genre films, and comic books. A single trait or multiple traits may define character types. These may be physical, psychological, or social traits; tattoos and a shaved head identify a character as one type (a "skinhead" or punk, perhaps), while another character's use of big words and a nasal accent may represent another type (a New England socialite, perhaps).

We might recognize the singularity of Warren Beatty's performance as Clyde in *Bonnie and Clyde* (1967), yet as we watch more movies and compare different protagonists, we might come to recognize him also as a character type who–like James Cagney as gangster Tom Powers in *The Public Enemy* (1931) and Bruce Willis as John McClane in *Die Hard* (1988)–can be described as a "tough yet sensitive outsider." Offering various emotional, intellectual, social, and psychological entrances into a movie, character types include such figures as "the innocent," such as Velvet Brown in *National Velvet* (1944); "the villain," such as Max Cody (played by Robert De Niro) in Martin Scorsese's remake of *Cape Fear* (1991); or the "heartless career woman," such as the imperious fashion editor played by Meryl Streep in *The Devil Wears Prada* (2006) [Figure 7.23]. These and other character types can often be subclassified in even more specific terms–such as "the damsel in distress" or "the psychotic killer." Usually character types convey clear psychological or social connotations and imply cultural values about gender, race, social class, or age that a film engages and manipulates. In *Life Is Beautiful* (1997), the father (played by director Roberto Benigni) jokes and pirouettes in the tradition of comic clowns from Charlie Chaplin and Buster Keaton to Jacques Tati and Bill Murray, outsiders whose physical games undermine the social and intellectual pretensions around them. In *Life Is Beautiful*, however, this comic type must live through the horrors of a Nazi concentration camp with his son, and in this context that type becomes transformed into a different figure, a heroic type who physically and spiritually saves his son [Figure 7.24].

Film characters are also presented as *figurative types*, characters so exaggerated or reduced that they no longer seem at all realistic and instead seem more like abstractions or emblems, like the white witch in *The Chronicles of Narnia: The Lion, the*

▶ **VIEWING CUE**

What kinds of social hierarchies are suggested by the character groupings in the film you've just viewed?

▶ **VIEWING CUE**

Turn your attention to the film's most important minor characters. What do they represent?

7.24   *Life Is Beautiful* (1997). The "comic" character type transformed into hero, depicted by Roberto Benigni in his role as a prisoner in a Nazi concentration camp.

Witch, and the Wardrobe (2006). In some movies, the figurative character appears as an **archetype**, a reflection of a spiritual or abstract state or process, such as when a character represents evil or oppression. In *The Battleship Potemkin,* a military commander unmistakably represents social oppression, while a baby in a carriage becomes the emblem of innocence oppressed. In different ways, figurative types present characters as intentionally flat, without the traditional depth and complexity of realistically drawn characters, and often for a specific purpose: for comic effect, as with the absentminded professor in *Back to the Future* (1985); for intellectual argument, as in *The Battleship Potemkin*; or for the creation of an imaginative landscape, as in *The Wizard of Oz* and *The Princess Bride* (1987).

When a film reduces an otherwise realistic character to a set of static traits that identify him or her in terms of a social, physical, or cultural category—such as the "mammy" character in *Imitation of Life* (1934) **[Figure 7.25]** or the vicious and inhuman Vietnamese in *The Deer Hunter* (1978)—this figurative type becomes a **stereotype**. Although Louise Beavers's role and performance in *Imitation of Life* are substantive enough to complicate the way the role is written, the role is an example of how stereotypes are offensive even when not overtly negative, because they tend to be applied to marginalized social groups who are not represented by a range of character types.

The relationship between film stars and character types has been a central part of film history and practice. For nearly one hundred years of film history, the construction of character in film has interacted with the personae of recognizable movie stars. Rudolph Valentino played exotic romantic heroes in *The Sheik* (1921) and *Son of the Sheik* (1926) and his offscreen image was similarly molded, with his enthusiastic female fans differentiating little between character and star. In such recent films as *Meet the Fockers* (2004), Robert De Niro's character draws on familiar aspects of his tough-guy persona—for example, his role as a young Vito Corleone in *The Godfather: Part II* or as Travis Bickle in *Taxi Driver* (1976)—to humorous effect. Our experience of stars garnered through publicity and promotion, television appearances, and criticism resembles the process by which characters are positioned in narratives. Elements of characterization through clothing or personal relationships, perceptions of coherence or development all factor in to our interest in stars and, in turn, how aspects of stars' offscreen image affect their film portrayals (see p. 76). One way to contemplate the effects of star image on character types is to imagine a familiar film cast differently. Would *Cast Away*'s (2000) story of everyman encountering his environment be the same if, instead of Tom Hanks, Jack Nicholson or Beyoncé Knowles played the lead?

Character Development

As we have seen, characters as presented in film narratives are a product of certain physical, psychological, or cultural elements that we as viewers must attend to and recognize as we are encouraged to regard these characters as individuals. In addition, certain character types reflect recognizable traits and actions derived from cultural, historical and cinematic conventions. Finally, film characters usually change over the course of a realist film and thus require us to evaluate and revise our understanding of them as they develop. We are charmed by Jimmy Stewart's character George Bailey in *It's a Wonderful Life* (1946) not simply because of his boyish and awkward good looks or because he represents a type of clownish and compassionate everyman. We

7.25   *Imitation of Life* (1934). The "mammy" stereotype is identified by her social, physical, or cultural category.

also learn to admire and understand Bailey through the traumatic crisis he experiences and overcomes. Here our interest in the character may be related to notions of growth, stability, patience, and remorse—human qualities that we see tested and developed throughout the course of the film.

In a conventional story, characters are often understood or measured by the degree to which they change and learn from their experiences. Both the changes and a character's reaction to them determine much about the character and the narrative as a whole. We follow characters through this process of **character development**, the patterns through which characters move from one mental, physical, or social state to another in a particular film. In Hitchcock's *Rear Window* (1954), under the stress of a murder mystery the beautiful Lisa changes from a seemingly passive socialite to an active detective. In *Garden State* (2004), an emotionally alienated twenty-something man undergoes a process of self-discovery as he reconnects with life through a chance encounter with a free-spirited young woman; in *Juno* (2007), the drama of a bright, sardonic sixteen-year-old's newly discovered pregnancy becomes ironically less about a social or moral crisis in the community and more poignantly and importantly about her own self-discovery of the meaning of love, family, and friendship [**Figure 7.26**].

7.26 *Juno* (2007). A sixteen-year-old's unexpected pregnancy and its social or moral implications are less the focus of the film than is her self-discovery.

Character development follows four general schemes: external and internal changes, and progressive and regressive developments. *External change* is typically a physical alteration, as when we watch a character grow taller or gray with age. Commonly overlooked as merely a realistic description of a character's growth, exterior change can signal other key changes in the meaning of a character. As in *Pygmalion* (1938) and *My Fair Lady* (1964), the main character in *Pretty Woman* (1990), Vivian, is an uneducated and rather crass girl who changes into a sophisticated woman with fashionable clothing, better speech, and a stylish coiffure; these external changes become markers of other changes in the character's social and personal sense of self and ability to evaluate others. *Internal change* measures character changes from within, such as when a character slowly becomes bitter through the experience of numerous hardships or becomes less materially ambitious as he or she gains more of a spiritual sense of the world. In *Mildred Pierce* (1945), though there is minimal external change in the appearance of the main character besides her costumes, her consciousness about her identity dramatically changes—from a submissive housewife, to a bold businesswoman, and finally to a confused, if not contrite, socialite. Furthermore, as part of these external and internal developments, what we might call *progressive character development* occurs with an improvement or advancement in some quality of the character, whereas *regressive character development* indicates a loss of or return to some previous state or a deterioration from the present state. For most viewers of *Pretty Woman*, Vivian grows into a more complex and perhaps more powerful woman; Mildred Pierce's path resembles for many a return to her originally submissive role.

Using these schemes to understand character development can be a complex and sometimes even contradictory process. Some characters may seem to progress materially but regress spiritually, for instance. Other characters may not develop at all or may resist development throughout a film. Character development is frequently symptomatic of the larger society in which characters live. When the boy Oskar in Volker Schlöndorff's *The Tin Drum* (1979) suddenly refuses to grow at all, his distorted physical and mental development reflects the new Nazi society then being born in Germany [**Figure 7.27**].

text continued on page 247 ▶

7.27 *The Tin Drum* (1979). Oskar's arrested character development is a symptom of the new Nazi society.

Characters in *Casablanca* (1942)

The Academy Award–winning film *Casablanca* offers an unusually varied and accomplished group of actors and characters. Humphrey Bogart as Rick creates a memorable portrait of an American businessman whose nightclub in Casablanca, in the neutral French Morocco, is the meeting place for expatriates and the Nazi soldiers who quietly intimidate them. Weathered and tough looking in the mold of such previous Bogart heroes as Sam Spade in *The Maltese Falcon* (1941), rather than glamorously handsome, Rick acts and dresses like a successful nightclub owner: appropriately calm and careful and seemingly in control of all situations. This physical demeanor is both complemented and complicated by Rick's psychological character, which convincingly alternates between his cool cynicism (about life and people in general) and his understated but passionate idealism (related to his deep love for Ilsa, the former lover who arrives in town with her freedom-fighter husband) [Figure 7.28]. In fact, Rick develops a complex relationship between his physical character and our glimpses of his psychological make-up that adds considerable depth to his overall character.

Character realism in *Casablanca* is clearly both historical and cultural, creating characters that reflect American assumptions in 1942 about certain kinds of individuals. Not only might Rick's physical features, such as his hairstyle and gestures, seem outdated today, but his psychological and emotional behavior, like his rugged and restrained masculinity, might also seem like an archaic description of a male character to contemporary viewers. These historical and cultural differences can complicate or impede our identification with and understanding of a movie.

Rick and other characters in *Casablanca* effectively and skillfully dramatize the balancing of the two dimensions of the ordinary and the extraordinary. Although Rick presents himself as part of the heterogeneous crowd he oversees, it is clear to us that he is distinguished from them by his superior intelligence and his exceptional physical and mental strength. Ingrid Bergman as Ilsa is more sophisticated than the other women in the film (including the timid Bulgarian Annina, whom Rick saves from the clutches of Captain Renault). Ilsa stands out because of her stunning beauty and her extraordinary devotion to the noble cause of her resistance-leader husband, Victor Laszlo, an aristocratic European, and the pathos and romance of her character's victimization by the Nazis are deepened by elements of Bergman's persona, including her accent, which connotes "European" [Figure 7.29]. Yet a central crisis of the movie reveals Ilsa's deep love for the tough and unsophisticated Rick, so that a part of her character also includes the basic and enduring passion of all lovers. With minor characters less central to the story—such as Sascha the bartender and Major Strasser the Nazi commander—the balance between the ordinary and the extraordinary tends to swing

7.28 *Casablanca* (1942). Rick's psychological character alternates between the cynical and the passionate.

one way or the other, making these minor characters appear more simplistic and less interesting.

Particularly rich characters like Rick and Ilsa can be evaluated according to any one of the three models of character coherence described earlier in this chapter. Both characters exhibit many different character traits, some of which may seem contradictory: they are at once aloof and caring, loyal and suspicious, quick to anger and to reconcile. For some viewers, Rick may represent the universal values of quiet nobility and heroism, while Ilsa may stand for endurance and self-sacrifice. For still other viewers, these characters make sense only according to 1940s mores and social codes, when to protect their emotions, men acted tough and bitter and women acted haughty and defensive. Rick and Ilsa might also be explained by the elaborate relationship of their internal and external lives: they have had to develop two sides to their characters, one as public survivors and the other as private lovers. Although those two sides are never really brought together, they remain humanly coherent as two, albeit painfully coexisting, sides of the human character.

It is difficult to find an incoherent or divided character in *Casablanca* (although the changing allegiances of Captain Renault shade him in that way). But character groupings and hierarchies do play central roles in this film. For instance, the positive values in Rick's singularity come into view, both through his hostile relationship with his main antagonist, Major Strasser, and even more so through his barely visible competition with Victor. Moreover, the many secondary characters create a particularly dynamic field of groupings, including the local north Africans, the American and European refugees and expatriates, and the French colonialists. Signor Ferrari, Ugarte, Mr. and Mrs. Leuchtag, and, significantly, the African American character Sam (Dooley Wilson) are among a panorama of minor characters who act as background, establishing the social fabric of the film.

Much of the patriotic force of *Casablanca* lies in how these minor groupings give way to the larger distinction of Nazis versus resisters. Occasionally our engagement with the private drama of Rick and Ilsa shifts to the community of Rick's nightclub—such as when the resisters dramatically confront the Nazis by rising to sing the French national anthem, "La Marseillaise" [Figure 7.30]. Indeed, we can understand *Casablanca* as a drama of character by following Rick's transformation from a singular to a collective character ready to sacrifice his individuality for a larger political cause.

7.29 *Casablanca* (1942). Ilsa's beauty and devotion to her husband make her both extraordinary and real.

7.30 *Casablanca* (1942). The drama of a single character becomes a drama of a community resisting Nazi occupation.

Diegetic and Nondiegetic Elements

Most narratives involve two kinds of materials: those related to the story, and those not related to the story. The entire world that a story describes or that the viewer infers is called its *diegesis*, which indicates the characters, places, and events shown in the story or implied by it. The diegesis of Steven Spielberg's *Amistad* (1997) includes

7.31 *House of Sand* (2005). The omission of a broader diegetic context intensifies the narrative focus on the psychological and emotional plight of a single character.

characters and events explicitly revealed in the narrative, such as a rebellion on a slave ship in the first part of the nineteenth century and the subsequent defense trial featuring John Quincy Adams. However, the film's diegesis also includes viewers' knowledge of other unseen figures and events from American history, including a victorious war for independence and a near future that would erupt in the Civil War. The extent to which we find the film realistic or convincing, creative or manipulative, depends on our recognition of the richness and coherence of the diegetic world surrounding the story.

Some films intentionally leave the larger diegesis unclear or barely visible as a way of complicating viewers' understanding of the story. Andrucha Waddington's *House of Sand* (2005) tells the story of a woman taken to the remote and shifting dunes of Maranhão, in northeast Brazil, in 1910 [**Figure 7.31**]; there she remains isolated for fifty-nine years, barely catching glimpses of the major events of the twentieth century that exist outside her enclosed world. In this case, the very lack of a broader diegetic context serves to intensify the desperate loneliness of the woman but also to concentrate on her personal transformation.

The notion of diegesis is critical to our understanding of film narrative because it forces us to consider those elements of the story that the narration chooses to include or not include in the plot—and to consider *why* these elements are included or excluded. Despite the similarity of information in a plot and a story, the concept of *plot selection and omission* describes the exchange by which plot constructs and shapes a story from its diegesis. Consider a film about the social unrest and revolution in Russia at the beginning of the twentieth century: since the diegesis of that event includes a number of events and many characters, what should be selected and what should be omitted? Faced with this question for his film on the 1905 revolution, Sergei Eisenstein reduced the diegesis to a single uprising on a battleship near the Odessa steps and called the film *The Battleship Potemkin*.

Nondiegetic information in the narrative includes material used to tell the story that does not relate to the diegesis and its world, such as background music and credits. These dimensions of a narrative indirectly add to a story and affect how viewers participate in or understand it. With silent films, nondiegetic information is sometimes part of the intertitles—those frames that usually print the dialogue of the characters but can occasionally comment on the action—as when D. W. Griffith inserts a line appropriated from Walt Whitman, "Out of the cradle endlessly rocking," into his complex narrative *Intolerance* (1916) [**Figure 7.32**]. As discussed in Chapter 6, nondiegetic soundtracks are commonly musical scores or other arrangements of noise and sound whose source is not found in the story, as opposed to diegetic soundtracks whose source can be located in the story. Most moviegoers are familiar with the ominously thumping soundtrack of *Jaws* (1975) that announces the unseen presence of the great white shark: in this way, the story punctuates its development to quicken our attention and create suspenseful anticipation of the next event.

Credits are another nondiegetic element of the narrative. Sometimes seen at the beginning and sometimes at the end of a movie, credits introduce the actors, producers, technicians, and other individuals who

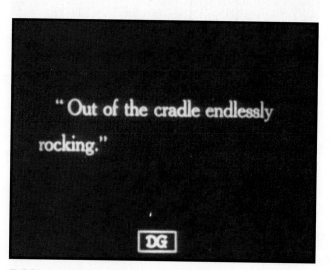

7.32 *Intolerance* (1916). In this complex silent film, nondiegetic information appears as an intertitle.

have worked on the film (with Hollywood movies to-day, the names of famous stars, the director, and the producers usually appear at the beginning, while the closing credits identify the secondary players and technicians). How this information is presented can often suggest ways of looking at the story and its themes as the story unfolds, or as we look back at it after it has ended. In *Se7en* (1995), for instance, the celebrated opening credits graphically anticipate a dark story about the efforts of two detectives to track down a diabolical serial killer. Filmed in a suitably grainy

7.33 *Se7en* (1995). The presentation of the credits in a film can suggest ways for viewing its story and its unfolding themes.

and fragmented style and set to the sounds of a pulsating industrial soundtrack, the opening credits depict the obsessive mind of a maniac as he crafts morbid scrapbooks, providing both atmosphere and expository narrative information [Figure 7.33].

Narrative Patterns of Time

Narrative films have experimented with new ways of telling stories since around 1900, the beginning of movie history. One of the first such films, Edwin S. Porter's *The Great Train Robbery* (1903), manipulated time and place by shifting from one action to another and coordinated different spaces by jumping between exterior and interior scenes. Since then, movie narratives have contracted and expanded times and places according to ever-varying patterns and well-established formulas, spanning centuries and traveling the world in Sally Potter's *Orlando* (1992) or confining the tale to two hours in one town in Agnès Varda's *Cleo from 5 to 7* (1962). For over one hundred years and through different cultures around the world, intricate temporal organizations and spatial shapes have responded to changing cultural and historical pressures to develop and alter the art of storytelling on film.

▶ **VIEWING CUE**

As you view the next film, identify the most important nondiegetic materials and analyze how they might emphasize certain key themes or ideas. ⏸

Linear Chronology

A narrative can be organized according to a variety of temporal patterns. Individuals and societies create patterns of time as ways of measuring and valuing experience. Repeating holidays once a year, marking births and deaths with symbolic rituals, and rewarding work for time invested are some of the ways we organize and value time. Similarly, narrative films develop a variety of temporal patterns as a way of creating meaning and value in the stories and experiences they recount.

Most commonly, plots follow a **linear chronology** in which the selected events and actions proceed one after another through a forward movement in time. The logic and direction of a linear plot commonly follow a central character's motivation—that is, the ideas or emotions that make a character choose a course of action. In these cases, a character pursues an object, belief, or goal of some sort, and the events in the plot are constructed according to some causal logic that follows a cause-and-effect pattern centered on that character's motivation. The linear chronology of the plot will thus show how that character's motivating desire affects or creates new situations or actions: put simply, past actions generate present situations, and decisions made in the present create future events. The narrative of *Little Miss Sunshine* (2006) structures its linear action precisely in this way: a family of offbeat and dysfunctional characters travels from New Mexico to California to participate in a beauty pageant, and on their drive toward this single goal, over the course of several days, they must overcome numerous, sometimes hilarious,

7.34 *Little Miss Sunshine* (2006). En route to California from New Mexico in this linearly organized plot, the characters find themselves in hilarious predicaments.

predicaments, obstacles, and personalities in order to complete their narrative journey and ultimately discover themselves anew [Figure 7.34].

Linear narratives most commonly structure their stories in terms of beginnings, middles, and ends. As a product of this structure, the relationship between the narrative opening and closing is normally central to the temporal logic of a plot. How a movie begins and ends and the relationship between those two poles explain much about a film. Sometimes this relation can create a sense of closure or completion, as happens when a romance ends with a couple united or with a journey finally concluded. Other plots provide less certain relations between openings and closings. Michelangelo Antonioni's *Blowup* (1966) begins with a photographer at work developing pictures and concludes with his retrieving an imaginary tennis ball for an imaginary tennis match played by mimes. From the opening, the film's narrative follows the photographer's search for reality (in photos that suggest a possible murder); the conclusion offers only ambiguity, suggesting perhaps the impossibility of that search [Figure 7.35].

The Deadline Structure

One of the most common temporal schemes in narrative films, the **deadline structure** adds to the tension and excitement of a plot, accelerating the action toward a central event or action that must be accomplished by a certain moment, hour, day, or year. These narrative rhythms can create suspense and anticipation that define the entire narrative and the characters who motivate it. In *The Graduate* (1967), Benjamin must race to the church in time to declare his love for Elaine and stop her from marrying his rival. In the German film *Run, Lola, Run* (1998), Lola has twenty minutes to find 100,000 Deutsche marks to save her boyfriend. This tight deadline results in three different versions of the same race across town in which, like a game, Lola's rapid-fire choices result in three different conclusions [Figure 7.36].

The deadline structure points to another common temporal pattern in film narrative: the doubled or parallel plot line. *Parallel plots* refer to the implied simultaneity of or connection between two different plot lines, usually with their intersection at one or more points. Quite frequently, a movie will alternate

7.35 *Blowup* (1966). The photographer's search for reality leads only to ambiguous closure.

7.36 *Run, Lola, Run* (1998). In three different versions of the same race against time, Lola is forced to make different choices.

between actions or subplots that take place at roughly the same time and that may be bound together in some way, such as by the relationship of two or more characters. One standard formula in a parallel plot is to intertwine a private story with a public story. *Jerry Maguire* (1996) develops the story of Jerry's efforts to succeed as an agent in the cutthroat world of professional sports; concurrently it follows the ups and downs of his romance with Dorothy, a single mother, and his bond with her son, Ray. In some crime films, such as *Underneath* (1995), a murder or heist plot (in this case, involving an armored car robbery) parallels and entwines with a torrid love story [Figure 7.37]. In addition to recognizing parallel plots, we need to consider the relationship between them.

7.37   *Underneath* (1995). The weaving together of the plot to rob an armored car and a torrid love story creates thematic and formal connections.

Plot Order

Despite the dominance of various versions of linear chronologies in movie narratives, most films deviate, to some extent, from straight linear chronologies to create different perspectives on events in order to lead viewers toward an understanding of what is or is not important in a story or to disrupt or challenge viewers' notions of the film as a realistic re-creation of events. *Plot order* describes how events and actions are arranged in relation to each other to create a chronology of one sort or another. Either within a linear chronology or as a variation of it, actions may appear out of chronological order, as when a later event precedes an earlier one in the plot.

One of the most common nonlinear plot devices is the narrative *flashback*, whereby a story shifts dramatically to an earlier time in the story. When a flashback describes the perspective on the whole story, it creates a **retrospective plot**, which tells of past events from the perspective of the present or future. In *The Godfather: Part II*, the modern story of mobster Michael Corleone periodically alternates with the flashback story of his father, Vito, many decades earlier; this counterpointing of two different histories draws parallels and suggests differences between the father's formation of his Mafia family and the son's later destruction of that family in the name of the Mafia business [Figures 7.38a and 7.38b]. Conversely and less frequently, a narrative chronology may *flashforward*, leaping ahead of the normal cause-and-effect order to a future incident. Thus a film narrative may show a man in an office and then flashforward to his plane leaving an

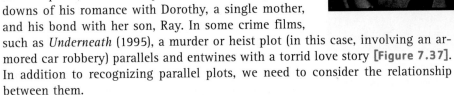

VIEWING CUE

In the movie you're currently studying, is there a double plot? If so, does one part of it have more force and meaning than the other?

7.38a and 7.38b   *The Godfather: Part II* (1974). A retrospective plot of a father's formation of his Mafia family woven into a contemporary tale of the son's later destruction of it.

7.39 *Eternal Sunshine of the Spotless Mind* (2004). The film's chronology attempts to recover what has been lost from the couple's story.

7.40 *Hiroshima Mon Amour* (1959). The nonlinear mix of past and present engages us in the main character's attempt to reconstruct an identity across a historical trauma.

airport before returning to the moment in the plot when he sits at his desk. In *They Shoot Horses, Don't They?* (1969), the plot flashes forward to a time when Robert, an unsuccessful Hollywood director during the Depression, is on trial; the unexplained scene creates a mysterious suspense that is not resolved until we later discover that he shoots Gloria, his partner in a marathon dance contest, at her request.

Other nonlinear chronological orders might interweave past, present, and future events in less predictable or logical patterns. In *Eternal Sunshine of the Spotless Mind*, the two main characters, Joel and Clementine, struggle to resurrect a romantic past that has been intentionally erased from their memories; the flashbacks here appear not as natural remembrances but as dramatic struggles to re-create a part of their narrative they have lost [**Figure 7.39**]. *Hiroshima Mon Amour* (1959) mixes documentary photos of the nuclear destruction of Hiroshima at the end of World War II, a modern story of a love affair between a French actress and a Japanese architect, and flashback images of the woman growing up in France during the previous war, when she had her first relationship with a German soldier [**Figure 7.40**]. Only gradually, and certainly not in chronological order, is the story of her past revealed. Conversations with her lover and images of Japan during World War II seem to provoke leaps in her memory; as the film narrative follows these flashbacks, we become involved in the difficulty of memory as it attempts to reconstruct an identity across a historical trauma. When a narrative violates linear chronology in these ways, the film may be demonstrating how subjective memories interact with the real world; at other times, as with *Hiroshima Mon Amour*, these violations may be ways of questioning the very notion of linear progress in life and civilization.

VIEWING CUE

How is time shaped in the film narrative you just viewed? What especially important instances of frequency or duration can you point to in this narrative's time scheme?

Narrative Duration and Frequency

Movie narratives also rely on various other temporal patterns, through which events in a story are constructed according to different time schemes. Not surprisingly, these narrative temporalities overlap with and rely on similar temporal patterns developed as editing strategies (see pp. 155–157). *Narrative duration* refers to the length of time an event or action is presented in a plot, whereas *narrative frequency* describes how often those plot elements are repeatedly shown. *Die Hard: With a Vengeance* (1995) features a now-standard digital countdown for a bomb that threatens to blow up New York City; the narrative suspense is, in large part, the amount of time the plot spends on this scene, dwelling on the bomb mechanism. Thus the thirty plot seconds for this event in the film narrative take much longer than thirty real seconds, the temporal duration being not simply a real but also an extended time. At the other end of the spectrum, a plot may include only a temporal flash of an action that really endures for a much longer period: in *Citizen Kane*, a series of short scenes lasting only moments describes the dissolution of Kane's first marriage over several years. Instead of representing the many complications that extend an actual duration of an event, the plot condenses these actions into a much shorter episode.

How often an event, person, or action is depicted by a plot—its narrative frequency—also determines the meaning or value of those events within a narrative. That is, when something is shown more than once, its value and meaning to the story increase. A movie may, for instance, return again and again to an exchange of glances between two specific characters, leaving no doubt that this relationship is central to the plot. In Eric Rohmer's *Claire's Knee* (1970), the witty plot returns again and again to the knee of the title, and the frequency of this return suggests both the main character's obsession with this part of the young woman's body and, at the same time, how potentially comic that obsession can become through time [**Figures 7.41a–7.41c**]. In repetitions like this, it is important to recognize narrative frequency as a way of drawing our attention to significant events, gestures, phrases, places, or actions.

7.41a–7.41c   *Claire's Knee* (1970). The frequency with which the knee is invoked becomes comical.

Narrative Space

In Louis Malle's strange and unusual film *My Dinner with Andre* (1981), story after story is told, but the narrative takes place in a single visible space. The film occurs at a dinner table, where Andre Gregory and Wallace Shawn exchange anecdotes and memories, dreams, and second-hand stories [**Figure 7.42**]. That this film infuses a single mise-en-scène with such energy testifies to the imaginative power of stories to use and transform space. Thus along with narrative patterns of time, plot constructions also involve a variety of spatial schemes, spaces constructed through the course of the narrative as different mise-en-scènes (see Chapter 3). These narrative locations—indoors, outdoors, natural spaces, artificial spaces, outer space—define more than just the background for stories. Stories and their characters explore these spaces, contrast them, conquer them, inhabit them, leave them, build on them, and transform them. As a consequence, both the characters and the stories usually change and develop not only as part of the formal shape of these places but also as part of their cultural and social significance and connotations.

7.42   *My Dinner with Andre* (1981). The film takes place at a dinner table, a single space across which multiple narratives are spread.

7.43   *Roman Holiday* (1953). During an exploration of Rome, a sense of human history emerges.

7.44   *Walk the Line* (2005). When Johnny Cash bonds with the inmates, the ideological significance of Folsom Prison emerges.

In conjunction with narrative action and characters, the cultural and social resonances of these spaces may be developed in four different ways: historically, ideologically, psychologically, and symbolically. Whether actual or constructed, the *historical location* abounds in film narratives as the recognized marker of a historical setting that can carry meanings and connotations important to the narrative. For example, in *Roman Holiday* (1953), a character visits the monuments of Rome, where she discovers a sense of human history and a romantic glory missing from her own life [**Figure 7.43**]. Films from *Ben-Hur* (1925) to *Gladiator* (2000) use the historical connotations of Rome to infuse the narrative with grandeur and wonder. An *ideological location* in a narrative describes spaces and places inscribed with distinctive social values or ideologies. Sometimes these narrative spaces have unmistakable political or philosophical significance, such as the Folsom prison where Johnny Cash bonds with prisoners in *Walk the Line* (2005) [**Figure 7.44**] or the oppressive grandeur of the czar's palace in Eisenstein's *October* (1927). Less obviously, the politics of gender can underpin the locations of a film narrative in crucial ideological ways: in *9 to 5* (1980), the plot focuses on how three working women successfully transform the patriarchal office space of their jobs into a place where the needs of women are met [**Figure 7.45**]. *Psychological location* in a film narrative suggests an important correlation between a character's state of mind and the place he or she inhabits at that moment in the story. In Sofia Coppola's *Lost in Translation* (2003), an American actor (played by Bill Murray) experiences confusion and communication difficulties while visiting contemporary Tokyo; these, along with his isolation in an expensive hotel, connect to deeper feelings of disaffection and disillusionment with his life back home [**Figure 7.46**]. Less common, *symbolic space* is a space transformed through spiritual or other abstract means related to the narrative. In different

7.45   *9 to 5* (1980). Three women transform the gendered politics of office space.

7.46   *Lost in Translation* (2003). The isolation of an American actor in Tokyo suggests a disaffected psychological space.

7.47 *Cast Away* (2000). The island as symbolic space becomes emblematic of the absurdity of the human condition.

7.48 *Mystery Train* (1989). Japanese tourists, ghosts of Elvis, and bungling drifters transform the space of a sleazy Memphis hotel into an offbeat carnival of loss and desire.

versions of the Robinson Crusoe story—from Luis Buñuel's *The Adventures of Robinson Crusoe* (1954) to *Robinson Crusoe on Mars* (1964) and *Cast Away* (2000)—the space of an island might become emblematic of the providential ways of life or of the absurdity of the human condition [Figure 7.47].

Complex narratives often develop and transform the significance of one or more locations, making this transformation of specific places central to the meaning of the movie. In *The Battleship Potemkin,* for example, the narrative infuses the Odessa steps with historical, psychological, ideological, and symbolic significance. In this case, the realistic mise-en-scène represents a famous location in the 1905 Russian Revolution, a psychological place of terror, an ideological location of oppression, and a symbol of the revolutionary uprising. In Jim Jarmusch's *Mystery Train* (1989), the narrative interweaves the stories of two Japanese tourists, an Italian woman on her way home to bury her husband, and three drifters who hold up a liquor store [Figure 7.48]. All happen to seek refuge in a sleazy Memphis hotel. Although they never meet, the narrative location of the hotel becomes gradually infused with the meanings of their individual dramas: the hotel becomes simultaneously a place of historical nostalgia for 1950s America and of blues music for the Japanese couple; a comically ritualistic and spiritual location for the Italian woman, who takes leave of her husband's ashes after meeting Elvis Presley's ghost; and a weird debating hall where the drifters discuss contemporary social violence.

Narrative Perspectives

Plots are organized by the perspective that informs them. Whether this perspective is explicit or implicit, we refer to this dimension of a narrative as its *narration*—the point of view that emotionally and intellectually shapes how plot materials appear and what is or is not revealed about them. Narration carries and creates attitudes, values, and aims that are central to understanding any movie. Sometimes narrations might reflect the attitudes clearly identified with a filmmaker. In movies like John Sayles's *Lianna* (1983), *The Brother from Another Planet* (1984), and *Lone Star* (1996), the narration moves around the fringes of society, quietly meditating on the loneliness and compassion that make individuals human. Tim Burton's *Edward Scissorhands* (1990) and *Ed Wood* (1994) also tell stories of isolation and longing, but his narrations assume a more exaggerated and often comic point of view, finding the human spirit in the most distorted actions

▶ VIEWING CUE

Identify the three most significant narrative locations in the movie you've just viewed. How does the narrative construct different meanings for each location?

7.49 *Edward Scissorhands*
(1990). The discovery of the human spirit in a character's distorted actions and figure.

and figures [**Figure 7.49**]. Sometimes these narrative perspectives suggest the historical period in which they were made; the narrations of 1930s Hollywood films re-create a theatrical point of view inherited from the New York stage. At other times, these narrative positions are cultural, as in the films of Yasujiro Ozu, whose slow explorations of family life show the traces of traditional Japanese conceptions of space and time.

Interestingly, film narration may be more transparent when we watch silent films, in which the narration must often speak through intertitles that provide both dialogue and commentary. When a narrative intertitle in *Foolish Wives* (1922) introduces a scene with the text "Woman's Vanity . . . Idle—Foolish—Wives," the narration speaks clearly the somewhat bitter and patriarchal prejudices that inform the perspective of the story. In *2001: A Space Odyssey* (1968), the narration covers thousands of years of human evolution, from apes to computer intelligence in outer space. It selects, as part of its narrative perspective, incidents that mark transitions in human knowledge, power, and perhaps violence: apes learning to kill to conquer land, and computers learning to kill to survive. Does this narration assume a position of divine wonder at the span of human development? Or could that narrative stance be better described as a satirical vision, mocking that history of human desire? Deciding which position controls the narrative will determine how we understand the movie.

Narrators and narrative frames are frequently used to signal the specific perspective of the narration. Both of these narrative elements describe formal tactics for drawing us into a story, and both direct the arrangement of the plot and create a specific position implying attitudes, standards, or powers. Additionally, they indicate certain cultural, social, or psychological perspective on events of the story. The most common narrative perspectives are first-person narration, omniscient narration, and restricted narration.

First-Person Narration

Some films, as noted earlier, use a narrator, a character or other person whose voice and perspective describe the action of a film from a point of view outside the story. A *first-person narrator* has some relation to the story he or she is telling, signaled by the pronoun "I" in written or spoken texts. Especially with first-person narrators, a standard device to mark the presence and perspective of that narrator is the voiceover commentary, a soundtrack commentary in which the narrator introduces the story and may occasionally make observations about it. First-person narration is an especially tricky notion for film narratives because this use of the voiceover to guide movie images can usually only approximate the full subjectivity of a first-person point of view. To attempt a literal first-person narration with film would require the film frame to become the narrator's eyes, re-creating only what the narrator sees. Narrated almost entirely through the first-person point of view of the detective Philip Marlowe, *Lady in the Lake* (1947) demonstrates how tiresome such a narration can become. The more common strategy is, accordingly, to signal a first-person narration through a voiceover narrator.

Appearing at the beginning and end of a narrative, a narrative frame is often a vehicle for introducing a first-person narration, but it serves many other narrative functions as well. A **narrative frame** describes a context or person positioned outside the story to bracket the film's narrative in a way that helps define its terms and meaning. Sometimes signaled by a voiceover, this frame may indicate the story's audience, the social context, or the period from which the story is understood. The frame may, for instance, indicate that the story is a tale told to children, that it is being told to a detective in a police station, or that it is the memory of a dying woman. In each case, the narrative frame indicates the crucial perspective and logic that define the narration.

In *Sunset Boulevard* (1950), the presence of the narrator is announced through the voiceover narration of the screenwriter-protagonist who introduces the setting and circumstances of the story [**Figure 7.50**]. His voice and death become the narrative frame for the story. Through the course of the film, his voiceover disappears and reappears, but we are aware from the start that the story is a product of his perspective; how we understand the story is at least as dependent on this narrator and his attitudes as it is on the story's events. For this reason, viewers realize that although the story and plot seem focused on a delusional movie star whose glory has long since passed, the narrative (as opposed to the story) is perhaps even more about this writer's experience of her. That we learn from the start that this first-person narrator is dead becomes an unsettling irony.

Ang Lee's *The Ice Storm* (1997) also uses a narrative frame. The narrator in this case is a young man whose commuter train has stopped en route to his home because of a heavy ice storm [**Figure 7.51**]. The narrative begins as he waits in the night for the tracks to be cleared of ice and debris, while he reflects on his family; this isolated moment and compartment frame the flashback narration that follows. Although he too disappears as a narrator until we return to the train and his voice at the end of the movie, his salient position as a narrator makes clear that this tale of a pathetically dysfunctional family in the 1970s is, most importantly, about this young man at a turning point in his life. Indeed, both these examples suggest a question to ask about narrators: does it make a difference if the narrator is seen as part of the story?

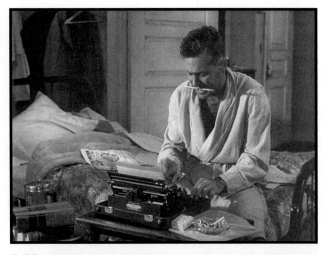

7.50   ***Sunset Boulevard*** (1950). The voiceover of the screenwriter-protagonist frames the narrative, an unsettling perspective as we know of the narrator's eventual death.

7.51   ***The Ice Storm*** (1997). When a storm stops his train, a young man's thoughts on his past become the film's narrative frame.

Omniscient and Restricted Narrations

Most film narrators are not so visible, and the majority of film narratives employ some version of a third-person narration. The standard form of classical movie narration is **omniscient narration**, a version of third-person narration in which all elements of the plot are presented from many or all potential angles. An omniscient narrative perspective not only knows all; it also knows what's important and how to arrange it to reveal the truth about a life or a history. A

▶ **VIEWING CUE**

Think about the first-person narration of a film like *Sunset Boulevard*. Does this perspective justify the narrator's actions in the story? How do the narrator's attitudes—cynical and fatigued—color the narration and hence inform the *story*?

7.52 *The General* (1927). Restricted narration limits the plot to the experiences of the main character, Johnny Gray, as he rescues his locomotive and his girlfriend from the Northern army during the Civil War.

limited third-person perspective, or **restricted narration**, organizes stories by focusing on one or two characters. Even though this narration also assumes objectivity and is able to present events and characters outside the range of those primary characters, it largely confines itself to the experiences and thoughts of the major characters.

The historical source of restricted narration is the novel and short story; as such, its emphasis on one or two individuals reflects a relatively modern view of the world (since the eighteenth century) that is mostly concerned with the progress of individuals, as depicted in Buster Keaton's *The General* (1927) **[Figure 7.52]**. Limiting the narration in this way allows the movie to attend to large historical events and actions (battles or family meetings, for instance) while also prioritizing the main character's—Johnny's—problems and desires. As a result, Johnny's ingenuity becomes apparent and seems much more honorable, and funny, than the grand epic of war that stays in the background of the narrative. With these and other restricted narrations, the logic and attitude of the narration determine why some characters receive more or less attention from the limited narrative point of view.

Reflexive, Unreliable, and Multiple Narrations

While omniscient narration and restricted narration are the most common kinds of classical narration, some films use variations on these models. **Reflexive narration** describes movies that call attention to the narrative point of view of the story in order to complicate or subvert their own narrative authority as a consistent perspective on the world. Robert Wiene's *The Cabinet of Dr. Caligari* (1919) is a well-known early example of reflexive narration that fractures the veracity and reliability of its narrative point of view when, at its conclusion, we discover that the narrator is a madman. Contemporary and experimental films commonly question the very process of narration at the same time that they construct the narrative. **Unreliable narration** (sometimes called *manipulative narration*) raises, at some point in the narrative, crucial questions about the very truth of the story being told: in *Fight Club* (1999), the bottom falls out of the narration when, toward the conclusion of the film, it becomes clear that the first-person narrator has been hallucinating the entire existence of a central character, around whom the plot develops.

Multiple narrations are found in films that use several different narrative perspectives for a single story or for different stories in a movie that loosely fits these perspectives together. The 1916 movie *Intolerance* weaves four stories about prejudice and hate from different historical periods ("the modern story," "the Judean story," "the French story," and "the Babylonian story") and could be considered a precursor to the tradition of multiple narration. Woody Allen's comedy *Zelig* (1983) parodies the objectivity proposed by many narratives by presenting the life of Leonard Zelig in the 1920s through the onscreen narrations of numerous fictional and real persons (such as Saul Bellow and Susan Sontag). More recently, *Babel* (2006) weaves together different stories from around the world (those of a Moroccan family, tourists visiting Morocco, a Mexican nanny living in the United States, and a deaf and mute Japanese teenager) that are coincidentally linked by an accidental shooting of an American tourist.

▶ **VIEWING CUE**

What narrative perspective features most prominently in the film you've just viewed? If the narration is omniscient or restricted, how does it determine the meaning of the story?

As these multiple narratives overlap and interact with each other, the film maps the struggle to find a common humanity and a common story in complex global society [Figure 7.53].

7.53 *Babel* (2006). Overlapping multiple narratives in a film about the search for a common humanity.

Compilation or anthology films, movies that feature the work of different filmmakers, such as *Germany in Autumn* (1978), *Two Evil Eyes* (1990), and *Four Rooms* (1995), are more extreme versions of multiple narratives. This type of movie features a number of stories, each made by a different film-maker. Although the stories may share a common theme or issue—a political crisis in Germany, adaptations of Edgar Allen Poe stories, or zany guests staying in a decaying hotel—they intentionally replace a singular narrative perspective with smaller narratives that establish their own distinctive perspectives.

The Significance of Film Narrative

In their reflections of time, change, and loss, film narratives engage viewers in ways that make time meaningful. Building on their relation with nineteenth-century novels, early films gravitated to historical events and characters for their subjects. Showing images of famous events and people soon led to more extended narratives about historical figures and actions, and even when fictional stories were the topic, film narratives grew increasingly fascinated with the many ways time and temporality could be organized. From *The Birth of a Nation* (1915) and *The New World* (2005) (historical epics) to *The Hours* (2002) (a film about crises in the daily lives of three women), narrative movies have been prized as both public and private histories, as records of celebrated events, personal memories, and daily routines.

Film narratives organize human experience through moving images and sounds in order to describe how individuals or communities change with time. Film, video, and computer narratives today saturate our lives with flashes of insight or events repeated again and again from different angles and at different speeds. As such, film narratives are significant for two reasons: they describe the different temporal experiences of individuals, and they reflect and reveal the shapes and patterns of larger social histories (of nations, communities, and cultures).

Shaping Memory, Making History

Film narratives shape memory by describing individual temporal experiences. In other words, they commonly portray the changes in a day, a year, or the life of a character or community. These narratives are not necessarily actual real-time experiences, as is partly the case in the 95-minute *Russian Ark* (2002), which explores, without a cut, St. Petersburg's Hermitage museum. However, they do aim to approximate the patterns through which different individuals experience and shape time: time as endurance, time as growth, time as loss. In *Drumline* (2002), for instance, narrative time becomes about anticipation and action. In this film that concentrates on the rise of a talented but brash drummer in a college marching band, the tense excitement of the movie is summarized by the

text continued on page 262 ▶

Narrative Space and Time in *The Searchers* (1956)

John Ford's *The Searchers* is a remarkable film narrative whose construction is as dramatic as it is unobtrusive. Its diegesis is quickly but clearly indicated: its world is the small settlements in a mostly open-range Texas not long after the Civil War, including the U.S. frontier where Ethan Edwards and Martin Pawley search for Edwards's nieces, Debbie and Lucy, who were captured by a renegade band of Comanche. There are a variety of minor characters within the story, such as Ethan's brother, Aaron, and sister-in-law, Martha; the feeble-minded Mose Harper; Reverend Samuel Clayton; and Ethan's Native American nemesis, Chief Scar. Additionally, some diegetic information not shown yet is part of the narrative: the facts behind Ethan's cloudy and perhaps criminal past, and his affectionately tense relationship with his brother's wife. Perhaps the most important part of the diegesis is the relationship between Debbie, the surviving white captive, and Scar, the Native American captor. Although this relationship drives the narrative and Ethan's vengeance, the story refuses to show it explicitly; we know very little about it, including whether it is consensual or not. More important, why is it not more directly addressed by the diegesis? Implied by the invisibility of this relationship is a historical fear of, and fascination with, miscegenation (interracial relationships) [**Figures 7.54a and 7.54b**].

The narrative of *The Searchers* features crucial nondiegetic material. The credits appear in a fairly standard manner: most prominently, the title and the names, in large letters, of the producer (C. V. Whitney), the star (John Wayne), and the director (John Ford). Yet three other features of these credits stand out: the titles are set against a drawing of a flat brick (probably adobe) wall, the final title pinpoints the time and place as "Texas 1868," and the overture song, "The Searchers," is introduced ("What makes a man to wander? . . ."). Minor though these details may seem, they announce *The Searchers* as being about the walls of home, with the weight of a precisely dated post–Civil War historical epic permeated by the existential questions of the cowboy ballad. The use of nondiegetic sound also supports our understanding of the narrative at other points. When serious encounters or revelations occur, such as Ethan's announcement that he will not return to the canyon where he discovered something unspeakable, sharp and ominous chords on the symphonic soundtrack punctuate his exclamation.

7.54a and 7.54b   *The Searchers* (1956). The invisible relationship between Debbie and Scar implies a fear of and fascination with interracial relationships.

The plot is clearly linear. The quest to find two young girls, Debbie and Lucy, kidnapped by Scar and his tribe, leads Ethan and Martin across the plains, where they must encounter and overcome various obstacles (hostile Comanche, the heat of the desert, winter hardships, and even Ethan's own tortured mind). After Lucy is found dead, Debbie becomes the sole object of their successful search, and through the condensation of several years, this linear chronology returns the two men to the home from which they began their quest. The resulting circularity of the linear plot suggests that even though the central character has moved forward through his quest, he has simultaneously circled backward.

Along the way, the plot introduces the precarious plight of the homesteaders, as well as extends the crisis of the kidnappings and Ethan's interior and exterior struggles through the majority of the film, and finally resolves that crisis with Debbie's rescue, her homecoming to her new family, the Jorgensens, and the successful reunion of Martin and the girl he left behind, Laurie. Framing this plot, the home lost at the beginning is figuratively restored at the end, although both these homes/houses are, somewhat disturbingly, associated with a darkened doorway. In *The Searchers,* some elements of the plot are necessarily shown: the attack on the homestead, various encounters along the trail as the men seek information about Scar's whereabouts, and the climactic battle with Scar and his men. Other elements omitted from or selected by the plot might seem more arbitrary and less obvious choices, yet it is often these choices that suggest most about the perspective and meaning of the narration. The omission of information about Ethan's past and his relationship with Martha, for instance, obliquely creates a "hero" with scars on his own moral character, thus complicating significantly his moral righteousness in pursuit of Debbie and Scar. Conversely, the inclusion of a sequence in which Ethan and Martin comically barter trinkets, mistakenly resulting in a Native American wife for Martin, seems, at least at first glance, a strange addition to the plot.

Although *The Searchers* may not seem determined by a deadline structure, such a temporal logic underlies it in two ways: (1) Martin must rescue Debbie before Ethan finds her if he is to save her from Ethan's plans to murder her, and (2) he must return home in time to marry Laurie and save her (and him) from the wrong marriage.

This deadline temporality of *The Searchers* points to another common temporal structure in film narrative: the parallel plot. The central plot of Ethan and Martin's relentless pursuit of Debbie and Scar is counterpointed by the romantic plot of the budding love between Martin and Laurie. Clearly, the two are related both thematically and temporally: the two plots cross paths as the search commences and continues, and in this film the search and restitution of social order must be completed before the personal romance can be resolved. The relationship of these two plot lines seems to suggest that Ethan's bitter need for vengeance must be stopped or redeemed if more compassionate and loving relations are to be allowed to develop.

Although *The Searchers* has a fundamentally linear plot, it does introduce an extended flashback within the linear chronology. As Martin's anxious girlfriend back home reads a letter from him in the present tense in the narrative chronology, the film narrative flashes back to earlier events retold in Martin's letter: his accidental acquisition of Look as a wife, a buffalo hunt in the deep of winter, the massacre of an Indian village by U.S. soldiers. Why this shift in the linear chronology of the plot? Perhaps it is a critical reminder of the domestic sanctuary of home and marriage that Martin has forsaken through his desperate drive toward a future goal. Though Martin's letter lasts only minutes, it is meant to describe many months of the story. Through this temporal condensation, Laurie's few minutes with the letter appear, on one level, to be more emotionally significant than Martin's many months of physical endurance on the plains.

Narrative frequency also becomes key to our understanding of *The Searchers*. Ethan's regular retort "That'll be the day!" may make that repeated comment more important than it seems, especially when he counters all its cynical expectations with the generosity of his final actions. More clearly central to the film's plot is the frequent return to the darkened threshold that opens and concludes the film, and that is re-created twice in the dark threshold of the cave into which Ethan, Martin, and, later, Debbie flee [Figure 7.55].

The narrative of *The Searchers* presents, develops, and coordinates a variety of central spaces. Most noticeably, the home of Aaron and Martha Edwards, with its domestic interiors, contrasts with the open expanses of the western frontier, with its stunning vistas and dramatic plateaus. Through the course of the narrative, moreover, the open spaces reveal a variety of different spatial connotations: the rugged terrain of deserts and valleys, river crossings, and snowy winter mountains. These open spaces then feature a number of more specific locations

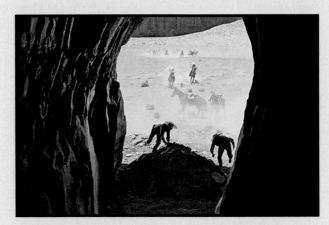

7.55 *The Searchers* (1956). The doorway and cave entrance describe the divide between presumed interior safety and exterior danger, a key theme in the film.

with more definite narrative significance: the cabin of the sinister traders, two different Native American encampments, the Mexican hacienda, and, most important, the cave in which Ethan and Martin hide and into which Debbie later flees. Thinking about the relation of these different geographies to the narrative, one might argue the following: the narrative of *The Searchers* explores these different places for the signs of a common humanity; the darkened cave, like the darkened doorway of the lost home, becomes that place where humanity is most threatened—possibly from within as well as from without—and where the troubled humanity of Ethan finally redeems itself in an act of forgiveness.

In *The Searchers,* Texas just after the Civil War—indeed, the entire U.S. frontier—works as a historical space central to the film's narrative. The many explicit narrative references to the history of this place make it the recognized site of a crossroads between European whites, Mexicans, and Native Americans, precisely at that time when U.S. identity attempted to recover from the national violence of the Civil War, fought in part over the racial divide between whites and blacks. Other places bear the marks of racial politics, such as the room where Ethan sees the white girls raised by Native Americans and notes that "they're not white anymore." Less intentionally, gender politics imbues various locations of this film (the washrooms of cabins, the teepees of Native Americans) that define women as subservient to men. Finally, the darkened cave and darkened doorway to the home both bear enormous psychological connotations in regard to Ethan and his darkened, alienated psyche.

The narration in *The Searchers* is far more complicated than it may first seem. Because the narrative point of view includes events both connected to Ethan's search and outside of it, the narration is technically third-person omniscient, capable of embracing all characters and actions within its purview. For most of the film, however, it develops a limited third-person or restricted focus on Ethan's and Martin's efforts to find Debbie. Even this dominant dimension of the narration becomes complicated because its limited concentration is implicitly divided between Ethan and Martin, characters with significantly different attitudes and goals. Within the main narrative, as we have seen, the film also interjects Martin's first-person narration as a letter to Laurie [**Figure 7.56**]. One way to think about this narrative mobility is to argue that the western epic here is told not as one person's story, but as a story stretched and experienced from competing perspectives. This would explain how the tone and logic of the film's narration skillfully alter its perspective from that of a determined quest to a more meditative inquiry.

7.56   *The Searchers* (1956). The first-person narration of Martin's letter and voiceover.

performances during a major marching band competition [**Figure 7.57**]. In the Dutch film *Antonia's Line* (1995), time becomes about women remembering and sharing experiences as their family expands in the years after World War II, about the generational bonds of the love between mothers and daughters.

Through their reflections on and revelations of social history, film narratives make history. Narratives order the various dimensions of time—past, present, and future events—in ways that are similar to models of history used by nations or other communities. Consequently, narratives create public perceptions of and ways of understanding those histories. The extent to which narratives and public histories are bound together can be seen by noting how many historical events—such as the civil rights movement or the first landing on the moon—become the subject for narrative films. But narrative films can also reveal public history in smaller events, where personal crisis or success becomes representative of a larger national or world history. A movie about J. Robert Oppenheimer and the Los Alamos detonation of July 16, 1945, Roland Joffé's *Fat Man and Little Boy* (1989) is a grippingly constructed account of the start of the U.S. atomic age. The tale of a heroic African

7.57   *Drumline* (2002). The narrative re-creates the familiar temporal experience of tense anticipation of a goal, climaxing in a final competition at the conclusion of the film.

American regiment, *Glory* (1989) [**Figure 7.58**], tells a history of the Civil War left out of such other narratives as *The Birth of a Nation* (1915) and *Gone with the Wind*. In these cases, film narratives are about cultural origins, historical losses, and national myths.

Narrative Traditions

Based on how movies can both shape memory and make history, two prominent styles of film narrative have emerged. The classical film narrative usually presents a close relationship between individual lives and social history, whereas the alternative film narrative often dramatizes the disjunction between how individuals live their lives according to personal temporal patterns and how those patterns conflict with those of the social history that intersects with their lives.

7.58   *Glory* (1989). A narrative of the heroic African American regiment that fought during the Civil War tells a different history.

Classical Film Narrative

Three primary features characterize the classical film narrative.

- It centers on one or more central characters who propel the plot with a cause-and-effect logic (whereby an action generates a reaction).
- Its plots develop with linear chronologies directed at certain goals (even when flashbacks are integrated into that linearity).
- It employs an omniscient or a restricted narration that suggests some degree of realism.

Classical narrative often appears as a three-part structure: (1) the presentation of a situation or a circumstance; (2) the disruption of that situation, often as a crisis or confrontation; and (3) the resolution of that disruption. Its narrative point of view is usually objective and realistic, including most information necessary to understand the characters and their world.

Since the 1910s, the U.S. **classical Hollywood narrative** has been the most visible and dominant form of classical narrative, but there have been many historical and cultural variations on this narrative model. Both the 1925 and 1959 films of *Ben-Hur* develop their plots around the heroic motivations of the title character and follow his struggles and triumphs as a former citizen who becomes a slave, rebel, and gladiator, fighting against the cruelties of the Roman Empire. Both movies spent inordinate amounts of money on large casts of characters and on details and locations that attempt to seem as realistic as possible. Yet even if both these Hollywood films can be classified as classical narratives, they can also be distinguished by their variations on this narrative formula. Besides some differences in the details of the story, the first version attends more to grand spectacles (such as the sea battles) and places greater emphasis on the plight of the Jews as a social group; the second version concentrates significantly more on the individual drama of Charlton Heston as Ben-Hur, on his search to find his lost family, and on Christian salvation through personal faith [**Figure 7.59**].

Two important variations on the classical narrative tradition are the **classical European narrative**, films made in Europe since 1910 and flourishing in the 1930s and 1940s (see pp. 384–387), and the **postclassical narrative**, a global body of films that began to appear in the decades after World War II and that strained but maintained the classical formula for coherent characters and plots (see pp. 411–421). This latter tradition remains visible to the present day. Although it is difficult to offer broad or definitive models for these two narrative forms, the European model tends to situate the story in large and varied social contexts that dilute the singularity of a central protagonist and is

VIEWING CUE

For the film you will watch next in class, what type of history is being depicted? What does the narrative say about the meaning of time and change in the lives of the characters? What events are presented as most important, and why?

7.59   *Ben-Hur* (1959). As the different versions of this film demonstrate, classical Hollywood narration can vary significantly through history—even when the story is fundamentally the same.

7.60 *Rules of the Game* (1939). Do classical European narratives, such as this one by Jean Renoir, tend to accentuate social contexts more than classical Hollywood narratives?

▶ **VIEWING CUE**

How would you describe the narrative tradition of the film you're now studying? What specific features of this film define it as part of one tradition or another?

7.61 *Taxi Driver* (1976). De Niro's character erupts into senseless violence and seems bent on his own destruction.

7.62 *Lost Highway* (1997). David Lynch's film is an example of an alternative narrative that upsets the audience's expectations about the characters' identities and linear stories.

usually less action-oriented than its U.S. counterpart. Thus in Jean Renoir's *Rules of the Game* (1939), a diverse milieu of many classes and social types (from servants to aristocrats) interact on a large estate to create a narrative that seems less like a single plot than a collage of many stories about sexual escapades and bankrupt social mores. An exchange between two characters summarizes the range of this satiric narrative: one character exclaims "Stop this farce!" and the other replies, "Which one?" **[Figure 7.60]**. Conversely, the post-classical model frequently undermines the power of a protagonist to control and drive the narrative forward in a clear direction. As a postclassical narrative, Martin Scorsese's *Taxi Driver* (1976) works with a plot much like that of *The Searchers*, but in Travis Bickle's strange quest to rescue a New York City prostitute from her pimp, he wanders with even less direction, identity, and control than his predecessor, Ethan. Bickle, a dark hero, becomes lost in his own fantasies. **[Figure 7.61]**.

Alternative Film Narrative

Most visible in foreign and independent film cultures, these movies tell stories while also revealing information or perspectives traditionally excluded from classical narratives in order to unsettle audience expectations, provoke new thinking, or differentiate themselves from more common narrative structures (see pp. 390–391). Generally, the **alternative film narrative** has the following characteristics:

■ It deviates from or challenges the linearity of the narrative.
■ It undermines the centrality of a main character.
■ It questions the objective realism of classical narration.

Both the predominance and motivational control of characters in moving a plot come into question with alternative films. Instead of the one or two central characters we see in classical narratives, alternative films may put a multitude of characters into play, with their stories perhaps not even being connected. In Jean-Luc Godard's *La Chinoise* (1967), the narrative shifts among three young people—a student, an economist, a philosopher—whose tales appear like a series of debates about politics and revolution in the streets of Paris. A visually stunning film, Abbas Kiarostami's *A Taste of Cherry* (1997) contains only the shadow of a story and plot: the middle-aged Mr. Badii wishes to commit suicide for no clear reason; after a series of random encounters and requests, his fate remains uncertain at the conclusion. Freed of the determining motivations of classical characters, the plots of alternative film narratives tend to break apart, omit links in a cause-and-effect logic, or proliferate plot lines well beyond the classical parallel plot. As an extreme example, David Lynch's *Lost Highway* (1997) seems to abandon its original story midway through the film when the protagonist inexplicably transforms into another character (played by another actor), leaving the audience unsure as to whether this change is actual, hallucinatory, or metaphorical **[Figure 7.62]**.

Many alternative film narratives question, in various ways, the classical narrative assumptions about an objective narrative point of view and about the power of a narrative to reflect universally true experiences. In *Rashomon* (1950), four people,

7.63 *Rashomon* (1950). Four different narrative perspectives tell a grisly tale that brings into question the possibility of narrative objectivity.

(a)

(b)

7.64 **(a)** *The River* (1951), **(b)** *Pather Panchali* (1955). Jean Renoir's *The River* influenced Satyajit Ray's adaptation of *Pather Panchali*, but the films differ markedly.

including the ghost of a dead man, recount a tale of robbery, murder, and rape four different ways, as four different narratives [Figure 7.63]. Ultimately, the group that hears these tales (as the frame of the narrative) realizes that it is impossible to know the true story.

By employing one or more of their defining characteristics, alternative film narratives have also fostered more specific cultural variations and traditions, including non-Western narratives and new-wave narratives. (With both these traditions, it should be noted, more state support and less commercial pressure have often abetted the experimentation with alternative narrative forms.) **Alternative non-Western narratives**, such as those found in the cinemas of Japan, Iran, and China, swerve from classical narrative by drawing on indigenous forms of storytelling with culturally distinctive themes, characters, plots, and narrative points of view. Indian filmmaker Satyajit Ray, for example, adapts a famous work of Bengali fiction for his 1955 *Pather Panchali* and its sequels, *Aparajito* (1956) and *The World of Apu* (1959), to render the story of a boy named Apu and his impoverished family. Although Ray was influenced by European filmmakers (he served as assistant to Jean Renoir on *The River* [1951], filmed in India), his work is suffused with the symbols and slow-paced plot of the original novel and of village life, as it rediscovers Indian history from inside India [Figures 7.64a and 7.64b]. **New-wave narratives** describe the proliferation of narrative forms that have appeared around the world since the 1950s; often experimental and disorienting, these narratives interrogate the political assumptions of classical narratives by overturning their formal assumptions. Italian new-wave director Bernardo Bertolucci's *The Conformist* (1970) is indicative: it creates a sensually vague and dreamy landscape where reality and nightmares overlap; through the mixed-up motivations of its central character, Marcelo Clerici, the film explores the historical roots of Italian fascism, a viciously decadent world of sex and politics rarely depicted in the histories of classical narrative [Figure 7.65].

text continued on page 268 ▶

7.65 *The Conformist* (1970). A new-wave narrative set within a dreamy landscape where reality and nightmares overlap.

Classical and Alternative Traditions in *Mildred Pierce* (1945) and *Daughters of the Dust* (1991)

Certainly many movies operate between the classical and alternative narrative traditions, and many other movies draw on parts of each tradition. Although pure examples may not exist, here we will examine *Mildred Pierce* and *Daughters of the Dust*, which employ the main features of these two traditions. Each film offers decidedly different ways to remember experiences and conceive of history.

Very much a part of the classical movie tradition, the narrative of Michael Curtiz's *Mildred Pierce* is an extended flashback covering many years—from Mildred's troubled marriage and divorce, her rise as a self-sufficient and enterprising businesswoman, and her disastrous affair with the playboy Monty. After the opening murder and the accusation of Mildred (its narrative frame), the narrative returns to her humble beginnings with two daughters and an irritating husband who soon divorces her. Left on her own, Mildred works determinedly to become a financial success and support her daughters [Figure 7.66]. Despite her material triumphs, her youngest daughter, Kay, dies tragically, and her other daughter, Veda, rejects her and falls in love with Mildred's lover, Monty. The temporal and linear progressions in Mildred's material life are thus ironically offset in the narrative by her loss along the way of her emotional and spiritual life.

In *Mildred Pierce* we find all three cornerstones of classical film form. The title character, through her need and determination to survive and succeed, drives the main story. The narrative uses a flashback frame that, after the opening murder, proceeds linearly, from Mildred's life as an obsequious housewife to a wealthy and vivacious socialite to her final sad awareness of the catastrophe of life. Finally, the restricted narration follows her development as an objective record of those past events.

7.66 *Mildred Pierce* (1945). A classical heroine with fatal ambitions.

Set in the 1940s with little mention of World War II, *Mildred Pierce* is not a narrative located explicitly in public history, yet it is a historical tale that visibly embraces a crisis in the public narrative of America. While focused on Mildred's personal confusion, the film delineates a critical period in U.S. history. In the years after World War II, the U.S. nuclear family would come under intense pressure as independent women with more freedom and power faced changing social structures. *Mildred Pierce* describes this public history in terms of personal experience; but like other classical narratives, the events, persons, and logic of Mildred's story reflect a national story in which a new politics of gender must be admitted and then incorporated into a tradition centered on the patriarchal family. *Mildred Pierce* aims directly at the incorporation of the private life (of Mildred) into a patriarchal public history (of the law, the community, and the nation): Mildred presumably recognizes the error of her independence and ambition and, through the guidance of the police, is restored to her ex-husband [**Figure 7.67**].

A very different kind of narrative, Julie Dash's *Daughters of the Dust* recounts a period of a few days in 1902 when an African American community prepares to move from Ibo Landing, an island off the coast of South Carolina, to settle in the North. The members of the Peazant family meld into a community whose place in time oscillates between their memories of their African heritage (as a kind of cyclical history) and their anticipation of a future on the U.S. mainland (where time progresses in a linear fashion) [**Figure 7.68**]. *Daughters of the Dust* avoids concentrating on the motivations of a single character. Instead it drifts among the perspectives of many members of the Peazant family—Nana (the grandmother), Haagar, Viola, Yellow Mary, the troubled married couple Eula and Eli, and even their unborn child.

7.67   *Mildred Pierce* (1945). Mildred's story reflects a larger national story about gender and labor.

For many viewers, the difficulty of following this film is related to its nontraditional narrative, which does not move its characters forward in the usual sense but instead depicts individuals who live in a time that seems more about communal rhythms than personal progress, where the distinction between private and public life makes little sense [**Figure 7.69**]. The plot of *Daughters of the Dust* is structured as a denial of the dramatic turn of events that organizes the three-part movement of a classical plot. A fundamental question or problem appears quietly at the beginning of the film: will the Peazant family's move to the U.S. mainland remove them from their roots and African heritage? Yet the film is more about presentation and reflection than about any drama or crisis emerging from that question. Eventually that question may be answered when some of the characters move to the mainland, where they presumably will

7.68   *Daughters of the Dust* (1991). Rather than focus on a single character, the narrative incorporates the perspectives of several Peazant family members.

7.69   *Daughters of the Dust* (1991). The narrative drifts between past and present merging history, memory, and mythology.

be recast in a narrative more like that of *Mildred Pierce.* But for now, in this narrative, they and the film embrace different temporal values.

In *Daughters of the Dust,* the shifting voices and perspectives of the narration have little interest in a unified or objective perspective on events [**Figure 7.70**]. Besides voiceovers by Nana and Eula, the narrative point of view appears through Unborn Child, a mysterious figure who is usually invisible to the other characters and who narrates as the voice of the future. Interweaving different subjective voices and experiences, the film's narration disperses time into the communal space of its island world, an orchestration of nonlinear rhythms. Certainly a public history is being mapped in this alternative film, but it is one commonly ignored by most other American narratives and classical films. Especially with its explicit reflections on the slave trade that once passed through Ibo Island, *Daughters of the Dust* maps part of African Ameri-

can history, perhaps best told through the wandering narrative patterns inherited from the traditions and styles of African storytellers.

7.70 ***Daughters of the Dust*** (1991). As a story narrated in many voices, the film resists a unified perspective on events.

Both these broad categories draw upon many narrative cultures that differ sharply from each other, and both suggest not so much a complete opposition to classical narrative as much as a dialogue with that tradition. In this context, Indian film narratives are very different from African film narratives, and the new waves of Greece and Spain represent divergent issues and narrative strategies. All, however, might be said to confront, in one way or another, the classical narrative paradigm.

CONCEPTS AT WORK

For most of us, narratives are the heart of our moviegoing experience as we seek out good films with interesting characters, plots, and narrative styles. All of these narrative elements and structures offer numerous possibilities for creating different kind of stories, invariably related to the cultural and historical contexts that help shape them. Characters range across a myriad of roles and functions in films, from coherent characters to collective characters, who can develop in many different and meaningful ways. The narrative perspective of a film may provide an omniscient view of the world or one restricted to the point of view of a single character, while a film's narration may organize the diegetic materials of a film according to various plots and patterns of time and space. While many film narratives follow a classical pattern of linear development and parallel plots, many others deviate from those patterns and explore different ways of constructing a story and of infusing

a film narrative with a larger significance. In all cases, film narratives allow us to explore and think about how time and history can be shaped as a meaningful experience.

Activity

Create a one-page treatment for your own film narrative, employing a classical narrative with parallel plots and five or six well-defined characters. As a commentary on your treatment, indicate the role of a particular narrative point of view in highlighting the themes of your narrative, as well as your goals in creating certain temporal and spatial schemes as part of your plot construction. Then create an "alternative narrative" of the same story, emphasizing the changes you would make in its major narrative features. How has this re-creation of the story through different structures changed the meaning of the story?

THE NEXT LEVEL: ADDITIONAL SOURCES

Bordwell, David, Janet Staiger, and Kristin Thompson. *The Classical Hollywood Cinema: Film Style and Mode of Production to 1960.* New York: Columbia University Press, 1985. A voluminous and detailed examination of Hollywood narrative style and its evolving historical, economic, and technological contexts.

Branigan, Edward. *Narrative Comprehension and Film.* New York: Routledge, 1992. Branigan offers an analytical account of the structures of narrative cinema and of how audiences learn to identify and process them.

Elsaesser, Thomas, and Adam Barker, eds. *Early Cinema: Space/Frame/Narrative.* London: BFI, 1990. Representing leading British, American, and European scholars, this collection of essays explores the first twenty years of the cinema, including the exciting multitude of filmic practices and experiments that fashioned early narrative cinema.

Fell, John L. *Film and the Narrative Tradition.* Norman: University of Oklahoma Press, 1974. This collection of essays traces the many different historical and cultural backgrounds of narrative cinema.

Gaines, Jane. *Classical Hollywood Narrative: The Paradigm Wars.* Durham: Duke University Press, 1982. A reinvestigation of the classical Hollywood paradigm, this collection of essays by leading film scholars describes how that paradigm has been challenged by television, new gender relations and other cultural changes.

Kawin, Bruce F. *Mindscreen: Bergman, Godard, and First-Person Film.* Princeton: Princeton University Press, 1978. In this deft and insightful study of self-conscious, or reflexive, narrative films, Kawin takes into account their literary heritage and philosophical/psychological underpinnings.

Turim, Maureen. *Flashbacks in Film: Memory and History.* New York: Routledge, 1989. This book is a complex theoretical investigation of how flashbacks have structured narratives from silent films to the present.

Representing the Real

Documentary Films

In 2001, at the site that is now known as Ground Zero, filmmakers Jules Naudet and Gédéon Naudet were working on a documentary about New York firefighters when Jules captured footage of an airliner striking the World Trade Center's North Tower. Thrown by chance into that monumental disaster, these directors found themselves making another documentary, now titled simply *9/11*. Following the firefighters in the center of the chaos, the film depicted with immediacy and authenticity a catastrophe that would haunt America for years. In the following years, many other documentaries would attempt to make sense of that tragedy, the events that led up to it, and the politics that surrounded it; this variety of perspectives calls attention to the spectrum of possibilities within documentary filmmaking. For example, three years later Michael Moore released *Fahrenheit 9/11* (2004). In this case, however, the film arguably crossed the line between fact and fiction, as Moore himself became a larger-than-life character in the film, satirizing the Bush administration and investigating a wide range of political and economic forces that, for Moore, led to the 9/11 events. If we assume documentary cinema is fundamentally about representing reality, *9/11* (2002), *Fahrenheit 9/11*, and the many other documentaries about that day remind us that documentary cinema can define and depict reality in very different ways and with very different goals.

F or most of us, the film experience is primarily about the suspense of a thriller, the humor of a comedy, or the intense emotions of a romance. Yet that experience may also be about the desire to be better informed about a person or an event, to engage with new and challenging ideas, or to learn more about what happens in other parts of the world. Indeed, these cinematic quests for information have persisted throughout film history. A movie that aims to inform viewers about truths or facts is commonly referred to as a **documentary** film, a term coined in 1926 by filmmaker John Grierson to describe a Robert Flaherty picture called *Moana* (1926) and its "visual account of events in the daily life of a Polynesian youth and his family." Broadly speaking, a documentary film is a visual and auditory representation of the presumed facts, real experiences, and actual events of the world. Documentary films usually employ and emphasize strategies and organizations other than those, such as plot and narration, that define narrative cinema. Later Flaherty would team up with German filmmaker F. W. Murnau to integrate the documentary world of *Moana* into the narrative film *Tabu: A Story of the South Seas* (1931) **[Figure 8.1]**, and this hybrid film raises key questions. How are documentary films different from narrative ones? What attracts us to them? How do they organize their material? What makes them popular, useful, and uniquely illuminating?

8.1 *Tabu* (1931). Following the documentary breakthrough of Flaherty's earlier *Moana,* Robert Flaherty and F. W. Murnau's new project combines a tragic love story with documentary images of Polynesian life.

KEY CONCEPTS

In this chapter, we will examine

- how documentary films are best distinguished as cultural practices
- how these films employ nonfictional and non-narrative images and forms
- how documentary movies make and draw on specific historical heritages
- how these films use particular formal strategies and organizations
- how documentary films have become associated with cultural values and traditions from which we develop filmic meaning

If narrative films are prominently about memory and the shaping of time, then documentary movies are about insight and learning—an enlarging of what we can know, feel, and see. The experiential core of the documentary film is educational and intellectual. Certainly narratives can enlarge and intensify the world for us in these ways as well, but without the primary task of telling a story, documentary movies—whether they are newsreels, theatrical films, or PBS broadcasts—can concentrate on leading our intellectual activities down new paths. For our purposes, intellectual insight describes how these films offer new facts and information. Entertainment and

artistry are of course not excluded from documentary films; a movie about the rise of skateboarding in southern California, *Dogtown and Z-Boys* (2001) communicates, on the one hand, ideas and facts about the birth of a sport and the individuals who helped develop it; on the other hand, it creates a poetic collage of still photos, music, and talking heads, capturing the emotional energy and visual ballet in skateboarding that many of us may not have previously appreciated [**Figure 8.2**].

If narrative films are at the heart of commercial entertainment, then documentary movies operate according to what we will call an *economics of information.* Many of the first films made in the 1890s and early 1900s, such as the traveling exhibitions and shows of Lyman H. Howe in America and Walter Haggar in England, were part of lectures, scientific presentations, or visual illustrations of the art of motion. Churches, schools, and cultural institutions supported and financially subsidized these presentations, usually in the name of intellectual, spiritual, or cultural development. Since then, documentaries have remained, to some extent, tied to and often financially dependent on private and public sponsorship, such as museums, government agencies, local social activists, and cultural foundations—from projects of the Works Progress Administration (WPA) that funded U.S. documentaries in the 1930s to the grants of the National Endowment for the Humanities (NEH) that support some nonfiction films today. In addition, many documentaries are made for television, a phenomenon that has increased since the 1980s, when the deregulation of the broadcast industry encouraged the proliferation of such cable channels as Discovery and History. For these channels, documentary programming has become a mainstay.

Although documentary films often claim and sometimes deserve the title "independent films," their survival has depended on a public culture that promotes learning as a crucial part of the film experience. Outside of or on the fringes of the commercial cinema, this "other" culture of films has endured and often triumphed through every period of film history and in virtually every world culture. In the following sections, we will explore the many ways these films have expanded how we observe, listen, and think.

8.2 *Dogtown and Z-Boyz*
(2001). Entertainment and artistry intermingle in this film on the facts and poetry of skateboarding.

VIEWING CUE

What three facts or realities are among the primary concerns of the film you just viewed? What specific information or knowledge is the film trying to communicate?

A Short History of Documentary Cinema

Through ancient government records to family home movies, through charts mapping new territories to school textbooks, we explain and learn about the world in ways that stories cannot fully explore. For example, the journals describing Marco Polo's travels through China or the early-nineteenth-century treatise by Sir Humphry Davy on

8.3 *President McKinley's Funeral Cortege at Buffalo, New York* (1901). Compelling images of events surrounding President William McKinley's assassination were recorded by motion-picture cameras. The Library of Congress has made these films available through the online American Memory Project.

the discovery of electricity have, in their own ways, recorded lost worlds, offered new ideas, or changed how we see society.

At the end of the nineteenth century, the search for empirical and spiritual truths produced new educational practices, technological tools, colonial expeditions, and secret societies—these were the vehicles to new experiences, pragmatic thought, and better worlds. In the midst of these trends, film was introduced in 1895 and used to illustrate lectures, offer cinematic portraits of famous people, and guide audiences through short movie travelogues. For many, film was not an art but a tool for investigating and explaining the physical and social worlds. The Edison Company stunned viewers in 1901 with a series of short films documenting the activities of President William McKinley on the day of his assassination, his funeral, and the transition of power to President Theodore Roosevelt [Figure 8.3]. Just as narrative films are rooted in cultural foundations and histories that preceded the cinema by centuries, so too are documentary films.

A Prehistory of Documentaries

For centuries, documentary cinema was anticipated by oral practices such as sermons, political speeches, and academic lectures; visual practices such as maps, photographs, and paintings; musical practices such as folk songs and symphonies; and written practices such as letters, diaries, poems, scientific treatises, and newspaper reports. The essay form appeared as a new kind of writing in the late sixteenth century, with Michel de Montaigne spearheading the new form and writing about personal and everyday subjects as a fragmented commentary on life and ideas.

Throughout the eighteenth and nineteenth centuries, journalism developed as a public forum for expressing ideas, announcing events, and recording daily happenings around town. Around 1800, Mary Wollstonecraft and Thomas Malthus wrote books, pamphlets, and lengthy essays describing the current state of society and insisting on practical ways that social science could improve people's lives. As the middle class moved to the center of Western societies in the nineteenth century, people demanded more information about the world.

Photography and photojournalism, evolving from new printing and lithographic technologies, became widespread and popular ways to record and comment on events. Unlike narrative practices, such as realistic novels or short stories, photojournalism presented virtually instantaneous and seemingly uncontestable records, factual representations of people and events frozen in time. One of the most dramatic combinations of social science and photography is Jacob Riis's *How the Other Half Lives* (1890) [Figure 8.4], which is part lecture, part photo essay; its pseudoscientific sermon exposes and condemns living conditions in New York City's tenement housing.

8.4 "Bandit's Roost," *How the Other Half Lives* (1890). Jacob Riis documents the squalor and danger of tenement life in nineteenth-century New York.

1895–1905: Early Actualities, Scenics, and Topicals

The very first movies appeared in 1895 and were frequently called **actualities**—that is, moving nonfiction snapshots of real people and events, with the most famous being Louis and Auguste Lumière's film *Workers Leaving the Factory*. This film captivated audiences with its recording and presentation of a simple everyday activity without explanation or storyline. **Scenics**, a variation of these early nonfiction films, offered exotic or remarkable images of nature or foreign lands. In Birt Acres's *Rough Sea at Dover* (1896), an immobile image shows waves crashing against a seawall, while other short scenics present views of Jerusalem or Niagara Falls. When these films captured or sometimes re-created historical or newsworthy events, they would be referred to as **topicals**, suggesting the kind of cultural, historical, or political relevance usually found in newspapers. Around 1898, for example, the ongoing Spanish-American War figures in a number of topicals, often with battle scenes depicting the sinking of the American ship *Maine*, which was re-created through miniatures. These factual and fabricated images of the war attracted large audiences [**Figure 8.5**].

The 1920s: Robert Flaherty and the Soviet Documentaries

Footage of distant lands continued to interest moviemakers and audiences even as narrative film became the norm after around 1910. American adventurers Martin and Osa Johnson documented their travels in Africa and the South Seas in such popular films as *Jungle Adventures* (1921) and *Simba* (1928). But it was Robert Flaherty, often referred to as "the father of documentary cinema," who significantly expanded the powers and popularity of nonfiction film in the 1920s, most famously with his early works *Nanook of the North* (1922) and *Moana* (1926). Blending a romantic fascination with nature and an anthropological desire to document and record other civilizations, Flaherty identified new possibilities for funding these noncommercial films (largely through corporations) and, with the success of *Nanook*, identified new audiences interested in realistic films that were exciting even without stories and stars.

At the same time, a very different kind of documentary was taking shape in the Soviet cinema. Filmmakers such as Dziga Vertov and Esfir Shub saw timely political potential in creating documentary films with strong ideological messages conveyed through the formal technique of montage. In *Fall of the Romanov Dynasty* (1927), Shub compiles and edits existing footage to show the historical conflicts between the aristocracy and the workers. In *The Man with the Movie Camera* (1929), which would become one of the most renowned "city symphony" documentaries, Vertov re-creates and celebrates the energy of the everyday people and the activities of a modern city (see pp. 296–298).

1930–1945: The Politics and Propaganda of Documentary

Even more definitively than it did in other film practices, the introduction of **optical sound recording** in 1927 catapulted documentary films forward, as it made the addition of educational or social commentary to accompany images possible in newsreels, documentaries, and propaganda films (see p. 198). Public institutions such as the General Post Office in England, President Roosevelt's Resettlement Administration, and the National Film Board of Canada, as well as private groups such as New York City's Film and Photo League, unhesitatingly supported documentary practices in the 1930s and 1940s. These institutions prefigure the more contemporary supporters of documentary film, including the American Public Broadcasting Service (PBS), the British Broadcasting Corporation (BBC), and the German ZDF television station.

Indeed, documentary film history can never really be divorced from these critical sources of funding and distribution. Perhaps the most prominent figure to forge and develop a relationship between documentary filmmakers and those institutions that would eventually fund them was British filmmaker John Grierson. From the late 1920s through the 1940s, as the first head of the National Film Board of Canada, Grierson not only promoted documentaries that dealt with social issues but also

8.5 *The Motion Picture Camera Goes to War* (1898). Films called topicals captured or re-created historical events; films produced between 1898 and 1901 depict the ongoing Spanish-American War.

established the institutional foundations that for years funded and distributed them. These concerns with government and institutional support for documentary cinema would proceed in a more troubling direction in the 1930s: in fascist Germany, Leni Riefensthal's *Triumph of the Will* (1935), commemorating the sixth Nazi rally in Nuremberg, represented the disturbing propagandistic power of documentary images as portrayed by government and other institutional agents [**Figures 8.6a–8.6c**].

1950s–1970s: New Technologies and the Arrival of Television

In the 1950s, changes in documentary practices followed the technological development of lightweight 16mm cameras (such as the Arriflex models), which allowed filmmakers a new kind of spontaneity and inventiveness when capturing reality. Most dramatic was the **cinema verité** movement that appeared in France at this time. Documentary filmmakers like Jean Rouch, with films like *Chronicle of a Summer* (1961), could now participate more directly and provocatively in the reality they filmed. This new mobile and independent method of documentary filmmaking leaped forward again with the development of portable magnetic sync-sound recorders in the late 1950s (specifically the Nagra system in 1958), and then again in 1968 with the introduction of Portapak video equipment. In conjunction with a lightweight camera, filmmakers now also had the ability to record direct sound and so document actions and events that previously remained hidden or at a distance. Frederick Wiseman's *Titicut Follies* (1967) has become a classic and highly controversial example of these new possibilities, as it explores the often shocking and disturbing world of the Massachusetts Institution for the Criminally Insane.

(a)

(b)

(c)

8.6a–8.6c From 1930 to 1945, politics became a defining topic and source for documentary and propaganda films like (a) Leni Riefensthal's Nazi film, *Triumph of the Will* (1935), (b) the U.S. government's *Japanese Relocation* (1943), or (c) the British documentary-style *The Lion Has Wings* (1939).

Sometimes referred to as the golden age of television documentary, the period 1950–1970 brought a rapid expansion of documentaries aimed at a new television audience. Merging older documentary traditions with television news reportage, these programs were often noted for their tough honesty and social commitment (most famously identified with the work of television journalist Edward R. Murrow, whose battles with Senator Joseph McCarthy's indiscriminate attacks on individuals set a new benchmark for news reporting). Perhaps the best-known example of the convergence of new technology, more mobile stylistics, and television reportage is Robert Drew's *Primary*, the 1960 film about the Democratic primary in Wisconsin between John F. Kennedy and Hubert Humphrey, produced for the documentary television series *Close-Up!* (1960–1961) by Drew Associates, the organization that would train many of the documentary filmmakers associated with the American documentary movement known as **direct cinema** [Figure 8.7]. Programming such as *The Undersea World of Jacques Cousteau* (1966–1976) also defined this era.

8.7   *Primary* (1960). This documentary about John F. Kennedy's presidential campaign took advantage of the mobility and immediacy produced by new camera and sound equipment.

1980–Present: Digital Cinema, Cable, and Reality TV

In the 1980s, the consumer video camera was taken up by artists and activists, such as the AIDS **activist video** collective Testing the Limits, as part of the democratization of documentary that would continue with the rapid shift to digital formats. With the introduction in the late 1980s of Avid's nonlinear digital editing process, documentary **shooting ratio** (the ratio of footage shot to footage used in the film), quickly increased exponentially (since editing became so much easier and less expensive), and *personal documentaries* became a rapidly growing subgenre that would eventually achieve theatrical exposure in such films as Morgan Spurlock's quirky tale of his weight-gaining quest, *Supersize Me* (2004) [Figure 8.8]. During this period, changes in the distribution and exhibition of documentary significantly impacted the availability and popularity of these films (See pp. 36–38).

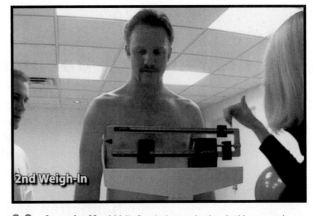

8.8   *Supersize Me* (2004). Spurlock at a checkup in this personal documentary on fast-food diets and their effects on American obesity.

In addition to increased festival and theatrical exposure and the expanding video rental market, cable and satellite television networks provide more and more opportunities for documentary projects. Under Sheila Nevins, premium cable channel HBO's documentary division has sponsored numerous powerful and acclaimed films, including *Born into Brothels* (2004) and *Baghdad ER* (2006). *Planet Earth* (2006), the eleven-part nature series co-produced by the BBC and Discovery Channel, garnered awards, critical praise, and wide audiences on TV and DVD for its state-of-the-art, high-definition cinematography and conservation message [Figure 8.9]. While The Sundance Channel and other cable channels provide more venues for independently produced documentaries that may otherwise have limited distribution, the relatively low production costs of nonfiction programming have encouraged many other channels to fill their schedules with reality television. From *Cops*

8.9   *Planet Earth: Jungles* (2006). This bird of paradise from the jungles of New Guinea attempts to impress a potential mate with his elaborate dance.

(a)

(b)

8.10 **(a) *American Idol*** (2002), **(b) *The Biggest Loser*** (2004). Just two examples of reality television shows that blur the boundaries among what is real, performed, and reenacted.

and MTV's *The Real World* to *American Idol* and *The Biggest Loser,* these formats feature real people in situations that blur the lines between actual events, theatrical performances, and reenactments **[Figures 8.10a and 8.10b]**.

The Elements of Documentary Films

For many, film served not as an art but as a tool for exploring and explaining the physical and social world. The documentary film, despite sharing elements of cinematic form with narrative and experimental films, very distinctly organizes its material, constitutes its authority, and engages the audience. The following section outlines these modes of discourse and organizations typical of the documentary film.

Nonfiction and Non-Narrative

VIEWING CUE

What historical precedents (scientific treatises? essays? news reports?) might explain the strategies used in the film you've just viewed?

Nonfiction and non-narrative, cornerstones of documentary films, are two key concepts that are often debated. Although documentary films and experimental films (see Chapter 9) can both be described as non-narrative, nonfiction has primarily been associated with documentary films. **Nonfiction films** present (presumed) factual descriptions of actual events, persons, or places, rather than their fictional or invented re-creation. In most cases, facts are malleable and debatable, much as every person's image of an attractive person differs slightly. Yet a basic distinction throughout human history (and thus film history) has been the difference between the inarguable truth of facts and the questionable truth of fiction.

The precariousness of this distinction has provoked heated debates throughout film history, but movie culture has nonetheless often assumed a fundamental distinction between, say, a PBS documentary about the life of Queen Elizabeth I of England and the feature film *Elizabeth: The Golden Age* (2007). The first film uses the accounts of scholars and historians, old paintings and artifacts, and the written accounts of her contemporaries to show the facts and complex issues in the life of one of the great women of history. The second film, a sequel to *Elizabeth* (1998), uses some of the same information but constructs it as an entertaining and easily comprehensible story. If nonfiction usually defines documentary films, it is important to recognize that it can be used in a variety of creative ways. For example, in *Enron: The Smartest Guys in the Room* (2005), Alex Gibney pursues a nonfictional, behind-the-scenes investigation of the cause behind the corporation's collapse through interviews with the actual participants and victims of the event [Figure 8.11]. In contrast, in *Of Great Events and Ordinary People* (1979), Raoul Ruiz turns an assignment to conduct nonfictional interviews in a Paris neighborhood into a complex and humorous reflection on the impossibility of revealing any truth or honesty through the interview process.

8.11 *Enron: The Smartest Guys in the Room* (2005). Alex Gibney's film is a nonfiction investigation of the corruption that led to the collapse of a powerful American corporation.

Non-narrative films are organized in a variety of ways that eschew or deemphasize stories and narratives, while employing other forms such as lists, repetitions, or contrasts as the organizational structure. Whether these films concentrate on abstract forms, events, objects, or individuals, they may choose—rather than to develop a story—to create a visual list (of objects found in an old house, for instance), to repeat a single image as an organizing pattern (returning to an ancient carving on the front door of that house), or to alternate between objects in a way that suggests different fundamental contrasts (contrasting the rooms, clothing, and tools used by the men and the women in that house). A non-narrative movie may certainly embed stories within its presiding organization, but those stories usually become secondary to the non-narrative pattern. In *Koyaanisqatsi* (1983), slow-motion and time-lapse photography capture the open vistas of an American landscape and their destruction against the drifting tones of Philip Glass's music: pristine fields and mountains, rusty towns, and garbage-strewn highways [Figure 8.12]. Through these images, one may detect traces of a story about the collapse of America in what the Hopi Indian title declares is "a life out of balance," but that simple and vague narrative is not nearly as powerful as the emotional force of the film's accumulating repetitions and contrasts. Diane Keaton's *Heaven* (1987) intersperses clips from old movies with angels and other images of heaven and presents a litany of faces and voices to answer such questions as "Does heaven exist?" and "Is there sex in heaven?" Although we may sense a religious mystery tale behind these questions and answers, this movie is better understood as a playful list of unpredictable reactions to the possibility of a life hereafter.

Nonfiction and non-narrative clearly suggest distinctive ways of seeing the world. Although they often overlap in documentary films, one form of presentation does not necessarily imply the other. A non-narrative film may be entirely or partly fictional, as when a pseudo-documentary movie pretends to be a scientific report about an undiscovered people. Conversely, a nonfiction film can be constructed as a narrative, as in a film about Eleanor Roosevelt that tells the story of her life from old photos, home movies, and newsreel film footage. Complicating these distinctions is the fact that both kinds of practices can become less a function of the intentions of the film than of viewers' perception of them; what may seem nonfictional or non-narrative in one context may not seem so in another. Keeping in mind the different meanings of nonfiction and non-narrative and how they can historically shift should, however, only make them more useful in judging the strategies of a particular documentary as part of changing cultural contexts.

text continued on page 281 ▶

8.12 *Koyaanisqatsi* (1983). A non-narrative catalogue of images contrasting America's beauty and decay.

Nonfiction and Non-Narrative in *Man of Aran* (1934)

Robert Flaherty's documentary film *Man of Aran* is an early, incisive example of how films employ, albeit in different ways, both nonfictional and non-narrative practices. *Man of Aran,* a documentary about a small community living on an island off the coast of western Ireland, does not identify the characters or explain their motivations; instead, it lists and describes the activities that make up their daily lives and records the hardships of living on a barren, isolated island. The members of this seemingly primitive community cart soil to grow potatoes on their rocky plots and struggle against the ferocious sea to fish and survive. In an important sense, the film is a historical and cultural record: it documents the routines of the residents' existence without the drama of a narrative beginning, climax, or conclusion. Adding to the distant atmosphere of a place that seems newly discovered by this film, the characters are not named and the force of the sea constantly overwhelms their meager attempts to create order and meaning in their lives [Figure 8.13]. Well beyond learning about the customs of a distant way of life, audiences find in *Man of Aran* a dignity of living far removed from common experience and knowledge.

Stories and narratives are not the primary organizational feature in *Man of Aran*. Instead, the film mostly accumulates, repeats, and contrasts images. The facts of the brutal lifestyle on the island are ordered as a list of tasks that contrast human activities with natural forces: images of people preparing meals, planting a garden, and repairing fishing nets alternate with images of crashing waves, barren rock coasts, and empty horizons.

Although they are subsumed under these alternative organizational patterns, traces of fiction and narrative are still visible in the film. Some situations are in fact fabricated, such as the episode in which the men are nearly lost at sea in the hunt for a basking shark (an activity that was part of

life two generations earlier but that, in 1934, no longer took place on the Aran Islands); the episode thus relies on the dramatic suspense that drives any good adventure story.

However innovative and distinctive this film is, it also reminds us of its cultural heritage. While explicitly working out of the tradition of an anthropological report, *Man of Aran* also adapts the tradition of the travel essay or travelogue, found in the works of writers from Henry James (1843–1916) to Bruce Chatwin (1940–1989). Whereas James describes the sights and sounds of his visits to Venice and Chatwin his encounters in Patagonia, Flaherty's film shows us a culture on the far reaches of the emerging modern civilizations of the twentieth century.

8.13 *Man of Aran* (1934). Inhabiting Irish islands unknown to many, nameless individuals fight for survival against the barren and harsh world.

Expositions: Organizations That Show or Describe

Narrative films might be said to merge science and art, as they shape the material realities of life into imaginative histories. Traditionally, however, documentary films have emphasized and developed a scientific and educational approach to life. A narrative film might tell the story of a young Thai girl longing to leave an isolated island and describe her adventurous escape to Bangkok. A documentary film, in contrast, might examine the details of her daily chores and intersperse those details with interviews in which she explains her frustrations and describes her hopes and wishes for another life. Whereas the narrative film relies on specific patterns that organize a plot around the actions and motivations of the girl, the documentary employs strategies and forms that resemble scientific and educational methods, presenting the girl according to a number of characteristics and behaviors. These various strategies alter our experience of the girl, thus making the character seem like two different people.

Documentaries are not always scientific investigations. Yet, however their borders may shift, we can identify the formal strategies used in documentary movies as *documentary organizations*. These organizations show or describe experiences according to a certain arrangement, logic, or order different from that of narrative organizations. These strategies may also appear in narrative films, but in documentary films they become the central, rather than the subsidiary, organizational form. Documentary films use expositional strategies to present information or perspectives without the temporal logic of narrative and with little explicit explanation or commentary. These are movies that observe the facts of life from a distance and organize their observations as objectively as possible to suggest some definition of the subject through the exposition itself. Here we will discuss three distinctive organizations of documentary films—the cumulative, the contrastive, and the developmental—as they might appear in different kinds of films or as they might be orchestrated through a single film. We will then describe how these formal practices, operating alone or together, are often presented through a presiding point of view or rhetorical position.

VIEWING CUE

Examine carefully the organization of the film you've viewed most recently. Does it follow a clear formal strategy? Explain.

Cumulative Organizations

Cumulative organizations present a catalog of images or sounds throughout the course of the film. It may be a simple series with no recognizable logic connecting the images. Joris Iven's *Rain* (1929) thus presents images from a rainstorm in Amsterdam, showing the rain falling in a multitude of different ways and from many different angles [Figure 8.14]. We do not sense that we are watching this downpour from beginning to end; rather, we see this rain as the accumulation of its seemingly infinite variety of shapes, movements, and textures. Although for most of us rain is a general, commonplace phenomenon, this film dissects and collects it as a collage of textures. *Thirty-Two Short Films about Glenn Gould* (1993) describes, as the title suggests, a series of performances and moving snapshots of the renowned pianist Glenn Gould. Although some viewers may expect a kind of biography of Gould, the film intentionally fragments his life into numerical episodes focused on his playing, on his acquaintances discussing him, and on reenactments of moments in his life [Figure 8.15].

8.14 *Rain* (1929). The accumulation of images of different kinds of rain showers gradually creates a poetic documentary of various shapes and textures.

8.15   *Thirty-Two Short Films about Glenn Gould* (1993). Rather than exposition, the film offers performance footage as a glimpse of the notoriously elusive genius.

8.16   *42 Up* (1998). Contrasting different faces through different generations.

Contrastive Organizations

A variation on cumulative exposition, *contrastive organizations* present a series of contrasts or oppositions meant to indicate the different points of view on its subject. Thus a film may alternate between images of war and peace or between contrasting skylines of different cities. Sometimes these contrasts may be evaluative, distinguishing positive and negative events. At other times, contrastive exposition may suggest a more complicated relationship between objects or individuals. Among the most ambitious versions of this technique is a group of films by Michael Apted, beginning with his documentary *7 Up* (1963) and followed by successive films made every seven years; the films track the changing attitudes and social situations of a group of children as they grow into the adults of *42 Up* (1998) **[Figure 8.16]** and *49 Up* (2005). With a new film appearing every seven years, these films contrast not only the differences among developing individuals in terms of class, gender, and family life but also the differences in their changing outlooks as they grow older.

Developmental Organizations

Developmental organizations present places, objects, individuals, or experiences through a pattern of development with a specific non-narrative logic or structure. For example, an individual or object may be presented according to a pattern that proceeds from small to large, as part of a developmental pattern from passive to active events, or as developing from the physical to the spiritual. With a script by W. H. Auden, *Night Mail* (1936) describes the journey of the mail train from London to Scotland, documenting and celebrating the many precisely coordinated tasks that describe this nightly civil service. With music from composer Benjamin Britten and poetry by Auden, the movement of this journey re-creates the rhythms of the train wheels as they accelerate, steady, and then slow in their developing path across England **[Figure 8.17]**. An early example of how a developmental organization can

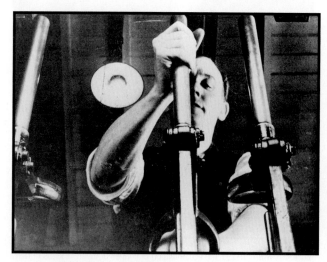

8.17   *Night Mail* (1936). Within the journey of mail from London to Scotland, a poetry of the everyday develops and progresses.

8.18   *Berlin: Symphony of a Great City* (1927). A city becomes a musical structure of events and people, streetcars and barges, moving forward from dawn to dusk.

emphasize abstract patterns of everyday activity to create a vibrant picture of city life is *Berlin: Symphony of a Great City* (1927). In this film, the daily comings and goings, the traffic, and the people of Berlin are arranged according to various movements, lines, and rhythms that remake the city as a musical structure developing from dawn to dusk [Figure 8.18].

Rhetorical Positions

Documentary organizations are often subject to the organizational point of view or rhetorical position that informs them. Just as narrative cinema uses narrators and narration, documentary and experimental films employ their own *rhetorical positions*, which shape those formal practices according to certain perspectives and attitudes. Sometimes these films avoid allowing a speaker to articulate the film's positions and attitudes and assume instead the neutral stance of the uninvolved observer—omniscient and neutral, sometimes referred to as the "voice of God" because of its assumed authority and objectivity. At other times, the point of view of the documentary assumes a more limited or even personal perspective. Whether clearly visible and heard, omniscient or personal, or merely implied by the film's organization, the rhetorical positions of documentary films generally articulate their attitudes and positions according to four principal frameworks:

- The first is associated with the effort to *explore* the world and its peoples.
- The second aims to *interrogate* or *analyze* an event or problem.
- The third assumes the stance of a *debater* or *polemicist* who attempts to convince the audience of a certain truth or point of view.
- The fourth foregrounds the presence and mediating activity of the film itself and/or the filmmaker in order to create a *reflexive* rhetorical position well aware of how the film "performs" and shapes a certain relationship with the world it describes.

Sometimes these frameworks will overlap in a single film. For example, the voice of Peter Davis's *Hearts and Minds* (1974) is both explorative and polemical as it tears apart, with strategically placed interviews and newsreel footage, the myths supporting the Vietnam War [Figure 8.19]. *Winged Migration* (2001) uses both very little commentary and a "bird's-eye view" to present the flights of migratory birds around the world, while at the same time it subtly promotes the natural mysteries of those activities. *Fahrenheit 9/11* (2004), a film about director Michael Moore's perspective on the war in Iraq and its relation to the U.S. oil industry, offers an often exaggerated performance as a clearly argumentative perspective meant to incite and arouse audiences and to sway opinion on that war.

Explorative Positions

Explorative positions mimic scientific points of view that announce or suggest that the driving perspective of the film is a search into particular social, psychological, or physical phenomena. Informed by this position, a documentary assumes the perspective of a traveler, explorer, or investigator who encounters new worlds, facts, or experiences and aims to present and describe these, often straightforwardly as a witness. While travel films were pervasive since the first days of cinema when filmmakers would offer short records of exotic sites such as Niagara Falls or the Great Wall of China, the first feature-length documentaries extended that explorative

8.19   *Hearts and Minds* (1974). A documentary explores the realities of the Vietnam War, while trying to convince its audience of the misguided decisions that led to the disaster it became.

8.20 *Nanook of the North* (1922). Many documentaries mimic the anthropologist's project of exploring other cultures, in this case the rituals and daily routines of an Inuit family.

8.21 *March of the Penguins* (2005). New technologies allow viewers to witness the delicate and unique exchange of the egg from mother to father.

curiosity as positioned somewhere between the anthropologist's urge to show different civilizations and peoples, as in Flaherty's *Nanook of the North* (1922) **[Figure 8.20]**, and the tourist's pleasure of visiting novel sites and locations, as in Jean Vigo's tongue-in-cheek wanderings through a French resort town in *Apropos of Nice* (1930). More recently, Academy Award winner and box-office success *March of the Penguins* (2005) assumes this traditional position but enhances it through the capabilities of new technologies to explore the migratory habits of Emperor penguins **[Figure 8.21]**.

Interrogative Positions

Interrogative or *analytical positions* rhetorically structure a movie either in terms of an implicit or explicit question-and-answer format or by other techniques that identify a subject as being under investigation. Commonly condensed in the interview format found in many documentary films, interrogative techniques can also employ a voiceover or an on-camera voice that asks questions of individuals or objects that do or do not respond to the questioning, much like television news. Frank Capra's *Why We Fight* series (1943–1945) explicitly formulates itself as an inquisition into the motivations for the U.S. involvement in World War II. With Trinh T. Minh-ha's *Surname Viet Given Name Nam* (1989), a question or problem may only be implied, and succeeding images may either resolve the problem or not. As a result, the film raises more questions than it answers. Harun Farocki's *The Interview* (1997) takes the logic of the interrogative position to a more reflexive level following unemployed individuals being trained to conduct themselves properly in a job interview. Interrogative and analytic forms may, in short, lead to more knowledge about an experience or may make the question of how we know the different cultures of the world the essential question of the film. One of the simplest and subtlest examples of the interrogative or analytical form is Alain Resnais's *Night and Fog* (1955), which offers images without answers **[Figures 8.22a and 8.22b]**.

8.22a and 8.22b *Night and Fog* (1955). As images of liberated survivors of the Nazi concentration camps alternate with contemporary images of the same empty camps, the complex organizational refrain of the film becomes, "Who is responsible?"

Persuasive Positions

Use of interrogation and analysis in a documentary film are often (but not always) intended to convince or persuade a viewer about certain facts or truths. *Persuasive positions* articulate a perspective that expresses some other personal or social position using emotions or beliefs and aim to persuade viewers to feel and see in a certain way. In *An Inconvenient Truth* (2006), former vice-president Al Gore positions himself like a professor before charts, graphs, and images in a sustained argument about the dangers of global warming [Figure 8.23]. When a movie attempts to persuade or convince, it may

8.23   *An Inconvenient Truth* (2006). Graphs, charts, and expert opinion help to persuade an audience of the dangers of global warming.

downplay the presence of the personal perspective and instead use images and sounds to influence viewers through argument or emotional appeal, as in propagandistic movies that urge certain political or social views. Leni Riefenstahl's infamous *Triumph of the Will* (1935) allows the grandiose composition of images to convince viewers of the glorious powers of the Nazi Party; meanwhile, Pare Lorentz's *The Plow That Broke the Plains* (1936) becomes an indictment of the lack of U.S. government planning that resulted in the environmental and social disaster in the West and Southwest known as the Dust Bowl. Persuasive forms can use the power of documentary images themselves, set up revealing contrasts (say, between certain images or between what is said and what is seen), or use voices and interviews in an attempt to convince viewers of a particular truth or cause. Frederick Wiseman's *Titicut Follies*, for example, exposes the treatment of and influences attitudes about the criminally insane without any overt argumentation [Figure 8.24]. With such movies, what we are being persuaded to do or think may not be immediately evident, yet it is usually obvious that we are engaged in a rhetorical argument that involves visual facts, intellectual statements, and sometimes emotional manipulation.

VIEWING CUE

Describe the presiding voice or attitude of the film you just viewed. Is the dominant technique appropriate to the subject? Can you imagine another way of filming this subject? Explain.

Reflexive and Performative Positions

Reflexive and *performative positions* call attention to the filmmaking process or perspective of the filmmaker in determining or shaping the documentary material being presented. Often this means calling attention to the making of the documentary or the process of watching a film itself. Certain films, like Laleen Jayamanne's *A Song of Ceylon* (1985), which references the classical documentary *Song of Ceylon* (1934) through meditation on colonialism and gender in Sri Lanka, can aim to remind viewers that documentary reality and history are always mediated by the film image, and that documentary films do not necessarily offer an easy access to truth. This attention to how the film performs itself can, moreover, shift from the filmmaking process to the filmmaker, thus emphasizing the personal or subjective participation of that individual as a kind of performer of reality. In Ross McElwee's *Sherman's March* (1986), the filmmaker sets out on a journey to document the famous Civil War general's conquest of the South; along the way, however, this witty film becomes more about the filmmaker's own failed attempts to start or maintain a romantic relationship with the many women he meets. Werner Herzog's *Grizzly Man* (2005) alternates between the self-performative videos of Timothy Treadwell and Herzog's documentary of Treadwell's unusual life in an Alaskan bear colony and his gruesome death. This back and forth makes the film a commentary on Treadwell, Herzog, and their different cinematic views of the world [Figure 8.25].

text continued on page 288 ▶

8.24   *Titicut Follies* (1967). Much of the film's power resides in shocking images of the institutional abuses of the prisoners.

8.25   *Grizzly Man* (2005). A documentary about another personal documentary, this film becomes a reflexive performance by filmmaker Herzog about the relation between images and nature.

Organizational Strategies and Rhetorical Positions in *Sunless* (1982)

Chris Marker's *Sunless*, perhaps better known by its original French title, *Sans Soleil,* is a global travelogue that moves through a dizzying catalog of different places and people, with commentary by a voice reading letters sent from the unnamed traveler to a friend in Europe. What makes this film such a beautiful and difficult movie is the precision and care with which different organizational strategies and rhetorical positions confront each other throughout the film, moving back and forth to parallel the correspondence between the traveler and his friend. On the one hand, the film explores, like social science or ethnography, the cultures of Japan and the African countries of Guinea-Bissau and the Cape Verde Islands. On the other, it enacts a reflexive meditation on different conceptions of time and memory in the twentieth century.

The film is unusually rich in organizational techniques. Indeed, the whole of *Sunless* can be considered a contrastive exposition of different cultures and peoples from around the world. As a kind of travelogue, the film moves, often abruptly, among Japan, Iceland, Guinea-Bissau, the Cape Verde Islands, Île-de-France, Okinawa, and the island of Sal. The contrasts that these places dramatize, however, are less about evaluations and surface differences than about differing senses of time and the commentator's efforts to comprehend them. As the commentator puts it, this is "not a search for contrasts but a journey to the two extreme poles of survival."

In *Sunless*, even conventional accumulative forms seem to have a twist or a sense of irony running through them. At one point, we see a series of more than twenty faces of African women. Each face has its own expression and shape, and as the series accumulates one face after another, each seems to shine forth with more individual personality and intensity: one stares, another turns away; one smiles, another glares hostilely. While the presentation appears to offer a collective representation of African women, almost a sampling of types of faces, the specific expressions undermine any generalities that might otherwise describe the exposition [**Figures 8.26a–8.26c**].

One of the central themes of *Sunless* is the power and isolated integrity of "things"—or in the voiceover's quotation of an eleventh-century Japanese woman writer, "things that quicken the heart." In one way, the film follows a cumulative organization by presenting different examples of these "things," from Japanese pachinko games to dogs on the beach. Yet in the film's meditation on this world of things, one possible and extremely subtle pattern that develops is the increasing intensity of objects and images as they grow more and more expressive of their own essence. Across its wide and varied exposition, *Sunless* moves from the many sleeping bodies on the ferry and the expressive faces of children to the abstract shapes of computer technology, where each thing becomes visual poetry in itself.

Just as it interrogates the scientific methods that have explored and colonized people of other cultures, *Sunless* also reflexively questions the methods used to romanticize those cultures, presenting images and simultaneously reflecting on them. Perhaps the most dramatic and important example occurs at the beginning and again toward the end of the film: at both points, the image of three children in Iceland appears, and the commentator, acting as the spokesperson for the unnamed letter writer, says about the effort to create a metaphor with this image, "He said that for him it was the image of happiness . . . and he has often tried to link it to other images but it had never worked." The image then becomes black and is replaced by three stationary U.S. fighter jets before the commentator continues, over another black image, with, "One day I'll have to put it at the beginning of a film with a long piece of black leader. If they don't see happiness in the picture, at least they'll see the

8.26a–8.26c *Sunless* (1982). A sampling of facial types represents the accumulation of individual expressions.

black." With this admittedly complex association, the film seems self-consciously to struggle to create or "perform" a meaning from one image of happiness and innocence that could attach itself to other experiences (in this case, perhaps the images of the entire film). But even in creating that meaning, the commentator seems to recognize that all film images disappear and fade to black as one image replaces the previous, sometimes fully alien, image.

Cats and owls permeate the film, sometimes appearing as images of patience and wisdom; at other times, they are simply described as the favorite animals of the traveler/commentator. Other cultural and cinematic objects also beckon in this film: a statue of a faithful dog in Tokyo or the spiral image that recurs in many forms, including in Alfred Hitchcock's *Vertigo* (1958) [**Figure 8.27**]. Certainly these figures become documents of time and history: how people devote themselves to time or how time turns us constantly in its twists. Yet in this film, the regular presentation of images is always about why and how we make, need, and perform ourselves through images—to help us anchor and explain living in a world so vexed by time and history.

Sunless thus makes continual references to the texture and structures of representation, film images, and other ways, such as rituals, that we try to organize our lives. One section of the film shows a group of images filled with television sets whose multiple rectangular patterns fill the

film frame [**Figure 8.28**]. In its most abstract moments, Marker's film shifts to abstract computer designs, or what the voiceover refers to as images from "The Zone," where previously real images are now translated into quivering colors and lines. Here the shift into abstract representation suggests an almost utopian purity or intensification that the real world will never have.

In *Sunless,* the voiceover is that of a commentator rather than a narrator. This is an intricate example of how powerful and complex a non-narrative voice can be—whether it is actually heard or is simply implied by the perspective of the film. The unidentified voice of a woman reads letters sent by another fictionalized person, Sandor Krasna (named only in the closing credits), who may be a camera person, the filmmaker, or simply a traveler. As these voices shift from one to another and merge one into another, they describe what they see, analyze its meaning, urge a certain understanding, or simply speak their amazement out loud. A scientifically inquiring voice moves through multiple questions and the unresolved analysis of these questions: What is the experience of happiness? What is memory? Is there a social politics to the experience of time? How can time be organized in life and on film? Meanwhile, the same voice grows poetically expressive and performative, providing

8.27 *Sunless* (1982). The recurring symbol of a spiral.

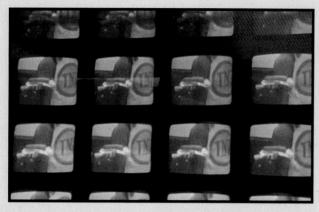

8.28   *Sunless* (1982). Images of other images verge on abstraction.

8.29   *Sunless* (1982). The layered voice of the film's commentator ruminates across images about a "poetry born of insecurity."

counterpoint to its more analytic questions with expressions of delight, meditative reflections, and occasional efforts at gentle persuasion. Sometimes the commentator verbally describes the emotionally drifting attitude of the film in its descriptions of its world: "poetry is born of insecurity . . . wandering Jews, quaking Japan . . . moving in a world of appearances, fragile, fleeting." At other times, the film silently describes that attitude: moving through still images of dead animals in the desert to frenetic and gay street festivals in Japan and Africa [Figure 8.29].

Sometimes frustrating and sometimes sublime, *Sunless* stands out as a remarkable orchestration of the many strategies and formal tools available to documentary filmmakers. If conventional documentaries reject the dominance of narrative organizations, Marker's movie rejects the distinctions that each of those two practices can claim in relation to the other. The result is a travelogue of a world that explodes into a collage of discrete particulars, which always fascinate us and elude our attempts to contain them.

The Significance of Documentary Films

Even more than narrative cinema, documentary films emphasize *meaning* and often make their appeal to audiences explicit. Although moviegoers have always been attracted to a film's entertainment value, from as early as the 1890s audiences have also appreciated the cultural and educational values of nonfiction movies. These films

8.30   *Leaving Jerusalem by Railway* (1896). Early film allowed audiences to experience the pleasure and education of visiting new lands and vistas.

presented sporting events, political speeches, and dramatic presentations of Shakespeare. In 1896, for instance, the Lumière brothers took audiences on an educational railway trip with the "phantom ride" of *Leaving Jerusalem by Railway* [Figure 8.30]. In 1898, Thomas Edison presented an early ethnographic film about Native Americans called *Wand Dance, Pueblo Indians.* According to these practices, then, the documentary as a movie form could presumably offer unmediated truths or factual insights unavailable through strictly narrative experiences. However much these views of the documentary may have changed during the next century, presenting presumed social, historical, or cultural truths or facts remained the foundations on which the different meanings for documentary films were built. Throughout the history of documentaries, in short, viewers have found these films most signficant in their ability (1) to reveal new or ignored realities not typically seen in narrative films, and (2) to confront assumptions and alter opinions.

As with narrative movies, the relationship between documentary films and the cultural and historical expectations of viewers plays a large part in how these movies are understood and what meanings we find in them. Some viewers might watch a film for scientific, social, or some other kind of conceptual information. Luis Buñuel's *Land without Bread* (1933) might seem to be a kind of travelogue about a remote region of Spain—Las Hurdes—but its bitingly ironic soundtrack commentary, which flatly understates the brutal misery, poverty, and degradation in the region, makes the film a searing political commentary on the failure of the state and church to care adequately for the people who live there. So unmistakable was the message of this film, in fact, that the Spanish government repressed it. Without its cultural context, this film might seem odd or confusing to some viewers today, reminding us that in order to locate the significance of a film, we often must understand the historical, social, and cultural context in which it was made.

▶ VIEWING CUE

What makes a documentary film you have recently seen important? How is it meaningful? How specifically does it achieve its aims and make its values apparent? **⏸**

Revealing New or Ignored Realities

Because narrative movies are the dominant ones, documentary films commonly have a differential value: successful documentary films offer different kinds of truth from what narrative movies can communicate or provide. Often this means to reveal new or ignored realities by showing people, events, or levels of reality we have not seen before, because they have been excluded either from our social experience or from our experiences of narrative films. To achieve these kinds of fresh insight, documentaries often question the basic terms of narratives, such as the centrality of characters, the importance of a cause-and-effect chronology, or the necessity of a narrative point of view, or they draw on perspectives or techniques that would seem out of place in a narrative movie.

Perhaps by showing us an object or a place from angles and points of views beyond the realistic range of human vision, such films will place us closer to a newly discovered reality: we see the bottom of a deep ocean through the power of an underwater camera or the flight of migrating birds from their perspectives in the skies. Perhaps the object will be presented for an inordinately long amount of time, showing minute changes rarely seen in our usual experiences: one movie condenses the gestation of a child in the womb, while another shows the dread and boredom experienced over one long night by a homeless person in Miami. David and Albert Maysles's *Grey Gardens* (1975) portrays the quirky extremes of a mother and daughter, relatives of Jacqueline Kennedy Onassis, living in a dilapidated mansion in East Hampton, Long Island. Slowly, by following their daily routines and dwelling on the incidentals in their lives, the film develops our capacity truly to see two individuals whose unique personalities and habits become less and less strange [**Figure 8.31**].

Confronting Assumptions, Altering Opinions

Documentary films may present a familiar or well-known subject and attempt to make us comprehend it in a new way. Some documentaries are openly polemical when presenting a subject: as an obvious example, documentaries about a political figure or a controversial event may confront viewers' assumptions or attempt to alter received opinions about the person or events. Other films may ask us to rethink a moment in history or our feelings about what once seemed like a simple exercise, as in *Wordplay* (2006), a documentary about crossword puzzles and how they inspire intellectual activity.

8.31 *Grey Gardens* (1975). The relationship between two quirky and unusual women becomes a touching and entertaining documentary about individualism and humanity.

With any and all of the formal and organizational tools available to a documentary, these films attempt to persuade viewers of certain facts, attack other points of view, argue with other films, or motivate viewers to act on social problems or concerns. An especially explicit example, Michael Moore's *Sicko* (2007) very visibly and tendentiously argues that the health care system in the United States is antiquated and destructive, and that it needs to be changed. Released the same year, the documentary *Manufacturing Dissent: Uncovering Michael Moore* (2007) takes Moore and his many films to task for fudging or misrepresenting facts. Such polemic is central to this tradition of documentary cinema, which is always about which reality we wish to accept and believe.

Serving as a Social, Political, Historical, and Cultural Lens

From the two primary agendas discussed above come two traditions of documentary cinema: the social documentary and the ethnographic film. While these two terms describe some of the main directions in and frameworks for understanding many documentary films throughout the twentieth century, more recent film practices such as personal and fake documentaries have developed other possibilities for creating and understanding documentary films.

The Social Documentary

Social documentaries examine and present both familiar and unfamiliar peoples and cultures as social activities from around the world. Using a variety of organizational practices, this tradition emphasizes one or both of the following goals: authenticity in representing how people live and interact, and discovery in representing unknown environments and cultures. Considered by some scholars and filmmakers the father of documentary, John Grierson made his first film, *Drifters* (1929), about North Sea herring fishermen; another early British filmmaker, Humphrey Jennings, continued this tradition with *Listen to Britain* (1942), a twenty-minute panorama of British society at war—from soldiers in the fields to women in factories. Indeed, the social-issue documentary tradition is long and varied, stretching from Pare Lorentz's *The River* (1937), made for the U.S. Department of Agriculture about the importance of the Mississippi River, through Indian filmmaker Pan Nalin's *Ayurveda: Art of Being* (2001), about the Indian system of holistic medicine. Two important spin-offs from the social documentary tradition are the political documentary and the historical documentary.

8.32 *The Spanish Earth* (1937). A celebration of the heroic resistance of fighters in Spain against an emerging fascist political machine.

The Political Documentary. Partially as a result of the social crisis of the Great Depression in the United States and the more general economic crises that occurred in most other countries after World War I, *political documentaries* aimed to investigate and to celebrate the political activities of men and women as they appear within the struggles of small and large social spheres. Contrasting themselves with the lavish Hollywood films of the times, these documentary films sought a balance of aesthetic objectivity and political purpose. Preceded by the films of Dziga Vertov and the Soviet cinema of the 1920s (such as the 1929 *Man with the Movie Camera*), political documentaries tend to take analytical or persuasive positions, hoping to provoke or move viewers with the will to reform social systems. Narrated by Ernest Hemingway, Joris Ivens's *The Spanish Earth* (1937) presents, for example, the heroic resistance of the "Loyalists" as they fight valiantly against the brutal forces of a fascist government [Figure 8.32]. While political documentaries such as these can sometimes be labeled *propaganda films* because of their visible efforts to support a particular social or political issue or group, they frequently use more complex arguments and more subtle tactics than bluntly manipulative documentaries.

Since World War II, political documentaries have grown more varied and occasionally more militant. In 1968, Argentine filmmakers Fernando Solanas and Octavio Getino produced *Hour of the Furnaces,* a three-hour-long examination of the colonial exploitation of Argentina's culture and resources that inspired heated political discussions and even demonstrations in the street. Emile de Antonio's *In the Year of the Pig* (1968) delivers a scathing attack on the Vietnam War. In recent decades, feminist documentaries, gay and lesbian documentaries, and documentaries about race (see pp. 424–449) have figured as prominent and important films in the traditions of political documentary as they explore the political issues and identity politics that have traditionally not been addressed by social documentaries. The variety of these films indicates the power and purpose of this mostly modern tradition. Focused on two sisters (who are later revealed to be actors) talking about their relationship with their mother, Michelle Citron's *Daughter Rite* (1979) expands as a much broader commentary on the development of female identity within the family. Robert Epstein and Richard Schmiechen's *The Times of Harvey Milk* (1984) describes the assassinations of the San Francisco mayor and of Milk, an activist who was the first gay supervisor elected in the city, and Jennie Livingston's *Paris Is Burning* (1990) explores the subculture of New York City drag balls, maintaining a serious, sympathetic, and witty tone throughout [**Figure 8.33**]. Spike Lee's HBO documentary *When the Levees Broke: A Requiem in Four Acts* (2006), about the government mishandling of the Hurricane Katrina disaster, is a worthy heir to a long tradition of documentaries that make the politics of race the centerpiece of the politics of the nation [**Figure 8.34**].

The Historical Documentary. Another form related to social documentary is the *historical documentary*, a type of film that concentrates largely on recovering and representing events or figures in history. Depending on the topic, these films are often compilations of materials, relying on old film footage or other materials such as letters, testimonials by historians, or photographs. Whatever the materials and tactics, however, historical documentaries have moved in two broad directions. *Conventional documentary histories* assume the facts and realities of a past history can be more or less recovered and accurately represented. Rooted in the journalistic movie series *The March of Time* from the late 1930s, these films assume a straightforward faith in the film medium to act as mirror to a historical truth (or as Oliver Wendell Holmes put it, "a mirror with a memory"). Thus *Atomic Café* (1982) is a rather satirical documentary that uses media and government footage to describe the paranoia and hysteria of the nuclear arms race during the Cold War

8.33   *Paris Is Burning* (1990). A sympathetic and witty portrayal of the subculture of drag balls in New York City.

8.34   *When the Levees Broke: A Requiem in Four Acts* (2006). Spike Lee's HBO documentary uses the medium as a powerful tool for political statements.

8.35   *Atomic Café* (1982). Employs the devices and material of conventional documentary history and uses them to satirize the paranoia of 1950s culture.

8.36   *Who Killed Vincent Chin?* (1988). Documents a local hate crime that resonates in larger historical terms; at the same time it reflects on the difficulty of communicating the full historical truth.

▶ **VIEWING CUE**

Identify a documentary film you've seen that can be considered a social documentary. What type of social documentary is it? Explain. ⏸

[Figure 8.35]. The films of Ken Burns, including the PBS series *The Civil War* (1990), *Baseball* (1996), and *The War* (2007) use a range of materials, techniques, and voices to re-create the layered dynamics of major historical and cultural events. *Reflexive documentary histories*, in contrast, adopt a dual point of view: alongside the work to describe an event (for instance, associated with a historical trauma such as the Holocaust or the nuclear bombing of Hiroshima) is the awareness that film or other discourses and materials will never be able to fully retrieve the reality of that lost history. Despite their vastly different topics (the Nazi death camps and the racist murder of a Chinese automotive engineer), Claude Lanzmann's *Shoah* (1986) and Chris Choy and Renee Tajima's *Who Killed Vincent Chin?* (1988) engage specific historical and cultural atrocities and simultaneously reflect on the extreme difficulty, if not impossibility, of fully and accurately documenting the truth of those events and experiences **[Figure 8.36]**.

Ethnographic Cinema

Especially after World War II, **ethnographic documentaries**, with roots in early cinema, become a second major tradition in documentary film. While social documentaries tend to emphasize the political and historical significance of certain events and figures, ethnographic films are typically about cultural revelations, aimed at presenting specific peoples, rituals, or communities that may have been marginalized by or invisible to the mainstream culture. Here we will highlight two practices within the ethnographic tradition: anthropological films and cinema verité.

Anthropological Films.   *Anthropological films* explore different global cultures and peoples, both living and extinct. In the first part of the twentieth century, these films often sought out exotic and endangered communities to reveal them to viewers who had little or no experience of them. *Grass* (1925), for example, features a Bakhtiari tribe in central Persia (modern-day Iran) on a remarkable migratory journey. Such documentaries generally aim to reveal cultures and peoples authentically, without imposing the filmmaker's interpretations, but in fact they are often implicitly shaped by the perspectives of their makers. In the 1940s and 1950s, such works as Jean Rouch's *The Magicians of Wanzerbé* (1949) transformed film into an extension of anthropology, searching out the social rituals and cultural habits that distinguish the people of particular, often primitive, societies. Robert Gardner's *Dead Birds* (1965) examines the war rituals of the Dani tribe in New Guinea, maintaining a scientific distance that draws out what is most unique and different about the people **[Figure 8.37]**.

The scope and subject matter of ethnographic documentaries have expanded considerably over the years, sometimes finding lost cultures in the West's own backyard. This contemporary revision of anthropological cinema investigates the rituals, values, and social patterns of families or subcultures such as the skateboard clan of *Dogtown and Z Boys* (2002), rather than directing its attention to cultures or communities that are "foreign" to its producers. Using found footage or archival prints of home movies made before 1950, Karen Shopsowitz's *My Father's Camera* (2001) argues that reality is sometimes best revealed by amateur filmmakers capturing everyday life though home movies and snapshots. *Capturing the Friedmans* (2003) also uses home videos and interviews to bring out the facts and contradictions in a Long Island family whose otherwise normal lifestyle is shattered when the father is accused of pedophilia [Figure 8.38].

8.37   ***Dead Birds*** (1965). Examines the war rituals of the Dani tribe in New Guinea, maintaining a scientific distance that draws out what is most unique and different about the people.

Cinema Verité and Direct Cinema. One of the most important and influential documentary schools related to ethnographic cinema is *cinema verité,* French for "cinema truth." Related to the Russian *Kino-Pravda* ("cinema truth") of the 1920s, cinema verité insists on filming real objects, people, and events in a confrontational way, in which the reality of the subject continually acknowledges the reality of the camera recording it. This film movement arose in the late 1950s and 1960s in Canada and France before quickly spreading to film cultures in the United States and other parts of the world.

Aided by the development of lightweight cameras and portable sound equipment, filmmakers like Jean Rouch created in their images a jerky immediacy to suggest the filmmakers' participation and absorption in the events they were recording. Rouch and Edgar Morin's *Chronicle of a Summer* (1961) is a se-

8.38   ***Capturing the Friedmans*** (2003). A domestic ethnography that reveals the social intricacies and psychological complexities of a troubled middle-class family.

ries of interviews with individuals on the streets of Paris; Rouch's *Moi un noir* (*I, a black*, 1958), filmed in Treichville, a neighborhood in Ivory Coast's capital city, portrays the everyday life of a group of young Africans accompanied by the voiceover narration of one who refers to himself as Edward G. Robinson (after the "tough guy" actor in American films of the 1930s). In this version of cinema verité, rules of continuity and character development are willfully ignored. Here reality is not just what objectively appears; reality is also the fictions and fantasies that these individuals create for and about themselves and the acknowledged involvement of the filmmaker as interlocutor. Moreover, unlike its American counterpart, French cinema verité draws particular attention to the subjective perspective of the camera's rhetorical position: in *Moi un noir,* the voiceover frequently makes ironic remarks about what is being shown; in *Chronicle,* the lingering camera seems consciously to provoke confessional admissions from its subjects.

The North American version of cinema verité, referred to as *direct cinema,* is more observational and less confrontational than the French practice. Its landmark film, *Primary* (1960), follows Democratic candidates John F. Kennedy and Hubert H. Humphrey through the Wisconsin state presidential primary. D. A. Pennebaker and the Maysles brothers, who were all involved in the making of *Primary,* continued to work in this tradition, gravitating toward social topics in which the identity of the subjects is inseparable from their role as performers. Pennebaker made numerous cinema verité–like films such as *Don't Look Back* (1967) [Figure 8.39],

8.39   ***Don't Look Back*** (1967). Direct cinema contemplates the inside of the celebrity world of Bob Dylan.

8.40 *A Healthy Baby Girl* (1996). Some documentaries, such as this one about the filmmaker and her mother, entwine the story of a personal life with larger issues, here a breach of medical ethics.

a portrait of the young Bob Dylan, and *The War Room* (1993), about the 1992 political campaign of Bill Clinton. In addition to *Grey Gardens,* Albert and David Maysles made many films in direct cinema style, including *Salesman* (1969), about itinerant Bible salesmen, and *Gimme Shelter* (1970), a powerful and troubling record of the 1969 Rolling Stones tour across the United States. Albert Maysles continues to be active, serving as an adviser to new generations of documentarians.

Personal Documentaries, Reenactments, and Mockumentaries

In recent years especially, the line between the documentary traditions of social documentaries and ethnographic films has wavered and shifted, as the foundational structures of narrative, non-narrative, nonfiction, and fiction have increasingly exchanged tactics and topics.

Increasingly common in recent years, **personal** or **subjective documentaries** create films that look more like autobiographies or diaries. In *Lost, Lost, Lost* (1976), Jonas Mekas portrays his fears and hopes in a diary film about his growing up as an immigrant in New York; counterpointing home movies, journal entries, and a fragmented style that resembles a diary, the rhythmic interjections of the commentator-poet express feelings ranging from angst to delight. In *A Healthy Baby Girl* (1996), filmmaker Judith Helfland explores the causes of her cancer diagnosis in her mother's use of the drug DES (diethylstilbestrol) during pregnancy, which was prescribed to prevent miscarriage. While the film exposes and indicts this breach of medical ethics and its impact on women's health, its primary focus is on the personal journey of the filmmaker and her family [Figure 8.40].

Questions about the truth and honesty of documentaries have shadowed this practice since Flaherty's reconstruction of "typical" events for the camera in *Nanook of the North* and his other films in the 1920s. Recently more and more documentaries have seized on the question of the veracity of the camera in order to complicate or to spoof documentary practices. Increasingly visible and debated today, documentary **reenactments** use documentary techniques in order to present a reenactment or theatrical staging of presumably true or real events. An early example of this blurring of boundaries, Sergei Eisenstein's fictional *Strike* (1924) uses documentary-style realism and avoids concentrating on individual characters in a narrative tale of a 1912 factory workers' strike in czarist Russia. *The Battle of Algiers* (1965) similarly depicts the Algerian revolt against the French occupation (1954–1962) as a recreation, a film about a real historical event that uses documentary techniques while developing the story with a script and actors [Figure 8.41]. Indeed, an opening caption boasts that no documentary footage is used in the film. Errol Morris's *The Thin Blue Line* (1988) is a documentary about a man, Randall Adams, convicted of killing a Dallas police officer in 1976, but it also becomes a mystery drama about discovering the real murderer. While it uses the many expository techniques of documentary film (such as close-ups of evidence and "talking-head" interviews), *The Thin Blue Line* alternates these with staged reenactments

8.41 *The Battle of Algiers* (1965). Reenacting historical realities.

8.42 *This Is Spinal Tap* (1984). Mockumentaries remind us that the authenticity of cinematic documentaries relies on the experiences and expectations of their audiences.

8.43 *Borat* (2006). Some of the most important assumptions about documentary integrity are violated in this film, perhaps as a way to satirize the pretensions of those assumptions.

of the murder evening, invented dialogue, an eerily musical soundtrack, courtroom drawings, and even clips from old movies. In the last decade, the popularity of and questions surrounding the practice of reenactment have grown so much that Rick Caine and Debbie Melnyk produced the documentary *Manufacturing Dissent* on Michael Moore's use of reenactments in his films.

At the other end of the spectrum, **mockumentaries** take a much more humorous approach to the question of truth and fact by using a documentary style and structure to present and stage fictional (sometimes ludicrous) realities. The mockumentary is an extreme example of how documentaries can generate different experiences and responses depending on one's knowledge of the traditions and aims of such films, and their viewing contexts. For example, with the initial release of *This Is Spinal Tap* (1984), some viewers saw and understood it as a straightforward rock-music documentary (or "rockumentary"), while most recognized it as a spoof on that documentary tradition. The two responses dramatize how people's different ideas of, knowledge about, and associations with documentaries can elicit very different interpretations of the "reality" of the film [Figure 8.42]. The popular and controversial *Borat* (2006) integrates a similar mockumentary style by following a fictional Kazakh television talking head as he travels "the greatest country in the world" in search of celebrities, cowboys, and the "cultural learning" found on the streets of America. Actor Sacha Baron Cohen mixes his impersonation of the character Borat with interviews of people who accept his persona as genuine. As such, the film raises questions about the boundary between a parody of viewers' assumptions about the truth and a dangerous distortion of the integrity of documentary values [Figure 8.43].

Closely related to the mockumentary but with more serious aims is the *fake documentary*, a tradition that extends from Buñuel's *Land without Bread* through Orson Welles's *F for Fake* (1974), a movie that looks at real charlatans and forgers while itself questioning the possibilities of documentary truth. A more recent film, Cheryl Dunye's *The Watermelon Woman* (1996), is a fictional account of an African American lesbian documentary filmmaker researching a black actress from the 1930s. The archive of photos and film footage she assembles for the film represents a lovingly fabricated work by the film's creative team—an imagining of a history that has not survived [Figure 8.44].

text continued on page 298 ▶

8.44 *The Watermelon Woman* (1996). As a serious use of a mockumentary tradition, this film suggests a history that has not survived—or perhaps not yet arrived.

Manufacturing Significance in *The Man with the Movie Camera* (1929)

Dziga Vertov's *The Man with the Movie Camera* appeared toward the end of the silent film era and amidst the most daring and powerful period in Russian cinema. At that time, Vertov's film theories and practices had moved in two directions, which, to a certain extent, culminated in this landmark movie. Vertov insisted on the use of actual people and events and the dynamics of daily living—what he called a function of the *Kino-Glaz* ("cinema eye")—and claimed that the cinema could extend the powers of the human eye to show the greater experiential and political truths of life—what he designated the power of *Kino-Pravda* ("cinema truth").

The Man with the Movie Camera is a documentary exploration of a generic Russian city (a composite of Moscow, Kiev, Odessa, and a region in Ukraine): a travel film that explores modern urban life, transforming it into a "city symphony" film. The beginning of the film intertwines three sets of images. First, a theater opens for an audience: empty seats flip down to welcome the crowd that will soon arrive, an orchestra prepares its instruments, and a projector is set up to show a film to the arriving audience. Second, the city awakens through a series of images: a woman stirs in bed; a sleeping man moves on a bench; and the immobile facades of buildings appear braced for activity. Finally, in the third part of this overture, a cameraman leaves a building, climbs in an open car, and begins his travels through the streets of the city, recording all the people and activities that describe the life of this city, from dawn until dusk [Figure 8.45]. This is not, in brief, a story; rather, it is a city coming to life,

and bringing that city to life for the viewer is a cameraman and his film.

From one point of view, this film is a breathtaking revelation of the variety and energy of modern urban life. Movement is everywhere. As the day breaks, we witness empty streets coming alive with more and more people until crowds appear in many different shapes and sizes: workers burst through the gates of a factory, crowds jostle through intersections, and athletes gather to race and test their skills. Trolleys crisscross; flocks of pigeons burst in the air; and coal miners push large carts through industrial yards. Interspersed with these sights of continual public life are a multitude of more personal activities: a woman climbs out of bed and dresses,

8.45 *The Man with the Movie Camera* (1929). Documentary in action as a cameraman and his film bring a city to life.

8.46 *The Man with the Movie Camera* (1929). An image of a revolving door links the urban environment to the ability of the camera's mechanical eye to imbue the world with motion.

8.47 *The Man with the Movie Camera* (1929). Film editor Yelizaveta Svilova constructs a vision at her editing table.

couples apply for marriage licenses, and groups gather at the end of the day for bubbling bottles of beer. A central theme of this Marxist film is "the people," rather than any one individual, and what *The Man with the Movie Camera* works most assiduously to reveal is that the people consists of individuals in all their many capacities to work and play together.

Alongside these revelations, the film challenges viewers to see this world with fresh eyes, to recognize the social and political multiplicities and harmonies that escape perceptions dulled by daily routines. At several points, an image superimposes a human eye on a camera lens (in which we can see the reflection of a cameraman), suggesting how both forms of vision see and embrace the city before them. In the film, everyday life becomes a work of art seen through the movie camera, allowing us to see and perceive more than just images of an imaginary Russian city in 1929. The rapid pace and dynamic movements of the film demand that we engage the raw energy and excitement of city life as a utopian vision of modernity, as a political ideal that we are capable of creating with our own eyes [Figure 8.46].

The Man with the Movie Camera can be seen as ethnographic in its depiction of a day in the life of a city's people, and as a social documentary exploring urban modernity. Both traditions would develop, often on different tracks, throughout the history of documentary. As an ethnographic documentary, this film attempts to show the essence of a 1920s society that, until the cinema, could never be fully represented in all its spatial and temporal dynamics. Its authenticity resides in the velocity of the life it represents and in the vast range of the everyday urban world it uncovers. After the awakening of this city, the speed of objects and people seems to accelerate according to the pace of modern life and the breadth of its new populace: a horse and buggy carrying refined women races the cameraman and his car, shoppers swing nonstop through a revolving door, factory machines and workers rapidly assemble cartons of cigarettes, and women run back and forth on a basketball court.

In addition to its place in the ethnographic tradition, *The Man with the Movie Camera* participates in the rise and centrality of social and political documentaries in the 1920s, which aimed to inform, agitate, and move people to action. Like other Russian political documentaries at this time, Vertov's film explores both how human vision moves and how the movies offer the unique means to capture and empower the mechanics and imagination of human vision in motion. Throughout, *The Man with the Movie Camera* transforms inanimate objects and routine activities into abstract visual patterns full of life and harmony: images of traffic splitting into two parallel, contrapuntal spaces; images of telephone operators constructing webs of lines and angles at their switchboards; and a collage of images of a streetcar twirling around in a whirlwind of lines and movements. Indeed, this futuristic intensification and activation of human vision is, as the film suggests regularly, available especially through the modern mechanics of the movies. At one point in the film, alternating with shots of the work of a seamstress, a woman (the film's editor, Yelizaveta Svilova) works at her editing table; she examines several images of faces and selects certain ones to insert into a crowd sequence before the flow of film begins again [Figure 8.47]. Just as the film constantly calls attention to its making of images of the city with a film camera, it also implies that people working together can reconstruct their lives and communities to be more efficient and humane

8.48 *The Man with the Movie Camera* (1929). The gigantic image of the cameraman looms over the city, the cinema, and modern life.

visions of the social world. A tiny figure of the cameraman rises from a glass of beer; elsewhere his gigantic image looms over masses of people moving through the city. The figure of the cameraman becomes the guiding angel for re-making a modern society through new eyes, a society in which individuals will work as a group and technology and machines will be the forces of social improvement and harmony [Figure 8.48].

The Man with the Movie Camera is a documentary in which new visions remake the realities of everyday people and activities into a utopian city. Crafted in a 1920s Russian society in which art and politics necessarily coexisted, the film demands viewers' involvement in its realities and dynamic techniques: at its beginning and end, viewers are welcomed into the movie theater and encouraged to participate in and re-create the world along with their guide, the man with the movie camera.

▶ VIEWING CUE

How does seeing a documentary in a different historical or cultural context distort or change the aims and assumptions of the film? Give an example. ⏸

As we have seen, documentary films create movie experiences markedly different from those of narrative cinema. While some of these experiences are non-narrative portraits that envision individuals in ways quite unlike the narrative histories of the same people, others are about the truth of events. Narrative movies encourage us to enjoy, imagine, and think about our temporal and historical relationships with the world and to consider when those plots and narratives seem adequate according to our experiences. Documentary movies remind us, however, that we have many other kinds of relationships with the world that involve us in many other insightful ways—through debate, through exploration, and through analysis.

CONCEPTS AT WORK

Documentary cinema has a history as long and rich as that of narrative cinema, and while the two different organizations sometimes overlap and exchange tactics, documentary films emphasize less the entertainment found in a good story than the educational pleasure of new information or insight about events, people, and even ideas. These films have accordingly developed their own strategies and formal features: from expositional organizations that contrast, accumulate, or develop facts and figures to rhetorical positions that work to explore, analyze, persuade, or even "perform" the world. What we often value about these films is their ability to reveal that world to us in new ways and to provoke us to see it with fresh eyes, outcomes that have generated numerous and complex traditions from the many types of social documentaries to the many kinds of ethnographic films.

Activities

- Choose what you consider to be a very specific and very pressing contemporary social issue as the topic for a documentary you will make. Describe the presiding point of view that the film will use (its rhetorical position). Then sketch some of the central scenes or images you intend to use. How will these be organized? Describe in detail one important sequence in the film.
- Imagine that you've been contracted to make a mockumentary film about a particular documentary practice such as a travelogue. Highlight three central scenes that will demonstrate an awareness of the formal and thematic features of the films you're parodying.

THE NEXT LEVEL: ADDITIONAL SOURCES

Barnouw, Erik. *Documentary: A History of Non-Fiction Film.* 2nd rev. ed. New York: Oxford University Press, 1993. This survey of major twentieth-century documentary films distinguishes kinds of nonfiction films by the rhetorical stances they initiate (such as those of "the explorer," "the prosecutor," and "the guerrilla").

Barsam, Richard M., ed. *Nonfiction Film Theory and Criticism.* New York: Dutton, 1976. One of the first and still most important collections on the aims and distinctions of nonfiction filmmaking, this book features essays by John Grierson, Joris Ivens, and others.

Bruzzi, Stella. *New Documentary: A Critical Introduction.* 2nd ed. London: Routledge, 2006. This book is a serious, polemical, and succinct introduction to practical and theoretical issues regarding documentaries, such as the changing roles of gender, spectatorship, and authorship.

Ellis, Jack C., and Betsy A. McLane. *A New History of Documentary Film.* New York: Continuum, 2006. A general introduction to the major trends in documentary film history, this book concentrates largely on English-language films from Flaherty's films of the 1920s through the changes and challenges of the contemporary era defined by digital technologies.

Nichols, Bill. *Blurred Boundaries: Questions of Meaning in Contemporary Culture.* Bloomington: Indiana University Press, 1994. This ambitious investigation explores the "blurred" middle ground between fiction and nonfiction films; its historical scope moves from Sergei Eisenstein's *Strike,* to the infamous Rodney King videotape, to the work of a host of exceptional contemporary filmmakers.

Renov, Michael. *The Subject of Documentary.* Minneapolis: University of Minnesota Press, 2004. Renov's collection of critical essays explores the various fashionings of self through different documentary traditions: from newsreels and autobiographies to domestic ethnographies and new interactive technologies.

Rosenthal, Alan and John Corner, eds. *New Challenges for Documentary.* 2nd ed. Manchester, England: Manchester University Press, 2005. Thirty-five essays by different authors address six sets of topics: documentary as genre, documentary producers and directors, ethics and aesthetics, documentary and television, representations of history, and docudramas.

OFFICIAL SELECTION
BERLIN
INTERNATIONAL FILM FESTIVAL
2007

OFFICIAL SELECTION
TORONTO
INTERNATIONAL FILM FESTIVAL
2006

OFFICIAL SELECTION
NEW YORK
FILM FESTIVAL
2006

"NUTTILY WONDERFUL!
One of the 10 BEST FILMS
of the year."
Manohla Dargis, NY TIMES

"UPROARIOUSLY FUNNY
and surprisingly touching.
A MAGICAL EXPERIENCE."
Michael Dwyer, IRISH TIMES

BRAND UPON THE BRAIN!

a film by
Guy Maddin

THE FILM COMPANY PRESENTS A GUY MADDIN FILM "BRAND UPON THE BRAIN"
SULLIVAN BROWN GRETCHEN KRICH MAYA LAWSON
ERIC STEELE MARIS KATHERINE E. SCHARHON
CASTING JOY FAIRFIELD COSTUME DESIGNER NINA MOSER PRODUCTION DESIGNER TANIA KUPCZAK
DIRECTOR OF PHOTOGRAPHY BENJAMIN KASULKE EDITED BY JOHN GURDEBEKE MUSIC BY JASON STACZEK
EXECUTIVE PRODUCERS JODY SHAPIRO AJ EPSTEIN PHILIP WOHLSTETTER PRODUCED BY AMY E. JACOBSON AND GREGG LACHOW
WRITTEN BY GUY MADDIN AND GEORGE TOLES DIRECTED BY GUY MADDIN

www.branduponthebrain.com

THE FILM COMPANY

9

Experimental Screens
Avant-Garde Film, Video Art, and New Media

The feverish imagery of Winnipeg-based auteur Guy Maddin's *Brand upon the Brain!* (2007) fuses memory, invention, and above all film history in a strange tale of the hero Guy's return to the isolated lighthouse where his mother once ran a bizarre orphanage. Twin teenage detectives, appalling science experiments, and expressionist paintings compound the mystery—and the fun. At festivals and special exhibitions, audiences could see this "silent" film accompanied by musicians, celebrity narrators (rock star Lou Reed or actress Isabella Rosselini), and sound-effects artists. Turning experimental film into a theatrical event, Maddin invigorates its long tradition for contemporary viewers as he "brands" his vision upon the audience's perception.

While narrative films relate to the human desire to order experience in terms of stories, and documentaries address the desire to see and understand the material world, other aspects of human experience—sensory states, intellectual puzzles, memories and dreams—are invoked by the range of non-narrative, non-realist practices explored in experimental film, video, and other media. Life encompasses a range of states beyond stories and direct observation. The sight of a child learning to ride a bike, for instance, may evoke childhood memories, or the contemplation of a work of art may conjure a wide range of emotions. In dreams, the act of remembering is linked to a process of abstraction, as unconscious memories and perceptions give rise to images often surreal and disjointed. This potent imagery of memory and dream lies at the foundation of experimental film.

Experimentation with form and abstract imagery has occurred across film history. Over the past century, many adventurous filmmakers have used film to go outside the bounds of traditional narrative and documentary forms, combining images of the seemingly mundane, the unusual, and even the bizarre in order to address and challenge their audiences in fascinating ways. In Michel Gondry's music video for Björk's song "Human Behavior," for instance, the strategies of such experimental classics as the surrealist *The Seashell and the Clergyman* (1928) and the abstract musical film *Allegretto* (1936) recur in a fusion of cryptic imagery and music [**Figure 9.1**]. This chapter explores experimental audiovisual media from its origins to the present day, giving you the necessary tools to watch and discuss some of film history's most complex, challenging, and rewarding cinematic endeavors.

9.1 **"Human Behavior"** (1993). Contemporary forms like music video are indebted to such experimental film traditions as surrealism. This video by Michel Gondry combines pop culture and the avant-garde, as does singer Björk's music.

KEY CONCEPTS

In this chapter, we will examine:

- how to distinguish experimental film and media as cultural practices
- how experimental works make and draw on aesthetic histories
- how these works interrogate the formal properties of their media
- how experimental media challenge and become part of dominant film forms and institutions
- how experimental traditions are related to technological developments
- how viewers can prepare themselves to watch and appreciate experimental works
- how the challenges of experimental media contribute another dimension of significance to the film experience

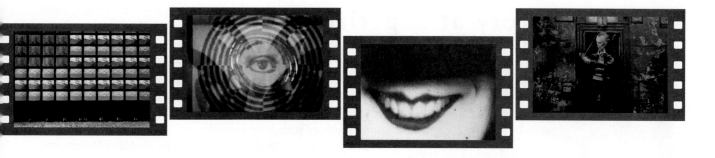

The word "cinema" is derived from the Greek word for movement, *kinema*. Arguably neither the storytelling ability of the medium nor its capacity to reveal the world is as basic to cinema as is the simple rendering of movement. So while narrative film defines the commercial industry and much of viewers' experience of the movies, and documentary builds on viewers' assumption of the camera's truth-telling function, experimental film focuses on the very properties that make film what it is—images in motion. Historically a variety of terms—notably **avant-garde cinema** (that is, advance guard or vanguard, derived from military terminology)—have been used to denote the works we discuss in this chapter. We have retained the more general term experimental precisely for its emphasis on the way filmmakers experiment with specific elements of film form for aesthetic expression or technical innovation. As we will see in many of this chapter's examples, which include experimental narratives and experimental documentaries as well as abstract films, experimental impulses do not respect boundaries.

Experimental films commonly reflect on the material specificity of the film medium and the conditions in which it is experienced by audiences—including such basic elements as film stock, sprocket holes, light, figure movement, editing patterns, and projection before an audience. Changes in technology bring changes in the form and object of these reflections. For example, filmmakers working in an amateur format like Super-8 may scratch directly on the film emulsion, as Su Friedrich does in *Gently Down the Stream* (1981), while a video artist might deliberately activate the vertical roll function to reflect on the medium of television, as Joan Jonas does in *Vertical Roll* (1972) **[Figure 9.2]**. The introduction of portable video equipment in the late 1960s and the shift to digital rather than analog formats, as well as the convergence of computers and cameras at the end of the twentieth century, expanded the resources of artists working in what can be broadly termed moving-image media.

Although this chapter primarily discusses the larger body and longer history of experimental film, we will also attempt to show how its histories and preoccupations are related to those of video art and **new media**, a term used in both information science and communications as well as the arts to refer to an array of technologies including the Internet, digital formats, video game consoles, cell phones, wireless devices, and the software applications and imaginative creations they support. Just as artists in the early twentieth century explored cinema's form and its place in modern life, many artists today use these technologies to reflect on life in the new millennium. The very fact that experimental films that were often difficult to see outside of urban arts or university contexts are now accessible through the Internet attests to a renewed energy in the realm of experimental moving-image media.

9.2 *Vertical Roll* (1972). Video artist Joan Jonas's piece reflects on the video medium, taking its name from a television malfunction.

A Short History of Experimental Film and Media Practices

(a)

(b)

9.3 **Nineteenth-century visual culture.** Nineteenth-century modernity celebrated visuality and technology (a) in Macy's window displays in 1884 and (b) at the Chicago World's Fair (1893), anticipating cinema's ways of seeing.

9.4 **Claude Monet,** *Water lilies* (c. 1916–1920). This panel from Monet's triptych anticipated experimental film in its energetic depiction of light.

The technology of experimental films and the vision they express have their roots in wider technological and social changes associated with **modernity**, a term that both names a broad period of history stretching from the end of the medieval era (with its primarily theological conception of the world) to the present, and identifies an attitude toward progress and science centered on the human capacity to shape history characteristic of our age [Figures 9.3a and 9.3b].

While modern society embraced progress and knowledge, some individuals rejected the scientific and utilitarian bias of the quest for facts. In the first half of the nineteenth century, Romantic poet Percy Bysshe Shelley proclaimed that poets were the unacknowledged legislators of the world. In the second half, Walter Pater, in *The Renaissance*, argued for the power of art to reveal the importance of the human imagination and create experiences unavailable in commerce and science: "To burn always with this hard, gemlike flame, to maintain this ecstasy," he claimed of art and poetry, "is success in life." New kinds of paintings—from the otherworldly visions of Pre-Raphaelites like Dante Gabriel Rossetti to the glimmering impressionist paintings of Claude Monet—expressed these aesthetic commitments to sensibility, creativity, and perception over factual observation [Figure 9.4]. Romantic aesthetic traditions influenced the emphasis on individual expressivity central to much experimental film practice [Figure 9.5].

The early twentieth century, when motion picture technology was perfected, saw rapid industrial and cultural change that was mirrored and questioned in developments in the arts. These artistic movements are known as *modernism*. New forms of painting, music, design, and architecture captured new experiences of

9.5 *The Garden of Earthly Delights* (1981). The work of prolific experimental filmmaker Stan Brakhage is indebted to the nineteenth-century tradition of Romantic poetry and its conception of artistic insight. This two-minute film was made by pressing actual flowers and leaves between strips of films and optically printing the images.

accelerated and disjunctive time, spatial juxtaposition, and fragmentation enabled by such technologies as the railroad, the telegraph, and electricity. Because cinema is literally made with machines, the medium was considered a central art of modernism, and experiments with space and time emerged early in the medium's history.

1910s–1920s: European Avant-Garde Movements

In the silent film era, numerous nations and movements embraced experimental film practices, which were often linked to other experimental art forms. In Germany, for instance, Dada and expressionism influenced the filmic rhythm studies of Viking Eggeling and Hans Richter [Figure 9.6] and the geometric set designs of *The Cabinet of Dr. Caligari* (1920). In 1920s France, avant-garde filmmakers such as Jean Epstein and Germaine Dulac (see pp. 409–411) drew on impressionism and cubism in painting as well as new musical forms in their work. At the same time, film artists explored cinematography and editing to develop the cinema as a unique art form. In *Ballet mécanique* (1924), French cubist painter Fernand Léger collaborated with American director Dudley Murphy in a celebration of machine-age aesthetics originally intended as a visual accompaniment to American composer George Antheil's musical piece of the same name (see Film in Focus, pp. 314–316).

One of the most significant experimental film movements in history occurred in the Soviet Union after the Russian Revolution in 1917. Vladimir Lenin declared cinema the most important of the arts, and Soviet filmmakers were inspired by the same principles as the constructivist movements that energized painting, theater, poetry, graphic design, and photomontage. Though avant-garde cinema flourished in these specific cities and countries, modernist filmmaking in the silent era was international in spirit, a characteristic that the introduction of sound (and hence language barriers) and the rise of fascism in Europe in the 1930s would inhibit. For example, the modern metropolis was paid tribute to in the transnational "city symphony" genre, examples of which hail from three different countries: Charles Sheeler and Paul Strand's tribute to New York City, *Manhatta* (1921) [Figure 9.7], Walther Ruttman's *Berlin: Symphony of a Great City* (1927), and Dziga Vertov's *The Man with a Movie Camera* (1929). In Britain, such internationalism was advocated by Kenneth Macpherson, Bryher, and the American poet h.d. in the pages of the film journal *Close Up* through the translation of writings by Soviet filmmaker Sergei Eisenstein, and in their strange and unique film, *Borderline* (1930). Featuring the

9.6   ***Rhythmus 21*** (1921). German artist Hans Richter's early abstract film explored the rhythm of shapes in motion.

9.7 *Manhatta* (1921). One of the first avant-garde films made in the United States, this tribute to the metropolis is echoed in European "city symphony" films.

9.8 *Borderline* (1930). The editors of the British film journal *Close Up* put their modernist ideas into practice in this experimental narrative featuring the American actor Paul Robeson.

▶ **VIEWING CUE**

What historical precedents might explain the strategies used in the film you just viewed? Does aligning the film with one or more historical precedents shed light on its aims? Explain. ⏸

politically outspoken African American actor Paul Robeson and his wife, Eslanda, *Borderline* evoked race and sexuality within the psychoanalytic theories of the era, all while challenging conventional narrative filmmaking [**Figure 9.8**].

1930s–1940s: Sound and Vision

While many experimental filmmakers continued to produce silent films long after the introduction of sound in the 1930s, some were immediately attracted to the formal possibilities sound introduced. Vertov incorporated his interest in radio and industrial sounds in *Enthusiasm* (1930). German animator Oskar Fischinger made abstract visual music in films such as *Allegretto* (1936), produced after he emigrated to the United States [**Figure 9.9**]. American ethnomusicologist Harry Smith produced dozens of short films to be accompanied by performances, records, or radio; artist Joseph Cornell re-edited a Hollywood B-movie to make *Rose Hobart* (1936) and played a samba record to accompany its projection. Playwright Jean Cocteau began making his influential poetic, surrealist films in 1930 with *The Blood of a Poet*, with music by Georges Auric [**Figure 9.10**].

9.9 *Allegretto* (1936). The films of animator Oskar Fischinger are intended as visual music.

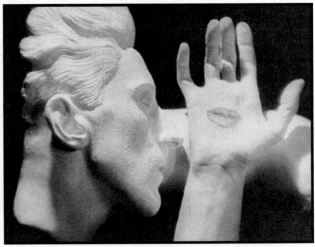

9.10 *The Blood of a Poet* (1930). Cocteau's first poetic experiment on film remains one of the best-known avant-garde films.

Most historians consider *Meshes of the Afternoon* (1943) by Russian-born Maya Deren and her Czech husband, Alexander Hammid (see "Film in Focus," pp. 326–327), the beginning of the American avant-garde's historical prominence. Lightweight 16mm cameras, introduced as an amateur format and widely used during World War II for reportage, were increasingly adopted by artists seeking more personal film expression. Deren's tireless advocacy for experimental film as a writer and lecturer, and the striking imagery and structure of her films, shaped the conditions for, and aesthetics of, American "visionary film," the term coined by scholar P. Adams Sitney for this movement.

1950s–1960s: The Postwar Avant-Garde in America

Stan Brakhage, a protégé of Deren's, is considered the most influential American avant-garde filmmaker, with four hundred 16mm and 8mm, mostly silent films in a career spanning almost half a century. While most of his films arrange imagery in sensual, abstract patterns, they also rely on very personal subject matter, such as the intimate images of his wife giving birth in *Window Water Baby Moving* (1959) [**Figure 9.11**]. Working with the film stock itself—painting, scratching, and even taping moth wings to celluloid in *Mothlight* (1963)—Brakhage emphasized the materiality of film and the direct creative process of the filmmaker. Establishing its own alternative exhibition circuit, centering in New York's Cinema 16, run by Amos and Marcia Vogel, and the Anthology Film Archives, founded and overseen to this day by Lithuanian refugee, filmmaker, and experimental film advocate Jonas Mekas, the American experimental film community fostered exchanges among artists and audiences that influenced later generations of filmmakers working with film as personal expression.

The countercultural impulses of many of the filmmakers of the 1960s were reflected in the preferred term **underground film**. In New York, pop artist Andy Warhol filmed hundreds of visitors to his studio in short *Screen Tests* between 1963 and 1966, incorporating some of these short films in such conceptual exhibition projects as the Exploding Plastic Inevitable. Warhol explored the properties of cinema as a time-based medium in his eight-hour view of the Empire State Building, *Empire* (1964), the five-hour *Sleep* (1963), and other films. He also created his own version of the Hollywood studio system at the Factory, whose "Superstars"—underground male and female devotees of glamour such as Viva, Mario Montez, and Holly Woodlawn—were featured in films he either directed or produced, including *Chelsea Girls* (1966) and *Flesh* (1968), respectively [**Figure 9.12**]. Warhol is only

9.11   *Window Water Baby Moving* (1959). The visceral impact of images of childbirth is tempered by silence and the play of light and water.

9.12   *Chelsea Girls* (1966). Nico in Andy Warhol and Paul Morrissey's legendary film. Composed of vignettes filmed in New York's Chelsea Hotel, the film was projected side by side on two screens.

9.13 **Jack Smith**. The legendary underground filmmaker whose *Flaming Creatures* was widely censored. *Courtesy Plaster Foundation.*

the most well known of a number of gay filmmakers whose sensibilities definitively shaped the underground film movement in New York. Jack Smith's work has been more difficult to see than Warhol's, as this eccentric artist incorporated his sublime and campy films and slides into erratically timed live performances in his downtown loft [Figure 9.13]. In one legendary incident, a screening organized by Jonas Mekas of Smith's film *Flaming Creatures* (1963) was shut down by the police for the film's provocative content—a rather listless pan-sexual "orgy".

The underground film movement frankly explored gender and sexual politics, but the increasing political radicalism of the period was more directly addressed at the border between documentary and experimental practice. African American actor, independent filmmaker, and documentarian William Greaves investigated the power relations on a film shoot in his feature-length *Symbiopsychotaxiplasm* (1968), made in Central Park [Figure 9.14]. Thirty-five years later, Greaves incorporated footage from the summer of 1968 with new scenes featuring the same actors in the sequel, *Symbiopsychotaxiplasm: Take 2 1/2* (2005), produced with the assistance of independent film stalwarts Stephen Soderbergh and Steve Buscemi.

While New York was an active site of experimental filmmaking and exhibition, San Francisco, at the heart of the counterculture and gay and lesbian rights movements, hosted its own vibrant avant-garde film scene, exemplified in the work of poet and filmmaker James Broughton and the prolific lesbian experimental filmmaker Barbara Hammer, who began her career in the Bay Area with such short explorations of nature and the female body as *Multiple Orgasm* (1976).

The final North American experimental film movement that emerged in this period was *structural film*, closely identified with the important Canadian filmmaker Michael Snow. Snow's explorations of space, time, and the capacity of the camera's vision to transcend human perception are epitomized in *La région centrale* (1971), in which a camera mounted on specially built apparatus pans, swoops, and swings to provide an unprecedented view of the mountainous Quebec region named in the film's title [Figure 9.15]. The avant-garde tradition is rich in Canada (whose arts funding has also fostered animation as an art form); some of its significant practitioners include Joyce Wieland (who was married to

9.14 *Symbiopsychotaxiplasm* (1968). A hybrid of fiction and documentary, Bill Greaves's film about making a film in Central Park in 1968 is a fascinating record of the counterculture.

9.15 *La région centrale* (1971). Michael Snow's 16mm camera moves wildly on a special mount, rendering the landscape abstractly through mechanized vision.

Snow), notable for films such as *Rat Life and Diet in North America* (1973), and, in the next generation, Bruce Elder, whose 36-hour cycle of films collectively titled *The Book of All the Dead* was completed in installments from 1982 to 1992.

1968 and After: Politics and Experimental Cinema

Outside North America, experimental film impulses have often been incorporated into narrative filmmaking and theatrical exhibition rather than confined exclusively to autonomous avant-garde circles. During the postwar period in Europe, Asia, and Latin America, innovative new-wave cinemas challenged and energized commercial cinemas with their visions and techniques. Such experimentation was spurred by the student unrest, Third World independence and decolonialization movements, and opposition to the American war in Vietnam that politicized film culture in Europe. Radical content and formal rigor characterized the films of Jean-Luc Godard and Chris Marker in France, Alexander Kluge in Germany, and the French-born Jean-Marie Straub and Danielle Huillet. Godard broke up the coherence of the image track with collage techniques, the use of printed texts, and voiceover quotations. The massive traffic jam depicted in his film *Weekend* (1968) foregrounds the collision of revolutionary rhetoric and consumerist culture as the consistent use of lateral tracking shots encourages viewers to keep an analytical distance [Figure 9.16]. Straub/Huillet's adaption of Kafka's unfinished *Amerika* is known by the unadorned title *Klassenverhältnisse/Class Relations* (1984), and Alexander Kluge, a central figure in the New German cinema, addressed the Nazi legacy through experimental means in such films as *The Patriot* (1979), in which a history teacher literally digs for the past with a spade. Much of this work was informed by Marxist intellectual traditions. Ideas were also central to experimental filmmaking in Britain; **poststructuralism**'s interrogation of how representations convey meaning influenced formalist filmmakers Malcolm Le Grice and Peter Gidal. Peter Wollen and Laura Mulvey drew on all of these currents, as well as psychoanalytic theory, in films and writings on cinema that interrogated the nature of narrative and the representation of women.

9.16 *Weekend* (1968). Godard's blistering critique of middle-class values is a famous example of the European avant-garde or counter cinema.

The cinema that emerged in the postrevolutionary, postcolonial contexts of such countries as Algeria, Cuba, and Senegal was also very concerned with intellectual currents and debates about the politics of representation. However, limited means and populist intentions meant that experimental techniques were used in conjunction with realist filmmaking strategies. Under the political repression of a military dictatorship, Argentine filmmakers Fernando Solanas and Octavio Getino called for a *third cinema* for the Third World, one that rejected both commercial cinema and "auteur," or art, cinema in order to engage directly with the people. Their epic documentary film *Hour of the Furnaces* (1968) covers the ongoing revolutionary struggles in Latin America and was intended to be exhibited and debated with audiences. Other examples of third cinema include Tomás Gutiérrez Alea's *Memories of Underdevelopment* (1968) [Figure 9.17], which depicts a European-identified intellectual's sense of displacement

9.17 *Memories of Underdevelopment* (1968). Documentary footage interrupts the musings of an alienated intellectual in postrevolutionary Cuba in this commonly cited exemplar of third cinema.

in the aftermath of the Cuban revolution, and Ousmane Sembène's *Black Girl* (1966), about an African domestic worker's alienation in France. The former incorporates experimental techniques such as unidentified documentary footage and an intermittent voiceover into its narrative, while some of the latter's innovation—such as the separation of sound as voiceover from the tableau-like images—arises from Sembène's lack of filmmaking resources (in particular, his inability to shoot synchronized sound). In *Perfumed Nightmare* (1978), Filipino filmmaker Kidlat Tahimik creates a witty parable of the clash between the "developed" world and the village of his birth by using a home movie aesthetic that incorporates cheap props and found footage.

Boundaries between experimental and documentary forms blurred during this period. In essay films by such filmmakers as Chris Marker (see Film in Focus, pp. 286–288) in France, Harun Farocki and Alexander Kluge in Germany, and Jonas Mekas and Jill Godmillow in the United States, the distinction between experimental and documentary form warrants interrogation. The "truth" of documentary is questioned through self-reflexive techniques, drawing on experimental film's ability to see referential imagery in new ways. These richly interactive traditions continue in explorations in video and computer-based media.

1980s–Present: New Technologies and New Media

While filmmakers continue to experiment using Super 8 and 16mm (and Super 16) formats, a radical shift to use and interrogate new technologies was driven by the introduction of consumer video formats. With the Sony Portapak in the late 1960s, video technology became available to artists for the first time. Such pioneers as Nam June Paik brought television into confrontation with the art world in video works that were often also works of installation art [**Figure 9.18**]. Inexpensive consumer video formats of the 1980s spurred growth in both activist video and video art. Exemplary of both is Marlon Riggs's *Tongues Untied* (1989), a personal and poetic depiction of black gay men and HIV [**Figure 9.19**]. On the other end of the commercial spectrum, the launch of MTV in 1981 brought many previously experimental techniques—such as rapid montage, use of handheld cameras, breaking of continuity rules, and juxtaposition of film stocks—into the mainstream, where they were quickly incorporated into commercials, television shows, and movies. Spike Jonze, for instance, developed the nonlinear narratives and inventive visuals of his commercial and music video work in the feature film *Being John Malkovich* (1999).

With the integration of computers and digital video in the 1990s, the lines between video and filmmaking traditions began to blur as formats were merged in the editing and exhibition processes. Commercial filmmakers used digital effects (for instance, the credit sequence of *Se7en* [1995] paid homage to Stan Brakhage), and video artists found new theatrical audiences for their work. At the same time, new media artists drew on moving-image traditions in computer-based work. The development of the ARPANET (Advanced Research Projects Agency Network) in 1968, which later grew into the Internet, and of hypertext (a data storage system that allows direct links to computer files, images, sounds, and related text) revolutionized

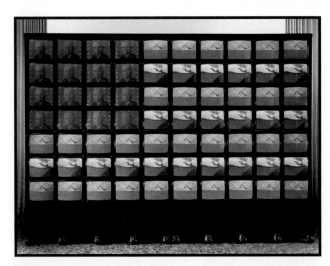

9.18 *Video Flag* (1985-1996). Nam June Paik's pioneering video art often incorporated multiple monitors.

9.19 *Tongues Untied* (1989). Marlon Riggs's *Tongues Untied* is one of the best known of the many experimental video works exploring issues of politics and identity that were facilitated by the availability of camcorders in the 1980s.

9.20 *A Movie a Day* (2007). Short films made available for downloading onto a user's iPod.

the potential for interactive art, in which the user determines the experience of the artwork by means of his or her participation. Lynn Herschman Leeson's work as a video and performance artist in the 1970s led to such pioneering interactive artworks as the networked installation *The Difference Engine #3* (1995-1998), which incorporates images of museum visitors and users logging onto the Internet to explore issues of identity and surveillance. The group Strange Company and other creators of the new media form **machinima** use video game engines to modify computer animation, creating new narratives from the game worlds. Midi Onodera's project *A Movie a Day* (2007) makes available daily short pieces for download onto a user's iPod [**Figure 9.20**]. Widespread access to computer technology has blurred the boundaries between artists and viewers, democratizing experiments with media forms and technologies.

The Elements of Experimental Media

According to one influential interpretation of the origins of cinema, the Lumière brothers' short scenes of everyday life and scenic views (such as *Baby's Breakfast* [1895]) represent the beginnings of the documentary tradition, and Georges Méliès's trick films (such as *Trip to the Moon* [1902]) represent the beginnings of narrative. But as film scholar Tom Gunning has pointed out, both types of film had a common objective—simply to solicit the viewer's desire to *see* something. He refers to early cinema as a "cinema of attractions" and locates its "look at me!" property in such ongoing film traditions as special effects, musical numbers, and comedy skits, and in the way the avant-garde cinema demands that viewers see with fresh eyes. Gunning's framework suggests that documentary and narrative forms have connections to, even origins in, experimental practice. From Émile Cohl's *Automatic Moving Company* (1910), which showed household items like spoons magically packing themselves away, to Douglas Gordon's *24-Hour Psycho* (1993), which slows down Hitchcock's 1960 film to play around the clock in a museum installation, experimental media have intrigued, delighted, and sometimes alienated viewers by getting them to see things anew.

Formalisms: Narrative Experimentation and Abstraction

Experimental film is often likened to poetry, with narrative film likened to fiction. Not only does this analogy underscore the lyrical impulse that often drives experimental work, but it also captures something of its economic marginality. Experimental work is made by individuals rather than by large crews or studios, and its audiences are small ones, comprising those who seek out such films and are motivated to engage with experimental strategies. Film, and later video and multimedia, have been embraced as means of artistic expression distinct from, but drawing upon, the other arts, whether these commonalities involve the properties of camera lenses shared with photography, the unfolding in time shared with music, or the presence in time and space shared with theater. Formal exploration of the qualities of light, the poetry of motion, and the juxtaposition of sound and image, as well as phenomenological inquiry into our ways of seeing, motivate many different experimental practices, from the camera-less film (made by exposing film stock) to video pastiche (made by re-editing television shows) to computer art (which depends on the user to determine the work's final form).

By nature, a great many experimental media works are **formalist**—concerned with problems of form over issues of content, and there are different kinds of formalisms. William Wees refers to the avant-garde film tradition as "light moving in time"; thus while Kenneth Anger's *Lucifer Rising* (1972) is on one level a film about esoteric ritual, on another it is an exploration of the principles of light (Lucifer is literally the light bearer). Chantal Akerman's films are formalist in their consistent use of a stationary medium shot to frame images as flat planes, although, as in her most widely praised film, *Jeanne Dielman* (1975), this formal concern is often joined to narrative. Tony Conrad's *The Flicker* (1966) is a formal exploration of editing (black and white frames) that extends to a phenomenological experience—the flicker effect to which the audience is subjected when the film is projected.

VIEWING CUE

Consider how abstraction is achieved and used in a film screened for class. How do repetition and variation contribute to the film's shape?

Many experimental films are *non-narrative* in that they lack well-defined characters or plots (see Chapter 7), and some are explicitly antinarrative, refusing what they see as the passive relationship the viewer has with the storytelling film. But the very dimension of time introduces the basics of narrative—beginning, middle, and end—and the play with narrative expectations can be central to experimental media. For some viewers, Alain Resnais's *Last Year at Marienbad* (1961) seems primarily a non-narrative study in the structural repetition and geometry of the rooms, hallways, and gardens of a baroque estate; for others, the film contains an elusive plot about a man's efforts to seduce a woman [Figure 9.21]. Similarly, an interactive art work can be thought of in terms of game strategy or narrative archetypes. Often the relationship to cultural as well as particular narratives can be one of the most fruitful routes of interpretation for experimental films.

Although formalism does structure some narrative films, it is central to one of the most fundamental impulses in experimental film—abstraction. **Abstract films** are formal experiments that are also nonrepresentational: they use color, shape, and line to create patterns and rhythms that are abstracted (that is, made more conceptual than concrete) from real actions and objects or created independently from recognizable figures to depict a more purely formal art. An abstract film might be constructed to be analogous to music, or to abstract

9.21 *Last Year at Marienbad* (1961). Experiments in time fracture the film's narrative.

9.22 *Third Eye Butterfly* (1968). Patterns emerge from natural and spiritual imagery in Storm De Hirsch's abstract film.

paintings that foreground the texture of paint and the shape of the canvas. It might explore the specificities of film as a time-based medium. Abstraction, which has been embraced by a range of movements from the 1920s' "absolute cinema," to the 1960s' psychedelic films such as Storm De Hirsch's *Third Eye Butterfly* (1968) [Figure 9.22], to current-day computer animation, can be explored through cinematography, through animation, or in the printing process.

Experimental Organizations: Associative, Structural, Participatory

While mainstream narrative films have predictable patterns of enigma and resolution, and documentaries follow one of a number of expository practices, experimental works organize experiences in ways that may defy realism and rational logic or that may follow strict formal principles. Whether experimental forms are abstract or in some way representational, and whether or not they draw on narrative, their organizations may be associative, structural, or participatory.

Associative Organizations

Freud used free association with his patients to uncover the unconscious logics of their symptoms and dreams. *Associative organizations* explore psychological or formal resonances, either through metaphorical images or symbolic concepts, and give many films a dreamlike quality that engages viewers' emotions and curiosity. *Surrealist film* is historically based in the artistic movement of the 1920s and its embrace of the unconscious. Later forms like music video, whose narratives follow a dreamlike logic of imagistic or psychological association or violent juxtaposition, draw on surrealist traditions. The most famous surrealist film, Luis Buñuel and Salvador Dalí's *Un chien andalou* (*An Andalusian Dog*, 1928), shocked viewers with an opening image of an eye being sliced with a razor blade. The film has since been widely alluded to and parodied (for example, in the song "Experimental Film" by They Might Be Giants). Associative organizations can be abstract, such as in musicologist Harry Smith's films that relate

VIEWING CUE

How are you as a viewer engaged by the film, video, or multimedia work screened for class— emotionally, intellectually, physically? Why and how?

text continued on page 316 ▶

Formal Play in
Ballet mécanique (1924)

Quick cuts transform a circle to a triangle and back again. The shapes are similar in scale and appear in white against a black background. Later in the film, the sequence repeats and the triangles appear to recede and approach (actually they change in size), exploring three-dimensional as well as two-dimensional space. Cinema allows such basic geometric patterns (including the square of the frame) to be explored temporally as well as spatially.

Fernand Léger made *Ballet mécanique* with filmmaker Dudley Murphy, and it explores principles similar to those addressed in Léger's paintings [Figure 9.23]. Léger was affiliated with the cubist painters who broke from realism in order to present the process of perception in their work, transforming the flat canvas with angular shapes and lines. A related visual arts movement from the same era, *futurism*, celebrated the machine age and its sleek designs, which Léger took up in his famous elongated shapes outlined thickly in black. Although black-and-white film lacked the primary colors used in his paintings, Léger used this emphatic black to explore the specificity of the film medium. He was among the first of many modernist visual artists in the 1920s who saw cinema as a perfect medium to explore dynamism—one of the primary properties of the new art and the new age.

The circles and triangles are introduced in *Ballet mécanique* by abstracted photographic images; a straw hat filmed from above is echoed in the circle, the back-and-forth of a woman on a swing describes a triangular shape. These recognizable images thus become less like references to reality or a story than part of a rhythmic chain. Further photographic images of moving parts—they could be gears, pendulums, or whisks—are even less identifiable. Not only are they filmed in motion and moved onscreen and offscreen by the

editing that associates one moving part with the next, but they are also refracted, mirror-like, by optical printing techniques so that they are repeated in multiple sectors within the frame itself [Figure 9.24]. The title's sense of a dance of mechanization is clearly figured in these groups of images.

The film's title also suggests that cinema could be regarded as a mechanization of what we know to be a human activity—ballet. As in all visual arts, the human form onscreen has a special attraction to the viewer; it orients us, invites our identification and narrative expectations: who is this person, what does she want, what will happen to her? Many modernist artists use the human figure in a notably different way, as an object rather than a subject, as an element like any other in

9.23 *Three Women (Le Grand Déjeuner)* (1921). Fernand Léger's paintings were inspired by mechanical forms, and their shapes—if not their colors—are carried over to his film.

9.24 *Ballet mécanique* (1924). Movement proliferates onscreen through refracted images of mechanical parts.

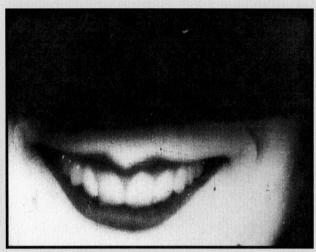

9.25 *Ballet mécanique* (1924). The fragmentation and abstraction of the female form is a common practice in modernist art.

the frame or as part of a machine. The swinging woman is the first image of the film, and we might think of the images that follow as her daydream, an interpretation supported by the final image of her smelling a flower. But we are also encouraged to abstract her image into one among many in a pattern of shapes and movements, as when the same footage of her swinging is shown upside down. The majority of the film is of non-human images, but these few command our attention, and they relate to the manner in which women's bodies are rendered as objects in the Dadaist and surrealist art of the period.

Indeed, one of the most notable ways that avant-garde art of the 1920s explored the connection between the human form and the machine is through fragmented images of modern women. For example, a second female form figures first as a pair of lips sharply outlined in lipstick (cosmetics were widely popularized during this period) and isolated in the frame by a black mask over the rest of the face [Figure 9.25]. The lips smile and relax, intercut with the image of the straw hat. The same woman is also made part of the patterns of the film in a later shot of the eyes, whose plucked eyebrows echo their curved shape so that a quick cut of the eyes upside down goes by almost undetected. We do eventually see the woman's full head in profile, but the bobbed hair and stylized pose make her a sculptural image rather than a character to identify with. A later "dance" of alternating images of manikin legs adorned with garters is at the same time a delightful visual joke and a slightly disturbing evocation of dismemberment. The male is treated differently in the film: a male head appears at the center of the refracted frame, perhaps signifying mind instead of body. Yet this image's closest visual rhyme is with a parrot framed in the same way, a surreal association that

prevents us from reading him as a guiding consciousness behind the film's succession of images.

Approaching an abstract film, or any experimental media work, is made easier by close description of its formal elements, identification of patterns, and synthesizing of its themes, as we have attempted here. An intriguing clue to the formal concerns of *Ballet mécanique* lies in the image that appears before the title: Hollywood silent film comedian Charlie Chaplin is rendered in a fragmented form very reminiscent of Léger's paintings. The film, the credit says, is presented by "Charlot," the French name for Chaplin. At the end of the film, the image does a little animated dance of its own, a mechanized ballet [Figure 9.26]. An actor's iconic film image is thus first paid tribute to by a painter in a graphic form, and then enfolded into the last of the

9.26 *Ballet mécanique* (1924). Charlie Chaplin animated by Fernand Léger.

film's sequence of everyday objects set in motion, demonstrating the vibrant crossing back and forth between cinema and the other arts in this period of modernist experimentation.

Before the introduction of synchronized sound would have an impact on the international appeal of cinema and of stars like Chaplin, the film shows the affinity between the cinema's patterns of edited imagery and musical structures. *Ballet mécanique*, George Antheil's original composition (which called for, among other things, sixteen player pianos, four bass drums, and three airplane propellers), originally intended to accompany this film, was too long to be played with it, and these outstanding works of the machine age were not brought together until 2001. Yet even "performed" on its own, *Ballet mécanique*, the film, with its combination of abstract and representational elements, brings the energies of the modernist art of the 1920s vividly to life.

shapes in succession or create resonances between objects and shapes or colors [Figure 9.27], but they are also used with representational forms, such as in numerous music videos.

Metaphoric associations link or associate different objects, images, events, or individuals in order to generate a new perception, emotion, or idea. In a film, this might be done by linking two different images, by indicating a connection between two objects or figures within a single frame, or by creating metaphors in the voiceover commentary as it responds to and anticipates images in the film. Juxtaposing images of workers being shot and a slaughtered bull, as Sergei Eisenstein does in *Strike* (1925), metaphorically describes the brutal dehumanization of those workers. Although metaphoric practices are typical to many movies, Derek Jarman's *Blue* (1993)—perhaps best described as an experimental autobiography—is a fully metaphoric meditation on the color of the title and its chain of associations in the life of a man (the filmmaker) dying of AIDS. Accompanying one single blue image, a voice drifts among associations: the blue flashes on a retina, the blue skies from youth, the blue moods of depression, and so on. Across this meditation, blue becomes associated with the "blue funk" created by a doctor's news, the "slow blue love on a delphinium day," and "the universal love in which all men bathe." Concrete images of decay—old films whose nitrate stock has deteriorated so that recognizable images and spaces blend into abstract splotches and blobs—form the image track of Bill Morrison's *Decasia* (2003) [Figure 9.28]. Metaphorical associations emerge in the dance of fleeting shapes, edited juxtapositions, and imagery called forth by Michael Gordon's symphonic soundtrack.

9.27 *Film #7* (1951). Famous for his collections of American folk music, Harry Smith also made inventive animations.

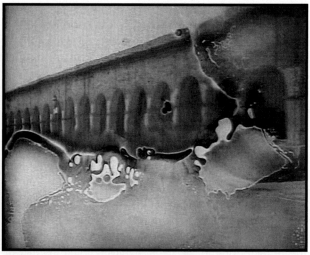

9.28 *Decasia* (2003). Patterns created by decaying nitrate film stock emerge on the surface of found footage.

Unlike the concrete associations that bind metaphoric images, *symbolic associations* isolate discrete objects or singular images that can generate or be assigned abstract meanings—either those already given those objects or images by a culture, or ones created by the film itself. The symbolic significance may be spiritual (as with the Christian cross) or political (such as the flag of a particular country), or it may be tied to some other concept that has been culturally and historically grafted onto the meaning of a person, event, or thing. In consciously poetic films, such as *Meshes of the Afternoon* or *The Blood of a Poet*, mirrors become symbolic of self-knowledge or self-confrontation. Building on his earlier work with puppet films, Czech filmmaker Jirí Trnka created a remarkable experimental film, *The Hand* (1965), around the symbolic weight associated with a hand: a puppet struggles against the domination of a single, live-action hand that demands he make only other hands and not flowerpots, symbolizing totalitarianism in Eastern Europe [Figure 9.29].

9.29 *The Hand* (1965). The hand symbolizes a figure of tyrannical power in this Eastern European film.

Structural Organizations

British filmmaker Peter Gidal theorized and practiced a rigorous development known as *structural/materialist film* that rejected the illusionism of narrative film. He challenged the audience's perceptions with a focus on the material fact of the film (its grain, sprockets, and journey through a projector past a beam of light) in such films as *Room Film* (1973). *Structural organizations* follow a particular logic or problem, and their principles inform a wide variety of media art works such as the stationary camera films of Andy Warhol, the video works of artist Bruce Nauman, and digital art works generated by algorithms.

Some filmmakers weave images, framings, camera movements, or other formal dimensions into patterns and structures that engage the viewer perceptually and often intellectually. Michael Snow's *Wavelength* (1967) is a forty-five-minute image that slowly moves across a room in an extended zoom-in and ends with a close-up of a picture of ocean waves [Figure 9.30]. Punctuated with vague references to a murder mystery, and accompanied by a high-pitched sound that explores another meaning of "wavelength," this movie is an almost pure investigation of the vibrant textures of space: as flat, as colored, as empty, and most of all, as geometrically tense.

Other films central to the structural film movement in the United States include Ernie Gehr's *Serene Velocity* (1970) and Hollis Frampton's *Zorns Lemma* (1970). *Serene Velocity* consists of images of the same hallway taken with structured variations in the camera's focal length, creating a hypnotic, rhythmic experience of lines and squares. In *Zorns Lemma*, a repeated sequence of one-second images of words on signs and storefronts arranged in alphabetical order creates a fascinating puzzle as they are replaced one by one with a set of consistent, though arbitrary, images [Figure 9.31]. The viewer learns to associate the images with their place in the cycle, in a sense relearning a picture alphabet. Such structural principles

9.30 **Filmstrip showing frames of *Wavelength*** (1967). An extended zoom-in for the duration of the film creates suspense through form.

9.31   ***Zorns Lemma*** (1970). Hollis Frampton's films are often organized around structural principles, as in this film's central alphabetical sequence.

9.32   ***Rapture*** (1999). Shirin Neshat is one of many contemporary artists who use film and video in gallery contexts.

are fascinating intellectually, but the most effective structural films also work on the viewer's senses.

Participatory Experiences

A third approach to experimental film emphasizes *participatory experiences*–the centrality of the viewer and the time and place of exhibition to the cinematic phenomenon. Often the film is part of a live performance by the filmmaker. *Nervous System* (1994), a film performance by underground filmmaker Ken Jacobs, uses two projectors, a propeller, and filters through which audiences view the work. In 1970, Gene Youngblood coined the term **expanded cinema** for such work and predicted that video and computer technology would allow moving image media to extend consciousness. Such pioneering video artists as Nam June Paik delivered on this prediction in conceptual pieces like *Video Fish* (1975), which combined video monitors displaying images of fish and aquariums containing real fish.

Many filmmakers working in the art world design their works around the audience's experience. *Rapture* (1999), an installation by Iranian-born Shirin Neshat, projects 16mm film footage of men and women on opposite gallery walls to signify their separation in Iranian society under Islamic law, with the viewer both mediating and separating these worlds **[Figure 9.32]**. Multimedia artists may produce CD-ROMs for museum installations or home use that rely on users' selections, the sense of touch, and interface design as crucial artistic components. For example, multimedia artist Shu Lea Cheang built several kinds of participatory experience into the design of *Bowling Alley* (1995). A museum installation and an actual bowling alley were linked to a Web site that gathered contributions by collaborating artists. The actions of the bowlers and the online participants affected what museum visitors experienced. Video blogs and the user-generated content on YouTube relate to these participatory traditions even when their content is not consciously artistic.

Styles and Perspectives: Surrealist, Lyrical, Critical

Although experimental films are often organized in associative, structural, or participatory ways, their very drive to innovate means that new forms will continually emerge. Behind this impulse are several stylistic orientations on the part of film artists. Experimental film, more than any other kind, can be attributed to the individual efforts and point of view of a filmmaker, who may shoot, edit, process, and project the film herself.

Defying the realist tendencies and narrative logic of the medium but building on both the basis in photographic reproduction and the unfolding of images in time, surrealist styles use recognizable imagery in strange contexts. One of the most influential avant-gardes, **surrealist cinema** was a driving force in Europe of the 1920s, especially in France. Early works include René Clair's *Entr'acte* (1924) and Germaine Dulac's *The Seashell and the Clergyman* (1928), based on a script by Antonin Artaud; but certainly the most renowned surrealist film is Salvador Dalí and Luis Buñuel's *Un chien andalou* (1928) [Figure 9.33]. Beginning with the shocking assault on the eye, the film teases the viewer with the possibility of a story about a woman and her relationship with one or more men, drifts among unexplained objects (like a recurring striped box), and never emerges from its dream state. Through the powers of film to manipulate time, space, and material objects, surrealist filmmakers confronted middle-class assumptions about normalcy and created a dream world driven by dark desires.

Since the 1920s, surrealism has had a great influence on animation, both directly, as in Dalí's unfinished collaboration with Disney, *Destino* (1945, 2003), which was recently completed and released [Figure 9.34], and more indirectly. Czech animator Jan Svankmajer's *Alice* (1988) and Japanese master Hiyao Miyazaki's *Spirited Away* (2001) both create utterly unique, surreal worlds. Outside the realm of animation, the original worlds of Terry Gilliam's *Brazil* (1985) and Michel Gondry's *Eternal Sunshine of the Spotless Mind* (2004) are shaped by surrealism. In Gondry's collaboration with Björk on the video "Human Behavior," an ethereal voice contemplates the vagaries of human behavior; someone in a goofy plush bear suit, stalked by a hunter, tromps around the forest. The woman singing eats a bowl of porridge, goes to the moon, floats down a river, and dances, suspended near a light bulb with a moth, only to finish her song from a small screen superimposed on the bear's stomach. Drawing on fairy tales and puppet animation, "Human Behavior" propelled Björk's international solo career and Gondry's idiosyncratic forays into feature filmmaking.

Lyrical styles express emotions, beliefs, or some other personal position in film, much as does the voice of the lyric poet. Lyrical films may emphasize a personal voice or vision through the singularity of the imagery or through such techniques as voiceovers or handheld camera movements. In his autobiographical film about his experience as an immigrant in New York, *Lost, Lost, Lost* (1976), Jonas Mekas portrays his fears and hopes. Home movies and journal entries are counterpointed in a fragmented style that resembles a diary, while the rhythmic interjections of the commentator-poet express feelings ranging from angst to delight [Figure 9.35].

Lyricism helped define postwar experimental cinema in the United States. Such work flourished in a climate of existential philosophy and with the help of lightweight 16mm cameras that the individual filmmaker could operate. As the movement's primary critic, P. Adams Sitney, argues, lyrical filmmaking carried forward traditions of inspiration and creativity based in Romanticism. These influences, together with an intimate community of viewers, helped create an unusually personal cinema that explored dreams, visions, and intricacies of human consciousness. Perhaps the most poetic and most prolific filmmaker of this movement, Stan Brakhage made films from the 1950s until his death in 2003. Topics include suicide (the 1958 *Anticipation of the Night*) and a Pittsburgh morgue (the 1971 *The Act of Seeing with One's Own Eyes*), while many films were abstract. Themes of insight and blindness

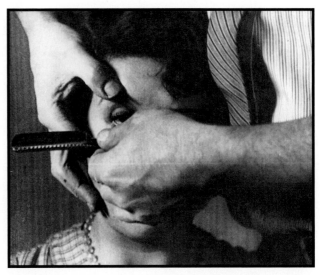

9.33   *Un chien andalou* (1928). The opening scene of an eye being slit by a razor exemplifies surrealism's use of shock and is arguably the most famous moment in experimental film history.

▶ **VIEWING CUE**

Consider the worlds constructed by music videos and ask whether surrealist traditions, impulses, or moods can be detected. If so, why does surrealism work within this format? ⏸

9.34   *Destino* (1945, 2003). Dalí's unlikely collaboration with Disney remained unfinished until its release in 2003.

9.35 *Lost, Lost, Lost* (1976). Jonas Mekas's diary-film represents the important tradition of experimental documentary.

9.36 *Fireworks* (1947). Kenneth Anger's lyrical reverie featuring images is one of the key early works of the American avant-garde.

run through many of his films, which range in length from the nine-second-long *Eye Myth* (1967) to the five-hour-long *The Art of Vision* (1965). Kenneth Anger's lyricism fuses homoeroticism, ritual, popular culture, and esoterica, from his landmark *Fireworks* (1947) **[Figure 9.36]** made when he was seventeen, to *Invocation of My Demon Brother* (1969). Brakhage and Anger represent just two of the many avant-garde filmmakers whose visions are so distinctive that their work is instantly recognizable.

Video art also draws on forms of lyricism. The installations of artist Bill Viola often use extreme slow motion to envelop the viewer and to approach religious contemplation. For example, in his projection-based installation *Going Forth by Day* (2002), viewers experience an array of five 35-minute sequences that reflect upon the cycle of birth, death, and resurrection.

Critical positions structure a film or media work through interrogation of their form, content, or communication with the viewer. In such work, experimental modes may overlap with documentary and narrative ones. In Jean-Luc Godard's *Two or Three Things I Know about Her* (1966), characters directly address the viewer, responding to questions such as "What is language?" whispered by the offscreen director. In Trinh T. Minh-ha's *Surname Viet Given Name Nam* (1989), Vietnamese women living in the United States act the roles of interviewees living in Vietnam, narrating their wartime experiences. The combination of this device, the filmmaker's voiceover text and other soundtrack elements, and unusual framings complicates the identities of these women and any effort to portray their experiences authentically or completely. As a result, the film raises more questions than it answers. A film may present images so layered and complex that they are difficult to explain. Bruce Conner's experimental film *A Movie* (1958) contrasts wild races and chase scenes with images of refugees, an execution, and air crashes in an elusive questioning of what it means to watch a movie. Yvonne Rainer's *The Man Who Envied Women* (1985) uses a range of collage-like devices to make viewers think about what they are seeing, from using several actors in the same role to a camera tracking over a wall hung with a variety of clippings (of war photography, advertising, editorials) while an unidentified voiceover analyzes them **[Figure 9.37]**. Many of these critical techniques are associated with political positions or with theoretical ones that take apart the assumed natural relationship between a word or image and the thing it represents.

▶ **VIEWING CUE**

Characterize the style of the film or media work you have viewed for class. What points to the artist's presence or position behind the work?

The assumption on the part of such critical film-makers is that audiences will take up similar critical positions by being exposed to formal experiments. Such aesthetic strategies are sometimes referred to as *political modernism*, and they are rooted in the social critiques of the late 1960s. One of the most interesting and influential approaches to the image-oriented society of consumer capitalism was advanced by Guy Debord in a book and film called *The Society of the Spectacle* (1967 and 1973, respectively). Identified with the 1960s' situationist movement that later influenced punk style, Debord argued that images themselves—taken out of context through a process called *détournement*—were the only way to transform the image-oriented society. Feminist filmmakers like Rainer and Laura Mulvey and Peter Wollen used critical techniques to question the representation of women in film. In *Riddles of the Sphinx* (1977), for instance, Mulvey and Wollen took great care to avoid using camera work that would objectify the young mother featured in the film (see Chapter 13, pp. 492–493). In the 1980s, video artists extended this critical function toward mainstream media, and new media today often demand that viewers ask how they are looking as well as what they are looking at.

9.37 *The Man Who Envied Women* (1985). Throughout the film, voiceovers analyze images pinned to a wall; the viewer of the film is similarly called upon to interrogate its images.

The Significance of Experimental Media

Perhaps more than any other form of media, experimental film and video asks viewers to reflect actively on the viewing experience. Experimental media contemplates the way human senses and consciousness function. Some of these works, in setting out to explore the phenomenon of vision (or perhaps hearing and touch), are *about* perception and its relationship to consciousness; some can even be about the experience of boredom. Whether we are challenged to figure out the meaning of symbolism or to relate a film to an artist's wider body of work or to a social context, we are always required to participate in some way. Setting out to entertain or inform, narrative and documentary films may offer a much less demanding film experience.

Just as the potential of the World Wide Web and other new technologies generates excitement and even utopian claims today, so did the invention of cinema a little more than a century ago. French filmmaker Jean Epstein enthusiastically anticipated the way that film could reveal secrets of the world: "slow motion and fast motion" teach us that "everything is alive," he claimed; and as we saw in the previous chapter, in *The Man with the Movie Camera* the Soviet Kino-Eye group led by Dziga Vertov celebrated the camera's capacity to see more and differently than the human eye. In the 1970s, Dara Birnbaum explored video art's basis in television technology in *Technology/Transformation: Wonder Woman* (1978–1979) in which the TV heroine's gestures are slowed and repeated in a ritualistic fashion as she transforms into her superhero persona [Figure 9.38].

Challenging and Expanding Perception

As part of a thorough examination of the medium, experimental works make meaning through challenging and expanding how viewers see, feel, and hear. Such films, videos, and other artwork press us to open our senses and our minds

9.38 *Technology/Transformation: Wonder Woman* (1978–1979). Dara Birnbaum was one of the first artists to explore the video medium's relationship with television by appropriating pop culture imagery. *Electronic Arts Intermix.*

in unaccustomed ways: for example, Hollis Frampton's *Lemon* (1969) presents only a single piece of fruit in changing light. For those who have seen this film, a lemon will never look the same again. An experimental movie might use unusual filmic techniques or materials, such as abstract graphic designs and animation, as vehicles for seeing and thinking in fresh ways. It might present a rapid series of images that seem to skip about randomly—much like the experience of a dream. Shirley Clarke's *Bridges-Go-Round* (1958) uses unexpected camera angles and zooms to turn the massive structures of various bridges into an ethereal dance.

Each new medium brings new perceptual possibilities. Web 2.0, the name that terms the Internet as not only an information source but also a site of social networks and massive, multiplayer games, has given rise to new kinds of experience. These experiences are based in representations of ourselves through avatars and connections with others whom we may never meet in the flesh. Works of art may explore these experiences by combining "old" and new media. For example, Lynn Hershman Leeson's film *Strange Culture* (2007) was exhibited at the Sundance Film Festival in the virtual, 3-D world known as Second Life **[Figure 9.39]**. This film documents the experiences of an artist whose possession of chemicals for use in his work led to his arrest as a bioterror suspect.

As with feature films or documentaries, the cultural and historical expectations of viewers play a large part in how experimental media are understood and what meanings are assigned to them. Education in ways of watching and artistic contexts plays a much greater part in the interpretation of experimental film, however, because of the difficulty and marginality of the medium or the technological platform.

Experimental Film Traditions

Old media were once new media. One paradox of the avant-garde is that it cannot remain a literal "advance guard" for very long. Innovations are absorbed into more dominant traditions, or artists' visions expand viewers' imaginations to encompass new forms. There are often historical precedents even for the most seemingly shocking, original, or technologically innovative works of art. Exploring these contexts not only is fascinating for its exposure of little known traditions, but it also enriches our experience of current works that often make reference to previous traditions. In its early decades, cinema was heralded as the "seventh art," and its practitioners and theorists were proud of incorporating practices from all the others.

Experimental traditions also have direct historical ties to politics—whether revolutions, resistance movements, or student unrest. Despite celebrating their independence, often through the formation of journals, clubs, and societies that share their ideas, experimental filmmakers also rely on cultural institutions such as museums, government agencies, and private corporations (as in the case of new media) for sponsorship.

9.39 *Strange Culture* (2007). New-media artist Lynn Hershman Leeson presented the first screening of this documentary in the online environment Second Life. The film is about the case of artist Steve Kurtz of Critical Art Ensemble.

Finally, audiences are essential to these traditions—not only for commercial viability but for the work of interpretation, advocacy, and aesthetic fulfillment. While all experimental works challenge their viewers, we can identify historical strains that emphasize personal expression and communication with the audience and strains that emphasize confrontation with audiences in the context of a wider social, political, or aesthetic critique.

Expressive Traditions

Impressionist painters used new techniques to render color and light as they were perceived, not as academic painting traditions prescribed. Cubist painters attempted to integrate spatial perception and temporal duration into their canvasses. These ways of seeing had a significant influence on the emergence of film art. In Paris in the late 1910s, Louis Delluc founded journals and cine-clubs that defined the impressionist film movement. Germaine Dulac, Jean Epstein, and his sister Marie Epstein made films, wrote articles, and lectured about the new film art. While some argued that film should be composed like music, others embraced narrative components and photographic realism.

In *poetic narratives*, a narrative organization exists but is subjected to (and often disappears within) the more abstract or imaginative shapes and experiences associated with experimental and avant-garde films. As early as René Clair's *The Crazy Ray* (1925) and later in Jean Cocteau's *Orpheus* (1950), movies used stories as mere skeletons on which to elaborate and explore novel cinematic techniques and special effects. Werner Herzog's *Heart of Glass* (1976) is based on a Bavarian legend about the death of a glassblower and the subsequent loss of a secret formula that supported the village industry; but with its characters wandering directionless and speaking in poetic non sequiturs, the heart of the film explores the hypnotic images floating through a world that has lost its sense of time. Stephen and Timothy Quay's *Street of Crocodiles* (1986), constructed through stop-motion photography and based on the memoirs of Polish author Bruno Schulz, is a dark tale of a porcelain doll trapped in a sinister, nightmarish environment of animate screws and threads. Here the remarkable life of thread and other objects—and not the thread of a story—shapes and organizes the film [Figure 9.40].

An expressive impulse is also at the heart of the American underground film. During the 1960s and 1970s, the American counterculture of "sex, drugs, and rock and roll" broke free of the perceived repressive social values, barriers, and gender roles of the 1950s. The San Francisco–based Kuchar brothers made campy films like *Hold Me When I'm Naked* (1966), while Marie Menken discovered a more personal expressive film language in such works as *Glimpse of the Garden* (1957). Subcultures—artistic and sexual—embraced filmmaking, and independent subcultures emerged around experimental filmmaking itself. A network of alternative cinemas and university screenings brought these works and their makers into contact with what became devoted audiences of filmmakers, critics, students, and other artists.

Expressive traditions also emerge from specific technologies and properties of the medium. For example, the small-gauge formats of 16mm and 8mm were developed in the 1920s and 1930s for the amateur film market and were taken up very early for artistic purposes. As video became more portable in the 1960s and was

▶ **VIEWING CUE**

Observe your own interpretative process. How are thought or the senses directly engaged by the experimental work you are viewing? What specific images or sounds solicit your attention? Are there devices that remind you of the elements of the medium?

9.40 *Street of Crocodiles* (1986). This poetic animated tale follows a puppet's adventures inside an old Kinetoscope.

introduced to the consumer market, it too became a medium for artists. Artists exploited the intimacies of these media, with the diaristic formula used by Jonas Mekas in the 1950s adopted by video artists in the 1970s and digital filmmakers today. One recent example is *Gina Kim's Video Diary* (2002), a feature-length collection of video diaries made by a young Korean woman who emigrates to the United States; it explores anorexia and family relationships with frank, startling imagery.

New media present a range of expressive possibilities. On the Web, YouTube is home to a plethora of user-generated content, as well as lively networks of self-identified experimental filmmakers. These moving-image artists use such sites to launch work that would otherwise have very limited chances of exposure. Although the vast majority of the work posted would not be associated with experimental film by their makers or viewers, the very technology that is being used and the expressive impulse fit very much into this tradition.

Confrontational Traditions

The shock of the modern—beautiful machines capable of terrifying accidents or brutal destruction; juxtapositions of commerce and art; time sped up and distances eliminated—was incorporated in the 1920s in a confrontational modernist impulse across the arts. Sometimes the urge was to "épater le bourgeoisie"—shock the middle class—as in *Olympia* (1863), the frank painting by Manet whose subject was clearly a prostitute, or the eyeball-slicing of *Un chien andalou* (see Figure 9.33, p. 319). Sometimes it was to document the democratization of art in a changing world, such as in Atget's photographs of Paris storefronts. As German cultural theorist Walter Benjamin argued in his famous 1936 essay "The Work of Art in the Age of Mechanical Reproduction," the very notion of artistic originality was challenged by the photograph and taken even further by film, which courted a mass, public audience. Artists saw their role anew, whether in embracing a machine aesthetic in architecture, design, or futurist paintings, or in making films suitable to the proletarian revolution in the Soviet Union. Such an attitude goes against Romantic traditions of artistic expressivity and shapes an alternative experimental film tradition of confrontation—of conventions, audiences, or expectations and associations.

Because cinema was seen as the quintessentially modern medium, artists active in other media, like Dada artist Marcel Duchamp, often ventured to make film experiments. *Anemic Cinema* (1926) alternated abstract images of rotating spirals of black and white with what might be called language spirals—not only were these nonsense mottos printed within circles that "rhymed" graphically with the spirals, but they also made language double back on itself in elaborate wordplay, of which the anagram in the title is an example.

The European avant-gardes of the 1920s were a conscious model for filmmakers like Jean-Luc Godard. Godard, along with many of the critics writing for the journal *Cahiers du cinéma*, began to make their own films in the late 1950s, fueling the French New Wave (see Chapter 12). His films of the 1960s were partly experimental, challenging commercial film conventions through unusual sound and image juxtapositions or by having actors go in and out of character. But as the critical and political environment of this period became more intense, the confrontational impulse of what became known as *counter cinema* went deeper. Godard started making consciously noncommercial films like *British Sounds* (1970) with collaborators under the name Dziga Vertov Group. In 1972, Godard and his partner, Jean-Pierre Gorin, made a film called *Letter to Jane* that scrutinizes a still photograph of liberal American actress Jane Fonda listening sympathetically on a visit to Vietnam. In voiceover, Godard and Gorin critique this image for its political naivete **[Figure 9.41]**. While prescient in its scrutiny of celebrity culture, the film is also misogynist and even cruel in its confrontational style. The radicalism of this period was hard to sustain, but the confrontational impulse informs all of Godard's work. For example, the intricate image and sound montages of the multipart *Histoire(s) du Cinema* (1988–1998) asks viewers to look at all the meanings images accumulate over time.

In the 1980s, *activist video*—particularly that produced around government indifference to the AIDS crisis—employed a confrontational style. While based in documentary in its presentation of information, it also used experimental techniques of editing, design elements drawn from advertising and propaganda, and self-conscious voiceover and personal reflection. Tom Kalin's *They Are Lost to Vision Altogether* (1987) combines elegiac imagery with footage of marches, portraying strategies

9.41 *Letter to Jane* (1972). The confrontational impulse of counter cinema is central to this film in which filmmakers Godard and Gorin critique a photograph of American actress Jane Fonda for the liberal—rather than radical—politics it represents.

of mourning and militancy employed by AIDS activists [Figure 9.42]. Also during this period, film and videomakers of color embraced experimental strategies in greater numbers than earlier, when documentary's directness was often preferred. In Britain, a government initiative funded and supported Black British cinema, fostering multicultural production for programming on Channel 4, Britain's independent television station. From this initiative came the collectively produced works of Sankofa and the Black Audio Film Collective. In the former's *Passion of Remembrance* (1986), political debate is combined with newsreel footage and home movies, and in the latter's *Handsworth Songs* (1986), footage of rioting and West Indian carnival traditions are juxtaposed with a voiceover that analyzes colonial history and the reasons for current racial unrest. In *Night Cries: A Rural Tragedy* (1989), Australian Aboriginal artist Tracey Moffatt uses stylized sets and sounds and disjunctive editing to tell a story about the assimilation policies that forced Aboriginal children to be adopted by white families through the 1960s. A grown daughter and her elderly mother's strained yet intimate relationship is conveyed without dialogue through the film's innovative sets, cinematography, and sound work [Figure 9.43]. Experimental works that confront the

text continued on page 327 ▶

9.42 *They Are Lost to Vision Altogether* (1987). Artist Tom Kalin conveyed competing impulses of mourning and militancy in response to the AIDS crisis in the elegiac imagery of this videotape.

9.43 *Night Cries: A Rural Tragedy* (1989). This film's depiction of the fraught relationship between a grown Aboriginal daughter and the white mother who adopted her as a child rejects realism in favor of emotional truth.

Avant-Garde Visions in
Meshes of the Afternoon (1943)

Maya Deren and Alexander Hammid's experimental film *Meshes of the Afternoon* forged a new American avant-garde cinema, drawing from Hammid's filmmaking experience in Europe and Deren's wide interests in poetry, dance and choreography, ritual, and psychoanalysis. Introspective and mysterious in its explorations of one woman's dream world, the film evokes symbolic associations and its sequences invite narrative speculations.

Meshes of the Afternoon opens with a brightly lit exterior shot of a flower in the street, then quickly lets us know it is about an interior reality of fantasies, fears, and unarticulated feelings when a hand reaches for the flower, and the latter disappears. A woman, played by Deren, enters a house with some difficulty and falls asleep in a chair. After images of her sleeping eyes alternate with a window to the outside world, we see such charged objects as a key, a knife, and a mirror begin to take on a life of their own. Gestures are repeated, with variation, but without explanation. A figure cloaked in black turns, showing a mirror where its face should be, carrying connotations of the double and of death. A man enters the house: a phone is off the hook, a phonograph record spins, the mirror breaks into shards on a bed. Are these images external or imagined? Is the broken mirror a symbol of violence or of insight? The woman sits down at a table—and is joined by two other figures of herself. Following the laws not of reality but of the imagination, *Meshes of the Afternoon* is a visionary exploration of a woman's consciousness that deploys symbols of the unconscious, a puzzle that never comes completely together as a clear picture.

The challenge of the film is that narrative is not its primary organizational feature. Instead, it accumulates, repeats, and contrasts images in associative chains that suggest symbolic meanings and follow internal patterns. The key to the door is dropped, reappears in the woman's hand, disappears [Figure 9.44]. The key suggests interpretation, but our interpretations of the film can never be definitive. The knife pertains to the domestic scene when it is used to cut bread; it may perpetrate domestic violence when the woman appears to be dead on a bed, or it may be the instrument of self-inflicted violence when she approaches her double with it in hand. The narrative tensions of the film contrast in-

9.44 *Meshes of the Afternoon* (1943). The central image of the key suggests the viewer's search for the key that will unlock the film's meaning.

terior and exterior as they define the woman's space, not only individually or unconsciously but also as a comment on women's historical relegation to the home and to film genres such as melodrama that depict this sphere. The black-caped figure's association with the exterior transforms it from a threatening to a beckoning figure.

Hints of a gothic narrative, as indicated by the caped figure, the knife, and the body on the bed, are also supported by formal reflections. Camera movement makes the woman's attempts to climb the stairs a journey into a harrowing vortex. Jump cuts transform presence into absence. The sound track (added for a later release of the film by Deren's second husband, composer Teiji Ito) underscores the subjective perspective of the film when the cuts are accompanied by sound and the phonograph is not.

The window, which represents the border between inside and outside, is a metaphor for the film frame [Figure 9.45]. The frame seems to suggest that Deren is trapped by domesticity. The woman who looks out is the filmmaker herself, who has shared her unique perspective in this film. *Meshes of the Afternoon* explores a woman's desires, fears, and struggle to escape through the work of the dream film. When one of the figures of the

9.45 *Meshes of the Afternoon* (1943). Deren looking out from the window has become an iconic image of this avant-garde film exploring women's subjectivity.

woman approaches her sleeping double with a dagger in her hand, each of the five different steps she takes is placed in a space that moves from outside to inside: a step by the ocean, another on the earth, the next on grass, the fourth on the pavement outside the house, and the last on the rug inside the room. As we discussed in Chapter 5, this editing transforms space and time (p. 149).

Meshes of the Afternoon infuses the emerging American avant-garde cinema with a deeply personal passion that Deren would bring to her future filmmaking, teaching, and writing. In it, we see a history of poetry and visionary painting that aims to transform reality through the interior power of the imagination. Like William Blake's illustrated poems about the dark side of the imagination or Odilon Redon's pictorial voyages into the subconscious, Deren's film explores the complex spaces of desire and fantasy. As individually expressive as the film is, however, it also subtly shows a critical perspective on conventional film traditions. After the film's title appear the words "Hollywood 1943." Made within miles of the film studios often referred to as the "dream factory," it left the industrial tradition behind to pursue a dream of film as art.

audience's complacency or histories of injustice and misrepresentation may be hybrids of documentary and narrative work such as these. Sometimes voices and visions that have been marginalized find less settled traditions like experimental film more fruitful areas to employ.

Confrontational tactics in new media are often about deflecting the messages of mainstream media. Groups like The Yes Men make fake Web sites offering corporate apologies for environmental degradation that mainstream news outlets sometimes pick up and report. As audiences become more diversified by cable network programming and Internet resources such as blogs and open-source media, confrontational media-making techniques are also multiplying.

▶ VIEWING CUE

Consider the film you've just viewed for class. Is it part of an expressive or confrontational tradition? Why?

CONCEPTS AT WORK

For the purposes of this chapter, we have distinguished experimental practices that are *alternative* to the commercial narrative cinema, to corporate- or state-sponsored documentary movements, or to the interests of software developers or game manufacturers. It is thus crucial to understand the institutions and networks that support this alternative culture. In recent decades in the United States, media artists have been able to make their work through modest financial assistance of cultural foundations and government agencies such as the National Endowment for the Arts (NEA) and through teaching. Many experimental filmmakers influenced new generations through their positions teaching at places such as Cal Arts and the Art Institutes of San Francisco and Chicago, the Rhode Island School of Design (RISD), Pratt Institute, and the School of Visual Arts. Museums like the Museum of Modern Art and the Whitney Museum of American Art have contributed to experimental film culture through their curatorial departments, collecting practices, and regular screening series. (Similar venues and networks exist in Britain, Canada, Germany, Japan, and elsewhere.) Other more traditional cultural institutions and funders, however, have resisted recognizing the media, sometimes suspicious of its commercial relations. Interestingly, it has been somewhat easier for video art and new media to find a home in the gallery or museum than it was for film, because their installation components are more compatible with both traditional sculpture and the habits of museum goers.

Experimental movies remind us that we are involved with the world through fantasy, aesthetic experience, and analysis as well as through stories and informational modes. While experimental forms are in some ways the least accessible forms of film and media, they have fundamental bearing on how we see; this chapter has explored some implications of the fact that the word "experience" shares the same root as the word "experiment."

Activities

- Experimental media texts are difficult to see. Research the venues and other institutions that support this media and consider what kinds of audience expectations go into encounters with it.
- Explore film's connection with music, architecture, painting, and sculpture by imagining the same set of elements in each of these different media.

THE NEXT LEVEL: ADDITIONAL SOURCES

Benjamin, Walter. "The Work of Art in the Age of Mechanical Reproduction." In *Illuminations*, edited by Hannah Arendt. New York: Schocken, 1969. This seminal essay written in Weimar-era Germany discusses how film and photography have transformed the work of art and contemporary ways of seeing.

Gunning, Tom. "The Cinema of Attraction: Early Film, Its Spectator and the Avant-Garde, *Wide Angle* 8.3–4 (1986): 63–70. Important theorization of early cinema's solicitation of the spectator and the implications of such a mode for non-narrative traditions including the avant-garde.

Hall, Doug, and Sally Jo Fifer, eds. *Illuminating Video: An Essential Guide to Video Art*. New York: Aperture, in association with the Bay Area Video Coalition, 1990. This is an authoritative study of video as an art medium before the advent of digital video.

James, David. E. *Allegories of Cinema: American Film in the 1960s*. Princeton: Princeton University Press, 1989. This study contextualizes underground and avant-garde cinema on the political and social movements of the period.

Le Grice, Malcolm. *Abstract Film and Beyond*. Cambridge: MIT Press, 1977. An important experimental filmmaker himself, Le Grice begins by comparing these films to avant-garde paintings and then maps their development from the futurist movement through various post–World War II movements in the United States.

MacDonald, Scott. *A Critical Cinema: Interviews with Independent Filmmakers*. 5 vols. Berkeley: California University Press, 1988–2006. One of the foremost scholars and advocates of experimental cinema interviews hundreds of filmmakers spanning several generations of the U.S. avant-garde in this vital series.

Manovich, Lev. *The Language of New Media*. Cambridge: MIT Press, 2001. Provocative and influential theorization of new media and their relation to old media.

Petrolle, Jean, and Virginia Wright Wexman, eds. *Women and Experimental Filmmaking*. Urbana: University of Illinois Press, 2005. This work is an anthology of new writings on filmmakers who are sometimes overshadowed in canonical accounts.

Rees, A. L. *A History of Experimental Film and Video*. London: BFI, 1999. Addressing subjects ranging from Jean Cocteau to Stan Brakhage and contemporary avant-garde video, this is a meticulous, smart, and readable account of twentieth-century experimental film and video.

Renov, Michael, and Erika Suderburg, eds. *Resolutions: Contemporary Video Practices*. Minneapolis: University of Minnesota Press, 1996. This is a comprehensive anthology of theoretical and historical essays on activist and art video.

Rieser, Martin, and Andrea Zapp. *New Screen Media: Cinema/Art/Narrative*. London: BFI, 2002. Features writings by a wide range of critics, theorists, and artists about the impact of new media forms on narrative and aesthetics.

Sitney, P. Adams. *Visionary Film: The American Avant-Garde, 1943–2000*. 3rd ed. Oxford: Oxford University Press, 2002. This classic text establishing the terminology with which the American avant-garde film and its key filmmakers were discussed for decades, originally published in 1974, now includes a new chapter surveying recent developments.

Wees, William C. *Light Moving in Time: Studies in the Visual Aesthetics of Avant-Garde Film*. Berkeley: University of California Press, 1992. Provides accounts of the aesthetics of many of the principal filmmakers of the North American avant-garde.

Rituals, Conventions, Archetypes, and Formulas

Movie Genres

Making a hasty escape from government agents and outraged neighbors after causing an environmental catastrophe in his hometown, Homer Simpson leads his family west. A log cabin sojourn and a wise Native American woman convince him to return and save Springfield. Invoking conventional settings, characters, and plot devices, this animated film also spoofs them: the pristine Alaskan wilderness is a travel poster stuck to the car windshield in one shot, only to be exactly replicated as a "real" location moments later. Since its debut in 1989, the long-running television series *The Simpsons* has played on nearly every popular genre in its verbal and visual satire while following the rules of the situation comedy, in which the lessons of one week are forgotten by the next. Finally making the leap to the big screen, *The Simpsons Movie* (2007) spoofs big-budget disaster movies and family films, among numerous other genres. The success of the humor in the film, as well as in the show, results from the fact that it often does not require us to have seen specific films, but simply to have a passing familiarity with their genre conventions. The show and the film both build on a knowing recognition of convention as a sign of the times.

A definition of **genre** can be derived from its root, meaning "kind." It is a category or classification of a group of movies in which the individual films share similar subject matter and similar ways of organizing the subject through narrative and stylistic patterns. This chapter argues that film genres are not merely formulaic categories but practices connected to the human need for archetypes (see pp. 337–338), rituals, and communication. The film industry has made this need part of an economic strategy in order to draw audiences back again and again to experience the genres they enjoy. Narrative, documentary, and experimental films have each created particular genres associated with their respective organizations, but in this chapter we will focus specifically on six narrative film genres: comedy, western, melodrama, musical, horror, and crime. For each genre, we will identify its primary formulas and conventions and consider how it reflects and regulates specific cultural and historical experiences.

| KEY CONCEPTS |

In this chapter, we will examine

- why film genres attract audiences
- how film genres spring from a long historical heritage
- how conventions and formulas identify a specific genre
- how genres function as cultural rituals that coordinate audience needs and desires
- how genres change over time
- how audiences' prescriptive and descriptive understanding of certain film types become ways of making meaning through genre

Why do so many movies repeat formulas and conventions? How do those repetitions affect our responses to films? Indeed, we sometimes choose to see a movie because we identify it with a particular genre, and we return to genre films because we know and appreciate them. Movies rely on repetitions and rituals that allow audiences to share expectations and routines. Grounded in audience expectations about characters, narrative, and visual style, a film genre is a set of conventions and formulas repeated and developed through film history. To some degree, our understanding of a movie is a function of genre expectations. We enjoy science fiction films—from the 1927 *Metropolis* to the 1958 and 1986 versions of *The Fly*—because we recognize and appreciate some version of a "mad scientist" who works in a mysterious laboratory in which new technology leads to strange and dangerous discoveries. One viewer may decide to rush out to see Danny Boyle's *28 Days Later* (2002) for the very same reason that another viewer may resolutely choose not to see it: because it is a horror film whose formulas and images—a catastrophic virus, deserted city streets, and frightening zombies—are part of a well-known genre designed to appeal to viewers' awareness of these conventions [**Figure 10.1**]. In an important sense, our different responses to particular genres define the film community to which we belong.

10.1 *28 Days Later* (2002). The genre formulas of the zombie film are recognizable but updated.

Genres also function as *cultural rituals*, the repetition of formulas that help coordinate our needs and desires. These rituals are both formal and ideological practices that can become a therapeutic means of responding to a crisis that is too traumatic, confusing, or irrational to resolve in a simple or pragmatic way. Many religions celebrate a child's coming-of-age (around the age of thirteen) through ritualized ceremonies involving family and friends. Some communities acknowledge the transition from autumn to winter by acting out serious and playful rituals—such as those associated with Halloween—that testify to the coming months of darkness and death. As we will learn in this chapter, film genres carry their own specific cultural values.

▶ **VIEWING CUE**

Identify the genre of the film you have just viewed for class. What specifically distinguishes this film as part of a genre?

A Short History of Film Genre

MGM's *Singin' in the Rain* (1952) reminds us more directly than most films that a film genre always carries the traces of an older and varied history. A musical comedy, it is as much about history as it is about music. It begins in 1928, with two silent film stars concluding one generic film, a historical romance in the model of a literary adaptation like *The Three Musketeers,* and follows them as they try, unsuccessfully, to adapt that genre to the new historical demands of "talking pictures" [Figure10.2]. In the narrative confusion, failures, and frustrations that follow this clash of genre and history, they re-create their movie as a different film genre, the musical. The fact that the title song, as well as "You Are My Lucky Star" and several others, are drawn from early MGM musicals adds another historical dimension to the film. As the story unfolds, a romantic melodrama involving the two protagonists, Kathy and Don, sneaks into the musical, while the wacky antics of Don's sidekick, Cosmo, recall the slapstick comedies of the Keystone Kops, Charlie Chaplin, and Harold Lloyd. *Singin' in the Rain* itself later became many viewers' reference point for the classical Hollywood musical; its awareness of genre history thus becomes incorporated in the history of film genres.

Historical Origins of Genres

Well before the advent of the movies, genres were used to classify works of literature, theater, music, painting, and other art forms. Tragedy was considered the most important genre in Aristotle's *Poetics* in 350 B.C., and more specific literary genres like poetic ballads, pastoral and epic poems, and dime novels were identified and refined in subsequent historical periods. Musical genres included classical sonatas and symphonies as well as popular love songs and children's lullabies. The seventeenth-century

10.2 *Singin' in the Rain* (1952). The film-within-the-film spoofs silent film genres.

King Lear (1916). This feature-
length version is only one of
several silent film adaptations of
the play.

Korol Lir (1971). Russian
filmmaker Grigori Kozintsev followed
his acclaimed *Hamlet* adaptation
with this black-and-white epic.

King Lear (1982). The BBC
television adaptations of
Shakespeare set standards for
prestige programming.

Ran (1985). Akira Kurosawa's last
great epic and his third loose
adaptation of a Shakespeare play.

Dutch painter Pieter de Hooch created genre paintings that depicted scenes of domestic life and daily social encounters. In the eighteenth-century and early-nineteenth-century paintings of David Wilkie, William Hogarth, and others, genre came to suggest an image of a "slice of life," or scenes aimed at familiarity, recognition, and shared (if heightened) human emotions **[Figure 10.3]**. This combination of domestic realism and theatricality linked genres to the stage, particularly to the staging of melodramas, the most popular genre of the nineteenth century. In these different forms, three functions for genre began to take shape:

1. to provide models for producing other works
2. to direct audience expectations
3. to create categories for judging or evaluating a work

For painters in the eighteenth century, for example, historical paintings would need to follow certain generic rules about what objects to include in a painting about a naval victory; classical audiences would learn to expect all epic poems to begin with a generic invocation to the gods or a muse.

Early Film Genres

Early cinema immediately employed genres, building on the lessons of its predecessors in photography, literature, art, and musical halls. Nineteenth-century portrait photography repeated standardized poses and backgrounds, and musical halls developed formulas that would, for instance, predictably alternate a musical number with a comic skit, both of which would often feature recognizable conventions and rhythms. Although the first films of the 1890s searched out new subject matter, objects, and events, rough generic patterns quickly developed. Common formulas for short films included panoramic views such as *Panoramic of Niagara Falls in Winter* (1899), historical events as in *Carrie Nation Smashing a Saloon* (1901), and, less often acknowledged, semi-pornographic scenes in "blue movies," such as *From Show Girl to Burlesque Queen* (1903) **[Figure 10.4]**. As the film industry and its audiences expanded through the 1900s, other types of films filled the catalog of early genres: scenes from the theater, sporting events, and slapstick comedies. And as outdoor filming increased, the first westerns became common subjects.

1920s–1940s: Genre and the Studio System

Since the beginning of film history, the importance of genre and the popularity of specific genres have waxed and waned depending on the historical period and culture. Film genres follow an economics of predictability—that is, the production, regulation, and distribution of materials—in ways that anticipate the desire for those materials and the efficient delivery of them. In this context, the movie industry's model for genre parallels the industrial model for the Ford Motor Company. Fordism, the economic model that defined U.S. industry through much of the twentieth century, increased the amount and quality of output (of a kind of car) through the division of labor and the mass production of parts. As a result of that increased output, cost would decrease and, ideally, consumption of the product would increase. Tied to a studio system that adapted this industrial system of mass production, film genres enabled movie producers to reuse script formulas, actors, sets, and costumes to create, again and again, many different modified versions of a popular movie. In the same way that a consumer might buy a Ford automobile in a new color or different style every seven years, an audience might return every Memorial Day weekend to see the latest version of a swashbuckler adventure film franchise like *Pirates of the Caribbean: At World's End* (2007).

Although films have used repeated subjects and formulas (such as Shakespeare plays and the chase, respectively) from their very beginnings, the rise of the studio system through the 1920s and 1930s provided extraordinarily fertile grounds for movie

10.3 *Shortly After Marriage* (1743), William Hogarth. Prominent English genre painter William Hogarth painted satirical views of everyday life and contemporary mores.

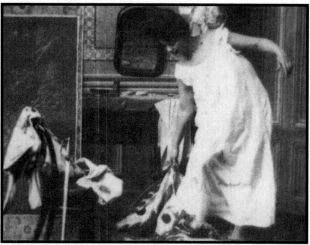

10.4 *From Show Girl to Burlesque Queen* (1903). Erotic "blue movies" emerged as an early film genre.

genres. The **studio system** describes the industrial practices of those large production (and, until 1948, distribution and exhibition) companies responsible for the kinds and quality of movies made in Hollywood and in other film industries around the world (see p. 380). The most famous Hollywood studios differed in size, strategies, and styles—from the smaller United Artists to the massive MGM—but each used a production system based on the efficient recycling of formulas and conventions, stars, and sets. The system was headed by a mogul who assigned a producer, who in turn oversaw those many moveable parts that a studio had at its disposal. In this environment, individual studios refined their production line techniques, established their association with specific genres, and used and refined that expertise to develop those genres. Thus, by the 1930s Warner Bros. was identified with gangster films, Paramount with sophisticated comedies, MGM with musicals and melodramas, RKO with literary adaptations, Columbia Pictures with westerns, and Universal with horror films.

(see p. 380)

▶ **VIEWING CUE**

Consider the historical precedents for the genre represented by the film screened in class. Do they come from literary or theatrical history? From a cultural or religious ritual?

1948–1970s: Postwar Film Genres

The *Paramount* decision of 1948, in which the Supreme Court ruled that the major studios violated antitrust laws by monopolizing the film business, undid the studio system and thus a cornerstone of movie genres. Without control of a distribution network of theaters to ensure the profitability of its production decisions, the studio system gradually began its decline and, with it waned the golden years of American film genres. Certainly, genre movies continued to be made and enjoyed. Some, like film noir, appeared during this waning, and others, like blaxploitation, came about in the ensuing fragmentation: the former, with its shadowy characters and violent crimes, reflected the cultural stresses and instabilities that followed World War II, while the latter, featuring African American urban life and often machismo stereotypes, developed in the 1970s against the background of turbulent race relations.

At the same time, independent and less formulaic movies started to challenge the supremacy of genre films. Finally, the popularity of many genre films in the 1960s and 1970s depended upon a recycling of genres through other cultures and within American culture. These revisionist genre films, like Robert Altman's western *McCabe and Mrs. Miller* (1971) **[Figure 10.5]** and

10.5 *McCabe and Mrs. Miller* (1971). Robert Altman and other New Hollywood filmmakers offered revisionist takes on Hollywood genres like the western.

10.6 *Rush Hour 3* (2007). Sequels and franchises cash in on the repetitive pleasures of genre formulas.

10.7 *Dilwale Dulhania Le Jayenge* (1995). Internationally successful, DDLJ (as it is known by fans) represents the globalization of national genres.

Wim Wenders's German film noir *The American Friend* (1977), often returned to the earlier conventions and icons but with an ironic and self-conscious perspective on those formulas and their relation to a changing world.

1970s–Present: New Hollywood, Sequels, and Global Genres

Jaws (1975) and *Star Wars* (1977) brought forth the era known as New Hollywood with film-school-educated directors drawing on established genres, special effects, and large advertising budgets to create blockbusters. Video and foreign sales helped such movies generate worldwide business, and the new corporate entities that owned the studios relied heavily on sequels and franchises, including those for blockbusters like *Star Wars*, to guarantee repeat successes. *The Godfather: Part II* (1974), for example, deepened the saga of the Corleone Mafia family and was hailed as a masterpiece, while contemporary sequels like *American Pie 2* (2001) and *Rush Hour 3* (2007) combine characters and plot elements with new situations to deliver familiar entertainment [**Figure 10.6**]. Franchises such as the live-action *Spider-Man* films (2002, 2004, 2007) spread genre elements into other platforms—for instance, video games.

Increasingly, the commercial movie business was not centered only on Hollywood. Hong Kong action films—for example, John Woo's *The Killer* (1989)—established a worldwide fan base by combining the successful national and regional genre of martial arts films with formulas of Hollywood action films, and they proved that films made outside Hollywood could be globally profitable. Mumbai (formerly Bombay)–based Hindi films, characterized by their extravagant song-and-dance sequences and megastars, deepened their popularity beyond the Indian subcontinent and South Asian communities abroad by relying on the Internet and DVD distribution. *Dilwale Dulhania Le Jayenge* (1995), a romantic comedy about second-generation Indians living in Britain who remain deeply attached to their cultural traditions and roots, set records in India and became widely distributed in the West (see pp. 415–416) [**Figure 10.7**].

As this section reveals, history renews some genres and demands the invention of new ones. Because genre is always a historical negotiation, an awareness of the vicissitudes of cultural history only makes movie genres more vital and meaningful.

The Elements of Film Genre

Genres identify group, social, or community activity and seem opposed to the individual creativity we associate with many art forms, including the art film (see Chapter 9). A film may work creatively and individually within its genre, but the work must begin within the framework of acknowledged conventions and formulas that audiences expect. Our recognition of these formulas represents a bond between filmmakers and audiences, determining a large part of how we see and understand a film. Film genres thus describe a kind of social contract, one that allows us to see a film as part of both a historical evolution and a cultural community. For instance, the western, which we might recognize by scenes of open plains and lone cowboys, engages

(a)

(b)

(c)

(d)

10.8 **(a)** *The Miracle Rider* (1935), **(b)** *My Darling Clementine* (1946), **(c)** *Bad Girls* (1994), **(d)** *Broken Arrow* (1996). Genres represent a bond between filmmakers and audiences that must be renegotiated by each genre film.

audiences' common knowledge of and interest in U.S. history and "how the West was won" in different ways and to different ends over time [Figures 10. 8a–10.8d].

 VIEWING CUE

For the movie you are about to watch for class, identify the genre and describe three conventions typically associated with this genre.

Conventions, Formulas, and Expectations

The most conspicuous dimensions of film genres are the conventions, formulas, and expectations through which we identify certain genres and distinguish them from others. *Generic conventions* are isolated properties or figures that identify a genre through such features as character types, settings, props, or events that are repeated from film to film. In westerns, cowboys often travel alone; in crime films, a seductive woman often foils the hard-boiled detective. Generic conventions also include **iconography**, images or image patterns with specific connotations or meanings. Dark alleys and smoky bars are staple images in crime movies; the world of the theater and entertainment industry is frequently the setting for musicals, as in *Hairspray* (2007) [Figure 10.9]. These conventions and iconographies can sometimes acquire larger meanings and connotations that align them with other social and cultural *archetypes*—that is, spiritual, psychological, or cultural models expressing certain virtues, values, or

10.9 *Hairspray* (2007). The set of the Corny Collins Show, around which much of the film revolves.

10.10   *The Last Wave* (1977). Archetypal imagery, such as the tidal wave shown here, underpins generic conventions.

10.11   *The Shining* (1980). Jack Nicholson as a writer who suffers a mental breakdown within the walls of a deceptively peaceful Colorado hotel.

▶ **VIEWING CUE**

While viewing the next film, consider whether the film relies on an identifiable genre iconography. Does it suggest certain archetypes or myths? ⏸

▶ **VIEWING CUE**

Reflect on the generic expectations that the film you've just seen triggers. What exactly creates those expectations? ⏸

timeless realities. Thus a flood may represent the end of a corrupt life and the beginning of a new spiritual life—an archetypal meaning used in some disaster films but not in others. A meditative version of this kind of film, Peter Weir's *The Last Wave* (1977) describes ominous visions of a tidal wave that will destroy Australia, according to the Aborigines who predict it, as part of a spiritual process [**Figure 10.10**].

When generic conventions are put in motion as part of a plot, they become *generic formulas,* the patterns for developing stories in a particular genre. While generic conventions depend on a principle of selection, generic formulas describe a principle of arrangement for organizing those conventions through a plot: some conventions may appear in a particular film and others may not, while generic formulas suggest that those elements can be arranged in a standard way or in a variation on the standard. With horror films, such as Stanley Kubrik's *The Shining* (1980), we immediately recognize the beginning of one of these formulas: a couple and their child decide to live alone in a large, mysterious hotel isolated in the mountains of Colorado [**Figure 10.11**]. The rest of the formula proceeds as follows: strange and disturbing events indicate that the house/hotel is haunted (and in *The Shining* the haunting begins to take over and derange the husband/father); the haunting leads to frightening visions and begins to destroy the characters, who flee into the night.

In some cases, these generic formulas can also become associated with *myths*—spiritual and cultural stories that describe a defining action or event for a group of people or an entire community. All cultures have important myths that help secure a shared cultural identity. One may celebrate a national event associated with a particular holiday, such as the Fourth of July; another culture may see the birth and rise of a great hero from the past as the key to its cultural history. From *Young Mr. Lincoln* (1939) and *Patton* (1970) to *Gandhi* (1982) and *Malcolm X* (1992), historical epics often re-create an actual historical figure as a cultural myth in which the character's actions determine a national identity—in these cases, a great nineteenth-century president who emancipated African Americans and a U.S. army commander who turned the tide of World War II [**Figure 10.12a**], a major political and spiritual leader of India who led the country's nonviolent independence movement, and a black American Muslim minister who served as spokesperson of the Nation of Islam and is often considered the father of the Black Panther movement in the United States [**Figures 10.12b and 10.12c**]. The formulas of other genres also participate in this mythic function: science fiction films, such as Stanley Kubrick's *2001: A Space Odyssey* (1968), frequently recount explorations or inventions that violate the laws of nature or the spiritual world. The narrative formulas of science fiction films can relate to broader myths, such as the Faustian myth of selling one's soul for knowledge and power or the story of Adam and Eve's eating from the tree of knowledge and their subsequent punishment.

Anthropologist Claude Lévi-Strauss suggests that myths help cultures reconcile the irreconcilable (life and death), justify the inevitable (the coming of winter) and explain the inexplicable (how life began). Similarly, film genres attempt to perform reconciliations, justifications, and explanations. Consider, for example, the zombies (or the "undead") that wander the sets of horror films, the coincidences that happen in a melodrama, or the aliens that invade the earth in science fiction films. These conventions allow films to function as modern myths similar to those Lévi-Strauss described.

Triggered by a film's promotion or by the film itself, *generic expectations* describe a viewer's experience and knowledge while watching a film that help to anticipate the

(a)

(b)

(c)

10.12   **(a)** *Patton* (1970), **(b)** *Gandhi* (1982), **(c)** *Malcolm X* (1992). Historical epics often use a heroic figure to build a national myth.

meaning of particular conventions or the direction of certain narrative formulas. Thus a narrative's beginning, characters, or setting can cue certain expectations about the genre that the film then satisfies or frustrates. The beginning of *Jaws* (1975), when an unidentified young woman swims alone at night in a dark and ominous ocean, leads viewers to anticipate shock and danger, participate in the unfolding of the genre, and respond to any surprises this particular film may offer. In the case of *Jaws,* the fact that much of the ensuing plot takes place on a sunny beach and open ocean, rather than in the darkened, confined houses of the usual horror film, is a clever variation that keeps the formula fresh and viewers' expectations attentive.

Indeed, generic expectations underscore the important role of viewers in determining a genre and how that role connects genres to a specific social, cultural, or national environment. Partly because of Hollywood's global reach and the extensive group of genre films it has produced, most audiences around the world will, for instance, quickly recognize the cues for a horror film or a western. Other non-Hollywood genres may not generate such clear expectations outside their native culture. Expectations about the formulas and conventions for a martial arts film are likely to be more sophisticated in China than the United States. Likewise, the religious films, or *cine de sacerdotes,* of the 1940s and 1950s were well known in Spain but may hardly be recognized by viewers from other cultures (even those international viewers familiar with Luis Buñuel's 1961 attack on this national genre, *Viridiana*) [Figure 10.13]. Indeed, even within a culture the popularity of certain genres depends on the shifting tastes and expectations of an audience: musicals proliferated in the United States in the 1930s during the Depression; film noir crime films flourished in the 1940s and early 1950s during and in the wake of World War II social upheaval; and the heyday of science fiction films came in the Cold War–era 1950s [Figure 10.14]. Audience expectations signal the social vitality of a particular genre, but that vitality changes as genres

text continued on page 341 ▶

10.13   *Viridiana* (1961). Audience reactions to Buñuel's film will vary according to their familiarity with the genre of films it attacks.

10.14   *The Day the Earth Stood Still* (1951). Science fiction films took over the Cold War era.

Conventions and Expectations in *The Gold Rush* (1925)

Made at the height of the silent film era, Charlie Chaplin's *The Gold Rush* signals this important star director's mastery of longer narrative films and anticipates much of the future course of film comedy. *The Gold Rush* takes place in the snowy and barren regions of the Yukon in the late nineteenth century. Structured as a series of vignettes or scenarios, the film begins with the arrival of Chaplin, the Lone Prospector, and proceeds through a series of misadventures as he seeks his fortune in gold, barely survives the dangers of the wilderness, and falls in love with a dance-hall girl, Georgia.

Conventions abound in *The Gold Rush*. Many of the characters are stereotypes: Georgia is the hardened bar girl with a heart of gold; Black Larsen is a "predatory scoundrel" whose massive and gruff appearance makes him the ideal counterpoint to the diminutive Chaplin; Chaplin's rival, Jack, is the handsome, suave bully whom he must battle for Georgia's heart. Here, as in many comic

films, the comic conventions can often be described as "gags," visual jokes based on incongruity or the mismatching of things, people, and places. A dapper little aristocrat in the hostile North, Chaplin and his clothing always seem out of place: his baggy pants, bowler hat, and cane fit him oddly and fit oddly into this rough mining town in the Yukon [Figure 10.15]. From this start, gag after gag follows. A bear arrives in his cabin kitchen; Chaplin mistakenly uses a rope with a dog tied to it as a makeshift belt during a dance; and no matter how Chaplin jumps and moves around Big Jim and Black Larsen's fight for a gun, the barrel always seems directly pointed at him.

The narrative of *The Gold Rush* describes a fundamental formula for film comedy: the triumph of life. Regardless of how out of sync Chaplin seems with his world, he manages to overcome all these incongruities through his casual grace: an old shoe becomes a sophisticated dining experience to the starving man; a

10.15 *The Gold Rush* (1925). Reinventing conventional gags.

10.16 *The Gold Rush* (1925). Comedy as the triumph of life.

cabin teetering on the edge of a cliff becomes the set of a clownish skit of slipping and sliding that, after a balletic escape, lands Chaplin and Big Jim on their lost gold mine; stood up at his own New Year's party, Chaplin turns two forks with potatoes into a remarkable little dance number [Figure 10.16]; and, however physically mismatched the couple may be, the Lone Prospector finally wins the heart of the beautiful Georgia. In the end, this particular version of the comic formula— about an "undaunted Lone Prospector . . . somewhere in that nowhere"—resonates with other myths of human endurance, like the tales of Sisyphus and Job, where humility and patience triumph against a hostile world.

Although Chaplin himself now represents a comic icon and, for some, an archetype, his character was built from a history of generic emblems and signs. Carried over from earlier films, Chaplin's "Little Tramp" character bears traces of earlier archetypes such as the Pierrot figure of the *commedia dell'arte* theatrical tradition that flourished from the sixteenth to the eighteenth centuries [Figure 10.17]. Even Shakespeare's fools and Picasso's many painted clowns are echoed in the Little Tramp and Lone Prospector: living on the edge of society, silly in most every way, Chaplin's clown, like those other theatrical, poetic, and painted clowns, represents a wisdom and

10.17 *Pierrot* (1857). Chaplin's character draws on this archetype of *commedia dell'arte*.

creativity that more powerful and conventional members of society lack. Through this and other films, Chaplin adds to an enduring archetype for comic films, whose heritage would continue, for all their differences, with the comic characters found in the films of Jacques Tati, Woody Allen, and Roberto Benigni.

Generic expectations are, naturally, crucial to this comedy. They are the foundation of the gag itself: an audience must recognize that a joke is coming in order to appreciate it. With the first appearance of a shuffling little man in the snowy wilderness, audiences sense a comic situation that determines their reactions throughout the film. Despite the larger men and more attractive women, expectations suggest that Chaplin will not be defeated. As in all genres, however, audience expectations direct our attention to how conventions will be varied in this individual film. Of course Chaplin will triumph, but the means and degree of his triumph become the source of our fascination. If the comic hero often wins the girl, the concluding surprise of *The Gold Rush* is that he wins not only his love but, unlike in his other comedies, his fortune in gold as well. Chaplin did not invent these comic conventions and formulas; rather, as in most successful genre films, *The Gold Rush* turns and twists those generic materials in ways that reinvigorate them with his personal touch.

move from culture to culture or between historical periods within a single culture. In this sense, genres can tell us a great deal about community or national identity.

Six Paradigms

From their first days, movies were organized as genres according to subject matter: films about a famous person, panoramic views, and so on. As movies became more sophisticated, however, genres grew into more complex narrative organizations with recognizable formal conventions. By 1923, one poll of high school students identified their two favorite movies as Rex Ingram's epic war story *The Four Horsemen of the Apocalypse* (1921) and the exotic romance *The Sheik* (1921), both featuring Rudolph Valentino. Two or three times a week these young people would

10.18 *The Rocky Horror Picture Show* (1975). A hybrid of horror film and musical comedy genres, this film also shares characteristics with other cult films.

▶ VIEWING CUE

Can you identify this film as a particular hybrid or subgenre?

go to the movies, attracted to the clearly identified generic preferences for westerns, comedies, detective stories, romances, and melodramatic tragedies. As films developed and differentiated stylistic and formal conventions, these generic preferences would change and grow.

Creating a list of movie genres can be more daunting and uncertain than it appears. Genres are a product of a perspective that groups individual movies together, sometimes in many different ways. To be extremely idiosyncratic and subjective, one could construct genres of "movies about Chicago" or "films with music tracks featuring David Bowie." For some scholars or viewers, for instance, film noir is an important movie genre that surfaced in the 1940s, whereas for others, it is less a film genre than a style that appears in multiple genres of the period. (For more discussion, see Chapter 13.) A particular genre designation may, moreover, offer unusually wide boundaries or unusually narrow ones: comedies might appear too grand a category for some critics, and screwball comedies may seem too limited a group to be termed a genre. Here we will focus on six important groupings of films that are generally talked about as genres: comedies, westerns, melodramas, musicals, horror films, and crime films. We'll aim to define each genre as it has appeared in different cultures and at different points in history, as well as how its social contract changes with different audiences.

Genres are to movies as constellations are to stars in the sky; they are multidimensional organizations that may be linked in different ways. To better understand this analogy, two terms that specify genre combinations or subdivisions are helpful: **hybrid genres** are those created through the interaction of different genres to produce fusions, such as romantic comedies or musical horror films [Figure 10. 18]. **Subgenres** are specific versions of a genre denoted by an adjective, for example, the spaghetti western (produced in Italy) or the slapstick comedy. Thus the idea of genres as constellations suggests how genres, as distinctive patterns, can overlap and shift their shape depending on their relation to other genres or as extensions of a primary field. *Blazing Saddles* (1974), for example, belongs both to the subgenre of comedic western and to the hybrid genre of western comedy; seeing that film from one perspective or the other can make a difference in how we appreciate it [Figure 10.19].

While hybrid genres and subgenres show the complexity of genres as constellations, it is also helpful to demarcate major genres. For each of our central six genres, we will highlight a selection of defining characteristics that have surfaced through film history, including

- the distinguishing features of the characters, narrative, and visual style
- the reflection of social rituals in the genre
- the production of certain historical hybrids or subgenres out of the generic paradigm

Although these generic blueprints will inevitably be reductive and the generic distinctions will overlap, they help isolate our responses to comedies, westerns, melodramas, musicals, horror films, and crime films. Maps of each of these paradigms can guide our explorations of specific films and of how they engage their audiences.

10.19 *Blazing Saddles* (1974). Comedic western or western comedy?

Comedies

Film comedy has flourished since the invention of cinema in 1895, as comic actors took their talents to the screen where they could be appreciated even without synchronized sound. Rooted in the *commedia dell'arte*, Punch and Judy, and the vaudeville stage acts that would produce Buster Keaton and a host of other early comedians, film comedy is one of the first and most enduring of film genres. Its many variations can be condensed into these main traits:

- central characters who are often defined by distinctive physical features, such as body shape and size, costuming, or manner of speaking
- narratives that emphasize episodes or "gags" more than plot continuity or progression and that usually conclude happily
- theatrical acting styles in which characters physically and playfully interact with the mise-en-scène that surrounds them

From the early comedies of producer Mack Sennett to the awkward and stumbling Woody Allen as Alvy Singer in *Annie Hall* (1977), comic characters stand out physically because of the shapes of their bodies, the expressions on their faces, or the gestures with which they move. Although comedies can develop intricate plots, their focus is usually on individual vignettes. In Sennett's *Saturday Afternoon* (1926), Harry Langdon balances between moving cars and hangs from telephone poles [Figure 10.20]. In *Annie Hall*, Alvy jumps around a kitchen chasing lobsters and later squirms at a family dinner table where he imagines himself perceived by others as a Hasidic Jew [Figure 10.21]. In these episodic encounters, the comic world becomes a stage full of unpredictable gags and theatrical possibilities.

Comedies celebrate the harmony and resiliency of social life. Although many viewers associate comedies with laughs and humor, comedy is more fundamentally about social reconciliation and the triumph of the physical over the intellectual. In comic narratives, obstacles or antagonists—in homes, marriages, communities, and nations—are overcome or dismissed by the physical dexterity or verbal wit of a character, or perhaps by luck, good timing, or magic. In *Bringing Up Baby* (1938), Katharine Hepburn is a flighty socialite who moves and talks so fast that she bewilders the verbally and physically bumbling paleontologist Cary Grant, who will inevitably forsake his scientific priorities for the joys of an improbable romance with her. In *Groundhog Day* (1993), Bill Murray plays a weatherman with many social and professional flaws who falls into a magical world where he relives the day again and again, with the ability to correct his previous errors and romantic blunders. The unlikely hero of *Knocked Up* (2007) finds in his own childishness a resource for impending fatherhood [Figure 10.22]. Perhaps the most obvious convention in comedies is the happy ending, in which couples or individuals are united in the form of a family unit or the promise of one to come. Very often, traditional comedies begin with some discord or disruption in social life or in the relationship between two people (lovers are separated, for instance); after various trials or misunderstandings, harmony is restored and individuals

10.20 *Saturday Afternoon* (1926). Classic silent comedies, such as this Mack Sennett film, depend on physical gags.

10.21 *Annie Hall* (1977). Alvy imagines himself as he thinks his non-Jewish hosts see him, a visual joke that only film comedy could deliver.

10.22   *Knocked Up* (2007). In this scene, slacker Ben, much like a child himself, proves his fatherhood potential.

10.23   *Home Alone* (1990). Comic resiliency appears in the form of a child who manages to foil the plans of two inept burglars.

are reunited. In *Home Alone* (1990), for example, a family going on a trip to Paris mistakenly leaves the youngest and most underappreciated boy behind. After the diminutive but clever child trips up a pair of gruff but inept burglars again and again, the family returns home to a happy reunion [**Figure 10.23**].

Slapstick, Screwball, and Romantic Comedies.

Historically, as the Hollywood film comedy responded to audience expectations in changing contexts, the genre itself endured numerous permutations and structural changes. Three salient subgenres emerged as a result: slapstick comedies, screwball comedies, and romantic comedies.

10.24   *Tillie's Punctured Romance* (1914). Slapstick comedies developed from shorts to features centered around physical humor.

Slapstick comedies, marked by their physical humor and stunts, comprised some of the first narrative films. In the 1910s, the initial versions of this subgenre used printed intertitles rather than spoken dialogue and ran from a few minutes to about fifteen minutes in length. Early films like those of Mack Sennett's Keystone Kops revolved around physical stunts set within fairly restricted social spaces. The feature-length slapstick that came later—Sennett's *Tillie's Punctured Romance* (1914) [**Figure 10.24**], Newmeyer and Taylor's *The Freshman* (1925), and Parrott's *The Music Box* (1932), to name a few—emphasized the humorous stunts and dexterity of characters. Harold Lloyd in *The Freshman* and Stan Laurel and Oliver Hardy in *The Music Box*, for instance, played figures who were able to maintain a balance despite the imbalance of their world.

By the 1920s, comedy had integrated its gags and physical actions into a story. This move allowed physical games to develop new twists and turns over the course of narrative time within a social arena. Yet even within these longer versions of slapstick comedy, the singular slapstick instants are what stand out. For example, unforgettable is the moment in *The General* (1927) when Buster Keaton misfires the cannon vertically into the air and manages to avoid disaster when the cannonball fortuitously misses him and just happens to destroy an enemy bridge. Slapstick comedies reemerged in the 1980s with such films as *Porky's* (1982) and *Police Academy* (1984). The ingenuity of physical comedy gave way in these films targeted at young male audiences to scatological and sexual jokes. In *Monty Python's The Meaning of Life* (1983) [**Figure 10.25**] and *Monty Python and the Holy Grail* (1975), slap-

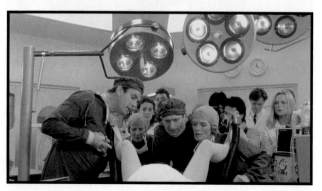

10.25   *Monty Python's The Meaning of Life* (1983). This birthing scene is an example of the metaphysical slapstick that fills this social satire.

(a)

(b)

10.26   (a) *There's Something about Mary* (1998), (b) *Austin Powers in Goldmember* (2002). Slapstick comedy has reinvented itself for new audiences.

stick becomes an ingredient of nonstop social satire. Today the genre is popular again, featuring comic stars such as Ben Stiller in *There's Something about Mary* (1998) and Mike Myers in *Austin Powers in Goldmember* (2002) **[Figures 10.26a and 10.26b]**.

In the 1930s and 1940s, **screwball comedies** transformed the humor of the physical into fast-talking verbal gymnastics, arguably displacing sexual energy with barbed verbal exchanges between men and women when the Production Code barred more direct expression. In effect, these films usually redirected the comic focus from the individual clown to the confused heterosexual couple. *It Happened One Night* (1934), *Bringing Up Baby, His Girl Friday* (1940), and *The Philadelphia Story* (1940) are among the best-known examples of screwball comedies; each features independent women who resist, mock, and challenge the crusty rules of their social worlds. When the right man arrives or returns, one who can match these women in charm and physical and verbal skills, confrontation leads to love. *My Best Friend's Wedding* (1997) revives some elements of this formula and its pleasures.

In **romantic comedies**, humor takes a second place to happiness. Popular since the 1930s and 1940s, romantic comedies like *Small Town Girl* (1936), *The Shop around the Corner* (1940) **[Figure 10.27]**, and *Adam's Rib* (1949) concentrate on the emotional attraction of a couple in a consistently lighthearted manner. This subgenre draws attention to a peculiar or awkward social predicament (in *Adam's Rib,* for example, the husband and wife lawyers oppose each other in the courtroom) that romance will eventually overcome on the way to a happy ending. More recent examples of the "rom-com," as its recent exemplars have come to be known, include Nora Ephron's *You've Got Mail* (a 1998 remake of Ernst Lubitsch's *The Shop around the Corner*), where the comic predicaments have contemporary twists—e-mail replaces the letters of the first version—but the formula and conventions remain fairly consistent. Stephen Frears's romantic comedy *My Beautiful Laundrette* (1985) suggests, however, the range of possibilities in the creative (and here political) reworking of any genre. In this case, the social complications include a wildly dysfunctional Pakistani family in London and the romance that blossoms between the entrepreneurial son and a white man, his childhood friend and a former right-wing punk **[Figure 10.28]**.

10.27   *The Shop around the Corner* (1940). In classic romantic comedy, true love triumphs over comic misunderstanding.

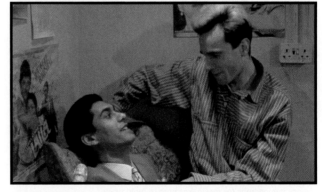

10.28   *My Beautiful Laundrette* (1985). Director Stephen Frears and writer Hanif Kureishi update romantic comedy to tell an interracial gay love story.

Westerns

Like film comedies, westerns are a staple of Hollywood, although their popularity has waxed and waned in different historical eras. This genre grew out of late-nineteenth-century stories, dime novels, and journalistic accounts of the wild American West [Figure 10.29]. With their reliance on visual iconography, these influences were more direct precursors of movie westerns than the frontier novels of James Fenimore Cooper. In the first years of the movie industry, the western began to take shape, acting as a kind of travelogue of a recent but now-lost historical period. From *The Great Train Robbery* (1903) to the HBO series *Deadwood* (2004–2006) [Figure 10.30], the western has grown over one hundred years into a surprisingly complex genre while also retaining its fundamental elements:

- characters, almost always male, whose physical and mental toughness separate them from the crowds of modern civilization
- narratives that follow some version of a quest into the natural world
- a stylistic emphasis on open, natural spaces and settings, such as the western frontier regions of the United States

According to this scheme, John Wayne as the Ringo Kid in *Stagecoach* (1939) has a physical energy and determination that find echoes in Paul Newman and Robert Redford as *Butch Cassidy and the Sundance Kid* (1969) [Figure 10.31]. Never at ease with the law or the restrictions of civilization, these men find themselves on vague searches for justice, peace, adventure, freedom, and perhaps a treasure that offers all these rewards. Taking them through a western landscape filled with natural and man-made violence (like marauding Native Americans), quests through wide-open canyons and deserts seem at once to threaten, inspire, and humble these western heroes.

Through the trials of a lone protagonist, rugged individualism becomes the measure of any social relationship and of the values of most western communities. Even when they are part of a gang, as in *The Magnificent Seven* (1960), these individuals are usually loners or mavericks rather than representative leaders. More than in historical epics, violent confrontations are central to these narratives, and this violence is primarily measured by the ability and will of the individual rather than the mass, nation, or community, even when it is directed against Native Americans. In *High Plains Drifter* (1972) [Figure 10.32], the moody Clint Eastwood must protect a frightened town from the vengeance of outlaws. When a violent showdown concerns two groups—as in the gunfight at the OK Corral between the Earps and the Clantons in John Ford's *My Darling Clementine* (1946)—the battle is often about individual justice or revenge (of sons and brothers) or about who has the rightful claims to nature.

Epic, Existential, and Political Westerns.
Like most film genres, westerns have responded to changing audiences. With several significant exceptions, including *The Covered Wagon* (1923), westerns were not a particularly respected genre in the 1920s and early 1930s. During the early twentieth century, they were popular among the mass audiences of early cinema and associated with such popular forms as Wild West shows. Since then, however, three hybrids or subgenres have distinguished the western: the western epic, the existential western, and the political western.

10.29 *Buffalo Bill's Wild West* (1899). At the end of the nineteenth century, William Cody's adventures as an army scout were reenacted in dime novels, stage melodramas, and in his wildly popular show, establishing cowboy iconography for movie westerns to build upon.

Within the constellation of westerns, the *epic western* concentrates on action and movement, developing a heroic character whose quests and battles serve to define the nation and its origins. With its roots in literature and epic paintings, this genre appears early and often in film history, foregrounding the spectacle of open land and beautiful scenery. An early instance of the epic, *The Covered Wagon* follows a wagon train of settlers into the harsh but breathtaking frontier, where their fortitude and determination establish the expanding spirit of America. Years later, *Dances with Wolves* (1990) describes a more complex struggle for national identity as a traumatized Civil War veteran allies himself with Native Americans [Figure 10.33].

10.30 *Deadwood* (2004–2006). The HBO series updates a genre whose popularity has waxed and waned over its hundred-year history.

In the 1950s, one of the most interesting decades for westerns, the *existential western* took shape. In this introspective version of the genre, the traditional western hero is troubled by his changing social status and his self-doubts. Here, too, the frontier tends to grow more populated and civilized, and the self-assurance and righteousness of the hero begins to suffer. *The Searchers* (1956), *The Furies* (1950), *Johnny Guitar* (1954), *Shane* (1953), and *The Left-Handed Gun* (1958) are existential westerns with protagonists who are troubled in their sense of purpose. The traditionally male domain of the West is now contested by women, evil is harder to locate and usually more insidious, and

10.31 *Butch Cassidy and the Sundance Kid* (1969). Paul Newman and Robert Redford incarnate western heroes for the 1960s.

the encroachment of society complicates life and suggests the end of the cowboy lifestyle. Even into the 1990s, this subgenre has endured, most notably with *Unforgiven* (1992): here the formerly unbendable Clint Eastwood is now financially strapped, somewhat hypocritical, and disturbingly aware that killing is an ugly business.

By the 1960s and 1970s, the *political western* had evolved out of the troubled territory of existential westerns: in this more contemporary and critical western, the ideology and politics that have always informed the genre are foregrounded; the heroism associated with individual independence and the use of violence naturalized in epic westerns become precisely what is questioned. In *The Man Who Shot Liberty Valance* (1962), the heroic myth of the American West is exposed as a lie.

10.32 *High Plains Drifter* (1972). The western hero is often a loner for whom violence comes naturally.

10.33 *Dances with Wolves* (1990). Costner plays a sympathetic Civil War veteran who commiserates with Native Americans in this modern epic western.

10.34 *The Wild Bunch* (1969). Sam Peckinpah's violent revisionist western depicts aging cowboys as "unchanged men in a changing land" according to the film's tagline.

With only communities rather than frontiers to conquer in *The Wild Bunch* (1969), aging cowboys are less interested in justice and freedom than in indiscriminate and grotesque killing [Figure 10.34]. More recently the western genre has remained visible in a variety of contemporary films, such as *There Will Be Blood* (2007) and *No Country for Old Men* (2007), where many of the conventional motifs and icons of violence and conquest reappear in more horrifying and exaggerated forms than ever before.

Melodramas

Movie melodramas are one of the more difficult genres to define because melodramatic characters and actions can be part of many other kinds of movies. The word itself indicates a combination of the intensities of music (*melos*) and the interaction of human conflicts (*drama*). Indebted to a nineteenth-century theatrical heritage in which social and domestic oppression created heightened emotional dramas, film melodramas arrived virtually simultaneously with the first developments toward film narrative. While the term "melodrama" was used in different ways by early film critics, the contemporary definition developed by film scholars includes these fundamental formulas and conventions:

- characters defined by their situation or basic traits rather than their deeds, who struggle, often desperately, to express their feelings or emotions
- narratives that rely on coincidences and reversals and build toward emotional or physical climaxes
- a visual style that emphasizes emotion or elemental struggle, whether in interior scenes and close-ups or in action tableaux

From D. W. Griffith's *Way Down East* (1920) to Kimberly Peirce's *Boys Don't Cry* (1999), the central character is restrained, repressed, or victimized by more powerful forces of society. These forces may pit a dominating masculinity against a weaker femininity. In Griffith's film, a city villain threatens an innocent virgin, and in *Boys Don't Cry*, Nebraska country boys assault and murder Brandon Teena when they discover that he was born female (and named Teena Brandon) and has been living as a male. In the first film, claustrophobic rooms dramatize this victimization [Figure 10.35], until a climactic chase over a frozen river brings the conflict between good and evil outside for the world to witness. In the second, medium shots and close-ups of the protagonist emphasize the strains and contradictions of identity [Figure 10.36]. In each of these films, true to the conventions of melodrama, the story reaches a breaking point with the threat of death: one character almost drifts away on ice floes; the other is senselessly shot and killed.

As social rituals, melodramas parallel and contrast with westerns. Individualism and private life anchor this genre as well, but the drama is not about conquering a frontier and finding a home; rather, it is about the strain on and often failure of the individual to act or speak out within an already established home and family. Melodramas thus develop a conflict between interior emotions and exterior restrictions, between yearning or loss and satisfaction or renewal. One or more women are typically at the center of melodrama, illustrating how his-

10.35 *Way Down East* (1920). Claustrophobic interiors represent the melodramatic heroine's victimization.

torically women have been excluded from or limited in their access to public powers of expression. Mise-en-scène and narrative space also play a major stylistic role in melodrama: for example, in Griffith's films, individuals, usually female, retreat into smaller and smaller private spaces while some obvious or implied hostile force, often male, threatens and drives them further into a desperate internal sanctuary. These rituals are often graphically acted out. In Elia Kazan's film version of *A Streetcar Named Desire* (1951), Blanche and Stella, confined in a run-down, claustrophobic home in New Orleans, also confine and repress their memories of a lost family history; their desires to escape are channeled through their sexuality. For Stella, that means accepting her husband Stanley's violent control of her; for Blanche, it means becoming a victim of Stanley's power and, after he rapes her, retreating into madness.

10.36 *Boys Don't Cry* (1999). Melodrama relies on close-ups to tell stories of contested identity—here the protagonist's expression of gender.

Physical, Family, and Social Melodramas. Whereas early melodramas followed formulas that depicted female distress and excessive emotions and entrapment in time and space, those formulas have grown subtler, or at least more realistic, over the years. Three subgenres of melodramas that usually overlap and rarely appear in complete isolation from one another can be distinguished: physical, family, and social melodramas.

   Physical melodramas focus on the physical plight and material conditions that repress or control the protagonist's desires and emotions; these physical restrictions may be related to the places and people that surround that person or may simply be a product of the person's physical size or color. One of the first great film melodramas, D. W. Griffith's *Broken Blossoms* (1919) is also one of the most grisly: in an atmosphere of drugs, violence, and poverty, a brutal boxer, Battling Burrows, hounds and physically terrifies his illegitimate and frail daughter, Lucy. He eventually beats her to death (as she retreats into smaller and smaller rooms) and is himself killed by Lucy's one friend, a Chinese immigrant (identified in the subtitles only as the Yellow Man), who then commits suicide. Although most melodramas do not so definitively emphasize the physical plight of the heroine, viewers can still recognize this generic focus on bodily or material strain in such melodramas as *Dark Victory* (1939), about a woman with a terminal brain illness; *Magnificent Obsession* (1954), about a blind woman whose vision is ultimately restored; and in *Boys Don't Cry* and Rainer Werner Fassbinder's *In a Year of Thirteen Moons* (1978), more contemporary melodramas about sexual identity and physical violence.

   Although physical arrangements play a part in them, *family melodramas* elaborate the confines and restrictions of the protagonist by investigating the psychological and gendered forces of the family. For many viewers, this is the quintessential form of melodrama, in which women and young people especially must struggle against patriarchal authority, economic dependency, and confining gender roles. In Douglas Sirk's *Written on the Wind* (1956), a Texas millionaire marries a beautiful but naive secretary and then tortures himself wondering whether the baby they are expecting is his or his best friend's (the man she should have married); the corruption and confusion of this household grow more intense and manic through the constant baiting and manipulations of a sister whose restlessness is expressed as sexual promiscuity. While the family melodrama came to prominence in the postwar period as gender and familial roles were being redefined, similar themes are found in soap operas and their popular nighttime serial counterparts such as *Dallas* (1978–1991) and *Desperate Housewives* (2004–). In *Ordinary People* (1980), an outwardly prosperous family is emotionally crippled by the loss of one son, the mother's withdrawal of affection from the other, and the

10.37 *The Namesake* (2007). Generations of an immigrant family struggle to find common ground in this transnational family melodrama.

father's powerlessness, while in Mira Nair's *The Name-sake* (2007), family melodrama becomes a generational and transnational affair as parents immigrated from India and a son raised in New York struggle to find common ground [Figure 10.37].

Social melodramas extend the melodramatic crisis of the family to include larger historical, community, and economic issues. In these films, the losses, sufferings, and frustrations of the protagonist are visibly part of social or national politics. Earlier melodramas fit this subgenre—for example, John Stahl's *Imitation of Life* (1934), remade by Douglas Sirk in 1959, makes the family melodrama inseparable from larger issues of racism as a black daughter passes for white. Modern melodramas also commonly explore social and political dimensions of personal conflicts: in Nair's *Mississippi Masala* (1991), the romance between an Indian woman born in Uganda and an African American man from Greenwood, Mississippi, must negotiate the family and cultural traditions of African Americans, South Asian immigrants, and local white Americans [Figure 10.38]. In *Brokeback Mountain* (2006), lovers are kept apart by social conventions (and arguably generic ones, as cowboys are not usually shown falling in love with each other) [Figure 10.39].

Musicals

As we noted in Chapter 6, when synchronous sound came to the cinema in 1927, the film industry quickly moved to design plots to highlight music. Before then, music had always surrounded movies through piano or orchestral accompaniments of a film's projection. With the new sound technology, however, films began to focus on music or to integrate music and song into the stories. Precedents for film musicals range from traditional opera to vaudeville and musical theater, in which songs either supported or punctuated the story. Since the first musicals, the most common components of the musical have been:

- characters who act out and express their emotions and thoughts through song and dance
- plots interrupted or moved forward by musical numbers
- spectacular sets and settings, such as Broadway theaters, fairs, and dramatic social or grand natural backgrounds, or animated environments

10.38 *Mississippi Masala* (1991). Negotiating multicultural family traditions through melodrama.

10.39 *Brokeback Mountain* (2006). The political melodrama of lovers kept apart by social and generic conventions.

In *Gold Diggers of 1933* (1933) and *The Sound of Music* (1965), groups of characters escape the complexities of the situation (Depression-era society and Austria threatened by Nazis, respectively) by breaking into song [Figure 10.40]. Whether on a Broadway stage or against the beauty of an Alpine setting, characters in musicals speak their hearts and minds most articulately through music and dance.

As social markers, musicals are the flip side of melodramas, highlighting the joy of expression rather than the pain of repression. With musicals, the tearful cries of melodrama give way to the beautiful articulations of music. Both focus on personal emotions, but in musicals, song and dance become the longed-for vehicles for the repressed and inexpressible emotions of the melodrama. In musicals, the present easily usurps the past. There are certainly romantic crises, social problems, and physical dangers in the narrative, but in most cases, these obstacles are secondary and any difficulties can be remedied or at least put into perspective by the immediacy of song, music, and dance. With more plot than most musicals, *West Side Story* (1961) features all the tragedy and violence found in Shakespeare's *Romeo and Juliet* (on which it is based) and a social commentary on Puerto Rican/white relationships in New York: gangs fight, lovers are separated, and horrible deaths happen. But even during the most troubling situations, a song and dance transform battle cries into gaiety ("The Jet Song") [Figure 10.41], patriotic idealism into comic satire ("America"), and even a tragic death into a peaceful vision ("Somewhere").

10.40 *The Sound of Music* (1965). The Nazi threat cannot dampen the spirit expressed through song.

10.41 *West Side Story* (1961). Social antagonisms are expressed through song and dance.

Julie Taymor's *Across the Universe* (2007), similarly rich with plot and narrative, weaves together the stories of several characters living in New York City during the turbulent 1960s. Musical enactments of Beatles' songs express the "free love" spirit and the darker, politically charged moments of the decade. "I Am the Walrus," parts of which were written by John Lennon while high on LSD, illustrates the drug-fueled art scene of the era, while "Let It Be" sums up the emotion and angst surrounding the tragic deaths of a brother and a boyfriend resulting from the 12th Street riot and the Vietnam War. "All You Need Is Love" is of course the song that pleads for an end to the turbulence and political and social strife that mark the period and the lives of the characters.

Theatrical, Integrated, and Animated Musicals. After the first feature-length musical, *The Jazz Singer* (1927), musicals adapted to reflect different cultural predicaments. Of the many types of musicals, we can identify three subgenres: theatrical, integrated, and animated musicals. Many examples of each subgenre are adaptations of Broadway musicals or other theatrical sources. No doubt the best known, *theatrical musicals* situate the musical convention onstage or "backstage"; here it is unmistakable that the fantasy and art of the theater supercede the reality

10.42   *42nd Street* (1933). The "Shuffle Off to Buffalo" number is presented as part of a Broadway show.

of the street. One of the finest early musicals, *42nd Street* (1933) is partly about the complicated love lives of its characters: a Broadway director who wants one last hit play, the starlet Dorothy Brock who juggles lovers offstage, and the chorus girl Peggy Sawyer who substitutes for the star and saves the show. What ultimately gathers all these hopes and conflicts is, of course, the musical show itself: through the remarkable choreography of Busby Berkeley and hit tunes like "Shuffle Off to Buffalo," jealousies and doubts turn into a spectacular celebration of life on Broadway [**Figure 10.42**]. Although theatrical musicals later waned in popularity, *All That Jazz* (1979) resurrected this subgenre as an exaggerated and even self-indulgent staging of the autobiography of choreographer Bob Fosse. In a recent resurgence, *Chicago* (2002) weaves the drama of abused and downtrodden women into an energetic musical in which the theatrics of song and dance burst open prison cells, and *Dreamgirls* (2006) dramatizes the story of Motown.

When musicals began to integrate musical numbers into more common situations and realistic actions, they became *integrated musicals*. Here the idyllic and redemptive moments of song and dance are part of everyday lives. In *My Fair Lady* (1964), the grueling transformation of a street girl into a glamorous aristocrat is described by song; in the case of numbers like "The Rain in Spain," songs actually assist that transformation. *Dancer in the Dark* (2000) and *Pennies from Heaven* (1981) are more ironic versions of this subgenre. In both films, musical interludes allow the characters (a blind woman accused of murder and a sheet-music salesman during the Depression, respectively) to unexpectedly transcend the tragedies and traumas of life.

Beginning with *Snow White* (1936) and increasing in popularity and frequency within the last decades, *animated musicals* use cartoon figures and stories to present songs and music. Moving in the opposite direction of integrated musicals, these films—from *Fantasia* (1940) and *The Yellow Submarine* (1968) to the Disney features *The Little Mermaid* (1989) [**Figure 10.43**] and *Beauty and the Beast* (1991) and Sylvain Chomet's offbeat *Triplets of Belleville* (2003) [**Figure 10.44**]—fully embrace the fantastic and utopian possibilities of music to make animals human, nature magical, or human life, as Mary Poppins says, "practically perfect in every way."

10.43   *The Little Mermaid* (1989). The resurgence of the animated musical highlights the utopian impulse of film genres.

10.44   *Triplets of Belleville* (2003). An offbeat animated musical takes advantage of the medium's possibilities.

Horror Films

Horror has been a popular literary and artistic theme at least since Sophocles' account of Oedipus's terrifying realization of his fate, the horrifying suicide of his mother, and his ghastly self-blinding. The supernatural mysteries of Gothic novels such as *The Monk* (1796) were followed in the nineteenth century by tales of monsters and murder, such as *Frankenstein* (1818) and *Dracula* (1897). Occasionally overlapping with science fiction, **horror films** have crossed cultures and appeared in various forms throughout film history. The fundamental elements of horror films include:

- characters with physical, psychological, and/or spiritual deformities
- narratives built on suspense, surprise, and shock
- visual compositions that move between the dread of not seeing and the horror of seeing

In Carl Boese's *The Golem* (1920) [**Figure 10.45**] and Ridley Scott's *Alien* (1979) [**Figure 10.46**], monstrous characters terrify the humans around them with their grotesque shapes and actions, lurking on the fringes of the visible world. Each film is infused with a nervous tension at the mere prospect of seeing a horror that exists just out of sight, a suspense that explodes when the creatures suddenly appear.

Horror films are about fear—physical fear, psychological fear, sexual fear, even social fear. The social repercussions of dramatizing what we fear are often debated, but regardless of whether showing horror on film has any effect on society, the genre's widespread popularity suggests that it is a central cultural ritual. Like scary stories around a campfire, horror films dramatize our personal and social terrors in their different forms, in effect allowing us to admit them and attempt to deal with them in an imaginary way and as part of a communal experience. Horror films make terror visible and, potentially, manageable. An eerie tale about alien invaders taking over bodies in an American town, *Invasion of the Body Snatchers* (1956) [**Figure 10.47**] acts out the prevalent fears in the 1950s about military and ideological invasion. The frightening story of a high school misfit with telekinetic powers, *Carrie* (1976) unveils all the anxiety and anger of female adolescence.

10.45 *The Golem* (1920). Horror takes monstrous physical form in this German expressionist film.

10.46 *Alien* (1979). Suspense and terror build as the grotesque creature lurks on the fringes of the visible, until finally bursting into view.

10.47 *Invasion of the Body Snatchers* (1956). Ordinary-seeming citizens are actually pod people in this 1950s horror classic.

10.48 *The Exorcist* (1973). Satan possesses a young girl in this 1970s masterpiece of supernatural horror.

10.49 *The Host* (2006). This Korean horror film was monstrously successful.

Supernatural, Psychological, and Physical Horrors. Within this genre, horror and fear have taken many shapes in many different cultures, addressing audiences in specific historical terms throughout the twentieth and into the current century. Here we call attention to three subgenres characterized by dominant elements: supernatural, psychological, and physical horror (slasher) films. In *supernatural horror* films, a spiritual evil erupts in the human realm, sometimes to avenge a moral wrong and sometimes for no explainable reason. This subgenre includes such movies as Henrik Galeen's *The Golem* (1915), an earlier film version of the myth of a clay monster brought to life to save the persecuted Jews; the Japanese film *Kaidan* (1964), which features four tales based on the writings of Lafcadio Hearn about samurai, monks, and spirits; and *The Sixth Sense* (1999), about a contemporary boy able to see the dead. In *The Exorcist* (1973), Satan possesses a young girl's body, deforming it into a twisted, obscenity-spewing nightmare **[Figure 10.48]**. *The Exorcist* is typical of supernatural horror in that how and why this evil has invaded the life of this modern and affluent family is never made entirely clear, but the character of Father Damien Karras, the exorcist, may hold the answer: doubting the real horrific presence of evil in a modern age, he and that age suffer its vengeance. Japanese horror films made in the aftermath of nuclear destruction featured supernatural figures like Godzilla; the contemporary Korean horror film *The Host* (2006) taps into political relations with the United States as well as into environmental issues **[Figure 10.49]**.

Another variation on the threat to modern life, *psychological horror* films locate the dangers and distortions that threaten normal life in the minds of bizarre and deranged individuals. While German expressionist films like *The Cabinet of Dr. Caligari* (1919) dealt with psychological themes, the modern cycle of such films begins with *Psycho* (1960). *Whatever Happened to Baby Jane?* (1962), *Don't Look Now* (1973), *The Stepfather* (1987), *The Hand That Rocks the Cradle* (1992) and *Birth* (2004) all participate in this subgenre **[Figure 10.50]**. *The Silence of the Lambs* (1991) is characteristic: although it features scenes of nauseating physical violence, it is Hannibal Lecter's diabolically brilliant mind and his empathetic bond with the protagonist, Clarice Starling, that make this film so mentally, rather than physically, horrifying.

Films in which the psychology of a character takes second place to the depiction of graphic violence are examples of *physical horror* films, a subgenre with a long pedigree and a consistent place in every cycle of horror film. Again, *Psycho* (1960) is an originator, this time of the contemporary horror films known as **slasher films**. *The Texas Chain Saw Massacre* (1974) **[Figure 10.51]**, the story of a cannibalistic Texas family who attacks lost travelers, *Halloween* (1978), the first of a sequence of films about ghastly serial killings that spawned many imitators, and the grisly *Saw* (2004) belong to this subgenre. Cut and banned in many countries, Tod Browning's *Freaks* (1932) testifies to both the longevity and the more intelligent potential of physical horror. A morality tale of rejection and revenge, *Freaks* features performers from actual carnival sideshows who, despite their shocking appearance and the repulsive revenge they perpetrate, ultimately act in more generous and humane ways than the physically "normal" villains.

10.50 *Birth* (2004). A woman is convinced that a young boy is a reincarnation of her dead husband in this psychological horror film.

Crime Films

Like other genres, crime films represent a large category that describes a wide variety of films. From the mysteries of Edgar Allan Poe and the tales of Sherlock Holmes to the pulp fiction of the 1920s, such as Dashiell Hammett's *Red Harvest* (1929), and Walter Mosley's ongoing Easy Rawlins series, crime stories have been a staple of modern culture. When early movies searched for good plots, criminal dramas that contained physical action and relied on keen observation were recognized as a genre made for the cinema, where movement and vision are central. A crime film's chief characteristics include:

- characters who live on the edge of a mysterious or violent society, either criminals or individuals dedicated to crime detection
- plots of crime, increasing mystery, and often ambiguous resolution
- urban, often dark and shadowy, settings

From *Underworld* (1927) to *The French Connection* (1971), the principal characters of crime movies are usually either criminals or individuals looking for criminals. In *Underworld,* gangster Bull Weed flees and then faces his relentless police pursuers in the mean streets of Chicago. In *The French Connection,* detective Popeye Doyle becomes entangled in New York's narcotics underworld. In the first film, the law triumphs but the tantalizing attraction of underworld life remains. In the second, legal victory is only partial and the glamour of the international drug market far outshines the tattered life of a New York cop [**Figure 10.52**].

10.51 *The Texas Chain Saw Massacre* (1974). This classic slasher film goes to extremes—cannibalism.

10.52 *The French Connection* (1971). The glamour of international crime is the film's dominant impression.

10.53 *The Godfather: Part II* (1974). Michael Corleone balances a life of organized crime and power with familial dedication and loyalty.

In crime films, deviance becomes a barometer of the state of society. If the outsider characters in horror films represent what we most physically and psychologically fear and repress, then the outsider characters in crime films describe what we socially reject as upholders of the status quo. As with horror films, the illegitimate groups and illegal behaviors of crime movies fascinate us as much as the savvy and determination of the detectives and other guardians of the law who track them. Perhaps the foundation for this fascination is that most people are capable of both social and antisocial inclinations at one time or another. Two of the most gripping and socially complex crime movies in film history, *The Godfather* (1972) and *The Godfather: Part II* (1974) offer a picture of twentieth-century America that culminates in the transformation of Michael Corleone from a respectable son and war hero into a ruthless mob boss willing and able to destroy any enemies or competitors [Figure 10.53]. The films reveal both sides of the Mafia cult: its familial dedication and loyalty, and its vicious thirst for power at any cost. Echoing this duality, these films suggest that U.S. society has grown from a struggling immigrant community into a rich and intimidating nation.

Gangster and Hard-Boiled Detective Films, and Film Noir. The different incarnations of crime films, from the 1920s to the present, include three prominent and popular subgenres: the gangster film, the hard-boiled detective film, and film noir. **Gangster films** are typically (but not necessarily) set in the 1930s, when underworld criminal societies thrived in defiance of Prohibition. In these films, criminal activity characterizes a social world continually threatened by the most brutal instincts of its outcasts. *Scarface* (1932) [Figure10.54] depicts a vicious mob war in which rivals coolly manipulate and shoot each other, while *The Public Enemy* (1931) follows Tom Powers's rise from a juvenile delinquent to a bootlegging killer who terrorizes Chicago. More recent versions of gangster films—the 1983 *Scarface*, *Goodfellas* (1990), and *Reservoir Dogs* (1992), for example—tend to escalate the violence and explore the peculiar personalities of the criminals or the strained rituals that define them as a subculture. The urban milieu of hip hop and so-called "gangsta" rap characterizes a cycle of African American crime films of the early 1990s, including *Boyz N the Hood* (1991), *New Jack City* (1991), and *Juice* (1992), in which the codes of loyalty and family are strained by the lure of fame, drugs, and cash. Japanese actor-director Takeshi Kitano has received wide acclaim for his reworking of the traditional Japanese gangster, or *yakuza*, film in *Hana-bi* (1997) and other films, while two Hong Kong films, the 2006 *Exiled* and the 2003 *Infernal Affairs* (remade in 2006 as Martin Scorsese's *The Departed*) demonstrate both the global reach of this genre and its ability to return from abroad to reshape Hollywood films [Figure 10.55].

10.54 *Scarface* (1932). A classic gangster film from the genre's heyday in the 1930s.

Moving their narrative perspectives more toward the side of the law, hard-boiled detective films focus on a protagonist who represents the law or a more ambiguous version of it, such as a private investigator. Usually these individuals must battle a criminal element (and sometimes the police) to solve a mystery or resolve a crime. In one of the most renowned films of this type, *The Maltese Falcon* (1941), detective Sam Spade pursues both a mysterious treasure (the falcon statue) and the murderers of his partner (killed for the statue). Suspected by the police, Spade embarks on a personal quest not so much for the treasure but, through his loyalty to his partner, for truth and integrity. Reinterpreted and reinvented in different cultures and with protagonists other than white males, this subgenre remains visible in such unusual movies as Jean-Luc Godard's meditation on crime detection, *Détective* (1985), and Lizzie Borden's feminist story of a sex crimes investigation in Georgia, *Love Crimes* (1992).

Although regularly discussed as a film style of shades and shadows, **film noir** can be considered a subgenre of crime films that emerged in the 1940s and distinctly elevates the legal, moral, and atmospheric ambiguity and confusion found in earlier examples of the genre. No longer simply about law versus crime or the ethical toughness of a detective, these films uncover darkness and corruption in virtually all their characters and never seem fully resolved. Orson Welles's *Touch of Evil* (1958) is one of the most powerful examples of film noir (see Film in Focus, pp. 474–476). Arriving in a Mexican town wild with drugs, prostitution, and murders, lawman Mike Vargas searches the dark alleys and filthy canals in pursuit of a murder mystery; he discovers that the heart of the corruption is Hank Quinlan, "a good detective but a lousy cop" [Figure 10.56]. In David Lynch's contemporary vision of a film noir world, *Blue Velvet* (1986), the naive Jeffrey Beaumont takes on the role of detective to solve the mystery of a decaying ear found in a field. Soon he finds himself a participant in the kinky sexual world of Dorothy Vallens [Figure 10.57]. His girlfriend, Sandy, wonders whether he is "a detective or a pervert." After his nightmarish wanderings through an underworld that he keeps returning to, Jeffrey can do no better than repeat that "it's a strange world, isn't it?"

text continued on page 359 ▶

10.55 *Exiled* (2006). Hong Kong gangster films such as this one are influencing recent Hollywood genre films.

10.56 *Touch of Evil* (1958). Orson Welles as Hank Quinlan, rotten with corruption in this classic example of film noir.

▶ VIEWING CUE

Identify the generic paradigm of the film you watch next in class. Which characteristics of this genre are most apparent?

10.57 *Blue Velvet* (1986). David Lynch makes the perversion at the heart of classic film noir explicit and surreal.

Generic *Chinatown* (1974)

Set in the 1930s Los Angeles of crime writers Dashiell Hammett and Raymond Chandler, Roman Polanski's *Chinatown* is a crime film that features elements of the gangster film, film noir, and especially the hard-boiled detective film. It opens in the offices of private investigator J. J. (Jake) Gittes, a location and a character that immediately recall such classics of the genre as *The Maltese Falcon* and *The Big Sleep* (1946). The room is scattered with light and shade from partially closed venetian blinds, and the tough but cool Gittes, wearing a white suit, controls the scene in every way [Figure 10.58], as he presents pictures of an unfaithful wife to the distraught husband who has hired him. A former police officer who worked the Chinatown district of Los Angeles, Gittes now operates between the legitimate law and the underworld, seeking out the seedy, dark side of human nature and exposing "other people's dirty laundry."

Familiar conventions and formulas are everywhere in this modern version of the crime-film plot; some of these conventions, including the exotic and mysterious connotations of the title, are clearly clichés (this one bordering on racism). Bitter, smart, and attractive, Gittes, played by Jack Nicholson, takes what he believes is an everyday assignment to follow a husband, Los Angeles Water Commissioner Hollis Mulwray, who is suspected of having a sexual affair. Gittes becomes entangled, however, in events that are more complicated and devious than he can quite understand, events that "half the city is trying to cover up." The woman who hired him to spy on Mulwray turns out not to be his real wife, and the real Evelyn Mulwray becomes the foil that both attracts Gittes and makes it clear that, in this case, he is no longer in control. Like other crime-film detectives who survive with their independent moral vision, Gittes gradually and painfully uncovers the twisted and complicated truth that underlies this plot: that Noah Cross, Mulwray's former partner and Evelyn's father, has killed Mulwray as part of a vast scheme to exploit the water shortage in Los Angeles. Indeed, it slowly becomes clear that the cryptic title of the movie refers to a section of urban life—and by extension, to all of life in this film—where conventional law and order have little meaning, where, in Gittes's words, "you can't always tell what's going on." As Cross tells him, "You may think you know what you're dealing with, but you don't." Shades and shadows, specialties of classic film noir, line the faces and spaces in this unclear world, and the addition of rich yellows, reds, and browns to the Los Angeles urbanscape creates a sickly, rather than sunny and natural, climate.

As in other crime films, the shadowy haze of corruption and violence appears also as a sexual darkness. Whereas in older crime films, sexuality regularly takes the form of a femme fatale whose aggressive sexuality threatens the men in the film, the sexual danger and disorder in *Chinatown* is far more horrifying. Here the femme fatale is Evelyn, who seduces the hard-boiled detective, Gittes, but the power of her sexuality poses little threat compared to the reality that he discovers behind it: that

10.58 *Chinatown* (1974). Jack Nicholson as Jake Gittes, the hard-boiled detective.

she has been raped by her own father, Cross, and that her daughter, the mysterious "other woman" involved with Hollis Mulwray, is also her sister. All these facts are climactically revealed in the dark streets of Chinatown when Evelyn is killed trying to flee with her daughter/sister [Figure 10.59]. True to the unsettling resolutions of this genre, the powerful and malevolent Cross walks away with his illegitimate daughter, the police stand idly by, and Gittes's only consolation is that "this is Chinatown." Although the resolutions of other crime films offer tentative and sometimes personal solutions to crime

10.59 *Chinatown* (1974). The dark streets of Los Angeles's Chinatown are the setting for this neo-noir.

and corruption, here the ambiguity is considerably darker and seamier.

Like the ending to *Chinatown,* many of the variations in these crime-film formulas may be the product of changing times. Although this mysterious world of crime and corruption seemed an appropriate generic barometer for 1930s America, in the 1970s its connection to social and historical contexts was less apparent. With the Great Depression, Prohibition, and urban crowding and unrest, the crime film of the 1930s acted out social instabilities through the marginal success of a marginal detective, like Sam Spade and others. In the 1970s, after the government corruption of Watergate, the moral ambiguities of the Vietnam War, and the confused sexual legacy of the 1960s, the genre returned with a new relevancy. In *Chinatown,* hard-boiled detectives are less confident than before, femmes fatales are more neurotic, and corruption is more sickly and widespread.

The Significance of Film Genre

Since the beginning of the twentieth century when chase films were an international fashion, the economics of the film industry were tied to the standardized formulas of film genre. Fashioned in accordance with the assembly-line productions of other industrialized businesses, these formulas, while meant to increase efficiency, also became the foundation for movie studios as they emerged through the 1920s. These studios would come to define themselves through the predictable scripts, sets, and actors of one or more genres. Gradually audiences learned what to expect from these genres and their associated studios. Although film genres have changed and spread considerably since the 1930s, they remain a critical measure of audience expectations as well as of the film's ability to satisfy or disappoint, and surprise or bore, the movie viewer.

Prescriptive and Descriptive Approaches

Broadly defined, genre represents a system of classification. Along with literary and visual arts, science organizes plants and animals according to generic groupings; similarly, human society characterizes individuals or activities as part of a class ("upper-middle-class"), gender ("a typically male response"), or region ("a Tuscan pasta specialty"). Similarly, film genres classify viewers' experience and understanding of a movie (as well as some directors' approaches to making a genre film). Specifically, a generic perspective on the movies may be prescriptive or descriptive. *Prescriptive approaches* assume that a model for a genre preexists any particular films in that genre; a successful genre film deviates as little as possible from that model; or a viewer can and should be objective in determining a genre.

Approaching a genre film prescriptively, a viewer might stand back from or outside of the many specific musicals that have been made and formulate, inductively and objectively, the main characteristics, rules, and conventions of that genre to determine "what this genre should be." With this model in mind, he or she can then evaluate any specific musical film in terms of whether it achieves or does not achieve that ideal. In this sense, Kenneth Branagh's *Love's Labour's Lost* (2000) may be seen as a terrific accomplishment, whereas *That's Entertainment* (1974) may be seen as a confused aberration of the prescribed terms of a musical.

With a *descriptive approach*, viewers prize genres for different reasons. From this perspective, a genre develops and changes over time; a successful genre film builds on older films and develops in new ways; or a viewer can and should acknowledge that his or her subjectivity helps determine a genre.

A filmgoer, looking at film descriptively, surveys the history of a particular genre—say, melodrama—and deduces how its chief characteristics have altered through history. Admitting that such an exercise will necessarily depend on a person's particular perspective (such as which films he or she has access to and the assumption that a particular genre exists), this viewer will value specific films for how they develop, change, and innovate within a generic pattern. From this perspective, a film like *Ali: Fear Eats the Soul* (1974), about the social prejudices that hound the relationship between a young Arab migrant worker and an older German woman, may be a remarkable variation on the melodramatic formula, which in the different cultural context of the 1950s produced Douglas Sirk's *All That Heaven Allows* (1955), a version of the story in which a gardener and a wealthy socialite fall in love. With Fassbinder's "remake" in mind, Todd Haynes's *Far from Heaven* (2002) then reshapes and develops that same basic story and generic formula into a contemporary film in which the melodramatic crisis turns on a married man's discovery of his gay identity and his wife's potential interracial affair with their gardener [**Figures 10.60a–10.60c**].

Both prescriptive and descriptive approaches can point viewers to particular readings of films. A studio, journalist, or filmmaker may, for instance, prescribe a particular genre as the framework for how a specific movie should be seen and evaluated. A studio may promote *In the Bedroom* (2001), a film about domestic violence and revenge, as a melodrama, whereas a journalist may urge audiences to see it as a murder mystery. Following one or the other of those prescribed genres will most likely result in different understandings of the film. Conversely, a movie historian may examine a number of similar films in order to describe the basic laws of a genre (say, science fiction), but if the body of films that generate his or her description is limited to Hollywood movies since 1950, that generic model will emphasize and overlook generic features that a wider survey (one including silent or Asian films, for example) might not. In both instances, the resulting model of a film genre reflects the perspective prescribing or describing the genre and generates meanings that limit or focus a viewer's understanding accordingly.

Classical and Revisionist Genres

The significance of particular movies' engagement with genre conventions and histories is shaped by their situation within classical or revisionist traditions. *Classical genre traditions* are aligned with prescriptive approaches that place a film in relation to a structural paradigm that transcends historical variations, a paradigm

(a)

(c)

(b)

10.60   **(a)** *All That Heaven Allows* (1955), **(b)** *Ali: Fear Eats the Soul* (1974), **(c)** *Far from Heaven* (2002). Melodrama's generic characteristics are both foregrounded and modified in loose remakes of Douglas Sirk's original by filmmakers Rainer Werner Fassbinder and Todd Haynes.

that a genre film either successfully follows or not. Classical generic traditions establish relatively fixed sets of formulas and conventions, associated with certain films or with a specific place in history. Proceeding from descriptive approaches, *revisionist genre traditions* see a film as a function of changing historical and cultural contexts that modify the conventions and formulas of that genre. A particular western, for example, will be understood differently from a classical perspective than from a revisionist one. Together these two traditions identify one of the central paradoxes of any genre: genres can appear to be at once timeless and time bound, to create patterns that transcend history and to be extremely sensitive measures of history.

Classical genres can be viewed as both historical and structural paradigms. A *historical paradigm* presumes that a genre evolved to a point of perfection at some point in history and that one or more films at that point describe the generic ideal. For some viewers and critics, John Ford's *Stagecoach* is the historical paradigm for the western that reached its pinnacle in the United States in 1939; for others, F. W. Murnau's *Nosferatu the Vampire* (1922) is the historical paradigm for the horror film, achieving its essential qualities in the climate of 1920s Germany **[Figure 10.61]**. A *structural paradigm* relies less on historical precedent than on a formal or structural ideal that may or may not be actually seen, in a complete or pure form, in any specific film. For example, regardless of the many variations on science fiction films, a viewer familiar with the genre

▶ **VIEWING CUE**

Place the next film you will watch in class in a generic tradition and discuss whether, how, and why it exemplifies classical or revisionist characteristics.

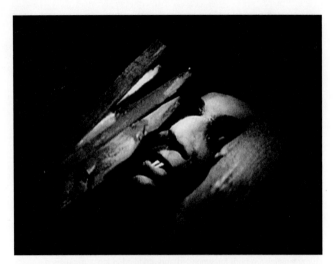

10.61 **Nosferatu the Vampire** (1922). A historical paradigm for horror films.

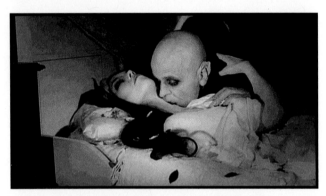

10.62 **Nosferatu the Vampyre** (1979). Generic reflexivity: re-creating and manipulating the paradigm.

may develop a structural paradigm for the classic science fiction film. After viewing a wide spectrum of films—from *The Day the Earth Stood Still* (1951) to *The Man Who Fell to Earth* (1976)—a viewer may understand that the paradigm for the genre requires a visual and dramatic conflict between earth and outer space, the centrality of special effects, and a deadline plot structure. Some films will then fit this paradigm easily, whereas others, such as the frolicking *Repo Man* (1984) (about teenage angst, the repossessing of cars, and a mad scientist), may seem less convincing participants in the genre.

With an alternative perspective on the same films, generic revisionism assumes that a genre is a product of historical and cultural flux, continually changing as part of a dialogue with films of the same genre. Seen as part of a *generic displacement*, films within a genre change to reflect different cultural and historical communities. From this perspective, Fred Schepisi's *Barbarosa* (1982) is as much a western as *Stagecoach*, but it is adapted to a contemporary climate that sees outlaws and their myths in a more fantastic light. More modern films may demonstrate *generic reflexivity*, that is, they are unusually self-conscious about their generic identity and clearly and visibly comment on the generic paradigms. *Young Frankenstein* (1974) and *L.A. Confidential* (1997) surely fit this model, the first a goofy look at one of the most famous models for a horror film and the second a serious self-conscious reworking of the crime film. Less obviously perhaps, Werner Herzog's *Nosferatu the Vampyre* (1979) does not simply re-create the original *Nosferatu*, but also returns to many of its conventions and icons as a way of commenting on the continuing relevancy of the vampire myth and how it still reveals much about contemporary society [**Figure 10.62**].

Local and Global Genres

Although major Hollywood genres may be the most recognizable, we also notice generic patterns in films connected to more specific times, places, events, and cultures—what we might call "local" genres. Modern American "teen films" such as *The Breakfast Club* (1985), *Heathers* (1989), *Clueless* (1995), *She's All That* (1999), and *Bring It On* (2000) [**Figure 10.63**] can be considered examples of a genre that relates in very particular ways to the characters, crises, and rituals of contemporary American youth.

In a sense, all genres are local because they first take shape to reflect the interests and traditions of a particular community or nation. Westerns are essentially an American genre, although they have traveled successfully to Australia, Italy, Spain, and many other countries. Although horror is now a global genre, horror films may have their roots in the expressionistic cinema of Germany around 1920.

Of the many local genres that have appeared around the world, two clearly stress the connection between genre and a particular culture: the Japanese *jidaigeki* films and the Austrian and German *heimat* films. Popular since the 1920s,

10.63 *Bring It On* (2000). This cheerleading film is part of the cycle of teen films prevalent since the 1980s.

10.64 *Ran* (1985). The classical Shakespearean story of King Lear retold in this essentially Japanese genre film.

the Japanese *jidai-geki* **films** are period films or costume dramas set before 1868, when feudal Japan entered the modern Meiji period. Movies such as *Revere the Emperor* (1927) and *A Diary of Chuji's Travels* (1927) work as historical travelogues to resurrect the customs and glory of times long past. Like most nations in relation to their preindustrial past, the Japanese view this period with curiosity, nostalgia, and pride, often seeing in these early films a kind of cultural purity that was lost in the twentieth century. Through the years, however, this genre, like all successful genres, has assimilated current affairs into its conventions and formulas: besides feudal courts and sword battles, *jidai-geki* films develop plots about class unrest and social rebellion. Akira Kurosawa's *Ran* (1985) is an interesting engagement with this essentially Japanese genre: a feudal Japanese costume drama replete with many of the *jidai-geki* conventions, it is a film adapted from Shakespeare's *King Lear* that, ultimately, describes the end of an ancient world [**Figure 10.64**].

Set in idyllic countryside locales, Austrian and German *heimat* **films** depict a world of traditional folk values in which love and family triumph over virtually any social evil, and communities gather around maypoles and sing traditional German folk songs. Hailed by Austrian and German audiences throughout the first half of the twentieth century, this genre thrived in both countries with films ranging from *The Priest from Kirchfeld* (1914) and *Heimat* (1938) to *The Trapp Family* (1956). As German filmmakers became more self-conscious about their historical background and the connection between this political history and the movies, modern films resurrected the *heimat* genre, now reinterpreted as complicit in the social history of Germany. Peter Fleischmann's *Hunting Scenes from Bavaria* (1969), Volker Schlöndorff's *The Sudden Wealth of the Poor People of Kombach* (1971), Edgar Reitz's sixteen-hour *Heimat* (1984) [**Figure 10.65**], and Stefan Ruzowitzky's *The Inheritors* (1998) are all explicit attacks on the mythology of this genre or reexaminations of its social meaning and power.

text continued on page 366 ▶

> **VIEWING CUE**
>
> Consider whether and how the cultural or historical context seems to shade and shape the generic formulas used in this film.

10.65 *Heimat* (1984). The traditional values of German home life are subjected to the conditions of postwar occupation.

The Significance of Genre History in
Vagabond (1985)

In *Easy Rider* (1969), two disaffected bikers go search-ing for "the real America" and ride, directionless, into violence, drugs, rock and roll, and eventually death. For some, this movie represents the historical center of the **road movie** genre. A prescriptive definition of the road movie would doubtless place automobiles or mo-torcycles at the center of a narrative about wandering or driven men who are or eventually will become bud-dies. Structurally, the narrative develops along a linear path, as a quest that episodically unfolds and is punc-tuated by traveling shots of open roads and land-scapes representing the stylistic heart of the genre. A descriptive definition would place at the center of this classically linear and episodic narrative an aimless odyssey toward freedom or an otherwise undefined place. If this structural paradigm can be found in *Easy Rider*, the genre has evolved and reappeared in numerous guises over the years.

The road movie genre has its origins in the 1930s, where the central motif of road travel occurs in such precursors as *Wild Boys of the Road* (1933), *You Only Live Once* (1937), and *The Grapes of Wrath* (1940), films that make traveling on the road the underpinning of the story. By the 1940s and 1950s, the more serious and existential dimensions of the road movie surface in *They Drive by Night* (1940), *De-tour* (1945), and *The Wages of Fear* (1953), in which a lone male or male ca-maraderie (frequently inflected with anger and violence) moves to the center of the genre [Figure 10.66]. This new dimension is summed up in the celebrated motorcycle movie *The Wild One* (1953), in which, iron-

ically, a road is rarely traveled. During the 1950s in the United States, the social turbulence associated with the road movie began to spread (especially to adoles-cents who sought for ways to express their angst against their families). That the automobile became the country's social and industrial backbone only added to the pertinence of the central convention of this genre.

The 1960s and 1970s featured both classical road movies like Monte Hellman's *Two-Lane Blacktop* (1971) and, more often, revisionist versions such as *Weekend* (1967), *Duel* (1972), *Paper Moon* (1973), *Badlands* (1973), *Road Movie* (1974), and *The Car* (1977). If *Two-Lane Blacktop* is a straightforward account of two

10.66 *The Wages of Fear* (1953). Clouzot's classic road movie centers on the tensions within and between men.

364

10.67 *Vagabond* (1985). Unconventional in form and content, this movie opens up the road movie genre.

young men racing across America to a romantically apocalyptic end, the latter movies revised those central themes and icons to reflect the changing times and styles: irony and pathos now permeate the adventure, and junk and garbage strew the highways. In the 1980s and 1990s, both displaced and reflexive versions of road movies appeared: *Mad Max* (1979), *Mad Max 2: The Road Warrior* (1981), *Paris, Texas* (1984), and *Thelma & Louise* (1991). In *The Living End* (1992), which resurrects the genre with searing relevancy, the two HIV-positive road buddies have more on their minds than the direction of the road. More recently, the witty and self-conscious *O Brother, Where Art Thou?* (2000) returns the genre to its historical roots, reappropriating its title and certain scenes from the 1941 comic road movie *Sullivan's Travels* as it remakes Homer's *Odyssey* into the frolicking road adventure of three escaped convicts.

As part of this historical development, French filmmaker Agnès Varda's feminist film, *Vagabond* (1985), is one of the most radical contemporary revisions of the road movie. At first glance, this film about a hitchhiking vagrant only partly resembles a road movie, lacking that prominent icon of a car, motorcycle, or other motorized vehicle. Moreover, rather than moving forward down the road, this film moves backward, beginning with the corpse of the female protagonist, Mona, in a roadside ditch. In order to explain how her body ended up there, the narrative presents

a series of flashbacks, tracing her wanderings as she hitchhikes through the French countryside [**Figure 10.67**]. It recounts forty-seven different episodes, eighteen of which describe individual meetings with Mona on the road. A migrant worker, a tree specialist named Landier and her assistant Jean-Pierre, a maidservant named Yolande, and her temporary boyfriend David are some of the different people who befriend Mona and try to stop her wanderings or just understand her. Throughout, Mona remains an enigma, often refusing help and companionship, explaining herself only with quips like "being alone is good" and "I move."

An undefined search for identity propels the protagonists of most road movies and usually leads to some version of self-knowledge. *Vagabond,* however, changes the terms of that search. Instead of following the protagonist's point of view as she searches the horizon or the rear-view mirror for some insight into her present and past self, the film assumes the points of view of the eighteen people along the road, hoping their roadside perspectives will provide the key to this road warrior. Again and again, Mona's movement confuses and angers them: she is physically repulsive to some, verbally unresponsive to most, and consistently impenetrable to all [**Figure 10.68**]. Her movement becomes a refusal to have an identity or a claim to a self, knowable either to herself or to others.

The key to the generic detours in this road movie is clearly that a woman has now taken the road traditionally

10.68 *Vagabond* (1985). A female road warrior.

claimed by men. Road movies commonly focus on male anxiety and desire; *Vagabond,* like the later American film *Thelma & Louise* (1991), alters that central feature and, with this change, maps a new road and explores different questions about identity. Men may attack Mona or be put off by her, but on this road they will not contain or control her. As in the classic road movie, the narrative and the film image continually move and progress in *Vagabond.* Here, however, progression and movement are the means of staying alive to the potential inherent in one's self, rather than a way to search for some uncertain goal at the end of the road. Like many other road movies, the end of the road here is death, but for this woman that ending reveals nothing about the journey.

CONCEPTS AT WORK

The six genres examined in the central section of this chapter are broad, but hardly all-encompassing. Depending on the level of specificity, one could expand this list of genres by a few entries, or by hundreds—as the mention of several among myriad local genres attests. Hybrid genres and subgenres extend the possibilities to the limits of generic frameworks, while many modern films try to bend the definition of one genre or another, or to defy definition altogether. Genres can blend into one another easily, as they should. Although classifying films by genre may seem like a way of restricting the entry of new ideas into the art form, forcing filmmakers to return to the same ideas time and again, nothing could be further from the truth. Identifying films by their genre simply helps to place them in their historical context by connecting them not just to other films, but to plays, books, and works of art that have come before. If a film is a dialogue between filmmaker and audience, then genre is an unspoken agreement on the language, one that is often made from a film's opening frames.

Activities

- As an example of the communicative power of genre conventions, examine a film trailer or teaser, preferably for a film you have not seen, and try to identify the film's genre as quickly as possible based on conventions and contextual clues. What visual and aural aspects indicate the film's genre? Trailers often attempt to establish a film as one genre to trick audiences into setting up particular expectations before suddenly introducing a generic shift. Does your initial assessment change by the end of the trailer/teaser?

- Choose a scene from a film that exemplifies that film's genre. For a horror film, this might be the moment when the killer finally steps out of the shadows. For a melodrama, this could be a scene of the heroine being physically or emotionally abused. Try to determine what subtle changes would need to occur to change this scene to one that would exemplify a different genre. Consider diegetic and nondiegetic sound, lighting, and mise-en-scène as you proceed.

THE NEXT LEVEL: ADDITIONAL SOURCES

Altman, Rick. *Film/Genre*. London: BFI, 1999. A balanced survey of genre theories since Aristotle, this study addresses the importance of film genres both for the industry and for movie audiences, examining the historical variations of genres and their relationship to social life.

Browne, Nick, ed. *Refiguring American Film Genres*. Berkeley: University of California Press, 1999. This collection features articles by many top scholars on film genre today and gathers pieces on particular films and genres (including the war film and the jury film) that develop new theoretical stands on film genre.

Clover, Carol. *Men, Women, and Chain-Saws: Gender in the Modern Horror Film*. Princeton: Princeton University Press, 1992. Clover's bold study of the slasher film argues that the "Final Girl" who survives the carnage is a figure of cross-gender identification for male fans.

Gledhill, Christine, ed. *Home Is Where the Heart Is: Studies in Melodrama and the Woman's Film*. London: BFI, 1987. This collection contains essays on silent melodrama, women's films of the 1930s and 1940s, and the family melodramas of the 1950s by some of the field's finest feminist theorists.

Grant, Barry, ed. *Film Genre Reader II*. Austin: University of Texas Press, 1995. An indispensable anthology of essays on film genre, this volume covers a range of theoretical issues and analyzes numerous film genres. Contributors represent a range of traditional and contemporary critical methods.

Kitses, Jim. *Horizons West: Directing the Western from John Ford to Clint Eastwood*. London: BFI, 2004. This new edition of a classic genre study first published in 1969 establishes the western at the center of American film genres and elegantly combines auteurist and genre criticism.

Neale, Steve. *Genre*. London: BFI, 1980. Neale's brief but intellectually provocative account of film genres emphasizes the institutional and textual contract between the movie industry and the audiences that genre films crystallize and require in order to create systems of meaning.

Shatz, Thomas. *Hollywood Genres: Formulas, Filmmaking, and the Studio System*. New York: Random House, 1981. A lucid and carefully organized introduction to how film genre operates as an organizing principle for movies, this work gives special attention to westerns, gangster and hard-boiled detective films, screwball comedies, musicals, and family melodramas.

PART 4
HISTORIES
Hollywood and the world

There is no single way to view the history of cinema. Like other histories, movie history takes many shapes and can include a variety of materials and information. In discussing film history we aim not only to present key information (such as important dates, names, and events), but also to indicate how our sense of history becomes richer and more insightful through an awareness of film **historiography**, the study of the methods and principles through which the past becomes organized according to certain perspectives and priorities.

In Chapters 11 and 12, we look at a selection of historical models used to understand the movies. One group, based in conventional models of history, is directed at Hollywood films, although any culture's films could be organized with these models. The other, based in inclusive historical approaches, extends the reach of film history beyond Hollywood to the rest of the world. Each of these models has its advantages and disadvantages; a sophisticated movie history is likely to combine several models. Determining a "correct" history of the cinema may be less important than recognizing the assumptions about film history that help shape our understanding and enjoyment of individual movies and film movements.

CHAPTER 11

Conventional Film History: Evolutions, Masterpieces, and Periodization

- Film history as evolution
- Film history as masters and masterpieces
- Film history as different styles and periods

CHAPTER 12

Global and Local: Inclusive Histories of the Movies

- History as global
- History as the recovery of film practices
- History as an examination of overlooked contexts

Conventional Film History

Evolutions, Masterpieces, and Periodization

The sinking of the luxury passenger liner *Titanic* on its maiden voyage in 1912 was covered extensively in the news media of the day, and film audiences learned details of the disaster from both newsreels and fiction films. Nearly a century after the ship's sinking, James Cameron directed the epic production *Titanic* (1997), and it became the highest grossing film of all time—a global box-office smash. Such enduring fascination with real events—footage of the ship's wreckage is included in Cameron's film—partly explains the appeal of historical films, but it was the technological sophistication, spectacle, and scale of *Titanic*, which echo elements of the state-of-the-art steamship itself, that really made history. How films represent history in a popular medium, as well as popular ways of recounting the history of film—its technical achievements, critical recognition, and epochal transformations—are the subject of this chapter.

I f our sense of film history shapes our experience of the movies, what are the best-known and most influential historical models for approaching and making sense of a film? With a focus on Hollywood film history, we will look at dominant histories that have determined why we value certain movies. We will also suggest some of the cultural assumptions that have supported these histories and examine both how these perspectives conceal certain complexities in specific films and the film industry and how they enrich our approach to both.

KEY CONCEPTS

In this chapter, we will emphasize three kinds of traditional or conventional movie history:

- history that describes the development of film as evolutionary growth
- history that focuses on the power of individuals and exceptional works
- history that concentrates on and distinguishes different stylistic periods

Since the first days of moving pictures, movies have attempted to make history— that is, to establish a correct history of the past or at least to document a history about which most of us can agree. At one end of the twentieth century, *The Birth of a Nation* (1915) was reportedly hailed by President Woodrow Wilson as "writing history with lightning." At the other end, *JFK* (1991) would claim to correct the assumed facts of the Kennedy assassination by presenting a new version of that infamous event on film. The first movies, with their remarkable ability to present events and individuals as living images, began immediately to record actual historical happenings or to re-create fictionalized versions of historical moments. Seeing a celebrated boxing match in *The Corbett-Fitzsimmons Fight* (1897) or a scene from the Spanish-American War in *Wreck of the Battleship "Maine"* (1898) astonished audiences with the illusion of witnessing or participating in history itself. Film history became, in one sense, the representation and actualization of true events. Since those early years, the cinema has become one of the most common and pervasive ways people encounter the figures of the past. From the tale of the eighteenth-century Russian monarch Catherine the Great in *The Scarlet Empress* (1934) [**Figure 11.1**] to the story of John Reed and the Greenwich Village leftist movement in *Reds* (1981), the history of the movies has so powerfully and convincingly reconstructed the past that it has become the dominant framework through which many of us see and understand it.

11.1 *The Scarlet Empress* (1934). History in the movies: Marlene Dietrich portrays a very glamorous Catherine the Great.

Just as the movies construct visions of history for us, how we look at film history is the product of certain

formulas and models. Most commonly, film cultures from around the world are described according to what we will call conventional models of movie history. These conventional histories claim traditional and logical formulas for connecting events or persons in a single course through time. Historical changes might thus appear as a function of economic forces or be seen as following the will of powerful individuals who, by their acts, determine the direction of history. Based on judgments of aesthetic value or inherited opinions about who and what is most important, historical perspectives such as these necessarily prioritize and omit people, films, and issues in favor of traditional assumptions or evaluations. The 1941 *Citizen Kane* will appear in virtually every conventional history of the movies; the 1941 *The Face behind the Mask* will probably never be found there.

Of the conventional film histories from around the world, Hollywood history has been the most dominant. Our focus on Hollywood history in this chapter should not be mistaken for a belief that "dominant" means most important. Rather, the Hollywood emphasis here is practical: because of its economic success, widely accepted artistic strategies, and global popularity, Hollywood cinema has provided the most universally recognized and influential framework for conventional histories of the movies. (Not surprisingly, these conventional histories invariably highlight films that perpetuate and perfect the classical Hollywood narrative examined in Chapter 7.) Here we will examine three of the most prominent ways that Hollywood history has been constructed: film history as evolution, film history as masters and masterpieces, and film history as periodization.

Film History as Evolution

The first movies to arrive in 1895 were already part of a historical evolution that developed from science, the arts, and other cultural precedents. They appeared as a revolutionary moment in that history, astonishing the world with two-dimensional images that suddenly could move. Seeking the shock of the new, in 1896, viewers flocked to see demonstrations of the new medium, including the race film *The Derby* [Figure 11.2]. Since then, each generation of films has identified its revolutionary and evolutionary moments. *The Jazz Singer* (1927) stunned audiences with talking images; *The Best Years of Our Lives* (1946) [Figure 11.3] rocked viewers with its hard realism; *The Godfather* (1972) confirmed the arrival of a Hollywood renaissance. This model of film history is one of gradual change, punctuated by dramatic and sweeping paradigm shifts.

11.2 *The Derby* (1896). A horse race depicted by R. W. Paul and Birt Acres stands at the beginning of cinema's evolution.

11.3 *The Best Years of Our Lives* (1946). William Wyler's wartime experience influenced the realism of his film about homecoming soldiers. First-time actor Harold Russell plays Homer, a serviceman fitted with prosthetic hands.

Both scientific and human history have, at least for the last two centuries, been drawn toward evolutionary models of development. Evolution, made famous in the nineteenth century by Charles Darwin, theorizes that all biological species develop from earlier forms by adapting to their environment. In the popular understanding, evolution is seen as a progressive "survival of the fittest." In societies, we often equate it with better lifestyles, more material comforts, and more sophisticated attitudes.

Given the wide impact of evolutionary thought, it is no surprise that one of the most common perspectives on movie history follows this formula. According to evolutionary film history, film culture develops through advancing forces that over time create more efficient, powerful, attractive, or sophisticated films. In this history, Hollywood films moved through the twentieth century by financially and artistically conquering or dominating all other film cultures because Hollywood supposedly has the most highly developed products and practices. This perspective on film history suggests that (1) movies have grown out of the primitive practices of optical toys and jerky film images to mature into the lavish special effects of today; and (2) movies attest to the survival and advancement of the best and most powerful film forms.

We admire early silent films like *A Trip to the Moon* [**Figure 11.4**] as defining the magic of movies. And yet its depiction of a rocket that hits the face of the man in the moon is crude and unsophisticated compared to the many artistic and technological advancements seen in *Star Wars* (1977) or in more recent high-tech movies such as *Cloverfield* (2007), with its headless Statue of Liberty.

Like scientific models of evolution, evolutionary film histories incorporate revolutionary events, punctuating slow progress with sudden disruptions and significant transformations. On the one hand, events or films proceed forward in a logical order that links one to the next, suggesting historical progression. On the other hand, that progress is often signaled by a disruptive or revolutionary change that directs movie advances in a particular way. The progress and disruptions of an evolutionary/revolutionary film history can involve any and all of the dimensions of movies: technological, economic, artistic, and so on. Using such a model, one can argue that movie history progresses through such revolutionary advances as the arrival of sound technology in 1927 and new acting styles in the early 1950s.

In this section, we will follow some of the ways evolutionary models have been used to organize movie history by (1) identifying different cinematic origins and (2) creating specific patterns of progression and conquest. Within these evolutionary origins and patterns, certain movies necessarily appear more valuable or important than others.

Points of Origin

Evolutionary movie histories establish points of origin—that is, movies or events that mark the beginnings of cinema. For these histories, beginnings often determine the essential nature and terms of the milestones that follow. Here we will highlight three kinds of historical origins commonly identified with early cinema: scientific and technological origins, artistic origins, and economic origins.

11.4 *A Trip to the Moon* (1902). Special effects in early cinema.

Scientific and Technological Origins

One influential path for an evolutionary history of the cinema begins with scientific and technological origins. With this kind of emphasis, the evolution of the cinema begins as a search for scientific knowledge (particularly in the field of optics) and proceeds on a path of ever-increasing technological proficiency. As early as 1640, Athanasius Kircher's magic lantern—a mechanical device for directing light and shadows to reproduce images of the world—appears as a precursor of cinematic technology. Over the next two hundred years, a stream of technological toys and scientific instruments demonstrated new ways to generate images. As the industry, science, and technology of the image expanded into the nineteenth century, more central and recognizable technological sources for the cinema emerged from those devices and experiments. In 1839, Louis Jacques Mandé Daguerre developed early forms of photography (almost simultaneously with William Henry Fox Talbot's photographic discoveries in the 1840s). By 1877, Eadweard Muybridge had demonstrated how a series of photographic images could create the illusion of movement. By 1892, Thomas Edison's and W. K. L. Dickson's work in the practical sciences took these experiments further to produce the Kinetoscope. Building on earlier experiments with a projection technology that ran a filmstrip with sprocket holes past the opening of a synchronized shutter, Edison's device allowed a single person to view continuously moving images through a peephole mechanism.

The first films of the brothers Auguste and Louis Lumière represent another major moment in the scientific origin of film. The Lumières rejected the peephole technology of the Kinetoscope to project movies for public viewings. On March 22, 1895, the brothers showed *Workers Leaving the Lumière Factory* to a small group of acquaintances. On December 28 of the same year, they projected a number of other short films for the public, including *Arrival of a Train at a Station*. For many historians, this is the beginning of cinema history proper (although some historians note that the German brothers Emil and Max Skladanowsky had projected movies publicly in Berlin in November of the same year). These and other films by the Lumière brothers documented small, seemingly incidental social and historical realities, sometimes with wit and humor. Although most of the movies that followed were associated more with the entertainment and artistic origins of cinema, these early scientific and documentary impulses are an important lineage throughout the evolution of film.

Artistic Origins

Another common historical narrative traces cinema's artistic origins. According to this perspective, cinematic images are foreshadowed in cave drawings, Egyptian hieroglyphics, and stories found on tapestries. Depicted on the famous Bayeux tapestry, for example, are scenes from the 1066 Norman invasion of England. In these origins, one witnesses the ritualistic, artistic, and entertainment powers that the movies would develop in later years. Through these artistic traditions, society represents itself and its world using beautiful images that honor that world, its myths, and its energy. These images reflect the creativity of individuals and societies and provide the pleasure of seeing human history re-created in pictures and words. Clearly, drama is part of this path, and theater begins to draw closer to the cinema in the nineteenth century when the public starts to seek not only theatrical spectacles but also dioramas and panoramas [**Figure 11.5**]. These exhibits, often presented in buildings especially constructed for this purpose, displayed large, sometimes circular paintings and relied upon special effects

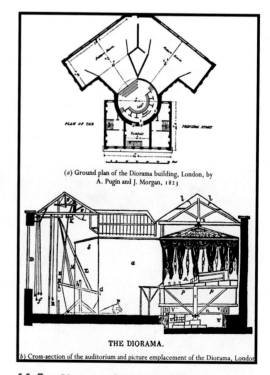

(*a*) Ground plan of the Diorama building, London, by A. Pugin and J. Morgan, 1823

THE DIORAMA.

b) Cross-section of the auditorium and picture emplacement of the Diorama, London

11.5 **Diagrams of the London Diorama.**
Dioramas, which presented elaborate visual spectacles to nineteenth-century visitors, were an important precursor of the cinema.

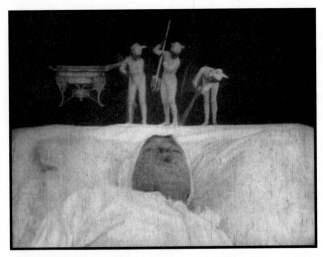

11.6 *The Dream of a Rarebit Fiend* (1906). Edwin S. Porter's special effects aided early cinema's shift toward artistry and imaginative storytelling.

▶ **VIEWING CUE**

Try to place the film you will watch next in class within a chronology of film history. How does it seem connected to particular origins of the movies?

to re-create great events of history, such as the defeat of Napoleon at Waterloo.

Original artistic and entertainment films followed fast on the heels of cinema's technological start in 1895 with short movies depicting theatrical scenes. By the beginning of the twentieth century, such movies as Georges Méliès's *The Impossible Voyage* (1904), the Pathé brothers' production of *Ali Baba and the Forty Thieves* (1907), and Edwin S. Porter's *The Dream of a Rarebit Fiend* (1906) [Figure 11.6], used various special effects and imaginative stories, thus demonstrating the artistic and entertainment possibilities of the cinema. By the time of the 1908 film *The Assassination of the Duke of Guise,* the French *film d'art* movement forcefully announced the unique potential of film as a creative art, absorbing painting, literature, and theater.

Economic Origins

A third starting point in an evolutionary history of cinema is its economic origins. Since the rise of a middle class in the eighteenth century, art, entertainment, and technology have had an important economic dimension. As popular entertainments expanded to address the rising middle class, cultural shows, books, and exhibitions generated more and more profits, which in turn attracted more and more economic investment. Throughout the nineteenth century, institutions such as vaudeville halls and popular literature identified a growing public appetite for amusements, encouraged by the increased leisure time and disposable incomes of the middle and lower classes. In 1893, in keeping with this trend, Edison started marketing his Kinetoscope, selling the machines for about two hundred dollars. Entrepreneurs then charged individuals twenty-five cents for admission to Kinetoscope parlors, where patrons could view short filmstrips of vaudevillian entertainment, historical tableaux, and re-created sporting events. In 1896, Edison began to employ Thomas Armat's and Charles Francis Jenkins's Vitascope [Figure 11.7], a projection system that competed with the Lumière brothers' public projector, the Cinématographe. With largely commercial aims, the Vitascope showed short vaudevillian subjects—like *Butterfly Dance* (1896) and *Skirt Dance* (1898)—in amusement halls to a public whose enthusiasm for new entertainments and curiosities seemed economically boundless.

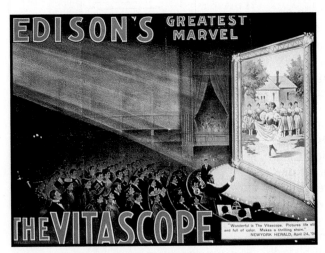

11.7 **Advertisement for the Vitascope.** Although he did not invent this projection system, Edison used his own name to promote it.

Progress and Conquest: More Reality, Money, and Sophistication

Along with points of origin, an evolutionary scheme requires progress through the conquest of old realities by new realities. According to this model of film history, movies get better with time because old problems are solved and former obstacles are overcome. Moving images become, it is assumed, more technologically proficient and entertaining, while the cultural force of movies becomes increasingly powerful. Here we will look at three ways Hollywood history can be mapped as an evolutionary series of improvements or advances: as an advancing realism, through its increasing economic importance as an entertainment industry, and in terms of the growing sophistication of its audiences.

Advancing Realism

A central notion about Hollywood history is that historical progress means an advancing realism, in which the depiction of reality on film becomes more accurate as film technology becomes more advanced. This evolutionary prejudice is something we experience with older films whose stories or portrayals seem antiquated or unrealistic to our contemporary eyes. For example, the representation of sexuality in classical cinema, when married couples were depicted in separate beds, appears unrealistic today. Otto Preminger defied the conventions of the time when he resolved to release *The Moon Is Blue* (1953), a comedy based on a hit play that contained the word "virgin," without the approval of the Production Code Administration. The film's sexual frankness seems mild indeed in relation to such contemporary onscreen depictions of sexuality as those in the espionage thriller *Lust, Caution* (2007) [Figure 11.8]. Like Preminger, this film's director, Ang Lee, refused to make cuts, and his film was denied an R rating. Standards of realism and standards of morality are conflated in both cases.

11.8 *Lust, Caution* (2007). Evolving representations of sexuality challenge evolving conventions of realism.

Once a mechanism had been developed to record real actions, one of the first major steps in the advancing realism of film was the development of more realistic characters and narrative actions to replace stagy scenes presented on artificial sets. The early films *The Lonedale Operator* (1911) [Figure 11.9] and *The Battle at Elderbush Gulch* (1914) employed such editing techniques as crosscutting, which convincingly approximates actions occurring simultaneously in two or more places, and alternating close-ups and long shots to depict the exchange of looks over a span of several minutes. From 1913 through the 1930s, Hollywood grew increasingly fluent with the language of narrative and the visual depiction of character psychology—no doubt, in part, because silent movies had to rely on images without dialogue. This path toward a greater realism has, moreover, continued to progress as movies explore a growing range of characters and stories. The 1895 *Feeding the Baby* provided a familial glimpse of a father (film pioneer Auguste Lumière) feeding his baby daughter, and the 1938 *You Can't Take It with You* follows the zany interaction of a single household. The 1996 *Lone Star* suggests a more elaborate family drama as it investigates the complex interracial bonds that twist and turn across two generations of Mexican American history [Figure 11.10].

11.9 *The Lonedale Operator* (1911). D. W. Griffith is credited with advancing film realism through editing patterns.

Along with the evolution of realistic narratives and characters, a major technical advance in cinematic realism was the arrival of realistic sound. As we discuss in Chapter 6, early silent movies often were accompanied by sound effects or live music; there were also numerous early experiments with sound, such as Edison's Kinetophone system, a combination of the Kinetoscope and the phonograph developed in the early 1890s. In 1926, however, Warner Bros. introduced the Vitaphone system, which synchronized sound on discs with the moving images on film. It was a significant advancement in the integration of the moving image and sound, and after a number of low-key releases, its triumph was announced with the

11.10 *Lone Star* (1996). Cultural complexity is captured in the familial and community relationships explored in John Sayles's film.

11.11 *A Clockwork Orange* (1971). Dolby sound was designed to enrich sonic realism in such films as Stanley Kubrick's violent cult classic.

premiere of *The Jazz Singer* on October 6, 1927. In the 1930s, the fascination with sound resulted in a cycle of musicals, from *The Broadway Melody* (1929) through *Gold Diggers of 1933* (1933) and *Top Hat* (1935), that hung their flimsy plots on musical numbers.

An unintended consequence of this new sound technology was impeded camera movement. Gradually, however, both the quality and mobility of sound recording equipment (from optical recording devices to magnetic to digital) improved, advancing the ways sound could promote realism in the movies. Synchronous sound could enhance visual realism (e.g., the sound of screeching tires as we see a car come to a sudden halt). As sound developed from the 1930s into the 1940s, asynchronous sound could create complex psychological realities (e.g., the sound of screeching violins as two bitter enemies meet in a room). By the mid-1960s, Dolby sound was used in films such as *A Clockwork Orange* (1971) to reduce noise and enrich sound in sophisticated ways [**Figure 11.11**]. In the twenty-first century, in keeping with an evolutionary scheme that insists that louder sound means more realism, films have been exhibited with increasingly sophisticated sound systems. Movies like *I Am Legend* (2007) use sound levels to increase the experience of being immersed in the film world [**Figure 11.12**].

Color processes began to appear in the 1920s. They offered, if not more reality, at least a greater range of visual realities, including those of fantasy worlds. Although hand-tinted color images had been used since early silent films and Technicolor had appeared in some movie sequences in the 1920s (such as DeMille's 1923 *The Ten Commandments*), the continual improvement of Technicolor processes in the 1930s set a new benchmark for cinematic realism. In 1935 *Becky Sharp*, adapted from William Makepeace Thackeray's novel *Vanity Fair*, became the first "three-color" Technicolor feature film. By the end of the decade, movies like *The Wizard of Oz* (1939) and *Gone with the Wind* (1939) fully established color as a powerful part of creating fantastic and historical realism. Although World War II slowed the advancement of color—in 1947 only 12 percent of feature films were in color—by 1954 more than half of the movies made by Hollywood were in color. Today color is so taken for granted that its reduction or elimination can be used to suggest greater realism. *The Man Who Wasn't There* (2001), a tribute to film noir style, challenges the progressive status of color by using a black-and-white format [**Figure 11.13**], and the muted color palette of *There Will Be Blood* (2007) references its setting in the 1910s.

11.12 *I Am Legend* (2007). Sound effects registered at high decibels enhance a sense of immersive realism.

Increasing Economic Importance of Entertainment

Along with the evolution of realism, it is commonly supposed that Hollywood history has evolved as both an entertainment and an economic venture. If the movies originally appeared as a simple amusement or novelty, their entertainment and cultural value increased enormously as they began to assimilate narrative forms. Here again, Georges Méliès is frequently

11.13 *The Man Who Wasn't There* (2001). This black-and-white film by the Coen brothers challenges color's progressive status.

credited with advancing this stage of movie history by developing film's ability to create illusions and present imaginative stories through such techniques as dissolves and stop-motion photography. His early films, like *Twenty Thousand Leagues under the Sea* (1907), construct fantastic or adventure tales taken from literature or current events. These films were immensely popular around the world and stimulated the transition of film from a novel distraction to an entertainment based in narrative forms. After 1905, nickelodeons, the small storefront theaters showing programs of short movies (each about fifteen minutes long), would expand their immigrant and working-class clientele to include middle-class viewers (see pp. 51–57). By 1910, films were drawing a larger audience on the basis of their ability to tell stories, which made movies appear to be a more respectable form of cultural entertainment. With new audiences and commercial possibilities before them, movies would develop their entertainment range by adapting great works of literature and, with movies like D. W. Griffith's *Intolerance* (1916), presenting themselves as a unique narrative form, able to entertain and enlighten on a level equal with other artistic forms. Between 1914 and 1920, movie palaces supplanted nickelodeons, and the movies evolved into an entertainment form at the center of American cultural life.

Special effects—methods of manipulating or adding new dimensions to the film image—have always been a part of the evolution of movies as entertainment (see pp. 120–121). Since the first movies, tricks with sets, cameras, film, and even projection techniques were used to create effects to startle audiences or impress them with new realities. In the first decades of the cinema, disasters at sea could be created in miniature or with matte paintings in the background. In the 1950s, however, special effects and new formats—from widescreen formats like CinemaScope to 3-D images—became increasingly important in distinguishing film from the newly arrived and more modest medium of television. Cinema-Scope, successfully pioneered in 1953 in both *The Robe* and *How to Marry a Millionaire,* used technology to claim greater image size, through more than doubling screen width [**Figure 11.14**]. The 3-D format, common between 1952 and 1954, was used in movies like *It Came from Outer Space* (1953) to present more realistic depth. Spectacular computer-generated imagery has led Hollywood's turn near the end of the twentieth century to a globally successful, effects-driven medium, with films like George Lucas's *The Empire Strikes Back* (1980) re-released in 1997 with more sophisticated effects [**Figure 11.15**]. Thus more and better special effects have served the historical advancement of films, each becoming the newest round in more astonishing big-budget entertainment.

As it developed, filmmaking grew into an increasingly large and complex economic force. The admission price of early movies was about a nickel, reflecting film's low production costs. As movie production began to emulate a factory system—with stars, directors, camera operators, and other workers participating in the rapid assembly of short films—the cost of making movies rose, and admission prices increased proportionately. Beginning around 1910, the star system (see pp. 43–44) marked a major shift in the history of cinema: it exploited the entertainment value of the movies to glamorize individual actors and later, to a lesser degree, directors. Since then, the economics of this system have accounted for enormous increases in the cost of movies:

11.14   *How to Marry a Millionaire* (1953). Widescreen technologies introduced in the 1950s enhanced Hollywood's entertainment value in the face of challenges from television.

11.15   *Star Wars: Episode V—The Empire Strikes Back* (1980). The 1997 special edition of the original Star Wars trilogy enhanced some effects, such as this view of the Wampa on the planet Hoth.

Atlanta's Fox Theatre, one of Fox's showpieces, opened in 1929.

Movietone News was produced weekly from 1929–1963.

Joseph Schenck (left) and Darryl F. Zanuck (right), Fox's studio chief and head of production, respectively.

A 2007 release from Fox Searchlight, a specialty division.

put simply, while star actors and directors require unusually large salaries, they draw large box-office profits that far exceed those salaries. The movies took full advantage of rising costs throughout the twentieth century to inflate the attraction of films. *Ben-Hur,* the costliest film of 1959 and winner of numerous Oscars, is superseded by *Titanic* (1997), whose costs far surpassed those of earlier films. *Titanic*'s Oscar total equals that of *Ben-Hur,* and its huge production costs paid off in its astonishing international box-office gross.

Crucial to the entertainment and economic history of Hollywood is its evolution into and out of the studio system. With the growth of film's power as commercial entertainment, financial competition intensified the stakes of evolutionary survival. In 1908, industry leaders organized a monopoly known as the Motion Picture Patents Company (MPPC) to claim and protect their patents and copyrights on film equipment and technology and to control movie production, distribution, and exhibition. The MPPC also quickly established standard pricing for films and quite effectively reduced foreign competition (before the organization was declared illegal by the Supreme Court in 1915).

From this early attempt to consolidate power, a variety of important studios emerged, many still prominent today. Following the movie industry's gradual move to Hollywood around 1910, Jesse L. Lasky and Adolph Zukor's Famous Players Film Company would unite to create the Lasky Corporation in 1916, eventually evolving into Paramount Pictures by 1935. In 1915, Louis B. Mayer began merging various production companies, establishing MGM (Metro-Goldwyn-Mayer) in 1924. William Fox's 1915 studio would become Twentieth Century Fox in 1935. Restructured from First National Pictures, Warner Bros. would come together in 1923. The smallest of the major studios, RKO (Radio-Keith-Orpheum) was formed in a 1929 merger. Three so-called minor studios also figure largely in the evolution of Hollywood as an economically powerful entertainment machine: Carl Laemmle formed Universal Studios in 1912; Columbia Pictures emerged in 1924; and competing with the studio goliaths was United Artists, formed by D. W. Griffith, Douglas Fairbanks, Mary Pickford, and Charlie Chaplin in 1919.

Identifying themselves with specific genres, stars, and styles that they could efficiently reproduce, these eight studios varied in size and strength, but they had enormous control over the kinds of movies made as well as how and where movies were seen. Thus, Warner Bros. developed a fast, modern style, claimed Bette Davis and Jimmy Cagney as trademark stars, and often produced films addressing social problems, whereas MGM created a rich, sumptuous style and was the home of Elizabeth Taylor, Clark Gable, and musicals. Especially for the major studios, a crucial feature of their power was block booking: in a system of **vertical integration**, the studios owned both the production companies and the theaters, and they could dictate that exhibitors book less desirable films in order to get the ones they wanted to show.

In 1948, the Supreme Court ruled in *United States v. Paramount* that Paramount had violated antitrust laws. As a result, studios were forced to divest themselves of their theater chains, dealing a major blow to the old studio system. As a result of new access to theater screens, independent film production increased dramatically, accounting for disturbing and sometimes challenging films like *Kiss Me Deadly* (1955). In the 1960s, another chapter in Hollywood history begins with the conglomerate takeovers of the traditional studios: Universal Studios was bought by MCA (Music Corporation of America) in 1962, Paramount by Gulf & Western in 1966, United Artists by TransAmerica in 1967, Warner Bros. by Kinney National Services in 1969, and MGM by business mogul Kirk Kerkorian in 1970. The profits from blockbuster movies drew these companies to the movies, and today the profits needed to maintain the interests of the media giants ensure the blockbuster's survival. All these remade entertainment companies pursue investments like the *Star Wars* trilogy, in which the $27 million invested returned well over $500 million by 1980, for a 1,855 percent profit.

Growing Audience Sophistication

A less common way to trace the evolutions and revolutions in classical Hollywood history is through the growing sophistication of audiences. When the word "primitive" is applied to early films and their audiences, it is not meant to be pejorative, but it does signal an evolutionary perspective, one that assumes movie viewers have advanced over the years as movies have grown more aesthetically and economically sophisticated. Presumably, movies historically progress as their audiences' knowledge and film literacy grow, each promoting the other.

11.16   *8 1/2* (1963). The European art cinema of the 1960s dramatically affected moviegoers' sensibilities.

It is frequently assumed that the first American audiences for the movies were predominantly working-class and immigrant viewers. While this is partly an overstatement, neglecting viewers from other classes and backgrounds, it is true that many early audiences were workers who sought out films for relief from tiresome jobs. Moreover, since many immigrants did not know English, silent movies provided an escape from the difficulties of negotiating life in a foreign language.

In 1922, the studios hired Will Hays to head the newly formed Motion Pictures Producers and Distributors of America (MPPDA). Commonly known as the Hays Office, it was intended to monitor the effects of movies on their growing audiences. By the 1930s, the average family attended films three times a week, suggesting the continuing social evolution of movies and their audiences into mainstream culture. Consequently, these audiences were carefully monitored by institutions like the Payne Fund, which studied movies' supposed deleterious effects on children, minorities, and women. The attempt to promote films as wholesome entertainment continued under the Production Code, enforced from 1934 to 1968.

By the late 1950s and 1960s, younger audiences came to the forefront of movie culture: drive-ins and teenage audiences are one example; another is the college and urban audiences of art films and other alternative cinemas that proliferated after 1960. By this time, movies could be considered complex artistic objects. With films like Ingmar Bergman's *The Seventh Seal* (1957) and Federico Fellini's *8 1/2* (1963) [Figure 11.16]—two very different meditations on existential questions—movies seemed to justify aesthetic appreciation and academic study by college students. The movie industry followed these students out of the classroom; in the mid-1980s, VCRs and other domestic viewing possibilities marked the beginning of another revolutionary phase of film literacy, intersecting with changes in the entertainment and technological histories of the movies.

> **VIEWING CUE**
>
> Does the film you just viewed stand out as part of a historical evolution or revolution?

From that period to the most recent developments in digital technologies, new viewing possibilities have allowed movie spectators more control over which movies they watch and how they watch them, thereby increasing the potential for viewer activity in unprecedented ways. Bonus materials included on DVDs address the audience's interest in and knowledge of a range of practices surrounding movie culture, from how movies are made (directors' commentaries) to how they were promoted (original trailers) to other possible histories (outtakes). Increasing access to and familiarity with different kinds of movies have also led to shifts in film language; films from *Shrek* (2001) to *Grindhouse* (2007) [Figure 11.17] make references to genre conventions or earlier types of filmmaking.

text continued on page 383 ▶

11.17   ***Planet Terror*** (2007). Robert Rodriguez's homage to zombie films, released as a double feature with Quentin Tarantino's *Death Proof* as *Grindhouse*, depends on audience familiarity with this film genre.

FILM IN FOCUS

Constructing Origins in *The Birth of a Nation* (1915)

D. W. Griffith's *The Birth of a Nation* exists at the intersection of the histories of cinema's increasing realism, economic impact, and audience reaction. However repugnant the racism of this adaptation of Thomas Dixon's *The Clansman*—the very source raises questions about the film's progressive status—Griffith's film pushed the evolution of cinema to a level that still defines the characteristics of classical narrative. This story of two families divided by the Civil War and the postwar reconstruction of the South has become the emblem for a major revolutionary turn in film history.

From an evolutionary perspective, *The Birth of a Nation* is part of the historical origin of mainstream cinema's technological, artistic, and economic sophistication. Technologically, it required an unprecedented number of sets and locations for its epic scale (and length), with both natural and artificial lighting techniques and special effects [Figure 11.18]. It also employed more than 1,544 separate shots, when even the most advanced films during this era commonly needed less than a hundred shots. Moreover, these technological leaps extended into the realm of sound. For *The Birth of a Nation,* Griffith worked with composer Joseph Carl Breil to create an elaborate musical score that included Wagner, Beethoven, Verdi, and a variety of American folk tunes. The score was performed by a live orchestra.

Building on its technological sophistication, *The Birth of a Nation* also marks an artistic turning point in the evolution of cinema. Setting new standards for longer, more complex narrative films, it serves as the most famous example of a historical origin for the Hollywood feature film. At a time when most feature films were made within a month, Griffith's movie was rehearsed for six weeks and filmed over another nine weeks. The result is considered an artistic landmark in film history for two main reasons. First, the film extended the reach and prestige of American film to encompass an epic subject: the purported birth of the modern United States, sprung from the violence and politics of the Civil War. Second, its narrative structure develops a complex parallel plot that intertwines U.S. history in the 1860s with the family dramas of the Camerons and the Stonemans, presenting a new spectrum of melodramatic emotions (ranging from intimate close-ups of women in distress to the tragic losses of lavish battle scenes) against a vast panorama of celebrated historical events. *The Birth of a Nation* also stands out as a major leap forward in the development of narrative structure and continuity editing. For example, it uses flashbacks to explain actions or a character's thoughts, framing devices such as irises to highlight information or perceptions, and varying shot lengths, angles, and distances to create emotional effects (as in a typical chase sequence) [Figure 11.19].

11.18   *The Birth of a Nation* (1915). A technological revolution in filmmaking craft, exemplified in this reenactment of Lincoln's assassination.

11.19 *The Birth of a Nation* (1915). Crosscutting builds narrative tension during the ride to the rescue.

11.20 *The Birth of a Nation* (1915). Griffith uses close shots and inserts to illustrate psychological states.

Economically, *The Birth of a Nation* signaled the start of movies as big business. Produced for the then-massive sum of $110,000, the film had an unprecedented run of forty-eight weeks, charged a two-dollar admission for the first time in film history, and within five years of its opening, returned more than $15 million, making it one of the top-grossing films of all time.

Although it appeared early in film history, *The Birth of a Nation* already represents an evolutionary advance in realism, entertainment, and audience literacy. Despite its grossly distorted depiction of African Americans (most of whom were portrayed by white actors in blackface), the film overwhelmed many viewers with the accuracy of its battle scenes (some shots were based on the Civil War photography of Mathew Brady), its re-creations of famous historical events (such as the assassination of Abraham Lincoln and the surrender at Appomattox), and the realistic representation of subjective emotions [**Figure 11.20**] (including the insert during a marriage proposal of an image of Margaret Cameron's dead brother to describe her psychological state).

Paralleling these advances in film realism, the status of movie entertainment also altered with *The Birth of a Nation*. After this film, the standard length of movies grew from about twenty minutes to over ninety, while films continued to identify themselves with a literary and artistic heritage that situated them within mainstream culture. For its public premiere, Griffith appropriately rented a Broadway theater, the Liberty, to reflect the newly elevated cultural status of the movies.

The original audiences for *The Birth of a Nation* were large and varied and located in every region of the country; most of them were seeing a visual spectacle of this size and magnitude for the first time. Their reactions to this film, moreover, were vocal and contentious, suggesting an awareness of how such a film impacts audiences and reverberates through society. Condemned by the newly formed National Association for the Advancement of Colored People (NAACP) for its racist portrayal of African Americans, *The Birth of a Nation* announced not only new film forms but also new audiences, ones more responsive to and engaged with the movies than ever before.

Film History as Masters and Masterpieces

A cinematic history of great individuals and their works is a history driven by human desires and ideas. It can be defined as a history of singular expression and achievement. History becomes humanized and dramatic, identified with specific people and the superlative artistic works they create. These acclaimed works then become recognized for their unique artistic value that transcends their historical context, their role as key moments in film history, or both.

11.21 *Citizen Kane* (1941). The film's place at the top of critics' polls indicates its status as a masterpiece as well as director Orson Welles's reputation as a genius.

In this context, Thomas Edison, D. W. Griffith, and Charlie Chaplin become some of the most prominent movers and shakers of early cinema history; Orson Welles and David O. Selznick reshape film culture in the mid-twentieth century; and today the future of the movies appears to be in the hands of such powerful and creative personalities as directors Steven Spielberg and the Weinstein brothers. This perspective assumes that the direction and achievements of film history are the product of individual wills and ideas, from which is generated a history of singular achievements, cinematic masterpieces that stand out from the mass of other movies.

To spotlight the filmmaker Orson Welles implies that his personal perspective altered the course of movie history. To designate *Citizen Kane* as a masterpiece is to claim that it stands above the many more common films made in 1941, or that it highlights the specific issues informing film culture at that time, such as leaps forward in camera technology or the shift to more complex narratives [Figure 11.21].

Despite the popularity and attractiveness of films featuring technological advancements and complex narratives (pp. 463–473), the tendency toward such films does romanticize the historical meaning of movies. Movies are, in fact, the products of many individuals—from technicians and writers, to stars and accountants—working together, so to designate one person as the primary source of a film is always a dubious proposition. Selecting a list of the best films is likewise a debatable and subjective task. The standards that produce those lists can vary considerably from list to list. For example, given Hollywood's mirroring of society as a whole and consequently its opportunities and prejudices, it should not be too surprising that histories of great works include few films by women or people of color.

Conversely, there are advantages to recording history through great individuals and work, especially in the willingness to differentiate and evaluate the achievements that have had the most impact on movie history. In this section, we follow a traditional history of masters and masterpieces, pinpointing films and filmmakers often considered as particularly accomplished or as uniquely important reflections of particular historical issues. While our survey is limited to a select number of commercial feature films that stand out in Hollywood history, remember that there are many masterpieces and masters outside that tradition; it is important to consider why certain films and filmmakers are included, while others are excluded.

Pioneers, Silent Masters, and European Influences: 1900–1920

At the origins of the cinema, pioneers such as Eadweard Muybridge, Thomas Edison, Auguste and Louis Lumière, and Georges Méliès were responsible for propelling the medium forward. Although their creativity and responsibility are sometimes overstated, these prominent individuals are credited with advancing the technology and art of the cinema to the next historical phase. Following them is Edwin S. Porter, noted for his achievements in *The Great Train Robbery* (1903) and many other films. Porter stands out as a transitional figure between the early experimenters with the film image and the makers of later narrative movies, and his film *The Great Train Robbery* represents one of the earliest and most successful developments of narrative form and cinematic language [Figure 11.22]. In this film about a group of outlaws holding up a train, Porter uses more shots and cuts from one scene to another so that the movie both follows and creates the narrative action, rather than simply showing the entire action in one scene and then moving on to the action in another scene.

As we have seen, the first masterpiece of American cinema is generally acknowledged to be *The Birth of a Nation*, and Griffith, often called the father of narrative film, is the most celebrated of the silent masters of Hollywood cinema (see Film in Focus, p. 382). Charlie Chaplin and Buster Keaton expand the group of prominent silent-film directors, with their slapstick vignettes and early narratives defining Hollywood's art in the 1920s. Although Chaplin and Keaton each created distinct styles and stories, both replaced the clownish and chaotic gymnastics of early film comedies (such as Mack Sennett's Keystone comedies) with nuanced and acrobatic gestures that dramatized serious human and social themes. Chaplin's *The Kid* (1921), the first of his many feature-length films, is a tale about his Little Tramp character befriending an impoverished orphan boy. It displays Chaplin's ingenious ability to make his seemingly awkward body a vehicle for poetic improvisation motivated by the human need for companionship [Figure 11.23].

11.22   ***The Great Train Robbery*** (1903). Edwin S. Porter's film represents a leap forward in film narrative.

Keaton's works contrast Chaplin's theatrical style with a more carefully considered use of the film medium. As would *The General* (1927) a few years later, Keaton's *Sherlock, Jr.* (1924) emphasizes his stoically subtle face and acrobatic body movements. This intellectually intriguing story is about a film projectionist whose ghostly image leaves his sleeping body and enters the action of a movie he's showing in the theater [Figure 11.24]. While Keaton uses many traditional comic falls and chases here, he incorporates the film image itself into this play, creating an almost philosophical depth as the character stumbles and wanders between the reality of film and the reality of life.

During the 1910s, a number of women worked as film directors, but few of them would see their careers extend into the 1920s. Lois Weber was particularly well known by audiences of the time; her films about social issues, including *Where Are My Children?* (1916), which advocated birth control and opposed abortion, remain striking. Better remembered are stars like Mary Pickford, who despite her little-girl image onscreen was a successful producer offscreen. She joined with Charlie Chaplin, D. W. Griffith, and her husband Douglas Fairbanks to found United Artists, and she enjoyed a long-term collaborative relationship with screenwriter Frances Marion [Figure 11.25], who wrote many of the films that made Pickford "America's Sweetheart."

Providing a bombastic counterpoint to silent comedies and dramas, Cecil B. DeMille's *The Ten Commandments* (1923) is a lavish spectacle that marks another direction in silent film history [Figure 11.26]. Extremely expensive to produce at that time (costing $1.5 million) and technically advanced (using an early Technicolor process), this film about Moses's biblical journey stands at the crossroads of 1920s film culture, when the excesses of movies began to provoke social concern about their ethics. Perhaps the most interesting balancing act in *The Ten Commandments* is in its portrayal of lurid sex and violence, scenes that are continually reframed by a clear and strong moral perspective.

11.23   ***The Kid*** (1921). Chaplin's feature represents the move from slapstick shorts to comic narrative features.

11.24 *Sherlock, Jr.* (1924). Buster Keaton's comic masterpiece reflects on the filmmaking medium.

11.25 **Mary Pickford and Frances Marion**. The producer and star and the screenwriter enjoyed a dynamic collaboration.

From the 1920s onward, European influences began to appear in Hollywood. The aesthetic visions of an older culture produced two especially important filmmakers in Hollywood history: Ernst Lubitsch and Erich von Stroheim. Lubitsch's adaptation of Oscar Wilde's *Lady Windermere's Fan* (1925) is one of many films displaying "the Lubitsch touch," a phrase indicating an urbane and world-weary visual and narrative style. In this film about upper-class social arrangements and manipulations, the sets and other elements of the mise-en-scène became elaborate, highly charged environments in which small details and gestures—a bedroom door closing or a furtive look—resonate with explicit meaning or symbolic overtones. In a similar vein, von Stroheim's *Foolish Wives* (1922) [Figure 11.27] presents a sordid vision of humanity in a drama about the seduction of wealthy Americans on the French Riviera. In addition, his monumental adaptation of Frank Norris's naturalist novel *McTeague,* retitled *Greed* (1925), is one of the most stunningly ambitious and creative works of silent cinema. Although surviving versions are less than half of its original 315 minutes, *Greed* retains much of its power and brilliance. Set in San Francisco, this epic account of a

11.26 *The Ten Commandments* (1923). Cecil B. DeMille's first version of the biblical story was a silent movie spectacular.

11.27 *Foolish Wives* (1922). Erich von Stroheim's Hollywood films were appreciated for their European sophistication.

dentist, McTeague, and his obsessive wife, Trina, painstakingly re-creates in naturalistic detail the social and psychological forces that lead to the characters' destruction. From the 1920s to today, directors from Europe, Asia, and other world cultures—Otto Preminger, Billy Wilder, Douglas Sirk, Louis Malle, Jane Campion, and Ang Lee, to name a few—have continued to distinguish themselves in Hollywood history.

Studio Classics and Classicists: 1930s

In the 1930s, an exceptional number and variety of studio classics and classicists emerged, making any list of greats reductive. With this group of masterpieces, the term "classical" suggests movies that work efficiently within established formulas while also infusing those formulas with unusual creativity and artistry. Of the many accomplished directors and celebrated films of this decade, three classicists and classics can be culled as representative: Lewis Milestone and *All Quiet on the Western Front* (1930), Frank Capra and *It Happened One Night* (1934), and John Ford and *Stagecoach* (1939).

Never truly within the mainstream of Hollywood, Lewis Milestone in *All Quiet on the Western Front* [Figure 11.28] created perhaps the greatest antiwar film of all time. Among the last of the silent films, this story of the horrors of World War I describes brutal trench warfare through mobile cameras and graphic images that make the drama seem like a documentary of human loss and political blindness in a wasteland of mud and darkness. Following the gaiety of the 1920s, this film is one of a multitude of movies that turned toward trenchant social issues with realism and honesty—for example, such dissimilar classics as William Wellman's *The Public Enemy* (1931), in which gangster violence and despair become a moral indictment of society as a whole, and German emigré Fritz Lang's *Fury* (1936), the dark tale of a lynch mob and a man wrongly accused of murder.

Of the many grand and popular movies made by Frank Capra—including *Mr. Deeds Goes to Town* (1936), *You Can't Take It with You*, *Mr. Smith Goes to Washington* (1939), and *Meet John Doe* (1941)—*It Happened One Night* is one of his first and best. The film tells a rollicking story of a rebellious socialite (Claudette Colbert) who flees her wealthy father and takes up, reluctantly, with a reporter (Clark Gable), who hopes to use her scandalous behavior as a news scoop. Despite their antagonism as they travel the back roads to hide from detectives, they eventually fall in love [Figure 11.29]. Like George Cukor's *The Philadelphia Story* (1940) in

11.28   *All Quiet on the Western Front* (1930). The first great antiwar film.

11.29   *It Happened One Night* (1934). Frank Capra's delightful screwball comedy is one of the quintessential 1930s Hollywood films.

11.30 *Stagecoach* (1939). Many consider this to be John Ford's perfect western.

its verbal and physical wit, *It Happened One Night* gathered much of the energy that was making its way in the 1930s from the New York theatrical stages to the Hollywood screen after the arrival of synchronized dialogue. The film's social allegory about common people correcting the greed and egotism of the rich would continue to define Capra's vision throughout this decade and into the 1940s.

Although John Ford worked successfully from the 1920s into the 1960s, *Stagecoach* is considered his watershed film. Followed soon after by *The Grapes of Wrath* (1940), an example of the ethical consciousness-raising undertaken by films in the 1930s, *Stagecoach,* as mentioned in Chapter 10, represents the structural perfection of the western [Figure 11.30]. The spare, tight narrative describes the plight of a group of stagecoach passengers traveling across a frontier plain who are threatened from without by Native Americans and from within by their social differences; the passengers include a corrupt banker, a prostitute with a heart of gold, and a remnant of the fragile gentry. With grand, sweeping vistas as its background and the Ringo Kid (played by Ford stalwart John Wayne) as its reluctant hero, *Stagecoach* documents the struggle for a national identity across a uniquely American terrain of violent frontiers and dramatic personal conflicts.

Many other movies stand out during these years. Although their artistic distinctions are debated, the 1939 triumvirate of *Gone with the Wind, The Wizard of Oz,* and *Young Mr. Lincoln* would certainly be part of many surveys, representing the astonishing diversity achieved within the rigorous standards of classic Hollywood cinema.

Transitional and Turbulent Visions: 1940s–1950s

In a period of transitional and turbulent visions from 1940 through the 1950s, some of the most celebrated work in film was produced. John Ford's westerns—from *My Darling Clementine* (1946) to *The Searchers* (1956)—continue to be regarded as historical barometers. *My Darling Clementine* re-creates the prototypical western as a meditation on the power of nature and a communal individualism to overcome evil. *The Searchers* is a morally ambivalent tale about where violence resides and how it troubles the motives of an older and darker John Wayne as Ethan Edwards (see pp. 260–263). Other important films of this dynamic Hollywood period include Preston Sturges's *Sullivan's Travels* (1941), William Wyler's *The Best Years of Our Lives* (1946), Elia Kazan's *A Streetcar Named Desire* (1951), and Billy Wilder's *Some Like It Hot* (1959). Spanning this variety, moreover, is the consistently brilliant work of Alfred Hitchcock, stretching from *Shadow of a Doubt* (1943) to the film many scholars and critics consider his greatest masterpiece, *Vertigo* (1958). In this section, we highlight only a few of the most salient masterpieces of these years.

Regularly canonized in film history's hierarchies are Orson Welles and *Citizen Kane,* a film admired in part because it challenges the realism, continuity, and clarity of classical Hollywood cinema. The film offers a parable of the great American individual through the story of Charles Foster Kane, whose idealism turns into egotism and greed, blinding him to the importance of the people around him. The narrative structure and style reflect the fragmentations and divisions of this character through the use of multiple points of view and complex shots that create tensions and contradictions within single images (see Film in Focus, pp. 54–55 and 514–516).

Although not as self-consciously coherent or formally complex, Michael Curtiz's *Mildred Pierce* (1945) and Howard Hawks's *The Big Sleep* (1946) both concentrate on this period's social and personal instability, most notably through questions surrounding female sexuality. As if reflecting their troubled characters and actions in their form, these films exhibit narratives that seem to lose their direction or offer visual styles overwhelmed with gloom. Along with its superb performances—notably Joan Crawford's Oscar-winning portrayal of the title role—and compelling narration, *Mildred Pierce* stands out in its trenchant depiction of a cultural crisis for 1940s women [Figure 11.31] (see Film in Focus, pp. 266–268). Hawks made a number of renowned screwball comedies including *Bringing Up Baby* (1938) and *His Girl Friday* (1940), and one of the charms of *The Big Sleep* is Humphrey Bogart's and Lauren Bacall's banter, a characteristic associated with those films. Bogart's and Bacall's electric characterizations of tough, independent individuals on the edges of right and wrong, along with a twisting story that's all the more powerful for its failure to remain focused, make this detective film one of the renowned classics of film history. [Figure 11.32].

The 1940s and 1950s also feature some of the greatest musicals in Hollywood history: Vincente Minnelli's *Meet Me in St. Louis* (1944, see Film in Focus, pp. 74–75) and Stanley Donen and Gene Kelly's *Singin' in the Rain* (1952). Set at the beginning of the twentieth century, Minnelli's film is a Technicolor musical tale of a happy family put in crisis by the possibility of having to leave their beloved St. Louis. Despite its lively and romantic tunes, the film also features darker elements, such as the melancholic lyrics of "Have Yourself a Merry Little Christmas," that suggest it is more than a nostalgic story. Although Donen and Kelly are usually not included among Hollywood's great directors, *Singin' in the Rain* figures on most lists of Hollywood masterpieces, both for its musical and choreographic ingenuity and the clever twists of a romantic plot set against the backdrop of 1927 and Hollywood's conversion to sound (see Film in Focus, pp. 194–196).

Appearing in the mid-1950s, Nicholas Ray's *Rebel without a Cause* (1955) and Douglas Sirk's *Written on the Wind* (1956) document in very different ways new tragedies at the heart of the American family. Perhaps Ray's most celebrated film, *Rebel without a Cause* gives a then-shocking depiction of a generational crisis in

11.31   *Mildred Pierce* (1945). This memorable look at gender roles in the 1940s is inflected with film noir style.

11.32   *The Big Sleep* (1946). The chemistry of Howard Hawks, Humphrey Bogart, and Lauren Bacall is palpable in this immediate postwar release.

America in which teenagers drift aimlessly beyond parental guidance [**Figure 11.33**]. Directed by German emigré Sirk, *Written on the Wind* presents the collapse of a wealthy family torn apart by violence and sex. Its exaggerated emotions and visual style both elicit and undermine the intense pathos at the heart of a lavish melodrama.

11.33   *Rebel without a Cause* (1955). Teenage angst and juvenile delinquency are on display in Nicholas Ray's CinemaScope classic.

Rebels and Visionaries, Dealers and Deals: 1960s–2000s

In the 1960s through the 1970s, rebels and visionaries move to the fore of our humanist history of powerful and influential filmmakers. Many of these young filmmakers learned their craft in film schools and went on to make movies steeped in the masterpieces and genres that preceded them. They include mostly men: Arthur Penn, Robert Altman, John Cassavetes, Stanley Kubrick, Francis Ford Coppola, Steven Spielberg, and George Lucas (with such women as Julia Phillips and Dede Allen working behind the scenes as producers and editors). From these and other directorial superstars came *The Graduate* (1967), *The Godfather* (1972), *The Godfather: Part II* (1974), *Jaws* (1975), and *Star Wars* (1977)—movies that redefined the masterpiece as an art film, a blockbuster, or both. Stylistically, these directors took chances with both content and form, exposing social hypocrisies and exploiting cultural fantasies and fears, while also experimenting with narrative structures, the reinterpretation of film genres, and new audiovisual technology.

Three 1960s films are regularly acknowledged as masterpieces among this decade's host of superior films: Arthur Penn's *Bonnie and Clyde* (1967), Stanley Kubrick's *2001: A Space Odyssey* (1968), and Sam Peckinpah's *The Wild Bunch* (1969). *Bonnie and Clyde* stands out for its timely exploration of naive Depression-era gangsters as modern anti-heroes and for its complex and jarring editing style, climaxing in the bloody ambush discussed in Chapter 5. *2001* startles its audiences with a tale of space exploration that soon becomes a searing investigation of the dark drive for power and the perils of technology in human history [**Figure 11.34**]. Just as *2001* dismantles the popular genre of science fiction, *The Wild Bunch* uses the genre formula for westerns to bring out the disturbing political undertones of America's westward expansion. Besides their powerfully contemporary themes and issues, each of these films brilliantly challenged expectations about narrative form, film genre, and imagistic composition.

As with other periods in this abridged history, our short list of contemporary masterpieces could and should be expanded to include other remarkable films and filmmakers. For example, the work of Martin Scorsese, extending from the 1970s through the present, includes several films that qualify as contemporary masterpieces: *Taxi Driver* (1976), *Raging Bull* (1980), *Goodfellas* (1990), and *The Departed* (2006) to name a few.

The most recent era of Hollywood movie-making, from about 1980 to the present, has been driven by deals and deal

11.34   *2001: A Space Odyssey* (1968). Combining art and intellect with science fiction, Kubrick's film became a 1960s classic.

makers, individuals whose commercial and entrepreneurial expertise, as much as, or more than, their artistic ability, accounts for the success of a movie. The central names and forces in this group are a combination of high-profile industry leaders and individuals traditionally marginalized from the center of Hollywood power. In the 1980s and 1990s, along with the continued rise and expansion of power for movie directors like Steven Spielberg and George Lucas, producers, agents, and studio CEOs like Michael

11.35 *Blue Velvet* (1986). David Lynch's wildly original film is an acknowledged contemporary classic.

Ovitz, Michael Eisner, and Sherry Lansing assert themselves as key makers of movies, without actually directing films. In this context, Spike Lee deserves special attention not only for directing and starring in a modern masterpiece, *Do the Right Thing* (1989), but also for his ability to use his reputation and business skills to create an important place for African American filmmakers in contemporary Hollywood.

Although recent history is always difficult to evaluate, we can propose three classics: Ridley Scott's *Blade Runner* (1982), David Lynch's *Blue Velvet* (1986) [Figure 11.35], and Quentin Tarantino's *Pulp Fiction* (1994). Each of these films is a dramatic visual and narrative experiment that investigates the confusion of human identity, violence, and ethics at the end of the twentieth century. In *Blade Runner,* Dekker (played by Harrison Ford) hunts down human replicants in a fascinatingly dark and visually complex dystopia where technology creates figures "more human than human." With *Blue Velvet,* Lynch fashions a nightmarish version of small-town America in which Jeffrey, the protagonist, discovers violence seething through his everyday community and his own naive soul. In *Pulp Fiction,* where violence is also a measure of human communication, the narrative unpredictably follows the twisted actions and reflections of two hit men who philosophically meditate out loud about the Bible, loyalty, and McDonald's hamburgers. In all three of these exceptional films, we find not only the imaginative quality of the movies themselves, but also the professional skill and innovativeness of the filmmakers in producing such daring and disturbing projects and successfully distributing them across mainstream film culture.

An important development in this recent Hollywood history of masters and masterpieces is the emergence of female and African American perspectives, upsetting the traditional hierarchy. Women directors have struggled to enter the traditionally male pantheon of mainstream film history, and the directorial work of women like Amy Heckerling, Barbara Kopple, Kathryn Bigelow, Martha Coolidge, Julie Dash, Karyn Kusama, and Gina Prince-Bythewood (pp. 425–428) ensures that Hollywood history will feature more than just white men. African American male directors, such as Spike Lee, John Singleton, the Hughes brothers, Carl Franklin, and others, came to prominence in the 1990s as part of this history of masters and masterpieces, highlighting both the limitations of, and important changes in, this tradition [Figure 11.36].

text continued on page 393 ▶

VIEWING CUE

Could the film you study next in class be considered a masterpiece of film history? Why or why not? Do you consider the director of this film one of the great American filmmakers? Why or why not?

11.36 *Do the Right Thing* (1989). In the 1980s, Spike Lee's artistically and socially important work opened up the history of Hollywood masterworks to include African American perspectives.

The Mastery of Alfred Hitchcock

The long career of Alfred Hitchcock parallels in many ways the history of Hollywood masters and masterpieces, emerging in the silent era of the 1920s and continuing into the rebellious innovations of the 1960s. Through this career, Hitchcock stands out as one of the most distinctive and flexible directors in cinema history. As a director, he reinvented his cinematic powers through a variety of different but equally accomplished films, calling attention to those powers by placing himself in his films through short cameo appearances. Indeed, beyond the notable achievements of the films, the director shrewdly assisted the cultural construction of "Hitchcock" as a cinematic master. From his self-promotion through his own television series and film advertisements to his famous book-length interview with French director François Truffaut, Hitchcock worked to create an image of himself to complement his filmic masterpieces. His artistic dexterity allowed him, perhaps more than any other filmmaker, to create a long line of cinematic achievements held together by his singular vision and personality. Of all the creative and prolific Hollywood filmmakers, Hitchcock claims the most films on lists of the greatest movies.

Even before he arrived in Hollywood from England, Hitchcock had created one of the first sound masterpieces of the 1930s, *The 39 Steps* (1935). Immediately identifying Hitchcock as a master of suspense, this espionage drama made the new cinematic technology of sound a key element in the mystery of the plot: a music-hall tune, screams, train whistles, and cryptic dialogue create the dense intrigue behind an assassination attempt. Even in this early phase of Hitchcock's career, his work demonstrates a remarkable ability to create carefully crafted stories that take unusual advantage of the formal and technological possibilities of film.

In the 1940s, Hitchcock made *Rebecca* (1940), *Suspicion* (1941), *Shadow of a Doubt* (1943), *Spell-bound* (1945), *Notorious* (1946), and *Rope* (1948), films that combine artistic achievement and box-office success with a very personal sensitivity to topical social issues. A literary tendency is pronounced through the 1930s and early 1940s, as subtle dialogue that often skims over the surface of a sinister reality. This device is used most obviously in Hitchcock's only Oscar-winning film, *Rebecca,* an adaptation of Daphne du Maurier's best-selling novel. Brilliantly attuned to the social and global unrest of the 1940s, each of Hitchcock's films concentrates on melodramatic situations vaguely connected to a political or public threat that will potentially corrupt traditional romantic, family, and community structures. In *Shadow of a Doubt*, for instance, the picture of a cozy, happy family begins to crumble when the mysterious Uncle Charlie visits. Shortly thereafter, his young niece, nicknamed Charlie,

11.37 *Shadow of a Doubt* (1943). Hitchcock masters the family movie.

begins to suspect that her favorite uncle is a serial killer [Figure 11.37].

Many film historians argue that Hitchcock produced his greatest films in the 1950s and early 1960s: *Strangers on a Train* (1951), *Dial M for Murder* (1954), *Rear Window* (1954), *Vertigo* (1958), *North by Northwest* (1959), *Psycho* (1960) [Figure 11.38], and *The Birds* (1963). Throughout this period, Hitchcock's work continues to explore turbulent worlds and minds beneath the surface of normalcy, but gradually those explorations begin to shape his plots and characters into more radical and rebellious figures. Especially in the later films, Hitchcock begins to appear less like a brilliant Hollywood classicist and more like a confrontational rebel aiming to shock audiences and twist traditional film forms. As early as *Rear Window*, he experiments with unpleasant subject matter, making a movie almost exclusively about voyeurism. Immobilized by a broken leg, a photographer spies on his neighbors' escapades as if watching them on a series of television sets; in the process, he discovers a murder—and the sordidness of his own imagination. By the time he made *Psycho*, Hitchcock had grown even more confrontational and visually complex. Halfway through this film, the main character is murdered in a short edited sequence that is recognized as one of the most memorable in film history.

11.38   *Psycho* (1960). Alfred Hitchcock's visual daring comes forward in his masterpiece of horror.

The sequence begins with a dramatic close-up of Norman Bates's eye spying on Marion Crane as she prepares to take a shower; it then explodes in a montage of rapid shots that, through the illusory power of editing, render Marion's murder in brutal detail. The sequence then concludes with a close-up of Marion's eye and the parallel image of water and blood washing down the hole of a drain. With stunning economy, the main character of the narrative is lost, and the audience's point of identification becomes strangely aligned with the murderous gaze of a psychotic killer.

Film History as Periodization

Another important and conventional way to organize film history is through historical **periodization**. With this method, we divide the timeline of Hollywood history into segments that describe groups of years during which movies share thematic and stylistic concerns. Cinemas other than Hollywood have often been described according to periods. For instance, the German expressionist period (ca. 1919–ca. 1926) encompasses films that address psychic horror and social chaos through artificial and exaggerated sets and lighting. The period of Italian neorealism (1945–1952) produced movies stripped of intricate plots and visual glamour that depicted the dark and bare social realities of postwar Italy. Both periods are discussed further in Chapter 12. Unlike a history of unique masterpieces and masters, periodization is a history of stylistic and thematic similarities, a history of the typical.

Like our other two conventional models of film history, organizing movies by periods has many precedents outside the cinema. Historians of English history describe the Renaissance period, the Augustan era, the Victorian period, and other periods that share a common ground in, for example, artistic practices, political leadership, or religious ideas. American history identifies such periods as the colonial age, the antebellum period, the Depression era and the Cold War period. In all these cases, there is an assumed or defined "spirit of the age"—such as the reign of a specific queen or an economic crisis—that either reflects a dominant event or institution or describes a cultural atmosphere made from the combination of various forces.

Two cornerstones of periodization are standardization and differentiation, suggesting that with Hollywood films especially, certain standard forms and styles become associated with a specific historical period or span of years. Furthermore, individual films can create variations on those standards as a way of differentiating themselves.

Most films made during the same period use not only historically recognizable themes, plot devices, characterizations, genres, and visual styles but also costuming, casting, editing, and sound practices. Often these filmic standards reflect an even wider range of cultural practices, such as trends in literature or television (for example, the rise of MTV-style editing in the 1980s) and social shifts (the effects of the feminist movement on the characterization of women in the 1970s). At the same time, an individual film works to differentiate itself within these period standards. For instance, even a masterpiece like *Citizen Kane* shares period standards employed by other films of the early 1940s, such as comic interludes and ominous lighting techniques. However, the film's radical reworking of these standards through its kaleidoscopic narrative, dramatic editing, and rich pictorial compositions clearly sets it off as exceptional within this period.

For each of the following periods in our survey—early, classical, postwar, and contemporary cinema—we will address telling social and industrial events that define the historical era inside and outside Hollywood. Within this context, we will highlight key formal shifts that provide the stylistic standards of that time, standards against which particular films might differentiate themselves.

As will become clear, a history of cinematic periods also has its risks as a historical model. It tends to draw historical boundaries that can appear too rigid. It also tends to homogenize a great variety of films as part of one period. Nonetheless, periodization offers a more equitable cross section of a period in film history than do other historical frameworks, defining a typical movie of the period rather than the revolutionary or exceptional film found in such other approaches as evolutionary or masterpiece history. Although historians frequently employ different dates and nomenclature for film periods (for example, referring to early cinema as preclassical or primitive, or to contemporary cinema as modern or postclassical), we use the four terms "early," "classical," "postwar," and "contemporary" to refer to the historical periods of Hollywood cinema.

Early Cinema

The early cinema period, stretching roughly from 1895 to 1913, was characterized by rapid development and experimentation in filmmaking before Hollywood settled into the more defined patterns of its classical period. In the United States, massive industrialization attracted large numbers of immigrants and rural Americans to urban centers, where the movie industry found many of its subjects and audiences. Traditional class, race, and gender lines began to shift, and these new openings in the social fabric of the country combined with expanding economic prosperity. The women's suffrage movement succeeded at the state level by 1890, the automobile arrived around 1900, and the first airplane left the ground in 1903. Besides encouraging new energies and visions throughout society, industrialization fostered the growth of leisure time and commercialized leisure activities. In the realm of this expanding free time, popular culture competed with the traditions of high culture as never before.

Although moving pictures themselves were the defining cinematic event of this early period in film history, we can identify several other significant industrial events, including: in 1895, the public exhibition of movies as part of the growing entertainment industry; in 1910, the rise of the star, or celebrity, system in the movies; and between 1907 and 1913, the beginning of the international dominance of Hollywood.

Beginning with the showing of *Workers Leaving the Lumière Factory* on March 22, 1895, the first movies, with their various subject matters, attracted and fascinated the public. Soon commercial and theatrical venues for showing movies to the general public arrived in the form of nickelodeon theaters. Actualities (early newsreels of everyday scenes), theatrical spectacles, and images of famous people constituted these first film programs. As the movies experimented with undefined possibilities, the subject matter and themes reflected a multitude of topics and interests. The characters in these short films were originally anonymous actors and actresses, but by 1911 the Biograph Girl became identified as the celebrity Florence Lawrence and Little Mary became the star Mary Pickford. These commercial personalities added to the growing cultural power of film. Finally, as American movies advanced in length and complexity, Hollywood quickly extended its reach around the world, producing half the films made worldwide in 1914.

Stylistically, the most important characteristics of early cinema are (1) the shift from scenes to shots and (2) the beginnings of continuity editing as an early elaboration of narrative form.

The first movies relied on the impact of a single shot of a specific scene or event, such as a man sneezing. But movies quickly moved to multiple shots of dramatic events and then to the dramatization of real or fictional events as a story told with many shots, logically connected in space and time. Released in 1903, *Uncle Tom's Cabin* presents a series of shots that isolate highlights of the famous story on which it is based. By 1911, however, Griffith's *The Lonedale Operator,* a short film about burglars threatening a telegraph operator, edited together numerous shots to re-create the characters' points of view, to establish different spatial relations between an office interior and its exterior, and to build narrative suspense through parallel editing.

Classical Cinema

Classical cinema is divided into two parts: silent and sound films. The first part encompasses Hollywood's classical silent period, from roughly 1913 to 1927, when the basic structures of classical narrative were put in place. With the devastation and resolution of World War I (1914–1918) at the start of this period, films often seemed a peculiar combination of energetic optimism and trembling fear. Many of the arts tested out new forms and visions during this time, such as F. Scott Fitzgerald's modernist novel *The Great Gatsby* (1925) and Edward Hopper's painting *Manhattan Bridge* (1927). The "roaring twenties" became shorthand for a decade of material and social liberality often slipping into decadence. Moreover, with New York City becoming the new cultural center of the world, the United States began to assert itself as both a powerful global force and the embodiment of the progressive promise of the twentieth century. This progress was climactically symbolized in the first nonstop flight from New York to Paris by Charles Lindbergh in 1927.

Hollywood itself came of age in the 1910s and 1920s with three major historical developments: the standardization of film production, the establishment of the feature film, and the cultural and economic expansion of movies throughout the society. As the Hollywood industry grew in size and proficiency, standardized formulas for film production took root, creating efficient teams of scriptwriters, producers, directors, camera operators, actors, and editors. One product of this standardization process was the establishment of a normalized running time of approximately one hundred minutes for a narrative movie. The feature-film model became the dominant commercial practice of the twentieth century and is still in place. Finally, along with their technological and economic growth, movies found more sophisticated subject matter and more elegant theaters for distribution, reflecting their rising cultural status and their ability to attract audiences from all

11.39 *Intolerance* (1916). D. W. Griffith intertwines stories set in four different historical periods in this landmark in the evolution of narrative film form.

corners of society. Internationally, Hollywood continued to extend its reach: while World War I wreaked havoc on European economics, Hollywood increased its exports fivefold and its overseas income by 35 percent.

The most pronounced and important aesthetic changes during the early classical period included (1) the full development of narrative realism as the center of film form, and (2) the integration of the viewer's perspective into the editing and narrative action.

Narrative realism came to the forefront of movie culture as the movies worked to legitimate themselves by adapting literary works and traditions. From Griffith's *The Birth of a Nation* and *Intolerance* [Figure 11.39] through King Vidor's *The Big Parade* (1925) and Buster Keaton's *The General,* narrative films learned to explore simultaneous actions, complex spatial geographies, and the psychological interaction of characters through narrative. As a significant part of this new formal complexity, movies developed point-of-view shots through camera movement and editing in order to situate viewers *within* the narrative action rather than at the theatrical distance (e.g., the view from a seat before a stage) found in early or preclassical films.

The second part of the classical cinema period, from about 1927 to 1945, brought sound to film and represents the golden age of Hollywood. The Great Depression, triggered in part by the stock market collapse of 1929, defined the American cultural experience at the beginning of the 1930s. In the midst of economic unrest and other strains, fascist and Marxist ideologies began to make inroads in the U.S., demanding major changes in the traditional way of life. Franklin Roosevelt's New Deal became the political antidote for much of the 1930s, pumping a determined spirit of optimism into society. The devastating conflict of World War II then defined the last four years of the classical period, in which the country fully asserted its global leadership and control.

The film industry followed these turbulent historical events with dramatic changes of its own, including the coming of sound in 1927, the empowerment of the Hays Office and the founding of the Production Code Administration in 1934, and the full definition and operation of an efficient studio system. The sensational

11.40 *The Jazz Singer* (1927). Sound comes to the cinema.

arrival of sound technology opened a whole new dimension to film form that allowed movies to expand their dramatic capacity: after *The Jazz Singer* (1927) [Figure 11.40], the "100 percent all-talkie" *Lights of New York* (1928) began a period of more complex soundtracks. With social issues more hotly debated and the movies gaining more influence than ever, the messages of films came increasingly under scrutiny. By 1934, the Hays Office, first established in 1927 with a set of guidelines, had evolved into the Production Code Administration, headed by Joseph I. Breen and empowered to enforce the Motion Picture Production Code of 1930. The code strictly enforced a conservative list of "Don'ts and Be Carefuls," primarily governing the depiction of crime and sex, that kept censorship efforts within the industry. During this time, the increasingly efficient movie studios produced more and better films out of generic molds that drew ever-larger audiences.

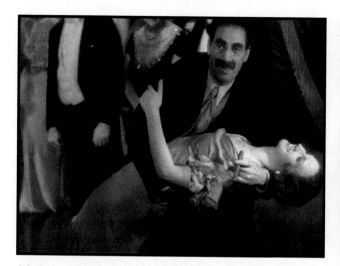

11.41   *Duck Soup* (1933). The introduction of sound brought dialogue and ushered in the comic talents of the Marx Brothers.

11.42   *The Little Foxes* (1941). Literary adaptations, such as William Wyler's film of Lillian Hellman's play, were a staple of quality production during Hollywood's classical period.

At this time, Hollywood films followed these industrial shifts with two important stylistic changes. First is the elaboration of movie dialogue and the concomitant growth of characterization in films. Second is the prominence of generic formulas in constructing film narratives.

With sound technology came more music and, of course, dialogue. Accomplished writers flocked to Hollywood, literary adaptations flourished, and outspoken characters became more verbally, psychologically, and socially complex. The rapid-fire witticisms of the Marx Brothers in *Duck Soup* (1933) **[Figure 11.41]** and the musically and verbally elaborate adaptation of Shakespeare's *A Midsummer Night's Dream* (1935) both reflected the new sound standards. Meanwhile, genres, always an important organizational dimension of the movies, were enlisted and explored as never before. Whether the movie was the melodramatic *Magnificent Obsession* (1935) or the literary *The Little Foxes* (1941), generic formulas became the primary production and distribution standard. In fact, they sometimes superseded the subject matter and actors in defining a film and expectations about it **[Figure 11.42]**.

Postwar Cinema

The postwar cinema period, which extended roughly from 1946 to 1965, is defined by several overriding historical events and motifs. In the wake of World War II, the inhuman nightmare of the Nazi concentration camps, and the atomic bombing of Hiroshima and Nagasaki in 1945, doubts about human nature and social progress shadowed the economic prosperity and surface optimism of this period in U.S. history. Unease permeated traditional institutions, especially the family and the sexual and social relationships associated with it. In addition, the Cold War with the Soviet Union and the Communist bloc began an extended period of tension and anxiety about national identity and security.

The civil rights movement began to challenge social injustice. Three key events defined postwar period in Hollywood as well. After the 1948 *Paramount* decision, for example, the traditional power of the studios dissolved. This was then followed by the arrival and rapid spread of television in the 1950s. Then, in 1968, the Production Code standards were relaxed and the ratings system was introduced.

11.43   ***The Best Years of Our Lives*** (1946). The darker realism of William Wyler's Oscar-winning film reflected the difficult postwar period.

As noted earlier in this chapter, the power of the studios began to erode with the *Paramount* decision of 1948. Widescreen movies, drive-in theaters, and other new cinematic strategies appeared to combat the allure of television, which threatened to undercut the cultural centrality of the movies. As society turned more to television, restrictions and censorship began to fade, and film practices began to test new themes, genres, and variations on the models of classical cinema, often in radical ways.

The movies themselves grew more daring and darker as they loosened or challenged the formulas of classical Hollywood, most notably by exploring more controversial themes and issues as part of a new standard of realism and developing a more self-conscious and exaggerated sense of image composition and narrative structure.

By the end of the war, a new, darker realism pervaded even Hollywood as the events of World War II settled into the national consciousness. Beginning with *The Best Years of Our Lives* (1946) and its layered tale of postwar trauma in small-town America [Figure 11.43], films opened doors into such subjects as family betrayal, alcoholism and drug abuse, sexuality, racial injustice, and psychological breakdowns. These topics led naturally to more unstable and unpredictable characters and narratives as well as to sometimes subversive and violent visual styles, as in *Touch of Evil* (1958) [Figure 11.44] and *Psycho* (1960). Although many examples of traditional heartwarming, epic, glamorous, or comedic entertainment, such as *White Christmas* (1954), arose during this era, even these more upbeat entertainments exhibit a self-consciousness about film form, entertainment and its relation to society, or the dangers of violence underlying the story.

▶ **VIEWING CUE**

How does the content of the film you just viewed identify it as part of a particular period? Which formal characteristics of this film seem common to this era? What distinguishes it from the standards of this era? ⏸

Contemporary Cinema

We designate the most recent period in Hollywood history, beginning around 1965 and continuing through the present, contemporary cinema. While the social anger and confusion of the Vietnam War colored the early part of this era, new pressures emerged when that war ended in 1975. Even as the United States seemed to fragment and split its national identity over this war, the sexual and drug revolutions extended the familial and gender anxieties of the 1950s well into the 1980s and beyond. Racial and gender politics, which had informed the strains and shifts of the 1950s, became a defining part of the American landscape. The relaxing of some global tensions (most visibly with the fall of the Berlin Wall in 1989 and the dissolution of the Soviet bloc in the 1990s) seemed to bring attention to tensions around domestic issues such as immigration, multiculturalism, gender inequities, and sexual orientation.

The movie industry shifted noticeably in response to four forces: youth audiences becoming the dominant group of moviegoers, European art films becoming an increasing influence in Hollywoods, globalization, and the arrival of conglomerates, blockbusters, cable, and home video.

11.44   ***Touch of Evil*** (1958). The baroque visual style of Orson Welles's crime drama captured the transition from the stable forms of studio-era Hollywood to a more dynamic cinema influenced by postwar European film.

In keeping with the times, Hollywood turned some of its power over to young filmmakers, who began to address the teenage audiences that made up larger and larger portions of the moviegoing public. *The Godfather* [Figure 11.45] and *Taxi Driver* are part of a remarkable series of films from the so-called New Hollywood. Influenced by European art cinemas, it took imaginative risks in form and narrative. This courtship of youth with experimentation changed significantly, however, when conglomerate enterprises began to assimilate and shape Hollywood. Corporate Hollywood would redirect youthful energy toward more commercial blockbusters and global markets. Finally, VCRs, cable, television, and later domestic technologies such as DVDs and personal electronics disseminated movies in ways that offered viewers more variety and control.

11.45   *The Godfather* (1972). Perhaps the key text of the New Hollywood, Francis Ford Coppola's film was an economic and a artistic success.

Amid so many cataclysmic changes in film culture, two trends dominate the contemporary period: the elevation of image spectacles and special effects, and the fragmentation and reflexivity of narrative constructions. On the one hand, contemporary movies frequently drift away from the traditional focus on narrative and instead balance or override the narration with sensational mise-en-scène or dramatic manipulations of the film image. In this context, conventional realism gives way to intentionally artificial, spectacular, or even cartoonish representations of characters, places, and actions. Playful films like *Who Framed Roger Rabbit* (1988) [Figure 11.46] allow cartoon characters and actions to interact with human ones, whereas a more serious drama like *The King of Comedy* (1983) shows an obsessive fan replacing the real world with strange fantasies. On the other hand, contemporary movies that do fully engage narrative traditions often intentionally fragment, reframe, or distort

11.46   *Who Framed Roger Rabbit* (1988). Cartoon characters interacting with actors exemplifies an interest in spectacle and a self-consciousness about film form.

the narrative in ways that challenge its coherence. *Mystery Train* (1989) portrays several interlocking tales that converge in a Memphis hotel haunted by the spirit of Elvis Presley. *Memento* (2000) reconstructs narrative through its continually changing retrospective perspectives, all subject to the narrator/protagonist's lack of short-term memory; the result is a series of overlapping episodes that eventually leads back to the murder that started the film. *Adaptation* (2002) describes the crisis of a fictionalized screenwriter, Charlie Kaufman (also the film's real writer's name), hailed for his earlier film *Being John Malkovich* (1999) (the real Kaufman's debut screenplay), as he struggles to adapt a script from Susan Orlean's nonfiction book *The Orchid Thief*. The film folds Kaufman into a tale of drugs and murder that becomes the film *Adaptation* [Figure 11.47]. In *Babel* (2006), an international coproduction directed by Mexican director Alejandro González Iñárritu, interlocking story lines unfold in multiple languages and on several continents. This new narrative complexity may relate to viewers' familiarity with game worlds and their ability to watch and rewatch these complex works on DVD to piece together narrative strands.

text continued on page 402 ▶

11.47   *Adaptation* (2002). Contemporary Hollywood narratives are frequently willing to experiment with temporality and different levels of narrative exposition.

Periodization and *Taxi Driver* (1976)

One reason Martin Scorsese's *Taxi Driver* remains such a powerful and rich film today is its keen self-consciousness about its place in film history and the complex historical references it puts into play. *Taxi Driver* is suffused with the historical events that colored and shaped U.S. society in the 1970s and shares many characteristics with other contemporary films. At the same time, it echoes and recalls Hollywood's classical and postwar periods, suggesting that one of the defining features of contemporary film is its awareness of its cinematic traditions and the legacy of past eras. For instance, Scorsese commissioned the film's haunting score from composer Bernard Herrmann, best known for his collaborations with Orson Welles on *Citizen Kane* and Alfred Hitchcock on *Vertigo, Psycho,* and other films. The darkness lurking in these classical and postwar films is fully embraced in *Taxi Driver* and resonates in its music.

The story, written by Paul Shrader, focuses on a New York cabdriver, Travis Bickle (played by Scorsese regular Robert DeNiro), and his increasing alienation from the city in which he lives and works. As he cruises New York locked in the isolated compartment of his cab, his voiceover narration rambles and meditates on his entrapment in a world that has lost its innocence and seems to be progressing only toward its own destruction. Travis decries the filth and decadence of the city and considers violent and apocalyptic solutions like assassinating a politician. Attempting to break out of the bitter routines of his existence, he imagines himself the savior of Iris, a young prostitute, and attracts the ire of her pimp. The film ends with a ghastly bloodbath in which Travis murders the pimp and the unsettling announcement that Travis has become a media hero.

The issues and atmosphere of 1970s U.S. society pervade *Taxi Driver.* Flagged by Travis's veteran's jacket and the traumatized personality associated with young soldiers returning from the Vietnam war, the specter of that war haunts the film. Travis's violent personality echoes a whole decade of U.S. violence: the assassinations of John F. Kennedy and Martin Luther King Jr. and, as an explicit source for the film, Arthur Bremer's attempted assassination of Alabama governor George Wallace. The violence in *Taxi Driver* associates it with many other films of the contemporary period. These range from *A Clockwork Orange* (1971) to *Natural Born Killers* (1994), in which modern life and identity are tied to the psychological and social prevalence of violence, and graphic and often unmotivated violence becomes a desperate means of expression for lost souls. Five years after its release, *Taxi Driver* remained a barometer of modern America. When John Hinckley Jr. tried to assassinate President Ronald Reagan in 1981, he claimed to have been inspired by *Taxi Driver* and had hoped, in killing a president, to "effect a mystical union with Jodie Foster," the star who played Iris.

As a part of its modern consciousness about the burdens of the past, the film's plot explicitly recalls John Ford's *The Searchers* (1956) and implicitly recalls other classical westerns, such as Ford's *Stagecoach* (1939) (suggested perhaps by the Mohawk haircut Travis acquires midway through the film and the Native American look of the pimp Travis kills). Like Ford's Ethan (John Wayne) in *The Searchers,* Travis becomes alienated from most social interaction, yet he yearns, through his determination to "save" Iris, to restore some lost form of family and community. He wants to be a hero in an age when there is little possibility for heroic action. Yet the recollection of earlier periods of Hollywood history and the plots and characters they produced only highlights the historical differences of

11.48   *Taxi Driver* (1976). The windshield functions as a frame for Travis Bickle's limited point of view.

11.49   *Taxi Driver* (1976). The famous scene in which the main character, Travis Bickle, confronts his mirror image demonstrates a divided and shifting identity.

this film: this Travis is a fully modern antihero, one with no frontier to explore and only imaginary heroics to motivate him. New York is not the Wild West, and Travis clearly lacks the proud, clear vision and the noble purpose of a western hero like the Ringo Kid in the classical *Stagecoach.* That a younger, more cynical audience became the primary target of and the vehicle for the success of *Taxi Driver* indicates that the changing social tastes and attitudes of audiences play a large part in determining the differences in historical periods and the films of those periods.

Stylistically, *Taxi Driver* is unmistakably contemporary, consistently suggesting a high degree of self-consciousness about its narrative organization and images. In this regard, two formal patterns are typical: an exaggerated or hyper-realistic cinematography and a self-conscious, often interiorized, narrative perspective. Both of these patterns suggest the influence of French New-Wave directors on Scorsese and on such other films of this period as *Apocalypse Now* (1979) and *Goodfellas* (1990). As a version of that contemporary imagistic style, *Taxi Driver* paints New York City through hyper-realistic images that seem to be the product of either a strained mind or a strained society. Shots of New York at night gleam and swirl with flashing colors, creating a carnivalesque atmosphere of neon and glass. Frames (like those of the cab window and its rearview mirror) constantly call attention to a subjective, partial point of view [Figure 11.48]. This attention to the frames through which we see and understand the world then crystallizes in one of the most renowned shots of the movie. Midway through the film, Travis equips himself with various guns, and while he poses before a mirror, he repeatedly addresses himself with the famous line, "You talkin' to me?" As he watches himself in the

mirror, identity appears to split, one image of self violently confronting the other [Figure 11.49]. This line becomes almost an anthem of contemporary movies on divided identity.

Similarly, the first-person narration of *Taxi Driver* transforms the realism of the film into an almost psychotic staging of Travis's personal desires and anxieties. "One day, indistinguishable from the next, a long continuous chain," Travis rambles on through the private voiceover. This drifting interior narrative jumps from one psychological state and illogical action to another: Travis tries, for instance, to court a woman with a date at a pornographic movie, and later he plans to assassinate her employer, a politician running for office, for no apparent reason. When Travis initiates his final bloody attack on Iris's pimp, the narrative takes its most unpredictable turn: despite the bizarre motivation for this event (to rescue a young woman who does not wish to be rescued) and the shockingly graphic slaughter that leaves a trail of shredded bodies, Travis becomes a community hero, celebrated in newspapers for his rescue of Iris. At this moment of anticipated closure, narrative logic becomes strained to the point of fracturing. A "happy ending" to a narrative motivated and shaped by a quirky, narcissistic, and unbalanced mind seems to subvert the possibility of a traditional narrative logic in *Taxi Driver*—and possibly in this modern world.

Like many contemporary films, *Taxi Driver* acts out the signs of its times, socially and artistically. More than many others, however, this film demonstrates that recent cinema also bears the burden of its historical past. Being true to its historical present requires unusual awareness of the dramatic changes and fissures that distinguish the film from its historical heritage.

Film Preservation and Archives

Histories of Hollywood cinema depend upon the records of the past, including the films that survive and are available to researchers. Scholars and general audiences today are able to encounter an expanding number of films from the silent era to the recent past because of preservation and archiving efforts as well as new digital technologies. Sometimes a film is re-released in theaters because lost scenes have been put back in or because the sound quality has been corrected or adjusted. A DVD release of an older film can mean the resurrection of a movie that would have otherwise been unavailable for viewing. In cases like these, audiences experience an important and growing dimension of film culture, one that aims to preserve or resurrect pieces of film history that are in danger of being lost.

The importance of archives and preservation is especially vital to silent film history. Scholars estimate that more than 80 percent of the films made before 1930 have disappeared, being routinely destroyed (movies were considered as ephemeral as newspapers) or simply neglected (the chemical instability of film's cellulose nitrate base means that films can self-combust or deteriorate quickly if not properly cared for).

Preserving film history takes many forms, some less satisfactory than others. For a short period in the 1980s, classic Hollywood films were "colorized" in a misguided attempt to make them appealing to contemporary viewers. Obviously this practice does not restore the original format. Videotape archiving has drawbacks because the medium deteriorates even more quickly than film and never adequately duplicates the qualities of celluloid. Preserving the original film with a cellulose acetate base is preferable, although doing so is expensive and complicated and cannot fully halt eventual deterioration. Digital imaging has offered an invaluable way to copy works in danger of deteriorating, but this process can alter the color tones of the original film and obviously does not preserve the physical object.

Kevin Brownlow and David Gill's 1981 restoration of Abel Gance's *Napoléon* (1927) is a complex and particularly sensational example of restoration. Frustrated with the tattered versions of this silent French classic in circulation, Brownlow pursued the confused history of the film, searching out different versions from private and public archives and eventually patching together an accurate reproduction of the film. More recently, contemporary filmmakers, in recognition of the fragile history and heritage of film, have supported restoration efforts for American and foreign classics. In 2001, Martin Scorsese presented a restored version of *Night of the Hunter* (1955)—a dark, offbeat tale of a religious con man pursuing his two stepchildren and a hidden stash of money—as part of a larger film-preservation effort he has helped to propel [**Figure 11.50**]. Films from Jean-Luc Godard's *Contempt* to F. W. Murnau's *Tabu* have been recent recipients of the efforts of specialty distributors to gratify audiences' interests in seeing film classics the way they were meant to be seen.

Film archives, which are key to the efforts of film preservation, became central institutions beginning in the 1930s. Most prominent has been the work at the Cinémathèque Française by Henri Langlois and at New York's Museum of Modern Art by Iris Barry. As early as 1898, Polish scholar Boleslaw Matuszewski argued the need for film archives, and today more than 120 archives dedicated to the preservation and proper exhibition of films and their study constitute the International Federation of Film Archives (FIAF), itself founded in 1938.

The consequences of such efforts to resurrect or preserve older films are heartening. Each fall, scholars flock to Pordenone, Italy, to see restored international classics of the silent film era. Several DVD initiatives have resulted in the distribution of rare movies that viewers previously had not been able to

11.50 *Night of the Hunter* (1955). This dark fable was restored with the support of Martin Scorsese.

see. For instances, the five-disc collection *The Movies Begin: A Treasury of Early Cinema,* released in 2002 by Kino International, offers a variety of restored films from 1894 to 1913. In addition, since 2000 the National Film Preservation Foundation has tapped U.S. archives to make available such fascinating films as James Sibley Watson's *The Fall of the House of Usher* (1928) and Zora Neale Hurston's ethnographic footage of the 1930s. More publicized, different versions of older films—such as Fritz Lang's *M* (1931) or Orson Welles's *Touch of Evil* (1958)—pieced together from materials found in archives and collections, are generating debates about which is the authoritative version. Indeed, an interesting question is whether some movies even exist in a definitive version or whether the original experience of a particular film can ever be accurately re-created.

CONCEPTS AT WORK

Historical knowledge helps our thinking about any subject, and movies are no exception. When watching films made in another era, we must consider them, to some degree, as documents whose style and subject matter need a historical context in order to be appreciated. For example, without a sense of film history, contemporary viewers of James Whale's *Frankenstein* (1931) might find its story simplistic, the acting clumsy, and its audiovisual style primitive. With a historical perspective on acting styles and techniques in the 1930s, however, such viewers could understand the film as a product of particular historical constraints and possibilities.

It is the films themselves that are key to any approach to film history; as we have indicated, film archiving and preservation can play a major role in a viewer's film experience by determining the quality and range of what audiences see. Priorities for film preservation may be different depending on what methods of constructing film history are employed. If only masterpieces are archived, we will lose a sense of the conventions they borrowed from, as well as those they challenged. If only the existing contents of national archives are preserved, then comparisons to alternative traditions may be hindered. In the next chapter we elaborate on the questions of value that shape historiography by looking at film histories outside evolutionary, masterpiece, periodizing, and Hollywood models.

Activities

- Looking at a group of works selected for your course syllabus (or for a screening series on television or at a cultural institution), try to connect the films using the three conventions of film history described in this chapter.
- Discuss the connections between a film and its historical period in political, technological, industrial, economic, and cultural terms.

THE NEXT LEVEL: ADDITIONAL SOURCES

Allen, Robert C., and Douglas Gomery. *Film History: Theory and Practice.* New York: Knopf, 1985. A successful combination of theoretical savvy and pragmatics, this study is a rare look at the different ways film histories can be constructed and used to illuminate individual films.

Beauchamp, Cari. *Frances Marion and the Powerful Women of Early Hollywood.* Berkeley: University of California Press, 1997. A lively and readable history of the women screenwriters, producers, and stars active in the early years of Hollywood's influence.

Bordwell, David, Janet Staiger, and Kristin Thompson. *The Classical Hollywood Cinema: Film Style and Mode to 1960.* New York: Columbia University Press, 1985. An extensively researched and detailed exploration of U.S. film history based on industrial standards that, according to the authors, have altered little in sixty years.

Cook, David A. *A History of Narrative Film,* 4th ed. New York: Norton, 2004. Large and exact, this excellent history of world cinema moves from the original to recent movie cultures. A superb source of information and dates that is punctuated by analysis of film masterpieces.

Harpole, Charles, general ed. *History of American Cinema.* 10 vols. New York: Scribner's, 1990–2002. With each volume edited by a different scholar, this monumental history provides a decade-by-decade compendium of details and facts that map the industrial, social, and stylistic development of American movies.

Sklar, Robert, and Charles Musser, eds. *Resisting Images: Essays on Cinema and History.* Philadelphia: Temple University Press, 1990. A collection of essays by contemporary film scholars and critics that examines the relationship between cinema history and social history through such topics as "Soviet worker clubs of the 1920s" and the "politics of Israeli cinema."

WHAT IMPRISONS
DESIRES OF THE HEART?
JULIANNE MOORE
DENNIS QUAID
DENNIS HAYSBERT
A FILM BY TODD HAYNES
FAR FROM HEAVEN
TF1 INTERNATIONAL PICTURES AND VULCAN PRODUCTIONS PRESENT IN ASSOCIATION WITH FOCUS FEATURES A KILLER FILMS/JOHN WELLS/SECTION EIGHT PRODUCTION
A FILM BY TODD HAYNES JULIANNE MOORE DENNIS QUAID DENNIS HAYSBERT "FAR FROM HEAVEN" PATRICIA CLARKSON CASTING BY LAURA ROSENTHAL
MUSIC BY ELMER BERNSTEIN ASSOCIATE PRODUCERS DIDIER SAPAUT JEAN CHARLES LÉVY COSTUME DESIGNER SANDY POWELL EDITED BY JAMES LYONS PRODUCTION DESIGNER MARK FRIEDBERG DIRECTOR OF PHOTOGRAPHY EDWARD LACHMAN, A.S.C.
CO-PRODUCERS BRADFORD SIMPSON DECLAN BALDWIN EXECUTIVE PRODUCERS JOHN WELLS ERIC ROBISON TRACY BRIMM JOHN SLOSS EXECUTIVE PRODUCERS STEVEN SODERBERGH GEORGE CLOONEY
VULCAN PRODUCTIONS
PRODUCED BY JODY PATTON PRODUCED BY CHRISTINE VACHON WRITTEN AND DIRECTED BY TODD HAYNES
SOUNDTRACK AVAILABLE ON VARÈSE SARABANDE CDs
TF1 INTERNATIONAL
killer films
www.farfromheavenmovie.com
ARTWORK: ©2002 FOCUS FEATURES, LLC. ALL RIGHTS RESERVED.

Global and Local

Inclusive Histories of the Movies

Three films retell the same story at different points over nearly fifty years of film history: *All That Heaven Allows*, a Hollywood melodrama made in 1955 by German émigré director Douglas Sirk; *Ali: Fear Eats the Soul*, directed in 1974 by German filmmaker Rainer Werner Fassbinder; and *Far from Heaven*, made in 2002 by American independent Todd Haynes. The first, starring Rock Hudson and Jane Wyman in a romance between a middle-class widow and her gardener, is a tale of social prejudice in small-town U.S.A. The second, concentrating on the love affair between an older cleaning-woman and a young Arab guest worker, tells a story about age, class, and immigration in modern Germany. The third remakes the love story into a film about the coming-out of a gay husband and his wife's interracial romance, shattering the facade of a typical 1950s family. Informed by three separate film histories, these very different films are also deeply connected as critical remakes of the same basic plot.

n 1998, to commemorate the first one hundred years of cinema, the American Film Institute (AFI) released a highly publicized list of the "100 Greatest American Movies of All Time." This list raised the AFI's profile and generated instant credibility for, and renewed public interest in, all of its entries, none more so than Orson Welles's *Citizen Kane* (1941)–the film in the number-one spot. Many critics and viewers disagreed, however, with the list's claim to be "timeless," as it tended to reproduce current, dominant tastes. Only four silent movies made the list (*The Birth of a Nation* and three Charlie Chaplin films), for example, and works by African American and female filmmakers were all but absent. Even the beloved musicals of Fred Astaire were missing **[Figure 12.1]**. While the AFI list may have been geared toward Hollywood films with mass appeal rather than films that may have greater artistic or historical significance, this does not mean the list should be dismissed. Rather we must consider the criteria and values that went into the list's creation, as well as its restriction to American films.

Our view of film history would be sorely incomplete if we were to ignore the rich traditions of filmmaking beyond Hollywood. This chapter will examine film cultures from around the world—some as old as Hollywood and some just beginning to emerge—as well as lesser-known film cultures within the United States.

In this chapter, we will examine three historical models that differ from conventional Hollywood histories:

- film history as global, emphasizing the distinctive shape of different national cinemas as well as transnational influences
- film history as a recovery of film practices, filmmakers, and audiences marginalized by traditional Hollywood-centered history
- film history as an examination of the various political, social, and cultural contexts that surround the movies

Various lists of "great movies" highlight different values. Whether creating a myth of a nation's film history through a lens of nostalgia and patriotism like the AFI list, establishing a record of a nation's distinctive film culture like the Library of Congress's registry, or tracking the rise and fall of global film aesthetics like the poll conducted every decade by the film journal *Sight and Sound*, lists draw attention to the films they feature. The films that appear on these lists are likely to become top rentals from Netflix and other rental sources and will also find new life on television. Lists create film heritage and shape film's future. But if an appearance on one of these prestigious lists breathes new life into a film, what happens to the films that never make the cut?

As a counterpoint to the conventional Hollywood histories of Chapter 11, this chapter introduces ways of using history to explore questions typically excluded from the study of Hollywood films. The models of movie history discussed in the preceding

chapter inevitably omit important traditions, films, filmmakers, and cultural debates. Other ways of looking at film history can illuminate these omissions while also offering more inclusive, alternative accounts.

Film History beyond Hollywood

Film history began well before the purchase of cheap California real estate started a colony called Hollywood. Moreover, early film developments in areas such as patents, equipment, the standard length of films, and exhibition protocols—as well as stylistic innovations in staging, camera, lighting, and cutting styles—were distinctly international. While much early activity was concentrated in Europe, vigorous film cultures sprang up in such countries as Brazil, Egypt, India, China, and Japan. It is not surprising that the movies had a multinational beginning. The emergence of cinema depended on technological innovations and the corresponding social changes wrought by rapid industrialization at the end of the nineteenth century. Countries became tied together in many new ways, and these global transformations provoked the emergence of new forms of international mass culture. Thinking globally—rejecting the simplistic model of "the West and the rest"—has transformed the pursuit of film history just as it has transformed politics, economics, and other cultural practices.

▶ **VIEWING CUE**

Scan local film listings, noting how many different countries are represented. If the range is limited, why do you think this is so? If you have located foreign films, what kinds of venues or channels show them?
⏸

Film History before World War II

Despite the dominance of Hollywood, movie history is a world affair involving many countries and films. Here we will highlight some of the most important national cinemas that have challenged a narrative centered on Hollywood. These are merely capsules, part of larger and more intricate histories.

The earliest years of motion-picture history involved competing and overlapping developments in equipment, style, and storytelling in France, England, and the United States. One of the earliest public film projections was the Lumière brothers' 1895 exhibition in France. Without language barriers, movies produced in Italy and Denmark circulated internationally in the 1910s. American audiences watched imported films, and the immigrants among them were often able to see images of their homelands. Early films were not necessarily fiction films, but films that delighted in the new medium's capacity to simply show things—actualities showing real events, scenic views, and

12.1 *Top Hat* (1935). This classic musical did not make the American Film Institute's 100 Greatest American Movies list.

12.2   *Panorama of the Eiffel Tower* (1900). Exciting locales, such as this view of the Eiffel Tower and the Paris Exposition, characterize the early "cinema of attractions."

brief skits [**Figure 12.2**]. The theater environment, including boisterous audience behavior, was as central to the experience as what was shown on the screen. This era, dubbed the "cinema of attractions" by historian Tom Gunning, was not a false start on the way to a more sophisticated storytelling form. Instead it saw a flourishing of equally important spectacular aspects of the cinema that survive today in special effects and other astonishing aspects of the movies.

Soviet Silent Films

The early internationalism of the cinema allowed stylistic innovations in one country to have an impact elsewhere. From about 1917 to 1931, Soviet silent films provided a major break with the entertainment history of the movies. That this movement developed out of the Russian Revolution of 1917 suggests its distance from the assumptions and aims of the capitalist economics of Hollywood, resulting in (1) an emphasis on documentary and historical subjects and (2) a political concept of cinema centered on audience response.

Dziga Vertov, a seminal theoretician and practitioner in this movement, established a collective workshop to investigate how cinema communicates both directly and subliminally. He and his colleagues were deeply committed to presenting everyday truths rather than distracting fictions. Yet Soviet filmmakers recognized that cinema is not a transparent image of the world but one that elicits different ideas and responses according to how images are structured and edited. Thus they developed a montage aesthetic suited to the modern world into which the Soviet people were being catapulted. In the spirit of these theories, Vertov's creative documentary *The Man with the Movie Camera* (1929) records not only the activity of the modern city but also how its energy is transformed by the camera recording it. Moving rapidly from one subject to another; using split screens, superimpositions, and variable film speeds; and continually placing the camera within the action, this movie does more than describe or narrate the city. It introduces the viewer to the movement and power of a dynamic community (see Chapter 5, pp. 140–141, and Chapter 8, pp. 296–298).

Although Soviet cinema at this time produced many exceptional films, Sergei Eisenstein's *The Battleship Potemkin* (1925) quickly became the most renowned film outside the U.S.S.R. In one sense his film is a document about the uprising of oppressed sailors on the ship that heralded the coming revolution; however, its elevated place in film history derives from its brilliant demonstration of how conflicting or unrelated images can be linked together, using what Eisenstein called **dialectical montage**, to generate an emotional, intellectual, and political understanding of the real events. In the powerful Odessa steps sequence analyzed in Chapter 5, images alternate tensely between the descending soldiers and the ascending protesters; the action itself describes a horrible massacre, but the construction and editing of the images also work to provoke outrage in the viewer. The film's extraordinary international and critical success enabled Eisenstein to travel throughout Europe, and in 1930, he arrived in Hollywood—with a contract from Paramount Studios that was quickly terminated. Invited by painter Diego Rivera, he began shooting an ambitious project in Mexico. When his sponsors cut off his funds, Eisenstein returned to the Soviet Union, where, under Joseph Stalin, socialist realism had become the official program in filmmaking. Consequently, the careers of Eisenstein and the other major experimental filmmakers of the revolutionary period suffered.

German Expressionistic Cinema

During the early decades of film history, **German expressionist cinema** (1918–1929) also detoured the movies from their realist drive, with aims to (1) concentrate on the dark fringes of human experience, and (2) represent irrational forces through lighting, set, and costume design.

Like the *film d'art* movement in France (1908–1912), German cinema first distinguished itself through imaginative interpretations of literature, such as theater director Max Reinhardt's adaptation of Hugo von Hofmannsthal's *The Strange Girl* (1913). After a national film industry was centralized toward the end of World War I, German films made under the postwar Weimar Republic began to compete successfully with Hollywood cinema. The most prominent achievements of the giant Universal Film AG, or UFA, studios exemplified the expressionist movements. Expressionism (in film, theater, painting, and the other arts) turned away from realist representation and toward the unconscious and irrational sides of human experience.

12.3 *The Cabinet of Dr. Caligari* (1919). Expressionist sets make this one of the most visually striking films in history.

Weimar-era cinema differed from Hollywood models in that it successfully integrated a commitment to artistic expression into a nationalized industry. The most famous achievement of the expressionist trend in film history is Robert Wiene's *The Cabinet of Dr. Caligari* (1919), a dreamlike story of a somnambulist who, in the service of a mad tyrant, stalks innocent victims [Figure 12.3]. Along with its story of obsessed and troubled individuals, the film's shadowy atmosphere and strangely distorted artificial sets became trademarks of German expressionist cinema. The two most important Weimar-era filmmakers are Fritz Lang, director of *Dr. Mabuse: The Gambler* (1922), *Metropolis* (1926–1927), and *M* (1931), and F. W. Murnau, director of *Nosferatu: A Symphony of Horror* (1922) and *The Last Laugh* (1924). In *Nosferatu,* Murnau re-creates the vampire legend within a naturalistic setting, one that lighting, camera angles, and other expressive techniques infuse with a supernatural anxiety. In his much more realistic *The Last Laugh,* Murnau nonetheless uses a dramatically subjective camera to disturb realism. Camera pans, tilts, and other innovative movements express the subjective horror of an aging doorman who loses his job and sees a hostile world collapsing around him. Other notable *street films*—so called for their exterior urban settings—are G. W. Pabst's *The Joyless Street* (1925) and Josef von Sternberg's *The Blue Angel* (1930). In both, the grim realities of the streets become excessive, morbid, and emotionally twisted. In the early sound film *The Blue Angel,* simultaneously filmed in German, French, and English versions, Marlene Dietrich plays her breakthrough role as a cabaret singer who seduces an aging professor. His decadent decline under her erotic spell plays out the grim and seedy brilliance of German expressionism. During the rise of Nazism, much of the Weimar cinema's creative personnel emigrated to the United States, where they introduced expressionist formal elements and moral ambiguities to such Hollywood films as Fritz Lang's *The Woman in the Window* (1944).

French Impressionist Cinema and Poetic Realism

Among the many remarkable periods in French cinema history, the one extending from French impressionist cinema through French poetic realism (1920–1939) is among the richest. In the beginning of this period, directors conducted radical experiments with film form. As in contemporaneous visual arts like impressionist painting, **French impressionist cinema** destabilized familiar or objective ways of seeing and revitalized the dynamics of human perception.

Representative of the early impressionist films are Germaine Dulac's *The Seashell and the Clergyman* (1928), Jean Epstein's *The Fall of the House of Usher* (1928), Marcel L'Herbier's *L'Argent* (1929), and Abel Gance's three daring narrative films, *I Accuse* (1919), *The Wheel* (1923), and *Napoléon* (1927). Dulac's surrealist film illustrates the daring play between subject matter and form that these films deploy. Scripted by avant-garde writer Antonin Artaud, *The Seashell and the Clergyman* barely has a story: a priest pursues a beautiful woman. Instead, it concentrates on the consciousness of the central character, who remembers, hallucinates, and fantasizes within a dream logic of split screens and other strange imagistic effects [**Figure 12.4**]. Also linked to this movement (see p. 323) are Spanish-born director Luis Buñuel's famous avant-garde collaboration with surrealist painter Salvador Dali, *Un chien andalou* (*An Andalusian Dog*) (1928), and the films of Jean Cocteau, such as *The Blood of a Poet* (1930).

Developing out of these avant-garde films in the 1930s are the more narrative and commercial examples of poetic realism by such directors as René Clair, Jean Vigo, Marcel Carné, and Jean Renoir. These directors integrated poetic innovations into traditional movie realism to unsettle perceptions in a way that exhibits a socially conscious perspective. These filmmakers and their films brought the perceptual freedoms of the avant-garde to a realistic narrative field in which the aesthetics of seeing informed the politics of living.

One film, Renoir's *The Rules of the Game* (1939) [**Figure 12.5**], deserves special mention as one of the most applauded films in history. Like Renoir's *The Grand Illusion* (1937), discussed in Chapter 4, *The Rules of the Game* appears to be a realistic account of social conflict and disintegration. A tale of aristocrats and their servants gathered for a holiday in the country, the film is a satirical and often biting critique of the social hypocrisy and brutality of this microcosm of decadent society. The film's insight and wit come from lighting, long takes, and framing that draw out dark ironies not visible on the surface of the relationships. One of the film's most noted sequences features a hunting expedition in which the editing searingly equates the slaughter of birds and rabbits with the social behavior of the hunters toward each other.

To see such films in terms of their cultural and national context means viewing them somewhat differently than we view Hollywood films. For instance, Jean

12.4 *The Seashell and the Clergyman* (1928). In a surreal image from Germaine Dulac's film, the main character sees his own head in the seashell.

12.5 *The Rules of the Game* (1939). Jean Renoir's masterwork of French cinema is known for its fluid style and social critique.

Vigo's *Zero for Conduct* (1933) takes up the themes of rebellion and social critique by depicting tyranny at a boys' boarding school. The spirit of rebellion in the boys is conveyed in a combination of realistic narrative and lyrical, sometimes fantastical, images. These images dramatize the wild and anarchistic vision of the young boys: at one point a pillow fight erupts in the dormitory, and the subsequent whirlwind of pillow feathers transforms the room into a paradise of disorder.

In the first decades of the twentieth century, film flourished around the globe, keeping pace with the accelerated sense of time and the contracted feeling of space particular to modernity. Recent inquiries have begun to fill in film histories centered in countries whose cinematic influence later declined. For example, Scandinavian cinema played an important role in advancing the international language of cinema before World War I, and the golden age of Chinese cinema occurred in 1930s Shanghai [**Figure 12.6**]. Both of these cinemas flourished in favorable economic situations; they declined because of such geopolitical events as war and revolution. As a result, Hollywood's dominance became firmly established.

12.6 *The Goddess* (1934). One of China's most popular actresses of the period, Ruan Lingyu, stars in this affecting melodrama.

Film History after World War II

Choosing World War II to divide our global film history makes historical sense. The war marks the virtual midpoint of the century, and it reshaped world geography and politics. It also makes cultural sense because in the wake of the conflict, filmmaking changed dramatically.

Italian Neorealism

The relatively short history of **Italian neorealism** (1942–1952) does not adequately suggest its profound historical impact. At a critical juncture of world history, Italian cinema revitalized film culture by (1) depicting postwar social crises, and (2) using a stark, realistic style clearly different from the glossy entertainment formulas of Hollywood and other studio systems.

Earlier in the century, Italian film spectacles such as *Quo Vadis?* (1912) and *Cabiria* (1914) had created a taste for lavish epics, and the films produced at the Cinecittá ("cinema city") studios under the fascist regime were glossy, decorative entertainments. In 1942, screenwriter Cesare Zavattini called for a new cinema that would forsake entertainment formulas and promote social realism instead. Luchino Visconti responded with *Ossessione* (1943), and Vittorio De Sica directed Zavattini's screenplays in such classics as *Bicycle Thieves* (1948). Perhaps the best example of the accomplishments and contradictions of this movement is Roberto Rossellini's *Rome, Open City* (1945), shot under adverse conditions at the end of the war [**Figure 12.7**]. Set during the Nazi occupation of Rome (1943–1944), the film intentionally approximates newsreel images of the strained and desperate street life of the war-torn city. The plot likewise employs the harsh reality of life in

▶ **VIEWING CUE**

Find a film festival program on the Web, and describe its range of programming. What countries are represented? What does your knowledge of the cinemas of those countries lead you to expect?

12.7 *Rome, Open City* (1945). Roberto Rossellini's film exemplifies Italian neorealism in its use of war-ravaged locations.

the city, as it tells of a community trying to protect a resistance fighter being hunted by the German S.S. and of the tragic deaths of those caught in between. One of its most shocking scenes shows the torture of one of these individuals. Despite the melodrama of its plot about lovers and families torn apart, the grim realism of *Rome, Open City* sounded a note that reverberated through postwar movie cultures, from the later work of Italian director Pier Paolo Pasolini through realist movements of the 1950s and 1960s, including the films of Senegalese director Ousmane Sembène (discussed later in this chapter). Subsequent Italian cinema—including the work of directors Michelangelo Antonioni, Vittorio and Paolo Taviani, Marco Bellocchio, Bernardo Bertolucci, and even Federico Fellini—follows from this neorealist history even when it introduces new forms and subjects.

European New Wave Cinemas: France and Germany

Significantly influenced by Italian neorealism, a particularly rich period of cinema history occurs from the 1950s through the 1970s, when numerous daring film movements, often designated as "new-wave cinema," appeared in such countries as Brazil, Czechoslovakia, England, France, Germany, and Japan, among others. Despite their exceptional variety, these different new waves share two common postwar interests that counterpoint their often nationalistic flavor: (1) a break with past filmmaking institutions and genres and (2) the use of film to express a personal vision.

The first and most influential new-wave cinema was the **French New Wave**, whose filmmakers came to prominence between 1945 and 1960 and were inspired by Italian neorealism. Following the momentum created in the 1950s with an exceptionally rich variety of films from such diverse French filmmakers as Robert Bresson and Jacques Tati, the year 1959 brought three definitive films: Jean-Luc Godard's *Breathless,* François Truffaut's *The 400 Blows,* and Alain Resnais's *Hiroshima, Mon Amour.* Although the style and subject matter of these films are extremely different, they each describe (1) the struggle for personal expression, and (2) the investigation of film form as a communication system.

The vitality of these films made a break with the past and an immediate impact on international audiences. Indeed, this vitality was often expressed in memorable stylistic innovations, such as the freeze frame on the boy protagonist's face that ends *The 400 Blows,* the jump cuts that register the restlessness of the antihero of *Breathless,* and the time-traveling editing of *Hiroshima, Mon Amour.*

Much of the inspiration for the French New Wave filmmakers sprang from the work of film critic and theoretician André Bazin. In 1951, Bazin helped establish the journal *Cahiers du cinéma,* a forum from which emerged some of the most renowned directors of the movement, including Eric Rohmer and Claude Chabrol [**Figure 12.8**] as well as François Truffaut and Jean-Luc Godard. The revitalization of film language occurred in conjunction with the journal's policy of auteurism, which emphasized the role of the director as an expressive author. Writing and directing their own films, paying tribute to the important figures emerging in other national cinemas—like Michelangelo Antonioni, Ingmar Bergman, and Akira Kurosawa—and rediscovering the work of Hollywood directors newly dubbed "auteurs," the young French filmmaker-critics helped shape the perspective and culture that elevated film to the art form it is today.

12.8   Claude Chabrol, 1980. Along with François Truffaut, Jean-Luc Godard, and Eric Rohmer, Claude Chabrol was both a critic for *Cahiers du cinéma* and one of the directors associated with the rise of the French New Wave. He has made more than forty films, many of them thrillers influenced by Alfred Hitchcock, about whom he and Rohmer published a book in 1957.

Of comparable international reputation to the French New Wave, **New German cinema** was launched in 1962, when a group of young filmmakers declared a new agenda for German film in a film festival document called the Oberhausen Manifesto. By 1982, when the movement's most celebrated and prolific director Rainer Werner Fassbinder died of a drug overdose, the movement's momentum was dispersing. In the interim, a unique mix of government subsidies and international critical acclaim, together with domestic television and worldwide film festival exposure, established New German cinema as an integral product of West Germany's national culture.

This extraordinarily vital and stylistically diverse cinema can nevertheless be characterized by (1) a confrontation with Germany's Nazi and postwar past, approached directly or through an examination of the current political and cultural climate, and (2) an emphasis on the distinctive, often maverick, visions of individual directors.

Alexander Kluge, one of the political founders of New German cinema, uses modernist film practices to question the interpretation of history in *Yesterday Girl* (1966). Fassbinder's varied body of work includes a trilogy of films about postwar Germany. In the first, *The Marriage of Maria Braun* (1979), he adapts the Hollywood melodrama to tell of a soldier's widow who builds a fortune in the aftermath of the war. Helma Sanders-Brahms takes an autobiographical approach to the World War II period in *Germany, Pale Mother* (1979). By 1984, Edgar Reitz's sixteen-hour television series *Heimat,* in part a response to the American television miniseries *Holocaust,* demonstrated that the cultural silence about the Nazi era had definitively been broken.

In the collective project *Germany in Autumn* (1978), nine filmmakers, including Kluge, Reitz, and Fassbinder, responded to the divisive events of their own historical moment, notably the deaths in prison of members of the leftist terrorist group Baader-Meinhof, which had become a symbol of political unrest. The story of one of its leaders, Ulrike Meinhof, was fictionalized in *Die Bleierne Zeit* (*Marianne and Juliane*, 1981) The film's director, Margarethe von Trotta, was one of many women active in New German cinema [**Figure 12.9**]. However, these women tended to receive less international attention than did their male counterparts.

Other filmmakers responded to the social movements of the period. Helke Sander's feminist film *Redupers: The All-Around Reduced Personality* (1978) deals with the challenges in the life of a single mother and socially committed photographer—a woman like the filmmaker—in the context of a divided Berlin. Radical gay filmmaker Rosa von Praunheim's prolific output includes the early activist documentary *It Is Not the Homosexual Who Is Perverse, but the Society in Which He Lives* (1970). While Fassbinder's several gay-themed films might share this social diagnosis, their stories are much more pessimistic. Internationally, gay German cinema made a mark when Frank Ripploh's *Taxi Zum Klo* (1981) became an unexpected hit.

On the international stage, however, the hallmark of New German cinema was less its depiction of historical, political, and social questions than the distinctive personae and filmic visions of its most celebrated participants. Wim Wenders's films, including *Alice in the Cities* (1974) and *Wings of Desire* (1987), are philosophical

12.9   **Margarethe von Trotta**. One of the many women directors who revitalized contemporary German cinema.

reflections on the nature of the cinematic image and the encounter between Europe and the United States. Werner Herzog's *Aguirre: The Wrath of God* (1973) and *Fitzcarraldo* (1982) are bold depictions of extreme cultural encounters set in Latin American jungles. Hans-Jürgen Syberberg produced extravagantly anti-naturalist historical epics such as *Ludwig: Requiem for a Virgin King* (1972) and the six-hour *Hitler: A Film from Germany* (1977). Literary adaptations like Volker Schlöndorff's *The Tin Drum* (1979) helped elevate the cultural status of film, as did the concept of *Autorenfilm,* or "author's cinema," that was used to market these filmmakers' work as artistically significant. The visionary Wenders, the driven Herzog (whose monomania is presented in the 1982 documentary *Burden of Dreams*), and the enormously productive, despotic, and hard-living Fassbinder were easily packaged as auteurs with outsized personalities. Several of the most successful directors began to work abroad; with wider social shifts and changes in cultural policy in Germany, the heyday of new German cinema came to an end. In reunified Germany, where many of these filmmakers continue to work, interesting new directions are indicated by Tom Tykwer's international hit, *Run, Lola, Run* (1998), Fatih Akin's films exploring Turkish-German culture, including *Edge of Heaven* (2007), and Florian Henckel von Donnersmarck's Academy Award–winning *The Lives of Others* (2006), set in the former East Germany.

▶ **VIEWING CUE**

View an important film from a national cinema that you know little about. Would knowing the cultural context help you better understand the film? Does the film speak to members of that culture, to outsiders, or to both? ⏸

Postwar Cinemas outside Europe: Japan and India

In the 1950s, a new consciousness of film's role in national and cultural life, along with the great changes and challenges wrought by World War II and its aftermath, breathed vitality into cinemas globally. Long-established non-Western cinemas came to the forefront at European festivals through the works of significant auteurs. *Japanese cinema*, which has a long and varied tradition characterized by a greater output of feature films than most Western countries, has used distinct perceptual and narrative forms. Even though many Japanese films increasingly incorporated Hollywood forms and styles after World War II, these films tend to (1) allow character rather than action to be the center of a narrative and (2) emphasize the contemplative aspect of images.

Kenji Mizoguchi, Yasujiro Ozu, Akira Kurosawa, Nagisa Oshima, and Juzo Itami are among the most celebrated names in Japanese cinema. Ozu's distinguished career began even before the coming of sound. By the time he made his midcareer masterpiece, *Tokyo Story* (1953), his exquisite sense of the rhythms of everyday life emerged in a distinctive style, conveyed through carefully composed frames, long takes, and a low camera [**Figure 12.10**]. The energies of postwar cinema are especially evident in Kurosawa's *Rashomon* (1950), which uses multiple, contradictory narrations of the same event. The film won the top prize at the Venice Film Festival, the oldest international festival, thereby marking Kurosawa and Japanese cinema in general as part of the emerging international postwar art cinema. Oshima helped define Japan's new wave with the violence and sexuality of his controversial *In the Realm of the Senses* (1976) [**Figure 12.11**]. Itami's *Tampopo* (1985) cannily bridges the culturally specific and the culturally shared with its depiction of the pleasures of noodle eating. Finally, one of the most widespread influences on contemporary transnational cinema today is *anime*, Japanese animation. The distinctive style and

12.10 *Tokyo Story* (1953). Carefully composed images suggest the rhythms of everyday life.

complex plots of such anime as *Ghost in the Shell* (1996) and *Ghost in the Shell 2: Innocence* (2004) have won worldwide audiences and influenced Hollywood productions.

Indian cinema provides a good case study in film historiography because it can be recorded in at least two different ways. A perspective that looks mainly at critically prized films with a presence on the world stage would focus on the work of the most acclaimed Indian director, Satyajit Ray. His modest black-and-white film *Pather Panchali* (1955) has been heralded internationally as a masterpiece of realist style. This film, together with the two subsequent features in the "Apu trilogy" (named after their main character), is rooted in Bengali landscape and culture. Yet the strong stamp of the individual artist's vision urges that Ray, like Bergman or Kurosawa, be viewed as unique, rather than as a representative of Indian national cinema. This is an example of how the conventional historical model of masterpieces and unique individuals can be used to talk about film histories outside of Hollywood.

Approached as a national popular cinema, Indian cinema is the most prolific film industry in the world, dominating the domestic box office and accounting for almost 75 percent of the movie attendance in the Asia-Pacific region. Since the 1950s, Bombay (now Mumbai) studios have produced hundreds of Hindi-language melodramas annually. Although they represent only one part of Indian cinema and do not account for the many regional cinemas in India, *Bollywood* films, as they are often referred to, are a dominant cultural form notable for (1) rootedness in Hindu culture and mythology, and (2) elaborate song-and-dance numbers erupting in almost any genre.

With an episodic narrative form based in theatrical traditions that accommodate musical numbers, many Hindi films highlight star performances. Nargis plays the title role of Mehboob Khan's *Mother India* (1957) [Figure 12.12]; the phenomenally successful action star Amitabh Bachchan was featured in the most popular Bollywood film of all time, *Sholay* (1975) [Figure 12.13]; and

12.11   *In the Realm of the Senses* (1976). Widely regarded as an erotic masterpiece, Nagisa Oshima's film was censored in the United States and Japan.

12.12   *Mother India* (1957). Nargis in the iconic role of a mother who withstands hardship and becomes an allegorical figure of an independent India.

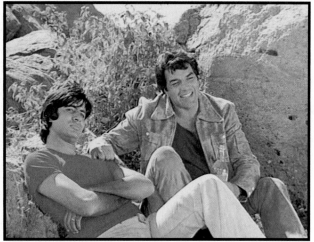

12.13   *Sholay* (1975). Amitabh Bachchan stars in the most popular Bollywood film of all time.

12.14 *Lagaan: Once Upon a Time in India* (2001). This epic centering on a cricket match between Indian villagers and their colonizers was a crossover success with non-Asian audiences.

Shahrukh Khan attracts audiences to such contemporary hits as *Dilwale Dulhania Le Jayenge* (1995). Not only are these and other stars massively popular in India, but they are also well known in Africa, the Middle East, and Southeast Asia and among South Asian audiences in the United Kingdom, Canada, the United States, and other parts of the world. Playback singers, who prerecord the songs that the film stars lip-sync, and music directors such as A. R. Rahman also enjoy celebrity status. The film *Lagaan: Once Upon a Time in India* (2001) [**Figure 12.14**] capitalized on the huge international popular base of Indian cinema to bid for attention from more mainstream art-house critics and audiences in the United States and the United Kingdom. The transnational dimension of Indian film can increasingly be seen in movies directed by filmmakers of the diaspora (that is, people scattered outside their homeland). For example, Gurinda Chadha's *Bride and Prejudice* (2004), an adaptation (with musical numbers), of Jane Austen's *Pride and Prejudice*, and Mira Nair's award-winning *Monsoon Wedding* (2001) employ many of the visual and narrative tropes of Bollywood cinema.

Third Cinema: Latin America and Cuba

The growing influence of film festivals in the decades after World War II helped foster film art and commerce internationally. In addition, another aspect of global film culture emerged in the politicized atmosphere of Third World decolonization in the 1960s. Manifestos such as "Towards a Third Cinema," written by Argentine filmmakers Fernando Solanas and Octavio Getino in 1969, championed revolutionary films in opposition to Hollywood and to state-dominated film cultures elsewhere (which they dubbed "first cinema") and in response to the sterile aesthetics of auteurist art cinema ("second cinema"). A term coined to echo "Third World," **third cinema** united films from many countries under one rubric, including some made by Europeans, such as *The Battle of Algiers* (1966), directed by Italian Marxist Gillo Pontecorvo in cooperation with the victorious Algerian revolutionary government. In Latin America, Solanas and Getino's *The Hour of the Furnaces* (1968) incited political opposition and cultural renewal in Argentina, and *Black God, White Devil* (1964) by prominent Brazilian *cinema novo* director Glauber Rocha embraced cultural diversity and violence. Third cinema aimed to (1) reject technical perfection in opposition to commercial traditions and (2) embrace film as the voice of the people.

These goals often entailed combining modernist techniques drawn from Soviet montage and from filmmakers like Jean-Luc Godard—such as fragmented formal structures and analytical voiceovers—with populist documentary subject matter and traditions. The creation of the film institute ICAIC (Instituto Cubano del Arte e Industria Cinematográficos, or Cuban Institute of Cinematographic Art and Industry) in postrevolutionary Cuba provided the ideal testing ground for integrating film with an emerging nation's cultural identity. Tomás Gutiérrez Alea's *Memories of Underdevelopment* (1968) is one of the best-known examples of third cinema. Its story of a middle-class intellectual contemplating the changes in postrevolutionary society is innovatively filmed and politically engaged [**Figure 12.15**].

As we have emphasized, World War II changed political, economic, and cultural history, and the cinema played an important role in the geopolitics of the

▶ **VIEWING CUE**

Compare a Western and a non-Western film. What differences exist in the narrative or visual elements?

Cold War and beyond. Many nations set up state-run or subsidized film industries to foster domestic production in the face of U.S. imports, thereby promoting serious film art or promulgating state ideology. Communist countries produced and exchanged sanctioned films, while hybrids such as *spaghetti westerns*, 1960s Italian films that breathed new life into a genre that had been exclusively American, testified to the cultural collisions in free-market nations.

Contemporary Global Cinema: Africa, China, and Iran

The contemporary post–Cold War context of globalization, which describes the movement of finance, information, commodities, and people across international lines, is characterized by an interdependent world film culture and the aesthetic and economic emergence of a range of new national and regional cinemas. Three such cinemas have attracted particular attention from critics and scholars: African, Chinese, and Iranian.

12.15 *Memories of Underdevelopment* (1968). With its political concept of third cinema, this Cuban film is linked to films from Latin America, Africa, and Asia.

African cinema encompasses an entire continent and, hence, many nations, languages, styles of government, and levels of economic development. An initial distinction can be made between the Arabic-language cinema of North Africa and the sub-Saharan African cinema. The *North African cinema* has a long history, beginning with the Egyptian premiere of the Lumières' Cinématographe in 1896. After the introduction of sound, a commercial industry developed in Egypt that still dominates the movie screens of Arab countries today. Youssef Chahine, working both in popular genres and on more political and personal projects (in which he sometimes appeared), was a cosmopolitan presence in Egyptian cinema from the 1950s to the present. His filmed autobiographical trilogy, beginning with *Alexandria . . . Why?* (1978), is notable for its humor, its frank approach to sexuality, and its inventive structure. In recent Tunisian production, art films predominate, several of which are directed by and/or tell the stories of women. Moufida Tlatli's *The Silences of the Palace* (1994) opens in the postindependence period and follows a young woman singer as she remembers her girlhood as a palace servant.

Taking shape in the 1960s after decolonization, and often linked to third cinema, *sub-Saharan African cinema* encompasses the relatively well-financed francophone, or French-language, cinema of West Africa; films from a range of anglophone, or English-speaking, countries; and films in African languages such as Wolof and Swahili. Although it is difficult to generalize about this rapidly expanding film culture, some of its most influential features and shorts have been united by (1) a focus on social and political themes rather than commercial interests, and (2) an exploration of the conflicts between tradition and modernity.

At the forefront of this vital development is the most respected proponent of African cinema, Senegalese filmmaker Ousmane Sembène, who in 1966 directed sub-Saharan Africa's first feature film, *La noire de . . .* (*Black Girl*), with extremely limited technical and financial resources. Already recognized as a novelist, Sembène realized that he could reach more of Senegal's predominantly illiterate population through cinema. Although he made only eight features before his death in 2007, each of Sembène's films is remarkable for its moral vision, accessible storytelling, and range of characters who represent aspects of traditional and modern African life without becoming two-dimensional symbols.

12.16 *Black Girl* (1966).
Simple long shots depict the young woman's sense of entrapment and alienation.

Black Girl follows a young woman who travels from Dakar, Senegal, to Monte Carlo to work with a white family as a nanny but soon becomes disillusioned and feels trapped in the home, cooking and cleaning. Her French voiceover records her increasing despair. Simply composed long shots depict her as enclosed and restricted by her surroundings. Her alienation is also illustrated by the traditional African mask hanging on the wall [**Figure 12.16**]. A brief newspaper item recording the suicide of just such an immigrant woman was Sembène's impetus to make the film.

Decades later, Sembène featured another female protagonist in the more affirmative *Faat Kiné* (2000). The film's heroine is a vibrant, outspoken businesswoman with children on the verge of adulthood. Her perspectives on sex, economics, family, and male inadequacy are practical and funny. The service station she runs becomes a metaphor of cultural resilience and connectedness in a film whose leisurely pace establishes an alternative to plot-driven narratives. Sembene's final feature, *Moolaadé* (2004), took on the controversial issue of female genital cutting.

As noted earlier, francophone cinema (sometimes financed in part by France) is responsible for the great majority of sub-Saharan filmmaking. Internationally known filmmakers include Souleymane Cissé (*Yeelen*, 1987; *Finye*, 1982) and Abderrahmane Sissako (*Life on Earth*, 1998; *Bamako*, 2006) from Mali and Idrissa Ouedraogo (*Tilai*, 1990) from Burkina Faso. Yet filmmakers are emerging all over the continent—in Ghana, Congo, Zimbabwe, and South Africa. Nigeria is known for popular genre films shot on digital video; the industry, known as *Nollywood*, is driven by the hunger of audiences for images of themselves and their lives.

A number of filmmakers outside Africa bring African motifs and themes to their work, creating a distinctive cinema of the diaspora. Ethiopian-born filmmaker Haile Gerima's U.S.-made *Sankofa* (1993) deals with the legacy of chattel slavery through the story of a contemporary African American woman whose visit to Africa prompts a travel back in time. With *Lumumba* (2001), Haitian filmmaker Raoul Peck produced a searing biographical film about Congo leader Patrice Lumumba, who was assassinated in 1961 [**Figure 12.17**].

One of the biggest hurdles to the development of cinema in Africa is not only the lack of financial and technical resources for film production but also the lack of distribution and exhibition infrastructure that would enable African audiences to see African-made films. The Pan-African Film and Television Festival of Ouagadougou (also known as FESPACO) in Burkina Faso is vital in this context. Filmmakers from all over the continent and the African diaspora meet at the festival, view each other's work, and strategize about how to extend the cinema's popular influence. Each edition of the festival launches a variety of new and promising films such as 2007's best feature, *Ezra*, a French-Nigerian co-production by Newton Aduaka, and Djamila Sahraoui's *Barakat* (2006), a French-Algerian co-production that won best first film the same year.

Chinese cinema poses its own challenge to models of national cinema because it includes films from the "three Chinas"—mainland China, Hong Kong, and Taiwan. Each of these areas developed under a different social and political regime and differs greatly in terms of its commercial structure, the role of government oversight, audience expectations, and even language. Yet they are all culturally united and increasingly economically interdependent. In mainland China after the 1949 Communist Revolution, cinema production was strictly limited to propaganda purposes. It was further disrupted during the Cultural Revolution in the 1960s, when leader Mao Zedong referred to American films as "sugar-coated bullets." It was not until

12.17 *Lumumba* (2001). Raoul Peck's critically acclaimed portrayal of self-taught Congo nationalist Patrice Lumumba.

12.18 *Raise the Red Lantern* (1991). Gong Li became an international art-film star in the films of Fifth Generation Chinese director Zhang Yimou.

the 1980s that a group of filmmakers emerged who were interested both in the formal potential of the medium and in critical social content. The renaissance was led by the so-called *Fifth Generation* filmmakers, who entered the recently reopened Beijing Film Academy in the same class. The enthusiastic reception given *Huang tu di* (*Yellow Earth,* 1984) at international film festivals made director Chen Kaige and cinematographer Zhang Yimou the most acclaimed filmmakers of the movement. *Yellow Earth* and other Fifth Generation films are notable for their (1) austere rural settings observed with an almost ethnographic eye, and (2) metaphorical stories critical of current society.

The strong aesthetic vision of these films, stemming from the filmmakers' experiences growing up as marginalized artists during the Cultural Revolution, made a critical statement in its own right. Essentially art films, this body of work did not reach for China's vast popular audiences. But with Zhang Yimou's turn to directing came a series of lush, sensuous films featuring Gong Li, an unknown actress who later became an international film star. Zhang's films *Ju dou* (1990) and *Raise the Red Lantern* (1991) **[Figure 12.18]** were the targets of censorship at home and the recipients of prizes and cofinancing offers abroad. Later forays into *wuxia*, or martial arts films—*Hero* (2002) and *House of Flying Daggers* (2004)—and his participation in the Beijing Olympics in 2008 established Zhang as a commercially successful, breathtaking visual stylist. The so-called *Sixth Generation* of directors from the People's Republic of China explored urban settings and controversial themes such as homosexuality. In *The World* (2006), Jia Zhangke captures the uprooted lives of young employees at a Beijing theme park in heartbreaking, wry compositions.

After the phenomenal international success of low-budget Hong Kong kung-fu films in the 1970s, the *Hong Kong new wave* led by producer-director Tsui Hark introduced sophisticated style, lucrative production methods, and a canny use of Western elements to the genre. Director John Woo became internationally known for his technical expertise and visceral editing of violent action films such as *The Killer* (1998). Along with legendary stunt star Jackie Chan, featured in the *Rush Hour* series (1998, 2001), Woo brought the Hong Kong style to Hollywood in such films as *Face/Off* (1997) **[Figure 12.19]**.

12.19 *Face/Off* (1997). Director John Woo successfully marries Hollywood and Hong Kong style in this thrilling action movie.

The more avant-garde work of Wong Kar-wai made an impact with its quirky stories of marginal figures moving through a postmodern, urban world, photographed and edited in an utterly distinctive style that finds beauty in the accidental and the momentary. *Happy Together* (1997) is the ironic title of a tale of two men drifting in and out of a relationship, set in a Buenos Aires that is not so different, in its urban anomie, from the men's home of Hong Kong. Wong's *In the Mood for Love* (2000) is set in the 1960s among cosmopolitan former residents of Shanghai, who are trying to establish a pattern of life in Hong Kong [**Figure 12.20**]. Contemplative family sagas by acclaimed auteurs, such as Hou Hsiao-hsien's *City of Sadness* (1989) and Edward Yang's *Yi yi* (2000), reflect on the identity of contemporary Taiwan, positioned between mainland China, where much of its population comes from, and the West.

While many Chinese films have achieved strong commercial as well as critical success internationally, *Iranian cinema* is notable for its many festival prizes and critical acclaim. The art films of this Islamic nation are characterized by (1) spare pictorial beauty, often of landscapes or scenes of everyday life on the margins, and (2) an elliptical storytelling mode developed in response to state regulation.

Interestingly, this influential national cinema grew up in a country where, following the 1978 Islamic Revolution, the cinema was attacked as a corrupt Western influence and movie theaters were closed. But by the 1990s, under a more moderate regime, both a popular cinema and a distinctive artistic film culture developed. The latter came to be seen as a way of enhancing Iran's international reputation. Films by such directors as Abbas Kiarostami and Mohsen Makhmalbaf became the most admired and accessible expressions of contemporary Iranian culture as well as some of the most highly praised examples of global cinema. In Kiarostami's *A Taste of Cherry* (1997), beautiful, barren landscapes are the settings for wandering characters' existential conversations [**Figure 12.21**]. Jafar Panahi's popular *The White Balloon* (1995) depicts a little girl's search for a goldfish. Rural settings and child protagonists helped filmmakers avoid the censorship from religious leaders that contemporary social themes would attract. These strategies also evaded strictures forbidding adult male and female characters from touching—a compromise that at least avoided offering a distorted picture of domestic and romantic life. More recently, however, filmmakers have used the international approval accorded Iranian films to tackle volatile social issues such as drugs and prostitution in portrayals of contemporary urban life, and they have tested the limits of the government's tolerance. Panahi's *The Circle* (2000), banned in Iran,

12.20 *In the Mood for Love* (2000). In this film by Wong Kar-wai, stylish characters make chance connections amid the urban alienation of Hong Kong.

12.21 *A Taste of Cherry* (1997). Abbas Kiarostami's rural settings avoid direct depictions of social problems and help his films avoid censorship by religious leaders.

focuses on the plight of women, some of whom find prison a refuge; Makhmalbaf's *Kandahar* (2000) depicts the situation of neighboring Afghanistan just before that country became the focus of international attention and the target of a U.S.-led military campaign [Figure 12.22].

One of the most interesting apparent contradictions in Iranian cinema is the prominence of women filmmakers. Strict religious decrees require female characters to keep their heads covered and forbid a range of onscreen behaviors including singing. Nevertheless, behind the camera many Iranian women filmmakers—such as Tahmineh

12.22   *Kandahar* (2000). Makhmalbaf's film explores the volatile social issues in Afghanistan just prior to the U.S.-led military campaign there.

Milani, who was arrested for her film *The Hidden Half* (2001), and Samira Makhmalbaf (daughter of Mohsen Makhmalbaf), whose first feature film *The Apple* (1998) was made when she was only eighteen, have achieved more than their contemporaries in many Western countries. Similar themes are more explicitly treated in the French animated film *Persepolis* (2007) by Vincent Paronnaud and Marjane Satrapi, based on the latter's graphic novel about her girlhood in Iran.

In each of these emergent cinemas, national identities are in the process of being defined in relation to postcolonial and postrevolutionary realities. Cinema serves an important role in shaping such definitions because of the strong appeal of its images and narratives. A global perspective looks at cinema in the context of multiple and overlapping political and cultural histories. At the same time, it emphasizes film history's role in constructing identity both within and outside a culture.

It has been impossible to be fully inclusive in this survey of global film history. We have selected examples of unique contributions and important trends, although the national cinemas of Argentina, Canada, Korea, Hungary, the Netherlands, and many other countries deserve much more attention than can be provided here. New cinemas regularly leap to prominence on the global scene, and the economy of global film production and distribution reinforces the tendency toward international coproductions that join personnel and entities from different countries to make films. By focusing on national or regional cinemas, we have also overlooked individuals who do not easily fit within certain national cinemas, who work in exile, or who may work in a country whose cinema lacks a distinctive global presence. This has been the case from early in film history, when Danish director Carl Theodor Dreyer made his extraordinary *The Passion of Joan of Arc* (1928) in France [Figure 12.23], to the postwar art cinema, which featured such unique auteurs as Ingmar Bergman (Sweden) and Luis Buñuel (Spain). More recently, directors like Pedro Almodóvar (Spain), Theo Angelopoulos (Greece), Chantal Akerman (Belgium), Kristof Kieslowski (Poland), Manoel de Oliveira (Portugal), Raoul Ruiz (Chile), Lars von Trier and the Dogme 95 directors (Denmark), Apichatpong Weerasethakul (Thailand), and Béla Tarr (Hungary) have helped define a truly global film culture.

text continued on page 424 ▶

► **VIEWING CUE**

Compare at least two films from the same country and film movement (such as Italian neorealism or Hong Kong new wave). Do the characteristics discussed in this chapter apply?

12.23   *The Passion of Joan of Arc* (1928). Carl Theodor Dreyer's striking depiction of the trial of Saint Joan was an early international art-film success.

Global Cinema in *The Apple* (1998)

Modest films from emerging national cinemas can strike outside viewers with their freshness and at the same time reveal their affinity with filmmaking traditions from other periods and countries. The promise of global cinema is exemplified in such discoveries, which reward close attention to their production and audience reception, as well as to their form and subject matter. Samira Makhmalbaf's *The Apple* is among the films that have made recent Iranian cinema such an exciting contribution to world film culture. *The Apple* speaks volumes about the society from which it emerges while telling its specific story simply and directly. It builds a fictional scenario on a real-life situation, recalling the innovations of Italian neorealist cinema in the mid-twentieth century.

The film's protagonists, played by their real-life counterparts, are the twelve-year-old twin girls Zahra and Massoumeh [Figure 12.24], who had been confined by their father and blind mother in their home in Tehran since birth. After neighbors reported the situation, the girls were briefly removed by social services, then returned to their parents. When she saw a report of the situation on the news, eighteen-year-old first-time director Makhmalbaf persuaded her father, one of Iran's most prominent filmmakers, to collaborate with her on a film about the girls. *The Apple* opens with the neighbors' letter to the authorities and with videotape footage taken just before the girls were returned to their home. The remainder of the film is scripted, structured around such simple scenes as a visit from the social worker or from the boy who sells ice cream. But it is shot on location with the actual family, social worker, and neighbors, within days of the girls' return home. The result is an extraordinary account of the girls' emergence into the world and a striking use of documentary techniques within a fictional frame. In the course of the filming, the girls acquire communication skills, delight in running down neighborhood streets (which are themselves walled in), and learn to shop and play. They have their first taste of ice cream. The curious gazes that greet these discoveries include those from the film's audience.

This unique film does share significant characteristics with other Iranian films. It avoids direct political critique by focusing on everyday life and on children. After

12.24   *The Apple* (1998). Eighteen-year-old Iranian director Samira Makhmalbaf's debut film tells the story of two young girls (portraying themselves) who survive abuse.

12.25 *The Apple* (1998). A father is locked in to prevent the confinement of his daughters.

12.26 *The Apple* (1998). The film's haunting final image of the girls' mother.

the girls are returned to their family, their father again locks them up. We see them behind bars from their courtyard. Little boys climb the high walls to peer down at them. The imagery of incarceration is powerful, with the camera confined to the small spaces in front of or behind the gate or in the narrow streets. Finally, the female social worker resorts to locking the father in the home to prevent the girls' confinement. She borrows a saw from a woman in the neighborhood and instructs him to use it if he needs to get out before her return [Figure 12.25]. The film ultimately emerges as a strong indictment of both poverty and the fate of girls and women under Islamic law. Like other Iranian films, *The Apple* employs simple poetic imagery. The girls are given handheld mirrors, and their play with these objects generates metaphors of seeing and discovery as well as interesting camera compositions. Although it is illuminating to discuss *The Apple* in relation to other examples within the artistically coherent Iranian cinema, the film contributes something that has never been seen before in its characters and situation.

Without didactic commentary, *The Apple* strongly argues for women's freedom. The women of the neighborhood speak out about the girls' fate; yet even as they do so, they are largely restricted to their homes, dooryards, and chadors (the garments that cover most of their heads and bodies). The social worker is a figure of strength, repeatedly confronting the girls' father directly. We see Zahra and Massoumeh, physically impaired and almost mute when the film begins, quickly grow more communicative and animated. Their progress is a metaphor for women commanding language and physical space. At the same time, the film's treatment of the parents is extraordinary. The father's cooperation with the project makes it impossible to completely condemn him for his cruelty. Their home is opened up to the camera,

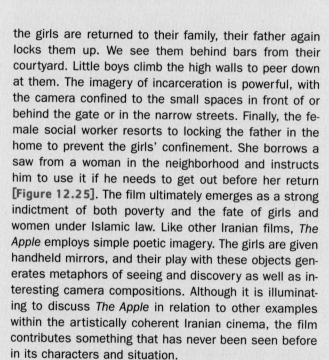

the young female director, and her crew. The portrayal of the mother is the film's most chilling: she keeps to the dark recesses of the home, always wrapped in her chador, often softly muttering and swearing. Without forcing the mother's participation in the film, the director achieves a potent symbol of the distortions that a patriarchal society has inflicted on the lives of this woman and her children.

In the film's final images, the blind mother, covered head to toe in her chador, is taunted by a neighborhood boy who dangles an apple on a string to tempt the girls with a taste of life outside. He bumps the apple against the mother's head and as she extends her hand, the frame freezes [Figure 12.26]. Is she ridding herself of an annoying obstacle in her path or reaching toward an image of freedom? As a contribution to global cinema, the film may seem minor. It is not a commercial film, and it operates not on an explicitly political level but rather as a personal and social tragedy, ultimately imbued with humor and hopefulness. Yet the film's ambiguous status on the borderline between fiction and "real life" is one way in which it suggests the function of cinema as political catalyst. The camera's presence in these girls' lives is not directly acknowledged, but it is decisive. The filmmaker's access to image-making comes through her father; although her films represent her confident voice, in a way her situation mirrors the twins' in their eagerness and determination to begin to explore the world on their own terms. After screening her film at the Cannes Film Festival, Samira Makhmalbaf said she was asked, "What kind of country is Iran? Is it a place where twelve-year-old girls are incarcerated or where eighteen-year-old girls make movies?" Her film shows that this contradiction itself is a part of what makes contemporary Iranian film such a rich contribution to global cinema.

The Lost and Found of American Film History

Lois Weber (1881–1939). One of the most important directors of the silent era.

Maya Deren (1917–1961). Pioneered U.S. experimental film-making in the 1940s.

Ida Lupino (1914–1995). Actress turned independent director, writer, and producer.

Julie Dash (1952–). Pathbreaking independent African American filmmaker.

Mira Nair (1957–). Prominent Indian–American director, writer, and producer.

One important model for studying movie history excavates histories outside the mainstream. This effort can be particularly difficult in the United States given the dominance of the commercial film industry. Tim Burton's movie *Ed Wood* (1994), itself a studio film, is a clever and insightful rediscovery of the story of a filmmaker whose work many would consider rightfully excluded from mainstream history. The film's subject, eccentric director Edward D. Wood Jr., made bad movies with great enthusiasm. A parodic barroom conversation depicts the completely marginal Wood arguing comparable status with acknowledged genius Orson Welles. Yet Wood's importance can be reassessed if we change our framework. In what are now considered cult classics, *Glen or Glenda?* (1953) and *Plan 9 from Outer Space* (1959), his deliberate, sincere imitation of movie genres exposes how preposterous Hollywood conventions can be and illuminates the alternative economics of the exploitation film industry.

Standards of quality are not timeless or universally shared, and divergences may be more than a matter of difference of opinion. Often what is deemed culturally valuable is determined by those who are empowered by a culture. Is it possible to write histories that remove the element of biased selection? One approach to an inclusive history is to try to be as thorough as possible, to strive for objectivity by letting the historical record speak for itself. A random sampling of Hollywood's yearly output will yield a very different chronology than will a history of masterpieces; the former will also tell us something different about the norms of filmmaking. Yet another approach is to excavate the cinematic past in order to uncover devalued contributions and traditions and perhaps discover the unacknowledged antecedents of some of today's diverse film practices. Such corrective film history does not argue that rediscovered films should replace or even be put on a par with previously lauded masterpieces. Rather, a *corrective history* tries to (1) consider different questions about the past and its artifacts and (2) uncover which version of the past has been accepted and supplement this version with missing perspectives.

Debates about criteria of inclusion and exclusion are familiar in literary studies, where the accepted list of essential great works is called the *canon*. Strictly used, the term designates irrefutable church law or scripture. To refer to a film canon gives a cultural weight to the movies, which, as a form of popular entertainment, they rarely attain. Using the term also sets up individual films and filmmakers as authoritative, obscuring the overall experience of cinema—from production to reception. Inclusive histories aim to acknowledge the benefits and drawbacks of evaluative criteria. Excavating film history might mean introducing new films to the canon and thus transforming the values of selection, or it might mean giving up on the idea of selectivity in favor of making strategic arguments. While forgotten works have not had the same influence as those that have never been lost from view, they may be worth studying precisely for the alternative vision of film history they afford. This looking at the past from a disadvantaged point of view, or "history from below," yields insights about how things could have been different.

In the shadow of canonized filmmakers and films, many others have been denied major status despite their significant historical contributions. Of the many important omissions, we will sketch three traditions that are central to a full historical understanding of U.S. movies: a history of women filmmakers, a history of African American cinema, and an introduction to "orphan films," ephemeral or noncommercial films that, despite their lack of traditional cultural value, have survived to yield fascinating glimpses of the past.

The Women Who Made the Movies

The movie industry remains male dominated, with women directing only 7 percent of the 250 top-grossing films in the United States, according to a 2006 study. In independent and experimental filmmaking, access for women is less prohibitive, but their participation is still unequal. And because history so frequently overlooks the significant contribution of women, contemporary women filmmakers have been cut off from an important past. Especially in the early years of a wide-open industry, women entered film history in great numbers as assistants, writers, editors, and actresses and soon turned to directing or producing. Alice Guy Blaché, who made what some consider the first fiction film, *La fée aux choux* (*The Cabbage Fairy*) for Gaumont studios in 1896 in France, set up her own U.S. company and turned out hundreds of films from a New Jersey studio [**Figure 12.27**]. Lois Weber, an actress turned writer, director, and producer, was one of the most important and highly paid American filmmakers in the 1910s, when she was almost as well known as fellow directors Cecil B. DeMille and D. W. Griffith. She directed scores of movies, often on social issues. *Where Are My Children?* (1916), for example, opposed abortion but advocated birth control [**Figure 12.28**]. Nevertheless both Alice Guy Blaché and Lois Weber are excluded from most mainstream histories of the cinema.

Screenwriter Frances Marion got her start with Weber and went on to write screenplays for more than 150 films. She is best known for her partnership with silent-movie star Mary Pickford, who, like another great star of the period, Lillian Gish, also tried directing herself. By the 1920s, as the movies became established in Hollywood as big business, most women who were active in the early U.S. industry encountered difficulties. Only writers and editors continued to work in any notable numbers.

The most prominent and, for a considerable period, the only active female director in sound-era Hollywood was Dorothy Arzner [**Figure 12.29**]. Her films *Christopher Strong* (1933) and *Dance, Girl, Dance* (1940) feature strong heroines

12.27 **Alice Guy Blaché in 1915.** The earliest and most prolific woman director in history has barely been acknowledged in mainstream film histories.

> ### VIEWING CUE
>
> Research a "lost and found" tradition in American cinema. Examples include Latino film, Asian American film, documentary, and exploitation films. In what ways does this particular tradition challenge mainstream film history?

12.28 *Where Are My Children?* (1916). The film by Lois Weber deals with the controversial social issues of birth control.

12.29 **Dorothy Arzner.** Arzner was the only woman to direct Hollywood films in the 1930s, the heyday of the studio system.

12.30 *The Bigamist* (1953). A well-known film star, director Ida Lupino retained her glamour both in front of and behind the camera, while she directed low-budget dramas about contemporary social problems.

played by top stars, and they portray significant bonds between women The next woman to achieve director credit in Hollywood, Ida Lupino, used her prominence as a movie star to help her get started as an independent filmmaker in the 1940s. She directed hard-hitting, low-budget films such as *Hard, Fast and Beautiful* (1951), about a mother who pushes her daughter to succeed in a tennis career, and *The Bigamist* (1953), in which Lupino appears as one of the wives [**Figure 12.30**]. She later had a successful directing career in television, which was easier to break into. Since their rediscovery by feminists in the 1970s, Arzner and Lupino have been the focus of rewarding scholarship on what it meant to be a woman director in the male-dominant power structure of the studio system.

Women in the Avant-Garde Movement

Because of their position outside the Hollywood mainstream and because their films require less money and equipment, the experimental and avant-garde movements have been more accessible to women filmmakers than has feature filmmaking. Probably the best known American avant-garde filmmaker is Maya Deren. A Russian immigrant, Deren began making poetic, inventive films that incorporated dance and music in the early 1940s. She not only appeared *in* her classic films *Meshes of the Afternoon* (1943) and *At Land* (1944), but she also often appeared *with* them, traveling around the country, organizing networks, and publishing articles to promote the experimental cinema of which she is rightly considered a founder. Deren paved the way for other avant-garde filmmakers, some of them women. Shirley Clarke made both abstract films and the remarkable interview film *Portrait of Jason* in 1967. Yoko Ono pursued filmmaking in addition to music and other areas of artistic expression, producing the humorous *Film No. 4 (Bottoms)* (1966) and the harrowing *Rape* (1969).

In the late 1960s and early 1970s, an explicitly feminist avant-garde movement emerged with such filmmakers as Carolee Schneeman, who filmed herself and her husband making love in *Fuses* (1966), and Yvonne Rainer, who incorporated her work as a dancer in the experimental *Film about a Woman Who . . .* (1974). Through the 1990s Rainer continued to make socially engaged films using collages of images and language, as in *MURDER and murder* (1996), which confronts breast cancer. Barbara Hammer uses experimental film language to explore lesbian identity and eroticism, as well as other questions of representation in more than eighty short films produced since the early 1970s. Lizzie Borden's *Born in Flames* (1983), scripted with a (mostly nonprofessional) ensemble cast, imagined a not-too-distant future in which women were still unequal citizens despite a progressive government. In this film, which uses an innovative structure while presenting a more accessible narrative than is typical of experimental films, coalitions of women fight together across lines of race, class, age, and sexual orientation [**Figure 12.31**]. Bette Gordon's *Variety* (1983) is notable for exploring themes of sexuality and voyeurism that parallel feminist concerns of the period. Trinh T. Minh-ha's films, such as

12.31 *Born in Flames* (1983). In this widely regarded independent film, a multiracial group of New York women rebel in the not-too-distant future.

Reassemblage (1982) and *Surname Viet Given Name Nam* (1989), critique the traditions of representation that render women from non-Western cultures as silent objects. Much of this work, as well as that of experimental feminist filmmakers outside the United States, such as Belgium's Chantal Akerman, England's Sally Potter, and France's Marguerite Duras, was analyzed and fostered in the then-burgeoning critical work by feminist film theorists; they looked both at the representation of women in mainstream film and the specific challenges to traditional film form advanced by these experimental filmmakers.

Women in Independent Film

Women frequently work in noncommercial traditions, such as documentary and short filmmaking, where the influence of feminism and other social movements is often felt. Prominent among documentarians is Barbara Kopple, whose cinema verité account of a strike in *Harlan County, U.S.A.* (1976) earned an Academy Award, as did her later documentary on a strike among meatpackers, *American Dream* (1990). Christine Choy has produced many documentaries on social issues, including *Who Killed Vincent Chin?* made with Renee Tajima (1988). African American filmmaker Ayoka Chenzira uses an animated format for *Hairpiece: A Film for Nappyheaded People* (1984). Julie Dash's influential short film *Illusions* (1982), the story of a black woman who "passes" as white in order to enter the motion-picture business during World War II, was followed by her feature *Daughters of the Dust* (1991). These and many other women filmmakers' works circulate outside theatrical exhibition structures and still have a considerable influence on audiences and scholars.

Independent features by women writers, directors, and producers are appearing in ever greater numbers. Allison Anders makes films based on her own experiences, such as *Gas Food Lodging* (1992), and on those of other girls and women, such as *Mi Vida Loca* (1993), about Chicana gang members. As an independent feature film producer, Christine Vachon has been responsible for bringing to the screen daring and acclaimed works by a number of female directors, including Rose Troche and Guinevere Turner's lesbian romance *Go Fish* (1994); Mary Harron's portrait of Valerie Solanas, *I Shot Andy Warhol* (1996) [Figure 12.32], and her *The Notorious Bettie Page* (2006); and Kimberly Peirce's drama based on the murder of Brandon Teena, *Boys Don't Cry* (1999) [Figure 12.33]. Several members of a diverse group of young women filmmakers negotiating feature filmmaking (often working in television as they get projects off the ground) include Lisa Cholodenko (*High Art*, 1998; *Laurel Canyon*, 2002), Gina

12.32   *I Shot Andy Warhol* (1996). Lili Taylor as the radical feminist Valerie Solanas who shoots Andy Warhol after he rejects her screenplay.

12.33   *Boys Don't Cry* (1999). First-time writer-director Kimberly Peirce's film about the tragic death of the transgendered Brandon Teena reached unexpectedly wide audiences.

Prince-Bythewood (*Love & Basketball*, 2000), Angela Robinson (*D.E.B.S.*, 2004; *Herbie Fully Loaded*, 2005), and Karen Kusama (*Girlfight*, 2000; *Aeon Flux*, 2005), who has teamed with writer Diablo Cody on a new project, *Jennifer's Body*.

Women in Contemporary Hollywood

Women entered contemporary Hollywood production slowly, with some of the first inroads to the prestigious position of director made by actresses who already had industry clout: Elaine May, Barbra Streisand, Penny Marshall, and Jodie Foster, for example. Few contemporary women are associated with cinematic masterpieces, and therefore most are excluded from histories that focus on prestige films. Indeed, women have often more readily been hired as directors in such genres as youth films and romantic and family comedies. Notable Hollywood women filmmakers who have made interesting statements in these genres include Amy Heckerling with *Fast Times at Ridgemont High* (1982), *Look Who's Talking* (1989), and *Clueless* (1995); Penny Marshall with *Big* (1988), *A League of Their Own* (1992), and *Riding in Cars with Boys* (2001); and Penelope Spheeris with *The Decline of Western Civilization* (1981) and *Wayne's World* (1992). Women who moved into Hollywood from independent production during the 1980s used such projects as a springboard to more personal feature films, and many of them fill out their directing careers with television assignments. Martha Coolidge's *Valley Girl* (1983), a successful youth film, was followed by *Rambling Rose* (1991), a sensitive portrait of a young woman's sexuality, and *Introducing Dorothy Dandridge* (1999), a made-for-television biopic of a key figure in women's film history. Susan Seidelman wrote and directed the New York–based comedy *Desperately Seeking Susan* (1985), giving Madonna her first film role, and directed the pilot episode of the television comedy *Sex and the City*. Mira Nair's *Mississippi Masala* (1991) explores patterns of immigration through the romance between an African American man and a South Asian woman in the Mississippi Delta. Nair's *The Namesake* (2007) is an adaptation of Indian American novelist Jhumpa Lahiri's acclaimed novel [Figure 12.34]. Another voice among the still small number of African American women making feature films is Kasi Lemmons, who with her debut *Eve's Bayou* (1997) brought a regional tale narrated by a young black girl to the screen. Lemmons continues to explore African American lives in such subsequent features as *Talk to Me* (2007).

On a bigger scale, writer and director Nora Ephron is associated with a more formulaic attention to women in such romantic comedies as *Sleepless in Seattle* (1993) and *You've Got Mail* (1998); Nancy Meyers (*Something's Gotta Give*, 2003) was also well established as a writer and producer before turning to directing. A director specializing in traditionally male genres, Kathryn Bigelow has made films like *Near Dark* (1987), a bizarre vampire film; *Blue Steel* (1990), a police drama; and *Strange Days* (1995), a futuristic thriller. Mimi Leder's feature debut with *Deep Impact* (1998) is also significant for not typecasting the director in a so-called woman's genre such as romantic comedy or family films.

The rediscovery of forgotten women filmmakers and the advocacy for increased participation of women in all levels of film production have been undertaken by scholars, activists, programmers, and audiences in conjunction with the women's movement since the early 1970s. However, thinking about women's role in film history goes

12.34 **The Namesake** (2007). Vivid images of India in this tale of generations and migration.

beyond the recovery of forgotten names and films. It also involves the following issues: What is the significance of a film's having been directed by a woman? Are women employed in other technical capacities? Whose story is told? How is the female image used in this work? Are women viewers specifically addressed by the film's characters, story, sounds, and images? If so, are some women included while others are not? Adjusting the historical record involves assessing the present and shaping the future. The more we know about how women's talents have been eclipsed, the more effective the challenge to remaining inequities can be. Our perspective toward contemporary efforts and future possibilities is enriched by evaluating historical continuities and discontinuities, exceptions and omissions.

VIEWING CUE

View and compare two films directed by women. How would you characterize and distinguish the filmmakers' perspectives behind the camera?

African American Cinema

The dominant American cinema has afforded only a limited range of representation for African, Asian, Hispanic, and Native Americans. When not absent from the screen altogether, these groups have traditionally been present in a small repertoire of often demeaning stereotypes. The role of people of color behind the screen has historically been even more restricted. Still, because film is a popular medium, it registers the diversity of U.S. culture even while sometimes distorting it. In particular, the portrayal of African Americans has been crucial to evolving representations of American identity. Historian Michael Rogin has pointed to the prominence in American cinema of films that deal centrally with race, although in a biased way. In this perspective, *The Birth of a Nation* (1915), *The Jazz Singer* (1927), and *Gone with the Wind* (1939) show that the legacy of slavery and the symbolic meanings of blackness and whiteness are of crucial though underacknowledged importance to America's understanding of itself. Such mainstream representations have been challenged by the alternative perspectives put forward in films made by African Americans. To evaluate the movies' historical role in perpetuating and shifting racial inequities, we will look at how African Americans have been depicted in Hollywood movies before surveying the long history of cinema produced by African Americans.

Some of the earliest U.S. films featured racial themes, usually drawn from the egregious stereotypes circulating in such forms of popular culture as minstrel shows. Later, African American performers such as Lena Horne were highlighted in specialty numbers in Hollywood musicals but were denied starring roles except in films with all-black casts. An important critical perspective on mainstream representations is provided by scholar Donald Bogle in his *Toms, Coons, Mullatoes, Mammies, and Bucks* (1973, revised 2001). Bogle analyzes these common stereotypes and shows how the African American performers who interpreted them often transcended the limitations of their supporting roles. Spike Lee's *Bamboozled* (2000) revisits this terrain: in order to expose his white boss's hypocritical appropriation of African American culture, a contemporary black television producer proposes a modern-day television minstrel show, replete with stock nineteenth-century stereotypes of subservient, caricatured African Americans [Figure 12.35]. The protagonist is stunned by the enormous success of the show, which even starts a fad for blackface. Besides the historical legacy that spawns such racist representations, the film implies that the success of the show is due to the enormous talent the performers channel into the songs and dances. Featuring the brilliant dancer

12.35 *Bamboozled* (2000). Spike Lee's aggressive and historically informed film confronts the legacy of racist stereotyping in American entertainment.

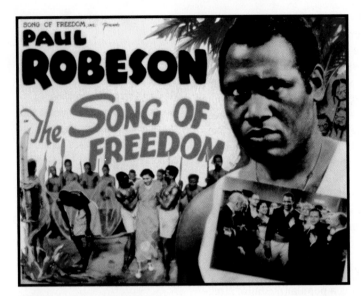

12.36 The "race movie." Such films depicting African American lives and concerns were targeted at black audiences during segregation.

Savion Glover, Lee's film acknowledges the genius of such historical performers as African American blackface artist Bert Williams and dancer Bill Robinson, the latter known for his pairings with Shirley Temple.

Lee's own body of work, which extends well beyond mounting a critique of mainstream films, illustrates decisively the importance of the intervention and participation of people of color in making films. In the past few decades, alternative representations by Asian American, Native American, Latino, and African American filmmakers have emerged in conjunction with *identity politics*, the practice of putting social (racial, ethnic, gender, or sexual) identity at the center of political and cultural activity. Such work is often by, about, and for members of the American film audience who have never before seen their lives and images reflected on the screen. African American cinema provides an important case study because of its historical scope and contemporary breadth as well as its economic impact. In addition, African American identity bears a symbolic weight in a nation that is increasingly willing to acknowledge its historical conflicts in terms of black and white (while often still marginalizing the images and voices of other people of color).

Early Independent African American Cinema

African American film production extends back to segregation and the silent film era, intensifying in the last few decades of the twentieth century as its significance began to match that of black urban cultural styles in music and fashion. Early African American film culture represents a distinguished and even heroic alternative to Hollywood history. An independent cinema arose in response to various phenomena, from the "race consciousness" of African American audiences cultivated by the burgeoning literature of the Harlem Renaissance and recordings by black musicians, to the realities of racism and segregation in the South. Opposition to the inflammatory depictions of blacks in *The Birth of a Nation* was a significant impetus for claiming film as a medium for self-representation. So-called *race movies* featured African American casts and were circulated to urban African American audiences in the North and shown in special segregated screenings in the South (including late-night screenings known as "midnight rambles") [Figure 12.36]. These films often billed their stars by capitalizing on mainstream Hollywood personalities: Lorenzo Tucker was "the black Valentino." Some race movies were produced by white entrepreneurs, but several prominent production companies were owned by African Americans. As early as 1910, for example, Bill Foster founded the Foster Photoplay Company in Chicago, while in 1916, actor Noble Johnson formed the all-black Lincoln Motion Picture Company in Los Angeles with his brother and other partners [Figure 12.37].

The most important figure in early independent African American cinema is the novelist, writer,

12.37 *The Realization of a Negro's Ambition* (1916). The Lincoln Motion Picture Company's first release, featuring co-founder Noble Johnson in the leading role, was a success with African American audiences.

producer-director, and impresario Oscar Micheaux, who directed the first African American feature film [Figure 12.38]. Micheaux owned and operated his own production company from 1918 to 1948, producing nearly forty feature films on extremely limited budgets. Micheaux's inventiveness in fund-raising and in film-making was legendary. He fashioned a distinctly non-Hollywood style whose "errors" have been interpreted as an alternative aesthetic. His most controversial film, *Within Our Gates* (1920), which realistically treated the spread of lynching, was threatened with censorship in Chicago, which had just seen its worst wave of race riots. Later, in *Body and Soul* (1925), Micheaux teamed up with actor, singer, and activist Paul Robeson in a powerful portrait of a corrupt preacher.

Another important writer-director-actor, Spencer Williams contributed considerably to African American film history and aesthetics with his religious films. The pictorial beauty of his *The Blood of Jesus* (1941) is echoed in scenes from Julie Dash's *Daughters of the Dust*. Although Williams contributed to sound-era cinema, and Micheaux continued to make films through the 1940s, the era of race movies peaked before the introduction of sound. By World War II, the participation of African Americans in the war effort led to increased expectations of equality in other sectors, including the Hollywood film industry. The studios themselves were eager to improve relations with audiences and journalists by updating the stereotyped images of the 1930s. Paradoxically, an agreement between the studios and the National Association for the Advancement of Colored People (NAACP) to enhance the portrayal of blacks contributed to the waning of the vibrant alternative culture of films about, for, and often by African Americans. Hollywood typically showcased black actors rather than creative personnel, though sometimes it made room for the voices of African American cultural producers, as with the major studio adaptation of Lorraine Hansberry's nuanced portrait of a black family, *A Raisin in the Sun* (1961). Actor Sidney Poitier, who appeared in the film, defined the era with his charismatic and dignified onscreen presence, but was too often restricted to playing overly idealized characters.

12.38   Oscar Micheaux. One of film's most resourceful figures, Micheaux wrote, produced, and directed feature films for African American exhibition networks from 1918 to the 1940s.

Blaxploitation and Commercial Leaders

After the studio system waned in the 1960s, new audiences for specialized films were sought by Hollywood, and the genre known as **blaxploitation** emerged. Although the term cynically suggests the economic exploitation of black film audiences (particularly an urban market likely to attend films about streetwise African American protagonists), the genre was also made possible in part by the black power movement. Many blaxploitation films were made by white producers, but some African American filmmakers turned the genre to their own purposes with significant impact. The immensely successful *Shaft* (1971) was directed by noted photographer Gordon Parks. Melvin Van Peebles wrote, directed, scored, and starred in *Sweet Sweetback's Baadasssss Song* (1971), which incorporates revolutionary rhetoric in a kinetic tale of a black man pursued by racist cops [Figure 12.39].

In the final two decades of the twentieth century, the commercial and artistic leader of the resurgence of African American cinema production was Spike Lee. With his debut feature *She's Gotta Have It* (1986), Lee helped revive independent cinema aesthetically and financially through a sophisticated use of cinematic language and

12.39 *Sweet Sweetback's Baadasssss Song* (1971). Melvin Van Peebles's militant blaxploitation hit.

▶ **VIEWING CUE**

View a race movie that has been rediscovered and released on video. Does the film offer a creative response to limited resources? Do some of its references or actions indicate that the filmmakers had an African American audience in mind? ⏸

engaging storytelling. Working through his production company, 40 Acres and a Mule, Lee addresses important topics in African American history in the biopic *Malcolm X* (1992) **[Figure 12.40]** and explores personal issues in *Mo' Better Blues* (1990). He has also directed documentaries, such as *4 Little Girls* (1997) and the four-part *When the Levees Broke* (2006) produced with HBO. In addition, he produced the work of many other young filmmakers of color, including women like Darnell Martin (*I Like It Like That*, 1994). Lee's success spurred an African American film boom in the early 1990s, centered on a wave of "gangsta" films about young men in urban settings. These included, for example, John Singleton's *Boyz N the Hood* (1991), Mario Van Peebles's *New Jack City* (1991), and the Hughes brothers' *Menace II Society* (1993). Yet these youth-marketed films often obscure less commercially successful works by independent African American film-makers, such as Julie Dash's *Daughters of the Dust* (1991) and Charles Burnett's *To Sleep with Anger* (1990). Dash's film takes on African storytelling traditions in the narration of a multigenerational family saga, while Burnett's film makes interesting use of a trickster figure.

Although African American cinema has achieved greater visibility due to the economic viability of an early independent film network and the emergence of a large "crossover" audience later on, films by and for other racial and ethnic groups have been made throughout U.S. film history and have increased in number as people of color obtained greater access to the means of film production. Each of these histories is fascinating, but we are able to cite only several important films and movements here. Yiddish-language cinema, much of it produced in Eastern Europe and enjoyed by Jewish immigrants in the United States, flourished in the years between the two world wars. With the fostering of independent feature filmmaking in general and with more emphasis on the multicultural nature of U.S. society, Chinese American Wayne Wang launched his significant filmmaking career with *Chan Is Missing* (1982), and playwright and director Luis Valdez brought important stories from Chicano history to the screen with *Zoot Suit* (1981) and *La Bamba* (1987). It was not until 1998 that a feature by and about Native Americans was produced: director Chris Eyre and writer Sherman Alexie's breakthrough film *Smoke Signals* (1998) received wide critical and popular acclaim.

Often these works emerge from strong critiques of mainstream representations of people of color and of underrepresentation in the film industry. In addition to these feature films and journalistic and scholarly work on race and representation, other kinds of community and art world–based media have appeared. Each year film festivals dedicated to Asian-Pacific American

12.40 *Malcolm X* (1992). Spike Lee argued that a big-budget biographical film about the slain leader should be directed by an African American.

and Latin American cinema showcase hundreds of short films, videos, and documentaries, as well as feature-length films from Asian and Latin American countries. All of these traditions expand the concept of American cinema beyond the genres, personalities, and stories that Hollywood has promoted.

Rewriting Film History

As we consider the different ways that film history can be regarded, it is important to remember that the very idea of reflecting on our film heritage is a relatively recent one. Precisely because film and photography capture the fleeting moment, they have been regarded as ephemeral and of little long-term value. In relation to more durable arts such as architecture, painting, and sculpture, film is also materially ephemeral. Because the earliest nitrate-based film stock was extremely flammable, negatives and prints of countless titles are now destroyed. Film prints that were once in circulation have been altered by censors, damaged in transit and projection, and improperly stored. Approximately 85 percent of our silent-film heritage has been lost. The later format of video, which deteriorates over time, has suffered a similar fate, with television stations routinely recording over the only records they have of earlier programs. Even some films that were celebrated and successful in their day no longer exist and so cannot be consulted by contemporary historians or shared with new audiences.

Orphan Films

The historical record looks as it does because of lucky accidents—informed and not-so-informed decisions about what to keep and what to throw away—and rare acts of foresight. The Library of Congress requested copies of all film materials submitted for copyright consideration and thus has records of the very first movies. The Museum of Modern Art, under the leadership of its first curator of film, Iris Barry, made the decision to treat film as a modern art and collected prints and stills beginning in 1935. Most Hollywood films that survive today were stored in vaults by the film studios that produced them; later owners of these companies discovered a new source of revenue in the preservation and re-release of old movies on television, video, or DVD. Films that have survived but have no commercial interests to pay the costs of their preservation are called **orphan films**, and it is no accident that these films tend to be rare or marginal for other reasons. Often these works are "orphans" because they have entered the public domain—no one claims them. At times, however, the word "orphan" is used to emphasize films that have been neglected by canonical film histories and need to be recovered materially as well as critically. Dorothy Arzner's *Working Girls* (1931), for example, was an orphan until its recent restoration through the UCLA Film and Television Archive; almost all surviving race movies are also orphans. Charles Burnett's MFA student thesis film, *Killer of Sheep* (1977) (see Chapter 2, p. 42), was finally released theatrically in 2007 when funds were available to clear the music rights. Despite having garnered numerous film festival awards in the early 1980s and being placed on the National Film Registry in 1990, this remarkable film was very difficult to see until it was restored by the UCLA Film and Television Archive.

Orphan films is a recent category devised by those interested in film preservation—including scholars, archivists, filmmakers, and collectors—to help draw attention to an eclectic range of films and their plight: newsreels, industrials, amateur films. Today, it is up to those who discover orphan films to evaluate what they have to tell us about the past: they function like time capsules of cinematic history and of history in general. For example, a 1952 informational film about

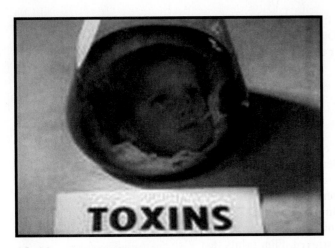

12.41 *What You Should Know about Biological Warfare* (1952). The U.S. government instructs citizens in Cold War protocol.

biological warfare conveys the anxieties of the government and citizens of the United States during the Cold War **[Figure 12.41]**. Looking carefully at the variety of forms, styles, and uses of orphan films helps us understand how central film was to the twentieth century, and how taken for granted it was. Although orphans are a worldwide phenomenon, rescuing such films is a particular challenge in the United States because of the volume and commercial concentration of film.

We are accustomed to thinking of certain films as twentieth-century classics on par with great paintings or novels—*Gone with the Wind* (1939), *Lawrence of Arabia* (1962), and *Schindler's List* (1993), as well as the non-Hollywood films *The Battleship Potemkin* (1925), *The Rules of the Game* (1939), *8 1/2* (1963), and *Tokyo Story* (1953). Interestingly, many of these historically significant works are about history themselves. However, most films that grace best-films lists—annual or regular polls of critics' and/or filmmakers' opinions—survive because they have been profitable. Copyrights have been renewed, new prints struck, high-quality digital transfers made, soundtracks remastered, DVD extras added, and "making of" movies produced, all driven by the potential to make more money from the property in an ancillary market, such as foreign sales, pay television, cable, or home video. Nearly all the other films—those with little or no box-office clout and which may not even be intended or able to be shown in theaters—are orphans.

What else is out there? Among others, a variety of amateur movies, avant-garde films and performance materials, censored materials, commercials, educational films, ethnographic footage, found footage, independent documentaries and features, industrials, home movies, medical imaging, newsreels, outtakes, shorts, stock footage, student films, surveillance footage, trailers, and training films exist as orphans. The term orphan films is a deliberate catchall, defined by what is normally excluded and by what is interesting to varied groups of people. This diversity is important in its own right because of what it tells us about the criteria used to construct historical narratives. When we consider the reach of this definition, we get a glimpse of how daunting, and costly, the task of saving all the orphans might be.

Let us consider newsreels, which are usually of more interest to conventional historians than, say, old student films. In the early decades of film, audiences expected newsreels to appear before the feature film at every showing. Think of the trove of information they offer historians—glimpses of past events just as the people of that era saw them presented. Such images were often actual records of events, a priceless view of a bustling city street or other such fleeting moments in history that only film can record. However, because of the sheer volume of footage, preserving newsreels presents problems in cost and storage.

Another important category of orphans is films of the silent era. Much of the surviving worldwide output of these three decades in film history is orphaned. Because film industries were not yet centralized, materials were scattered in random archives, prints were modified by exhibitors and review panels in individual states and countries, and print conditions have deteriorated irreversibly. Because copyright has expired on many silent films, there is little economic interest in their preservation, leaving this art form seriously endangered.

Other films become orphaned because they are made outside the commercial mainstream and may even threaten its norms. Avant-garde and experimental works are rarely commercially viable; in addition, they may use unusual gauges or substances that require extraordinary preservation methods, such as Stan Brakhage's

Mothlight (1963), which used actual moth wings. Political documentaries and features that never find commercial distributors or that are shelved by studios are also orphaned.

Preservation

Some orphans—from ethnographic footage to medical films and screen tests—have special needs that raise interesting questions about the goals of preservation. Do we want to keep all of these films? With the vast storage capacities computers have for digital media, it may not seem like we have to make such choices. Indeed, given today's technology, it can seem absurd that so many orphan films are inaccessible. But it is also important to preserve the materials in their original format. Objects created and used in the past are part of material culture that deserve our attention. Numerous reasons exist for saving as much as possible, and various constituencies have different roles to play in the preservation effort:

- Archivists can research, catalog, store, and make available to researchers original negatives, prints, soundtracks, documentation, and so on.
- Preservation experts can begin to restore prints to as close to their original condition as possible.
- Film historians and curators can have access to as wide a range of images as possible.
- Social and cultural historians can have access to images from particular times, places, and institutions.
- Filmmakers can ensure that their work survives and even attracts new viewers.
- Other filmmakers may use orphan films as sources for their work, such as compilation films or historical documentaries.
- Specialists in computer technology can devise new restoration and access methods.
- Specialists in information technology can organize a wide range of materials.
- Audiences can have new educational, eye-opening, and outrageous film experiences.

As we have seen, orphan film is a productive category that addresses a number of different reasons films disappear: what they are made of can be ephemeral; who made them might be unknown or lacking in means or influence; what they were made for has served its purpose; what they were about is now out of favor, disapproved of, or extremely specialized; where they were made or ended up was not in Hollywood. Undoubtedly, we have made a good deal of progress in considering films not only as documents of history but also as having a history in their own right, one that is worth preserving. Orphan films remind us that conventional notions of film history also preselect what is worth saving. That a research and preservation category can be based largely on the criteria of commercially untenable movies shows us how pervasive economic interests are in the construction of film history. Many of these films were not made for commercial purposes, while others, such as sponsored films, have outlived those purposes [Figure 12.42]. Although preservation is so costly as to rarely be motivated by the desire to generate revenue, it is nevertheless likely that the orphans receiving the most attention will be those that have some commercial potential.

text continued on page 438 ▶

▶ VIEWING CUE

View an "ephemeral film" on the Internet archive at www.archive.org/details/ephemera. What does it tell us about history?

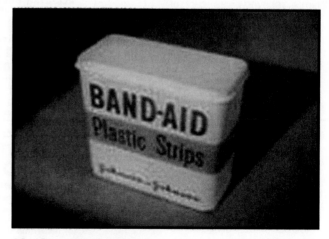

12.42 Band-Aid commercial (1948). Early television commercials can function like time capsules.

Lost and Found History: *Within Our Gates* (1920)

Oscar Micheaux's *Within Our Gates* is a crucial film in the counter-history of American cinema because of its content, its circumstances of production and reception, and its fate [Figure 12.43]. Produced independently in 1919 and released in 1920, it is the earliest surviving feature film by an African American filmmaker. Despite its historical significance, however, the film was lost for decades. Greeted with controversy upon its initial release, it came back into circulation in the 1990s after the Library of Congress identified a print titled *La Negra* in a film archive in Spain as Micheaux's lost film and then restored it. The film's recovery was part of the efforts of film historians and black cultural critics to re-investigate the vibrant world of early twentieth-century "race movies" and the remarkable role Micheaux played in this culture. The picture of African American life and politics in the North and South offered by Micheaux's film is completely missing from Hollywood films of the same era, as is any concept of the audience that Micheaux addressed. The film's long absence from the historical record deprived generations of viewers and cultural producers of a countertradition upon which to build.

Within Our Gates is important to an alternative film history because it offers a corrective view of a devastating historical phenomenon, the lynching of African Americans, which had reached epidemic proportions in the first decades of the twentieth century. When the film was returned to circulation in the 1990s, viewers immediately saw it as a countervision to Griffith's *The Birth of a Nation,* which boldly uses cinematic techniques like parallel editing to tell the inflammatory story of a black man pursuing a white virgin, who commits suicide rather than succumb to rape. The Klan is formed to avenge her death, and the would-be rapist is captured and punished in what the film depicts as justified vigilante justice. Micheaux offers an equally visceral story that counters the myth of lynching as a justified reaction to black male violence by presenting a testament to white racist mob violence against African Americans. In his film, after an African American ten-

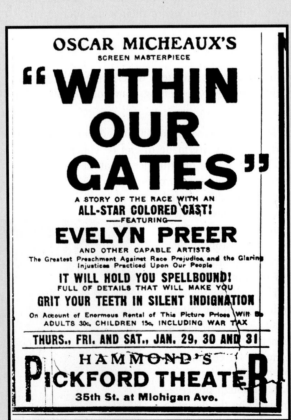

12.43 **Poster for *Within Our Gates*** (1920). Oscar Micheaux's rediscovered film about the lives and philanthropic work of middle-class African Americans includes dramatic scenes of lynching.

12.44   *Within Our Gates* (1920). In the framing story of Oscar Micheaux's film, the heroine speaks with Dr. Vivian.

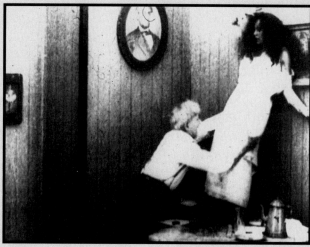

12.45   *Within Our Gates* (1920). A last-minute coincidence saves the heroine.

ant farmer, Jasper Landry, is unjustly accused of shooting the wealthy landowner Girdlestone (the guilty party is actually an angry white tenant), a lynching party attacks Landry's family. *Within Our Gates* poignantly depicts the lynching of the mother and father and the last-minute escape of their small son as a public spectacle attended by the townspeople, including women and children, a historically accurate depiction of lynching. If race movies are often considered to have been spurred by the misrepresentations of *The Birth of a Nation,* this powerful sequence stands as perhaps the strongest cinematic rebuttal to that celebrated film's distortion of history. It uses the power of the visual to make history, just as Griffith's film does. Finally, as a director, Micheaux offers an important contrast to Griffith. Whereas Griffith has been consistently heralded as a father of American cinema, Micheaux's diverse talents, his unique approach to film language, his business savvy, and his modernity have waited decades for full recognition.

The structure of Micheaux's film also rewards historical inquiry because it requires viewers to look with fresh eyes and think about how certain modes of storytelling become naturalized. Although *Within Our Gates's* treatment of lynching is its most noted feature, this controversial material, which threatened to prevent the film's exhibition in Chicago where racial tensions had recently erupted in rioting, is buried in an extensive flashback. The flashback fills in the past of Sylvia Landry, described by a title card as someone "who could think of nothing but the eternal struggle of her race and how she could uplift it." The language of racial uplift directly addresses the racially conscious, middle-class black audiences for Micheaux's film. Sylvia's

quest to raise funds for a black school in the South, her romance with the politically active Dr. Vivian [Figure 12.44], and several side plots featuring less noble characters, make the lynching story at the film's heart feel even closer to the historical record. The story serves a didactic purpose in the film: the demonstration of the racial injustice that propels Sylvia's struggle. But the film does not spare melodramatic detail. We learn that Sylvia, the Landrys' adopted daughter, escapes the lynch mob only to be threatened with rape by landowner Girdlestone's brother [Figure 12.45]. The attack is diverted when the would-be rapist notices a scar that reveals she is actually his daughter. The film's inclusion of white male violence against black women is another rebuttal of the distortions in *The Birth of a Nation.* The unlikeliness of the rescue scenario can be understood as the use of melodramatic coincidence to right wrongs that cannot easily receive redress in other ways. In other words, Micheaux uses the form of the movies to imagine social reality differently.

Micheaux's films were made with extreme ingenuity on low budgets. Their sometimes random-seeming narrative structures and their lack of conformity with the rules of continuity editing mark the historical existence of film practices unassimilated to the classical tradition. When Micheaux's affecting melodrama of African American hardship and determination disappeared from film history, a great deal was lost. The film's subject matter was not undertaken in mainstream cinema. The perspective of African American filmmakers was absent in Hollywood, and black audiences were not addressed by its films. The title *Within Our Gates* speaks to the film's own status—a powerful presence within American film history too long unacknowledged.

12.46 *Triumph of the Will*
(1934). Leni Riefenstahl's documentary
is ideological in form and content.

▶ **VIEWING CUE**

Research an event in the history of
cinema—such as the introduction of
the drive-in theater or the DVD
format. What cultural influences
resulted in this development?

Film, History, and Cultural Context

A film such as *Saving Private Ryan* (1998) depicts a historical topic—in this case, the invasion of Normandy, which marked the beginning of the end of World War II in Europe. Much of the film's promotion and reception centered around its historical fidelity, and its investment in realism made its scenes seem accurate to veterans of the campaign as well as to younger audiences who had no reference point beyond other movies depicting the war. Seeing *Saving Private Ryan* in a cultural context, however, requires embedding it in the late 1990s. The circumstances of its production, release, and reception include the enormous cultural and economic clout of filmmaker Steven Spielberg; the business practices that made it possible to produce, advertise, and distribute a big-budget film worldwide; the aesthetic standards that value realism; technological innovations, such as CGI (computer-generated imagery), that served those aesthetic standards; and reviewing protocols in the press that elevated the film to a cultural reference point. The historian might seek to understand how the film's version of events in the 1940s was shaped by U.S. sentiment at the end of the century, including nostalgia for the "good war" and a new role as the world's only superpower. In this example, we speak of the context for the *telling* of history as well as the context for the *events* of history.

Contextual analysis of individual films and of film history itself may be conducted in many different ways. Here we will focus on three particular contexts:

- ideology and film, with a focus on the "Red Scare" in Hollywood
- lesbian and gay representation and subcultures
- indigenous films and their challenge to traditional ethnographic filmmaking

Ideology and Film: Celluloid Communism

The most overt example of a film's ideological influence is a propaganda film, which sets out to persuade the audience that a particular view or way of life is correct or desirable. Leni Riefenstahl's documentary of the Nazi party congress, *Triumph of the Will* (1934), is one of the best-known and most effective examples of film propaganda. From camera angles to editing, the film uses aesthetic means to characterize and glorify fascism [**Figure 12.46**]. A close connection between the media and the government, such as existed in Riefenstahl's case (despite her equivocation about her affiliation with the Nazi party), assures that ideological messages are relatively clear. Still, even in the United States, where movies are autonomous from the state, government interests can be expressed in films. *Mrs. Miniver* (1942), a Hollywood drama about one woman's courage during the bombing of London in World War II, helped clinch the support of the U.S. public for entering the war [**Figure 12.47**]. *Song of Russia* (1943), an effort made in cooperation with the Roosevelt administration in support of the Russian allies, was later attacked by cold warriors as subversive.

Ideological effects may be less intentional. The stereotypes perpetuated in Hollywood westerns have

12.47 *Mrs. Miniver* (1942). William Wyler's film ideologically
supported American involvement in World War II.

indelibly shaped ideas about Native Americans and distorted their culture and political grievances. *Mississippi Burning* (1988) is a mainstream film about the civil rights era, but by showing the perspective and story of white activists in the South, it risks sending the ideological message that these characters' struggles are more easily identified with than those of the African American civil rights leaders, and the people whose lives the movement sought to better **[Figure 12.48]**.

12.48   Mississippi Burning (1988). The choice to focus on white protagonists in a civil rights-era drama may have a subtle ideological impart.

Film theorists also use the concept of **ideology** to discuss a film's critical, compliant, or contradictory attitude toward the status quo, or dominant ideology, an attitude that may come through even in the absence of overt political content. For example, in *Bigger Than Life* (1956), a melodrama about a postwar suburban father's addiction to prescription drugs, director Nicholas Ray makes use of formal elements (such as framing, camera angles, and mise-en-scène) to depict the social confinement and rigid role expectations that lead to his protagonist's dreams of grandeur. The film thus critiques the period's dominant ideology of conformism by showing the cracks in the facade.

The American cinema of the postwar period arose from and spoke to a country whose surface calm and prosperity belied insecurity and enormous change in the making. The participation of African American men in the military and of women, both black and white, in the wartime workforce helped sow the seeds of the civil rights and women's movements soon afterward. In 1956, the year *Bigger Than Life* was made, Martin Luther King Jr. led the Montgomery bus boycott **[Figure 12.49]**. At the same time, anxiety about national security and internal stability was fed by fear of atomic weapons, the arms race with the Soviet Union, and decolonization of Third World countries in the wake of wartime upheaval.

▶ **VIEWING CUE**

What was happening in the world or the nation when the film screened in class was released? How did the history show itself in the film?

Amid the social and political turmoil of postwar America, the film industry was targeted for its capacity for ideological influence. The congressional investigation of Communist infiltration of the motion-picture business in the late 1940s and 1950s represents a specific historical context in which film played an unusually significant role. In 1946, Congress held its first hearings on Communist influence in Hollywood; the Taft-Hartley Act (1946) restricted organized labor's power to strike; and crackdowns on Communists in the unions included motion-picture industry workers. Hollywood was undergoing many changes at this time and, as a result, would never again function as the stable studio system it had been for several decades. Antitrust laws, new technologies and new tastes, and the arrival of foreign art films led to an increase in independent productions that bypassed the studios. During this period, movies interacted with political ideology in various ways—ranging from the discontent and anxiety expressed in *Bigger Than Life,* to the paranoia about the atomic bomb that fueled the imagination of low-budget science fiction films made for the new drive-ins, to the overt anti-Communist messages of such films as *My Son John* (1952). Most notably, the film industry itself came under more direct political scrutiny than ever before.

12.49   Martin Luther King Jr. Larger social movements such as the beginnings of the civil rights movement are an important context of postwar American cinema.

The Blacklist Era.   In the years after World War II, the government investigation into Communist infiltration in the motion-picture business was part of the postwar Red Scare associated with Senator Joseph McCarthy

12.50   Senator Joseph McCarthy. McCarthy's anti-Communist fervor planted the seeds for the blacklisting of numerous progressive film personnel, including directors, screenwriters, and actors.

[Figure 12.50]. It was also evidence of the unique role Hollywood played in depicting the United States to itself. The film industry served as a high-profile target in the sensationalist hearings conducted by the House Un-American Activities Committee (HUAC), an episode that deserves to be recounted in some detail. Amid the Cold War hysteria, accusations of present or past Communist Party affiliation devastated Hollywood's creative pool and led to the blacklisting of more than three hundred screenwriters, directors, actors, and technical personnel, among them significant numbers of politically progressive Jews and African Americans. Only a few actual films, such as the U.S. government–supported wartime film *Mission to Moscow* (1943), were scrutinized in the congressional hearings. Nevertheless, the dynamics of power, intimidation, and resistance in these hearings involved many other dimensions of film history, including labor relations, the self-regulation of the industry, the status of writers, and constitutional claims to freedom of expression. A conventional film history that looks at the period in terms of common style or content cannot fully illuminate the unfolding of what became a witchhunt. It was not until much later that this event in U.S. political history was fully documented and condemned.

During Franklin D. Roosevelt's administration in the 1930s, facing the Great Depression and opposing fascism in the Spanish Civil War, many Hollywood screenwriters, actors, and others embraced leftist politics. But the postwar mushrooming of anti-Soviet sentiment that would culminate in the Cold War cast suspicion on the left. In 1944, a group of right-wing Hollywood personalities, including Walt Disney, Gary Cooper, John Wayne, and Barbara Stanwyck, established the Motion Picture Alliance for the Preservation of American Ideals. With a mission "to fight . . . any effort . . . to divert the loyalty of the screen from the free America that gave it birth," the group became a key ally in the congressional intimidation effort. In 1947, under the leadership of anti–New Deal Republican J. Parnell Thomas, HUAC invited the alliance to testify about its efforts to purge the industry. Other "friendly" witnesses, such as eventual Screen Actors Guild president and later U.S. president Ronald Reagan and studio head Jack Warner, testified before the committee, naming names of Communists and "fellow travelers," names the committee already seemed to have on its lists. Eric Johnston, president of the Motion Picture Association of America, who was also called to Washington to testify, asserted that the political views of Communists employed in the industry did not have any influence on the films that were produced.

During the second week of these hearings, nineteen suspected Communists were called as "unfriendly" witnesses. A group of liberal industry luminaries calling themselves the Committee for the First Amendment formed in their support. Headed by director John Huston and including director William Wyler, producer Walter Wanger, and actors such as Katharine Hepburn, Humphrey Bogart, Lauren Bacall, and Groucho Marx, the committee organized a highly publicized contingent to fly to Washington, carrying five hundred signatures in support of First Amendment rights.

The testimony of the "unfriendly witnesses," however, was more eventful than the Hollywood supporters had anticipated. Congressman Thomas abruptly suspended the hearings after only eleven of the nineteen witnesses had taken the stand. Among them was Bertolt Brecht, who, having fled Nazi Germany, would now flee the United States after denying any Communist affiliation. The remaining ten "unfriendly witnesses" refused to answer the committee's question, "Are you now or have you ever been a member of the Communist Party?" The week began with John Howard Lawson, Screenwriters Guild founder and president. When he was denied permission to read a prepared statement, he protested vociferously and was removed from the chamber and cited for contempt of Congress. A similar pattern was repeated with the remaining witnesses: Alvah Bessie, Herbert Biberman, Lester Cole, Edward Dmytryk, Ring Lardner Jr., Sam Ornitz, Adrian Scott, and Dalton Trumbo. These writers and directors, known as the "Hollywood Ten," were eventually convicted for contempt and served short prison terms [**Figure 12.51**].

Although HUAC's charges remained unconfirmed, its intimidation tactics were influential. Industry leaders, privately convened by Eric Johnston at the Waldorf-Astoria Hotel, attempted to control the repercussions of the hearings by issuing the so-called Waldorf Statement, condemning the actions of the Hollywood Ten and declaring that the industry would not "knowingly employ" Communists or subversives. Three hundred names were included in the statement; the blacklist era thus began. While some redress was achieved when Dalton Trumbo, one of the Hollywood Ten, received screenwriting credit for *Exodus* and *Spartacus* in 1960, the careers of many others were irreversibly affected. Although the industry had initially dismissed and resisted the tactics of HUAC, a fearful ideological climate, epitomized by the rise to prominence of the red-baiting Senator McCarthy, prevailed.

In 1951, with the blacklist in place, a second round of HUAC hearings into Hollywood Communists was dominated by the ritual of naming names. Former and suspected Communist Party members cooperated in an attempt to save their own careers. One of the most notable of these witnesses was director Elia Kazan, whose groundbreaking films *Gentleman's Agreement* (1947) and *Pinky* (1949) had brought issues of anti-Semitism and racism to the screen. Kazan provided the committee with the names of eleven Communist Party members, an action that his Academy Award–winning *On the Waterfront* (1954), about an informer, is often construed as an attempt to vindicate [**Figure 12.52**]. Another noteworthy cooperative witness was director Edward Dmytryk. One of the Hollywood Ten, Dmytryk was able to resume his career after naming fellow Communists before HUAC.

Today, it may appear that it was the committee rather than its witnesses that engaged in "un-American" activities, punishing political beliefs and violating constitutional rights. But why did the cultural context of the early Cold War encourage such efforts at direct ideological control? And why were movies targeted for expressing political differences, which pervaded many other sectors of American life?

One reason is that the film industry depends on stars' names to sell its products. In some sense, HUAC, in emphasizing an almost ritualistic practice of naming names, was using celebrities to publicize its own efforts. Throughout the hearings, the movies were invoked as an unparalleled medium for influencing public opinion, and the government claimed to be justified in regulating them to prevent any hints of what were considered unspeakable political views from circulating. Because fiction films are not usually used as political platforms, however, postwar movies depict this anxious cultural context through what *is* specific to them—genre conventions, storytelling, and visual and aural means of expression.

12.51 **The Hollywood Ten**. Refusing to answer HUAC's questions, these ten directors, screenwriters, and producers were jailed for contempt of Congress.

12.52 **On the Waterfront** (1954). Director Elia Kazan was widely criticized for "naming names" during the Communist witchhunt.

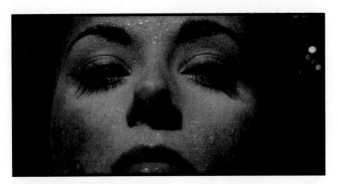

12.53 *Invasion of the Body Snatchers* (1956). A chilling story of small-town Americans who lose their identities provides a compelling if ambiguous political allegory.

Fear of the unknown—encompassing fear of annihilation as well as of "others," from immigrants to children to Third World countries—was expressed in films of the postwar period in surprisingly creative and ambiguous ways. The newly energized science fiction genre provided adaptable metaphors for a familiar world now out of control. In *Invasion of the Body Snatchers* (1956), inhabitants of a small California town become convinced that their nearest and dearest are, literally, not themselves. In fact, the residents of the town are being taken over, one by one, by emotionless replicas that arrive in giant seed-pods. Among the most stylish of the genre, this film can be seen as an anti–Red Scare movie. In this nightmare world, the hero, who refuses to conform, is persecuted by irrational mobs. His girlfriend turns into a pod and blows his cover, a truly chilling moment that suggests a condemnation of the betrayals of McCarthyism. She also becomes more sensual when she changes, an anxious conflation of the unfamiliar with a sexual threat [Figure 12.53].

At the same time, the vivid nightmare of *Invasion of the Body Snatchers* can be read as participating in the paranoia of the Red Scare—you can't tell who is a Communist or recognize your nearest and dearest by looks alone. The metaphor is consistent with fears of Communist infiltration (as is the collective agriculture the pods undertake). As a story with great visual impact, the film works less as a decipherable political allegory than as a symptom of the many fears and aspirations of its cultural context. *Invasion of the Body Snatchers* (1978), a remake, presents Cold War issues differently. This film's metaphors of lack of recognition and threats from nearby resonate with the 1970s, a historical juncture that includes the cultural context of feminism and the disillusionment and alienation felt in the aftermath of the Vietnam War.

More overtly anti-Communist films of the 1950s—in *My Son John* (1952), for example, the hero played by Robert Walker is suspected by his mother of Communist party membership—appear less effective today precisely because they lack the ambiguity of *Invasion of the Body Snatchers*. The producers' assumption that viewers will be homogenous and share a particular response to a film underestimates how ideology works in fictional representations in specific media. In film, messages come as much from genre, character, mise-en-scène, and filming and editing styles as from didactic content. With its sensual immediacy and offers of identification and closure, cinema can be a powerful tool for consensus.

However, film can also speak in an oppositional voice. Under the conditions mentioned earlier for the emergence of independent production in the late 1940s and 1950s, *Salt of the Earth* (1954)—sometimes characterized as the only U.S.-produced Communist film because it was made by blacklisted personnel, including director Herbert Biberman, one of the Hollywood Ten—integrates politics with narrative and formal choices. The film's production and its reception over the years show the importance of cultural context in film history (see "Film in Focus" on pp. 450–451).

Lesbian and Gay Film History

Looking at a specific culture or subculture across a longer span of time offers a second way to consider film history. Lesbian and gay film history provokes reflection on the relationship between representation and sexuality in general. Images help us define our desires and sexual identities. The history of sexuality in the twentieth century was shaped by the mass production and circulation of images. Examples include the largely but by no means exclusively female fan cult enjoyed by film star Rudolph Valentino in the 1920s [Figure 12.54]; such television shows as the *Newlywed Game*; and the boom in pornography fostered by the availability of home video in the 1980s. Looking at lesbian and gay film history can tell us not

VIEWING CUE

For any one of the films you recently viewed for class, research or speculate about who the audiences for the film were. What did the contemporary press say about it? Was the film successful? Why or why not?

only about changing representations of same-sex desire, but also about continuity and discontinuity in definitions of any form of sexual identity and community—as well as about the social regulation of sexuality and its representations. This history has become more accessible since the 1990s, when mainstream images of lesbians and gay men became much more common and less stigmatized, provoking interest in the images of the past.

Because its very definition is negotiable, lesbian and gay film history presents fascinating questions for historiography. Three approaches to the topic will be discussed here:

- films by gay men and lesbians
- films that include explicit or encoded representations of same-sex desire or lesbian/gay/bisexual identification
- films that are made for self-identified lesbian and gay communities or that such audiences have embraced (these films may have no explicit lesbian or gay content)

Our "by, about, and for" model can be used to discuss the cinema in relation to most underrepresented groups. Unique to lesbian and gay film history is the fluidity of lesbian and gay identity or content, a factor that affects all three categories. Rather than taking this looseness of definition as a liability, it can be made into a source of strength.

12.54 *The Son of the Sheik* (1926). Cult star Rudolph Valentino's final film before his tragic early death, which prompted hysteria and even suicides among his fans.

Films Made by Lesbians and Gay Men.

Looking for films made *by* lesbians and gay men is a model of historical recovery, an effort to locate a past that has been denied. The contributions of lesbians and gay men as filmmakers, technicians, and actors to film production are especially easy to erase or overlook because of the closet mentality that non-normative sexual orientation should be kept secret or the presumption that most people are straight. In intolerant or untested contexts, filmmakers and especially actors often pass as straight—that is, they do not correct such assumptions and/or they actively cultivate a heterosexual public persona. It is important to recognize that, like any identity, the sexual orientation of a filmmaker does not necessarily have any specific impact on his or her work. However, knowing whether a filmmaker identified himself or herself as lesbian, gay, bisexual, or transgendered, or whether there is significant biographical evidence of same-sex erotic attachments or activities, does make a difference in two contexts:

- when his or her sexual identity arguably affects the filmmaker's subject matter or aesthetic approach
- when withholding information about a filmmaker's sexual identity erases a specific historical legacy

In the first context, filmmakers may be explicit about their identity and affiliation with the gay and lesbian community or movement in order to make films for a social cause or for a specific audience or because they consider sexuality an integral part of their experience and vision as artists. The first lesbian and gay activist movie was made in 1919. *Anders als der Anderin* (*Different from the Others*) was produced in Germany amidst the social tolerance and cultural ferment of the period between the two world wars. Dramatizing the risk of blackmail to a prominent citizen because of his sexual preference, the film advocates the decriminalization of male homosexuality (no statute specifically prohibited lesbianism) and features a lecture

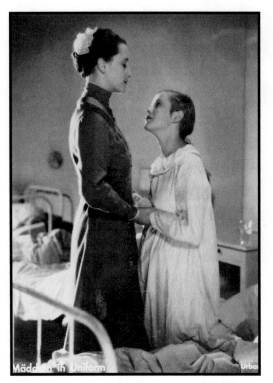

12.55   *Mädchen in Uniform*
(1931). This Weimar-era film about a
student's crush on her teacher features
an all-female cast and was written and
directed by women.

by Magnus Hirschfeld. The writings of this pioneering doctor, a leader of this early movement for lesbian and gay rights, were burned by the Nazis when they came to power, and the film he appeared in was butchered. Another famous Weimar-era film, *Mädchen in Uniform* (1931), was written by lesbian author Christa Winsloe and based on her own play [**Figure 12.55**]. Featuring an all-women cast and directed by a woman, Leontine Sagan, the film depicts a young woman's boarding-school crush on a sympathetic teacher. It achieved international success despite its censorship in the United States.

The rise of the gay rights movement during the 1970s was documented in *Word Is Out* (1978). Director Rob Epstein went on to make the award-winning *The Times of Harvey Milk* (1984) and, with Jeffrey Friedman, a series of acclaimed documentaries on lesbian and gay issues, including *The Celluloid Closet* (1995), based on Vito Russo's book about the depiction of lesbians and gay men in film. The 1980s saw an explosion of activist video advocating for money for AIDS research. At the same time, British director Derek Jarman produced a significant oeuvre, including such lyrical and subversive interpretations of historical and literary subjects as *Caravaggio* (1986) and *Edward II* (1991). Probably the most internationally celebrated gay filmmaker, Jarman became one of many talented artists lost to AIDS.

By the early 1990s, gay-themed works had prepared critics and audiences for a crop of commercially successful, aesthetically innovative films by an impressive group of young gay and lesbian filmmakers. The trend, dubbed New Queer Cinema, arose from a cultural moment when the lesbian and gay movement had become more militant in response to the AIDS crisis, embracing the formerly pejorative term "queer" for its connotations of going against the norm; the best of these films were "queer" in relation to cinematic as well as gender and sexual norms. Jennie Livingston's documentary *Paris Is Burning* (1990) [**Figure 12.56**] and fiction films such as Todd Haynes's *Poison* (1991) and *Safe* (1995), Gregg Araki's *The Living End* (1992), and Rose Troche and Guinevere Turner's *Go Fish* (1994), won awards and critical acclaim [**Figures 12.57 and 12.58**]. The industry took notice and big-budget dramas like *Philadelphia* (1993) and comedies like *In and Out* (1997) addressed gay issues more openly than ever before. Because the access of lesbians and gay men to filmmaking has mirrored the gender and race imbalances of the industry as a whole, the critical and commercial success of the harrowing drama *Boys Don't Cry* (1999) is notable. Preceding and accompanying these feature films' recognition is the burgeoning of independent lesbian and gay film and video produced for non-theatrical exhibition, notable examples of which include Pratibha Parmar's *Khush* (1991), about South Asian lesbians and gays, and Marlon Riggs's acclaimed video *Tongues United* (1989), about African American gay men.

Withholding information about a filmmaker's sexual identity can sometimes erase a specific historical legacy. We recognize that gay men and lesbians worked in almost all periods and styles of film and had a particularly significant presence in avant-garde and experimental filmmaking, drawing creativity from an otherwise marginal status. But even in Hollywood, gay presence was a significant story that has until recently been excluded from dominant film histories. Knowing that Dorothy Arzner shared her life with a female partner and maintained a

12.56   *Paris Is Burning* (1990). This documentary about New York City drag balls won critical acclaim, but it was shut out of the Oscars, possibly due to what was deemed its unconventional subject matter.

12.57 and 12.58 *The Living End* (1992) **and** *Go Fish* (1994). These two critically acclaimed independent films from the New Queer Cinema paved the way for studio-produced films that openly addressed lesbian and gay themes.

personal style as a director that did not conform to expectations of feminine behavior gives a deeper picture of the only woman who had a successful career as a director in Hollywood's heyday.

Asserting that it makes a difference to a given film that its director was gay or lesbian is an auteurist argument (see Chapter 13)—that is, a critic's construction of a director's distinctive style, rather than something objectively measurable in the work. Take as a test case George Cukor, the MGM studio director whose classic films include *The Women* (1939) and *A Star Is Born* (1954), among many others. Cukor was often called a "women's director" because of the excellent performances given by such female stars as Greta Garbo, Judy Garland, Katharine Hepburn, and Judy Holliday under his direction. The term was also intended as a euphemism, often pejorative, for gay, and Cukor was even replaced as director of *Gone with the Wind* at the behest of macho star Clark Gable. But this characterization of Cukor can be the basis of a more nuanced auteurist reading, taking into account the professions and means of expression that were open and attractive to gay men in the first half of the twentieth century. Such an exploration might also highlight how specific codes arose in the worlds of theater, cinema, fashion, and design to communicate a shared subcultural aesthetic sensibility when overt gay content was prohibited.

Another important example of how a historiography sensitive to gay presence can illuminate film's past can be found in the underground films of the 1960s. Chroniclers of the films of Jack Smith, Andy Warhol, and Kenneth Anger sought to have them taken seriously as art, describing their outrageous transvestite actors and transgressive sexual content but failing to mention that the directors themselves were gay. Both social history and film interpretation are enhanced by correcting this omission.

An attempt at an inclusive historiography began during a period when nearly two hundred film festivals showing lesbian and gay work sprang up worldwide. The festivals reflected the growing social and cultural presence of lesbians and gay men and featured documentaries, new short works on both film and video, and mainstream and independent films. They also made history, with retrospectives of such gay film giants as Luchino Visconti, Rainer Werner Fassbinder, and Pier Paolo Pasolini and reinterpretations of the distorted and sometimes fascinating ways gay men and lesbians were objectified in films made for general audiences in the past.

VIEWING CUE

What models or types of sexuality appear in one of the films you've recently seen? How does its historical moment shape these models?

12.59 *The Children's Hour* (1961). Lillian Hellman's 1936 play was finally faithfully adapted to the screen when the Production Code was relaxed in the 1960s, but by then its depiction of a lesbian's suicide was dated and damaging.

Lesbian and Gay Images. If we try to reconstruct a history of lesbian and gay images onscreen, we face different obstacles and challenges, most notably censorship. In 1934, the U.S. motion-picture industry began to strictly enforce self-imposed restrictions on film content. The document known as the Production Code stated that "homosexuality and any inference to it are prohibited." In this instance, cultural context matters greatly, because it is virtually impossible to eliminate "inferences" for contemporary audiences. Lillian Hellman's play *The Children's Hour* dealt with the consequences of a malicious child's lies about the lesbian relationship between the two headmistresses of her school. The play was a hit on Broadway in 1936, but the 1937 movie version, *These Three,* implied that the child's gossip was about one teacher's heterosexual affair with the other's fiancé, a change that was transparent to the many members of the audience who were familiar with the play or the publicity surrounding it. Strictures on the theme of homosexuality finally relaxed in the 1960s, in part due to a Supreme Court decision declaring that the movies were entitled to constitutional protections of freedom of speech. One of the first films to capitalize on this shift was William Wyler's remake of *The Children's Hour* (1961) **[Figure 12.59]**. However, nearly a quarter of a century later, and with the feminist and gay rights movements just around the corner, the film's depiction of one teacher's suicide (when the child's accusations provoke her recognition of her own desire for her friend) had a negative impact. The trend of dead or murderous gay characters continued in mainstream treatments for a considerable period, including the notorious examples *Cruising* (1980) and *Basic Instinct* (1992). The vocal protests surrounding both films' perpetuation of stereotypes were probably more instrumental in achieving lesbian and gay visibility than were the films themselves. Also during the 1980s, mainstream heterosexual stars began to appear in films offering so-called positive or complex images of gay men and sometimes lesbians, such as William Hurt's award-winning performance in *Kiss of the Spider Woman* (1985). By the 1990s, many such films were in circulation. Gay actors Harvey Fierstein, Rupert Everett, and Nathan Lane gained considerable fame, while gay director Gus Van Sant was able to make *My Own Private Idaho* (1991), banking on the stature of his mainstream stars River Phoenix and Keanu Reeves **[Figure 12.60]**.

12.60 *My Own Private Idaho* (1991). Gus Van Sant is one of the most successful gay directors of feature films.

Lesbian and Gay Audiences and Niche Marketing. Films like *My Own Private Idaho* addressed themselves to general audiences as well as to lesbians and gay men, a group Hollywood was beginning to recognize as a market niche. This brings us to the third component in the approach to lesbian and gay film: audience. In a legacy of absence and distortion, many of the films that are most cherished by gay and lesbian subcultures have no gay and lesbian content or characters at all, a phenomenon that deserves attention. Films featuring cross-dressing and mistaken identity may eventually resolve themselves with heterosexual coupling while offering many opportunities to play with the possibilities of same-sex pairs along the way. *Peking Opera Blues* (1986), a Hong Kong martial arts movie, and *Yidl mitn Fidl* (1936), a Yiddish-language musical from the 1930s, show the worldwide reach of such story conventions. Musicals have historically been popular in some gay subcultures (as well as among many other audiences), not only for their unabashed pleasure in color, song, and dance, but also for their lack of realism. Musicals offer a vision of a more harmonious world that can appeal to gay men who have been marginalized from the privileges and promises of the world as it is. (Such lyrics as "Somewhere over the rainbow" or "There's a place for us . . . somewhere" make this a theme.) Identification with Hollywood heroines, who carry the emotional weight of such films, and with the stars who pull off such convincing impersonations, is historically a hallmark of gay male subculture. Vulnerable, plucky divas such as Judy Garland, perfectionists such as Barbra Streisand, and unapologetically excessive personalities such as Joan Crawford and Diana Ross have had enormous gay followings. An overall recognition of artifice has shaped the sensibility of *camp*, a humor found in the exaggeration or outdatedness of conventions or in failed attempts at serious art. Horror films such as *Frankenstein* (1931) often side with misunderstood monsters, another way that gay stories have been *coded*, or told indirectly, when direct depiction is prohibited. *The Rocky Horror Picture Show* (1975) successfully exploited camp for an audience that was gay and straight, appealing to another "outsider" group—young people. It is important to stress that there is nothing about gay people that predisposes them to particular tastes in movies; subcultural codes are learned, and they vary among communities and across time.

Censorship itself often leaves traces in the movies it affects. Greta Garbo's 1933 film *Queen Christina* shows the Swedish monarch kissing a lady-in-waiting affectionately on the lips; the character is based on a woman at the real queen's court with whom her biographers have romantically linked her. The film's main storyline, however, concerns the monarch's romance with a male ambassador, a story with no basis in history. "Reading against the grain," a tactic advocated in modern literary studies that acknowledges the reader's participation in making meaning and notes that any text has its own omissions and contradictions, has been fine-tuned by lesbian and gay audiences. In 1993, women applauded *Thelma & Louise* for hitting the road together and rerouting the road movie genre [**Figure 12.61**]. Lesbian audiences saw an erotic commitment between Thelma and Louise, even though the script includes just the one kiss good-bye, right before the women choose death rather than a return to (male) civilization.

Inevitably such interpretations will be debunked by viewers who object to "reading things into" films, but just as the historical archive will never be without a gap, so also are our experiences of the movies never complete—or identical. There is always something that each viewer fills in for himself or herself, and a little piece of the present in the past that we encounter in film history. Lesbian and gay film history is thus illuminating for film historiography in general because it shows that what is invisible is just as important as what is visible.

Representing Culture: Indigenous Media

A third way to understand film history in terms of cultural context is to examine the role that film plays in defining and transmitting a particular culture and in shaping encounters between cultures. In this example, we emphasize the anthropological sense of the term "culture"—that is, culture as the ensemble of customs, relationships, and practices that comprise the way of life of a group of people.

12.61   *Thelma & Louise* (1991). The heroines are not a couple, but the romance of the road and their good-bye kiss has led lesbian audiences to imagine them as such.

Although it is now understood expansively, anthropology arose as the study of the cultures of so-called primitive people.

The medium of film and the history of the discipline have had an important connection. One of the earliest uses of film was to record the ways of life of other cultures for exhibition to audiences in the West. Thomas Edison's early films included some whose purpose was, at least in part, to observe other cultures. In the first decades of film history, little distinction was made between science and sensation: Ernest B. Schoedsack and Merian C. Cooper, the team that made *Grass* (1925), a record of an Iranian migration, went on to make *King Kong* (1933), whose premise, it is sometimes forgotten, is a moviemaking expedition to Sumatra. But with the increased specialization of anthropology, a distinct practice of ethnographic film—the use of film to document cultures for others to study—emerged as an indispensable tool.

Film can record rituals in a way that written ethnographies cannot. Videotaping daily life or festivities can help bypass the traditional ethnographer's preselection of what to document. Filming interviews minimizes the mediation of an interpreter by capturing the subject's own words and gestures through the lens. (The value of objectivity associated with the camera is implied in the French word for lens: *objectif.*) However, the camera can never grant complete access to a cultural context. In a culture that does not use cameras, the equipment can hardly be invisible or neutral. Filming a ritual is necessarily intrusive; moreover, some rituals are not meant to be witnessed by nonparticipants. An on-camera interview is still a performance. The editing of an ethnographic film provides many ways of shaping its message. But because it can capture conversations and gestures, sounds and settings, time and space, film can give a strong impression of documenting a culture despite such mediations.

Nowhere do claims of film as an impartial record become more loaded than in the filming of indigenous people by Western observers, and not until recently have indigenous groups been able to appropriate video and film technology to tell their own stories. Deploying a technology like the movies in such a cultural encounter means claiming the power to represent others and their history. The camera conveys a profound feeling of presence that puts the viewer in the place of the observer or "expert."

Widely considered the first feature-length documentary film and certainly one of the most influential movies ever made, Robert Flaherty's *Nanook of the North* (1922) is a record of the lives and customs of the Inuit people of the Canadian Arctic. The isolation of the people in a harsh environment, and the duration of Flaherty's stay among them, required that the film be produced in close collaboration with its subjects. In the film, Nanook (played by the uncredited Allakariallak), his family, and others engage in traditional behavior, including an exciting seal hunt and the construction of an igloo. These activities were performed and modified for the purposes of the film—the igloo was missing a wall to accommodate the camera, and the struggle of a harpooned seal was represented by men pulling at Nanook's line off camera—but they were "real" records of Inuit people carrying out Inuit hunting and building techniques **[Figure 12.62]**. Part of *Nanook of the North*'s impact at the time lay in the use of a still relatively new technology to deliver an image of a technology-free universe, so that the viewer marveled at both.

Flaherty's claims that he presented an accurate representation of Inuit life are compromised by the reenact-

12.62 *Nanook of the North* (1922). Robert Flaherty re-created traditional activities for the camera, but his images are nevertheless striking records of the Inuit.

ments and by his having paid his subjects. Nevertheless, it is important to realize that Flaherty's supposed blurring of the line between documentary and fiction occurred before such a line had been drawn—that is, before the concept of documentary truth had been defined. The film is also often *primitivist*, using contemporary stereotypes of non-Western people as simple, childlike, and outside the process of history. For example, Nanook is shown trying to eat a gramophone record, yet he and other native collaborators were familiar with modern technology and worked as Flaherty's (uncredited) crew, operating the film cameras and developing the footage. The complex legacy of this film is explored in the video *Nanook Revisited* (1988), which returns to the village where Flaherty's classic was made to take on the myths and realities surrounding his great film among the people whose ancestors participated in its making. *Nanook Revisited* gives a glimpse of another side to the story of the conjunction of "camera" and "primitive," one that characterizes the end of the twentieth century.

12.63   *The Spirit of TV* (1990). Amazon Indians, such as the Waipai, have used video to record their culture and express their rights.

The introduction of video technology to indigenous people, such as the Kayapo and Waipai Indians in the Amazon Basin of Brazil, has resulted in considerable output that has several empowering uses. These include the preservation of traditional culture for future generations; video activism for rights and the environment; and a new form of visual expression in a culture that has always relied on pictorial communication.

In 1985, a Brazilian filmmaker and several anthropologists gave the Kayapo video cameras to use for documenting aspects of traditional culture [Figure 12.63]. As Kremoro, a Kayapo chief, testifies, "In the past, many photographers came here and took our pictures, but they never gave us anything in return. They never attempted to teach anything. Now we, the Kayapo, we are recording our rituals for our children." Soon the Kayapo were also using their cameras to communicate among their villages and to carry on their political struggles with the Brazilian state for land rights. Kayapo videomakers received considerable publicity, including a *Time* magazine cover story. While the Kayapo are entering a new historical moment by employing this technology, the video work's primary purpose is to preserve the past.

Communication strategies were also important to the broadcasting initiatives of indigenous people in Canada, who left behind their legacy as objects of ethnographic film and campaigned for self-representation. Organized activism resulted in the licensing of the Inuit Broadcasting Network in 1982, featuring programming by, for, and about native Canadians. In 1999, the Canadian government ordered cable companies to carry the Aboriginal Peoples Television Network, bringing this culture and its video productions to the whole country. A new phase of indigenous media-making was marked by the historic release of *Atanarjuat: The Fast Runner* (2001). Shot in digital video, this extraordinary film, directed by experienced Inuit filmmaker Zacharias Kunuk, appropriately enough deploys the genre of epic to explore a people's past [Figure 12.64]. But it portrays a cultural legend, not a factual past. Although at first it resembles an ethnographic film, *Atanarjuat* is set a millennium ago. By setting its depiction of the traditional way of life in the mythic past, the film represents an

text continued on page 452 ▶

12.64   *Atanarjuat: The Fast Runner* (2001). Shot on digital video in the Canadian Arctic, this epic is the first feature made in the Inuktitut language by Inuit filmmakers.

Historical Context and
Salt of the Earth (1954)

A film about a successful miners' strike, *Salt of the Earth* (1954) impresses us today as a modest and straightforward picture of the lives of working people, surprising perhaps for its compelling performances and rare focus on Chicano and especially Chicana voices. At the time it was made, however, the film was at the center of violence and controversy. Due to its subject matter, its marginal status vis-à-vis the film industry, or perhaps its limited initial release, it has been ignored in many histories of American cinema. Nonetheless, *Salt of the Earth* provides an excellent case for the study of the cultural contexts of film because political circumstances of its era profoundly shaped its form, its subject matter, and its reception.

Salt of the Earth is one of very few films of its time to focus on the lives of people of color. The story of an actual 1951–1952 miners' strike, the film was shot on location in Silver City, New Mexico, and features Chicano union members playing themselves. As the film acknowledges, the land they now mine for an East Coast company was originally part of Mexico. Adding even more depth to this attention to race and ethnicity is the fact that the film is told from the perspective of a woman. Esperanza Quintero (played by Mexican actress Rosaura Revueltas), the wife of the union local's president, opens the film with a voiceover. *Salt of the Earth* thus chronicles not only the strike, but also Esperanza's emerging consciousness of her own political voice [Figure 12.65]. This consciousness is shown to be rooted in her experience as a woman, a mother, and a working-class resident of the community, called Zinc Town in the film. In the beginning of the film, the pregnant Esperanza (whose name means "hope" in Spanish) is reluctant to join the other women, who argue that proper sanitation is just as important as safety in the miners' demands. Then, at a crucial juncture in the film, she speaks for the women at a union meeting, to the shock and displeasure of her husband, Ramon (Juan Chacón). Ramon's ultimate acknowledgment of her right to speak out and of the equal

status of her concerns parallels the successful resolution of the strike, bringing the film to a hopeful conclusion on both personal and political levels.

Esperanza's story is interwoven with the events of the strike throughout the film, setting up a relationship between the women's and men's struggles that can be described as dialectical, because taken together the two seemingly opposed perspectives create something much stronger. For example, Esperanza is disappointed when she realizes Ramon has forgotten her birthday, but after her son reminds him, the neighbors come by to celebrate in a scene of community life that anticipates the solidarity the families will show during the strike. Later, the silent presence of the neighbors outside her home prevents her family's threatened eviction. During the strike, women start out by bringing coffee to the picketers and end up taking over the lines when the men are barred by a court order. When the women

12.65 *Salt of the Earth* (1954). Rosaura Revueltas as Esperanza, the film's central consciousness.

are jailed, the men must take their turn at household chores. In another cinematically effective dialectical sequence, images of Esperanza giving birth are crosscut with shots of Ramon being brutally beaten by strikebreakers. Their parallel pains show triumph through struggle and link them as partners in their eventual victory.

Salt of the Earth stands in an interesting relationship to Hollywood films of its era that take on social issues, such as Elia Kazan's Gentleman's Agreement. Like them, it translates public conflicts into personal terms. Unlike them, it translates these concerns back out to a broader context so that we are left with more than regrets for the injurious effects of prejudice on individuals. Esperanza's personal journey results in her finding a public voice that is echoed in the cinematic device of the voiceover.

Aesthetically, Salt of the Earth draws on the traditions of Italian neorealism, as it was shot on location with a mostly amateur cast. Dramatically, it conforms to the style of socialist realism, in which an individuated hero stands in for the problems of a class of people. His or her growing consciousness is meant to be echoed by that of the viewers, who are thereby convinced of the justness of a political cause—in this case, that of the striking miners. One particular sequence, in which union members across the country send their dollars to ensure that the workers' families can hold out until the union's demands are met, is intended to solicit our identification and participation.

Salt of the Earth is unique—many of its filmmakers were Communist Party members who turned to independent production when they were blacklisted after the HUAC hearings. Director Herbert Biberman was one of the Hollywood Ten jailed for contempt of Congress. Producer Paul Jarrico had written the script for Song of Russia (1943), one of the HUAC's targets. Oscar-winning screenwriter Michael Wilson (A Place in the Sun, 1951) would later defy the blacklist by writing the pacifist drama Friendly Persuasion (1956). For Salt of the Earth, Wilson visited the miners and wrote his script in consultation with the film's participants, who read or attended readings of the work in progress, giving their input. Juan Chacón, the union president, was cast in that role in the film, giving an unforgettable performance. Nearly all the cast members were actual participants in the strike. The exceptions were Mexican actress Revueltas and several white actors in secondary roles, including blacklisted actor Will Geer as the sinister sheriff. Later, the film was used as a labor-organizing tool, bringing its involvement with working people full circle.

The production was fraught with difficulties. Members of the Hollywood union of technical workers, SMPTE (Society of Motion Picture and Television Engineers), were forbidden from working on the film, and so blacklisted personnel were employed instead, including a number of African American crew members. The publicity surrounding the film was inflammatory. Shooting was sabotaged. Juan Chacón was physically attacked. When Revueltas was de-

tained at the Mexican border and later deported, several scenes had to be shot around her.

The film's exhibition history was also eventful. The projectionists' union forbade its members from showing the film. Opening briefly in New York and Toronto, Salt of the Earth was attacked in the press: respected critic Pauline Kael condemned it as "extremely shrewd propaganda for the urgent business of the USSR." The film was pulled from U.S. distribution and subsequently screened mainly by film societies and at union events. (It has, however, been seen by more people than most Hollywood films because official sanction by the Communist government meant decades of screenings to the vast population of the People's Republic of China.) While this reception sensationalized its content, Salt of the Earth, with its Chicana working-class heroine and narrator, was an unprecedented treatment of class, race, and gender in American film history; arguably, few narrative films made since have addressed their intersection more sensitively.

A specific product of its social and political context, the film did not come out of nowhere. Indeed, its message, in both form and content, is about how a specific context demands particular responses. A brief review of events of the year of the film's release, a time of conflict and contradiction, provides a backdrop for its concerns as well as for the resistance with which it was met. In 1953, the Korean War ended in compromise, with Korea divided into Communist and capitalist nations. Protests in the United States failed to avert the execution of Ethel and Julius Rosenberg, accused of spying for the Soviets. Gender roles were hotly contested, as evidenced by two publication events that year: the first issue of Playboy and the English translation of Simone de Beauvoir's The Second Sex. Puerto Rican nationalist Lolita Lebron, along with three others, opened fire in the U.S. House of Representatives to draw attention to their cause. But hopefulness about racial cooperation was encouraged when the Supreme Court ended school segregation in the landmark case Brown v. Board of Education.

Salt of the Earth's concern with gender and with the relationship of the United States with other nations in the Americas, and the virulence with which its pro-labor message was met, were unique responses to this cultural moment. At the opposite end of the spectrum of production and exhibition, Hollywood released its first films in CinemaScope and 3-D the same year. These entertainments were also consistent with their times, relying as they did on technological innovation for a sense of well-being, as did home appliances and the arms race. As an independently produced film, Salt of the Earth nevertheless drew on the expertise of personnel who had worked within Hollywood. Biberman, Jarrico, Wilson, and Geer had been forced out of the industry by the red scare, an event that is unthinkable today. However, one wonders whether the ideological convictions that their film represents would be compatible in the entertainment cinema of our current cultural context.

Inuit claim to self-representation on several levels. The film's use of amateur actors lends an "authenticity" to the scripted scenes, and its script represents the longest text ever written in the Inuit language. Its images also implicity acknowledge and respond to the beauty as well as the ideological dimensions of a film like *Nanook of the North*.

Atanarjuat reflects many dimensions of its cultural context. The film incorporates traditional Inuit narrative modes, myths, and customs as well as contemporary Inuit activism, which led to the establishment of a native state in the Canadian north. Canada's official policy of multiculturalism allocates funds for artists of color, including media artists, which enabled the filmmakers to receive training and cultivate their ideas in the field. The technological development of digital video made the production possible. Historical cinematic influences, including neorealism and the rich tradition of Canadian documentary, and patterns of distribution and reception, ranging from community screenings to a prize at the Cannes International Film Festival, mark the film's journey. If Steven Spielberg offered us a historical myth in *Saving Private Ryan*, Kunuk and his collaborators offer us a mythical history, both in the content of their film and as the first feature-length film made by an Inuit filmmaker and crew.

▶ **VIEWING CUE**

View a film that depicts another culture. What questions do you have about what you are seeing? How would you put the film in context in order to answer those questions? ⏸

CONCEPTS AT WORK

In this chapter, we have explored inclusive and disjunctive accounts of film history. Alternatives to traditional, selective methods that strive for order and completion, these methods interrupt the certainty of a continuous history. Looking, however cursorily, at global histories, we have attempted to move beyond a single evolutionary progression to multiple sites on the map and beyond stylistic periods to a more dynamic sense of the interaction of national history and film. By introducing films and filmmakers that have been hidden from American film history, we hope to have prompted new explorations of the past. Finally, we have discussed orphan films, lesbian and gay film history, and the representation of indigenous people as questions of, and in, cultural context to show how interdependent representation and reality can be, cautioning us to remember both meanings of the phrase "making history."

Activities

- Good filmmakers know film history; they know which historical tradition they belong to and which ones they reject. Often this implicit knowledge allows a filmmaker to build on those other histories or to distinguish his or her own film against the background of other histories. How would you involve film history as part of your own filmmaking project?
- Sketch a treatment for a different version of an older, perhaps Hollywood, film (such as *Rebel without a Cause* [1955] or *The Graduate* [1967]), remaking it according to a specific contemporary cultural context or that highlights a different historical tradition (such as a political or sexual orientation). How does this new film connect with other inclusive histories? How has this new historical context altered the film?

THE NEXT LEVEL: ADDITIONAL SOURCES

Bruno, Giuliana. *Streetwalking on a Ruined Map: Cultural Theory and the City Films of Elvira Notari.* Princeton: Princeton University Press, 1993. Focusing on the fascinating career of a woman producer of early films in Italy, Bruno makes an argument about gender, cities, and the new experiences of space and time offered by the film medium and the institution of cinema in the context of modernity.

Cripps, Thomas. *Slow Fade to Black: The Negro in American Film,* 1900–1942. New York: Oxford University Press, 1977. A richly detailed social history of the representation of African Americans in U.S. films until World War II that continues in the author's *Making Movies Black* (1993).

Elsaesser, Thomas. *New German Cinema.* New Brunswick: Rutgers University Press, 1989. This definitive study maps the historical and cultural contexts of this influential film movement.

Grant, Catherine, and Annette Kuhn. *Screening World Cinema.* London and NY: Routledge, 2006. This anthology of contemporary essays on transnational cinema explores many of the most current theoretical issues (for instance, the relation of modernity to international cinema) and also discusses some of the most important national cinemas to emerge in recent years (such as the Iranian, Chinese, and Latin American cinemas).

Hansen, Miriam. *Babel and Babylon.* Cambridge: Harvard University Press, 1991. Looking at the specific contexts of U.S. silent film reception as well as at such examples as the popularity of Rudolph Valentino, this book argues that audiences found a new public experience of the modern world at the movies.

Hill, John, and Patricia Church Gibson. *World Cinema: Critical Approaches.* NY: Oxford University Press, 2000. A wide-ranging collection of essays by film scholars from around the world, the book features some general essays on topics such as "Concepts of National Cinema" and "Issues in European Cinema," as well as case studies on individual film cultures, including "East Central European Cinema" and "Taiwanese New Cinema."

Nowell-Smith, Geoffrey, ed. *The Oxford History of World Cinema.* New York: Oxford University Press, 1996. A comprehensive volume featuring contributions from experts on periods, topics, and regions of world cinema.

PART 5

REACTIONS
reading and writing about film

Often our feelings and thoughts about a particular film linger well after we leave the theater, eject a DVD, or turn off our iPods. We may puzzle over a film's meanings or over why it has managed to move us so deeply. We may then seek out reviews, essays, or books about the film, its director, or the country where it was made and become interested in film criticism, theory, and analysis. Reading such film scholarship offers some of the most complex, challenging, and rewarding experiences of the movies. In addition to reading about films, we can also be inspired to write about them. Whether this writing springs from a personal desire or from an assignment given in class, writing about film allows us to develop, articulate, and organize our feelings and perceptions about a movie.

In the next two chapters, we will explore and explain how reading and writing about film deepens and enriches our experience of the movies. We will introduce theories of film, examine different critical methods that have evolved over the years, and map the steps and procedures for turning our initial perceptions about a movie into a sophisticated essay. Through speculation, research, and critical analysis, the film experience grows and develops in as many directions as we are willing to take it.

Reading about Film: Critical Theories and Methods

- ■ Models of cinematic specificity
- ■ Authorship and genre as comparative models
- ■ Classical film theory
- ■ Contemporary film theory

CHAPTER 14

Writing a Film Essay: Observations, Arguments, Research, and Analysis

- ■ Reviews and critical essays
- ■ Taking and organizing notes
- ■ Topic selection
- ■ Thesis and argument development
- ■ Research
- ■ The polished essay

chapter

13

Reading about Film
Critical Theories and Methods

The opening shot of Michael Haneke's *Caché* (2006) depicts a closed doorway on a quiet street. The image appears to conceal nothing; yet slowly the realization dawns on the viewer that this is surveillance footage of the entrance to the main characters' home. At least three distinct points of view are thus implied by the shot: that of the person who has taped the footage; that of the couple to whom the video has been sent; and that of the viewer, who is thus uncomfortably split between characters who solicit empathy and an anonymous other who scrutinizes those characters' lives.

Such complex ways of seeing lie under the surface of all films. Writings about the cinema from the early days of the medium to the present explore both the aesthetics of sound and image and the visceral, ethical, and historically situated encounters between viewers and images that the plot of *Caché* goes on to explore. Readings in film theory help bring hidden dimensions of the film experience into critical view.

At the dawn of a new millennium, audiovisual technologies are more prevalent and more integrated with our experience than ever before. When television was introduced in the mid-twentieth century, and later when home video and computer games became popular, predictions abounded that moviegoing would be eclipsed by the new leisure forms. However, these pronouncements on the death of cinema were premature. What is it about the film experience that resonates so meaningfully with modern life? This question, which emerged with the first projected moving images, continues to be considered today. Such reflection on the nature and uses of the medium is the province of film theory.

KEY CONCEPTS

In this chapter, we will explore

- models of cinematic specificity and formal analysis
- how comparative models such as authorship and genre help us think about the movies
- major problems in classical film theory, including montage and realism
- schools and debates within contemporary film theory, including semiotics, structuralism, and Marxism; poststructuralism; cultural studies, feminism, and race and representation; film and philosophy; and postmodernism and new media

Precisely because cinema is so accessible and familiar, theorizing about it makes some viewers skeptical. Yet with avid moviegoing comes knowledge about the movies. Such knowledge can be the foundation of a theoretical position. Every time we go to the movies, we evaluate elements about the film beforehand: when we choose drama or comedy, we invoke genre; if we choose to see a film because it is made by Steven Soderbergh, we have considered some element of auteurism, the idea that movies are the creative responsibility of a single individual. If we elect, despite the dismissive quality of the term, a "chick flick," we invoke some understanding of reception theory, which focuses on how different kinds of audiences regard different kinds of films. In other words, we recognize that female audiences have related similar types of films to their own experiences in the past. When we speak of the fictional world of *The Godfather* (1972) **[Figure 13.1]** as if it were real, we invoke the concept of *verisimilitude,* the sense of "having the

13.1 *The Godfather* (1972). Audiences accept the verisimilitude of the world of the Corleone crime family.

quality of truth" (see Chapter 5, p. 149). When we select a seat at the movie the-ater, implicit in our choice is an ideal vantage point from which the film illusion will be most complete.

Throughout this book we introduce questions that are explicitly and sys-tematically taken up by film theory. Moreover, theoretical perspectives underpin our discussions of film form, narrative, and genre. Film theory can be defined as a sustained interrogation of propositions about the nature of the medium, the features of individual films, or the interaction between viewers and films. Here we will make explicit the theoretical issues that remain implicit in previous chapters and put this discussion in the context of more specific histories of film theory.

Concepts and Methods in Film Theory

A theory is an explanatory model. *Merriam-Webster's Collegiate Dictionary* (11th ed.) defines *theory* as "the analysis of a set of facts in their relation to one another." In the natural sciences, a theory is verified by experimental work. In a humanistic in-quiry like the study of cinema, a theory cannot be verified in the same manner; rather, it is used to relate and illuminate observed and repeatable phenomena.

The very word "theory" has an interesting resonance in the context of cinema studies. It is derived from the Greek word *theoria*, meaning "a looking at, a con-templation." If theory is "a looking at," as film viewers we know that our eyes can sometimes be deceived. Theories may not be absolute truths, but they do generate understanding. In this section, we will consider what a theory is and what it does.

A theory begins as a hypothesis, a proposition about a phenomenon that awaits verification. Next, as concrete evidence is gathered, the theory may undergo modi-fication. Certain criteria will be enlisted by some theories that would not be consid-ered by others. For example, if we were to postulate that watching a movie resembles dreaming, we would consider such factors as the darkened room, the rel-ative immobility of the viewer, and the way that edited images flow as evidence to be used in confirmation of our hypothesis. We might also conclude from this re-semblance to dreams that movies affect us at a deep, unconscious level. This theory would relegate to the background the more social aspects of attending the movies, such as eating popcorn, chatting with friends, or emulating movie-star fashions. Our "film viewing is like dreaming" theory would also gloss over the fact that movies are produced by many individuals and represent complicated mediations—that is, they do not spring from our individual mental functioning as dreams do. In turn, the alternative theory that films have a particularly strong capacity for realism would exclude evidence supporting the "films resemble dreams" hypothesis. It might instead garner evidence from statements by technicians about how they attempt to approximate reality and from the coherence conveyed by continuity editing. In short, every theoretical approach to cinema foregrounds some elements and relegates others to the background.

Consequently a single theory cannot account for everything about its subject. Indeed, several competing theories can be valid. They may engage in direct debate or be derived from different traditions that are not in dialogue with each other at all. The theory that the cinema inherently strives toward realism may not be exhaustive, but it may still be a useful way to approach a particular film or technological development. It is helpful to think of theories as part of the tool kit of the cultural critic. Sometimes a wrench is required; at other times, a hammer. This metaphor also implies that theoretical inquiry is not only about taking something apart but also about building models and connections.

Besides looking at different aspects of the experience, film theories vary in their level of analysis, selecting different features to address. Some theories regard the cinema as a mass phenomenon that needs to be approached on the basic level of the significance and organization of the institution of cinema, from the industry to the broad-based reception of films, while others are concerned with formal principles alone. Before we present an overview of the history and debates of film theory, it is helpful to situate some important concepts in relation to two general types of theoretical inquiry and the methods that correspond to them. *Concepts of specificity* address the characteristics of the medium as such or the inner workings of a specific film. *Comparative methods* study films in relation to other films in set categories such as auteur films and genre films.

As we have implied, film theory encompasses many different kinds of writing addressed to different problems and readers. Because cinema is relatively new, it has not attracted the internally consistent body of commentary that we see in art or literary criticism. Therefore the field of film theory is wide open, and attempts to give it continuity can be misleading. Another drawback of an introductory text like this one is that the reader does not experience theories and theorists in their own words. A paraphrase does not perform the same function as the theoretical work itself, in whose actual language, rhetoric, and context much of the argument resides. Reading this chapter in tandem with the theoretical texts themselves will give a more complete picture of the range and depth of film theory.

VIEWING CUE

Compare a scene from a film you have viewed in class with a passage from the book from which it was adapted. What elements are specific to the film?

Concepts of Specificity: The Cinematic Medium and Film Form

Theories of an artistic medium often begin by trying to define their object. "What is cinema?" asks French film theorist André Bazin in his classic book of the same title. In philosophy, this is called the question of ontology or being. Ontology is a logical starting point, for many other questions can be derived from the "What is . . . ?" question. One way theorists debate the definition of the cinematic medium is by characterizing its relationship to the world: does the cinema represent or copy reality, or is it fundamentally artistic?

The Cinematic Medium

Sometimes theorists approach film ontologically in an attempt to define the specificity of the medium in relation to other artististic media. How does cinema differ from painting, for example? Both use pictorial imagery. But film differs from painting and drawing because it is composed of photographic images captured with a camera (even if the images are of drawings, as with traditional animation). Film differs from photography in that its images are displayed to give the illusion of motion, a property that it shares with television. Unlike television, but like architecture, cinema involves an experience of spatial immersion. Like performed music, film unfolds in a specific period of time. Yet most musical performances are live, whereas film is recorded. As a storytelling medium, cinema borrows from the novel; yet the way it associates images with emotions resembles poetry. Each of these comparisons can and has been extended considerably and productively. Theorists hope that from ever more precise statements of its properties, they will arrive at the genuine specificity of cinema.

Probably the most persistent and generative comparison in film theory is that between cinema and theater. Both present a perceptual phenomenon, emphasizing sound and vision above the other senses, to an assembly of spectators. However, at the movies, what spectators see and hear is in some sense not really there. There are no actors—or in the case of sound film, musicians—present during the performance. The so-called "liveliest art" (see Arthur Knight's book of that title) can be seen as rather ghostly. Film takes place, in the words of theorist Christian Metz, in an "elsewhere" and an "elsewhen." Theorists contemplating the nature of absence in cinema postulate that viewers overcompensate for it. They invest in the characters and their fates, respond to the rush of colors and sounds, and really *believe* in the film or at least engage in the *suspension of disbelief*. Some theorists regard this attitude of the spectators as a characteristic of cinematic specificity, one that distinguishes film from theater and even from television, which is viewed in a more distracted manner and does not provoke such a strong sense of illusion.

Other theories of cinematic specificity isolate the two-dimensionality, "framedness," rectangular shape, and enhanced size of the moving image as defining characteristics. Still others focus on its material specificity, what the film is made of: light projected through celluloid. Recent technological developments—from videotape playback and virtual reality to computer-generated imagery (CGI), digital cinematography, and digital projection—raise profound ontological questions about cinema. Altering the properties of the image itself by making it smaller or rendering it electronically, rather than capturing or generating it optically, undoubtedly changes the materiality of the image. Other practices challenge film's established relationship to space, time, or the real or phenomenal world—that is, what we can perceive. A photographic image refers to another space, another time, and an actual object whose image is captured by rays of light striking the film emulsion and causing a chemical reaction. A computer-generated image, however, does not have a real-world reference; the image *is* the thing [**Figure 13.2**].

Indeed, the theoretical questions that swirl around new media today recall the period of cinema's inception, when it attracted similar—and almost instantaneous—speculation. André Bazin's question, "What is cinema?" resulted in hundreds of answers. Film "is" many things, in part because film theory has been drawn from many different disciplines—philosophy, psychology, art history, literary theory, history, and sociology—as well as from the many different practices of cinema itself.

Film Form

One advantage of honing a definition of cinema to its specifics is that theorists who accept that definition can then share terms

13.2 *Final Fantasy: The Spirit Within* (2000). The nature of the film image—its ontological status—is challenged by computer-generated imagery (CGI), as in this first film to feature human "actors" produced entirely through CGI.

of analysis and point to concrete elements as the basis for interpretations. Although some theorists might postulate that cinema is defined by some ineffable essence, most would characterize it by its *form*, the configuration of its specific parts. *Formalism* is a method of analysis that considers a film's form, or its structure, to be primary. The theoretical precept behind formalism is that meaning is to be found in the work itself. We do not need to know anything else in order to interpret it—not the identity of the filmmaker, not what setup was used for a particular shot, not the fact that a film's landscape provided the backdrop for other westerns—although such factors might provide context. Of course, most critical approaches include some focus on the work itself, but formalists isolate form as the primary level of interpretation. Like the formalist art historian, the film analyst examines how elements such as light, color, and composition are used in a particular film. Likewise, elements unique to cinema, such as camera movement and distance, shot duration and rhythm, will provide further insights into the film's effectiveness.

Formalist approaches to specific film texts are often called *close readings*. As the term implies, this technique is derived from literary studies. Close readers analyze texts by isolating, naming, and considering the effects of individual elements and of their interrelationships. In the 1920s, formalist critics in the Soviet Union sought to define criteria for the "literariness" of works of literature. Close reading was also central to the practice of new criticism, which developed in the United States in the 1930s. New critics isolated diction, rhyme scheme, punctuation, repetition, and metaphors to speak of *how* a poem means as a crucial component of *what* it means, setting aside speculation about an author's intentions and historical and biographical information about the work. This formalist approach, very influential in the humanities in the United States, has been carried over to university film studies based in English and modern language departments. The theoretical orientation of formalism is toward the autonomy of the work of art, a relatively familiar way to discuss works considered part of high culture, such as symphonies and oil paintings. However, applying formal criteria to commercial cinema requires theorists to make an argument for film's aesthetic specificity.

Although formalism looks at the work in and of itself, it also varies in context. The Russian formalists codified criticism through an elaborate nomenclature, striving for a scientific standard of objectivity that was political in aim. If interpretations of artworks could be accomplished through the application of specific techniques, they would no longer be the province of a privileged few who based their "appreciations" on ultimately impressionistic criteria. But formalism is just as often apolitical. Attempting to sever the connection between literature and social context was an expressed purpose of new criticism. Applied loosely, formalism accompanies almost any serious treatment of works of art in terms of their media, and it is a pervasive element in contemporary film studies.

However, in adapting literary techniques to film studies, several problems arise. First, the vocabulary of literary analysis is well established, whereas film studies must introduce terms and make them widely accepted. The terminology of filmmaking—jump cut, three-point lighting, over-the-shoulder shot—is available to help critics identify the properties of a shot or sequence, but sometimes new terms must be invented. Literary interpretation uses words to talk about words. In the case of film analysis, words must be used to describe images and sounds. Formalist approaches to film can borrow language from traditional art and music criticism to discuss color and composition, melody and rhythm. But film has an added temporal dimension, and its moving images are difficult to pin down without distorting the viewer's perception. Theater criticism can help in the discussion of performance and mise-en-scène. But the very act of referring to these elements in a particular film presents its own unique problems. Historically, it has been impossible to "quote" the cinematic "passage" one is analyzing, precisely because it literally passes by in an instant. One can say a great deal about a single image, but during the viewing of a film, there are twenty-four discrete images per second. Stopping the film to look closely means that the *cinematic* experience disappears—"cinema" means movement. New technologies can facilitate critics' references to moving images, allowing analysts to "capture" clips or still frames. Here a problem of methodology—how to refer—has theoretical implications.

One method of close reading is to look at a segment of film shot by shot. This technique of *textual analysis* is exemplified in the work of French film theorist Raymond Bellour. Bellour's detailed studies of films by Alfred Hitchcock, Howard Hawks, and others are accompanied by charts listing all the shots in the sequence to be analyzed as well as such variables as camera distance or movement. From such a chart, the analyst notes and interprets the interrelations among different formal elements and their patterns of development. For example, how do variations in camera distance correlate with camera movements in a given sequence? What effect do these variations have? Borrowing from semiotics and communication studies, analysts such as Bellour refer to elements such as shot duration, camera movement, and lighting as **codes**. A code is essentially a rule, and it structures a particular act of communication, a *message*. The code must be shared by the sender and the receiver for the message to be understood. For example, viewers understand that the shadows in a shot from *The Big Heat* (1953) signify a threat because they recognize the code of film noir lighting [**Figure 13.3**]. Familiarity with the codes of film music allows us to understand such connotations as the time and place the movie is set in as well as the concept of "this is the introductory sequence." The textual analyst draws conclusions from the interactions of these codes over a series of shots. For instance, dark shadows and threatening music reinforce each other to connote danger. Some codes used in cinema, such as lighting and dialogue, are shared with theater. Other codes, such as framing, camera movement, and shot duration, are specific to film. One of the striking features of textual analyses is that they have no apparent stopping point: there is always something more to interpret. Book-length studies have analyzed a single feature film. Textual analyses are an especially effective way to train oneself to look—and listen—to the movies more closely.

13.3 *The Big Heat* (1953). Low-key lighting is a code that gives viewers the message that this is a film noir.

▶ **VIEWING CUE**

Closely analyze the first scene of the last film you viewed for class. Enumerate the shots. What categories or codes will yield the most interesting results when applied to each shot?

Comparative Methods: Authorship and Genre Theories

In order to test propositions about how films work, critics and theorists have found ways to classify films. Two of the primary categories for exploring groups of films in order to generate hypotheses about their commonalities and divergences are *authors* or *auteurs* and *genres*. These two groupings are also commonsense ways of looking at the movies. Today names of directors are even used as adjectives, as in a "Lynchean universe" and a "Spike Lee shot" [**Figure 13.4**].

13.4 *Do the Right Thing* (1989). Recognizing the head-on close-up as a "Spike Lee shot" shows our everyday understanding of auteurist theory.

13.5   *Hannibal* (2001). Director Ridley Scott crowds his frame with details, using mise-en-scène to reflect his characters' plights in a thriller . . .

13.6   *Blade Runner* (1982). . . . and in a science fiction film.

We refer to genre when we discuss what kind of film we are interested in seeing. Because authors and genres are such widespread classificatory schemas, we do not always realize that they are based in part on *theories* about film.

Authorship

The theory of film authorship, or **auteur theory**, holds that a film bears the creative imprint of one individual, usually the director, whether or not it is considered a great work of art. A so-called auteur film, from the French word for author, is taken to reveal the personality of its director. The film *Citizen Kane* (1941) is rarely invoked without mention of the film's cowriter, director, and star Orson Welles. However, many, if not most, films generate no such immediate association with a creator. Viewers often remain oblivious to the director's name or simply consider other aspects of a film to be more immediate.

Ridley Scott's *Hannibal* (2001) **[Figure 13.5]** is likely to be first identified as the sequel to Jonathan Demme's *The Silence of the Lambs* (1991). Fans of the novelist Thomas Harris will think of it as part of a series of films adapted from his novels that feature the character Dr. Hannibal Lecter. However, *Hannibal* can be contextualized in terms of director Ridley Scott's authorship. In the film's emphasis on an enveloping mise-en-scène, one might detect visual similarities to Scott's otherwise very different *Gladiator* (2000) and *Blade Runner* (1982) **[Figure 13.6]**. One might find interesting parallels in the director's depiction of violence in *Hannibal*, a thriller, and in his war film *Black Hawk Down* (2001), which was made in the same year. Another argument about authorship would emphasize the thematic link between the strong female character played by Julianne Moore in *Hannibal* and the heroines of Scott's *G.I. Jane* (1997), *Thelma & Louise* (1991), and *Alien* (1979).

These examples show that authorship is not only a matter of crediting an individual with a film's artistry but also a way of meaningfully relating works within a filmmaker's corpus. Films grouped by author reveal something about the personal style and preoccupations of that filmmaker. For example, John Ford's westerns, produced over several decades, often show an individual in conflict with a community's ethos.

Chapter 11 looks at film history in terms of a theory of authorship; notions of masters and masterpieces employ value judgments. In this framework, great films and great individuals make history. Authorship is a concept drawn from literary studies, and with that field comes canons and rankings. Because great literature is considered "culture," in the sense of appealing to cultivated taste, borrowing the literary concept of authorship helps lend prestige to the medium of cinema, rendering it indisputably worthy of study. (Somewhat paradoxically, the "author" role is usually reserved for directors rather than screenwriters—although directors who write their own scripts are especially revered.) However, the concept of value itself is relative. Alfred Hitchcock made his name known to audiences through devices such as cameo appearances [Figure 13.7] when most directors remained anonymous. But because he worked in the thriller genre, he was critically dismissed as an entertainer who was only later considered a prestigious author. Elia Kazan, a theater director whose films, including *Gentleman's Agreement* (1947), deal with social issues, was accorded greater respect in his day. Yet among film enthusiasts today, Hitchcock is granted higher status—evidence of changing values.

13.7 *Strangers on a Train* (1951). Alfred Hitchcock's cameos assisted popular recognition of his authorship.

Hitchcock's self-promotion is not without precedent. In the first few decades of film, directors like D. W. Griffith made their creative role a selling point for their films. The intertitles of Griffith's films bore his initials, and he banked on his name recognition when he joined stars Mary Pickford, Douglas Fairbanks, and Charlie Chaplin (also a director) in the founding of United Artists. Griffith's contemporary Lois Weber was also known to her audiences by name, although her reputation was eclipsed until recent interest in women directors led to her rediscovery. Woody Allen is one of the most recognizable of American auteurs because he writes, directs, and appears in his films, which often use the same actors and contain recurrent themes.

Increasingly, marketing and promotion identify films by their directors. That a film is directed by Quentin Tarantino, Clint Eastwood, the Coen brothers, or Ang Lee is often considered its most salient feature. Tarantino's name has even been used to "present" other directors' work, such as Wong Kar-wai's *Chungking Express* (1994). International names such as Ken Loach, Zhang Yimou, Claire Denis, and Aki Kaurismäki attract art-house and festival audiences. These filmmakers draw on the tradition of postwar art cinema, which made the filmgoing public aware of film directors' names. Such filmmakers' idiosyncrasies are an important marker of this type of authorship; in contrast, the name recognition of directors such as Chris Columbus is more like that of a commercial novelist. Certainly there are many films whose directors we could not name. *The Brady Bunch Movie* (1995) was marketed on the name recognition of the 1970s television show. Nevertheless, the use of authorship as a critical approach reveals that this film was directed by a woman, Betty Thomas. Because female directors in Hollywood are still a small minority, this knowledge might be significant. It should be clear from these examples that a theory of authorship, or auteurism, is not an inevitable way to see films, although it is frequently intuitive and often very useful.

> **▶ VIEWING CUE**
>
> Watch another film by the director of the last one you viewed. What stylistic features appear in both films? What aspects of auteur theory does your comparison reveal? **⏸**

The History of Auteur Theory. Authorship as a critical construct has a history; it is often invoked strategically; and it is not free from the economics of filmmaking and film promotion. This history became visible in the 1950s when specific directors were vocally championed by French critics. The retention of the French term "auteur" in English marks this origin. Not only does the French word refer to a critical tradition, but simply by being French it carries connotations of cultural value for English speakers. In the 1950s, writers for the new film magazine *Cahiers du cinéma* promoted what they called "*la politique des auteurs*," a "policy" or doctrine of singling out for praise certain filmmakers, such as Orson Welles, Fritz Lang, Samuel Fuller, and Robert Bresson, whose distinct styles made their films immediately identifiable. The criticism written by young filmmakers like François Truffaut was a rebellious gesture against commercial French filmmaking of that time, which they felt lacked vitality and currency. The journal and its

13.8 **Jean-Luc Godard**, auteur.

polemics—impassioned paeans to the greats and denigration of those who lacked vision—attracted a great deal of attention and debate in the United States and Britain.

As noted in Chapter 12, in the post–World War II period, film culture was energized by Italian neorealism, whose immediacy allowed for the expression of filmmakers' personal visions. Italian filmmaker Roberto Rossellini and Swedish art-film director Ingmar Bergman stood out in this period as true "authors" who wrote and directed their films. The *Cahiers* critics themselves aspired to be and soon emerged as significant auteurs, defining the *nouvelle vague,* or French New Wave. Besides François Truffaut, among their number were Jean-Luc Godard **[Figure 13.8]**, Eric Rohmer, Jacques Rivette, and Claude Chabrol, all of whom continue to make films. These *cineastes,* or film aficionados, wrote fervent appreciations of European directors like Rossellini, whose works clearly reflected his individual vision of humanity and the prospects for postwar renewal. Yet *Cahiers du cinéma*'s concept of authorship was also applied to a group of filmmakers for whom the idea of such conscious and consistent creative artistry seemed less appropriate: directors working in the heyday of the Hollywood studio system. In the critics' minds, the efforts of such filmmakers were extraordinary because they each left their unmistakable mark on even routine assignments. Despite the constraints on their artistic autonomy and the primacy of market considerations, Hollywood auteurs such as Raoul Walsh and Howard Hawks emerged as artists who left their signature on their films in the form of characteristic motifs or striking compositions. The elevation of these directors' reputations glorified the task of the critics as well. Their writings in praise of B-filmmakers like Budd Boetticher, known for his films about bullfighting, were impassioned polemics. Debates arose over whether a particular director should be classified a true auteur or a mere **metteur en scène** (French, "director," derived from theatrical usage), a label that conveyed technical competence without a strong individual vision. When the *Cahiers* group began writing and directing their own films at the end of the 1950s, they combined the influences of their European and Hollywood idols into distinct auteurist styles of their own (see Film in Focus, pp. 30–32 and Chapter 12, pp. 412–414).

The *politique des auteurs* was imported to the American context and popularized by critic Andrew Sarris of *Film Culture* and the *Village Voice.* In his 1968 collection *The American Cinema: Directors and Directions, 1929–1968,* Sarris lists his pantheon of directors, such as Howard Hawks, whose films often center around strong male bonds, and deflates the reputations of Academy Award winners such as William Wyler. In Sarris's hierarchy of Hollywood talent, the judgment of the critic prevails in assigning relative status to a wide array of directors based on their personal signature. Like that of the French critics, Sarris's work depends on a deep **cinephilia,** or love of cinema, and an almost exhaustive knowledge of the films—major and minor—released throughout the previous several decades. Sarris's rendering of *la politique des auteurs* as auteur theory is somewhat misleading; it is less a fully worked-out theory than a method, and the political connotation is lost in translation. Defining the approach, Sarris isolates as criteria of value the director's "technical competence" and "distinguishable personality" as well as the quality of "interior meaning" that makes the director's films art. Challenged even at the time but exerting a wide influence on film education, Sarris's work stands as a humanist appreciation of cinema that helped elevate film to significant cultural status. Certainly the popularization of auteur theory saved many Hollywood studio productions from historical obscurity and critical neglect.

Critiques of Auteur Theory.

Critiques of Auteur Theory. A cluster of contradictions lies at the heart of the auteurist approach: cinema is a collaborative, commercial, and highly technologically mediated form. Making a film is not as personal as authoring a poem. It might make sense to call U.S. independent filmmaker Su Friedrich an author, since she writes, directs, produces, shoots, and edits most of her films. But because so many individuals usually contribute to a film, it can be hard to assign credit to a single authorial vision, especially in studio-produced work. Critic Pauline Kael counters Sarris's position in one famous instance, asserting that writer Herman Mankiewicz rather than Orson Welles should be credited for coming up with *Citizen Kane*'s original structure and that cinematographer Gregg Toland's work is what distinguishes the film's look. Often it makes sense to speak of a body of work in terms of creative personnel other than the director. The film *42nd Street* (1933) is meaningfully grouped with the work of choreographer Busby Berkeley, even though it was directed by Lloyd Bacon. In commercial cinema, a producer, studio, or franchise may be more important than a director. Today a credit such as "a Tom Cruise film" or even "an Oliver Stone film" may be more a matter of contractual obligations and financial arrangements than of authorship. Finally the technology involved in film production intervenes between the author/visionary and the final product in a way that can again be contrasted with the example of poetry. Indeed, the equally strong mystique that the camera simply captures what is put before it detracts from crediting an author's vision. Yet the theory of film authorship remains strong, identifying one person as having primary responsibility for the artistic merits of a film.

Another contradiction of auteur theory is that it extended some of the cultural prestige of the literary "genius" to filmmakers at the same time literary critics were calling this traditional notion into question. In a 1968 essay, French literary critic Roland Barthes declared "the death of the author." The artist's conscious intention and biography were set aside to consider the formal qualities of the work itself and to give play to the inventiveness of the activity of interpretation. The new perspectives on authorship had their roots in **structuralism**, an approach to linguistics and anthropology that, when extended to literary and filmic narratives, looks for common structures rather than originality. In the case of films, these common structures might be plots or characters that recur across works. Because the cinema depends so heavily and so obviously on standard formulas, the structuralist method was very productive when applied to film. The attribution of authorship to filmmakers began to be reevaluated in light of this new work.

In his influential 1972 book, *Signs and Meaning in the Cinema*, Peter Wollen advocates a structural approach to authorship: "The *auteur* theory does not limit itself to acclaiming the director as the main author of a film. It implies an operation of decipherment; it reveals authors where none had been seen before." "Decipherment" puts the activity on the side of the critic. Wollen places the film author's name in quotation marks to designate a critical construct rather than a biographical individual. For example, John Ford's films return again and again to the antinomy, or opposition, between garden and wilderness. One can see this common "Ford" structure developed differently from *My Darling Clementine* (1946) to *The Man Who Shot Liberty Valance* (1962). Through his approach, Wollen attempts to reconcile the contradiction between the heralding of artistry that always informs criticism and the skepticism toward individual creative intention that is characteristic of structuralism.

13.9 *The Portrait of a Lady* (1996). Auteurist approaches to Jane Campion's work take her films' representations of female social identity into account.

Today, although informed writing about film for a general readership relies heavily on references to directors, most theorists would not admit to being auteurists, whose main business is to recognize and applaud intentional artistry. Crediting directors as the source of meanings in their films can seem too naive or biased, too much like a fan's approach to film. Yet no matter how pure one's theoretical approach, one cannot deny that individual creativity plays a role in filmmaking. Theorists concede this when they choose to write about films by directors they particularly admire.

Identity Politics and Auteur Theory.

Directions in criticism that came after structuralism and poststructuralism offer new reasons to retain the concept of authorship. Although the biography of a filmmaker may not be directly reflected in his or her films, such theories argue, aspects of social identity do have an important impact on a filmmaker's vision. In criticism using authorship, the stakes have shifted, from debating where a particular film should be ranked in John Ford's oeuvre to exploring, for example, writer-director Jane Campion's conceptualization of restrictions on female identity in such films as *The Piano* (1993) and *The Portrait of a Lady* (1996) [Figure 13.9]. Spike Lee asserted that as an African American filmmaker he was more qualified to make the biographical film *Malcolm X* (1992) than a white director would have been. Filmmakers whose group identities have been marginalized or deemed irrelevant throughout the history of cinema may now find their work being admitted to the canon. The criteria for evaluation is changing to consider racial, ethnic, and gender identity alongside the elusive qualities of "distinguishable personality."

Identity categories can certainly receive too much emphasis. Filmmakers can be slotted by studios into a particular subject matter, or their achievements can be diminished by such phrases as "woman filmmaker." But identity categories are not irrelevant even when they are invisible. Generally more readily thought of as individuals than as representatives of a group, white male filmmakers are entrusted with large-budget films with universal themes and stories—for example, the sinking of the *Titanic* told as a love story. In a different way, director Steven Spielberg claimed his Jewish heritage with his film about the Holocaust, *Schindler's List* (1993), and used his prominence and that of the film to establish the Survivors of the Shoah Visual History Foundation.

Still, social identity does not necessarily leave an imprint on a work. Even when it does, it is often difficult to determine exactly what that imprint is. Whether it is important that Jane Campion is a woman filmmaker depends on the critic's argument. More conventional auteurist arguments may or may not touch on aspects of social identity—for example, Hitchcock's Britishness. Feminist and antiracist literary critics have pointed out that just when more women and people of color were receiving recognition as authors, "the death of the author" declared that authorial identity was irrelevant. If one can be excluded from making films because of one's identity, then critical accounts of the work of those who do succeed are justified in taking the social identity and struggles of the author into account.

As we have argued, authorship is a methodology that finds elements of commonality in films by the same individual. One can surely find unifying elements among the films of a particular composer, producer, or costume designer, but because a director oversees all creative elements, he or she is usually touted as the author. Although various theories of authorship exist, they all attribute elements in the film to the filmmaker, whether they argue that these are intentional features, unconscious preoccupations, or traces of social experience. In any case, it is important to realize that because the set of common traits is advanced by the critic, authorship itself is a critical construct.

Genre

Thinking of films in terms of genre is a fundamental way of classifying and theorizing about them. As noted in Chapter 10 on film genres, "genre" means kind or classification. Characters, story, iconography, a happy or sad ending—these are elements that films in a particular genre have in common. Yet the concept of genre is not a simple one. As we have suggested, what constitutes a specific genre is open for interpretation, as is the function genres serve for filmmakers, audiences, and critics. Whereas Chapter 10 emphasized the formal and cultural shapes of different film genres, here we will concentrate on theoretical approaches to the concept.

As a comparative method, the employment of genre in film theory is influenced by literary approaches dating back to Aristotle's *Poetics*. However, the contemporary use of the term often refers less to the category of the aesthetic than to mass-produced cultural artifacts as distinguished from works of art. Artworks are thought to exhibit the artistic originality of their creators; they are anything but generic. This is a tension similar to one we uncovered in our earlier discussion of authorship. Because films are products of an industry, associating them with authors tends to raise them above genre. The term "genre film" designates a type of movie that is quickly recognizable, but it may also carry pejorative connotations of lacking originality. Because unique works of art have traditionally been invested with cultural value, genre films have less prestige. For example, it was a surprise when *The Silence of the Lambs* won an Academy Award for Best Picture because it is a thriller, a somewhat devalued popular genre.

In some ways it makes more sense for an expensive, entertainment-oriented product like film to rely on the category of genre than it does for literature to do so. Genre distinctions are used within the film industry both to differentiate its products and to promote new films in relation to a known quantity. Genres ebb and flow according to audience response: musicals and westerns have been prominent in some periods and "box-office poison" in others. Specific film types, such as killer-couple-on-a-rampage films, might become a genre when audiences respond well to one such film. Kung-fu or surfer films are marketed in specifically generic terms.

Critics of mass culture contend that audiences are given films that follow formulas so that the market will remain predictable. This position does not acknowledge any real need or preference on the part of the audience to which a genre responds. Other commentators believe that the cycle of definition and demand is more reciprocal. For the genre contract to work, it must be honored at the points of production and reception—that is, producers and audiences must agree on what to expect from a certain kind of film. Spoofs such as *Airplane!* (1980), *Scary Movie* (2000), *Date Movie* (2006), and their sequels acknowledge just how practiced film audiences are at recognizing genre conventions. Far from playing to the lowest common denominator, genre films actually depend on and often reward audience sophistication. *Scream 2* (1997) calls attention to the conventions of its genre—for example, that someone who leaves the room in a horror film is unlikely to return—and still satisfyingly fulfills them. Is it with the conventions or the variations that our pleasure lies? Most commentators agree that it is both. The viewing of a genre film resembles a ritual in that the participants already know the rules, but the particular enactment is a strategic use of those rules.

Myth and Genre. One explanation for the appeal of genres is that they function like myths. In anthropologist Claude Levi-Strauss's terms, myths are stories that mediate or manage contradictions in social life and that cultures use to explain the inexplicable, justify the inevitable, or reconcile the irreconcilable. Many studies have focused on varieties of U.S. studio-produced films in the heyday of the Hollywood system, not only as products being sold to audiences as consumers, but also as modern myths.

Westerns are popular examples for genre theory. The stark outlines of the western's opposition between good and evil and the outcome that favors the cowboys and settlers' victory over indigenous Americans are ways of justifying as inevitable the course of a history now decided. The western appeared in turn-of-the-century American culture in dime novels and Wild West shows just at the time when there was no more land to settle. The genre serves as a way to keep the closed frontier open in the imagination. When we go to see a western, we know what we are getting: horses, open horizons, good guys in white, bad guys in black. Or do we? Critics have documented how genres evolve and cultural myths shift. During the Cold War in the 1950s, the need for identifiable bad guys can be associated with the U.S. attitude toward the Soviet Union. From such an easy identification of good guys and bad guys, we end up with more complicated moral scenarios in existential westerns: *The Searchers* (1956), in which John Wayne's character's racism is evident, and *Unforgiven* (1992), in which violence seems pointless [**Figure 13.10**]. We see westerns featuring independent women in *The Quick and the Dead* (1995) and African American cowboys in *Posse* (1993). These films may redefine our notions of history and heroism. That an epic western can be transposed to an outer-space setting in *Star Wars* (1977) suggests ways in which the geography of the western United States that the genre usually features may itself be an imaginary space. Different genres work out different cultural questions or problems; hence, their emergence and decline in particular periods. Critic Thomas Schatz, in his book *Hollywood Genres*, for example, sees musicals as celebrating cultural integration, often symbolized by the couple coming together, whereas westerns require the establishment of a home, one that the wandering hero cannot himself enjoy.

As we can see from these examples of the western, a genre is both a cultural form that works as if through shorthand and a pervasive, diverse phenomenon. The common structures that genres use allow a conflict to be posed in an immediately recognizable form. The variety among films in a genre allows the conflict to be revisited with some complexity, perhaps to challenge the inevitability of a social "fact" such as Native American genocide. Genre is conservative because it uses fixed structures, but it can also register social change or dissent. The repetition so basic to genre testifies that a society needs to "solve" the same problems and open the same contradictions again and again, which evidences a measure of critique of the status quo. For example, the horror film allows for the eruption of repressed, antisocial impulses. Genre thus serves an important social function, and audiences' immediate and enthusiastic response supports this claim.

13.10   ***Unforgiven*** (1992). Clint Eastwood's existential western revived the genre in the 1990s.

Genres and Contexts. Like auteur criticism, genre criticism was invigorated by the film culture of post–World War II France. American films that had not been released during that country's occupation by Germany were finally exhibited all at once, making commonalities easy to identify. Also, like auteur criticism, genre criticism depends on cinephilia because making generalizations based on only a few films would be imprudent. Sometimes genre criticism is considered at odds with auteurism. Geniuses could not make run-of-the-mill films—or if they did, it was an exception in their oeuvre. But keeping the history of criticism in mind, we can see that auteurist approaches actually developed in tandem with genre perspectives. It was often the mark of the auteur on a genre that distinguished him. This is certainly the case with John Ford and the western. The critic would consider how the artist's intentions intersected with the set rules of genre.

13.11 *His Girl Friday* (1940). Howard Hawks made classics in disparate genres, including westerns, musicals, adventure films, and comedies such as this one.

Auteur criticism also praised the handling of different genres by a particularly gifted auteur. Critic Robin Wood looks at the elaboration of Hawksian themes in both Howard Hawks's male adventure films and his screwball comedies and finds them to be related to the same concerns [**Figure 13.11**]. A contemporary auteur such as Quentin Tarantino is known for his self-conscious use of martial arts, blaxploitation, and crime film genres. Ridley Scott made an utterly original film in *Blade Runner* while respecting science fiction conventions. Steven Soderbergh set out to make a genre film with *Out of Sight* (1998) as well as to "tweak" crime film conventions. The critical rehabilitation of the popular cinema, especially Hollywood movies, that auteurism began to bring about in the 1950s was carried on through genre criticism more directly and without auteur theory's dependence on the literary analogy.

As we have intimated, genre is a category that must be analyzed across texts. While we might be able to designate a single film as a western, it is only because we have seen westerns before. This repetition of formulas leads to a complicated **intertextuality**, the dependence of one text on other texts for its full meaning. For example, the intertexts of *The Dark Knight* (2008) include the other Batman movies; the comic book from which the characters are derived; the 1960s television series; the toys, games, and Halloween costumes featuring the characters; and similar feature films based on other superheroes. The audience is the place where all of the intersecting intertextual meanings come together. Bringing their prior experiences with them to the movie theater, audiences have agency, or control, in determining meaning.

What defines a genre is a key question for theorists. The extremely useful categories of film noir and melodrama pose interesting problems for genre criticism. The term "film noir" was coined by French critics for 1940s and 1950s American films that shared a dark sensibility and a dark lighting style, such as *Double Indemnity* (1944) and *The Big Heat*. In this case the Hollywood studios did not set out to produce a distinct genre to sell its products; rather, critical comparison brought out similarities. Some theorists related common aesthetic elements to a postwar society characterized by insecurity about gender roles, the economy, changing definitions of race, and nuclear technology. Others were concerned with whether film noir actually qualified as a genre. Many film noirs belong to the existing genre of crime films, and film noir–type lighting also appeared in occasional westerns or even musicals in the 1940s and 1950s. Some critics designated film noir a cycle, a term intended to demonstrate a closer tie to

13.12   ***Bound*** (1996). Film noir conventions are updated with a wink to the audience.

a specific historical moment than did the more adaptable and ahistorical notion of genre. Many films made in the 1970s and after pay homage to this style, from *Chinatown* (1974) and *Body Heat* (1981) to *Bound* (1996) **[Figure 13.12]**; they are sometimes referred to as *neo-noir*. At its simplest, film noir was a category that critics used to make sense of a group of films by comparing them with each other. But debates about its parameters indicate that the ambiguity and confusion at the heart of film noir are precisely what has generated theoretical interest in the category.

"Melodrama" is a theatrical term used long before the advent of cinema, and film theory has introduced further meanings. Historically, film reviewers and studios referred to many kinds of films as melodrama, but we would not necessarily include them in the category today. Melodramatic feeling infuses a range of genres, from thrillers to historical dramas such as *Gone with the Wind* (1939). Critics sometimes refer to melodrama as a mode rather than a genre because it is so pervasive, informing film history from most silent-era dramas through to a film like *Brokeback Mountain* (2005). Family melodramas of the 1950s and early 1960s by such directors as Douglas Sirk (*Written on the Wind,* 1956), Nicholas Ray (*Rebel without a Cause,* 1955), and Vincente Minnelli (*Home from the Hill,* 1960) were championed by film scholars for their stylistic critiques of the social and familial norms that constrained their protagonists. Such interpretations identified a critical function in apparently mainstream Hollywood films. Again, the critical definition of a category of films allowed a specific theoretical position to emerge. This position, which saw social critique in apparently escapist films, influenced contemporary independent filmmaker Todd Haynes's film *Far from Heaven* (2002) **[Figure 13.13]**, which emulates the subject matter and style of such 1950s melodramas as Sirk's *All That Heaven Allows.*

Westerns and gangster films attracted attention from the first practitioners of genre criticism. Genres concerned with the role of violence and the status of the outsider, they also have historically appealed primarily to men and have emphasized male characters and issues. One of the cultural problems genre attempts to address is a gender question—in this case, the viable forms of male identity. The so-called **woman's picture**, a genre produced for and marketed directly to women, received attention somewhat later in the development of film studies when feminist issues came to the fore. A type of melodrama branded by the film industry for its appeal to female audiences, the woman's picture, or "weepie," has been understood by theorists as a cultural refuge, a forum for dealing with problems of female social identity. This does not mean that romance and motherhood, the concerns of these films, are the only dimensions of female experience, or that the sacrifices these films so often depict are to be applauded or emulated. Rather, the genre addresses the contradictions of the status quo, and women's pictures and their soap-opera offshoots are centered in some of the most restrictive aspects of women's

▶ **VIEWING CUE**

View another film of the genre of the one you have just watched. Draw up a list of features the two movies share. What differences can you identify? Does your comparison of these films reveal aspects of genre theory? ⏸

13.13   ***Far from Heaven*** (2002). Todd Haynes's tribute to the domestic melodrama of the 1950s.

lives [**Figure 13.14**]. Identifying the specific gendered or national dimensions of genres challenges the idea of their mythic function as timeless and unchanging. Such theoretical insights are in fact behind some of the most successful revisionist genre films: *Thelma & Louise* (1991), for instance, a road movie that makes a powerful equation between freedom and driving, is geared toward women.

In sum, genre is a powerful way to organize our experience of the cinema. We respond to the ritual of genre in unconscious ways, while also consciously recognizing its conventions and appreciating its stylistic and ideological variations. Film theory that focuses on genre enables us to appreciate both aesthetic features and audience experience. Genre criticism is a way to relate individual films to a flexible set of shared rules. Approaches looking abstractly at the nature or ontology of the film medium, close readings, or genre and auteur criticism all operate on different levels of inquiry but are often combined in practice, as the Film in Focus on *Touch of Evil* (1958) (pp. 474–476) shows. Film theorist Stephen Heath's elaborate and influential close reading looks at how each segment of the film engages and elaborates specific formal and narrative codes. According to Heath, the prominence of the code "light" references the film's status as a representative of the crime film genre with its shadowy mise-en-scène, while the code "author" is especially meaningful because writer-director Orson Welles appears as the film's antihero. In fact, Welles's imposing figure casts its shadow on most accounts of this film, even those that use it to illustrate the category of film noir.

13.14 *Stella Dallas* (1937). This classic "weepie" makes maternal sacrifice seem subversive.

Film Theory and Historical Context

The concepts and methods reviewed so far were formulated over time in the work of major film theorists, and they are still discussed and practiced by contemporary scholars. An overview of film theory allows us to contextualize and historicize important thinkers and to understand how key principles and terms have been defined and debated. There are no clear boundaries to the field, however. Film theory, and the emerging theories that address new and related audiovisual media, will undoubtedly take on new questions in the future. These concerns will be shaped by an intellectual history of considerable longevity and complexity.

Early Film Theory

"Last night I was in the Kingdom of Shadows. If you only knew how strange it is to be there," wrote the Russian novelist Maxim Gorky after attending a film screening in 1896. When movies were new, observers searched for metaphors to describe the experience of seeing them. Struck by movies' magical properties, viewers attempted to pinpoint what was distinctive about the medium. This reflection on the nature of cinema has continued throughout the more than one hundred years of its existence. Some early critics considered moviegoing a social phenomenon, a new form of urban entertainment characteristic of the dawning twentieth century. Others viewed the cinema in aesthetic terms, heralding it as the "seventh art."

text continued on page 476 ▶

FILM IN FOCUS

Genre and Authorship in *Touch of Evil* (1958)

Touch of Evil is a police thriller based on the novel *Badge of Evil* by Whit Masterson, who specialized in books of this genre. Set in an unnamed, unsavory town on the U.S.-Mexico border, the film follows the power struggle between the Mexican official Vargas (Charlton Heston), recently married to an American woman named Susie (Janet Leigh), and the corrupt American detective Quinlan (Orson Welles). In the very first shot—a remarkable mobile tracking shot—a wealthy American and his girlfriend are killed, and the film leads us from the crime investigation into an investigation by Vargas of Quinlan's long history of witness intimidation and evidence tampering. Meanwhile, Susie is assaulted and then framed for drug use and homicide by the Grandi family, the border town's small-time criminal mob. It turns out that Quinlan is behind the attack on Susie, and in the end he is shot and killed by his formerly loyal sidekick, and Vargas and Susie are happily reunited.

Elements of story, setting, and character quickly establish *Touch of Evil* as a crime thriller that can be rewardingly discussed in comparison to other films of the genre and period shot in a film noir style. The plot follows the investigation. Generic characteristics include "criminal" locations such as nightclubs and bars, cheap motels, and deserted streets and alleyways. Most of the important scenes take place at night. The characters include a range of recurrent generic figures: a taciturn streetwise hero, Vargas; and a physically and morally monstrous villain, Quinlan. The two principal female characters suggest, even as they complicate, the common division between good girl and bad in the film noir. Susie is an all-American blonde bride, and Tanya, a woman from Quinlan's past, is a dark-haired, ethnically indeterminate fortune-teller, who runs a suspect establishment on the Mexican side of the border. Yet Susie spends most of the film, however inadvertently, in sleazy motels that associate her with the femme fatale stereotype. Meanwhile, Marlene Dietrich's

Tanya almost caricatures the inscrutability of the femme fatale. An eccentric denizen of the night, she has seen everything but reveals very little. Secondary characters, such as Quinlan's sidekick Menzies, the upright U.S. attorney who helps Vargas, and the corrupt Grandis, are familiar types from similar genre films. The plot is convoluted, and characters' motives are often cynical. Beyond these narrative characteristics, there also are unmistakable stylistic marks of the film's genre.

Stylistically, *Touch of Evil* displays and exaggerates the conventions associated with film noir. It is shot in black and white, and the extremely effective low-key lighting produces sharp contrasts that emphasize the sinister quality of people and places and the mysteriousness of unfolding events. Unbalanced composition and figures lit from below produce distortions in everyday perceptions that frighten or unsettle [Figure 13.15]. The film's score by Henry Mancini reflects the incorporation of jazz in film noir's urban night world.

By the time *Touch of Evil* was made at the end of the 1950s, the film noir cycle had nearly run its course. *Touch of Evil* supports genre theorist Thomas Schatz's contention

13.15 *Touch of Evil* (1958). Low-key lighting and unbalanced composition characterize the film noir mise-en-scène.

13.16 *Touch of Evil* (1958). The drugged Susie wakes up to this shocking point-of-view-shot. Wide-angle lenses increase distortion in the images.

that the end of a genre's life span is characterized by "self-conscious formalism"; the film's style is so baroque that it overtakes the story. Consider, for example, the grotesque low-angle shot, taken from Susie's point of view, of Grandi after he has been strangled [Figure 13.16]. The film's cynicism takes the pessimistic values of film noir to the extreme. In the exaggerated rottenness of Quinlan, the law itself is shown to be corrupt. Although the film's good characters, Vargas and his wife, experience a happy ending, at the end of the film they are pictured in a convertible, a sinister echo of the couple who had been blown up by a car bomb in the first shot.

In fact, the strangeness of *Touch of Evil* made it difficult to market. At the other end of the spectrum from the one-of-a-kind superproductions that were beginning to be produced in Hollywood, *Touch of Evil* was intended as the kind of low-budget film that uses genre to let audiences know what to expect. Welles seems to have violated such expectations; the industry publication *Variety* called it a "confusing, somewhat 'artsy' film" with "so-so prospects." Interestingly, however, it is precisely as a genre film that *Touch of Evil* supports an assessment of Orson Welles's greatness as an auteur, for he certainly made the most of his "routine" assignment. In sharp contrast to his unprecedented (and short-lived) autonomy when he first arrived in Hollywood to make *Citizen Kane* in 1941, *Touch of Evil* was not designed as "an Orson Welles film." It was offered to Welles to direct at the behest of the film's star, Charlton Heston.

Welles's almost accidental participation mitigates against assigning too much original intention to him as an author. Universal agreed to allow him to adapt the screenplay and to direct because they thought he would make an interesting Quinlan. Welles's appearance in the film enforces his authorship, drawing our attention to his character and away from his foil, the ostensible "good guy" protagonist Vargas. Welles's flamboyant presence and his willingness to play a remarkably unappealing character reference his performances in films he directed, most

notably *Citizen Kane,* whose hero is also larger than life— and flawed. One could read authorship in *Touch of Evil* allegorically, as Welles's commentary on the corruption and eventual sorry fate of a maverick coming into conflict with the system.

Auteurism, of course, goes beyond the visual presence or "signature" of the author. It is a way of connecting stylistic and thematic similarities across a group of an individual's films. Welles had been known for stylistic excess since making brilliant innovations in camera, sound, lighting, acting, and composition in *Citizen Kane.* Many of these techniques are used in *Touch of Evil.* For example, low-angle shots, which can make a figure appear strong and powerful, provide ironic commentary on Quinlan's status by emphasizing his unsightly corpulence [Figure 13.17]. In *Citizen Kane,* Welles uses low-angle shots ironically, showing Kane just as he loses the gubernatorial election [Figure 13.18]. The use of deep-focus cinematography, so characteristic of *Citizen Kane* and *The Magnificent Ambersons* (1942), results in menacing and distorted images as the edges of the frames stretch. Wide-angle lenses include more in the frame,

13.17 *Touch of Evil* (1958). Orson Welles's presence in the film is emphasized by unflattering low-angle shots.

13.18 *Citizen Kane* (1941). In his earlier film, Orson Welles uses low-angle shots ironically to depict Kane's election defeat.

allowing a shot to run longer without cutting, for naturalistic or virtuosic effects. An example of the latter is *Touch of Evil*'s famous opening shot, which lasts approximately 2.5 minutes; it covers a great deal of territory and ultimately explosive action. French critics were particularly admiring of this "sequence shot," so named because a whole sequence unfolds in one continuous camera take; after they saw the film, these critics helped canonize Welles as Hollywood's greatest auteur. Truffaut wrote, "You could remove Orson Welles's name from the credits and it wouldn't make any difference, because from the first shot, beginning with the credits themselves, it's obvious that Citizen Kane is behind the camera."

Because of Welles's fame, today it is almost impossible to consider the film outside of an auteurist framework. Although *Touch of Evil* is revived in series surveying film noirs, its reputation as a classic is owed to its being a sleazy police film directed by a genius. The 2000 release of the restored "director's cut" of *Touch of Evil* demonstrates the importance of the auteurist perspective on the film. This version is not a recovered copy of the film Welles originally submitted. Rather, the restoration team construed his intentions by referring to an extensive memo that Welles wrote upon viewing Universal's cut of the original release. The story of the artist's vision being sacrificed to the studio's wishes helps construct Welles's authorial persona as a misunderstood artist. Readings of *Touch of Evil* based on genre or authorship demonstrate how film theory goes beyond abstraction, using concrete evidence to test the usefulness of propositions about how films work.

While today film theory is considered part of an academic discipline, earlier writers on the topic came from many contexts and traditions, making any overview of the history of film theory a disjunctive one. A few early theorists wrote books, yet equally important theoretical contributions have been made in journal articles and other forms. Writers on film might be critics of other art forms or scholars in other disciplines. Or they might be filmmakers who share their ideas and excitement about the developing medium with each other in specialized publications.

Some of the questions film theorists have examined include the following:

- What is the specific nature of the medium?
- Is the cinema an art form?
- How does it relate to photography, painting, theater, music, and other art forms?
- How does film resemble language?
- Is film's primary responsibility to tell a story?
- How does film relate to the phenomenal world (the world perceptible to the senses)?
- What is the place of film in the modern world that fostered its development?
- What is the nature of the viewer's encounter with film?

Film theorists have attempted to answer these questions in many different ways.

Intellectuals began to comment on cinema after the first public exhibitions of films by Thomas Edison and the Lumière brothers. Two noteworthy books on movies appeared in the United States in the 1910s. Although they did not strongly determine the course of film theory, the questions they raised have persisted and their claims have piqued the interest of contemporary theorists. Poet Vachel Lindsay's *The Art of the Motion Picture* (1915) responded enthusiastically to the novelty and the democratizing potential of the medium. "I am the one poet who has a right to claim for his muses Blanche Sweet, Mary Pickford, and Mae Marsh," he gushed, invoking the popular movie stars of the day. In his idiosyncratic but suggestive book, Lindsay likened film language to hieroglyphics. The metaphor of picture writing suggests cinema's promise of universality, which excited many early observers.

A more systematic elaboration of ideas about cinema was contributed by Harvard psychologist Hugo Münsterberg in *The Photoplay: A Psychological Study* (1916).

For Münsterberg, viewing films was linked to the subjective process of thinking. The properties of the medium that distinguished it from the physical reality to which its images referred were what made it of interest aesthetically and psychologically. Unlike watching a play, watching movies requires specific mental activities to make sense of cues of movement and depth. "The photoplay tells us the human story by overcoming the forms of the outer world, namely, space, time, and causality, and by adjusting the events to the forms of the inner world, namely, attention, memory, imagination, and emotion," wrote Münsterberg. His ideas thus emphasized the viewer's interaction with the medium. Decades later, theories of spectatorship would do the same. "Many a controversy must come before a method of criticism is fully established," wrote Lindsay, and his words aptly characterize the course of film theory. Lindsay's work praised specific films, whereas Münsterberg referred to the photoplay in general. In a sense, their works mark the division between criticism, which reflects on a given aesthetic object, and theory, which is more abstract.

Outside the United States, much early writing about cinema came from filmmakers themselves. Although movies immediately became commercial, it is important to remember they emerged in the context of modernist experimentation in the arts—music, writing, theater, painting, architecture, and photography—especially in Europe. Because film was based on new technology, many considered it an exemplary art for the machine age. Film influenced new approaches to established media, such as cubism in painting and the "automatic writing" of the surrealists. In turn, filmmakers adopted avant-garde practices, and painters like Hans Richter took up filmmaking, exploring graphic and rhythmic possibilities [Figure 13.19]. Modernist intellectuals debated cinema's aesthetic status and its relationship to the other arts.

In the 1910s and 1920s in France, the first avant-garde film movement, impressionism, was fostered by groups known as ciné-clubs and by journals dedicated to the new medium. In one of these publications, *Cinéma*, Louis Delluc coined the term *photogénie* to refer to a particular quality that distinguishes the filmed object from its everyday reality. Jean Epstein elaborated on this elusive concept in such poetic writings as "Bonjour Cinéma" and in *The Fall of the House of Usher* (1928) [Figure 13.20], his film adaptation of Edgar Allan Poe's story. Germaine Dulac compared film to music in her extensive writings and lectures. Film theory and practice continued to develop in tandem in the period between the world wars.

Soviet Film Theory: Montage

Perhaps most systematic in its relationship with artistic modernism and certainly most influential in world film history was the school of filmmakers working in the Soviet Union during the 1920s. After the 1919 revolution, these artist-intellectuals set about defining an artistic practice that could participate in revolutionary change. Like the avant-garde graphic and set designers, painters, and composers who were their comrades, they were eager to incorporate the materials of industrial modernity in their art. The cinema, with its industrial base and its populist reach, provided a perfect medium. Lev Kuleshov's teaching at the state film school put the theory of montage at the center of Soviet filmmaking, and as our discussion in Chapter 5 indicates, his ideas went well beyond the world of film theory to influence filmmaking worldwide. Montage involves directing spectators' experience through the organization of fragments, inviting them to make meaning from a juxtaposition or chain of shots. Editing experiments showed that audiences formed interpretations based on montage alone, a phenomenon known as the Kuleshov effect. The same neutral shot of an actor's face could signify "hunger" or "joy"

13.19 *Film Study* (1926). Frames of Hans Richter's early abstract film.

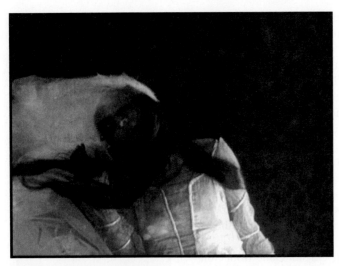

13.20 *The Fall of the House of Usher* (1928). An impressionist film by Jean Epstein.

when juxtaposed with shots of a bowl of soup or a baby, respectively.

Vsevolod Pudovkin and Sergei Eisenstein, Kuleshov's students, elaborated the theory of montage in their own writings and films. In Pudovkin's *Mother* (1926) **[Figure 13.21]** and other films, montage is a way of breaking down a scene to direct the spectator's look and understanding. Eisenstein's theories emphasized the effects of collision between shots. He correlated the exponential increase of meaning to be gained by the juxtaposition of shots to the dialectic, a philosophical concept that Karl Marx adopted and incorporated in his theory of historical materialism. Simply defined, a dialectic consists of a thesis that is countered by an antithesis, or opposing element, which results in a synthesis of both that is more forceful and truthful than either element on its own. Eisenstein's extensive body of writing, amply illustrated with examples from his celebrated films, spans several decades and constitutes the most significant contribution to film theory by a filmmaker.

Filmmaker Dziga Vertov also wrote film theory in the form of manifestos signed by the Kinoki, or Kino-Eye group **[Figure 13.22]**. Resisting systemization in his poetic, avant-garde writings, Vertov rejected the fiction film and emphasized the possibilities of sound. Eisenstein denounced Vertov's trick shots as "formalist jackstraws"; Vertov scorned Eisenstein's "filmed theater." The polemics and practices of these two great filmmakers were later championed by the 1960s generation of critic-filmmakers in France.

In 1919, revolutionary leader Vladimir Lenin pronounced film "the most important of the arts." Film was seen as a vital force within the revolutionary culture of the early Soviet Union, one that could bring the masses, many of them illiterate, into modernity. The intensity of discussion about the properties and potential of the medium contributed as much to the cinema's importance as did the films themselves; at this time and place, theory was an indispensable part of film culture. Above all, the concept of montage survived as one of the central theoretical and practical concerns of cinema. It is as significant to film analysts as it has been to filmmakers from Alfred Hitchcock to Soviet editor Slavko Vorkapich, who lent his name to the "montage sequences" he supervised for classical Hollywood films.

Classical Film Theories: Formalism and Realism

While integral to the historical context in which they emerged, Sergei Eisenstein's writings were also taken up by thinkers and academics outside the Soviet Union as film history progressed. Today they form part of a corpus referred to as **classical film theory**. Europeans Béla Balázs, Rudolf Arnheim, André Bazin, and Siegfried Kracauer are also central figures in classical film theory, which spanned the shift from silent to sound filmmaking (and the periods before and after World War II). This momentous technical development was accompanied

13.21 *Mother* (1926). Like other Soviet filmmakers, Vsevolod Pudovkin emphasized montage.

by ontological speculation: does sound allow film to fulfill a mission to reproduce the world as it is, or does sound hinder cinema's visual expression?

One of the organizing debates of classical film theory centers around the appeal to **realism** made first by photography and then by film. Realism is not a simple or unitary term; generally speaking, it relates to mimesis, or imitation of reality, in the arts. The mimetic quality has been valued in the Western artistic tradition since ancient Greece. However, the term "realism" itself only came into use in the nineteenth century to designate a style—developed in the most important genre of the era, the novel—that embraced subject matter drawn from the experience of everyday life. Realist style was highly descriptive, a function that the photographic basis of cinema fulfills by its very nature. For theorists such as Bazin and Kracauer, film's ability to refer to the world through images that resemble and record the presence of objects and sources of sounds sets it apart as a realist medium. In contrast, theorists such as Arnheim and Balázs emphasize film form as fundamental; for them, realism is only a style that uses form in a particular way.

Viewers and commentators addressed the question of cinematic realism from the beginning, and digital media theorists pose it anew today. Stories of the presentation of the Lumière brothers' first films at the Grand Café in Paris invariably tell how audiences shrank from the arriving train or feared they would be splashed by the waves of the sea. Whether or not these stories are true, they characterize cinema as lacking the aesthetic distance of the other arts. For many, film seems too "natural" to be a vehicle for making meaning or an object to which traditional aesthetic criteria apply. The French and Soviet modernists were concerned primarily with cinema's status as an art, distancing themselves from the impression it gives of reproducing the world, perhaps because the artist's role is downplayed by such a notion.

Before laying out the thinking of individual theorists, a brief overview of **semiotics**—the study of signs—will give us some useful vocabulary for discussing the divergent opinions about realism within film theory. Although this vocabulary was introduced later in the history of film theory, it illuminates what is at stake for classical theorists. Semiotics considers words and images as different kinds of signs or ways of making meaning. Words designate the things that they refer to, which are known as their *referents*, according to conventions that are arbitrary. (One easy way to think about this is to note that different languages designate the same referent completely differently.) In the terminology of the late nineteenth-century American philosopher C. S. Peirce, who helped develop semiotics, a word is a *symbolic sign*. Photography and film, in contrast, use *iconic signs*, which look like their referents; this resemblance often gives the impression of a natural connection. Finally, since photographic images are a product of a process in which light, reflected from an object, produces an image that is fixed by the chemical emulsion on film, these images are also *indexical signs*, Peirce's third type of sign. In other words, a direct relationship exists between the sign and the object depicted, a relationship that can be likened to pointing or indicating, implied by the word "index." A footprint indicates that a person has walked in a particular path; a weathervane points in the direction the wind blows. Both are indexical signs. In most cases, an impression is left on film because a real object has been photographed. Marks can even be made

13.22 **Poster for *The Man with the Movie Camera*** (1929). This poster by the Stenberg brothers shows the close relationship between the graphic arts and cinema of the period.

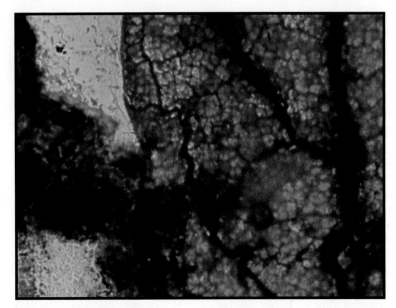

13.23 *Mothlight* (1963). Stan Brakhage's challenge to the usual practice of indexical imagery; rather than photographs of wings and leaves, he used the objects themselves to make this film.

▶ **VIEWING CUE**

From the last film you viewed for class, identify a scene that illustrates the arguments of (1) Béla Balázs about the close-up or (2) Rudolf Arnheim about the two-dimensional screen. ⏸

13.24 **Asta Nielsen as** *Hamlet* (1921). Theorist Béla Balázs believed the close-up could reveal the soul onscreen and wrote eloquently about Danish silent film star Asta Nielsen's face in close-up.

directly on the filmstrip; Stan Brakhage's *Mothlight* (1963), for example, challenged the usual practice by pasting moths' wings on celluloid [Figure 13.23]. The referential relationship strengthens cinema's claim to represent the world as it really is. Considering cinema as a reflection of the natural world is almost automatic, yet cinematic images and sounds are constructed signs. Computer-generated film imagery, which does not have a direct referent—it is iconic but not indexical—is changing our assumptions about cinematic realism.

Formalism: Béla Balázs and Rudolf Arnheim

Whether their positions argued for or against realism, all classical film theorists were concerned with the nature of filmic reference. In addition to Sergei Eisenstein, two key authors associated with modernism, Béla Balázs and Rudolf Arnheim, were especially interested in how film became an art form precisely by transcending its referential qualities. They elaborated formalist theories of film.

Béla Balázs, a Hungarian screenwriter and film critic, published his first book on film in 1924, making him one of the earliest important film theorists. Later, his writings were published in the influential volume *Theory of the Film*. Balázs was passionate about the new ways of observing the world that cinema made possible, and he defended the medium against highbrow critics who simply dismissed it as entertainment. For Balázs, film was a new "form-language" that broke with the language of theater. In particular, Balázs wrote eloquently on the power of the close-up, an element of film art impossible to approximate on stage: "by means of the close-up the camera in the days of the silent film revealed also the hidden mainsprings of a life which we had thought we already knew so well" [Figure 13.24]. Balázs also explored the crucial phenomenon of identification in cinema as an aspect of film language, describing how in watching a movie, "we look up to Juliet's balcony with Romeo's eyes and look down on Romeo with Juliet's." Thus for Balázs, film was able to reveal aspects of reality that could not otherwise be seen. He also championed the pursuit of film theory itself, arguing that the new form-language required systematic elaboration.

German art historian Rudolf Arnheim argued even more strongly for a formalist position in his 1933 study *Film,* which was later revised for English publication as *Film as Art*. For Arnheim, the quest for film realism was misguided, a betrayal of the unique aesthetic properties of the medium that equipped it to transcend the imitation of nature. He set out to "refute the assertion that film is nothing but the feeble mechanical reproduction of real life." For example, in his view the two-dimensionality of the screen image was not a limitation but an aesthetic parameter to be exploited by filmmakers and emphasized by theorists. The perception of lighting effects and various other artistic manipulations were what allowed film to go beyond mere duplication. Arnheim's position recalls Hugo Münsterberg's arguments about the distinctive properties and processes of film. Indeed, the two theorists were both interested in the psychology of perception and did not value the perception of resemblance above other responses.

Realism: André Bazin and Siegfried Kracauer

André Bazin saw film as quintessentially realist, a medium "in which the image is evaluated not according to what it adds to reality but what it reveals of it." One of the most prominent film theorists of the 1950s and 1960s, Bazin responded directly to the formalists who preceded him, and he serves as an important predecessor of contemporary film studies in turn. An instructive polarity in classical film theory pits Sergei Eisenstein, for whom montage was the quintessential tool of the medium, against Bazin. In "The Evolution of the Language of Cinema" Bazin expressed the view that cinema's ability to capture a space and event in real time is its essence. Montage interfered with this vocation, he argued, by altering spatial and temporal relationships. He advocated instead the use of composition in depth, made possible by deep-focus cinematography, which kept all planes of the image in view, making cutting between parts of the image unnecessary. A filmmaker like Jean Renoir, who staged scenes in depth using long takes, conveyed "respect for the continuity of dramatic space and, of course, of its duration." Why was this so important to Bazin? He saw the image not only as a reference to reality but also as a record of it—and ultimately as a means of transcending time. Preserving duration and the integrity of space paid tribute to the reality of the object filmed, stressing the indexical properties of the medium.

13.25 *Footlight Parade* (1933). Siegfried Kracauer cited the almost abstract patterns of chorus girls in performance as examples of "mass ornament."

Another influential and formidable thinker on film, Siegfried Kracauer, is, like Bazin, best known for his strong advocacy of realism. Kracauer's position evolved over time. In the 1920s, he began writing newspaper essays in Weimar Germany amid modernist experimentation with film form. In "The Mass Ornament," Kracauer explored the aesthetics of mass culture and the new rhythms of life it inspired [Figure 13.25]. After fleeing Nazi Germany, Kracauer settled in the United States. In *From Caligari to Hitler,* he wrote about how hypnosis and other themes of German expressionist cinema reflected the nation's growing acceptance of Nazi ideology. It was not until 1960 that he published his major work, *Theory of Film: The Redemption of Physical Reality,* in which he elaborated his views on film's capacity for realism. The cinematic medium "is uniquely equipped to record and reveal physical reality," Kracauer argued. It was not only that film provided a window on the phenomenal world. For Kracauer, it was crucial that film was able to preserve what would otherwise meet with destruction: the momentary, the everyday, the random.

> **▶ VIEWING CUE**
>
> Analyze from a realist position the last film you viewed for class. Identify a scene that corresponds with André Bazin's ideas about the long take or Siegfried Kracauer's ideas about the photographic basis of the medium. **⏸**

Modernity and Cinema: Walter Benjamin

Walter Benjamin, Siegfried Kracauer's Weimar-era contemporary, was particularly interested in how cinema participated in the transformation of perception in the modern world. Benjamin wrote about cinema as well as photography in a famous, though difficult, essay, known in English as "The Work of Art in the Age of Mechanical Reproduction." For Benjamin, the comparison of photography and film with painting did not hinge on their relative artistic value or even their technique. Rather, they differed because these new art forms did not produce unique objects

13.26 *Germany Year Zero* (1947). For André Bazin, Roberto Rossellini's film puts its "faith in reality."

with the "aura" of an original artwork. Instead, film captured the sense of accelerated time and effortlessly traversed space typical of contemporary urban life. Benjamin regarded the distracted state of the film viewer as the characteristic mode of perception of the medium and of the historical moment. Written in 1935 as the Nazis rose to power, Benjamin's essay closed with an epilogue critiquing fascism's manipulation of the masses through traditional aesthetics. Benjamin did not survive the war, and his writings on cinema remained too sparse to put him at the center of classical debates in film theory. His influence on contemporary theorists, however—particularly his description of the transformation of the senses by twentieth-century modernity—has been great.

Postwar Cinema, Bazin, and *Cahiers du cinéma*

In many ways World War II divides film culture—both filmmaking and film theory—into two periods. The theoretical issues we have outlined, in particular the defense of realism, can be illuminated by a historical perspective. Siegfried Kracauer's experience as a German Jewish refugee certainly influenced his views on the value of realism as a kind of historical evidence. André Bazin, a Catholic and French Resistance activist, invested cinema with similar redemptive properties in his post–World War II writings. The trauma and destruction of the war seemed to add urgency to the argument for film's ability to preserve the natural world. Bazin had a high regard for the postwar Italian neorealist movement [**Figure 13.26**]. With its amateur actors and location shooting, the movement demonstrated what Bazin called "faith in reality," which he valued above films by directors who put their "faith in the image." The postmodernist postulate that our only access to the world is through representations might make the defense of realism seem outmoded. However, such positions were far from naive and responded to their historical context. Bazin and Kracauer well understood the artistry involved in creating a film, as well as the fact that a technical process intervened between the world and the image.

Bazin's interest in cinema's ontology, or being, was explored in his posthumously published two-volume work appropriately titled *What Is Cinema?* A transitional figure between classical and contemporary film theory, Bazin cofounded *Cahiers du cinéma* in 1951. For many film buffs, the distinctive yellow cover of *Cahiers du cinéma* in the 1950s is as iconic an image of film history as that of Fay Wray in King Kong's hairy palm [**Figure 13.27**]. Under Bazin's mentorship, the magazine published the criticism of the young cineastes who would shape the French New Wave. The journal and its writers' films, widely cine-literate and iconoclastic, energized world film culture and influenced the emergence of the discipline of film studies in universities. Eventually, *Cahiers du cinéma* also catalyzed the resurgence of theory in film culture in the early 1970s.

13.27 *Cahiers du cinéma*. The journal featured an iconic yellow cover in the 1950s.

The Role of Film Journals

Film journals have played an indispensable role in the history of film culture. They have published early works of film theory, contributed to the emergence of film studies as an academic discipline, and at times influenced the kinds of films that were made. Journals were particularly central to avant-garde film movements. Sergei Eisenstein published in such Soviet cultural journals as *Novy Lef* ("New Left") before his essays were gathered into books of film theory. Interest in film in France during the 1910s was heightened by the circulation of publications such as *Le Film*, edited by the film club organizer Louis Delluc. Emulating the French, from the late 1920s to the early 1930s, the British *Close Up* published opinion and analysis pieces as well as English translations of Eisenstein's writings. Eclectic and partisan, *Close Up* discussed such topics as psychoanalysis, the representation of race, and the negative effects of censorship, all of which would become current in film theory decades later. Starting in the 1950s, the avant-garde and underground film movements in the United States were chronicled in the pages of curator and experimental filmmaker Jonas Mekas's magazine, *Film Culture* [Figure 13.28].

After the cultural upheaval provoked by general strikes in France in May 1968, *Cahiers du cinéma* became more political and theoretical. In its pages, films from *Hiroshima mon amour* (1959) to *Young Mr. Lincoln* (1939) were analyzed, Godard praised Nicholas Ray, and Jean-Pierre Oudart developed the concept of *suture*. Rival journals in France, *Positif* and *Cinéthique,* also flourished, and the polemics energized film enthusiasts.

The same goes for English-language publications. In the 1970s, writers for the British journal *Screen* introduced the Marxist, semiotic, and psychoanalytic language and ideas that would permeate Anglo-American cinema studies for more than a decade, in part by translating French material. Meanwhile, *Sight and Sound,* the British Film Institute's venerable magazine, reviewed every film released in Britain. Refurbished in the 1980s, the publication targets a film-literate readership with pieces by scholars, including Thomas Elsaesser, Peter Wollen, and Ginette Vincendeau. U.S. scholarly journals, such as the feminist *Camera Obscura* and *The Velvet Light Trap*, have roots in the politicized film culture of the late 1960s and early 1970s. *Projections*, edited by filmmaker John Boorman, includes writings by and about contemporary filmmakers. Currently a number of online scholarly journals, from *Senses of Cinema* to *Kino* and *Flow*, are timely sources of commentary on contemporary audiovisual culture.

By emphasizing contexts, such as journals, we have shown that film theory has always been more of a public conversation than a realm of solitary reflection. Contemporary film theory, which we will discuss next, is more elaborated and diverse than classical film theory. As film culture has expanded, ways of contemplating the medium have become more numerous. Journals are just one of the social institutions that shape and contextualize film theory; others include festivals, archives, Web sites, blogs, and of course, scholarly publishing and college classes. Individuals interested in film—from moviegoers to students doing course work and filmmakers planning new works—avail themselves in many forms.

text continued on page 485 ▶

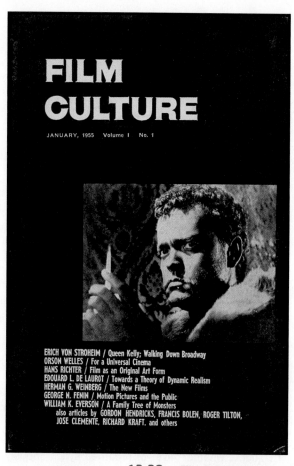

13.28 *Film Culture*. The first issue of the influential U.S. film magazine.

▶ **VIEWING CUE**

Read several issues of one of the journals mentioned in this section. Characterize its perspective on film culture by giving concrete examples.

FILM IN FOCUS

Coding Time in *Timecode* (2000)

In its heyday—from roughly the 1920s to 1960—classical film theory sought to describe our experience of a medium distinguished by specific characteristics:

- the use of photographic means to capture images, generally those depicting "live action," on film
- the recording of images in rapid sequence so that when passed at equivalent speed before a beam of light, they produce the illusion of movement
- the accompaniment of the moving images with sound, whether "live" or recorded synchronously
- the presentation of the image on a large flat rectangular screen in a darkened room to a collective audience that normally pays money to attend

Many of these basic requirements are no longer met by the phenomenon we call the movies. Mike Figgis's *Timecode* did not use photographic means to record its images, but was shot on digital video. Like almost all recent theatrical films, *Timecode* is just as likely to be viewed individually—at home, on a small screen, or in an electronic format such as video or DVD—as it is to be seen projected on 35mm film onto the big screen in the company of a paying audience. These differences raise ontological questions. In addition, *Timecode* can be used to illustrate one of the most critical dichotomies in classical film theory: that between Sergei Eisenstein's championing of montage as the most specific attribute of cinema and André Bazin's advocacy of the long take. This dichotomy hinges on how much priority is given to film's referential capacity and thus to the pursuit of an aesthetic of realism.

Is *Timecode* a realist film? It is organized as four continuous ninety-three-minute takes running simultaneously onscreen in four quadrants of uniform size and shape, accompanied by a soundtrack edited to highlight each of four interrelated stories at different moments. The continuous takes extend Bazin's "sequence shot" to the full

capacity of video technology and result in a "sequence film." (Film, in contrast, is limited in the duration of individual takes by the size of the magazine and camera.) Bazin championed qualities of democracy and ambiguity—no one tells us where to look or what to think or feel about what we see in long takes featuring composition-in-depth. Do those qualities apply here? Certainly it is the viewer who chooses where to look, and this decision making is multiplied by having to choose among the four images onscreen. Yet the handheld camera can emulate editing strategies that direct our gaze through close-ups and eyeline matches, and the soundtrack we hear is co-ordinated with only one of the four images at any given time. What about film's propensity to reference the reality before the camera (the profilmic event) that Bazin prized? The film's actors are almost all stars, rather than the amateurs who appeared in neorealist films. They are, however, *really* acting for a full ninety minutes, mainly improvising their lines, which upholds a certain value of referentiality. It is unlikely Bazin would see anything particularly laudatory in *Timecode*'s respect for the unfolding of real time, however, because the activities of the cast are characterized by pettiness and *self*-referentiality. The story interweaves threads about aspiring starlets, callous film producers, jaded directors, and exploitative story ideas.

Given the film's embrace of façades, is *Timecode* more illustrative of Eisenstein's advocacy of montage as constructing meaning? Certainly, the four quadrants illustrate his concept of each frame of film as a montage cell. Eisenstein advocated the contrapuntal, or contrastive, use of sound. The film's editing of dialogue is always in sync with one of the four stories, while its continuous score arguably provides parallelism with all four. The dialogue is technically in counterpoint with the three stories we are not following on the audio track at any given moment, but this technique is also an example of image-sound parallelism because it encourages us to look at the story we also hear. Moreover, sound generally reinforces the narrative. We hear one character talking about her husband and see him simultaneously cheating on her. Rather than contrasting images and ideas whose juxtaposition raises us to a new level of critical insight and potential decisive action, *Timecode* paralyzes the viewer in a hall of mirrors. One character pitches to the team of producers a movie whose premise is that of the one we are watching. He is peremptorily dismissed: "That is the most pretentious crap I've ever heard." This is far from the state of moral reflection that Bazin would have us glean from open-ended films.

Timecode's title is a reference to the numerical counter that runs continuously in the corner of the image on uncut video footage. Time code is used to log footage so that a particular shot or fragment of a shot can be located when one wants to edit out the boring sections, which tend to accumulate due to video's inexpensive stock and extreme mobility. While a rapid montage style that can ultimately be traced back to Eisenstein would seem to be the most prevalent editing code of our video-transformed era, the unblinking eye of surveillance footage is probably equally characteristic. Indeed, this is what *Timecode*'s quadrants reference, as it becomes apparent that all four stories converge at the same time in the same building. The film's continuous takes ultimately capture a contemporary reality that is always potentially exposed to the camera. "Faith in reality" and "faith in the image" are no longer clearly distinct.

Critical Questions in Contemporary Film Theory

The idea that film theory can be spoken about as a unified or distinct body of knowledge comes from a position within the academic discipline of film studies. The study of film in higher education began as early as 1926, with a course taught by Terry Ramsaye at the New School in New York City. Although there was resistance from curricular traditionalists, by the 1970s, film studies had become an established discipline in the United States and some other countries. The discipline had strong footholds in English and art history programs as well as in its own academic departments, societies, and journals. Film studies has been fostered in the context of a wider culture of film enthusiasts who read about American, European, and non-Western films, festivals, and directors in such publications as *Film Comment* and *Film Quarterly.* In the United States, film culture also has been characterized by the growth of art-houses and film societies showing foreign films as well as by the emergence of exciting American filmmakers—from independents like John Cassavetes to the first generation of Hollywood directors who had been educated in film schools, including George Lucas, Paul Schrader, Francis Ford Coppola, and Martin Scorsese.

Most of the writing published in film magazines has been *criticism*, which aims to illuminate a particular work or body of work for a general or more expert readership. U.S. film theory, which takes the more general properties of the medium as its object, has become the domain of academics. In countries such as France, film theory has also been pursued by public intellectuals, well-known individuals whose writings and lectures are aimed at a public beyond students and scholars. In the 1970s, the vocabulary of film theory became very specialized as the discipline gained a foothold in the academy. Theorists were interested in a more systematic approach to cinema than was offered by the often subjective and impressionistic legacy of film criticism.

The following necessarily partial overview of contemporary film theory is organized according to the major critical schools within the discipline. There are important interrelationships among these schools: often one set of questions grows out of another; feminism overlaps with psychoanalytic theory on the one hand, and with cultural studies on the other. However, it is important to trace the terms and evolution of broad issues before discussing more specific ones.

Semiotics, Structuralism, and Marxism

The academic discipline of film studies has been heavily influenced by European thought, especially by several currents converging in postwar France, including semiotics, structuralism, and Marxism. At first glance, these ideas may seem to have little to do with film, but in fact such iconoclastic systems of thought are well suited to questioning a medium of comparable freshness and vitality.

A word on the encounter with such theory may be appropriate here. Beginning film students often find the work of French theorists, and the English-speaking theorists influenced by them, quite baffling until they grasp both the questions that these thinkers are trying to illuminate and something of the context in which they have worked. When theories are understood as part of intellectual history, they yield new perspectives on contemporary problems. We will be frustrated if we look to theoretical writings for universally valid truths. Rather, it is helpful to think of these writings as stories, as more or less compelling versions of the way things work. Sometimes what is most compelling about film theory is the language in which it is elaborated, which can be speculative, poetic, even contradictory. To preface a discussion of contemporary theory this way is not to authorize its dismissal. Rather, we hope to encourage the curiosity that accompanies intellectual inquiry even when there are no set answers.

Semiotics

In order to introduce semiotics (also called semiology) and structuralism, we must understand that a language model, one that compares a given object or system to the structure of language, is central to 1970s film theory. This might at first seem curious. After all, films consist predominantly of pictures. But the influence of linguistics was pervasive in French thought of the 1960s, and it can be traced back to the work of Ferdinand de Saussure in the early part of the century. Saussure used linguistics as the most exemplary case of a new science of signs he called semiology, which could include pictures, gestures, and a wide range of other systems of communication or perception. A **sign**, for Saussure, is composed of a *signifier*, the spoken or written word, picture, or gesture, and a *signified*, the mental concept it evokes. Together, the signifier "c-a-t" and the signified mental image of a domesticated feline form a sign, and the two parts cannot be imagined without each other. In a particular instance of discourse, the sign "cat" might refer to a specific tabby, which would be its *referent*.

The importance of Saussure's distinctions cannot be overestimated. Any system of communication substitutes signs for objects, and such naming is more than a natural process. Language, whose use distinguishes humankind, is a purely social convention.

As noted earlier, pictures, especially photographs and film or video images, give a much stronger impression of identity with their referents than do words, whose connection to what they designate is purely arbitrary. In René Magritte's painting *The Treachery of Images*, the words "*Ceci n'est pas une pipe*" ("This is not a pipe") seem absurd because we take them to refer to what is unmistakably a picture of a pipe [**Figure 13.29**]. But a picture of a pipe is not a pipe. There is no essential nature of an object that is captured in a sign, of whatever kind. Semiotics is antiessentialist, stressing human invention and social convention rather than essential qualities. The scientific methodology devised by linguistics to describe these conventions

13.29 *The Treachery of Images* (1928–1929). René Magritte's painting contrasts verbal and visual signs. Neither the picture nor the word is an actual pipe.

has been useful to theorists attempting to approach cinema systematically, rather than relying on subjective evaluations such as beauty and truth.

However, some film theorists question the use of the linguistic sign as a starting point for cinematic analysis. For example, philosopher Gilles Deleuze returns to the contributions of C. S. Peirce, who in his conception of semiotics defined the sign as that which "stands for something to someone in some respect or capacity," a formulation that emphasizes the mental process of association. Earlier in the chapter, we introduced Peirce's three varieties of signs: *icons* refer through resemblance, *indices* refer through a trace of the object, and *symbolic signs* such as words are purely arbitrary. Although Saussure's linguistics-based semiology is the more dominant influence in film as well as literary and narrative theory, today his term is more or less interchangeable with Peirce's preferred term, "semiotics."

The comparison of film and language is by no means new. Throughout film history, filmmakers and theorists touted film's universality, its ability to transcend linguistic barriers. Classical film theorists—from Vachel Lindsay to Sergei Eisenstein and Belá Balázs—have used linguistic metaphors of hieroglyphics, rhetoric, and grammar in their writings, and filmmakers like D. W. Griffith sought a visual Esperanto, or common language. But contemporary theorists, most notably Christian Metz in books like *Film Language,* use the analogy even more systematically. Eisenstein had concluded that a shot was more like a sentence than it was like a word, in that a shot could be subdivided again and again and its components would still "make sense." Yet, is there a cinematic grammar? Metz wanted to know. One can combine shots in an infinite number of ways, so on that level no film grammar exists. But in narrative filmmaking, there are many similarities among types and sequences of narrative units. Metz gives names to the limited number of units in use, such as "scene," "sequence," and "alternating **syntagma**" (a crosscutting sequence), to build something like a narrative grammar of film.

VIEWING CUE

How does the juxtaposition of shots begin to build a sequence or syntax?

Structuralism

The legacy of linguistics has been felt more generally in theories of film narrative. French anthropologist Claude Lévi-Strauss titled his important 1957 work *Structural Anthropology,* building on Ferdinand de Saussure's structural linguistics. Lévi-Strauss studied thousands of myths and discovered that they share basic structures that profoundly shape cultural life. In a number of disciplines, structuralism arose as an attempt to identify common structures within empirical data. Russian folklorist Vladimir Propp noticed a similar unity in his study of folktales. There are a limited number of what he called character functions (eight) and plot elements (thirty-one), and certain kinds of plot events always occur in the same order. From hundreds of tales he discerned basic plots, which are, moreover, echoed in many other narrative films. *Narratology*, the study of narrative forms, is a branch of structuralism that encompasses stories of all kinds, including films. Are there a limited number of basic plots available to filmmakers? Are genres like myths? Because movies are so formulaic and so strikingly similar to myths and folktales even when not explicitly based on them, narratological studies had fruitful results. The characters in the *Star Wars* series, for example, closely match the heroes, antiheroes, magical helpers, princesses, and witches of the folktales Propp studied.

The linguists known as the Russian formalists, contemporaries of Sergei Eisenstein and Vladimir Propp, have contributed the important distinction between *syuzhet* (plot) and *fabula* (story) to the study of narrative. *Syuzhet* refers to the way events are arranged in the actual tale or film and *fabula* to the chronologically ordered sequence of events as we rationally reconstruct it. The distinction gives us a helpful tool for discussing an individual text. A detective story's *syuzhet* follows the detective's progress through the investigation. Its *fabula* commences with the circumstances leading up to the committing of the crime. The story of *The Lord of the Rings: The Fellowship of the Ring* (2001) resembles that of the first volume of J. R. R. Tolkien's novel. But the plot is different. Not only are incidents omitted from the film, but also the means of telling the story is language in one version and moving pictures and sounds in the other. Here the question of adapting films from literary works arises as a theoretical issue. In response to the common plaint "The book was better," theorists point to distinctions between these two means of expression.

Structuralist theorists reduce narrative to its most basic form: a beginning situation is disrupted, a hero takes action as a result, and a new equilibrium is reached at the end. The novel, the distinctive middle-class cultural form of the nineteenth century, gave that hero psychological depth and a realistic field of action. The novel's basic narrative form is adopted by motion pictures, just as many famous novels were adapted for the screen. Film theory and film practice have challenged whether this classical narrative cinema is necessarily the norm. According to its critics, classical narrative form affirms values of middle-class culture, such as the agency of the individual, the transparency of realism, and the inevitability of the status quo, through processes of identification, verisimilitude, catharsis, and closure. *Modernism* favors a more fragmented human subjectivity, a foregrounding of style, and an open-ended narrative. *Postmodernism* mixes and matches different kinds of narratives and formal approaches. The disjunctive incidents of surrealist films, Dziga Vertov's kaleidoscopic urban documentary *The Man with the Movie Camera* (1929), abstract films by avant-garde filmmakers such as Maya Deren and Michael Snow, and murky postmodern tales such as *Blade Runner* and *Fight Club* (1999) intentionally reject classical narrative characteristics adopted from the realist novel. These include cause-and-effect linearity, rounded or even identifiable protagonists, and neat happy endings. Non-narrative films reference film's *materiality* when celluloid, movement, sprocket holes, or light becomes their subject matter as well as their means. In such work, film language is no longer based on an analogy with the verbal, and narrative, such as it is, is stripped of its structural stability.

▶ VIEWING CUE

Compare *The Wizard of Oz* to a fairy tale. Do they share a similar narrative structure?

Marxism

In many of the preceding examples, the rejection of narrative is based on an ideological argument against the naturalization of conventions and the mystification of how things work. Marxism is most immediately understood as a political and economic discourse, one that looks at history and society in terms of unequal class relations. In contemporary U.S. political discourse, Marxism may even be considered marginal or dated. But it can still be used to approach wider social questions through the lenses of economic realities and class hierarchies and to interrogate the cultural structures and material realities that underpin exploitation. Historically varieties of Marxism have been prominent among international intellectuals, with Marxist approaches to film and mass culture exerting a profound influence long before the 1970s, when they had such a determining role in shaping film theory. As we have seen, in the Soviet Union, the work of Sergei Eisenstein, Dziga Vertov, Vsevolod Pudovkin, and other practitioner-theorists was made possible by a Marxist state. Walter Benjamin also theorized film in a Marxist frame when he welcomed the democratization of culture made possible by "the age of mechanical reproduction." At the same time, the Frankfurt School, a group of thinkers based in Frankfurt, Germany, with whom Benjamin was associated, critiqued film and other forms of mass culture for reinforcing the capitalist social structure. Theodor Adorno and Max Horkheimer's essay "The Culture Industry," written in the United States in 1944 but not widely read until its republication in 1969, greatly influenced postwar academic and popular perceptions that mass culture duped its viewers, churning out movies in the same manner as it did new cars or brands of toothpaste, with only superficial differences among the products.

The approach to mass communication in the United States in the 1960s and 1970s tended to follow the thesis of "The Culture Industry." At the same time, a different strain of Marxist thinking became prominent in French film theory, which was catalyzed by the radical social disruptions, political protests, and intellectual currents of the late 1960s. One of the most important theorists to influence contemporary film studies, French Marxist Louis Althusser approaches the traditional Marxist question of the nature of **ideology**—a systematic set of beliefs that is not necessarily conscious—with a new understanding of the structures of representation. He wants to explain how people come to accept ideas and conditions contrary to their interests. Althusser defines ideology as "the imaginary representation of the real relations in which we live." According to him, real relations, such as paid work that contributes to the profits of others, disempower working people in the interests of the ruling class, and our imaginary representations (that this is the way it is supposed to be, according to the evening news and the fashion magazines) make this powerlessness seem inevitable and tolerable.

For the critics at *Cahiers du cinéma,* film is an important test of Althusser's theories about ideology. Jean-Luc Comolli and Jean Narboni open their 1969 editorial "Cinema/Ideology/Criticism" by acknowledging that their own work as critics is "situated fairly and squarely inside the economic system of capitalist publishing." They then look at varieties of film practice and classify them according to their relationship with the "dominant ideology." They most highly value films that break with this ideology, not only on the level of content (portraying decolonization and the conflict over U.S. involvement in Vietnam) but also on the level of form—for example, experimental films that disturb easy viewing processes. Jean-Luc Godard's obscure political film *Le Vent d'est* (*Wind from the East*) (credited to the Dziga Vertov Group, 1969) was heralded by leftist critics of the period.

But Comolli and Narboni's editorial set an even more lasting agenda for film theory. In an alphabetical list of types of films to study, they use category "e" to designate films that seem to uphold the status quo but register, in their formal excesses or internal contradictions, the stresses and strains of trying to make ideology work, thus exposing it to close viewers as a representation rather than an unchangeable reality. Soon other critics followed Comolli and Narboni's lead to read films in this way, such as those made by studio-era auteur Douglas Sirk. Sirk's 1950s melodramas, including *All That Heaven Allows* (1955), were considered too color-coordinated, his characters too hysterical, and their environments too crammed with artificial commodities to be taken at face value [**Figure 13.30**]. These glossy surfaces were seen to be cracking under the brittle hypocrisies characterizing prosperous, Eisenhower-era America, including anti-Communist hysteria, repression of civil rights movements, and enforcing of gender roles and sexual

▶ **VIEWING CUE**

Does the film you are watching put forth a clear ideological position? Are there ways to see conflicting positions in it? ⏸

codes that had been challenged during the war. Sirk's films are *progressive texts*; the uneasy feeling they leave us with critiques dominant ideology. This subtle, and sometimes wishful, approach is known as *symptomatic reading*, a fruitful legacy of Louis Althusser's Marxist influence on contemporary film theory.

Poststructuralism: Psychoanalysis, Apparatus Theory, and Spectatorship

As the term implies, *poststructuralism* is the intellectual development that came after structuralism and in some sense supplanted it. Poststructuralism calls into question the

13.30 *All That Heaven Allows* (1955). Critics regarded Douglas Sirk's melodramas as "progressive texts" whose formal excesses and improbable situations showed the cracks in Eisenhower America's facade of prosperity and social consensus.

rational methodology and fixed definitions that structuralists bring to their various objects of study. Because the term is not descriptive but relational, it is versatile enough to include many areas of thought, from psychoanalysis to postcolonial and feminist theory. In some sense it is unfortunate that the term "poststructuralism" has stuck because it builds obscurity into its very name. If you don't know what structuralism is, how can you understand poststructuralism? Regrettable as this situation is, the question is part of the point. Poststructuralism is a position of critique, asking us to reconsider everything we take for granted, including attitudes that we might hold without recognizing the names others have given them. For example, our implicit standard that a satisfying film ties up all its loose ends is a structuralist position that posits closure as a basic narrative element. Poststructuralism stresses the open-endedness of stories: what if we daydream about the characters we have been introduced to or pick up on the relationship between a film and topical events? Closure is a relative quality.

Structuralism attempted to be more rigorous than common forms of humanist criticism by introducing scientific protocols into the study of literature. It tried to be systematic with empirical observation by looking for transhistorical patterns into which specific data would fit (for example, anthropologists compared dozens of creation myths; film critics compared westerns). Poststructuralism, in turn, questions the assumption of objectivity and the disregard for cultural and historical context. Hence, it is a whole lot messier as an intellectual movement. A shorthand definition might be: structuralism + subjectivity = poststructuralism. Most of contemporary film theory is poststructuralist in orientation, although some schools refer to the thinkers and tenets identified with structuralism and poststructuralism more explicitly than others. Key movements in poststructuralist film theory include psychoanalysis, apparatus theory, and spectatorship.

Psychoanalysis

Louis Althusser's work has been central to poststructuralist currents in film theory. His elaboration of how an individual comes to believe in ideology as "imaginary representation" refers to **psychoanalysis** and in particular to the French psychoanalyst Jacques Lacan's definition of the imaginary. In his teachings from the 1950s through his death in 1981, Lacan spoke of three domains of psychic experience: the *imaginary*, the *symbolic*, and the *real*. The Lacanian imaginary is not simply opposed to "reality"—in fact, "the real" in Lacan's thought is a domain akin to trauma that cannot be directly represented. Rather, the imaginary realm deals in images, and the symbolic realm is the domain of language. The human subject relates to pictures in a particularly powerful way, rooted in one of the earliest images to leave an impression on us, our own reflection in the mirror. In the mirror stage, the infant comes to recognize himself or herself as a human individual. But this recognition is also a "misrecognition," for the image is really an illusion. Lacanian film theorists liken this early sense of self, which is both powerful and illusory, to the experience of viewing a film and "believing" in its world. We are immobile and surrounded in darkness when we watch, and a grandiose image appears lit up on the wall. Moreover, films are peopled with stars and characters with physical powers superior to ours and with whom we identify [Figure 13.31].

13.31 *Casino Royale* (2006). Star Daniel Craig's physical prowess and that of his character represent idealized objects of identification.

Apparatus Theory

In Plato's ancient parable of the cave, people chained underground watching shadows on the wall had no way of knowing that what they saw was not real. Film theorists followed Althusser in understanding the cinema as an *apparatus*, an ideological mechanism based in a physical set of technologies, with the power to convince us that an illusion is real. If the everyday world we live in is a collection of images imbued with capitalist ideology, how much more saturated with dominant ways of thinking are movies, whose images are selected and combined by filmmakers working for huge entertainment companies? The essays of Jean-Louis Baudry use the term "apparatus" to argue that the arrangement of equipment, such as the hidden projector and the illuminated screen, influences our unconscious receptivity to the image and to ideology—as if we too were trapped in Plato's cave. **Apparatus theory** explores the values built into film technology through the particular context of its historical development. The camera's monocular (single-eyed) view and use of perspective incorporate the values of human-scaled Renaissance art. Such art posits a viewer standing at the point where perspective lines converge. This viewer-addressee is in the same position as the camera and can thus imagine himself or herself as the originator or possessor of the illusion on the canvas or the screen. Anthropocentrism (human-centeredness), individualism, possession, and the primacy of the visual are all particular cultural values. It goes without saying, we may think, that a camera depends on perspective. But what "goes without saying" is one way to define ideology. A culture that did not put the possessive individual at the center of representation—a culture that valued empty space, inanimate objects, and animals as well as people; multiple subjects or scrolls instead of frames in pictorial depictions; or senses other than sight in the arts—might never have developed the technology of photography.

Poststructuralist theory claims that the position constructed by the representation preexists the human subject that will later assume it, and thus the representation constructs that subject as a *subject of vision*. In other words, an individual who stands in front of a Renaissance painting or who watches a classical Hollywood movie is "subjected" to the apparatus's positioning and understands his or her "subjectivity" in pre-given terms. Theorists argue that subjects are constituted through language or through other acts of signification (meaning-making), such as film. For example, the word "I" has no definite meaning until it is used by someone in a sentence. It will then designate the person saying "I," and its meaning will shift as a conversation progresses and each speaker uses "I" to refer to himself or herself in turn. Although viewers cannot "talk back" when they watch a film (as they can with video games, Web sites, and interactive films), they can be said to be constituted as the object of the film's address: they are meant to laugh, cry, or put clues together as the film unfolds.

Spectatorship

The topic of how subjects interact with films and with the cinematic apparatus is known as the theory of **spectatorship.** As suggested earlier, spectatorship has been a concern in film theory since Münsterberg, who used psychology to explain the mind's role in making sense of movies. Theorists such as Sergei Eisenstein were also interested in the viewer's interaction with images and sounds. In the poststructuralist theory of the 1970s, however, spectatorship stood at the convergence of theories of language and subjectivity, psychoanalysis, and Marxism.

Christian Metz, one of the most prolific and influential contemporary theorists, has also been at the center of spectatorship theory. He refers to linguistic and psychoanalytic terminology in the title of his influential book *The Imaginary Signifier* (1977), which argues that film's strong perceptual presence makes it an almost hallucinatory experience, gratifying to our voyeurism (our love of looking without being seen ourselves) and to our unconscious self-image of potency. The work of Metz and other French theorists began to appear in translation in the English journal *Screen* in the early 1970s; the theory of spectatorship refined there by English and American contributors is sometimes known as *screen theory* or *gaze theory*.

▶ **VIEWING CUE**

Consider your experience as a spectator of the film screened most recently for class. Did you relate to the point of view of a particular character? Were you aware of the apparatus (the camera, the projection)?

13.32 *And God Created Woman* (1957). Brigitte Bardot's character exemplifies what Laura Mulvey calls woman's "to-be-looked-at-ness."

Theories of Gender and Sexuality

The poststructuralist concern with spectatorship and subjectivity remains abstract if spectatorship is generalized and the nature of subjectivity is not questioned. Psychoanalytic theory revolves around the issues of desire and identification. These issues and the questions of gender and sexuality to which they are related soon became key to film theory's exploration of how subjectivity is engaged by and constructed in cinema.

Feminist Film Theory

Feminism began to have wide social and intellectual currency during the 1970s. Commentators point out that the female image is treated differently from the male image in film—as well as in advertising, pornography, and painting [**Figure 13.32**]. The objectification of the female image seems to solicit a possessive male gaze or female identification. In film theory, feminist critics note, the spectator is envisioned in a similarly gendered way. "Is the Gaze Male?" asks E. Ann Kaplan in an essay of that title, noting that vision is often associated with ownership and power in our culture.

British theorist and filmmaker Laura Mulvey's "Visual Pleasure and Narrative Cinema," published in *Screen* in 1975, is one of the most important essays in contemporary film theory. Arguing that psychoanalysis offers a compelling account of how the difference between the sexes is culturally internalized and valued, Mulvey observes that the glamorous and desirable female image in film is also a potentially threatening vision of difference, or otherness, for male viewers. Hollywood films repeat a pattern of visual mastery of the woman as "Other" by attributing the on-screen gaze to a male character who can cover for the camera's voyeurism—its capacity for looking without being seen—and stand in for the male viewer. Film narratives also tend to domesticate or otherwise tame the woman, Mulvey shows, offering analyses of Alfred Hitchcock's *Vertigo* (1958) and *Rear Window* (1954), whose stories are driven by voyeurism and female makeovers. In another primary example, Mulvey uses the psychosexual concept of fetishism to explain the effect of the elaborately controlled presentation of Marlene Dietrich's image in the films of Josef von Sternberg [**Figure 13.33**]. In Freudian theory, fetishism is a denial of, by way of overcompensation for, female lack, with "lack" defined as difference from masculinity, or castration.

Although generations of students have resisted Mulvey's emphasis on such questionable psychoanalytic concepts as castration, most have also agreed with her formulation of the standard dichotomy in Hollywood film: "woman as image / man as bearer of the look." Mulvey's essay is polemical: she champions "a political use of psychoanalysis" and a new kind of filmmaking that would "free the look of the camera into its materiality in time and space" so that it could not be ignored through assimilation to the viewer's or characters' perspective. In their film *Riddles of the*

13.33 *The Devil Is a Woman* (1935). Marlene Dietrich's image invites the viewer's fetishistic gaze, according to feminist theorist Laura Mulvey.

Sphinx (1977), Mulvey and Peter Wollen use 360-degree pans, with the camera positioned at about waist level, to emulate the circularity of a young mother's rhythms of work and to avoid objectifying her body in a centered, still image [Figure 13.34]. The film deliberately sets out to destroy conventional visual pleasure and narrative satisfaction. Like many theorists of this period, Mulvey and Wollen believed that making spectators think about what they were seeing was the first step toward a critical perspective.

Building on Mulvey's provocative argument, other feminist critics raise the question of female spectatorship. If narrative cinema so successfully positions the viewer to take up a male gaze, why are women historically often the most enthusiastic film viewers?

13.34 *Riddles of the Sphinx* (1977). Laura Mulvey puts her own theories about images of women into practice in a film made with Peter Wollen.

One way to approach this question is to consider films produced with a female audience in mind. During Hollywood's heyday, women's pictures featured female stars who had a strong appeal to women, such as Bette Davis and Joan Crawford. At first glance, women's pleasure in these films seems self-defeating because what these heroines do best is suffer. However, feminists argue that a film like *Now, Voyager* (1942) enables female spectators to explore their own dissatisfaction with their lives by fantasizing a more fulfilling version of that existence. The movie shows Davis as a dowdy spinster taking control of her life—through psychoanalytic treatment and new clothes! In this way, the contradictions of women's situations are revealed, while no satisfactory solutions are posited. Perhaps no easy solutions exist, the films imply. Today's commercial films aimed at women are not that different from those of the 1940s. *Divine Secrets of the Ya-Ya Sisterhood* (2002) reveals similar contradictions to *Now, Voyager*: mother-daughter bonds are both destructive and primary. Many feminist critics argue that women's pleasure in these complicated, mixed-message movies should be taken seriously. Because film is a mass medium, it will never radically challenge existing power relations, but if it speaks to women's dilemmas, it is doing more than much official culture does. Sometimes filmmakers succeed in evoking these emotions and mass cultural traditions in more reflexive and satisfying ways, such as in Pedro Almodóvar's revisiting of maternal melodramas in *All about My Mother* (1999) and *Volver* (2006) [Figure 13.35].

Still other feminist scholars turn to the work of past women filmmakers. The political and aesthetic options and strategies of contemporary feminist filmmakers—from Kathryn Bigelow in the United States, Ann Hui in Hong Kong, and Márta Mészáros in Hungary—differ greatly from those of Matilde Landeta, a Mexican director working in the 1940s, or Larisa Shepitko, a Soviet filmmaker of the 1950s. (See our discussion of American women filmmakers in Chapter 12.) Nevertheless, there are important continuities and common questions to ask about the conditions under which these women work, the sources that inspire them, and the cinematic languages they draw on and develop. Overall, feminism has had more of an impact on the

13.35 *Volver* (2006). Pedro Almodóvar revisits the maternal melodrama to empower female characters.

▶ **VIEWING CUE**

Describe the interrelated issues of gender representation and gendered spectatorship in a film you viewed recently. ⏸

relatively young discipline of film theory than on many more established ones. Arguably, gender in film cannot be ignored. As Mulvey's work suggests, cinema—certainly entertainment film but also the avant-garde—depends on the stylized images of women for its appeal. Moreover, the cinema, because it is part of the fabric of daily life, necessarily comments on the everyday, private sphere. In the private sphere, women's role is pervasive, if sometimes undervalued. Feminism's significant inroads in film theory have laid the groundwork for related, though not always parallel, critiques of cinema's deployment of sexuality, race, and national identity.

Lesbian and Gay Film Studies

Feminist and psychoanalytic theory stress that unconscious processes of desire and identification are at play when we go to the movies. Our everyday ways of talking about stars and films acknowledge how strong the element of fantasy is in our viewing. Despite the sexist historical legacy of psychoanalysis, many feminists find its focus on subjectivity, gender, and sexuality very useful. Like cinema itself, however, psychoanalysis historically concentrates on heterosexual scenarios (such as the Oedipus complex) and pathologizes gays and lesbians (as cases of "arrested development," for example). *Lesbian and gay film theory* critiques and supplements feminist approaches that use psychoanalysis. According to this theory, films allow for more flexible ways of seeing and experiencing visual pleasure than are accounted for by the binary opposites of male versus female, seeing versus seen, and being versus desiring that are the basis of Mulvey's influential model of spectatorship.

The gender of a member of the audience need not correspond with that of the character he or she finds most absorbing or most alluring. Marlene Dietrich, Mulvey's example of a "fetish" or mask for male desire, cross-dressed for songs in many films and even kissed a woman on the lips in her first American movie, *Morocco* (1930) **[Figure 13.36]**. Dietrich's gender bending is more than theoretical. Her onscreen style borrows directly from the fashions of the lesbian and gay subculture of Weimar-era Germany, where her career began. Dietrich thus appealed on many different levels to lesbian and gay viewers, as well as to heterosexual women and men. In fact, this multiplicity could be seen more generally as a key to cinema's mass appeal. Although movies tend to conform to the dominant values of a society—in this case, to heterosexuality as the norm—they also make unconscious appeals to our fantasies, which may not be as conformist; anyone may identify with or desire a character of either gender in a particular movie. Moreover, films leave room for viewers' own interpretations and appropriations, such as when fan writers continue the adventures of particular mainstream characters or celebrities and share them on the Internet. Spectators positioned at the margins, such as gay men and lesbians, often "read against the grain" for cues of performance or mise-en-scène that suggest a different story than the one onscreen, one with more relevance to their lives. An interest in stars may extend beyond any particular film they are cast in and ignore those films' required romantic outcomes. For example, Dietrich's and Jodie Foster's strong images have historically appealed to lesbian viewers. Lesbian and gay portrayals in and responses to the cinema constitute one of many areas that have demanded fresh concepts in film theory.

13.36 *Morocco* (1930). Lesbian and gay theorists interpret Marlene Dietrich—here kissing a woman—in a different way than feminist theorist Laura Mulvey does in her influential essay, "Visual Pleasure and Narrative Cinema."

New Directions in Film Studies

In this section, we will broadly consider three new directions in film studies. *Cultural studies* scrutinizes aspects of cinema embedded in the everyday lives—of individuals or groups—at particular historical junctures and in particular social contexts; it does not analyze individual texts or theorize about spectatorship in the abstract. The phenomena cultural studies addresses can range from the reception of film stars to the transformations of postcolonial societies; it is thus impossible to encompass all applications of its methods in a brief discussion such as this one. Another new direction in film studies, one that critiques poststructuralist film theory explicitly, comes from scholars rigorously exploring philosophy and film as well as the cognitive processes involved in viewing and comprehending movies. Finally, characteristics of contemporary society designated by the term *postmodernism,* and the potential and uses of *new media* technologies that are altering the place of cinema in the twenty-first century, have also emerged as important concerns in recent film theory. These three new directions in film study address questions left open by poststructuralist models, bringing theory in touch with present-day viewers' diverse experiences.

Cultural Studies

A useful way of understanding the fresh approach that cultural studies takes toward cinema lies in a shift in the very definition of "culture." Instead of defining culture as great works produced by transcendent artists and appreciated by knowledgeable patrons, cultural studies uses an anthropological definition: culture as a way of life, including social structures and habits. In other words, it is how movies are encountered, understood, and "used" in daily experience that interests cultural studies scholars. **Cultural studies** is a loosely defined set of approaches drawn from the humanities and social sciences and united by the refusal to isolate an artistic text from the processes of production and consumption. Social critics at the influential Birmingham Center for the Study of Contemporary Culture in England were among the first to use the term, in studies of youth culture and of television audiences in the 1970s. The way social background and education influence taste, legal decisions on monopoly practices or censorship in film, how films were exhibited in the first decade of cinema, the reception of particular films by particular groups at particular times, and the activities of movie fans are all topics that have been pursued under the rubric of cultural studies. We will look at a few key examples of cultural studies: reception, stars, and race and representation.

Reception Theory

One of the most important approaches used by cultural studies of film is termed **reception theory** because it focuses on how a film is received by audiences, rather than on who made a film or on its formal features or thematic content. As suggested throughout this book, audiences are at the center of the film experience. The global reach of contemporary films should persuade us that any theory that does not take audiences into account would give a limited picture of film culture. Composed of actual individuals whose habits and preferences may be researched through surveys and testimonies, audiences provide a concrete basis for theorizing. Collecting information about audience composition or preferences is not itself film theory—the film industry is as interested in audience demographics as is the sociologist, and the studios themselves have initiated some of the best viewer surveys. Cultural studies goes further, theorizing that a work's meaning is only achieved in its reception. This implies a theory of audiences as active rather than passive. Obvious examples are participatory viewing practices such as the costumes and call-and-response of *The*

13.37 *The Rocky Horror Picture Show* (1975). Participatory audiences and repeat viewers are studied by reception theory.

Rocky Horror Picture Show (1975) fans and the imaginative play inspired by kids' viewing [**Figure 13.37**]. In addition, films from the past may be received by today's audiences in entirely new ways. We might have a response that roots for the Native Americans rather than the cowboys or that enjoy a supporting character's subversive wit rather than investing in the romance of a pair of bland leads. Studying reception details the complexity of viewer-text interactions.

Beyond the idiosyncrasies of personal history and circumstances, aspects of our *cultural identity*—for instance, age, immigration status, and educational background—can predispose us toward particular kinds of reception. The gay subtext of *Rebel without a Cause* is likely to be more salient to an audience knowledgeable about the subculture. Such an audience is referred to as an *interpretive community* because its members share particular knowledge, or *cultural competence*, through which a film is experienced and interpreted. The panoply of West African–derived hairstyles in *Daughters of the Dust* (1991) is more likely to be enjoyed and recognized by black women than by other audience members; indeed, filmmaker Julie Dash intended this special gratification as part of the movie's *address,* or vision, of its ideal audience. Viewers who have read the book on which a movie is based, such as Ian McEwan's *Atonement*, have different competences from those who have only read reviews of the film [**Figure 13.38**].

The responses of particular viewers to cultural phenomena are considered *situated responses*; that is, readings that are influenced, though not predetermined, by geography, age, gender, wealth, and a host of other contingent factors. *Shrek* (2001) is appreciated by children for its simple fairy-tale story and for the expected pleasures encountered through repeat viewings, whereas Eddie Murphy's fans appreciate his performance of the donkey's voice, and those interested in technology scrutinize the advances in animation. Theorists see these multiple ways of interacting with a text as confirmation that individuals actively make meaning even in response to otherwise homogenous mass media.

The methodologies associated with reception theory include comparing and contrasting the protocols of reviews drawn from different periodicals, countries, or decades; conducting detailed interviews with viewers; tracking commodity tie-ins, the goods that are marketed with the "brand name" of a particular film or characters; and studying fan activity on the Web. Here we focus on two kinds of reception studies: *ethnographic* and *historical.*

Ethnographic Reception Studies.
The word "ethnography," literally meaning "people" plus "writing," is adopted from anthropology. As noted in Chapter 12, ethnographic film is a way of documenting a culture's daily life. Ethnographic reception studies focus on film users and are often based on surveys or interviews. They may look at a cross section of an audience, but they are often designed to illuminate the behavior and situation

13.38 *Atonement* (2007). Viewers who have read the book bring different knowledge to the movie.

of a particular group (an "ethnos") that is socially nondominant and lacking cultural power. Advocating for social change that extends rights and recognition to such a group is part of identity politics. Reception is an important dimension of identity-based critiques of mainstream cinema.

Because social out-groups are often denied access to the creation of representations that reflect their lives, members of such groups may find meaning and creativity in their own kind of consumption of popular forms. To give an example, African American audiences might enjoy Paul Robeson's performance in *Show Boat* (1936) while critiquing aspects of the film's racial politics. Reception differs from spectatorship in that it deals with actual audiences rather than a hypothetical subject constructed by the text. Reception studies thus address both actual responses to movies and the behavior of groups; spectatorship is concerned with the unconscious patterns evoked by a particular text or by the process of film viewing in the abstract. British cultural studies scholar Stuart Hall has argued that groups respond to mass culture from their different positions of social empowerment. They may react from the position the text slots them into, a *dominant* reading; offer a *negotiated* reading that accommodates different realities; or reject the framework in which a dominant message is conveyed through an *oppositional* reading. Ethnographic studies can map these three positions. Social identity considerably complicates the picture of subjectivity offered in poststructuralist film theory.

Historical Reception Studies.

Historical Reception Studies. In historical reception studies, critics remind us that our understandings of films from the past are incomplete if they do not consider the meanings those texts carry with them from the contexts in which they were produced and consumed. Control of film production is much more entwined with economic incentives than are other forms of art-making, but popular media are not devoid of the spirit of the people, a spirit that resides in reception. Scandalous films, exhibition circumstances in different communities, scrapbooks and other artifacts, mentions of films in works by contemporary writers—these all help fill in the texture of historical experience. For example, the reception of the countercultural film *Easy Rider* (1969) changed the kinds of films Hollywood produced.

The Birth of a Nation (1915) is fascinating to study textually; it used more shots, more close-ups, more editing, and more scoring innovations than had ever been seen in film. But its reception is also a defining event of both film history and of the politics of race in America. The NAACP gathered prominence as an organization through opposition to the film's racism. The African American independent cinema, discussed in Chapter 12, was catalyzed by D. W. Griffith's film. But *The Birth of a Nation* was also screened at a Ku Klux Klan rally as recently as in 1978— though not without protesters. Concretely, the historian looks at ad campaigns as well as contemporary reviews and commentaries in newspapers and publications of different orientations. The historian might also research the film's reception by interviewing moviegoers who saw it during one of its many re-releases. Each film is embedded in personal and cultural memories, including those of the students who study it in contemporary film studies classes.

Topics ranging from the impact of protests against *Year of the Dragon* (1985) on Asian American political organizing to the patent wars that shaped the early film landscape yield insights into film's reception history. Methodologically, historicizing means looking at nonfilm, or **extratextual**, sources in one's research: laws governing where films could or could not be shown, the design of buildings that exhibited films, studies of immigrant populations, import tariffs, equipment patents, records of censorship boards, and the like. Historians of reception regard films as social events whose meaning can only be determined by understanding and decoding the many forces that intersect with them.

> **▶ VIEWING CUE**
>
> Conduct a reception study of the film you just viewed by surveying your classmates about which characters and situations they responded to most favorably. Compare and contrast their opinions with those of film reviewers. ⏸

Star Studies

An important component of reception is our response to *stars*, performers who become recognizable through their films or who bring celebrity to their roles. In addition to analyzing how a star's image is composed from various elements—not only film appearances but also promotion, publicity, and critical commentary—theorists are interested in how audience reception helps define a star's cultural meaning (see pp. 72–76). Although one of the most pervasive aspects of cinema, stars may seem one of the least likely topics to be considered in a theoretical approach. After all, stars are the province of entertainment and newsmagazines, tabloid journalism, and online chats. In fact, textual critics can have difficulty dealing with stardom, which is fundamentally an intertextual phenomenon. In contrast, familiar and ephemeral sources such as fan magazines have an important place in cultural studies, as do the responses of fans themselves. One understands a film in relationship to what one knows of its stars outside the world of the film's fiction. From Judy Garland to Lindsay Lohan, stars with troubled offscreen lives are perceived differently in wholesome onscreen roles [**Figures 13.39a and 13.39b**].

(a)

(b)

13.39   ***Mean Girls*** (2004). Lindsay Lohan's wholesome character (a) contrasts with viewers' knowledge of her troubled offscreen life (b).

Beyond the range of roles that a star becomes familiar for playing, other discourses about stars—including promotion (studio-arranged exposure such as Web sites and television appearances), publicity (romances, scandals, and political involvement), and commentary (critical evaluations and awards)—help construct their images. Star images become texts to be read in their own right. Sean Penn's promise as a teen star was associated with "acting" rather than cosmetic appeal. His brief marriage to Madonna and his arrest for assaulting a photographer, his portrayals of a condemned man in *Dead Man Walking* (1995) and of a mentally disabled father in *I Am Sam* (2001), and his work as an independent director in films like *Into the Wild* (2007) construct him as an individualist, even an "outlaw," a persona that carries connotations of "authenticity" [**Figure 13.40**]. Even when a particular star is billed as "just an ordinary guy," like Tom Hanks, or "the girl next door," like 1950s star Doris Day, this image is carefully orchestrated. Hence, the fascination of so many paperback star biographies that purport to look behind the façade.

We will never have access to the star as a real person. Instead, we experience his or her constructed image in relation to cultural codes (including age, race, class, gender, region, fashion, and more) and according to filmic codes (genre, acting, and even lighting). For example, the silent film star Lillian Gish was sometimes lit from above as she stood on a white sheet. The reflected light enhanced her pallor and the radiance of her blonde hair, connoting a virginal whiteness that was an important component of her star image in her films with D. W. Griffith. We use aspects of star images as a kind of cultural shorthand: For example, Sidney Poitier stands in for a particular aspect of 1950s and 1960s American race relations. A wishful image of overachieving middle-class black men disguised aspects of everyday and structural racism and encoded some of the gains of the contemporary civil rights movement. We also construct our own identities and communities through stars whom we will never know, and this is not necessarily a negative aspect of the phenomenon. Young girls who patterned themselves after plucky singing star Deanna Durbin in the 1940s or Madonna in the 1980s incorporated the quality of independence they embodied and identified themselves in solidarity, rather than in competition, with other girls who shared their appreciation.

Stars are often considered the embodiment of types. For example, John Wayne connotes rugged individualism; Meg Ryan, perky romanticism; Morgan Freeman, quiet dignity; Robin Williams, manic mayhem. Different film roles, such as Robin Williams's creepy stalker in *One Hour Photo* (2002), add new inflections to these personas. In recent years, critics attempted to theorize the phenomenon of stardom and to illuminate not just the sociological significance of particular types but also how stars' images contribute to a film's meaning. Judy Garland became a teenage star when she appeared in *The Wizard of Oz* (1939). Her later troubles with drugs, partly a result of her "grooming" by the studio, lend irony to the image of girlish innocence she projects in the film classic.

According to critic Richard Dyer, who urges us to consider stars' images in general in terms of contradiction, Marilyn Monroe's phenomenally successful image reconciled innocence and sexiness. At the root of the star phenomenon, Dyer argues, is a basic conflict between the ordinary and the extraordinary. Stars are not better people than the rest of us, which facilitates our identification with them. And yet they are a breed apart.

One kind of research we might undertake to examine the contributions of stars' images to films involves looking at fan magazines, a type of publication that emerged early in the twentieth century. Such magazines show how films were pro-

13.40   **Sean Penn**. Star images are approached seriously in cultural studies of film.

moted and received as star vehicles. Star discourse is a particularly revealing and useful critical approach to cinema because it is based in our everyday experience as fans. We have many immediate and unexamined responses to stars, from crushes to antipathies. But we also appreciate stars in nuanced ways that yield considerable critical understanding. Cultural studies of stars often begin with viewer testimonials, taking them not at face value but using them as a starting point for a more sociological analysis. What ethnic groups are represented in a nation's most popular stars? Do popular female stars transgress the boundaries of what is considered proper female behavior? Are people of color limited to supporting roles? Stars are powerful forces for gathering up what is important to a culture at any given moment. They represent conflicts that are not necessarily worked out.

Race and Representation

The concept of race—for race is not an objective fact but a socially constructed category based on historical experiences and valuations of perceived difference—intersects with the film experience on many different levels, raising questions about the possibilities for cross-racial identification and other aspects of spectatorship. Cultural studies of film offer ways to address these questions. The psychoanalytic models for understanding gender in film have provided inadequate explanations of race. What might be called the fetishism of whiteness in Hollywood movies, a dominance and idealization of representations of one race, left people of color out of the picture and squirming in their seats at the cinema for decades. It is helpful to distinguish in this area two senses of the term "representation": (1) the *aesthetic sense*, whereby we may speak of representations of African Americans in the films of Spike

▶ **VIEWING CUE**

Research the star of the film you are about to watch for class. What does your previous knowledge of this star bring to your viewing? Is the role at odds with his or her established image?

13.41 *The King and I* (1956). Colonialism becomes a charming musical romance told from a white Englishwoman's perspective.

Lee versus those of *Gone with the Wind,* for example, and (2) the *political sense* of standing for a group of people, as an elected representative does. Both senses are at play in the cinematic representation of race. Cultural studies models are flexible enough to address racialized images, such as stereotypes and their reception by diverse audiences, as well as how discourses of imperialism, colonialism, and nationalism, often related to racial representations, are embedded in film stories, genres, and star images. Recent theories of exile and homeland, cultural hybridity and diaspora, and the global and the intercultural have added to the store of explanatory frames we have for looking at race and representation in cinema. Here we can only introduce issues that will reward further exploration.

If gender and sexual identifications are more mobile in cinema than they might at first appear, identification across race is a fraught and often obligatory process for nonwhite viewers because of the historical lack of racial diversity onscreen. Cinematic history reinforces the assumption of a white, western, "unmarked" spectator-subject. In classical Hollywood films, nonwhite characters are relegated to the periphery of the action as villainous or comic or sometimes noble, but always secondary, characters. Colonialism, the assumed primacy of Western values, peoples, and power over people from other parts of the globe, pervades such genres as the western and the adventure film. It even appears in the musical *The King and I* (1956), in which one white Englishwoman proves to be a match for the Siamese king and his entire court [Figure 13.41]. In *Unthinking Eurocentrism* (1994), theorists Robert Stam and Ella Shohat show how a Western gaze and voice are reproduced in such popular films as the *Indiana Jones* series, in which ancient cultures provide colorful backgrounds for the exploits of a Western hero. They also discuss how non-dominant cultures are marginalized by casting, when white actors play other races [Figure 13.42], and even by sound, when everyone speaks English in films set in another country or when jazz scores are used in films in which all the characters are white. But Stam and Shohat's examples show that American cinema often reflects a multicultural society in other ways. The importance of the western as a genre, or of the plantation as a motif, gives evidence of a cultural preoccupation with racial difference and conflicts. Although stereotyped in such film representations, people of color stand at the center of the nation's definition of itself. Recent Hollywood films often incorporate multiculturalism as part of the very definition of America.

The increasing success of filmmakers of color in the United States has paralleled theoretical explorations of alternative aesthetics, which are closely linked to literary and other artistic movements. The trickster figure of West African tradition, which appears in *To Sleep with Anger* (1990) by Charles Burnett and in *Zajota and the Boogie Spirit* (1989) by Ayoka Chenzira, is an expression of the identification of these African American filmmakers with the diaspora, a scattered community of people who share an original homeland. Finally, aesthetic expressions of politics are a major concern in postcolonial cinemas that have emerged around the world. *Third cinema*, discussed in Chapter 12, is one theorization of this conjuncture. The term, derived from "Third World," names film practices that are politicized in relation to the dominant cinemas of the West (first cinema) and the artistic films that still remain disengaged from social contexts and popular audiences (second cinema). These works often use

13.42 *West Side Story* (1961). The film's Puerto Rican heroine is played by white actress Natalie Wood.

narrative forms more in keeping with specific cultural traditions or political ideas than the linear cause-and-effect structures of Hollywood films. Humberto Solás's *Lucía* (1969), for instance, uses a three-part structure to link the fates of three Cuban women in different historical moments [Figure 13.43].

By arguing that there is room for agency and divergence in our spectatorial and reception experiences, and in opening up the kinds of films and related cinematic phenomena that are deemed worthy of theoretical attention, critics associated with cultural studies take apart the unity and inevitability that characterized poststructuralist film theory in the 1970s. Cultural studies is less concerned with the specific film text or with the generalized film apparatus than with concrete dimensions of cinematic experience. For example, the advertising practices that surround films, the costumes designed for them and related retail schemes, censorship campaigns, and fan clubs all might be considered in a cultural studies approach. With roots in sociology, cultural studies takes a broader approach to contemporary media than film studies based in the humanities often do, shifting scholars' attention to the even more pervasive media form of television. Concepts of "the gaze" and the spectator do not translate directly to the case of television, with its much more interactive and everyday mode of consumption. Comparison of these media has opened up space to address the distinctiveness of new media, such as computer-based art, as well as the many social and economic transactions that surround cinema today, from the viewing of works on cable, tape, or disc to the incorporation of movie franchises into our daily lives.

13.43 *Lucía* (1969). Humberto Solás's film uses formal innovation to reflect on Cuban history.

Film and Philosophy

While cultural studies critics reject the overt formalism as well as the abstractions of 1970s film theory, film philosophers critique the same dominant school for its lack of empirical support and theoretical rigor. As we have described, the film theory of the 1970s draws on a closely linked body of works from Marxist, psychoanalytic, and linguistic traditions. In doing so, it produces an account of the film experience in which an abstractly conceived spectator is "subjected" (in the double sense of "ruled by" and "given subjectivity") to a system that equates vision with truth and possession. This dominant school has been dubbed "grand theory" because of its sweeping claims and its failure to distinguish among the effects of specific films.

To some extent all film theory is related to philosophy and characterized by a search for underlying principles and a logical argument. However, some film theorists identify more strongly than others with philosophical methods. In *Mystifying Movies*, Noël Carroll carefully and gleefully debunks the analogy of film to dreams; other scholars point out the flawed reasoning in using linguistic models to describe sounds and images. David Bordwell, one of the most prolific and well-respected film scholars, advocates a cognitivist approach to the medium. Cognition is the overall process of knowing, including perception, memory, and judgment. *Cognitivist film theory* understands our response to film in terms of rational evaluation of visual and narrative cues. Based in psychological research, it advocates verifiable scientific approaches. Rejecting analysis that invokes unconscious fantasy or employs idiosyncratic interpretation, cognitivism claims that we respond to the visual stimuli of the moving image with the same perceptual processes we use to respond to visual stimuli in the world—adjusting film images for lack of depth, perceiving the identity of objects that are moving and changing in time. Not simply a backlash against the obscure terminology and French-influenced syntax of poststructuralist theory, cognitive film theory argues for a less metaphorical, more scientific, and historically verifiable definition and practice of theory. In another important strand of film theory, American philosopher Stanley Cavell, in *The World Viewed* (1971) and subsequent works, discusses the aesthetic experience of watching films as a philosophical encounter in its own right, one related to the rhetorical tradition of philosophy.

Phenomenology, which stresses that any act of perception involves a mutuality of viewer and viewed, has also had a profound effect on film theory. Jacques Lacan and Christian Metz derived their emphasis on the gaze from phenomenologists, but the psychoanalytic concept of the unconscious drew away from the more embodied consciousness that phenomenology described. More recently, Vivian Sobchack returns to the phenomenology of perception in accounting for the film experience as an intersubjective one.

French philosopher Gilles Deleuze has made an important contribution to recent film theory, building on the semiotics of C. S. Peirce and the work of other philosophers. More than the writings of almost any other film theorist, Deleuze's work must be studied on its own terms because he develops ideas through specific interrelated terminology. But the investment is rewarding. In his two books on cinema, Deleuze distinguishes between two types of cinema that correspond roughly to two historical periods. The "movement image," prevalent in the cinema of the early twentieth century, reflects what might be called a cause-and-effect view of the world. The physical comedy of Buster Keaton and the collision at the heart of Sergei Eisenstein's montage represent action and a linear or dialectical forward movement that provoke a response in the viewer. The "time image" is displayed in films by such masters as the neorealist Roberto Rossellini and the more metaphorical Michelangelo Antonioni, both working in the wake of the disillusionment and uncertainty of postwar Italy. In such movies, images and sounds do not give clear signals of spatial connection or logical sequence; instead, they represent the open-endedness of time and the potentiality of thought [Figure 13.44]. Deleuze's philosophy of film goes beyond the specific films and directors he uses as examples to suggest new ways of imagining the relationship between images and the world. *Referentiality*, the idea that filmic images refer to actual objects, events, or phenomena, is no longer a basic tenet of film theory. For Deleuze, the film image is not a representation of the world; it is an experience of movement or time itself. For other thinkers, referentiality is no longer a tenet of film theory because neither film nor the world is what it used to be.

Postmodernism and New Media

Obviously, film is no longer the only medium that organizes our audiovisual experience. At least since the 1940s, when television was rapidly adopted into U.S. homes, other moving-image media have challenged cinema's dominance. Many predict that digital media will soon replace film stock. However, such developments also suggest that this book's title is more apt than ever before: film has so thoroughly transformed our overall experience that it has prepared us for the integration of digital media and other image technologies in our lives. Rather than defining film more narrowly, we can think of it more broadly.

The predominance of visual media is characteristic of the culture of postmodernism. As we have mentioned, the term "modernism" refers both to a group of artistic movements (from atonal music to cubist painting to montage filmmaking) and the period in which those movements emerged and to which they responded (generally, the first half of the

13.44 *L'Avventura* (1960). According to philosopher Gilles Deleuze, this classic art film presents "a direct image of time," in part through its unpredictable editing patterns.

twentieth century). Similarly, **postmodernism** has two primary definitions:

1. In architecture, art, music, and film, postmodernism incorporates many other styles through fragments or references in a practice known as *pastiche*. That is, it is a triumph of style itself.
2. Historically, postmodernism is the cultural period in which political, cultural, and economic shifts engendered challenges to the tenets of modernism, including its belief in the possibility of critiquing the world through art, the division of high and low culture, and the genius and independent identity of the artist.

13.45   *The Matrix* (1999). "What is the matrix?" the film's ad campaign asked. Postmodern theorist Jean Baudrillard is quoted in the film.

The most important thinkers on postmodernism have addressed both aspects of this definition. Fredric Jameson defines postmodernism historically as "the cultural logic of late capitalism," referring to the period in postwar economic history when advertising and consumerism, multinational conglomerates, and globalization of financing and services took over from industrial production and circulation of goods. Stylistically, postmodern cinema represents history as nostalgia, as if the past were nothing more than a movie that could be quoted.

For Jean Baudrillard, the triumph of the image in our cultural age is so complete that we live in a *simulacrum*, a copy without an original, of which Disneyland is one of his most illuminating examples. In *The Matrix* (1999) and its sequels, the characters' belief that they live in the "real world" is mistaken: the city, food, intimate relationships, and physical struggles are all computer-generated **[Figure 13.45]**. This lack of referentiality is frightening in that it represents the absence of any overarching certainty to ground postmodern fragmentation. But on the hopeful side, the "real" is now open to change. When *The Matrix* shows a (fake) book written by Baudrillard, the film is both making an in-joke and illustrating postmodernism's feeling that there is nothing new in the world.

It is no accident that the postmodern world is most vividly presented in a movie because movies themselves are simulations. Film theorist Anne Friedberg notes that the way we consume film images can be generalized to a society characterized by image consumption and mobility. But the variety of "looks" one finds by window-shopping or identifying with other characters at the movies has a positive side. The postmodern breakdown of singular identity has as its corollary a recognition of identities—of African Americans, women, immigrants, and other "others"—formerly relegated to the margins of society.

In the context of today's postmodern society, film theory must meet the challenge of new technologies such as computer-generated imagery, which literally does not have a referent. Extinct species can be brought to life through modern science—not through biology as *Jurassic Park* (1993) imagines, but through digital technology in the form of the film itself.

Our survey of the history of contemporary film theory evokes the auspicious institutional climate of the academic discipline of film studies in Anglo-American universities, which has consolidated and developed ideas from France and elsewhere since the late 1960s. This story of the origins of contemporary film theory can be told fairly smoothly, and that should make us suspicious. Fields of knowledge tend to advance by active questioning and dissent. As we have noted, cultural studies and cognitivism have challenged the orthodoxies that began to emerge in film theory by the 1970s, and their pluralism and skepticism add a welcome perspective on ideas that might otherwise become rote and ossified, simply "applied" to new cases. Scholars continue to draw on the legacies of previous inquiries in order to identify the salient questions our contemporary audiovisual experience raises and to develop tools with which to address those questions.

text continued on page 505 ▶

Clueless (1995) about Contemporary Film Theory?

Let us assume that the issues debated within an academic discourse such as film theory are important issues of the times. This is not to say that the term "referent" will turn up on the evening news. Nevertheless, when the Supreme Court rules that virtual pornography must be considered constitutionally protected speech because it does not involve actual photographs of subjects posing, the problem of referentiality is of critical social importance.

Theoretical questions will be present in all the sites that a culture uses for debate and conversation, including popular films. Although the title of the 1995 film *Clueless* would seem to disclaim any form of knowledge whatsoever, many theoretical issues are raised by the film. *Clueless* helps "clue us in" to the concerns of postmodern cinema and is also of particular interest to feminist and cultural studies critics.

Clueless takes place in Los Angeles, a city whose freeways, location, cultural diversity, entertainment industry, commercial and artistic gems of pastiche architecture, and rampant consumerism have made it exemplary for theorists of postmodernism. The film's main character is a high school student, and thus marginal in terms of social power. But as a blonde, white, rich girl, she represents the relative power of consumerism. A "remake" or update of Jane Austen's novel *Emma,* the film could be considered a nostalgic but inauthentic citation of the culture of another era. The main character's name, Cher, is another citation, this time of the "inauthentic" culture of the recent past (pop star Cher is known for her costumes and transformations). The multiculturalism of postmodern Los Angeles is signaled by Cher's group of school friends. Yet this is a tongue-in-cheek depiction because Cher's African American best friend, Dionne, is as fabulously wealthy as she is: the girls are worlds apart in socioeconomic terms from Cher's Latina housekeeper, for example.

The film opens with a montage of fresh-faced teenagers, and with postmodern irony Cher's voiceover compares it to the montage of an acne-product commercial. The definition of identity as a matter of surface appearance is underscored in the next set of images: Cher "tries on" different outfits using a computer program containing simulations of the ample contents of her closet [Figure 13.46]. Cher does undergo a transformation in character during the course of the film. Nevertheless, she still understands social problems in commodity-culture terms: she donates her skis to the homeless. Appropriately, while window-shopping, Cher finally realizes what she truly wants as bits of the film replay in her mind, a thorough confusion of "real" and cinematic perception that perfectly illustrates what Anne Friedberg calls postmodernism's "mobilized virtual gaze."

Admittedly, the description thus far makes the film seem as if it is concerned only with the trivial. But feminist

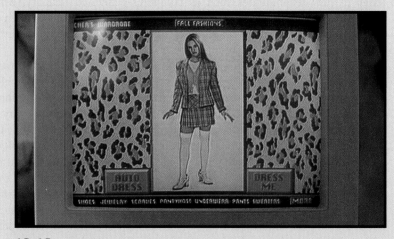

13.46 *Clueless* (1995). Postmodern style and attitude in a film that found a welcome reception among young women.

theorists point out that women's consignment to the domestic sphere with its "trivial" concerns of shopping and romance has a direct effect on the public sphere, which was as true in Jane Austen's day as it is in our own. Cher's ostensibly minor concerns have important consequences in her world. Moreover, the film portrays her subjectivity by her voiceover and her optical point of view, which gives her perspective validity. The film was directed by a woman, Amy Heckerling, who has specialized in youth genre films that pay special attention to young women's perspectives; Austen, too, was consigned to a circumscribed genre within which she made enduring works of art.

Viewers might find *Clueless*'s romantic ending predictable, even disappointing in that it undermines what has so far been the film's most important relationship— the one between Cher and Dionne and the other girls—by conflating plot closure with heterosexual coupling. But this convention is also derived from traditionally female genres, and like earlier examples, it represents the triumph of the young woman's concerns over other, usually more culturally valued, agendas. In fact, the film winks at the happily-ever-after convention, ending with a wedding and suggesting for a moment that it is Cher's. "As if!" her voiceover exclaims: two schoolteachers she helped fix up are getting married. She escapes the strictures of the plot with postmodern irony.

To viewers familiar with the film, an analysis of its visual system is somewhat beside the point; what is most remarkable about it is its reception. *Clueless* successfully addressed a teenage interpretive community, both in and outside the United States, which quickly adopted the film's styles in fashion and slang. Young women's "use" of the film was generally positive. *Clueless* validated and enabled (coded) communication among young girls, who, far from being treated yet again as know-nothings, were now the only ones fully "clued in." Multiple viewing makes for an open-ended text; *Clueless* sums up the complexity of postmodern simulation in a succinct "as if!"

CONCEPTS AT WORK

This chapter has aimed to demystify the field of film theory, which is not to imply that readers will not have to struggle with theory or do some work to understand film on a more abstract plane. Because film theory is a notoriously difficult discourse, any summary gives it much more continuity than it warrants. In reading and picking apart theorists' work, it is important to recall that referring to "theory" in the abstract is misleading. The term is a useful, shorthand way to refer to a body of knowledge and a set of questions. We study this corpus to gain historical perspective, to acquire tools for decoding our experiences of particular films, and above all, to comprehend the hold that movies have on our imaginations, desires, and experience.

Activities
- Do a shot-by-shot analysis of the opening sequence of a film. What codes—of lighting, camera movement, framing, or figure movement—are used to create meaning?
- Compare reviews of a film from a number of different sources. Pay particular attention to the time and place those reviews appeared. What does the range of reviews tell you about the film's reception context(s)?

THE NEXT LEVEL: ADDITIONAL SOURCES

Andrew, Dudley. *Concepts in Film Theory*. Oxford: Oxford University Press, 1984. A thoughtful introduction to issues taken up in contemporary film theory.

Braudy, Leo, and Marshall Cohen, eds. *Film Theory and Criticism*. 6th ed. New York: Oxford University Press, 2004. This anthology brings together important essays from classical and contemporary theorists from Hugo Münsterberg to Laura Mulvey.

Dyer, Richard. *Stars*. London: British Film Institute, 1979. 2nd ed. 1998. Foundational study of how stars function in film and culture.

Hill, John, and Pamela Church Gibson, eds. *The Oxford Guide to Film Studies*. Oxford and New York: Oxford University Press, 1998. Introduction to the field, with strong sections on classical and contemporary film theory as well as film history and culture.

Kaplan, E. Ann. *Feminism and Film*. Oxford and New York: Oxford University Press, 2000. Collection of many significant contributions to feminist film studies, covering authorship, genres, spectatorship, race, sexuality, and more.

Lehman, Peter, ed. *Defining Cinema*. New Brunswick: Rutgers University Press, 1997. Essays and contemporary commentaries on five major theorists, from Sergei Eisenstein to Metz.

Stam, Robert. *Film Theory: An Introduction*. Malden: Blackwell, 2000. A concise, vivid account covering contemporary classical contributions and including fresh examples from global traditions.

Stam, Robert, and Ella Shohat. *Unthinking Eurocentrism: Multiculturalism and the Media*. London: Routledge, 1998. Rich with examples from many film traditions, this book is a theoretical intervention that also opens up Western thinking about the cinema.

A film by
SALLY POTTER
ORLANDO
TILDA SWINTON BILLY ZANE
ADVENTURE PICTURES
PRESENTS A CO-PRODUCTION WITH
LENFILM MIKADO FILM RIO
SIGMA FILMPRODUCTIONS
WITH THE PARTICIPATION OF
BRITISH SCREEN
DEVELOPED WITH THE SUPPORT OF THE
EUROPEAN SCRIPT FUND
A FILM BY
SALLY POTTER
BASED ON THE BOOK BY
VIRGINIA WOOLF
ORLANDO
TILDA SWINTON
BILLY ZANE
LOTHAIRE BLUTEAU
JOHN WOOD
CHARLOTTE VALANDREY
HEATHCOTE WILLIAMS
AND QUENTIN CRISP
COSTUME DESIGN
SANDY POWELL
PRODUCTION DESIGN
BEN VAN OS JAN ROELFS
MUSIC COMPOSED BY
DAVID MOTION
AND SALLY POTTER
MUSIC SUPERVISOR
BOB LAST
EDITOR
HERVE SCHNEID
DIRECTOR OF PHOTOGRAPHY
ALEXEI RODIONOV
PRODUCED BY
CHRISTOPHER SHEPPARD
WRITTEN AND DIRECTED BY
SALLY POTTER
Read the HARCOURT BRACE book
DOLBY STEREO
PG-13 PARENTS STRONGLY CAUTIONED
SONY PICTURES CLASSICS™
©1993 Sony Pictures Entertainment, Inc.

Writing a Film Essay

Observations, Arguments, Research, and Analysis

Based on British novelist and critic Virginia Woolf's celebrated novel, Sally Potter's *Orlando* (1993) is a film about reading, writing, and imaginative self-expression. Leaping through time from the seventeenth to the twentieth century, Orlando encounters poets and writers such as Jonathan Swift and Alexander Pope and changes historical—and even gender—identities as if walking through different film sets of history. Throughout, the poet-writer Orlando reflects on experience, relationships, and cultures in an effort to find and define a personal voice that is expressive, creative, and critical. In a sense, Orlando's journey through history mirrors that of all good writers.

Writers can be found everywhere in films and film history. In modern movies alone, famous and not-so-famous writers populate and drive many kinds of stories about many kinds of experience. *Mishima* (1985) describes the intense blend of radically conservative politics and restless creativity in the life of Japanese author Yukio Mishima. In *Central Station* (1998), a middle-aged woman, Dora, sets up a stand in the middle of a crowded railroad station where illiterate people go to have her write letters to their friends and loved ones. And in Cameron Crowe's semiautobiographical *Almost Famous* (2000), a young music reviewer, William Miller, encounters rock journalist Lester Bangs **[Figure 14.1]**, who gives Miller the advice that motivates his life: "Write honestly and mercilessly."

| KEY CONCEPTS | This chapter will explain |

- how to distinguish between reviews and critical essays
- how to take notes on films
- how to organize those notes
- how to choose a topic and develop it into a thesis and argument for a paper
- how to conduct research and integrate sources
- how to turn your work into a polished essay

Writing about film has been a significant part of film culture since the beginning of movies. Almost simultaneously with the arrival of the cinema, writers debated the function and value of this new art form. In the first few decades of film history, film critics such as Vachel Lindsay (in his 1915 book *The Art of the Moving Picture*) and Dorothy Richardson (in the 1920s art magazine *Close Up*) wrote passionately about movies. Since then, movie reviews, scholarly essays, and philosophical books—by writers including James Agee, Pauline Kael, Trinh T. Minh-ha, and Umberto Eco—have debated the achievements of individual films and the cultural importance of movies in general. As with other arts and cultural activities, movies inspire a common and fundamental human need to explain one's feelings about and responses to a significant experience. In this chapter, we will see how writing about film develops from these needs and inspirations, and we will show how it can become a rich extension of our fundamental film experiences.

14.1 *Almost Famous* (2000). Lester Bangs's advice to a young music reviewer is to "Write honestly and mercilessly."

Writing an Analytical Film Essay

Writing extends the complex relationship we have with films by challenging us to articulate our feelings and ideas and to communicate our responses convincingly. In 1915, early reviewers and critics often focused on the dangerous or uplifting effects that movies might have on women or children. In the 1960s, film was frequently discussed in terms of its political impact or social meaning. Today's writers focus on a range of topics—from characters, stars, and stories to new film technologies or historical questions, such as how 1930s censorship influenced film content or how 1950s teenage audiences encouraged the making of certain kinds of films.

Personal Opinion and Objectivity

Writing about a film usually involves a play between subject matter and meaning. The subject matter of a film is the material that directly or indirectly comprises the film, whereas the meaning is the interpretation a writer discovers within that material. In *Crouching Tiger, Hidden Dragon* (2000), for instance, the subject matter includes the five main characters and their adventures in feudal China. The warrior Li Mu Bai returns to a town where he encounters his soul mate, Yu Shu Lien, the vengeful Jade Fox, and her ferocious but naive companion Jen Yu, and Jen Yu's lover, the desert fighter Lo. The interaction of these characters describes a journey through China that ends in love and death. The subject matter's meaning, however, is more complicated than any simple description; the meaning will depend on the film's style and organization, the historical and cultural significance of those techniques, as well as the experience and thinking of the viewer responding to it. Other films certainly use the subject matter of martial arts combat or the trials of love and honor in ancient China, but *Crouching Tiger, Hidden Dragon* creates and elicits more specific meanings for those who have seen it. For some writers, this martial arts tale of love and honor weaves subtle and often complex points about women and their desires and about the importance of love over mastery [Figure 14.2]. For other writers, the film transforms its Asian subject matter into a Western take on self-knowledge and sacrifice.

The meanings a writer finds in a film are not simply personal and arbitrary. No film can mean whatever one chooses to make it mean, and useful and insightful writing always balances opinion and **critical objectivity**. *Opinion* or *subjectivity* indicates

14.2 *Crouching Tiger, Hidden Dragon* (2000). Discovering the more complex meaning behind deceptively simple subject matter.

14.3   _Crouching Tiger, Hidden Dragon_ (2000). Is the interpretation of this final leap as suicide or liberation a matter of opinion?

► VIEWING CUE

Examine a short critical essay about a film you have seen in class. What subjective or objective claims does the writer make about the film? What evidence from the film does he or she provide? Be specific.

personal responses and evaluations. Critical objectivity, however, refers to a more detached response, one that offers judgments based on facts and evidence with which others would, or could, agree. Good writing about film is a balance of both: your personal views and opinions are where insights and evaluations usually begin, but for your essay to make sense to others, you must convince your readers that your insights have a larger, more objective truth. An essay that hides behind personal opinion—constantly stating "I feel" or "In my opinion"—will seem too personal to have any value for others. Writing about _Crouching Tiger, Hidden Dragon,_ a writer may attempt to hide behind a lack of certainty about the meaning: "In my opinion, Jen's final leap off the mountainside is very ambiguous. I think her decision was probably a suicide, but it seemed to me to be a strangely beautiful act" [**Figure 14.3**]. Conversely, flat descriptive statements fail to interest readers in an essay's argument and often miss the subtleties of a film: "Jen's leap off the mountain is a suicide. It is not a liberating act." Balancing opinion and critical objectivity, as in the following passage, results in writing that engages and convinces the reader that your insights could be useful revelations for most viewers of the film:

> The conclusion of _Crouching Tiger, Hidden Dragon_ is both shocking and uplifting, a combination that disturbs and confuses me, as it probably does most viewers. This confusion about Jen's motives is, however, part of the strange and mysterious beauty of the film because it asks us to recognize a central theme: the possibility that love and passion can transcend any physical limitations when we have faith in that love.

Identifying Your Readers

Knowing or anticipating your readers is central to writing about film and indeed to all writing, often guiding a writer in balancing opinion and objectivity. If we think of writing about film as an extension of conversations or arguments we have with friends about a film, we realize that the terms and tone of these discussions change with different people. A conversation between two knowledgeable fans of war films would likely presume that they have both seen many of the same films and know a great deal about special effects. Their discussion might thus get quickly to the finer points about how successful the portrayal of a famous battle between the Japanese and the Americans during World War II was in _Letters from Iwo Jima_ (2006), told from the perspective of Japanese soldiers [**Figure 14.4**]. In talking about Ken Loach's _Raining Stones_ (1993) with an American film buff, a British viewer might have to provide some political and social background—about Manchester, England, where the film is set; about the government of then prime minister Margaret Thatcher; or about the particular cultural complications of the protagonist's being a Catholic in this British industrial town.

14.4   _Letters from Iwo Jima_ (2006). Clint Eastwood portrays one of World War II's fiercest battles from the perspective of the Japanese.

14.5a and 14.5b   *The Bourne Ultimatum* (2007). The various cityscapes through which Jason Bourne travels might be the basis of an argument about the film.

Possessing an awareness of your readers is like knowing the person you are talking with: it helps determine the amount of basic information you need to provide, the level of complexity of the discussion, and the kind of language you should use. The following four questions are useful guidelines in gearing your essay to certain readers: (1) how familiar are your readers with the film being discussed? (2) what is your readers' level of interest in the film? (3) what do your readers know about the film's historical and cultural contexts? and (4) how familiar are your readers with the terminology of film criticism and theory?

For most critical essays, anticipating your readers' knowledge of the film means assuming they have seen the film at least once and thus do not require an extensive plot summary. Such readers are not primarily concerned with whether a movie is good or bad or with other general observations. Rather, they want to be enlightened about a specific dimension of the film (such as the opening shot) or about a complicated or puzzling issue in the film (for instance, why the different cityscapes in the *The Bourne Ultimatum* [2007], carry specific thematic points important to the action of the film) **[Figures 14.5.a and 14.5b]**. An effective writer works to convince readers that their interests can be deepened and enriched by following the writer's argument about a film.

Knowledge of a film's historical and critical contexts refers to how much your readers know about the place and time of the film's appearance. If the film was made in the United States in the 1920s, would information about that period help your readers better understand the film? Finally, determining your readers' level of familiarity with the terminology of film criticism and theory allows you to choose language that can efficiently and clearly communicate your argument. Can you assume that a term like *continuity editing* will be easily understood, or do you need to define it? In making these decisions, keep in mind that overly simplistic language or dense jargon can equally undermine your analysis.

In most college-level film courses, your audience will be not only your professor but also your peers: intelligent individuals who have seen the film and who share information and knowledge about film criticism, but who are not necessarily experts. For this audience, you can concentrate on a particular theme or sequence that may have been overlooked by a critical viewer. Note that your writing style and choice of words should be more rigorous and academic than in the typical movie review.

▶ **VIEWING CUE**

Prepare to write an analytical essay about a film you have seen in class. First, consider your readers. What defines them? What are their interests? What do they need or want to know about the film?

Elements of the Analytical Film Essay

Two common forms of film writing are film reviews and **analytical essays**. Aimed at a general audience that has not seen the film, a film review tends to be a short essay that describes the plot of a movie, provides useful background

14.6 *O Brother, Where Art Thou?* (2001). Three escaped convicts: the focus for a precise analysis.

information (about the actors and the director, for example), and pronounces a clear evaluation of the film to guide its readers. In contrast, the **analytical essay**, distinguished by its intended audience and the level of its critical language, is the most common kind of writing done by film students and scholars. It typically focuses on a particular feature or theme of a film, provides an interpretation of that material, and then gives a careful analysis to prove or demonstrate that interpretation. Unlike the writer of a movie review for a magazine, the writer of an analytical essay presumes that readers know the film and do not require an extensive plot summary or background information. Although a clear and engaging style is the goal of any kind of writing about film, the writer of an analytical essay often chooses words and terms that can effectively communicate complex ideas.

Consider this passage from a hypothetical essay about *O Brother, Where Art Thou?* (2001), written for a college film course [**Figure 14.6**]. Whereas a newspaper review might summarize the plot, offer some background information, and employ more casual language, note how this analytical essay concentrates on a specific and perhaps less obvious argument:

> Joel and Ethan Coen's *O Brother, Where Art Thou?* (2001) is much more than a musical comedy loosely structured around *The Odyssey*. Woven through the distinctive soundtrack, the plot set in Depression-era America, and the comic exaggerations of its characters, is a sharp ideological critique of race and class in modern America. Regularly mistaken to be African Americans, the three escaped convicts, Everett, Pete, and Delmar, learn quickly that their lower-class white status binds them most importantly to the fate of the black men and women they encounter, and from this predicament the film explores the economic and political power structures that then and now make poverty color-blind. Two sequences in particular dramatize this less noticed but more provocative dimension of the film: the arrival of the prisoners at a church to see a movie (a direct reference to Preston Sturges's film *Sullivan's Travels,* in which the Coens found the title for their movie) and the Ku Klux Klan rally where the fugitives rescue their black comrade Tommy.

▶ **VIEWING CUE**

Examine the language of your essay or of another analytical essay. Which words and phrases best identify the intended audience? The level of the analysis? Where could the language be improved or clarified? ⏸

Here the essay's focus is relatively refined and sophisticated. It assumes its readers have seen and know the film, and it concentrates not on general information, but on a specific thesis about race and class [**Figure 14.7**]. Along with its choice of a polemical thesis (an analysis directed at two particular sequences that viewers may not have carefully considered), this critical essay employs terms suited to academic writing, such as "ideological critique."

14.7 *O Brother, Where Art Thou?* (2001). An analytical paper on race and class in this comic film can be shaped around two specific sequences.

Preparing to Write about a Film

Despite some common ground, an effective film essay does differ from a casual conversation or a debate about a movie. Few writers can dash off a perceptive commentary on a film with little preparation or revision. Instead, most writers gain considerably from anticipating what they will write about and later reviewing carefully what they have written. Few could watch *The Sorrow and the Pity* (1970), a powerful documentary about fascism in France during World War II, and then immediately type a brilliant paper on Marcel Ophuls's use of documentary strategies to expose certain myths about French history or the French Resistance. Like all good writers, you must follow certain steps in preparing to write an essay.

Asking Questions

First, try to identify your own interests *before* you view the film. Ask yourself, How does the film relate to my own background and experiences? What have I heard about the film? Am I drawn to technology or to questions about gender? To a particular filmmaker or period in movie history? To a certain national cinema? In what direction of inquiry does my interest point? In Howard Hawks's 1938 *Bringing Up Baby,* Katharine Hepburn plays an audacious heiress, Susan, whose pet leopard Baby becomes the foil in her zany relationship with a bumbling paleontologist, David, played by Cary Grant [Figure 14.8]. Perhaps you've seen other films by Hawks, like *His Girl Friday* (1941), or other films with Hepburn, like *The Philadelphia Story* (1940). Might you consider comparing the two Hawks films or Hepburn's two different roles?

This sort of preparation is not meant to preclude your being drawn to new ideas and in unexpected directions when you view the film. Surprising discoveries are certainly one of the bonuses of approaching films with an open mind. While watching *In the Bedroom* (2001), one viewer might become puzzled by how the film seems to suddenly change direction: after depicting the excruciating pain of two parents who have lost a son, the movie then becomes a revenge tale in which the father seeks out and murders his son's killer. For the viewer, what seems at first a slow meditation on inexpressible grief becomes a tense thriller. How do the two parts work together? Does loss always require retribution? Does violence always beget violence? By asking these kinds of questions, you can intellectually interact with a film, sharpening your responses and shaping the direction of your essay.

Taking Notes

Note taking, an essential part of writing about film, stimulates critical thinking and generates precise and productive observations. Whereas most students find it natural to take notes on a biology experiment or on their reading of a Shakespeare play, annotating a film is both awkward and unnatural; it is difficult to write while watching a movie in a darkened room, and most films ask that we constantly attend to them so that we do not miss information that passes *text continued on page 516* ▶

▶ **VIEWING CUE**

Before viewing your next film, jot down three or four questions you want to direct at the film. While viewing, ask three or four more about specific shots or scenes. Later, attempt to answer all of your questions as precisely as possible. ⏸

14.8   *Bringing Up Baby* (1938). Katharine Hepburn's role as an audacious heiress involved with a blundering paleontologist could start a writer's critical thinking about the film.

Analysis, Audience, and *Citizen Kane* (1941)

For more than sixty years, viewers have responded to Orson Welles's *Citizen Kane* with a seemingly endless variety of opinions. Some find it fascinating; others feel it is boring or confusing. The character of Susan Alexander fascinates some viewers; the final sequence in which the camera surveys a large room full of Kane's many acquisitions intrigues others. Any of these opinions about, or reactions to, *Citizen Kane* could be developed into a provocative essay about the film, but only if those ideas can be substantiated or proven useful, true, and important—that is, only if they can be shown to have objective accuracy. One such viewer decides to write a review of *Citizen Kane* for his college newspaper in anticipation of the film's upcoming appearance at the college art house. Despite the celebrity of the film, the writer presumes that many of his potential readers have not yet seen it and need both information and balanced opinions. He proceeds with a clear sense of what his readers already know, don't know, and need to know about the film.

Citizen Kane is one of those movies that everyone talks about but few have ever seen. When it first appeared in 1941, the film was surrounded by enormous hype about the debut of the "boy genius" Orson Welles and his ballyhooed transition from the New York stage to the Hollywood screen. Before the film even appeared, rumors also connected *Citizen Kane* to the life of William Randolph Hearst, the U.S. newspaper mogul, and this too made the movie something of a fascinating scandal. In the six decades since its release, *Citizen Kane* has appeared at the top of almost every list of the "greatest movies ever made," and it appears in practically every film course in the world.

Be prepared for a bit of a disappointment. The story is simple enough: played wonderfully by Welles himself, Charles Foster Kane grows, with the help of a windfall fortune, from a boy torn from his childhood home in Colorado into a lonely man obsessed with power and possessions. For me, the story is melodramatic and overblown, and Kane never becomes a very likeable character. What redeems *Citizen Kane*, however, is the construction of the story: different parts of Kane's story are told through the eyes of his friends and acquaintances, and these shifting perspectives create a kind of visual puzzle that the movie never really solves, enlivening an otherwise dull tale.

This black-and-white film is a continuous series of stunning (and famous) shots, such as the opening sequence of dark shots that takes viewers past a No Trespassing sign to Kane's deathbed. In our age of digital technology and new-wave television commercials, these images will probably seem less surprising and innovative than they did when the movie first appeared. Yet *Citizen Kane* remains a film to see—if only to judge for yourself whether it is among the "greatest movies ever made."

The same writer later chooses to compose the following critical essay about *Citizen Kane* for a film history course. In this case, his readers are his professor and the other students in the class, readers who are familiar with the film and have even read other material about *Citizen Kane*. Note this student's inclusion of images from the film. These images do not serve merely as a visual embellishment for the paper but as concrete and precise evidence in support of his argument.

In the many critical essays on *Citizen Kane*, three different perspectives on its meaning dominate: analyses that focus on the mythic character of Kane, discussions of the kaleidoscopic narrative structure that shapes the story, and detailed interpretations of the stylistic compositions (such as the use of deep-focus and dramatic editing techniques). Engaging all three analytical perspectives, I will examine a single, early scene in *Citizen Kane* that demonstrates the legendary visual power of the film. In this scene, *Citizen Kane* crystallizes a family drama of loss and division that is inseparable from a life lived in dense and complex spaces and perceived from many points of view.

In this tale of Charles Foster Kane's rise to a position as one of the richest and most powerful men in America, the scene in question sets the stage for the entire film. It succinctly describes the sudden wealth of Kane's mother, who receives an unexpected windfall from a deed to a gold mine (mistakenly presumed useless), and her subsequent decision to send Charles to be educated on the East Coast. The scene's setting is the rustic family cabin in Colorado, with glimpses of the snowy yard outside where the child, Charlie Kane, plays.

In this scene, one shot begins by showing Charles making snowballs in the field; then it moves back to show his mother in the foreground watching from inside and, through an open window, the boy building a snowman in the background [CK.1]. Here the window frame within the film frame calls attention to how a point of view can control perspective, specifically the point of view on the child Kane. As the shot pulls back further, the frame expands to include the central conversation about the boy and the money, while the original subject of the shot, Charlie, becomes a much smaller, background figure in the action and the frame.

The shot pulls back even further, following the mother's movement away from the window, and the frame creates visible tensions and conflicts among the individuals. Mrs. Kane's stern face and upper body dominate the center of the image, flanked by the banker Thatcher, while Charlie's father drifts along the edges of the frame, complaining, "You seem to forget

CK.1   *Citizen Kane* (1941). Framing emphasizes the point of view.

CK.2   *Citizen Kane* (1941). This famous shot uses reframing, along with deep focus, to convey the drama of Charles Foster Kane's boyhood.

CK.3   *Citizen Kane* (1941). Describing and interpreting Kane's obsession with the power of images.

I'm the boy's father." Moments later, Thatcher and Mrs. Kane sit at a table in the foreground of the image and prepare to sign papers authorizing the child's departure, while the father protests in vain in the middle ground and Charlie remains barely visible in the far background, playing outside in the snow [Figure CK.2]. The rectangular shape of the frame crowds these characters within a tight visual space, even including the ceiling on the top of the frame as a way of further drawing in the space. Positioned between the adults but in the far background is the diminutive shape of Charlie, the subject of their quarreling and plans to remove him from the home. Visually it is fairly clear how power and control are being distributed through this frame: the mother and Thatcher visually overwhelm the father, and the tiny figure of Charles is the impotent object of exchange.

In *Citizen Kane*, Charles Foster Kane grows up to become obsessed with the power of images, such as paintings, newspaper pictures, and images of himself [Figure CK.3]. This obsession perhaps acts out his semiconscious struggle to replace the image of his lost childhood and family. Throughout the remainder of his life, Kane struggles to create, own, and control the people and things around him by imposing his perspective on them—just as the perspective of others controlled him early in his life. The film is also a narrative constructed around the multiple points of view of Kane's friends, wife, and associates, all of whom dramatize how points of view can attempt to frame a man's life as a way of understanding or interpreting that life. The irony and tragedy of Charlie Kane's life is that no one, not even Kane himself, is able to reconstruct the complete picture and harmony that were lost in that early childhood scene.

quickly. Note taking is, however, absolutely necessary to writing about film because a good analytical essay must include concrete evidence to support its argument—and precise notes provide that support. The three general rules for annotating a film are (1) take notes on the unusual—events or formal elements that stand out in the film; (2) take notes on events or techniques that recur with regularity; and (3) take notes on oppositions that appear in the film.

For instance, most viewers of *Bringing Up Baby* would agree that the sequence involving David and Susan at the local jail, with Hepburn pretending to be a hardened gangster's moll, stands out as one of the funniest and most unusual moments in the film. Equally important, however, are those actions or images whose repetitions suggest a recurring theme or pattern, such as David's repeatedly losing his clothes or glasses. Oppositions can be equally illuminating, such as the contrast between the rival women: the goofy Susan and David's staid fiancée, his scientific assistant.

Each writer develops his or her own shorthand for taking notes on films. The trick is to jot down information about the story or characters that seems significant while also recording visual, audio, or other formal details. Some common abbreviations for visual compositions include the following:

es: establishing shot	**la:** low angle	**mls:** medium long shot
ha: high angle	**trs:** tracking shot	**nds:** nondiegetic sound
ct: cut	**ls:** long shot	**vo:** voiceover
cu: close-up	**ds:** diegetic sound	
mcu: medium close-up	**ps:** pan shot	

More specific camera movements and directions can often be re-created with arrows and lines that graph the actions or directions. The following drawings suggest the movements of the camera:

low camera angle ↗   high camera angle ↙   tracking shot ∿

For example, part of the jailhouse sequence in *Bringing Up Baby* [**Figures 14.9 and 14.10**] might be annotated as follows to indicate cuts, camera movements, or angles.

— mcu of constable and Susan through bars
— ct mcu David

Later, these notes would be filled in, perhaps by again reviewing the sequence for more details—for example, pieces of the hilarious monologue of "Swinging Door Susie." Drawings of shots can supplement such details. Critical comments or observations might also be added—for instance, about how the organization of the shot composition and editing provides the contrast between the officious and tongue-tied sheriff and the zany and loquacious Susan.

Selecting a Topic

After taking and reviewing your notes on the film, you need to choose the topic for the paper. Because there are so many dimensions of a film to write about—character, story, music, editing—selecting a manageable topic can prove daunting.

VIEWING CUE

Which events, sounds, or shots in the film just viewed stand out as unusual? As most important? As examples of a pattern of repetition? Describe clearly and concretely one or two events, sounds, or shots from the film.

VIEWING CUE

For any film you've viewed for class, select one key scene or sequence to annotate as precisely as possible. Consider the position of the characters, camera, and frame, and note any sounds, including dialogue. Support your description with a rough sketch.

14.9 *Bringing Up Baby* (1938). "Swinging Door Susie" engages the sheriff . . .

14.10 *Bringing Up Baby* (1938). . . . and baffles her cellmate, David.

Even a lengthy essay will suffer if it attempts to address too many issues. Narrowing your topic will allow you to investigate the issues fully and carefully, resulting in better writing. In a five- or six-page essay, a topic such as "fast-talking comedy in *Bringing Up Baby*" would probably need to rely on generalities and large claims, whereas "gender, order, and disorder in the jailhouse" would be a more focused and manageable topic.

Formal Topics

Although good critical analysis usually considers different features of a film, we can distinguish two sets of topics for writing about film: formal and contextual. Formal topics, which concentrate on forms and ideas within a film, include character analysis, narrative analysis, and stylistic analysis. As a formal topic, **character analysis** focuses its argument on a single character or on the interactions between two or more characters, while **narrative analysis** deals with a topic that relates to the story and its construction. **Stylistic analysis** concentrates on a variety of topics that involve the formal arrangements of image and sound, such as shot composition, editing, and the use of sound.

Although writing a character analysis may appear easier to do than other kinds of analyses, a good essay about a character requires subtlety and eloquence. Rather than write about a central character, like Susan in *Bringing Up Baby* or the tormented musician Johnny Cash in *Walk the Line* (2005) **[Figure 14.11]**, an essay might concentrate on a minor character, such as Susan's aristocratic aunt or Cash's wife Alicia. Similarly, a narrative analysis should usually be refined so that the paper addresses, for instance, the relation of the beginning and end of the film or the way a voiceover comments on and directs the story. A paper that deals with a stylistic topic will be more controllable and incisive if, for instance, it isolates a particular group of shots or identifies a single sound motif that recurs in the film. One student may find a topic for a paper by examining the role of the various narrators in Terrence Malick's *The Thin Red Line* (1998). Another student may choose to look more carefully at repeated editing patterns in *The Battleship Potemkin* (1925) or at the use of framing in Yasujiro Ozu's *Tokyo Story* (1953). Any one of these topics will grow more interesting and insightful if you continue to ask questions during the writing process: How is the character David in *Bringing Up Baby* shaped by costuming or shot composition? How do the various narrators in *The Thin Red Line* reflect different attitudes about war?

14.11 ***Walk the Line*** (2005). Character analysis of a primary role, the tormented musician Johnny Cash, played by Joaquin Phoenix, risks the obvious.

Contextual Topics

Contextual topics, which relate a film to other films or to surrounding issues, include comparative analysis and historical or cultural analysis. A **comparative analysis** evaluates features or elements of two or more different films or perhaps a film and its literary source. A comparative analysis might thus contrast Susan in *Bringing Up Baby* with one or more heroines in more recent films, such as Julia Roberts's character Tess in *Ocean's Twelve* (2004) **[Figure 14.12]**.

14.12 ***Ocean's Twelve*** (2004). The heroine Tess as played by Julia Roberts becomes a rich subject of a comparative analysis.

A comparative analysis always calls for some common ground in order to link what you are comparing and contrasting. Conversely, **historical** or **cultural analysis** investigates topics that relate a film to its place in history, society, or culture. Such a topic might examine historical contexts or debates that surround the film and help explain it—for example, the social status of women or the importance of class in 1938 America. With historical or cultural analysis, the pertinence of the topic to understanding the film is crucial (in our example, the role of women is obviously important; the historical status of leopards probably is not).

Once a topic has been selected (the more specific, the better), the writer should view the film again. This second viewing allows the writer to refine and build on those initial notes, now that he or she has a topic in mind. The writer who comes to *Bringing Up Baby* with a vague interest in how it portrays the battle of the sexes might, after seeing the film again, find that he or she wishes to refocus the topic on how the leopard becomes a metaphor for that battle.

VIEWING CUE

Review your notes for possible topics to write about. Look for different categories of topics. For example: character analysis, narrative, stylistics, and historical or comparative issues.

Elements of a Film Essay

With notes in hand and a topic clearly in mind, writing a film essay becomes a less daunting task. The next step, composing a first draft, will be less cumbersome because the writer has prepared for the task. Ideally, the writer should view the film once again while working through the following stages of the writing process, in order to sharpen the analysis and confirm details from the film. When a topic leads to a clearly defined thesis, focus, and argument, this additional viewing of the film inevitably reveals other useful details and leads to new or better formulated ideas and interpretations.

Interpretation, Argument, and Evidence

Whether your topic is a formal analysis of a sequence or a comparison of the narrative point of view of a novel and its filmic adaptation, it needs to be honed and shaped into a precise interpretation and argument. Your interpretation is your explanation of what the film or a part of it means. In addition, a good essay must construct a logical argument by presenting **evidence** from the film—concrete details that convince readers of your point of view—and then analyzing that evidence. Although different audiences may interpret all or part of a movie somewhat differently, a valid and interesting argument distinguishes itself by how well the analysis of evidence supports the interpretation. Without good evidence, precise analysis, and logical argument, an essay will appear to be simply one viewer's impression or opinion.

VIEWING CUE

Sketch an argument for your essay. What is the logic of its development? What conclusions do you foresee making?

Thesis Statement

Perhaps the most important element in a good analytical essay is the **thesis statement,** a short statement (often a single sentence) that succinctly describes the interpretation and argument and anticipates each stage of the argument. The following pages of the essay should prove that thesis with evidence. As a significantly refined version of the topic, the thesis statement identifies clearly the writer's critical perspective on the film; it should indicate what is at stake in the argument and perhaps how that argument is important to understanding the film. A strong thesis anticipates each stage of the argument that will follow in the paper. Usually this statement, which appears in the first paragraph of the essay, undergoes various revisions

text continued on page 524 ▶

VIEWING CUE

Write a precise thesis statement. Is your thesis specific enough, or does it need refinement? Is it sufficiently interesting to encourage readers to continue reading your essay?

FILM IN FOCUS

Analyzing Character as Image in Sally Potter's *Orlando* (1993)

Sally Potter's *Orlando* (1993) surprises many first-time viewers. Perhaps most unsettling, the character Orlando time-travels through numerous periods of British history. From court life in 1610 and 1650 to the political and social drawing rooms of 1700 and 1750 [Figure 14.13], and from romantic landscapes of 1850 to World War I and the 1990s, Orlando appears without aging. Complicating this time travel, Orlando, at first a man, unexpectedly becomes a woman. More than in other films, questions come fast and furious: How does one account for the jumps between historical periods and the gender transformation of the main character? What is the movie saying about gender and identity?

Sketching the story might be the writer's first note-taking task for *Orlando*. After that, the film features so many unusual shots and actions [Figure 14.14] that the writer would need to choose carefully which ones are most important or suggestive. Among the most powerful moments in the film, for example, is Orlando's discovery, as she sees herself in a mirror, that she has transformed from a man into a woman; she casually comments, "Same person, different sex." In addition, the brilliant red hair and alabaster face of actress Tilda Swinton as Orlando [Figure 14.15] become more and more significant through repeated close-ups; these create a series of images whose

14.13 *Orlando* (1993). As a figure of history, Orlando gazes back at—and resists—the images of his patriarch.

14.14 *Orlando* (1993). An unusual action: the queen washes her hands in a finger bowl.

520

14.15   *Orlando* (1993). Orlando, in close-up, repeatedly addresses the camera, linking the film's historical episodes.

14.16   *Orlando* (1993). Scene from the film's dramatic beginning.

radiant beauty seems to supersede the changing of historical place and gender. One writer immediately notes the dramatic beginning of the film [Figure 14.16.]:

— mls: centered tree, Orlan. Reading/track back and forth/vo: "There could be no doubt about his sex. . . ."
— cu: Orlan. staring right/vo: "but when he . . . "/quick glance at camera—"That is, I"

Later, the writer, Anna Lee, fills in these annotations—from memory and from another viewing—and formulates a succinct description of the scene.

The opening shot of Sally Potter's *Orlando* shows Orlando reading in a field beneath a single oak tree; as Orlando walks back and forth, the medium long shot tracks back and forth in the opposite direction. After the Elizabethan youth sits down to continue his reading, a close-up shows his profile staring off to the right, while a commentary describes his situation in life. As the female voiceover continues, "But when he . . . ," the luminously pale and red-haired Orlando suddenly turns and looks directly into the camera and corrects the commentator, "That is, I."

During this process, the writer begins to consider topics for her paper. "The meaning of history in *Orlando*" seems far too grand and would most likely need to rely on generalities and large claims. She also considers "the image of the oak tree in *Orlando*" and a comparison of the film with the Virginia Woolf novel on which it is based. Her personal interests lead her to questions about gender, politics, and history, and she is struck by how Orlando's passionate self-expression seems to complicate those issues in fascinating ways. In the end, she gathers her notes and thoughts around a sophisticated character analysis of gender and expression in *Orlando*.

Anna Lee   Lee 1
Professor Corrigan
Film 102
3 November 2008

Expression, Gender, and Character in Sally Potter's Orlando

In the opening shot of Sally Potter's *Orlando*, the title character reads in a field beneath a single oak tree. As Orlando (Tilda Swinton) walks back and forth, the medium long shot tracks back and forth in the opposite direction of his movements. He sits down under the tree, and a close-up shows his profile staring off to the right, while the commentary describes his current situation in life as a privileged member of the Elizabethan aristocracy. As the female voiceover continues, "But when he . . . ," the luminously pale and red-haired Orlando suddenly turns and looks directly into the camera and corrects the commentator, "That is, I." The film then shifts to a series of shots illustrating a grand court ceremony: a medium long shot shows Queen Elizabeth (Quentin Crisp) arriving by torchlight in a regal barge, while close-ups focus on small, expressive details, such as the queen washing her hands in a silver finger bowl. In later historical eras, similarly rich and dynamic shots, created through erratic tracking and shifting angles, re-create Orlando's perspective on a British history and culture moving through rapid changes. History becomes a pageant of images, and stylistically, both the narrative and specific shots and edits describe this pageant as an abundant and luxurious activity through which the character of Orlando becomes a carnival of changing identities. Unlike a documentary or a more conventional fiction film, the pageant of this history is the drama of a character relentlessly looking for self-expression in every moment.

Certainly the most remarkable feature of the film's plot, Orlando's character radically changes identities many times throughout the film—and even changes gender. In the beginning, Orlando lives as a male youth in Elizabethan England, but by the eighteenth century he has become a glamorous "she." In the nineteenth century, Orlando transforms into a romantic heroine, and with the twentieth century, she flies through the horrors of World War I to survive as a single mother with a daughter of her own.

Through the course of this history, social and cultural formulas continually threaten to define and reduce the character of Orlando or to re-create him or her within the strict framework of a single time and place. After his father dies, for example, a medium shot shows Orlando from behind, looking at a large portrait of that man on the wall, an austere and traditional image that displays his father's dignity, wealth, and aristocratic stature. When Orlando turns toward the camera and assumes the same pose as his father, the figure in the painting takes on the stance and look of Orlando, suggesting that generational history might re-create Orlando in the social image of his father. This image is quite important because the remaining film acknowledges the power of heritage and history to capture and control an individual—in terms of class, gender, or other social positions—while working to liberate Orlando from those defining powers (and the original patriarchal power). The power of social and historical perspectives to frame and determine the character of Orlando is thus at the heart of this cultural drama, but in situation after situation Orlando's identity rejects or overcomes these historical images of what he/she *should* be.

Orlando's character wrestles with the social forces of history primarily through the force of passionate self-expression. Early in the film the male Orlando falls deeply in love with the young Russian woman Sasha, despite the clear disapproval of British society and despite the language barrier. As a determined poet and incurable romantic, Orlando reenacts this kind of rebellious encounter in many forms and with many people, writing poems, seeking exotic

Lee 3

adventures, and leaping fully into different romantic trysts. Whether in eigh-teenth-century Turkey or nineteenth-century England, Orlando is a character who passionately loves life and who seeks passionately to express an identity through love.

In *Orlando*, character is thus a combination of historical conditions and the passionate resistance of the self to those conditions. Out of this conflict arises perhaps the most important quality of character in this film: self-consciousness, or self-awareness. From the beginning of the film, Orlando continually reflects on her/his own character and its place in the cultures through which he/she passes; Orlando comments on the relation between identity and social place, and he/she creates an ironic distance between the expression of his/her character and its historical situation. During one conversation in the eighteenth century, a medium shot pans back and forth behind Lady Orlando to reveal a group of famous writers (including Alexander Pope and Jonathan Swift) demeaning the importance of women. Orlando's perspective both reveals and debunks the mean-spirited interro-gation by the celebrated wits. Indeed, this kind of distance and analysis of Orlando's self and its social context occurs most clearly when Orlando turns and addresses the camera, usually in close-up. When Orlando examines the mirror image of herself as a man suddenly turned into a woman, she turns and wryly comments, "Same person. . . . different sex." Later, amid her ecstatic embrace with the Byronic Shelmerdine, she self-consciously claims the romantic force of this moment by looking into the camera and saying, "I think I'm going to faint. I've never felt better in my life." Orlando's identity and character appear and evolve, consequently, through the complementary activities of both perceiving and reflecting, demonstrating how an individual's passion and love for life can and should engage self-consciously with values and choices about how to live that life.

Whether as a man or a woman, a sixteenth-century nobleman, or a rebel-lious twentieth-century mother, Orlando champions the vibrancy of human pres-ence, moving above and beyond all those historical and cultural differences, beyond all those defining frames. In the last sequence of the film, Orlando, now a modern woman lounging under the aged oak that opens the film, becomes the object of her own daughter's video recorder. As the child runs toward her mother, we see Orlando in a bouncing handheld shot that closes in on her face as a tilted out-of-focus image. As the culmination of so many images of Orlando across four centuries, the framed image now seems to deny its own ability to control and capture this character: Orlando is a presence that will not be constricted by her own daughter, nor by the most technologically modern images of her or him.

Although *Orlando* is based on a novel by Virginia Woolf, Sally Potter's stunning adaptation re-creates the essence of the novel as a drama of percep-tion, visual and social frames, and passionate self-assertion. Like other Woolf novels, *Orlando* presents individual character and historical change embracing each other in the changing intensities of human expression. Like other Woolf characters, Orlando is defined not by social or sexual status but rather by the quality of the consciousness through which Orlando perceives and lives life.

14.17   *Traffic* (2000). A character destroyed by drug abuse presents an abundance of issues for analytical writing.

14.18   *My Beautiful Laundrette* (1985). The climactic mise-en-scène of the laundrette.

during the writing process. Having a *working thesis*, a rough version of a thesis, in mind as you begin your first draft, however, will help anchor your argument. In its final form, a precise and assertive thesis statement is likely to engage readers' interest in the essay.

As with most films, Steven Soderbergh's *Traffic* (2000) and Stephen Frears's *My Beautiful Laundrette* (1985) both offer a wide variety of topics that could be developed into specific arguments and thesis statements. For *Traffic,* a film about the drug trade that flows from Mexico into various U.S. communities, one student writer considers analyzing either the cinema verité camera movements used in the Mexican settings or the transformation of the central character, a U.S. drug czar who sees his daughter destroyed by heroin [Figure 14.17]. For *My Beautiful Laundrette,* a contemporary romance between a young Pakistani man and a male friend involved with right-wing British gangs, the writer weighs the advantages of two possible topics: the developing sexual relationship of the two main characters or the mise-en-scène of the laundrette where the climactic scenes take place. After reflecting on these topics and seeing the films again, the student opts for the second film and develops a thesis statement that demonstrates clear and specific direction: "*My Beautiful Laundrette* looks at contemporary British politics from numerous angles: family politics, sexual politics, racial politics, and economic politics. In the end these various motifs coalesce and climax in a single space that is both practical and fantastic, the mise-en-scène of the laundrette" [Figure 14.18]. As clear and intelligent as it is, this proposed thesis statement will no doubt be revised for the final draft of the paper, as the writing will certainly generate new insights and possibly new issues.

Outline and Topic Sentences

Although some writers prefer other methods of organization, preparing an **outline** results in a valuable blueprint of an essay, allowing the writer to see and examine the different parts and overall development of the argument as it proceeds out of a strong thesis. An outline can consist of a simple list of ideas to address or shots and scenes to highlight—such as "weak father figures," "house squatting as metaphor for identity," and "description of the laundrette"—or a more complete (and more useful) list that includes subheadings and perhaps full sentences, which can be used as topic sentences (see p. 525) in the essay.

Here is an excerpt from the detailed outline prepared by the student working on the essay about *My Beautiful Laundrette.*

 VIEWING CUE

Formulate a specific interpretation for the film you are writing about. Why is that interpretation important? What new light does it shed on the film for your readers?

The Politics of Laundry in *My Beautiful Laundrette*

Working Thesis: *My Beautiful Laundrette* looks at contemporary British politics from numerous angles: family politics, sexual politics, racial politics, and economic politics. In the end these various motifs coalesce and climax in a single space that is both practical and fantastic, the mise-en-scène of the laundrette.

    I. Family politics: the most immediate and complicated type

        A. Fathers and authority

        B. Family traditions and repression

   II. Sexual politics: underpins family situations in way that exposes hypocrisy
- A. Heterosexual politics: Nasser, his wife, and his mistress Rachel
- B. Feminist politics: Tania, Nasser's daughter
- C. Gay politics: Johnny and Omar

  III. Racial politics: nearly lost in this drama is the way they permeate all other relationships
- A. Johnny, race, and right-wing politics (National Front)
- B. Papa, race, and left-wing politics

  IV. Economic politics: where the other confrontations are—presumably and ironically—resolved
- A. Papa as businessman
- B. Salim as drug dealer
- C. Johnny and Omar as laundry entrepreneurs

   V. These political motifs coalesce and climax in a single space that is both practical and fantastic: the mise-en-scène of the laundrette
- A. Detailed description of mise-en-scène of laundrette
- B. Pragmatics meet fantasy
- C. Analysis of climactic gathering

As this example illustrates, a detailed outline allows the writer to review the structure of the essay and note any problems with the scope or logic of the argument or with the transitions from one section to another. At this stage the topic should be focused on a specific thesis whose parts develop as logical steps in the body of the paper.

Whether or not you work from an outline, a clear organization and structure—most notably, coherent paragraphs introduced and linked by topic sentences—are paramount for an effective essay. Well-developed paragraphs, which tend to consist of several sentences, demand coherence and evidence. Critical to a good paragraph is the **topic sentence,** usually the first sentence, which announces the central idea to which all other sentences within the paragraph are related. The remainder of the paragraph develops the idea stated in the topic sentence and provides evidence from the film as support.

In this excerpt from the essay on *My Beautiful Laundrette*, note how the strong and lucid topic sentence opening the paragraph is then supported by evidence:

> In *My Beautiful Laundrette,* the drama of the characters is invariably about space, territory, and most importantly, home. In the first sequence, Salim and a henchman evict Johnny and another squatter from an abandoned tenement, and for the rest of the film the metaphor of squatting describes the characters' unstable and temporary relations to the places in which they live and with which they interact. Although most of the characters are driven by the idea that, as one character puts it, "people should make up their minds where they want to live," places and homes are never more than shifting locations, foreign territory where one lives uncomfortably. In this sense, "home" is at best a dream and usually just a temporary convenience. Nasser's daughter Tania wants to be anywhere but with her family, and she is willing to have either Johnny or Omar as a lover, depending on who will take her away from her home. In the end, Nasser watches from a window as a medium shot shows Tania being visually swept off the platform by a series of trains that rush off the screen, on her way to another home that she will define for herself.

▶ **VIEWING CUE**

Create a detailed outline of your essay. Does your outline include subsections that can later be developed with details and evidence from the film?

▶ **VIEWING CUE**

Begin each section of your outline with a topic sentence that summarizes the issues you will address. Do your topic sentences relate to each other? Do they accurately describe the logic of the essay?

Revision, Manuscript Format, and Proofreading

VIEWING CUE

In your draft, look for consistent errors and troublespots that you need to pay special attention to during revision.

A completed first draft of an essay is not a completed essay. The final stage in writing about film requires at least one revision of the paper, with special attention to manuscript format and proofreading. Last-minute corrections should be kept to a minimum and should be clear and simple.

A good revision begins by reading the essay with fresh eyes, achieved best by allowing time away from the first draft—at least a few hours and at best a few days—before returning to work on the revision. A revision should examine, clarify, and rewrite word choice, sentence structure, paragraphs, the logic and organization, and the coherency of the ideas; it should improve the presentation and the efficiency of the argument and analysis. In addition, carefully check manuscript format, including margins, title position, footnotes, and other mechanics. Typically, the format for a film essay should follow these guidelines, which are based on recommendations by the Modern Language Association.

- Put your name in the top left-hand corner of the first page, along with your instructor's name, the course title and number, and the date of submission. Your title should be centered on the next line.
- The entire essay, including quotations, should be double-spaced.
- Quotations running more than four lines should be indented ten spaces at the left margin and reproduced without quotation marks.
- Leave one-inch margins at the top, bottom, and sides of each page. Indent paragraphs five character spaces or one-half inch.
- Put your last name and the number of each page (including the first) in the upper right-hand corner.
- Be certain quotations and documentation are in the proper format.

Note: For more information, see the *MLA Handbook for Writers of Research Papers,* 6th ed. (2003).

Once your final revision is completed, proofreading—checking the revision for grammatical and structural errors, typos, or omissions that can be easily corrected—is essential. With any kind of writing, the presentation helps determine how your reader views your work, and an accurate, professional look will promote an accurate, professional reading of it. Typographical mistakes and other small goofs do not ruin a good essay, but they do undermine it by creating an impression of carelessness.

While not all writers about film precisely follow the guidelines for outlining, formulating a thesis statement, revising, proofreading, and so on, experienced writers almost always do so, even if unconsciously or in abbreviated ways. Keeping a checklist of these mechanics in mind can alleviate much of the anxiety about writing, providing a working framework that leads to stronger and more interesting essays.

Using Film Images in Your Paper

VIEWING CUE

Locate areas in your essay where an image might improve your argument. Are there technical aspects, such as the use of lighting or types of camera movements, that could be further explained with an illustration?

With computer and Internet technologies, film images are increasingly available to incorporate into a critical essay. Now writers can easily transpose an image from a DVD to illustrate a part of an argument and analysis. Being able to "quote" from a film to support an interpretation or insight can be quite important since such images can provide the evidence that underpins a strong argument.

Many instructors prefer that students avoid using images since often these images function simply as ornaments and distractions from the real work of the writing. If, however, film images are used in an essay, they should be used judiciously to support a key point in the argument. As with the example from the paper on *Citizen Kane* (pp. 514–516), use a specific image or series of images that illustrates important visual information (about image composition or editing, for example) that your text discusses. If useful, provide a short caption that encapsulates what you wish your reader to see in the images.

Writer's Checklist

As you grow more confident as a writer, you will be able to write about films in a fluid motion: watching the film, taking some notes, sketching an outline, and writing the first draft and final essay. Even the most competent writers, however, pause to reflect on their work by consulting a checklist like this one.

1. Review your notes, filling in details where you can. Ideally, view the film one more time.
2. Try to summarize the most important themes or motifs in the film.
3. Formulate a working thesis and argument for the essay.
4. Outline the argument. If possible, use full sentences for headings because they can then become your topic sentences.
5. Develop the central idea of each paragraph using details from the film that support that paragraph's topic sentence.
6. Rewrite your thesis statement to reflect any changes or refinements in your thinking that occurred while you were writing your first draft.
7. If you are writing a research essay, be sure to use the correct documentation format for in-text citations and the Works Cited list (see pp. 534–535 and 541–542).
8. Revise your essay, checking for such problems as vague or illogical organization, and proofread for surface errors in spelling and grammar.
9. Select a title that reflects the main argument of your paper.
10. Print out the essay and correct any remaining typographical errors.

 VIEWING CUE

After writing your first draft, revise your thesis statement to reflect changes in your thinking. Be sure to sharpen your thesis statement to better describe your argument.

Researching the Movies

While in some critical film essays writers aim simply to convey a personal response to a film based on critical distance and careful reflection, in other essays they want or need to use research in order to sharpen and develop their interpretation of a film. Research enables writers to identify significant issues surrounding a film and to contribute their opinions and ideas to the ongoing critical dialogue about it. A student intending to write about Jean Cocteau's *Orpheus* (1950), for example, may be intrigued by the film but uncertain about his or her specific argument. With some reading and research about Cocteau, his relation to the surrealist movement, and his work as a poet and painter, the student discovers a more specific argument about the complicated role of poetry in the film and the relevance of the Orpheus myth to Cocteau's vision of the modern artist [Figure 14.19].

Distinguishing Research Materials

Whether limited or extensive, research helps determine why your essay is important and what critical questions are at stake in writing it. Various kinds of materials qualify as research sources for a film essay, including primary, secondary, and Internet resources.

14.19 *Orpheus* (1950). Researching this film may also mean researching the poetry of the surrealist movement.

text continued on page 532 ▶

Interpretation, Argument, and Evidence in *Rashomon* (1950)

After reviewing his notes on Akira Kurosawa's *Rashomon,* a student writer considers some possible topics. He begins by thinking about the film's unusual narrative structure: as three men, including a priest, seek shelter from a rainstorm under an ancient city gate, they hear the tale of a murder and rape through four different points of view—those of a bandit, the woman, the ghost of the dead man, and a woodcutter. The narrative tension in the film, the writer realizes, develops around the discrepancies in these competing points of view; the result is a dark ambiguity about the truth of this violent and tragic event. After seeing the film again and trying to refine his thinking about it, the writer develops the following thesis, a clear interpretation of the film.

> In Akira Kurosawa's *Rashomon*, four different perspectives present four different versions of the truth about a violent attack. At the conclusion of the film, after we have seen and heard these various perspectives and have been presented with the evidence, the opening confusion of the three men is even more pervasive, setting the stage for the only possible response to a world defined by egotism and uncertainty: compassion.

The student's next step is to sketch an outline, one in which he uses topic sentences to mark the development of the argument and the places where key evidence will appear.

Rashomon: Beyond Understanding and Evidence

Thesis statement: *Rashomon* is a drama of evidence and interpretation.

I. Central to this film is the drama of interpretation and evidence.
   A. Four accounts of same horrifying event
   B. The opening focus on evidence
II. Although more evidence appears through the perspective of the different witnesses, that evidence does not always agree and seems to befuddle a clear interpretation.
   A. Overlaps and inconsistencies in describing the facts
   B. The dagger as key piece of evidence

III. The heart of the fragmented narratives of *Rashomon* is the egotism that fashions the various perspectives.
    A. The bandit's violent sexual desire and the crime
    B. His story of conquest and surrender
IV. Both the wife's and the husband's perspectives are likewise mostly about themselves
    A. The wife's tale of a helpless woman
    B. The husband's tale of honor and self-sacrifice
V. The woodcutter's narrative is more problematic, but equally locked into its own needs for self-justification and protection.
    A. His revised vision: a base and cowardly world
    B. His acknowledging stealing the evidence of the dagger
VI. Each of these perspectives is distorted by the ethical failures of the individuals telling them, indicating the horrifying indeterminacy of a world determined by isolated egos, as well as the corruption of these perspectives by human egotism.
    A. Natural disaster and moral depravity
    B. Editing and shot compositions add considerably to this sense of confusion, disorientation, and failure to see facts and events clearly.
VII. Although the humane conclusion of the film seems unexpected (and somewhat sentimental), its unexpectedness is what makes the film so engaged with modern times.

After writing his first draft, the writer sets the paper aside for three days before undertaking a careful revision. He proofreads a printed version of the essay and then submits his final copy, which follows.

Fred Stillman   Stillman 1
Professor White
Film 101
10 October 2007

Beyond Understanding and Evidence:
The Surprise of Compassion in *Rashomon*

The setting that opens and closes Akira Kurosawa's *Rashomon* is the collapsed Rashomon gate in the ancient city of Kyoto. Amidst a torrential rainstorm, a woodcutter, a commoner, and a priest huddle together, and the first recounts a horrifying tale of rape, murder, and possibly suicide told through four different perspectives that structure the narrative of the film. Seen through the eyes of a criminal, the female victim, the dead husband, and a woodcutter, each of these perspectives offers a contrasting version of events and the truth of what happened, and each introduces pieces of evidence to support that particular version. Despite having heard these witnesses, however, the priest can only murmur, "I don't understand." At the film's conclusion, moreover, the uncertainty of the men is more pervasive than ever, setting the stage for the only possible response to a world defined by egotism and uncertainty: compassion.

Rashomon is a drama of evidence and interpretation. As the priest and woodcutter explain to the commoner, the original staging of the different testimonies was a police court trying to gather evidence about a horrible crime in

R.1   ***Rashomon*** (1950). The mystery of a horrifying death.

which a noblewoman and her husband were attacked in the wilderness—she was raped and he was killed. Appropriately, the first point of view presented is that of the woodcutter, who follows a trail of evidence through the woods—a woman's hat, a man's hat, a belt, and an amulet case—to the sudden discovery of the dead body of the samurai nobleman, his stiffened arms and hands stretched grotesquely toward the horrified woodcutter in a low-angle shot [**Figure R.1**]. Shortly thereafter, a man describes how he captured the bandit Tajomaru, emphasizing the discovered evidence of the samurai's horse as well as "seventeen arrows" and a "Korean sword" found on the criminal. Yet this seemingly incontestable claim and evidence become subject to doubt when the bandit suddenly denounces and denies the man's interpretation of certain details.

Although more evidence is given through the perspective of the other witnesses, that evidence does not always agree, and it seems to befuddle a clear interpretation. Most importantly, the significance of a pearl-handled dagger, the weapon that supposedly killed the husband, changes dramatically in the different narratives, acting as an evidential marker to distinguish the interpretations of events.

Focused on the shifting place of the dagger, the heart of the fragmented narratives of *Rashomon* becomes the egotism that informs each perspective. Or more exactly, each version becomes more about the personal desire and greed of the person explaining what happened than about the factual events and evidence. What initiates the horrendous crime is the violent sexual desire of the bandit, who happens to witness—in a sharp-shot/reverse-shot exchange beginning with his awakening eyes—the exposed face and feet of the wife. After that, his entire account emphasizes greed and desire: he deceives and entraps the nobleman by suggesting he will sell him riches from an old tomb, and his leering gaze at the young woman turns quickly to a brutal sexual attack. Not surprisingly, in the bandit's version, his desires and demands fulfill the woman, and she becomes the mirror image of his greed and lust when she ecstatically surrenders to his assault. At this moment, the critical object, the dagger, drops passively from her hand, according to the bandit, who claims to then kill the husband "honestly."

Both the wife's and the husband's perspectives are likewise mostly about themselves. From the beginning, she appears discreet and demure, partly hidden by veils and white makeup and barely moving as she rides her horse through the forest. In her account, she becomes a "poor helpless woman" whose husband turns viciously on her after the assault. Unable to bear his hateful stare, she claims to have fainted—only to later discover her dagger in her husband's chest. The husband's narrative, in contrast, paints a picture of his suffering devotion and lost honor, weeping from the grave as he recounts killing himself with the controversial dagger. Light and shadow fill the images of this account, suggesting an ambiguity and lack of certainty even in this testimony by a dead man.

Finally, the woodcutter's narrative is more problematic, but equally locked into its own needs for self-justification and protection. After introducing the story at the beginning of the film, he returns to offer a final version that reveals deceptions and lies in his first account. Now he admits to having

Stillman 3

witnessed the entire scene. His subsequent description of the part-clownish, part-terrified fighting of the two men shows a world that is fundamentally base and cowardly, a reflection of his own base and cowardly position in failing to intervene or fully disclose the truth of what he saw. Most disturbing perhaps, he tacitly acknowledges stealing the crucial piece of evidence, the dagger, in order to sell it for personal gain.

That each of these perspectives is distorted by different degrees of ethical failure on the part of the individual indicates the source of the horrifying indeterminacy and chaos of this world [Figure R.2]. This is a world described by the priest in the opening as full of "war, earthquake, wind, fire, famine, plague . . . each year full of disaster . . . hundreds of men dying like animals." Stylistically, the stunning editing and shot compositions of *Rashomon* dramatize this world of confusion and disorientation, in which seeing and understanding seem to constantly combat each other. Witnesses are introduced with a wipe that crosses the screen in one direction or the other, almost violently wiping out the perspective of the preceding account. Within the different accounts, rapid tracks and flash pans re-create the desperately unsettled struggle to discover facts through perspectives that dart across surfaces blocked by branches and leaves.

R.2   *Rashomon* (1950). Trying to make meaning in a chaotic world.

Within all this moral darkness and despair, however, the conclusion of *Rashomon* suggests a possible way out of the terror and blindness that results from so much visual and narrative ambiguity. In this final sequence, the threesome who tell and hear that tale of violence discover an abandoned baby in the ruins of the gate. The commoner urges them to steal the baby's blankets and clothing because "you can't live unless you're what you call selfish." At this point, a dramatic turn occurs: in a head-to-head confrontation in the rain, the commoner accuses the woodcutter of hiding his theft of that crucial piece of evidence, the dagger. In dazed silence, the priest and woodcutter stand against a wall. As the rain stops, the commoner suddenly insists on taking the child home with him to his already crowded family. Despite his shame about his selfishness and despite the missing evidence of the stolen dagger, a glimmer of human value returns to the world. Compassion overcomes the evidence of mistakes, and as they all depart, the sun gleams through the clouds and the saved child becomes the emblem of a new future. During this sequence, the priest shouts the fundamental truth so often lost in this violent courtroom: "If men don't trust each other, then the world becomes a hell."

Although this conclusion seems unexpected (and somewhat sentimental), its unexpectedness is what makes the film so engaged with modern times. Danish philosopher and theologian Søren Kierkegaard uses the term "leap of faith" to describe the only possibility for a spiritual faith in modern times. What his term implies is that both spiritual and human faith—the grounds for ethical behavior— often occur *despite* the evidence before our eyes and *despite* the failure of human reason to understand it. As in *Rashomon*, truth and morality may need to leap over the confusion of facts and logic in order simply to do what is right.

14.20 *Invasion of the Body Snatchers* (1956). Watching a film closely and following its script allow a student to analyze it with precision and depth.

▶ **VIEWING CUE**

For your next film essay identify several primary research sources. List the sources that would be appropriate for your research topic and explain why these sources would be helpful. ⏸

Primary Research

Primary research sources—such as 16mm films, videotapes, DVDs, and film scripts—have a direct relationship with the original film. Some of these materials are readily available in libraries, including the many classic scripts now published as books; others, such as 16mm films, can be far more difficult to locate, except in film archives. A student planning to write a research essay on Don Siegel's *Invasion of the Body Snatchers* (1956) might first view a 16mm or DVD projection of that film, and then access other primary sources, such as a script, as follow-ups to the first screening [**Figure 14.20**]. With primary sources, however, keep in mind that they may approximate, but not duplicate exactly, the look of a film when seen in a theater (see pp. 51–57). Videotapes may format images differently from the format used in theatrical screenings, while scripts may represent a simple blueprint from which the actual film dialogue deviates.

Secondary Research

Secondary research sources—including books, critical articles, Web sites, supplementary DVD materials, and newspaper reviews—contain ideas or information from outside sources such as film critics or scholars. The student researching *Invasion of the Body Snatchers* might include film reviews published at the time of release, scholarly essays on Siegel's work, and perhaps a book on 1950s American cinema. Even in our electronic age, libraries and their databases remain the most reliable places to find solid secondary materials. Check such databases as the Humanities Index, Lexis-Nexis, and Comindex for essays and books on your subject, and don't underestimate the more conventional approach of exploring the library's shelves. Annual bibliographic indexes and their electronic versions identify journal articles and books that may support and broaden your thinking, including especially *The Readers' Guide to Periodical Literature,* the *MLA International Bibliography,* and the *Film Literature Index.* Once you have a topic and a working thesis, you can search for sources relevant to your topic and argument. After checking general categories like "film," "cinema," and "movies," a more precise topic, such as "contemporary Australian cinema" or "sound technology and the movies," will lead you more quickly to pertinent research materials.

In addition to databases and bibliographic indexes, specialized encyclopedias, which identify important topics and figures in film studies, are useful resources for initiating research on a film. Examples include Ephraim Katz's *The Film Encyclopedia,* Pam Cook's *The Cinema Book,* Leonard Maltin's *The Whole Film Sourcebook,* Ginette Vincendeau's *Encyclopedia of European Cinema,* and Amy Unterburger's *The St. James Women Filmmakers Encyclopedia.* Film guides such as these provide factual information about and short introductions to a subject. The entries typically do not offer the sort of detailed analysis or arguments required for a good research paper, but they can suggest pertinent information and issues that can lead you to more research and a refined argument.

Internet Sources

The Internet offers useful discussion groups, access to various library and media catalogs, and numerous other information sites. However, with so many Web sites available, the writer must be careful to consult the three kinds of reputable Internet sources for film studies:

- sites and databases that provide basic facts about a film and the individuals involved with that film, including biographical facts about the director, the running time of a film, and the like
- sites that offer reviews or essays from academic film journals, such as *Film Comment, Jump Cut,* and *Sight and Sound*
- film-specific sites that provide information ranging from production facts to gossip as well as reviews and interviews. Almost every major film now has its own Web site, as do the studios and distributors.

While the Internet is an important source of information of all kinds, film researchers and writers must be cautious about the quality of the material found there. For one thing, it can be difficult to determine the authenticity of some Internet-based information. Unlike material published in academic journals or books, Internet essays and articles may not have been through a review process to determine their value. Virtually anyone can post on a Web site any opinion or "facts," often without substantial evidence. When using the Internet for research, therefore, writers need to differentiate substantial and useful material from chat and frivolous commentary. Especially with Internet sources, there are three important rules to follow.

- Determine the quality of the Internet source. Does it provide reliable information and a carefully evaluated argument supported by research? Is the source a refereed publication (one whose material is evaluated by experts) or a reputable institution? Is its information supported by references to other research? What are the credentials of the authors?
- Define your search as precisely as possible. Instead of just the title of a film, focus your search on, for example, "lighting in *Double Indemnity*" or "politics and Iranian cinema." Pursue your topic through the advanced search option.
- Explore links to other sites. Does your research link you to sites on other films by the same director or to such related issues as the film genre or the country in which the film was made?

Here is a short list of Web sites useful for film research:

- *All Movie Guide* (www.allmovie.com): film and video reviews and production credits, cross-referenced by actor, director, and genre.
- *American Film Institute* (www.afi.com): recent industry news, events, educational seminars, and reviews.
- *Berkeley Film Studies Resources* (www.lib.berkeley.edu/MRC/): a growing collection of online bibliographies and sources for film and media studies.
- *Cinema Sites* (www.cinema-sites.com): a comprehensive listing of links to hundreds of sites.
- *The Criterion Collection* (www.criterion.com): DVD distributor of well-known masterpieces of international art cinema, Hollywood classics, and often overlooked gems from film history.
- *EarlyCinema.com* (www.earlycinema.com/index.html): a solid introduction to the filmmakers, technologies, and social environments for early cinema, including suggestions for further research.
- *Film Literature Index* (webapp1.dlib.indiana.edu/fli/index.jsp): an index, with more than two thousand subject heads, of the publications in 150 film and media journals.
- *Film-Philosophy* (www.film-philosophy.com/): an international journal that features a wide range of book reviews, theoretical essays, and sophisticated analyses of individual films.
- *FilmSound.org* (www. filmsound.org): covers all topics related to film sound—including definitions of terms, links to scholarly articles, and interviews with sound designers—and is useful for students and practitioners.

VIEWING CUE

Locate at least five secondary research sources for your essay topic. What are the most recent books on the film or topic? Find at least two relevant scholarly articles on this topic.

VIEWING CUE

Search the Internet for information about your film and topic, and locate at least one useful source. What distinguishes this source from other online information about your topic?

- *History on/and/in Film* (wwwmcc.murdoch.edu.au/ReadingRoom/hfilm/contenth1.html): conference papers and scholarly essays on a range of film history topics.
- *Internet Movie Database* (www.imdb.com): plot summaries, links to reviews, and background information on individual films.
- *Kino International: The Best in World Cinema* (www.kino.com): DVD distributor of many of the most important films from throughout film history and around the world.
- *Library of Congress Motion Picture & Television Reading Room* (lcweb.loc.gov/rr/mopic/): the library's catalogue, the national Film Registry preservation list, and the American Memory Collection of online early films.
- *Offscreen* (www.offscreen.com): an extremely well organized online film journal that covers genres, directors, and individual films, along with reviews of festivals and other journals.
- *ScreenSite* (www.tcf.ua.edu/ScreenSite/contents.htm): provides data on films, film conferences, archives, and useful links to other academic cinema sites.
- *Society for Cinema and Media Studies* (www.cmstudies.org/): academic society dedicated to the scholarly study of film, television, and new media.
- *Ubuweb* (www.ubu.com/): allows users to download rare and remarkable documents from literary, film, video, and music history, such as a Dadaist magazine from 1917 or a documentary on Andy Warhol.
- *Vectors: Journal of Culture and Technology in a Dynamic Vernacular* (www.vectorsjournal.org): A cutting-edge journal that combines scholarship and analysis with new design and delivery technologies.
- *Yale University Library Research Guide in Film Studies* (www.library.yale.edu/humanities/film/): an introductory guide to conducting library and Internet research in film studies.

Using and Documenting Sources

Writers gather research material in a variety of ways: some record paragraphs and phrases on handwritten note cards, while others prefer to type that material directly into their computers, allowing them to sort, move, and insert text easily. In either case, the bibliographic information for quotations should be double-checked for accuracy. It should include all of the publication data required for the Works Cited list (and sometimes the Works Consulted section) of your research paper. Just as sloppy technical errors—such as a boom microphone appearing in a frame—can undermine a film's look and effect, so too can inaccurate or careless source documentation make a research paper look amateurish.

Integrating research material into the text of your paper requires both logic and rhetoric. Sometimes research can be used to describe how your argument differs from prevailing positions on a film or issue. In this case, the writer frequently identifies one or more opposing positions as a way of highlighting how the essay will distinguish itself: "While Annette Michelson has claimed that Kuleshov's films are best understood as part of a debate with Eisenstein, this paper argues that the French films of Jean Epstein are equally important to Kuleshov's development." Conversely, research can be used to support and validate a point or a part of the overall argument: "Both Patrice Petro and Judith Mayne have produced complex feminist readings of silent-era German films that support my interpretation of *Mädchen in Uniform* (1931)." Yet another possibility is to use research sources to back up the validity of facts or critical frameworks necessary for introducing an argument: "In *The Zero Hour: Glasnost and Soviet Cinema in Transition*, Andrew Horton and Michael Brashinsky convincingly show that Russian cinema after 1985 returned to the center of the world stage, an argument that will provide the background for my claims about the importance of *Little Vera* (1988) in Europe and America."

▶ **VIEWING CUE**

How will you collect the research you need to formulate and present your argument? What sources will you use? Keep a detailed list of each for later documentation.

Direct Quotations and Paraphrasing

Once research material has been gathered, selected, and integrated into an essay, all of the sources used must be properly documented. There are two kinds of research material that require documentation: (1) direct quotation from a secondary source, and (2) paraphrasing, in which the writer puts the idea or observation from another source into his or her own words. When information is considered common knowledge and is well known to most people, there is no need to document where you found it. If, however, there is any doubt about whether the observation is common knowledge, always document the source so as to avoid any suspicion of plagiarism. For example, a critic's remark that Ousmane Sembène is one of Africa's premier filmmakers and that his films work in a realist tradition would be considered common knowledge by many seasoned filmgoers. But a writer new to Sembène's work may feel more comfortable documenting the source of that information, and like all writers, should *never* risk the charge of plagiarism. Quotations of dialogue from a film usually do not require documentation.

Documentation Format

There are various documentation formats for listing authors, titles, and publication data. Here we will describe the format advocated by the Modern Language Association (MLA) and widely used in the humanities. (See the *MLA Handbook for Writers of Research Papers,* 6th ed. [2003].) The primary components of the MLA format are in-text citations and the Works Cited list. An in-text citation is required wherever the writer refers to, or quotes from, a research source within the essay's text. The in-text citation includes the author's name and the page number, enclosed in parentheses. Note that "p." and "pp." are not used.

> Filmmakers such as Stan Brakhage and Jonas Mekas "appropriated home-movie style as a formal manifestation of a spontaneous, untampered form of filmmaking" (Zimmerman 146).

When the author's name appears in the discussion that introduces the quotation, only the page number or numbers are given.

> As Patricia Zimmerman has noted, filmmakers such as Stan Brakhage and Jonas Mekas "appropriated home-movie style as a formal manifestation of a spontaneous, untampered form of filmmaking" (146).

The same citation formats are used whether the material is quoted directly or paraphrased.

> Much of the American avant-garde movement experimented not so much with the techniques of modern art but with the spontaneous actions associated with home movies (Zimmerman 146).

When you use two or more sources by the same author in your essay, you must distinguish among them by including an abbreviated version of the title. The title can be part of the introductory text, as in "Zimmerman writes in *Reel Families* . . ." or in the parenthetical citation: "(Zimmerman, *Reel Families* 146)." Each source cited in the text must also appear in the Works Cited section with full bibliographic detail.

Another type of annotation is the content note or **explanatory note,** which may or may not include secondary sources. These notes offer background information on the topic being discussed or on related issues, suggest related readings, or offer an

text continued on page 540 ▶

▶ **VIEWING CUE**

As you prepare to integrate research into your essay, think about a particular quote or critical position you will argue against. What factual or historical material will support your argument? Note passages you can use to bolster a central part of your essay.

FILM IN FOCUS

From Research to Writing about
The Cabinet of Dr. Caligari (1919)

A writer researching an essay on *The Cabinet of Dr. Caligari* probably has more sources and materials than can ever be read in a reasonable period of time. Responding to the strange look and feel of this silent film from Germany and looking for some basic information, one student writer, for instance, starts his research by examining the introductory material in David Cook's *History of Narrative Film* (2004) and in two film guides, Richard Roud's *Cinema: A Critical Dictionary* (1982), and Ginette Vincendeau's *Encyclopedia of European Cinema* (1995). In the indexes of these books, he checks various headings, such as "German cinema" and "Weimar cinema," as well as the title of the film and the name of its director, Robert Wiene. Next, he searches the Internet by entering the title of the film in a search engine, which results in dozens of different Web sites containing reviews, plot summaries, stills, and even images of early posters. *Carafax Abbey: The Horror Film Database, Internet Source for Early German Cinema,* and *Das Kabinett des Doktor Caligari* by Damin Canon are a few of the sites he investigates. Although much of the Internet information is too general, he keeps a list of his Web sources and their bibliographic details, noting one particular site that provides early reviews of the film. Even this preliminary research starts to shape his thinking about a topic involving the period known as the Weimar era.

Following this preliminary work, the writer then checks the databases at his college library for more substantial critical books and essays on the Weimar period in German history. This initial search leads him to dozens of books and critical articles, but he selects *The Weimar Republic Sourcebook* (1994) because it is a relatively recent publication and seems quite comprehensive. He then decides to concentrate on books that deal with films made during the Weimar period; he discovers numerous scholarly studies devoted to this particular film culture and even whole books devoted to *The Cabinet of Dr. Caligari*. He reads and takes notes on appropriate sections of well-known books, such as Siegfried Kracauer's *From Caligari to Hitler* (1947) and Lotte Eisner's *The Haunted Screen* (1973), works he has seen mentioned frequently by other writers. He also consults two recent scholarly books, Michael Budd's *"The Cabinet of Dr. Caligari": Texts, Contexts, Histories* (1990) and Thomas Elsaesser's *Weimar Cinema and After* (2000).

Armed with information about how the Weimar era became the prelude to fascism and the rise of Hitler, the writer realizes he needs to refine his topic so that he has a more focused thesis. He reviews the film on videotape and begins to concentrate on the social violence that seethes beneath the surface of *The Cabinet of Dr. Caligari.* This is not a simple horror film, he realizes, but one in which the violence and horror seem connected to the social context of a prefascist Germany. As his thesis about social violence begins to take shape, he returns to the library, where he finds a good recent study of film violence, Stephen Prince's edited collection, *Screening Violence* (2000).

With each step, the writer makes notes, double-checks quotations for accuracy, and makes certain to record accurate bibliographic information on all the sources he consults. As he formulates his thesis statement and constructs an outline, he tries to indicate where the different parts of his research would be most effective in directing and supporting his argument. His final essay, reproduced here, clearly demonstrates the important contribution that careful research makes to writing about film.

Thompson 1

Steven Thompson
Film Criticism 101
Professor Corrigan
10 Dec. 2008

History, Violence, and *The Cabinet of Dr. Caligari*

In his detailed study of *The Cabinet of Dr. Caligari* (1919), Michael Budd
identifies the complex cultural history of the film's arrival in the United States,
an arrival that intentionally obscured the origins of one of Germany's most famous movies. When the film premiered in New York on April 3, 1921, it followed
a well-crafted promotion and distribution campaign that stressed *Dr. Caligari's*
novelty, global appeal, and generic formulas. One 1921 poster identifies the film
as "a mystery story that holds the public in suspense every minute," while another describes it as "thrilling, fantastic, bizarre, gripping." However accurate
these descriptions may be, these promotions, as Budd notes, intentionally present the film "out of context, [with] its origins both cultural and national deliberately obscured" (56–58). That obfuscation has continued to dog *The Cabinet
of Dr. Caligari* in the many decades since its initial release, so that American and
other viewers have remained less attuned to the specific historical and social realities dramatized in the film than to the psychological mysteries played out in
its thrills, fantasies, and horror.[1] Exploring the social drama of *Dr. Caligari* reconnects the film more concretely to its original German context and makes clear
that this film is about national unrest and violence, both of which are far more
historically tangible than the usually acknowledged fantasy of the film's mad-
men and monsters.

The film's story tells of the hypnotist Dr. Caligari who comes to a town with
a carnival [**Figure CDC.1**]. In his sideshow act, Caligari presents Cesare, a somnambulist who can supposedly see the future. At the same time, a series of murders occurs in the town. Francis, a student who discovers that Caligari and Cesare are
behind the killings, pursues Caligari to an insane asylum. The final twist occurs
when the narrative shifts its perspective and we discover the truth: Francis has
been the narrator of the tale, he is in fact the mad patient in the asylum, and Caligari is the kind director of the hospital allowing Francis to tell his delusional tale.[2]

Background research clearly sets
up the writer's argument.

The thesis statement
announces the argument.

This summary paragraph assumes
readers know the film, but re-
freshes their memory of its story
and plot.

A content note provides additional
information about a point raised in
the text.

CDC.1   ***The Cabinet of Dr. Caligari*** (1919). The malevolent or
benevolent Caligari.

An image that shows a main character, followed by a caption that
identifies a key question in the film
and the student's argument about
that character.

While watching this film, many (if not most) viewers understandably fixate on the exaggerated sets and backdrop paintings. These factors, together with the twisted narrative that turns the story into the vision of a madman, place this film squarely in the cultural and aesthetic tradition of expressionism, a movement in which unconscious or unseen forces create a world distorted by personal fears, desires, and anxieties. According to this position, Cesare acts out the evil unconscious of Caligari, while the violence and chaos associated with that unconscious spread through the entire community.

Many critics have, in fact, made intelligent connections between the psychological underpinnings of expressionism and the German society that, bereft of so many fathers after the devastation of World War I, gravitated toward malevolent authority figures. Most famously, Siegfried Kracauer's *From Caligari to Hitler* offers the most direct statement of Dr. Caligari as the unconscious of a social history predicting the imminent arrival of fascism **[Figure CDC.2]**. He writes that Caligari becomes "a premonition of Hitler" (72):

> Whether intentionally or not, *Caligari* exposes the soul wavering between tyranny and chaos, and facing a desperate situation: any escape from tyranny seems to throw it into a state of utter confusion. Quite logically, the film spreads an all-pervading atmosphere of horror. Like the Nazi world, that of *Caligari* overflows with sinister portents, acts of terror and outbursts of panic. (74)

Although *Dr. Caligari* certainly responds to readings like this, which see the film as part of an expressionist aesthetic or a projection of the unconscious of the German masses around 1920, the more concrete social realities informing the film frequently get overlooked. In *The Weimar Republic Sourcebook*, Anton Kaes, Martin Jay, and Edward Dimendberg have assembled a compendium of documents on this period in German history, and many of the topics for this cultural history of Germany from 1918 to 1930 could act as a social blueprint for the thematic history that permeates *Dr. Caligari*. Three topics stand out as especially pertinent: the traumatic legacy of war (creating a fatherless generation), economic upheaval and social instabilities (that rattled almost every social institution at the time), and the rise of fascism (through repressive authority figures). With traces of each of these three motifs throughout the film, *Dr. Caligari* becomes, from one angle, a study of social violence within the interpersonal relationships and the cultural institutions of Weimar Germany.

At the heart of *Dr. Caligari* is a social melodrama concentrated on conscious sexual activities that quickly turn violent. According to Thomas Elsaesser, "It is essentially the tale of a suitor who is ignored or turned down" (qtd. in Budd 184). The threesome at the center of the story—Francis, Alan, and Jane—suggests both male bonds and a heterosexual romance that moves toward the conventional outcome of marriage. However, like Jane's anxious worry over "her father's long absence," each member of this standard social group seems physically and emotionally handicapped by a missing parental or patriarchal figure. Essential to the plot is the rivalry that creates a tension among the three characters, with Alan and Francis competing for the affections of Jane. That seemingly normal and playful tension, however, turns dark when Cesare becomes a stand-in for the simmering violence implicit in this group, murdering

---

The marginal annotations:

This overview of a major scholarly position establishes the writer's authority and prepares readers for what will distinguish his argument.

A succinct quotation sums up a complex critical viewpoint. Because it is more than four lines in length, the quotation is presented without quotation marks in the block (indented) format.

Against the backdrop of these other critical positions, the writer reasserts and develops his thesis.

The writer refines and focuses his thesis as three motifs in the film.

A strong topic sentence presents the first motif, supported by a secondary source.

An exact quotation from the film's dialogue provides supporting evidence for the writer's claim.

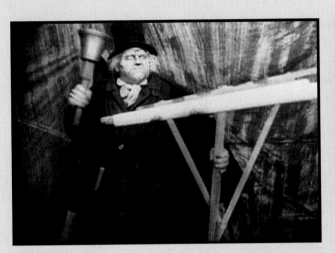

CDC.2   *The Cabinet of Dr. Caligari* (1919). A premonition of Hitler?

CDC.3   *The Cabinet of Dr. Caligari* (1919). Horror, or a romance gone awry?

Francis's rival Alan and seducing and abducting Jane. In the midst of these events, the dazed Jane can only mutter that "we queens may never choose as our hearts dictate," and Francis goes mad [**Figure CDC.3**]. If heterosexual melodramas take many forms through history and in different cultures, here a common love triangle suddenly and inexplicitly erupts with unusual violence, suggesting that the problem may be less about Caligari and Cesare than about the enormous social stress and strain within this fundamental social grouping.

The violent stress and strain of this heterosexual drama spreads and appears through every social institution in *Dr. Caligari*. If the home is where the melodrama explodes, the film identifies this violence with three other social spaces: the city government, the carnival, and the mental hospital. With the first, an officious town clerk is murdered on a whim for enforcing restrictions that annoy Dr. Caligari. With the second, entertainment turns ominously threatening when a sideshow amusement tells Alan, "You die at dawn." With the third, a traditional institution for healing becomes a prison to subjugate or control human beings who have lost all ability to interact socially. In each case—and most notably in the hospital where the narrative pretends to return to a normal world—the visual disturbances of the graphically twisted walls and out-of-kilter windows become a measure of not merely an unbalanced expressionistic mind but, more importantly, of the social violence that surrounds all individuals as part of the institutions in which they must live.

If violence has always been an ingredient and attraction of films, the brand of social violence in *Dr. Caligari* is clearly linked to a specific time and place, a Weimar Germany from which the Nazi regime would soon spring. In "Graphic Violence in the Cinema" from *Screening Violence*, Stephen Prince correctly argues that "screen violence is deeply embedded in the history and functioning of cinema" and the "appeal of violence in the cinema—for filmmakers and viewers—is tied to the medium's inherently visceral properties" (2). Although Prince claims that "screen violence in earlier periods was generally more genteel and indirect" (2), there is nothing genteel about the social violence of *Dr. Caligari*, even if it lacks the physical excess of contemporary movies. With the crucial insights of historical hindsight, this violence should not be relegated

A smooth transition from the previous paragraph to the second motif about "social institutions," analyzed here as three different "social spaces."

Visual details strengthen the argument.

The third motif builds on a more general secondary source on "screen violence."

merely to the unconscious and the psychological distortions of dark fantasies, but should be recognized as the shadow of a historical and social reality. In its original historical context, the melodramatic violence in the relationship of Alan, Francis, and Jane maps a frustrating and often desperate problem with heterosexual romance in a fatherless Germany, while the troubled, anxious, and repressive interactions at town halls, carnivals, and hospitals refer to a real political and structural crisis in the social arenas of post–World War I Germany. If the social violence of *Dr. Caligari* seems tame (to modern eyes accustomed to Technicolor bloodbaths), there is no doubt that such violence reverberates with more extensive, if less intensive, implications for the state of German society in 1920.

Many viewers without a precise sense of German history and *Caligari*'s original cultural context can still appreciate its dark tale, striking visual effects, and unsettling frame tale. The psychological dimension that permeates this murder mystery is, moreover, an undeniable and critical component to its disturbing plot and expressionistic mise-en-scène. Yet, in the wake of World War I, the nightmarish violence of the film resonates with particular historical and social meaning that cannot be explained as fantasy. *The Cabinet of Dr. Caligari* will always be a specific cultural space whose violence remains historically tangible.

> The assertive conclusion restates the central thesis.

[1]A fascinating and rich source of information about the reception of *The Cabinet of Dr. Caligari* is the Web site at www.filmgeschichte.de/film/caligari.htm. Besides numerous early reviews of the film (in German), this site offers information about the many films, plays, and books that describe or are based on the original film.

[2]In *A History of Narrative Film,* David Cook notes that it was the great German director Fritz Lang who urged this frame tale: "Lang correctly thought that the reality frame would heighten the expressionistic elements of the mise-en-scène" (110).

---

aside. They should be placed on a separate page after the text (but before the Works Cited list) or as footnotes at the bottom of the page. Thus a writer discussing horror films and Brian De Palma's *Carrie* (1976) might include this text and content note:

Although *Carrie* focuses on female anxiety and violence, it is difficult to pinpoint a specific audience for this film.[1]

[1]Especially since *Psycho,* horror films seem fixated on violence against women, but there is good reason to consider how both female and male audiences identify with these films. An important discussion of this issue is Carol Clover's *Men, Women, and Chain Saws* (3-21).

Full documentation for every source cited in your essay should be included in the **Works Cited** section, positioned on a separate page immediately after the last page of the essay text. Sources that have been consulted, but not cited in the text or notes of the essay, can be included in an optional **Works Consulted** section, which follows on a separate page after the Works Cited list. (Note that for reasons of space, we do *not* show the Works Cited and Works Consulted sections as separate pages in the essay beginning on p. 537.) Punctuation of the different entries must be absolutely correct. Titles should be typed either in italics or underlined, according to your instructor's preference.

Examples of some of the most common types of Works Cited entries follow.

[According to MLA, begin new page here.]   Thompson 5

Works Cited

Budd, Michael. *"The Cabinet of Dr.Caligari": Texts, Contexts, Histories*. New Brunswick: Rutgers UP, 1990.

Cook, David A. *A History of Narrative Film*. 4th ed. New York: Norton, 2003.

Elsaesser, Thomas. "Social Mobility and the Fantastic: German Silent Cinema." *"The Cabinet of Dr. Caligari": Texts, Contexts, Histories*. Ed. Mike Budd. New Brunswick: Rutgers UP, 1990. 171–90.

Kaes, Anton, Martin Jay, and Edward Dimendberg. *The Weimar Republic Sourcebook*. Berkeley: U of California P, 1994.

"Das Kabinett des Doktor Caligari." 7 Dec. 2001 <www.filmgeshicte.de/film/caligari.htm>.

Kracauer, Siegfried. *From Caligari to Hitler: A Psychological Study of German Film*. Princeton: Princeton UP, 1947.

Prince, Stephen. "Graphic Violence in the Cinema: Origins, Aesthetic Design, and Social Effects." *Screening Violence*. Ed. Stephen Prince. New Brunswick: Rutgers UP, 2000. 1–46.

The Works Cited list starts on a new page at the end of the research essay.

[According to MLA, begin new page here]   Thompson 6

Works Consulted

Carroll, Noel. "The Cabinet of Dr. Kracauer." *Millenium Film Journal* 1.2 (Spring/Summer 1978): 77–85.

Eisner, Lotte. *The Haunted Screen: Expressionism in the German Cinema and the Influence of Max Reinhardt*. Berkeley: U of California P, 1973.

Elsaesser, Thomas. *Weimar Cinema and After: Germany's Historical Imaginary*. London: Routledge, 2000.

The Works Consulted list, when included, starts on a new page following Works Cited.

Book by One Author

Zimmerman, Patricia. *Reel Families: A Social History of Amateur Film*. Bloomington: Indiana UP, 1995.

Book by More Than One Author

Bordwell, David, Janet Staiger, and Kristin Thompson. *The Classical Hollywood Cinema: Film Style and Mode of Production to 1960*. New York: Columbia UP, 1985.

Edited Book

Cook, Pam, and Mieke Bernink, eds. *The Cinema Book*. 2nd ed. London: British Film Institute, 1999.

Article in an Anthology of Film Criticism

Gaines, Jane. "Dream/Factory." *Reinventing Film Studies*. Eds. Christine Gledhill and Linda Williams. London: Arnold, 2000. 100–13.

Journal Article

Spivak, Gayatri. "In Praise of *Sammy and Rosie Get Laid*." *Critical Quarterly* 31.2 (Summer 1989): 80–88.

Articles in Daily or Weekly Periodical

Corliss, Richard. "Suddenly Shakespeare." *Time* 4 Nov. 1996: 88–90.

Interview (Printed)

Seberg, Jean. Interview with Mark Rappaport. "I, Jean Seberg." *Film Quarterly* 55.1
(Fall 2001): 2–13.

Article in an Online Journal (including Access Date)

Firshing, Robert. "Italian Horror in the Seventies." *Images Journal* 8 Nov. 2001. 23
July 2003 <www.imagesjournal.com>.

Information from an Online Site (including Access Date)

Magnolia: The Official Movie Page. 1999. New Line Productions. 14 Nov. 2003
<www.magnoliamovie.com>.

Information from a Videocassette or DVD

Always identify whether you are referencing a videocassette or a DVD. Include the
director, main performers, and original release date of the film, followed by the
video/DVD distributor and year.

Fearless. Dir. Peter Weir. Perf. Jeff Bridges, Isabella Rossellini, Rosie Perez. 1993.
DVD. Warner Home Video, 1999.

Always remember to keep in mind that plagiarism—using sources without giving the proper credit to them—is one of the most serious offenses in writing and research. For more information on attribution formats for other types of sources,
consult the *MLA Handbook for Writers of Research Papers,* 6th ed. (2003).

CONCEPTS AT WORK

In this chapter we've examined both the aims and mechanics of good writing about film. Some of the important preliminary steps in this kind of writing include
identifying an audience, balancing subjective and objective perspectives, taking notes, and sketching an outline
that develops a particular argument and interpretation.
The actual writing requires a clear and detailed thesis,
strong topic sentences, and concrete evidence from the
film, and is always followed by a series of revisions of
first drafts that work to clarify the argument, its ideas,
and its presentation. Careful proofreading then follows
final revision, double-checking mechanics such as
spelling and punctuation. Students should beware of in-
discriminately using images from a film if they are simply ornamental; if used, images should provide precise
and detailed evidence for a part of your argument and
be connected to that argument with a short caption that
reinforces that connection. Finally, we have discussed
both why research can be crucial to a strong critical paper and how that research can be pursued and integrated
into the writing.

Activity

- Many filmmakers, such as François Truffaut and
Peter Bogdanovich, also work as fine film critics and
scholars, and much of the work of making a film—
research, planning, organizing, and revising—can
resemble the work of writing a critical essay. Not
surprisingly, an important film practice has been
films that act as critical commentaries: films about
films, films about writers, films about art. Try your
hand at an "essayistic film" by sketching the opening of a movie that critically engages another film
of your choice, a film that analyzes and comments
on the achievements or failures of another movie.

THE NEXT LEVEL: ADDITIONAL SOURCES

Donald, James, Anne Friedberg, and Laura Marcus, eds. *Close Up, 1927–1933: Cinema and Modernism*. Princeton: Princeton University Press, 1998. Featuring some of the earliest and best writers about film—such as Dorothy Richardson, Harry Potamkin, and H. D., who still have much to tell contemporary writers about style and substance—this volume collects relatively early, passionately serious, and still important reviews and essays on the art of film as it moved from the silent to the sound era.

Lant, Antonia, ed. *Red Velvet Seat: Women's Writings on the First Fifty Years of Cinema*. London: Verso, 2006. While filmgoing was one of the most important cultural activities for women throughout the twentieth century, this collection of writings is the first widely inclusive survey of the many ways women wrote about film. The book features not only the writings of actresses, filmmakers, and writers, such as Virginia Woolf and H. D., but also social activists such as Jane Addams and Barbara Deming.

Lopate, Phillip, ed. *American Movie Critics: From the Silents until Now*. New York: Library of America, 2006. A wideranging anthology of American film criticism, this recent collection spans the history of cinema, from Vachel Lindsay's prophetic writings in 1915 to Roger Ebert's modern reviews, and it offers an exceptional range of voices and perspectives, from Manny Farber's 1930s writings to poet John Ashbery's contemporary reflections of the cinema.

Lopate, Phillip. *Totally, Tenderly, Tragically: Essays and Criticism from a Lifelong Love Affair with the Movies*. New York: Anchor, 1998. Opinionated and smart, Lopate mediates journalistic reviews and scholarly criticism across topics that range from Michelangelo Antonioni's *La Notte* (1960) to "Images of Children in Film."

Nichols, Bill, ed. *Movies and Method*. 2 vols. Berkeley: University of California Press, 1976, 1985. This two-volume anthology, a classic collection of film criticism and film theory, includes historical and recent writings. Although the material and arguments are largely scholarly and theoretical, the wide scope of topics suggests the many avenues students might follow in writing a critical film essay.

Rich, B. Ruby. *Chick Flicks: Theories and Memories of the Feminist Film Movement*. Durham: Duke University Press, 1998. Covering a range of topics and films that engage several decades of feminist film criticism, Rich writes as both a journalist and a film scholar, with each essay demonstrating a skillful balance of personal experience and intellectual argument.

Stam, Robert, and Toby Miller, eds. *Film and Theory: An Anthology*. Oxford: Blackwell, 2000. One of the most current collections of scholarly film essays available, this volume arranges its many essays around various topics, such as "questions of realism" and "class and the culture industry"; the selections are often demanding and theoretical, representing some of the most sophisticated and important writing in film studies today.

Note: MLA coverage in this chapter is based on the *MLA Handbook for Writers of Research Papers*, 6th Ed. (2003), as recommended for undergraduate students by the Modern Language Association. Our coverage will be updated in a reprint after MLA publishes the seventh edition of its handbook, anticipated for spring 2009.

Glossary

above-the-line expenses: A film's initial costs of contracting the major personnel, such as **directors** and stars, as well as administrative and organizational expenses in setting up a film **production**.

abstract films: Formal experiments that are also nonrepresentational. These films use color, shape, and line to create patterns and rhythms that are abstracted from real actions and objects.

academy ratio: An **aspect ratio** of screen width to height of 1.37:1, the standard adopted by the Motion Picture Academy of Arts and Sciences in 1931 and used by most films until the introduction of **widescreen ratios** in the1950s; similar to the standard television ratio of 1.33:1 or 4:3.

activist video: A confrontational political **documentary** using low-cost video equipment.

actor: An individual who embodies and performs a film character through gestures and movements.

actualities: Early **nonfiction films** introduced in the 1890s depicting real people and events through continuous footage; a famous example is Louis and Auguste Lumière's *Workers Leaving the Lumière Factory* (1985).

adaptation: The process of turning a novel, short story, play, or other artistic work into a film.

agents: Individuals who represent **actors**, **directors**, writers, and other major personnel employed by a film **production** by contacting and negotiating with writers, **casting directors**, and **producers**.

alternative film narrative: Film **narratives** that deviate from or challenge the linearity of **classical film narrative**, often undermining the centrality of the main character, the continuity of the plot, or the **verisimilitude** of the **narration**.

analytical editing: **Continuity editing** that establishes spatial and temporal clarity by breaking down a **scene**, often using progressively tighter **framings** that maintain consistent spatial relations.

analytical essay: The most common kind of writing done by film students and scholars, distinguished by its intended audience and the level of its critical language.

anamorphic lens: A **camera lens** that compresses the horizontal axis of an image or a projector lens that "unsqueezes" such an image to produce a widescreen image.

ancillary market: A venue other than theatrical release in which a film can make money, such as foreign sales, airlines, pay television, cable, or home video.

animation: A process that traditionally refers to moving images drawn or painted on individual **cels** or to manipulated three-dimensional objects, which are then photographed onto single frames of film. Animation now encompasses digital imaging techniques.

antagonists: **Characters** who oppose the **protagonists** as negative forces.

anthology films: See **compilation films**.

A picture: A **feature film** with a considerable budget and prestigious source material or stars or other personnel that has been historically promoted as a main attraction receiving top billing in a double feature; see **B picture**.

apparatus theory: A critical school that explores the cinema as an ideological phenomenon based on a physical set of technologies, including the camera and the arrangement of projector and screen, that reinforces the values of individualism and the transcendence of the material basis of the cinematic illusion.

apparent motion: The psychological process that explains our perception of movement when watching films, in which the brain is actively responding to the visual stimuli of a rapid sequence of still images exactly as it would in actual motion perception.

archetype: An original model or type, such as Satan as an archetype of evil.

art director: The individual responsible for supervising the conception and construction of the physical environment in which the **actors** appear, including sets, locations, **props**, and costumes; see **production designer** and **set designer**.

art film: A type of film produced for aesthetic rather than primarily for commercial or entertainment purposes, whose intellectual or formal challenges are often attributed to the vision of an **auteur**.

aspect ratio: The width-to-height ratio of the film frame as it appears on a movie screen or television monitor.

asynchronous sound: Sound that does not have a visible onscreen source; also referred to as **offscreen sound**.

auteur: The French term for author; the individual credited with the creative vision defining a film; implies a **director** whose unique style is apparent across his or her body of work; see **auteur theory**.

auteur theory: An approach to cinema first proposed in the French film journal *Cahiers du cinéma* that emphasized the role of the **director** as the expressive force behind a film and saw a director's body of work as united by common themes or formal strategies; also referred to as *auteurism*.

automated dialogue replacement (ADR): A process during which **actors** watch the film footage and re-record their lines to be dubbed into the **soundtrack**; also known as **looping**.

avant-garde cinema: Aesthetically challenging, noncommercial films that self-consciously reflect on how human senses and consciousness work or explore and experiment with film forms and techniques. Avant-garde cinema thrived in Europe in the 1920s and in the United States after World War II.

axis of action: An imaginary line bisecting a **scene** corresponding to the **180-degree rule** in **continuity editing**.

backlighting: A **highlighting** technique that illuminates the person or object from behind, tending to silhouette the subject; sometimes called *edgelighting*.

below-the-line expenses: The technical and material costs—costumes, sets, transportation, and so on—involved in the actual making of a film.

blaxploitation: A **genre** of low-budget films made in the early 1970s targeting urban, African American audiences with films about streetwise African American **protagonists**. Several black **directors** made a creative mark in a genre that was primarily intended to make money for its **producers**.

block booking: A practice in which movie theaters had to exhibit whatever a studio/distributor packaged with its more popular and desirable movies; declared an unfair business practice in 1948.

blockbuster: A big-budget film, intended for **wide release**, whose large investment in stars, **special effects**, and advertising attracts large audiences and economic profits.

blocking: The arrangement and movement of **actors** in relation to each other within the **mise-en-scène**.

blue screen technology: A **visual effects** process that superimposes two images. **Actors** perform in front of a blue background screen; later the blue is keyed out and background images are superimposed. With the shift to digital technology, use of blue screen has become more prevalent.

boom: A long pole used to hold a microphone above the **actors** to capture sound while remaining outside the frame, handled by a *boom operator*.

B picture: A low-budget, nonprestigious movie that usually played on the bottom half of a double bill. B pictures were often produced by the smaller studios referred to as Hollywood's Poverty Row; see **A picture**.

camera lens: A piece of curved glass that focuses light rays in order to form an image on film.

camera movement: See **mobile frame**.

camera operator: A member of the film crew in charge of physically manipulating the camera, overseen by the **cinematographer**.

canted frame: **Framing** that is not level, creating an unbalanced appearance.

casting director: The individual responsible for identifying and selecting which **actors** would work best in a particular role.

cels: A transparent sheet of celluloid on which individual images are drawn or painted in traditional **animation**. These drawings are then photographed onto single frames of film.

character actors: Recognizable **actors** associated with particular **character types**, often humorous or sinister, and often cast in minor parts.

character analysis: A formal topic, concentrating its argument on a single character or on the interactions between more than one character.

character coherence: A quality created within a fiction of **characters** displaying behavior, emotions, and thoughts that appear consistent and coherent.

character depth: A quality created within a fiction of **characters** displaying psychological and social features that distinguish them as rounded and complex in a way that approximates realistic human personalities.

character development: The patterns through which **characters** in a particular film move from one mental, physical, or social state to another.

characters: Individuals who motivate the events and perform the actions of the **story**.

character types: Conventional **characters** (e.g., hardboiled detective or femme fatale) typically portrayed by **actors** cast because of their physical features, acting style, or the history of other roles they have played; see **stereotype**.

chiaroscuro lighting: A term that describes dramatic, high-contrast **lighting** that emphasizes shadows and the contrast between light and dark; frequently used in **German expressionist cinema** and **film noir**.

chronology: The order according to which **shots** or **scenes** convey the temporal sequence of the **story**'s events.

chronophotography: A **sequence** of still photographs such as those depicting human or animal motion produced by Eadweard Muybridge and Étienne-Jules Marey; the immediate precursors of the cinema.

cinematographer: The member of the film crew who selects the cameras, **film stock**, **lighting**, and lenses to be used as well as the camera setup or position. Also known as the director of photography or D.P.

cinematography: Motion-picture photography, literally "writing in movement."

cinema verité: A French term literally meaning "cinema truth"; a style of **documentary** filmmaking first practiced in the late 1950s and early 1960s that used unobtrusive, lightweight cameras and sound equipment to capture a real-life situation; the parallel U.S. movement is called **direct cinema**.

cinephilia: A love of cinema.

clapboard: A device marked with the **scene** and **take** number that is filmed at the beginning of each take; the sound of its being snapped is recorded in order to synchronize **sound recordings** and camera images.

classical film narrative: A style of **narrative** filmmaking centered on one or more central **characters** who propel the **plot** with a cause-and-effect logic wherein an action generates a reaction. Normally plots are developed with **linear chronologies** directed at definite goals, and the film employs an omniscient or a restricted **third-person narration** that suggests some degree of **verisimilitude.**

classical film theory: Writings on the fundamental questions of cinema produced in roughly the first half of the twentieth century. Important classical film theorists include Sergei Eisenstein, Rudolf Arnheim, André Bazin, and Siegfried Kracauer.

classical Hollywood narrative: The dominant form of **classical film narrative** associated with the Hollywood **studio system** from the end of the 1910s to the end of the 1950s.

claymation: A process that uses **stop-motion photography** with clay figures to create the illusion of movement.

click track: Holes punched in the film corresponding to the beat of a metronome that can help **actors**, musicians, and the composer keep the rhythm of the action.

close-up: **Framing** that shows details of a person or object, such as a character's face.

code: A term used in linguistics and **semiotics** meaning a system of **signs** from which a *message* is generated. In a communication act, a code must be shared by the sender and the receiver for the message to be understood. For example, traffic signals use a color code. Film analysts isolate the codes of **camera movement, framing, lighting,** acting, etc., that determine the specific form of a particular **shot, scene,** film, or **genre.**

color balance: Putting emphasis on a particular part of the color spectrum to create realistic or unrealistic palettes.

color filter: A device fitted to the **camera lens** to change the **tones** of the filmed image.

comparative analysis: An analysis evaluating features or elements of two or more different films, or perhaps a film and its literary source.

compilation films: Films comprised of various segments by different filmmakers; also known as **anthology films.**

computer-generated imagery (CGI): Still or animated images created through digital computer technology. First introduced in the 1970s, CGI was used to create feature-length films by the mid-1990s and is widely used for **visual effects.**

continuity editing: The institutionalized system of Hollywood **editing** that uses **cuts** and other transitions to establish **verisimilitude,** to construct a coherent time and space, and to tell stories clearly and efficiently. Continuity editing follows the basic principle that each **shot** or **scene** has a continuous relationship to the next; sometimes called **invisible editing.**

continuity script: A **screenplay** that presents in detail the action, **scenes,** dialogue, transitions, and often camera setups in the order planned for the final film.

continuity style: The systematic approach to filmmaking associated with classical Hollywood cinema, utilizing a broad array of technical choices from **continuity editing** to scoring that support the principle of effacing technique in order to emphasize human agency and **narrative** clarity.

costume designers: Individuals who plan and prepare how **actors** will be dressed for parts.

counter cinema: A cinematic style or movement with a confrontational impulse, challenging commercial film conventions of **narrative,** sound, image, or conventional practices of film **production, distribution,** and **exhibition.**

counterpoint: Using sound to indicate a different meaning or association than the image.

crane shot: A **shot** taken from a camera mounted on a crane that can vary distance, height, and angle.

credits: A list of all the personnel involved in a film **production,** including cast, crew, and executives, usually divided into *opening* and *closing credits.*

critical objectivity: Writing with a detached response that offers judgments based on facts and **evidence** with which others would, or could, agree.

crosscutting: An **editing** technique that cuts back and forth between actions in separate spaces, often implying simultaneity; also called **parallel editing.**

cue: A visual or aural signal that indicates the beginning of an action, line of dialogue, or piece of music.

cultural analysis: A formal topic that investigates the relationship of a film to its place in history, society, or culture.

cultural studies: A set of approaches drawn from the humanities and social sciences that considers cultural text and phenomena in conjunction with processes of **production** and consumption.

cut: In the **editing** process, the join or splice between two pieces of film; in the finished film, an editing transition between two separate **shots** or **scenes** achieved without **optical effects.** Also used to describe a version of the edited film, as in **rough cut, final cut,** or director's cut.

cutaway: A **shot** that interrupts a continuous action, "cutting away" to another image or action, often to abridge time.

deadline structure: A **narrative** structure that accelerates the action and **plot** toward a central event or action that must be accomplished by a certain time.

deep focus: A **focus** in which multiple planes in the **shot** are all in focus simultaneously; usually achieved with a **wide-angle lens.**

depth of field: The range or distance before and behind the main **focus** of a **shot** within which objects remain relatively sharp and clear.

dialectical montage: A concept developed in the theories and films of Soviet silent-film **director** Sergei Eisenstein that refers to the cutting together of conflicting or unrelated images to generate an idea or emotion in the viewer.

diegesis: A term that refers to the world of the film's **story** (its **characters**, places, and events), including not only what is shown but also what is implied to have taken place. It comes from the Greek word meaning "**narration.**"

diegetic sound: Sound that has its source in the **narrative** world of the film, whose **characters** are presumed to be able to hear it.

digital cinematography: Shooting with a camera that records and stores visual information electronically as digital code.

digital sound: Recording and reproducing sound through technologies that encode and decode it as digital information.

direct cinema: A **documentary** style originating in the United States in the 1960s that aims to observe an unfolding situation as unobtrusively as possible; related to **cinema verité**.

directional lighting: **Lighting** that may appear to emanate from a natural source and defines and shapes the object, area, or person being illuminated.

director: The chief creative presence or the primary manager in film **production**, responsible for overseeing virtually all the work of making a movie.

direct sound: Sound captured directly from its source.

disjunctive editing: A variety of alternative **editing** practices that call attention to the **cut** through spatial tension, temporal jumps, or rhythmic or graphic pattern so as to affect viscerally, disorient, or intellectually engage the viewer. Also called *visible editing*.

dissolve: An **optical effect** that briefly superimposes one **shot** over the next. One image fades out as another image fades in and takes its place; sometimes called a *lap dissolve* because two images overlap in the printing process.

distantiation: Derived from the work and theories of Bertolt Brecht, an artistic practice intended to create an intellectual distance between the viewer and the **performance** or artwork in order to reflect on the work's **production** or various ideas and issues raised by it.

distribution: The means through which movies are delivered to theaters, video stores, television and Internet networks, and other venues that make them available to consumers, or to educational and cultural institutions. The entity that performs this function is a *distributor*.

documentary: A **nonfiction film** that presents real objects, people, and events.

dolly shot: A **shot** in which the camera is moved on a wheeled dolly that follows a determined course.

duration: Denotes the temporal relation of **shots** and **scenes** to the amount of time that passes in the **story**.

edgelighting: See **backlighting**.

editing: The process of selecting and joining film footage and **shots**. The individual responsible for this process is the *editor*.

ellipsis: An abridgment in time in the **narrative** implied by **editing**.

establishing shot: Generally, an initial **long shot** that establishes the location and **setting** and that orients the viewer in space to a clear view of the action.

ethnographic documentary: An anthropological film that aims to reveal cultures and peoples in the most authentic terms possible, without imposing the filmmaker's interpretation on that experience.

evidence: Concrete details that convince readers of the validity of a writer's interpretation.

exclusive release: A movie that premieres in restricted locations initially.

executive producer: A **producer** who finances or facilitates a film deal and who usually has little creative or technical involvement.

exhibition: The part of the film industry that shows films to a paying public, usually in movie theaters.

expanded cinema: A term coined in 1970 by Gene Youngblood that describes how video and computer technology can allow moving-image media to extend consciousness; also designates a number of installation or **performance**-based **experimental film** practices.

experimental films: Films that explore film form and subject matters in new and unconventional ways, ranging from abstract image and sound patterns to dreamlike worlds.

explanatory note: Offers background information on the topic being discussed or on related issues, suggests related readings, or offers an aside.

extratextual: Characterizes aspects of the film experience available to the scholar that exist outside of the film itself, including **production**, **distribution**, **exhibition**, and reception.

extreme close-up (ECU): A **framing** that is comparatively tighter than a **close-up**, singling out, for instance, a person's eyes, or the petal of a flower.

extreme long shot: A **framing** from a comparatively greater distance than a **long shot**, in which the surrounding space dominates human figures, such as in distant vistas of cities or landscapes.

eyeline match: A principle in **continuity editing** that calls for following a **shot** of a character looking offscreen with a shot of a subject whose screen position matches the gaze of the character in the first shot.

fade-in: An **optical effect** in which a black screen gradually brightens to a full picture; often used after a **fade-out** to create a transition between **scenes**.

fade-out: An **optical effect** in which an image gradually darkens to black, often ending a **scene** or a film; see **fade-in.**

fast motion: A cinematic special effect that makes the action move at unrealistic speeds, achieved by filming the action faster than normal and then projecting it at standard speeds. See **slow motion.**

feature film: Running typically 90 to 120 minutes in length, a **narrative** film that is the primary attraction for audiences.

fill lighting: A **lighting** technique using secondary fill lights to balance the **key lighting** by removing shadows or to emphasize other spaces and objects in the **scene.**

film gauge: The width of the **film stock;** e.g., 8mm, 16mm, 35mm, and 70mm.

film noir: A term introduced by French critics (meaning literally "black film") to describe Hollywood films of the 1940s set in the criminal underworld, which were considerably darker in mood and **mise-en-scène** than those that had come before. Typically shot in black and white in nighttime urban **settings,** they featured morally ambiguous **protagonists,** corrupt institutions, dangerous women, and convoluted **plots,** and they used stylized **lighting** and **cinematography.**

film review: A short essay that describes the **plot** of a movie, provides useful background information (about the **actors** and the **director,** for example), and pronounces a clear evaluation of the film to guide its readers.

film shoot: The weeks or month of actual shooting, on **set** or on location.

film speed: The rate at which moving images are recorded and later projected, standardized for 35mm sound film at twenty-four frames per second (fps); also, a measure of **film stock**'s sensitivity to light.

film stock: Unexposed film consisting of a flexible backing or base and a light-sensitive emulsion.

filters: Transparent sheets of glass or gels placed in front of the lens to create various effects.

final cut: The final edited version of a film.

first release: A movie's original **exhibition,** also referred to as its *first run,* often limited to specific theaters in major cities.

flare: A spot or flash of white light created by directing strong light directly at the lens.

flashback: A **sequence** that follows images set in the present with images set in the past; it may be introduced with a **dissolve** conveying a character's subjective memory or with a **voiceover** in which a character narrates the past.

flashforward: A **sequence** that connects an image set in the present with one or more future images and that leaps ahead of the normal cause-and-effect order.

focal length: The distance from the center of the lens to the point where light rays meet in sharp **focus.**

focus: The point or area in the image that is most precisely outlined and defined by the lens of the camera; the point at which light rays refracted through the lens converge.

foley artist: A member of the sound crew who generates live synchronized sound effects such as footsteps, the rustle of clothing, or a key turning in a lock, while watching the projected film. Named after their inventor, Jack Foley, foley tracks are eventually mixed with other audio tracks.

following shots: A **pan, tilt,** or **tracking shot** that follows a moving individual or object.

formalist: A scholar who believes a work's form or structure is primary, and posits that objective meaning is to be found in the work itself and not in an outside source, such as the author's biography.

framing: The portion of the filmed subject that appears within the borders of the frame; it correlates with camera distance, e.g., **long shot** or **medium close-up.**

French impressionist cinema: The first of a series of radical experiments with film form between 1920 and 1939. This movement aimed to destabilize familiar or objective ways of seeing, and to revitalize the dynamics of human perception.

French New Wave: A film movement that came to prominence in the late 1950s and 1960s in France in opposition to the conventional **studio system;** designates films by a group of young writer/directors involved as critics with the journal *Cahiers du Cinéma* made with low budgets and young **actors** and shot on location. The films often used unconventional sound and **editing** patterns or addressed the struggle for personal expression.

frontal lighting: Techniques used to illuminate the subject from the front. Related terms are **sidelighting, underlighting,** and **top lighting.**

fullscreen: Format in which the image fills the entire screen. Widescreen films are sometimes converted to this using a **"pan-and-scan"** process.

gangster films: Films about the criminal underworld, typically (but not necessarily) set in the U.S. during Prohibition in the 1930s.

genre: A category or classification of a group of movies in which the individual films share similar subject matter and similar ways of organizing the subject through **narrative** and stylistic patterns.

German expressionist cinema: Film movement drawing on painting and theatrical developments that emerged in Germany between 1918 and 1929; expressionism depicted the dark fringes of human experience through the use of dramatic **lighting** and **set** and costume design to represent irrational forces.

graphic editing: A style of **editing** creating formal patterns of shapes, masses, colors, lines, and **lighting** patterns through links between **shots.**

graphic match: An edit in which a dominant shape or line in one **shot** provides a visual transition to a similar shape or line in the next shot.

grip: A crew member who installs **lighting** and dollies.

handheld camera: A lightweight camera (such as the 16mm Arriflex) that can be carried by the operator rather than mounted on a tripod. Such cameras, widely used during World War II, allowed **cinematography** to become more mobile and fostered the advent of on-location shooting.

handheld shot: A film image produced by an individual carrying the camera, creating an unsteady **shot** that may suggest the **point of view** of an individual moving through space.

hard lighting: A high-contrast **lighting** style that creates hard edges, distinctive shadows, and a harsh effect, especially when filming people.

***heimat* films:** Set in idyllic countryside locales of Germany and Austria, these films depict a world of traditional folk values in which love and family triumph over virtually any social evil.

high angle: A **shot** directed at a downward angle on individuals or a **scene**.

high concept: A short phrase that attempts to sell a movie by identifying its main **marketing** features, such as its stars, **genre**, or some other easily identifiable connection.

highlighting: Using **lighting** to brighten or emphasize specific **characters** or objects.

historiography: The writing of history; the study of the methods and principles through which the past becomes organized according to certain perspectives and priorities.

Hong Kong new wave: A movement in Chinese cinema led by producer-director Tsui Hark, which introduced sophisticated style, lucrative **production** methods, and a canny use of Western elements to the **genre**.

horror film: A film **genre** with origins in gothic literature that seeks to frighten the viewer though supernatural or predator **characters**; **narratives** built on suspense, dread, and surprise; and visual compositions that anticipate and manipulate shocking sights.

hybrid genres: Mixed forms produced by the interaction of different **genres**, such as musical **horror films**.

iconography: Images or image patterns with specific connotations or meanings.

ideology: A systematic set of beliefs, not necessarily conscious or acknowledged.

IMAX: A large-format film system that is projected horizontally rather than vertically to produce an image approximately ten times larger than the standard 35mm frame.

independent film: Films that are produced without initial studio financing, typically with much lower budgets; they include feature-length **narratives**, documentaries, and shorts.

Indian cinema: Approached as a national popular cinema, this is the most prolific film industry in the world. Indian cinema is notable for *Bollywood* films, as they are often referred to, as a dominant cultural form, and critically prized films with a presence on the world stage, such as those of Satyajit Ray.

insert: A brief **shot**, often a **close-up**, filmed separately from a **scene** and inserted during **editing**, that points out details significant to the action.

intercutting: Interposing **shots** of two or more actions, locations, or contents.

internal diegetic sound: See **semidiegetic sound**.

intertextuality: A critical approach that holds that a text depends on other, related texts for its full meaning.

intertitle: Printed text inserted between film images, typically used in silent films to indicate dialogue and exposition and in contemporary films to indicate time and place or other transitions.

invisible editing: See **continuity editing**.

iris-in: An **optical effect** used as an **editing** transition that gradually opens from a small, usually circular, portion of the frame to reveal the entire image. It is infrequently used in modern cinema.

iris-out: An **optical effect** used as an **editing** transition that begins by masking the corners of the frame in black and gradually reduces the image to a small circle. It is infrequently used in modern cinema.

iris shot: A **shot** in which the frame is masked so that only a small circular piece of the image is seen.

Italian neorealism: A film movement that began in Italy during World War II and lasted until approximately 1952 depicting everyday social realities using location shooting and amateur **actors**, in opposition to glossy studio formulas.

***jidai-geki* films:** Period films or costume dramas set before 1868, when feudal Japan entered the modern Meiji period.

jump cut: An edit that interrupts a particular action and intentionally or unintentionally creates discontinuities in the spatial or temporal development of **shots**.

key lighting: The main source of non-natural **lighting** in a **scene**. *High-key light* is even (the ratio between key and fill light is high); *low-key light* shows strong contrast (the ratio between key and fill light is low).

leader: A length of film attached to the beginning (head) or end (tail) of a film reel that is used to thread the projector.

leading actors: The two or three **actors**, often stars, who represent the central **characters** in a **narrative**.

letterbox: A format for video or DVD viewing that maintains the **widescreen ratio** of theatrical projection by masking the top and bottom of the frame with black bars.

lighting: Sources of illumination—both natural light and electrical lamps—used to present, shade, and accentuate figures, objects, spaces, or **mise-en-scène**. Lighting is primarily the responsibility of the *director of photography* and the *lighting crew*; see **key lighting**, **fill lighting**, and **highlighting**.

limited release: The practice of initially distributing a film only to major cities and expanding **distribution** according to its success or failure.

linear chronology: **Plot** events and actions that proceed one after another as a forward movement in time.

line producer: The individual in charge of the daily business of tracking costs and maintaining the **production** schedule of a film.

location scouting: Determining and securing suitable places besides studio **sets** to use for shooting particular movie **scenes**.

long shot: A **framing** that places considerable distance between the camera and the **scene** or person so that the object or person is recognizable but defined by the large space and background; see **establishing shot**.

long take: A **shot** of relatively long **duration**.

looping: An image or sound recorded on a loop of film to be replayed and layered.

low angle: A **shot** from a position lower than its subject.

machinima: A **new media** form that modifies video-game engines to create computer **animation**.

marketing: The process of identifying an audience and bringing a product such as a movie to its attention through various strategies so that they will consume (watch or purchase) it.

masks: Attachments to the camera or devices added optically that cut off portions of the frame so that part of the image is black.

match on action: A **cut** between two **shots** featuring a similar visual action, such as when a shot in which a character opening a door cuts to a shot depicting the continuation of that action, or when a shot of a train moving left to right cuts to a character running in the same direction.

matte shot: A **shot** that joins two pieces of film, one with the central action or object and the other with additional background, figures, or action (sometimes painted or digitally produced) that would be difficult to create physically for the shot.

media convergence: The process by which formerly distinct media, such as cinema, television, the Internet, and video games, and viewing platforms such as television, computers, and cell phones become interdependent.

medium close-up: A **framing** that shows a comparatively larger area than a **close-up**, such as a person shown from the shoulders up; typically used during conversation **sequences**.

medium long shot: A **framing** that increases the distance between the camera and the subject compared with a **medium shot**; it shows most of an individual's body.

medium shot: A middle-ground **framing** in which we see the body of a person from approximately the waist up.

melodrama: Theatrical, literary, and cinematic **narrative** mode often centered on individual crises within the confines of family or other social institutions, frequently characterized by clearly identifiable moral types, coincidences and reversals of fortune, and the use of music (*melos*) to underscore the action.

metteur-en-scène: French term for **director** (particularly a theater director); in **auteur theory** this term refers to a director who conveys technical competence without possessing a strong streak of individual vision, in contrast to an **auteur**.

mickey-mousing: Overillustrating the action through the musical score, drawn from the conventions of composing for cartoons. An example of mickey-mousing is accompanying a character walking on tiptoe with music played by plucked strings.

miniature model: A small-scale model constructed for use during the filming process to stage **special effects sequences** and complex backgrounds.

mise-en-scène: A French theatrical term meaning literally "put on stage"; used in film studies to refer to all the elements of a movie **scene** that are organized, often by the **director**, to be filmed and that are later visible onscreen. They include the scenic elements of a movie, such as **actors**, **lighting**, **sets**, costumes, make-up, and other features of the image that exist independently of the camera and the processes of filming and **editing**. A *naturalistic mise-en-scène* appears realistic and recognizable to viewers, while a *theatrical mise-en-scène* emphasizes the artificial or constructed nature of its world.

mix: The combination by the sound mixer of separate **soundtracks** into a single master track that will be transferred onto the film print together with the image track to which it is synchronized.

mobile frame: A property of a **shot** in which the camera itself moves or the borders of the image are altered by a change in the **focal length** of the **camera lens**.

mockumentary: A film that uses a **documentary** style and structure to present and stage fictional (sometimes ludicrous) subjects.

modernism: An artistic movement in painting, music, design, architecture, and literature of the 1920s that rendered a fragmented vision of human subjectivity through strategies such as the foregrounding of style, experiments with space and time, and open-ended **narratives**.

modernity: A term designating the period of history stretching from the end of the medieval era to the present, as well as the period's attitude of confidence in progress and science centered on the human capacity to shape history.

montage: The French word for **editing**. It can be used to signify any joining of images, but it has come to indicate a style that emphasizes the breaks and contrasts between images joined by a **cut**, following Soviet silent-era filmmakers' use of the term; also designates rapid **sequences** in Hollywood films used for descriptive purposes or to show the rapid passage of time. *Intellectual montage* was defined by Sergei Eisenstein as an intentional juxtaposition of two images in order to generate ideas. See **dialectical montage** and **disjunctive editing**.

motion capture: A **special effects** technology used to incorporate an **actor**'s physical features into a computer-generated character.

movement editing: An **editing** technique through which the direction and **pace** of actions, gestures, and other movements are linked with corresponding or contrasting movements in one or more other **shots**.

multiple narrations: Found in films that use several different **narrative** perspectives for a single **story** or for different stories in a movie that loosely fits these perspectives together.

music supervisor: The individual who selects and secures the rights for songs to be used in films.

narration: The telling of a **story** or description of a situation; the emotional, physical, or intellectual perspective through which the **characters**, events, and action of the **plot** are conveyed. In film, narration is most explicit when provided as asynchronous verbal commentary on the action or images, but it can also designate the storytelling function of the camera, the **editing**, and verbal and other **soundtracks**.

narrative: A **story** told by a **narrator** or conveyed by a narrational **point of view**; see **plot**.

narrative analysis: A formal topic that concentrates on the **story** and its construction.

narrative frame: A context or person positioned outside the principal **narrative** of a film, such as bracketing **scenes** in which a character in the **story**'s present begins to relate events of the past and later concludes her or his tale.

narrative frequency: How often certain **plot** elements are repeated.

narratology: The study of **narrative** forms, encompassing stories of all kinds, including films. From Russian narratology are derived the terms *fabula* (**story**), all the events included in a tale or imagined by the reader or viewer in the order in which they are assumed to have occurred, and *syuzhet* (**plot**), the ordering of narrative events in the particular narrative.

narrator: A **character** or other person whose voice and perspective describe the action of a film, either in **voiceover** or through strict limitation of what is shown to a particular **point of view**.

natural lighting: Light derived from a natural source in a **scene** or **setting**, such as the illumination of the daylight sun or firelight.

naturalistic acting: An **actor**'s effort to embody the **character** that he or she is playing in order to communicate the essential self of the character.

negative cutter: The individual who conforms the negative of the film to the **final cut**. Release prints are then struck from the negative.

New German cinema: A film movement launched in West Germany in 1962, when a group of young filmmakers declared a new agenda for German film in a film festival document called the Oberhausen Manifesto. These films were known for their confrontation with Germany's Nazi and postwar past and their emphasis on the distinctive, often maverick, visions of **directors** whose creativity earned the movement the designation *Autorenfilm* within Germany.

new media: A term used in both information science and communications as well as the arts to refer to an array of technologies including the Internet, digital technologies, video-game consoles, cell phones, wireless devices, and the applications and imaginative creations they support.

niche market: A term referring to a segment of the audience with specialized tastes, which Hollywood increasingly has come to recognize as lucrative and to target with films and **marketing**.

nickelodeons: Early movie theaters, typically converted storefront or arcade spaces, where short films were shown continuously for a five-cent admission price to audiences passing in and out. They were prominent until the rise of the **feature film** in the 1910s demanded more comfortable settings.

nitrate: The highly flammable chemical base of 35mm **film stock** used until 1951.

nondiegetic insert: An **insert** that depicts an action, object, or title originating outside of the space and time of the **narrative** world.

nondiegetic sound: Sound that does not have an identifiable source in the **characters**' world and that consequently the characters cannot hear; see **diegetic sound** and **semidiegetic sound**.

nonfiction films: Films presenting (presumed) factual descriptions of actual events, persons, or places, rather than their fictional, or invented, re-creation.

non-narrative films: Films organized in a variety of ways besides storytelling; they employ organizational forms such as associations, lists, repetitions, or contrasts.

objective point of view: A **point of view** that does not associate the perspective of the camera with that of a specific character.

offscreen sound: A term used to distinguish **diegetic sounds** related to the action but whose source is not visible on the screen.

offscreen space: The implied space outside the boundaries of the film frame.

omniscient narration: **Narration** that presents all elements of the **plot**, exceeding the perspective of any one character; see also **third-person narration**.

180-degree rule: A central convention of **continuity editing** that restricts possible camera setups to the 180-degree area on one side of an imaginary line (the **axis of action**) drawn between the **characters** or figures of a **scene**. If the camera were to cross the line to film from within the 180-degree field on the other side, onscreen figure positions would be reversed.

onscreen sound: Sound with a visible onscreen source, such as when dialogue appears to come directly from the speaker's moving lips.

onscreen space: Space visible within the frame of the image.

optical effect: **Special effects** produced with the use of an **optical printer**, including visual transitions between **shots** such as **dissolves**, **fade-outs**, and **wipes**, or **process shots** that combine figures and backgrounds through the use of **matte shots**.

optical printer: The photographic equipment used by technicians to create **optical effects** in films by duplicating the already exposed image onto new **film stock** and altering the **lighting** or adding additional components.

optical sound recording: A **sound recording** process that converts sound waves into electrical impulses that then control how a light beam is projected onto film. The process enables a **soundtrack** to be recorded alongside the image for simultaneous projection.

orthochromatic: A property of black-and-white **film stock** used in the 1920s, sensitive to greens and blues but registering red light as black.

overhead shot: A **shot** that depicts the action from above, generally looking directly down on the subject; the camera may be mounted on a crane.

overlapping dialogue: Mixing two or more **characters'** speech to imitate the rhythm of speech; the term may also refer to dialogue that overlaps two **scenes** to effect a transition between them.

overlapping editing: An edited **sequence** that presents two **shots** of the same action; because this technique violates continuity, it is rarely used.

pace: The tempo at which the film seems to move. It is determined by the **duration** of individual **shots** and the style of **editing**, as well as by other elements of **cinematography** and **mise-en-scène** and the overall rhythm and flow of the film's action.

package-unit approach: An approach to film **production** established in the mid-1950s whereby the agent, **producer**, and **casting director** assembled a script, stars, and other major personnel as a key first step in a major production.

pan: A left or right rotation of the camera, whose tripod or mount remains in a fixed position that produces a horizontal movement onscreen.

"pan-and-scan" process: The process used to transfer a widescreen-format film to the standard television **aspect ratio**. A computer-controlled scanner determines the most important action in the image, and then crops peripheral action and space or presents the original frame as two separate images.

panchromatic: A property of a black-and-white **film stock** introduced in the 1920s that responds to a full spectrum of colors, rendering them as shades of gray, for a more nuanced and realistic image.

parallel editing: An **editing** technique that alternates between two or more strands of action in separate locations, often presented as occurring simultaneously; see **crosscutting**.

parallelism: An instance in which the **soundtrack** reinforces the image, such as synchronized dialogue or sound effects or a **voiceover** that is consistent with what is displayed onscreen; see **counterpoint**.

performance: An **actor's** use of language, physical expression, and gesture to bring a **character** to life and to communicate important dimensions of that character to the audience.

periodization: A method of organizing film history by groups of years defined by historical events and/or during which movies share thematic and stylistic concerns.

persistence of vision: The hypothesis, offered to explain the cinematic illusion of movement, that the eye briefly retains a visual imprint after an object has disappeared; this perception is now considered an effect of **apparent motion**.

personal or **subjective documentaries:** Documentary formats that emphasize the personal perspective or involvement of the filmmaker, often making the films resemble autobiographies or diaries.

perspective: The manner in which the distance and spatial relationships among objects are represented on a two-dimensional surface. In painting, parallel and converging lines were used to give the illusion of distance and depth; in film, perspective is manipulated by changes in the **focal length** of **camera lenses**.

phi phenomenon: The psychological illusion of motion when two or more still images of an object in different positions are shown in sequence; see **persistence of vision**.

pixilation: A type of **animation** that employs **stop-motion photography** (or instead simply cuts out images from a continuous piece of filmed action) to transform the movement of human figures into rapid jerky gestures.

platforming: The **distribution** strategy of releasing a film in gradually widening markets and theaters so that it slowly builds its reputation and momentum through reviews and word of mouth.

plot: The **narrative** ordering of the events of the **story** as they appear in the actual work, selected and arranged according to particular temporal, spatial, generic, causal, or other patterns; in **narratology**, also known by the Russian word *syuzhet*.

point of view: The position from which a person, event, or object is seen or filmed; in **narrative** form, the perspective through which events are narrated.

point-of-view (POV) shot: A subjective **shot** that reproduces a character's optical **point of view**, often preceded and/or followed by shots of the character looking.

postclassical narrative: A term used to characterize cinema after the decline of the **studio system** around 1960.

postmodernism: An artistic style in architecture, art, literature, music, and film that incorporates fragments of or references to other styles; or the cultural period in which political, cultural, and economic shifts engendered challenges to the tenets of **modernism**, including its belief in the possibility of critiquing the world through art, the division of high and low culture, and the genius and independent identity of the artist.

postproduction: The period in the filmmaking process that occurs after **principal photography** has been completed and usually consisting of **editing**, sound, and **special effects** work.

postproduction sound: Sound recorded and added to a film in the **postproduction** phase.

poststructuralism: An intellectual development that came after **structuralism** and in some sense supplanted it, calling into question the rational methodology and fixed definitions that structuralists bring to their various objects of study.

postsynchronous sound: Sound recorded after the actual filming and then synchronized with onscreen sources.

preproduction: The phase when a film project is in development, involving the preparation of the script, financing the project, casting, hiring crew, and securing locations.

primary research sources: These sources have a direct and close relationship with the original film, such as a DVD. Some of these materials are readily available in libraries, including the many classic scripts now published as books; others, such as 16mm films, can be far more difficult to locate, except in film archives.

principal photography: The majority of footage filmed for a project.

process shot: A special effect that combines two or more images as a single **shot**, such as filming an **actor** in front of a projected background.

producer: The person or persons responsible for steering and monitoring each step of a film project, especially the financial aspects, from development to **postproduction** and a **distribution** deal.

production: The industrial stages that contribute to the making of a finished movie, from the financing and scripting of a film to its final edit; more specifically, the actual shooting of a film after **preproduction** and before **postproduction**.

production designer: The person in charge of the film's overall look.

production sound mixer: The sound engineer on the production **set**; also called a *sound recordist*.

promotion: The aspect of the movie industry through which audiences are exposed to and encouraged to see a particular film; promotion includes advertisements, **trailers**, publicity appearances, and product **tie-ins**.

prop: An object that functions as a part of the **set** or as a tool used by the **actors**.

psychoanalysis: The therapeutic method innovated by Sigmund Freud based on his attribution of unconscious motives to human actions, desires, and symptoms; theoretical tenets developed by literary and film critics to facilitate the cultural study of texts and the interaction between viewers and texts.

protagonists: Individuals identified as the positive forces in a film; see **antagonists**.

rack focus (or **pulled focus**): A dramatic change in **focus** from one object to another.

reaction shot: A **shot** that depicts a character's response to something shown in a previous shot.

realism: An artwork's truthful picture of a society, person, or some other dimension of everyday life; an artistic movement that aims to achieve **verisimilitude**.

reception theory: A theoretical approach to the ways different kinds of audiences regard different kinds of films.

reenactment: Re-creating presumably real events within the context of a **documentary**.

reestablishing shot: A **shot** during an edited **sequence** that returns to an **establishing shot** to restore a seemingly "objective" view to the spectator.

reflected sound: Recorded sound that is captured as it bounces from the walls and **sets**. It is usually used to give a sense of space; opposed to **direct sound**.

reflexive narration: A mode of **narration** that calls attention to the **narrative point of view** of the **story** in order to complicate or subvert its own **narrative** authority as an objective perspective on the world.

reframing: The process of moving the frame from one position to another within a single continuous **shot**.

restricted narration: A **narrative** in which our knowledge is limited to that of a particular character.

retrospective plot: A **plot** that tells of past events from the perspective of the present or future.

rhythmic editing: The organization of **editing** according to different **paces** or tempos determined by how quickly **cuts** are made.

road movie: A film **genre** that depicts **characters** on a journey, usually following a **linear chronology**.

romantic comedy: A film **genre** that depicts the emotional attraction of a couple in a consistently lighthearted manner, popular since the 1930s.

room tone: The aural properties of a location that are recorded and then mixed in with dialogue and other tracks to achieve a more realistic sound.

rotoscoping: A technique using recorded real figures and action as a basis for painting individual **animation** frames digitally.

rough cut: The initial edited version of a movie in which an editor approximates the finished film.

safety film: Acetate-based **film stock** that replaced the highly flammable **nitrate** film base in 1952.

saturation booking: The **distribution** strategy of releasing a film simultaneously in as many locations as possible, widely implemented with the advent of the **blockbuster** in the 1970s. Also called *saturated release*.

scale: Determined by the distance of the camera from its subject.

scene: One or more **shots** that depict a continuous space and time.

scenics: Early **nonfiction films** that offered exotic or remarkable images of nature or foreign lands.

screenplay: The text from which a movie is made, including dialogue and information about action, **settings**, etc., as well as **shots** and transitions. Developed from a **treatment**. Also known as a *script*.

screenwriter: A writer of a film's **screenplay**; the screenwriter may begin with a **treatment** and develop the **plot** structure and dialogue over the span of several versions. Also called a *scriptwriter*.

screwball comedies: A comic **subgenre** of the 1930s and 1940s usually featuring humorous situations through which heterosexual **antagonists** are eventually romantically united; their characteristic witty banter is often taken as a displaced representation of the sexual expression forbidden by the Production Code of that era.

script doctor: An uncredited individual called in to do rewrites on a **screenplay**.

segmentation: The process of dividing a film into large **narrative** units for the purposes of analysis.

semidiegetic sound: Sound that is neither strictly **diegetic** nor **nondiegetic**, such as certain **voiceovers** that can be construed as the thoughts of a character and thus as arising from the **story** world; also known as **internal diegetic sound**.

semiotics: The study of **signs** and signification; posits that meaning is constructed and communicated through the selection, ordering, and interpretation of signs and sign systems, including words, gestures, images, symbols, or virtually anything that can be meaningfully codified. Also called *semiology*.

sequence: Any number of **shots** or **scenes** that are unified as a coherent action or an identifiable motif, regardless of changes in space and time.

sequence shot: A **shot** in which an entire **scene** is played out in one continuous **take**.

set: Strictly speaking, a constructed **setting**, often on a studio **soundstage**, but both the setting and the set can combine natural and constructed elements.

set designer: The individual responsible for supervising the conception and construction of movie **sets**.

set lighting: The distribution of an evenly diffused illumination through a **scene** as a kind of **lighting** base.

setting: A fictional or real place where the action and events of the film occur.

shallow focus: A **shot** in which only a narrow range of the field is in focus.

shock cut: A **cut** that juxtaposes two images whose dramatic difference aims to create a jarring visual effect.

shooting ratio: The relationship between the overall amount or length of film shot and the amount used in the finished project.

shot: A continuous **point of view** (or continuously exposed piece of film) that may move forward or backward, up or down, but not change, break, or cut to another point of view or image.

shot/reverse shot: An **editing** pattern that begins with a **shot** of one **character** taken from an angle at one end of the **axis of action**, follows with a shot of the second character from the "reverse" angle at the other end of the line, and continues back and forth through the **sequence**; often used in conversations. Also called *shot/countershot*.

Showscan: A projection system, developed by Douglas Trumbull and marketed in 1983, that projects at sixty frames per second (rather than twenty-four frames) and creates remarkably dense and detailed images.

sidelighting: Used to illuminate the subject from the side.

sign: Term used in **semiotics** for something that signifies something else, whether the connection is causal, conventional, or based on resemblance. As defined by Ferdinand de Saussure, a sign is composed of a *signifier*, the spoken or written word, picture, or gesture, and a *signified*, the mental concept it evokes.

slapstick comedy: Films known for physical humor and stunts; some of the first films were slapstick comedies.

slasher films: A **subgenre** of contemporary **horror films** depicting serial killers, often considered to have originated with *Psycho* (1960).

slow motion: A cinematic special effect that makes the action move at unrealistic speeds, achieved by filming the action slower than normal and then projecting it at standard speeds. See **fast motion**.

soft lighting: Diffused, low contrast **lighting** that reduces or eliminates hard edges and shadows and can be more flattering when filming people.

sound bridge: The term for sound carried over a picture transition, or a sound belonging to the coming **scene** playing before the image changes.

sound continuity: The range of scoring, **sound recording**, mixing, and playback processes that strive for the unification of film meaning and experience by subordinating sound to the aims of the **narrative**.

sound designer: The individual responsible for planning and directing the overall sound of a film through to the final **mix**.

sound editing: Combining music, dialogue, and effects tracks to interact with the image track in order to create rhythmic relationships, establish connections between sound and onscreen source, and smooth or mark transitions. Performed by a *sound editor*.

sound mixing: An important stage in the **postproduction** of a film that takes place after the image track, including the **credits**, is complete; the process by which all the elements of the **soundtrack**, including music, effects, and dialogue, are combined and adjusted; also called *re-recording*.

sound perspective: The apparent location and distance of a sound source.

sound recording: The recording of dialogue and other sound that takes place simultaneously with the filming of a **scene**.

sound reproduction: Sound playback during a film's **exhibition**.

soundstage: A large soundproofed building designed to construct and move **sets** and **props** and effectively capture sound and dialogue during filming.

soundtrack: Audio recorded to synchronize with a moving image, including dialogue, music, and sound effects, as well as the physical portion of the film used for recorded sound.

source music: Diegetic music; music whose source is visible onscreen.

special effects: A variety of illusions created during the filmmaking process through mechanical means, such as the building of models, or on-**set** explosions, or with the camera, such as **slow motion, color filters, process shots**, and **matte shots**. Sometimes used interchangeably with **visual effects**, which more often denotes digital effects added in **postproduction**.

spectatorship: The process of film viewing; the conscious and unconscious interaction of viewers and films as a topic of interest to film theorists.

spotting: The process of determining where music and effects will be added to a film.

star system: Employing one or more well-known **actors** (*stars*) whose appearance in movies builds on audience expectations and promotes the movie. In a **studio system** or a national film industry, the star system will often have a specific economic organization of contracts, publicity, and vehicles.

Steadicam: A camera stabilization system introduced in 1976 that allows a **camera operator** to film a continuous and steady **shot** without losing the freedom of movement afforded by the **handheld camera**.

stereotype: A character type that simplifies and standardizes perceptions that one group holds about another, often less numerous, powerful, or privileged group.

stinger: Sound that forces the audience to notice the significance of something onscreen, such as the ominous chord struck when the villain's presence is made known.

stop-motion photography: A process that records inanimate objects or actual human figures in separate frames and then synthesizes them on film to create the illusion of motion and action.

story: The subject matter or raw material of a **narrative**, or our reconstruction of the events of a narrative based on what is explicitly shown and ordered in the **plot**.

structural film: An **experimental film** movement that emerged in North America in the 1960s with filmmakers like Hollis Frampton and Michael Snow in which films followed a predetermined structure; developed into *structural/materialist* film in the United Kingdom in the 1970s.

structuralism: Derived from linguistics and anthropology, an approach to literary and filmic **narratives** that looks for common structures rather than originality.

studio system: The industrial practices of the large **production** (and, until 1948, **distribution**) companies responsible for the kinds and quality of movies made in Hollywood or other film industries. During the Hollywood *studio era* extending from the late 1920s to the 1950s, the five major studios were MGM, Paramount, RKO, Twentieth Century Fox, and Warner Bros.

stylistic analysis: Offers a wide variety of topics that engage the formal arrangements of image and sound, such as **shot** composition, **editing**, and the use of sound.

subgenres: A specialized **genre** that defines a specific, more limited version of a more general genre, often by refining it with an adjective, such as the spaghetti western or **slapstick comedy**.

subjective point of view: A **point of view** that re-creates the perspective of a **character**.

supporting actors: **Actors** who play secondary **characters** in a film, serving as foils or companions to the central characters.

surrealist cinema: One of the most influential of the **avant-garde** movements, surrealist films confronted middle-class assumptions about normality using the powers of film to manipulate time, space, and material objects according to a dreamlike logic.

suture: A term that refers to our sense of being inserted in a specific place in the film, from which to look at its fictional world through **editing** and **point of view**.

synchronous sound: Sound that is recorded during a **scene** or that is synchronized with the filmed images; as used by scholar Siegfried Kracauer, a term that describes sound that has a visible onscreen source, such as moving lips; also referred to as **onscreen sound**.

syntagma: A term derived from linguistics for sequential units of meaning and used by Christian Metz to refer to the smallest combinable **narrative** units of film—**sequences, scenes**, and autonomous **shots**.

take: A single filmed version of a **shot** during **production** or a single shot onscreen.

talking heads: An on-camera interview that typically shows the speaker from the shoulders up, hence "talking head."

Technicolor: Color processing that uses three strips of film to transfer colors directly onto a single image; developed between 1926 and 1932.

telephoto lens: A lens with a **focal length** of at least 75mm, capable of magnifying and flattening distant objects; see also **zoom lens**.

theatrical trailer: A promotional preview of an upcoming release presented before the main feature or as a television commercial.

thesis statement: A short statement (often a single sentence) that succinctly describes and anticipates each stage of an essay's argument. A *working thesis* is a rough version of a thesis used to draft an essay.

Third Cinema: A term coined in the late 1960s in Latin America to echo the phrase and concept "Third World," Third Cinema opposed commercial and auteurist cinemas with a political, populist aesthetic and united films from a number of countries and contexts.

third-person narration: A **narration** that assumes an objective and detached stance vis-à-vis the **plot** and **characters**, describing events from outside the **story**.

30-degree rule: A **cinematography** and **editing** rule that specifies that a **shot** should only be followed by another shot taken from a position greater than 30 degrees from that of the first.

3-D modeling: A computer imaging technique that uses software to create visual representations from three-dimensional models.

three-point lighting: A **lighting** technique common in Hollywood that combines **key lighting**, **fill lighting**, and **backlighting** to blend the distribution of light in a **scene**.

tie-ins: Ancillary products that advertise and promote a movie, such as T-shirts, CD **soundtracks**, toys, and other gimmicks made available at stores and restaurants.

tilt shot: An upward or downward rotation of the camera, whose tripod or mount remains in a fixed position, producing a vertical movement onscreen.

tone: The shading, intensification, or saturation of colors (such as metallic blues, soft greens, or deep reds) in order to sharpen, mute, or balance them for certain effects.

topicals: Early films that captured or sometimes re-created historical or newsworthy events.

topic sentence: Usually the first sentence of a paragraph that announces the central idea around which all other sentences within the paragraph cohere.

top lighting: Used to illuminate the subject from above.

tracking shot: A **shot** that changes the position of the **point of view** by moving forward, backward, or around the subject, usually on tracks that have been constructed in advance (see **dolly shot**); also called a *traveling shot.*

trailer: A form of promotional advertising that previews edited images and **scenes** from a film in theaters before the main **feature film** or on a television commercial or Web site.

treatment: A succinct description of the content of a film written before the **screenplay** or *script.*

two-shot: A **shot** depicting two **characters**.

underground film: Nonmainstream film, associated particularly with the **experimental film** culture of 1960s and 1970s New York and San Francisco, characterized by the intersection of **performance** and sexual subcultures.

underlighting: Used to illuminate the subject from below.

underscoring: A film's background music; contrasts with **source music**.

unit production manager: A member of a film's production team responsible for reporting and managing the details of receipts and purchases.

unreliable narration: A type of **narration** that raises questions about the truth of the **story** being told. Also called *manipulative narration.*

verisimilitude: The quality of fictional representation that allows readers or viewers to accept a constructed world, its events, its **characters**, and their actions as plausible; literally "having the appearance of truth."

vertical integration: The industrial organization of the major studios in the 1930s and 1940s, in which film **distribution** was controlled through production companies' ownership of theater chains.

viral marketing: A phenomenon in which consumers pass along a **marketing** message through word of mouth, electronic messaging, or other means.

visual effects: **Special effects** created in **postproduction** though digital imaging.

voice-off: A voice that originates from a speaker who can be inferred to be present in the **scene** but who is not visible onscreen.

voiceover: A voice whose source is neither visible in the frame nor implied to be offscreen; it typically narrates the film's images, such as in a **flashback** or the commentary in a **documentary** film.

walla: A nonsense word spoken by extras in a film to approximate the sound of a crowd during sound dubbing.

wide-angle lens: A lens with a short **focal length** (typically less than 35mm) that allows **cinematographers** to explore a **depth of field** that can simultaneously show foreground and background objects or events in focus.

wide release: The premiere of a movie at many locations simultaneously, sometimes on as many as 1,500 to 2,000 screens nationally.

widescreen processes: Any of a number of systems introduced in the 1950s that widened the **aspect ratio** and the dimensions of the movie screen.

widescreen ratio: The wider, rectangular **aspect ratio** of typically 1.85:1 or 2.35:1; see **academy ratio**.

wipe: A transition used to join two **shots** by moving a vertical, horizontal, or sometimes diagonal line across one image to replace it with a second image that follows the line across the frame.

women's picture: A category of films produced in the 1930s–1950s, featuring female stars in romances or **melodramas** and marketed primarily to women.

work print: The processed film that is cut during the **editing** process; after the editing process, release prints are made to show in cinemas.

Works Cited: List of sources cited in an essay, positioned on a separate page immediately after the last page of the essay text.

Works Consulted: Optional list of sources that have been consulted but not cited in the text or notes of an essay; appears on a separate page after the **Works Cited** list.

zoom-in: The act of changing the lens's **focal length** to narrow the field of view of a distant object, magnifying and **reframing** it, often in **close-up**, while the camera remains stationary; see **zoom-out**.

zoom lens: A lens with variable **focal length**.

zoom-out: Reversing the action of a **zoom-in**, so that objects that appear close initially are distanced and **reframed** as small figures.

Acknowledgments

Photo Credits

p. 3: (left) Courtesy Everett Collection; (right) Columbia/ Sony/ The Kobal Collection; **p. 4:** Courtesy Everett Collection; **1.1:** Odd Anderson/AFP/Getty Images; **1.2:** Mary Evans Picture Library/The Image Works; **1.3:** Rue des Archives/The Granger Collection, New York; **1.5a:** Image of Treasures from American Film Archives DVD courtesy of the National Film Preservation Foundation; **1.5b:** Image of More Treasures from American Film Archives DVD courtesy of the National Film Preservation Foundation; **1.6:** Seth Wenig/Reuters/Corbis; **1.7a:** J. R. Eyerman/Time Life Pictures/Getty Images; **1.7b:** Royalty Free/Corbis; **1.7c:** Guang Niu/Getty Images; **1.7d:** Jeremy Hoare/Alamy; **1.8a:** Sony Pictures/Courtesy Everett Collection; **1.8b:** Sony Pictures/Courtesy Everett Collection; **1.8c:** Lions Gate/Courtesy Everett Collection; **1.8d:** Doanne Gregory/Fox Searchlight/The Kobal Collection; **1.10:** Courtesy Everett Collection; **p. 14:** Columbia/Sony/The Kobal Collection; **2.2:** Photofest; **2.14:** Kevin Winter/Getty Images; **2.18:** Courtesy Everett Collection; **2.21:** Courtesy Everett Collection; **2.22:** Tristar Pictures/Courtesy Everett Collection; **2.26:** Anglo Enterprise/Vineyard/The Kobal Collection; **2.29:** Courtesy Everett Collection; **2.32:** © Weinstein Company/Courtesy Everett Collection; **2.36:** Biphoto/ Alamy; **2.42:** Columbia/The Kobal Collection; **2.47:** Courtesy of Milestone Film & Video; **2.49:** Photofest; **2.52:** AP/Wide World Photos; **2.60:** © New Line Cinema/Courtesy Everett Collection; **2.66:** Bettmann/Corbis; **2.67:** RKO/The Kobal Collection; **Transforming Film, p. 56:** (top to bottom) Courtesy Everett Collection; Bettmann/Corbis; J. R. Eyerman/Getty Images; Richard Levine/Alamy; Aurora/Getty Image; **p. 58:** Paramount/The Kobal Collection; **p. 59:** (left to right) Courtesy Everett Collection; © DreamWorks/Courtesy Everett Collection; Jan Chapman Productions/CIBY 2000/The Kobal Collection; **p. 60:** Paramount/The Kobal Collection; **3.4a:** Gianni Dagli Orti/Corbis; **3.4c:** Courtesy Everett Collection; **3.4d:** Buena Vista Pictures/Courtesy Everett Collection; **3.4e:** Warner Brothers/Courtesy Everett Collection; **3.6:** Courtesy Everett Collection; **3.8:** DDT Efectos Especiales; **Transforming Film, p. 81:** (a, b) Courtesy Everett Collection; (c, d, e) "The Lord of the Rings: The Two Towers" Copyright MMII, New Line Productions, Inc. ™ The Saul Zaentz Company d/b/a/ Tolkein Enterprises under license to New Line Productions, Inc. All rights reserved. Photo by Pierre Vinet. Photo appears courtesy of New Line Productions, Inc.; **3.35:** Courtesy Everett Collection; **p. 94:** Courtesy Everett Collection; **4.5:** Bibliotheque Nationale, Paris, France/Archives Charmet/Bridgeman Art Library International, Ltd.; **4.6:** Hulton-Deutsch Collection/Corbis; **4.8:** Henry Gutmann/Getty Images; **4.15:** The Kobal Collection; **4.16a:** Andrei Rublev Museum, Moscow, Russia/Bridgeman Art Library International, Ltd.; **4.17a:** Andy Kingsbury/Corbis; **4.22:** SGF/Gaumont/The Kobal Collection; **4.80:** Courtesy British Film Institute; **p. 134:** © DreamWorks/Courtesy Everett

Collection; **5.1a:** © Gianni Dagli Orti/Corbis; **5.1b:** Erich Lessing/Art Resource, NY; **5.1c:** 2004 Ki-hoon LEE, Seung-ypu CHO, DAIWON C.I. Inc. All Rights Reserved. First published in Korea in 2004 by Daiwon C.I. Inc. English translation rights in North America, UK, NZ, and Australia arranged by Daiwon C.I. Inc. through Topaz Agency; **5.2:** Etienne Jules Marey/Getty Images; **5.3:** Bridgeman-Giraudon Art Resource, NY; **5.5:** Edison/The Kobal Collection; **Transforming Film, p. 141:** (a) Hulton-Deutsch Collection/Corbis; (b) David Wells/The Image Works; © Jim Sugar/Corbis; **5.47:** Olympia-Film/The Kobal Collection; **5.57:** MTV/Photofest; **5.58a, 5.58b:** Courtesy the Everett Collection; **5.65b:** Courtesy Everett Collection; **Transforming Film, p. 175:** (top to bottom) Digital Image © The Museum of Modern Art/Licensed by SCALA/Art Resource, NY; Courtesy the Everett Collection; Posteritati; **p. 184:** Jan Chapman Productions/CIBY 2000/The Kobal Collection; **6.1:** Courtesy Edison Historic Site, NPS; **6.2a:** Courtesy Joseph Yranski; **6.2b:** Marnan Collection, Minneapolis, Minnesota; **6.2c:** Marnan Collection, Minneapolis, Minnesota; **6.4:** Photofest; **6.6:** Photofest; **6.10:** Banque d'Images, ADAGP/Art Resource, NY; **6.17:** Photofest; **6.18:** Courtesy Killer Films and Focus Features; **6.23:** Think Film/Courtesy Everett Collection; **6.26:** Photofest; **Transforming Film, p. 203:** (a) The Kobal Collection; (b) Courtesy Everett Collection; (c) Courtesy Everett Collection; (d) Sony Pictures/Courtesy Everett Collection; **6.33:** Courtesy Everett Collection; **6.34a:** "Shrek" ® & © 2001 DreamWorks Animation LLC. Used with permission of DreamWorks Animation LLC; **p. 224:** Sony Pictures/The Kobal Collection; **p. 225:** (left to right) Lions Gate/© Dog Eat Dog Films/Photofest; The Film Company; Matt Groening/20th Century Fox/The Kobal Collection; **p. 226:** Sony Pictures/The Kobal Collection; **7.1a:** Erich Lessing/Art Resource, NY; **7.1b:** The National Gallery, London; **7.2a:** Spider-Man: ™ & © 2008 Marvel Characters, Inc. Used with permission; **7.10a-7.10d:** Photofest; **Transforming Film, p. 240:** (a) Archival film materials from the collections of the Library of Congress; **7.26:** ™ & © Fox Searchlight. All rights reserved/Courtesy Everett Collection; **7.40:** Photofest; **7.42:** Courtesy Everett Collection; **7.64b:** Govt. of W. Bengal/The Kobal Collection; **p. 270:** Lions Gate/© Dog Eat Dog Films/Photofest; **8.1:** Courtesy of Everett Collection; **8.3:** Archival film and/or video materials from the collections of the Library of Congress; **8.4:** Jacob August Riis/Corbis; **Transforming Film, p. 275:** (second from top) Courtesy of Milestone Film & Video; (third from top) Resettlement Administration/The Kobal Collection; **8.5:** Archival film and/or video materials from the collections of the Library of Congress; **8.6a:** Contemporary Films Ltd./Photofest; **8.6c:** London Films/The Kobal Collection; **8.10a:** Frank Micelotta/™ and Copyright © 20th Century Fox Film Corp. All rights reserved, Courtesy: Everett Collection; **8.10b:** Dave Bjerke/NBCU Photo Bank; **8.15:** Rhombus Media/Telefilm Canada/The Kobal

Collection; 8.17: Courtesy British Film Institute; 8.24: Zipporah Films; 8.26b, 8.27: Photofest; 8.32: Courtesy of Everett Collection; 8.36: Milestone Film & Video; 8.37: Michael Rockefeller/ President and Fellows Harvard College; p. 300: The Film Company; 9.2: Courtesy of the Video Data Bank, www.vdb.org; 9.3a: The Granger Collection, NY; 9.3b: Hulton Archive/Getty Images; 9.4: Digital Image © The Museum of Modern Art/ Licensed by SCALA/Art Resource, NY; **Transforming Film, p. 305:** (second from top) Image of Interior New York Subway, 14th Street to 42nd Street courtesy of the National Film Preservation Foundation and the Museum of Modern Art; (third from top) Martha Cooper; 9.12: Courtesy the Everett Collection; 9.15: Courtesy of Michael Snow; 9.18: Hirshhorn Museum and Sculpture Garden, Smithsonian Institution, Holenia Purchase Fund in Memory of Joseph H. Hirshhorn, 1996; 9.20: Name of Film: "The Real Me," Year of Production: 2007, Photo Credit: Midi Onodera, website: www.midionodera.com; 9.21: Courtesy of the Everett Collection; 9.22: Third Eye Butterfly by Storm de Hirsch, 1968. Copyright Anthology Film Archives; 9.23: Digital Image © The Museum of Modern Art/Licensed by SCALA/Art Resource, NY; 9.30: Courtesy of Michael Snow; 9.31: Photo Courtesy of Anthology Film Archives, All Rights Reserved. Under License from Marion Faller; 9.32: Shirin Neshat, Untitled (Rapture Series-Women Pushing Boat) 1999, Gelatin silver print, 44 × 68 1/4 inches, Edition of 5, Copyright Shirin Neshat, Courtesy Gladstone Gallery; 9.33: Photofest; 9.34: Buena Vista Pictures/Photofest; 9.35: Photofest; 9.39: Courtesy Lynn Hershman; 9.43a: Women Make Movies Release. Courtesy of Women Make Movies www.wmm.com; 9.44: Courtesy of Anthology Film Archives. All Rights Reserved; 9.45: Courtesy of Anthology Film Archives. All Rights Reserved; p. 330: Matt Groening/20th Century Fox/The Kobal Collection; **Transforming Film, p. 334:** (top) Cambridge University Press; 10.03: Erich Lessing/Art Resource, NY; 10.15: Courtesy of Anthology Film Archives. All Rights Reserved; 10.32: MPI/Getty Images; 10.57: Photofest; p. 369: (left to right) 20th Century Fox/ Paramount/The Kobal Collection; Focus Features Courtesy the Everett Collection; p. 370: 20th Century Fox/Paramount/The Kobal Collection; 11.5: From "L.J.M. Daguerre: The History of the Diorama and the Daguerreotype" by Helmut and Alison Gernsheim (Dover, 1968); 11.7: MPI/Getty Images; **Transforming Film, p. 380:** (top to bottom) Franz Marc Frei/Corbis; Courtesy the Everett Collection; Time and Life Pictures/Getty Images; Fox Searchlight/The Kobal Collection; 11.23: Photofest; 11.25: General Photographic Agency/Getty Images; 11.26: Photofest; 11.40: Photofest; p. 404: Focus Features/ Courtesy the Everett Collection; 12.1: Photofest; 12.4: Courtesy British Film Institute; 12.5: Everett Collection; 12.6: Courtesy Kristine Harris; 12.8: Nancy R. Schiff/Hulton Archive/Getty Images; 12.9: The Kobal Collection; 12.15: Photofest; **Transforming Film, p. 424:** (top to bottom) The Kobal Collection; Photofest; Collection of Patricia White; Courtesy the Everett Collection; 20th Century Fox. All rights reserved/The Kobal Collection; 12.27: Ft. Lee Public Library, Silent Film Collection, Ft. Lee, NJ; 12.29: Photofest; 12.36: Courtesy the Everett Collection; 12.37: Courtesy the Everett Collection; 12.38: Photofest; 12.41: Courtesy Prelinger Archives; 12.43, 12.44, 12.45: Courtesy Oscar Micheaux Society, Duke University, with thanks to Jane Gaines; 12.49: AP/Wide World Photos; 12.50: AP/Wide World Photos; 12.51: AP/Wide World Photos; 12.55: Photofest; 12.63: Courtesy of DER from The Video in the Villages Series by Vincent Carelli; 12.65: Photofest; p. 455: (right) Posteritati; 13.09: Gramercy Pictures/Courtesy the Everett Collection; 13.22: Courtesy the Everett Collection; 13.27: Samuel Aranda/Getty Images; 13.28: Photo Courtesy of Anthology Film Archives, All Rights Reserved; 13.37: © Allen Eyestone/Palm Beach Post/Zuma Press; 13.39b: Steve Granitz/Getty Images; 13.40: Hubert Boesl/dpa/Landov; p. 506: Posteritati

Index

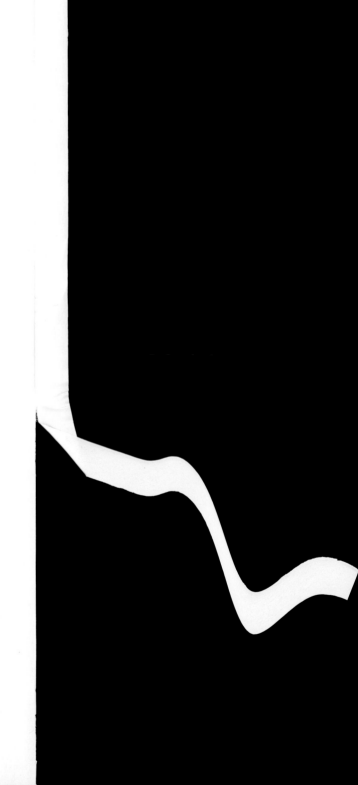

You get more.
bedfordstmartins.com/filmexperience

The companion Web site for *The Film Experience* offers a wealth of useful resources for both students and instructors that complement the main text. Key features include:

- **Chapter summaries** that review central film concepts.

- **Quizzes** that test and reinforce students' knowledge of film.

- **Film resource links** for additional information and research on specific film techniques, genres, important filmmakers, and more.

- **Glossary resources** that include an unabridged glossary covering all terms and definitions in the main text's glossary plus a chapter-by-chapter glossary that helps students understand how key terms relate to specific cinematic concepts.

- **Access to a vast store of research and writing resources** including *The Bedford Bibliographer, The Bedford Research Room,* and a powerful *Model Documents Gallery* that offers hundreds of student and professional essays and speeches on a wide range of topics.

- **Powerful instructor resources** that include a downloadable version of the Instructor's Resource Manual, a Quiz Gradebook that allows instructors to assess student quiz results, and access to a wealth of useful guidelines on helping students conduct research, cite sources, write polished essays, and avoid plagiarism.